WAR AND WARFARE IN LATE ANTIQUITY

LATE ANTIQUE ARCHAEOLOGY

VOLUME 8.2 – 2011

The titles published in this series are listed at brill.com/laa

WAR AND WARFARE
IN LATE ANTIQUITY

EDITED BY

ALEXANDER SARANTIS
AND
NEIL CHRISTIE

BRILL

LEIDEN · BOSTON
2013

Cover illustration: Interior visualisation of the Alacami (Richard Bayliss)

Library of Congress Cataloging-in-Publication Data

War and warfare in late antiquity / edited by Alexander Sarantis and Neil Christie.
    pages cm.—(Late antique archaeology, ISSN 1570-6893 ; 8)
    Includes bibliographical references and index.
    ISBN 978-90-04-25257-8 (hardback : alk. paper)—ISBN 978-90-04-25281-3 (hardback : v. 1 : alk. paper)—ISBN 978-90-04-25282-0 (hardback : v. 2 : alk. paper)—ISBN 978-90-04-25258-5 (e-book)
 1. Military art and science—Rome—History. 2. Rome—Military antiquities. 3. Europe, Eastern—Antiquities, Roman. 4. Military art and science—History—To 500. 5. Military art and science—History—Medieval, 500–1500. 6. Rome—History, Military—30 B.C.–476 A.D. I. Sarantis, Alexander Constantine, 1978–, editor. II. Christie, Neil.

    U35.W343 2013
    355.020937'09015—dc23

                                                                          2013022107

This publication has been typeset in the multilingual "Brill" typeface. With over 5,100 characters covering Latin, IPA, Greek, and Cyrillic, this typeface is especially suitable for use in the humanities. For more information, please see www.brill.com/brill-typeface.

ISSN 1570-6893
ISBN 978-90-04-25257-8 (hardback set)
ISBN 978-90-04-25281-3 (hardback vol. 1)
ISBN 978-90-04-25282-0 (hardback vol. 2)
ISBN 978-90-04-25258-5 (e-book)

MIX
Paper from
responsible sources
FSC
www.fsc.org   FSC® C004472

PRINTED BY DRUKKERIJ WILCO B.V. - AMERSFOORT, THE NETHERLANDS

CONTENTS

VOLUME 8.1

BIBLIOGRAPHIC ESSAYS

Literary Sources and Topography

The West

The Balkans

STRATEGY AND INTELLIGENCE

INFORMATION AND WAR:
SOME COMMENTS ON DEFENSIVE STRATEGY AND INFORMATION IN THE MIDDLE BYZANTINE PERIOD (*ca.* A.D. 660–1025)

John Haldon

Abstract

This article looks at the relationship between information about the land-scape and geography of Anatolia in the period from the 7th to 11th c. A.D., the practical strategic arrangements put in place by the eastern Roman gov-ernment in dealing with its enemies, and the communications which bound frontier or operational regions to their hinterlands, sources of supplies and reserves of manpower. It demonstrates the association between the physi-cal structures through which information was gathered and the types of information which were deployed, and suggests that Byzantine defensive arrangements could be both sophisticated and effective.

Successful warfare depends upon a number of factors, which may com-bine and re-combine in various ways—among them we might include an efficient logistical system, effective fighting units with good morale and discipline, intelligent leadership, reliable officers, good equipment and weaponry, flexible tactical structures, sensible strategic arrangements, along with many other factors. A fundamental aspect of Byzantine defen-sive and offensive warfare was intelligence gathering. Advance scouting parties were a part of every campaign army, of course, and combined with lookouts and border guards were responsible for providing a great deal of essential information about enemy movements, size and quality of raiding or invading forces, and so on. Information was also gathered by diplomatic envoys, travellers and merchants (10th c. A.D. military treatises recommended the employment of all these groups), and apart from the interrogation of deserters and sometimes the torture of prisoners for infor-mation, spies disguised as merchants or travellers were also employed to collect and pass on vital information.[1] In addition, visitors to Byzantine prisoners held in Muslim prisons were also exploited for the information they might be able to obtain. No doubt the quality and reliability of the

---

[1] For diplomatic exchanges, see Kaplony (1996); Rochow (2001) 305–25.

A. Sarantis, N. Christie (edd.) *War and Warfare in Late Antiquity: Current Perspectives*
(Late Antique Archaeology 8.1–8.2 – 2010–11) (Leiden 2013), pp. 373–393

information varied considerably, but it was regarded as an essential element in war-making and in the defence of the empire, and was organised
on a relatively sophisticated basis.[2]

Geographical knowledge of the terrain which was fought over and
the possibilities it offered, not just for fighting battles, but for supplying
armies, for eliciting support or at least neutrality from the resident population, was essential. This short paper will review some aspects of the
ways in which information of all sorts was collected, evaluated and disseminated in the eastern Roman world after the 6th c., both with a view
to pointing out continuities as well as to noting innovations and changes
in emphasis. Two main elements will be considered: geographical context and communications, and types of information and misinformation.
The ways in which information was understood or evaluated according to
social and cultural context is of course equally important, but represents
a somewhat different undertaking which I cannot accommodate within
the confines of this paper.

A good deal of work has been done on aspects of Late Roman practice
with respect to both the gathering and exploitation of information as well
as the physical structure of the various frontiers of the empire.[3] Rather
than repeat or attempt to emulate recent work on some of these issues,
this paper will look at the structures or systems through which information might be transmitted, and will be confined largely to the period from
the 6th–11th c. A.D., beginning with a few remarks on communications and
the possibilities for the movement of information.[4] The maintenance of
roads and the ability to transmit and receive information relevant to the
empire's territorial security was always a key concern of Roman govern-
ments, both at central and provincial level. This is highlighted, for example, in the course of the 6th c. when under Justinian, certain cost-cutting
measures in respect of the state postal system were instituted—Lydus'
account and Procopius' critical remarks on this from the *Anekdota* are

---

[2] For the nature and speed of movement of information under various conditions, see
the important discussion in Lee (1993) 149–65 and 166–84; and, for the Middle Byzantine
period, the advice and account regarding information-gathering in Const. Porph. *Three
Treatises* (B) 18–33; also Dagron and Mihaescu (1986) 248–54 on spies and other sources
of information. Intelligence gathering operations and methods are discussed by Koutrakou
(1995) and (1999–2000). See also Haldon (2013) commentary to Leo, *Taktika* 17.171–74 and
18.661–68.

[3] Lee (1993); Shepard (1985). The literature on the physical and organisational aspects
of Late Roman frontiers is vast, as reference to such journals as *Limes* will testify.

[4] For a general account of the evolution of Byzantine strategy across this period, see
Haldon (1999a) 34–66, 71–85.

well-known, even if the effects the emperor's policy is supposed to have had on some aspects of provincial economy remain the subject of debate among historians. In fact, it is clear that Justinian did very little to damage communications relevant to warfare on the eastern or Balkan fronts, even if substantial economies were made; and that certain key routes were maintained that had a specific relevance to these theatres.[5]

One of the recognised achievements of Roman armies up to the late 2nd c. A.D. was the construction of a network of major arterial roads suitable for the rapid movement of information, men and materials from the inner provinces to the frontiers, and connecting these provinces to one another and to major political centres. During the later 3rd c., this system was further expanded in certain frontier districts, linking military bases and forts to their sources of supply, for example, and facilitating the movement of small and larger bodies of troops to meet external threats. The network associated with the *Strata Diocletiana* in Arabia, for example, has received a great deal of attention from historians.

But there took place dramatic changes in these arrangements over the period from the later 4th–7th c. A.D., which we may reasonably characterise as a gradual decline in the standard of many—if not most—major public roads. The reasons remain unclear and under-researched: in terms of maintenance and upkeep, it seems in part to reflect a shift in priorities and in particular an unwillingness on the part of provincial cities to allocate the necessary resources. Already the *Codex Theodosianus* laws of the later 4th c. and early 5th c. regret the poor state of many roads.[6] A 5th c. historian notes that the western sections of the *Via Egnatia*—the major route westwards from Constantinople to the Adriatic coast—was in such a state of disrepair that travellers could barely pass along it; while in the last years of the 6th c., the General Comentiolus supposedly had to rely on an aged local man to find the military road leading south from the Danube plain through the 'Gates of Trajan'. While the latter event took place at a time when the government, either centrally or at local level, had little or no control over these regions, it illustrates how rapidly the physical fabric of the road system could degrade without regular upkeep.

---

[5] See Hendy (1985) 295, 605–609; Joh. Lydus, *Mag.* 3.61; Procop. *Anec.* 30.3–11.

[6] For the *Strata Diocletiana* and its strategic significance, see Eadie (1996) 72–82. For the general state of the roads by the late 4th and 5th c., see *Cod. Theod.* 15.3.4 (A.D. 412), which refers to 'the immense ruin of the highways' throughout the Prefecture of the East. Procopius describes a section of the *Via Egnatia* as almost impassable in wet weather: Procop. *Aed.* 4.8.5.

But the route was known and regularly used throughout the Byzantine period, and Constantine VII, in the 10th c., notes that it took an individual 8 days to travel from Thessalonica to Belgrade (Singidunum) along it (with pauses).[7] Even if the story of Comentiolus is exaggerated, it is indicative of what contemporaries thought about the road system in the region. In addition, the transformation in the role of urban centres during the Late Roman period must have had equally dramatic consequences for the upkeep of the provincial road systems, since it had been local municipalities which had borne the chief responsibility for maintaining the roads in their administrative territories.[8]

The change in the fortunes of the Roman road network seems also in part to reflect the availability, or non-availability, of the requisite engineering skills in the Army. Evidence about other aspects of Late Roman engineering and technical know-how would support the notion of a decline in high-level technical skills applied to military engineering: the move during the 5th–6th c. A.D. from torsion-powered artillery, which requires fairly complex construction techniques as well as highly-trained artificers, to tension-powered machines, is one example, although there are others.[9] Yet there is plenty of evidence from fortification and defensive architecture—quite apart from other secular and in particular ecclesiastical architecture—to show that a sufficient knowledge in engineering was available to maintain often very elaborate and sophisticated military building. Why less effort appears to have been invested in road maintenance—if that is indeed what the sources are telling us—remains an as yet unanswered question, and deserves greater attention from both historians (cultural and political) and archaeologists. Certainly, it would appear to be the case that Late Roman and Byzantine culture seems—as

---

[7] *Via Egnatia*: Malchus of Philadelphia, §18 (127); Comentiolus: Theoph. Sim. 8.4.3–8 (Whitby and Whitby (1986) 214). For Constantine's remark: Const. Porph. *DAI* §42.15–18. For rates of travel in the Byzantine period, see now Belke (2010) 50–56 with literature and sources. The differential between the speed of an individual and a body of soldiers is clear from the remark of Theophylact Simocatta in the early 7th c. that a somewhat shorter journey—from Drizipera in Thrace (between modern Lüleburgaz and Corlu) to Dorostolon (Dristra, mod. Silistra) on the Danube—for a field army could take 20 days: see Theoph. Sim. 6.6.5 (Whitby and Whitby (1986) 167).

[8] See Haldon (1997) 92–124.

[9] This concerns double-spring torsion weapons only, since the balance between the two springs is crucial. Horizontally-mounted single-spring torsion weapons, such as the *onager*, seem to have continued in use throughout the medieval world, although evidence for them is sparse. See the valuable discussion in Chevedden (1995); and for the (apparent) continued use of torsion machines in the non-Byzantine medieval world, see Nicolle (1996) I, 50, 99; II, 47, 85.

in other fields—to have invested its knowledge and intellectual wealth differently from the ways in which it did so during the previous period, relying upon, but not further developing, the inheritance of the Romano-Hellenistic past.

Whatever the cultural significance of these changes may be, only in the area of a few major cities—chiefly, in fact, around Constantinople—is there evidence for road maintenance or repair work undertaken by the state, and much of this comes from the middle of the 6th c. A.D., associated with the Emperor Justinian's building schemes. Procopius reports that efforts were made to re-surface short stretches of road along the *Via Egnatia* between Constantinople and Rhegion, for example, along the main highway from Bithynia to Phrygia, as well as on the road from Antioch in Syria northwards across the mountains into Cilicia (a dangerous route at the best of times, as Procopius notes). Justinian is also credited by Procopius with repairing or building several bridges—across the Sangarios and Drakôn rivers in Bithynia, or the Siberis in Galatia.[10] And there is a decent amount of epigraphic evidence from across the empire for work of this sort being carried on fairly regularly.[11] But, after this time, there is no evidence for any central direction of road-building or maintenance in the provinces, except on a purely *ad hoc* basis, even in the laudatory accounts of the building programmes of emperors such as Basil I in the second half of the 9th c.

Roads were, however, certainly maintained and, in the case of some bridges, newly constructed.[12] Some bridges survived well into the Middle Byzantine period in this way—several historians report the existence of the strategically vital bridge at Zompos (or Zompê) over the Sangarios in the 11th and early 12th c. A.D.[13] Late Roman and Byzantine sources make it clear that road and bridge maintenance was achieved through the compulsory duties imposed upon local communities by local military or provincial authorities, and sanctioned by the central government. Obligations

---

[10] Procop. *Aed.* 4.8.4–9; 5.2.12–14; 3.4–6, 8–10, 12–15; 4.1–4; 5.1–7. But there are a number of problems with Procopius' account, and his reports should not always be taken at face value. See Whitby (1985); and Greatrex (1994).

[11] E.g. Beševliev (1964) 2 no. 3 (an inscription from Serdica [Sofia] dated to A.D. 580 recording repairs to an aqueduct under a certain Julianus, bearing the rank of *candidatus*).

[12] For a good short survey of the key issues and literature, see Belke (2008) 295–308; and Hild (2010) 106–107.

[13] See Attaleiates, 145.20; Bryennios, 2.14 (169.8); Anna Comnena, 15.4 (Sewter (1969) 482).

in the 4th–6th c., such as *viarum et pontium sollicitudo*, known certainly from the 9th c. and probably before by a variety of terms such as *odostrô-sia* or *gephyrôsis*, occur in various sources from the Late Roman period, up to the 12th c. and beyond.[14]

But the results seem to have been patchy. Not all roads were of the same standard, nor were they constructed for the same purpose. Byzantine sources often differentiate between wide roads and narrow roads or paths, between paved and unpaved roads, and between roads that were suitable for wagons or wheeled vehicles and other roads. A 10th c. treatise on frontier warfare distinguishes 'public roads', maintained at least irregularly by the local administration through compulsory services imposed on local communities, from paths and tracks of a humbler nature. Other Middle Byzantine sources refer to 'public' as opposed to 'imperial' roads, sometimes combining or interchanging the two, suggesting a clear imperial involvement and association in their upkeep.[15] Procopius notes with pride the fact that the re-paved sections of road between the capital and Rhegion were wide enough to permit two wagons to pass each other.[16] Roads that were strategically important to the state may in general have been maintained more regularly, and by the means noted already. Yet the majority of these routes, even the major arterial roads, were often mere tracks, and even where formerly well-paved had generally decayed substantially by the 8th and 9th c. Basil I had to lay branches and logs along the back road leading out of Koukousos in A.D. 877 to make it passable.[17]

However degraded paved Roman roads became, a clearly-defined system of predominantly military routes, along which imperial and provincial marching camps were established, evolves from the 7th c. onwards in response to the transformed strategic situation of the empire. A similar pattern emerges also in the Balkans. While based in both cases on the pre-existing Roman network, the new emphasis reflects a specifically Byzantine strategic response to invasion in both regions. In many districts, the roads of the Late Roman period seem to have continued in use, in spite of their gradual dilapidation, at least until they became so pot-holed and

---

[14] See, for example, the imperial prescriptions incorporated into the 5th c. *Codex Theodosianus*, and repeated or replaced in the 6th c. legislation of Justianian: *Cod. Theod.* 9.16.15, 16.18, 15.3.6; *Cod. Iust.* 1.2.5; *Nov. Iust.* 131.5; repeated again in the early 10th c. codification, the *Basilika* 5.1.4; 5.3.6. For local military authorities responsible: Leo, *Taktika* 20.71 (Dennis ed. 560. 344–54).

[15] See Dagron and Mihaescu (1986) 219.

[16] Procop. *Aed.* 4.8. 4–9.

[17] Theoph., *cont.* 280.13–14; and Anderson (1896) 138–39.

irregular that even pack-animals and soldiers could not pass.[18] In addition, at least from the later 8th c. (although possibly before), a system of marching-camps or *aplekta* had evolved, which served as major supply-centres as well as points at which substantial forces could be assembled, and which lay at key points along the military road system leading to the Syrian frontier or the Armenian frontier of the empire in Anatolia.[19]

In both the Balkans and Asia Minor, these routes can be traced, to some extent at least, both by their description in a variety of sources, as well as by occasional material traces. This system of roads was then supplemented by the imperial post, a complex set of institutions derived from the Late Roman *cursus publicus* which, in the 8th c. and afterwards, incorporated both a rapid courier service as well as arrangements for dealing with the billeting of imperial officials, soldiers, provision of draught-animals and mounts.[20] Together, imperial military roads and courier service constituted the fundamental element in the state's intelligence and information activities, permitting the rapid movement of information from one part of the empire to another.

The process of gathering intelligence about enemy movements was fundamental, and it was not simply enemy movements that concerned the planners. We are informed about aspects of this from 9th and 10th c. documents. Exact information about the state of the roads or tracks to be followed by the army was required, about the availability of water and fodder for the animals, and about the crossing points of rivers or the various defiles through the mountains that the Army would have to negotiate.[21] In all cases, commanders were advised to send small parties well ahead of the main force to secure these against enemy action.[22] Especial emphasis was placed on the work and skills of the scouts sent

---

[18] Since their maintenance was a localised and infrequent matter, many must have become little more than paths or tracks unsuitable for any wheeled vehicles at all by the 6th and 7th c. For a good overview of the Roman road system in Asia Minor, see the map edited by Calder and Bean (1958); and for the later Byzantine situation, see the overview, with further literature and archaeological materials, by Belke (2008); for aspects of the Byzantine road system in the later 11th and 12th c., see Hild (2010).

[19] For discussion of Byzantine road networks in Anatolia, see Koder (2012); Const. Porph. *Three Treatises*, Introd. 62–65; text (A) and commentary at 155–57; Haldon (1999a) 150–51.

[20] For the operations of the postal system in the Middle Byzantine period, see Laurent (1981) 289–99, 487–97.

[21] Const. Porph, *Three Treatises* (B) 1–17, 39–42, (C) 116–20; *Campaign Organisation* §18; Nikephoros Ouranos, *Tactica* §63.1. For the 6th c., much of this is implicit or directly discussed in Books 7–11 of the *Strategikon*, ascribed to the Emperor Maurice.

[22] See, for example, *Campaign Organisation* §19.

out to check that water-supplies were adequate along the route, and those who planned and laid out the marching camps, the sites of which had to be chosen with regard to water, cover, defensibility and forage.[23] The need for good, reliable scouts with local knowledge of roads, passes and river crossings is constantly emphasised in both the military treatises and the historians' accounts, and highlights the uncertainty and difficulty attendant upon any military undertaking in a context in which both major routes and local tracks were generally of such poor quality.[24]

The final aspect of the physical context I want briefly to look at concerns the frontier and related installations through which the East Roman State attempted to keep an eye on its actual or potential enemies, and through which much of the information that the local or imperial military administration needed was collected or passed. Archaeologically, these arrangements have barely begun to be studied, but a few examples from which we may generalise throw light on the system in general. The first point to be made is that such systems were not static, that they evolved and continued to evolve across the history of the empire and on all fronts, and depended to a large degree less on the empire's military organisation than on its political strength or weakness and the effectiveness of its diplomacy.

In the Taurus and anti-Taurus frontier regions, for example, it is clear from both Byzantine and Arab sources that certain fortresses and installations were constant bones of contention—names such as Loulon, Koukousos, Podandos, Rhodandos, for example, recur endlessly through the histories and chronicles of the period. Hardly a decade passed across the period from the A.D. 660s to the 760s when these strong-points are not mentioned as targets for one side or the other—as soon as Arab forces had managed to seize or force the surrender of one, the imperial forces struck back, sometimes surprising the enemy in mid-winter, at other times, re-taking them as part of the regular spring and summer campaigning seasons. But these strongholds were supported by other sets of installations about which we have very little information—lookout posts at highpoints along the chain of mountains; and refuges to which local people with their movables could be evacuated. Some of this system can be traced, although hardly dated precisely—only the location of some places

---

[23] *Campaign Organisation* §§1, 6, 7, 30.
[24] The treatises on imperial expeditions note the importance of sending both an advance division to prepare the way and of employing suitably qualified scouts: see Const. Porph. *Three Treatises* (B) 116–21, (C) 564–65, and commentary with other sources, 171.

suggests the date, since this was a frontier region only from the later 7th into the early 10th c.

We obtain a glimpse of Byzantine attitudes to these installations in the 9th c. anonymous treatise on strategy. Traditionally considered a 6th c. text, it is becoming clear that, even if sections, possibly substantial sections, are derived from older treatises, much of the material reflects 9th c. conditions and assumptions.[25] Two sections in particular are relevant, Books 9 and 12, on forts (*phrouria*) and on building a 'city' (*polis*). The first thing that strikes the reader is that the 'city' in question is in fact a (small) fortress:

> Suitable sites for building a city, especially if it is going to be fairly close to the border, are those on high ground with steep slopes all about to make approach difficult. Also suitable, are sites with large rivers flowing around them or which can be made to do so, and which, because of the nature of the land, cannot easily be diverted. Finally, there are sites on a promontory in the sea, or in very large rivers connected to the mainland only by a very narrow isthmus. (*Strategy* 11.3–9).[26]

The section on *phrouria* is especially interesting. The text tells us that their function is to observe the approach of the enemy, to receive deserters, and to prevent people from fleeing to the enemy. Such installations should be near the routes they are meant to observe, but not obvious enough to attract attention. They should exploit natural features for their defence, they should have a small garrison without their families, and the troops posted there should be relieved at regular intervals. All these characteristics are repeated in the later, mid 10th c. treatise on shadowing or guerrilla warfare, where outposts should be situated on 'high and rugged mountains', some three or four miles apart, and relieved every two weeks. What is meant by the term *phrourion* thus becomes clear—a small, defended post with minimal facilities, relatively inconspicuous, easily abandoned, and recovered after the enemy have moved past, and essential for maintaining a watching brief on hostile incursions.[27]

---

[25] *Strategy*. For the re-dating, see Zuckerman (1990); Cosentino (2000); Rance (2007).

[26] Definitions of what a *polis* was varied by author and literary context, of course. Certainly by the 9th c., the terms *polis* and *kastron* were often employed synonymously, although it is also clear that some authors reserved *polis* for something more than a fortress. See Haldon (1999b); Brandes (1999).

[27] *Strategy* 9; *Skirmishing* 1. It is worth underlining the fact that the descriptions of a frontier context, of the forts and 'cities' which are situated there and their function in watching for enemy movements, and a number of related topics, all fit the context of the 8th-10th c. far better than that of the Late Roman period, thus reinforcing the arguments

Modern surveys of the Cappadocian frontier suggest at least three bands of forts and fortresses covering, first, the passes into Roman territory, second, the roads north of the Taurus and Anti-Taurus, and finally, those protecting the more important fortified centres. Along the fringe of imperially-controlled territory, fortresses such as Loulon, Podandos, Rhodandos and Lykandos stood as major obstacles and garrisons, each with a chain of minor forts covering them. In southern Cappadocia, the natural barriers represented by the Hasan Dağı and the Melendiz Dağları were strengthened by fortresses such as Argaios, Koron, Antigous and Nakida; and behind these, lay a further ring of forts and towers, as exemplified by the ruins at sites such as Hisn Sinan, Yenipınar, Neroassos and Kyzistra. And, finally, in inner Cappadocia, forts covered the major routes—the route from Sebasteia to Melitene; the road from Caesarea to Germanikeia; the road from Ankyra to Sebasteia; the road from Ankyra to Caesarea; and from Caesarea to Melitene. Even the most important of these strongholds or guard-posts was quite small. A fortress such as Loulon, for example, which also guarded the mines of the area, is a classic example. Perched on a rocky outcrop 2,100 m above sea-level, its walls encircle an area of approximately 40 × 60 m, within which shelter for the garrison as well as cisterns for their water-supply were accommodated.

The numerous fortified strongholds controlling key routes across the region, such as Kyzistra,[28] Semalouos *kastron*,[29] Podandos, Rhodandos (which also protected an iron-producing district),[30] and the many other outposts revealed by recent surveys, were of a very similar nature. These seem often to have been the seats of local military commanders—*tourmarchai*, for example—and thus also, probably by the early 8th c., centres of administration and justice. Saniana, for example, situated on a hill overlooking the Halys some 76 km south-east of Ankyra, was of similar size, and became the headquarters of a *tourma* in the later 9th c., having

put forward by Cosentino and Rance that this text is—at least in many of its sections—a product of the Byzantine rather than the Late Roman world.

[28] Hild and Restlé (1981) 219–20. Known as Dhu l-Qila' in the Arabic sources, Kyzistra controlled the road from the south—Podandos and Tyana—to Caesarea. Sited on a 1,557 m high eminence, its upper fort was some 40 × 30 m in area, with a lower fortress and defended outwork on the promontories below.

[29] For Semaluos, see Hild and Restle (1981) 276; and for Loulon, 223–24 (it was also the site of the first in the chain of fire-beacons which stretched across Asia Minor to Constantinople during the 9th c.: see Haldon comm. to Const. Porph. *Three Treatises*, 254–55). It overlooked the road from Caesarea to Ankyra, played a major role in the raiding warfare of the 7th–9th c., yet occupied an area of just 60 × 30 m.

[30] Hild and Restle (1981) 261–62 and 266–67.

served also as the base of Gazarenos Koloniates, one of the comrades-in-arms of Thomas the Slav in the A.D. 820s.[31] The anonymous treatise on Strategy notes that:

> The garrison in each fort should have a commanding officer entrusted with complete responsibility for the post. The men in the garrison should not have their wives and children with them . . . . . . Soldiers should not stay too long in these posts, but should be relieved at regular intervals . . . if a fort is extremely strong, so that there is no danger of its being besieged, and we can keep it provisioned without any problem, then there is no reason why the men cannot have their families reside with them . . . (*Strategy* 9.21–33).

We know next to nothing of what sort of 'officer' is meant. Provincial officers appear usually to have been responsible for maintaining the defences of such forts or fortresses, the labour habitually being provided through the imposition of the burden of *kastroktisia* on the local peasantry, although sometimes the central government stepped in where important defensive installations were concerned: an 8th c. inscription notes that a certain Symeon, imperial *spatharios*, was despatched by the Emperors Leo and Constantine to take charge of the repairs to the fortress of Rhodandos on the south-eastern frontier.[32] Life in such forts and outposts was always risk-laden, as the small fund of inscriptions from the frontier region for the 9th and 10th c. shows. Inscriptions from the region of medieval Barata (ancient Gaianoupolis, modern Maden Şehir) in Lykaonia, south-east of Ikonion, may be characteristic. The defended upper town at the site of a city of the Roman period was re-occupied from the 7th to 10th c., dated by several small churches, and suggests the sort of settlement to which much of the rural population of such a region would have recourse in time of attack. Inscriptions, probably 8th or 9th c., hint at the centrality of warfare in the lives of those who lived there: 'Here lies Mousianos, who endured many wounds', for example, or 'Here lies Philaretos Akylas, who died in the war on May 30th in the 4th indiction'. The simple reference to 'the war' is testimony enough to its endemic quality.[33]

The smaller fortified centres, almost exclusively situated on relatively inaccessible sites, well-protected by natural features, can be divided into two sub-types at least. Those alongside main routes into and across the

---

[31] Belke and Restle (1984) 222 with sources.

[32] Grégoire (1908) 434f.

[33] See Ramsay and Bell (1919) 525–26 and inscr. nos. 13, 42, 43. The dating of the inscriptions remains problematic, but sometime between the 8th and 10th c. is generally accepted.

empire must have had a defensive function, serving to police and protect the local populace, defend particular resources—for example, mines— and to guard strategic roads or routes, as well as serving also—depending on context—as refuges for the surrounding populace and their livestock. Typical sites include Neroassos, on the road from Koloneia (Aksaray) to Nakida in Cappadocia, defended by a single wall with towers and enclosing an area 100 × 50 m;[34] Alaman Kale, on a small route from Tzamandos and Malandara northwards to the Ankyra-Sebasteia road, of similar area; and Meşkiran Kalesi, on a secondary route through the mountains from Caesarea to Melitene, occupying an area of some 80 × 50 m, defended by a curtain wall and towers.[35] All have at least one defensive wall, often with traces of a *proteichisma* or outer defence, with towers and defended entrance, a cistern (often more than one) and evidence of internal structures suggestive of permanent or at least regular occupation. They would also have served as foci for the collection and further transmission of information.

Watchtowers and small guard-posts were a part of this system, although we have precious little evidence for them on the ground. A similar arrangement appears to have been operational in the Peloponnese for a while, as a 9th or 10th c. inscription on a signal-tower near Corinth attests.[36]

While the exact date of such structures is rarely certain, the architectural evidence suggests that they were occupied and in use during the period between the middle of the 7th and the 10th or 11th c., sometimes later. There are many such forts and outposts throughout Anatolia, particularly in what Ralph Lilie has suggested be seen as the second and third, or outer, defensive regions (as in fig. 1). Many of them are located on pre-Roman/pre-Hellenistic sites. Thus, places such as Kızılca Kale (a walled enclosure of approximately 50 × 35 m),[37] Bahçeli Kale,[38] Sığırlık Kale,[39] and Asar Kale,[40] all on the road from Attaleia northwards to Akrotiri in Pisidia; Asar kalesi on the *Via Sebaste* west of Ikonion;[41] Kızıl Kale on the

---

[34] Hilde and Restle (1981) 245–46. A search through the current volumes of the *Tabula Imperii Byzantini* for Anatolia will reveal scores of such sites.

[35] It is possibly to be identified with the fortress Phyrokastron mentioned in Basil I's campaign of A.D. 878: Hild and Restle (1981) 237.

[36] For the inscription, probably originally located at Acrocorinth, see Philippidis-Braat (1985) no. 41 (299–300).

[37] Belke and Mersich (1990) 306.

[38] Belke and Mersich (1990) 203.

[39] Belke and Mersich (1990) 383.

[40] Belke and Mersich (1990) 193.

[41] Belke and Mersich (1990) 93.

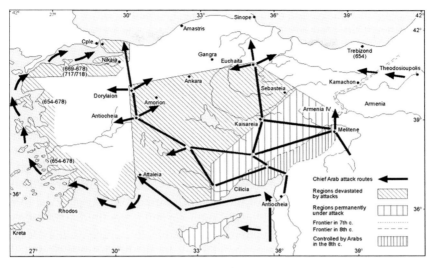

Fig. 1   Main directions of Arab attacks and strategic-defensive zones
ca. A.D. 660–740.

road from Amorion to Philomelion in Phrygia;[42] Zengicek Kale (a walled
area of *ca.* 60 × 50 m) on the road from Kongoustos to Perta in Lykaonia;[43]
or, much further north, Masıroğlu Kalesi, covering the approaches to Pom-
peioupolis in Paphlagonia,[44] are all representative. Some may have been
the headquarters of military units—Karanlı Kale in Galatia, for example,
with similar defensive features and on a similar site, has been identified
with the *topoteresia* or *bandon* of Eudokia, the headquarters for a unit of
local troops of between 50 and 300 men and commanded by a *komes*.[45]

     According to the later 10th c. treatise on shadowing or skirmishing war-
fare dedicated to the Phocas family, such places were essential elements
in the system for transmitting information about the movement of hostile
forces on imperial territory. Information was relayed from lookout posts
along the higher ground and covering the passes leading into Roman territory, posts which should be some three or four miles apart. The text
actually says:

> When they observe the enemy moving out they should quickly hurry off to
> the next station and report what they observed. In turn, those men should

---

[42] Belke and Mersich (1990) 306.
[43] Belke and Restle (1984) 245.
[44] Belke (1996) 251.
[45] Belke and Restle (1984) 186 with sources.

race off to the next station. In this way the information will eventually reach
the cavalry posts situated on more level terrain, and they will then inform
the general of the enemy incursion. (*Skirmishing* 1.8–17)

But the points at which scouts or lookouts were stationed were not always
fixed posts: the text continues: 'They should not stay in the same station
for a long time but should change and move to another place. Otherwise,
if they are too long in the same place, they will be recognised and might
easily be captured by the enemy', suggesting that in fact these scouts were
as much spies as regular scouts, who would move around the enemy concealing their military function—perhaps as merchants or peasants.

So much for the physical context. I want now briefly to turn my attention to types of information, or indeed misinformation that played a role
in determining imperial and local responses. Following the model established by Hellenistic and Roman military writers, Byzantine military texts
offer a full range of advice to the general. In all the theatres in which
Roman forces were engaged, their tactics needed to take account of the
different styles of fighting and tactical traditions of the peoples with
whom they were dealing, and the *Stratêgikon* is eloquent testimony to
the importance which Roman tactical thinking attached to understanding
one's enemy properly. The same sentiments were repeated in the *Tactica*
of Leo VI, and the later 11th c. *Stratêgikon* of Kekaumenos.

Both the *Stratêgikon* and Leo's *Tactica* describe the tactics, customs
and fighting styles of several barbarian peoples neighbouring the empire,
for example; and although Leo again derives much of what he has to say
from Maurice, he does attempt to update the information to take account
of more recent developments. During the days preceding battle, the commander should endeavour to collect and verify as much information as
possible about enemy intentions, numbers and dispositions, through spies
and scouts, enemy deserters and captured soldiers.[46] Familiarity with the
terrain was essential: only where it was favourable to the Roman forces
should battle be offered. Officers with local knowledge of roads, tracks
which might outflank major 'public' or 'imperial' routes, and sources of
water were to be preferred—local knowledge was at a premium. Commanders were urged to be aware of the state of the roads, of the pass-
ability of rivers and streams, of bridges and fords, of their own and enemy
strong-points, of where the enemy might post his own scouts and send his
spies. Information was to be collected on anything and everything that
might be relevant to hostile movement and the defensive response.

---

[46] For prisoners as spies, see Khouri al-Odetallah (1991); and esp. Patoura (1994).

Probably the best-known method of relaying information about an impending attack was the famous system of fire-signals or beacons, situated on prominences stretching from the fortress of Loulon in the Taurus, to the north of the Cilician Gates, across Asia Minor to the Bosphorus and the imperial palace itself, where a constant look-out was maintained. How long this system operated, how effective it was in practical terms, and when it was inaugurated is not clear: a 10th c. story (almost certainly spurious) maintains that it was closed down for economic reasons by the Emperor Michael III.[47] It may in fact have been closed down when it became redundant. But, local fire-signalling posts were maintained along key invasion routes on the eastern frontier regions into the 10th c., as the use of the terms *kaminobiglia*, 'watch-fires', and *kaminobiglatores*, 'watch-fire sentries', suggests. The 9th or 10th c. inscription on the watchtower in the Peloponnese noted above refers to a similar system.[48]

Finally, a word on types of information. So far I have talked about information that had specific tactical and strategic value relating to landscape, resources, roads and paths, water supplies and so forth. But information about the enemies an imperial army might face was also important, and the military handbooks as well as other texts devoted some space to this subject. The use of spies and informants was universal, and the treatises warn of the dangers of generals being misled by false information planted by spies of the enemy as well as of the problems of unreliable informants such as prisoners or deserters.[49] The late 6th c. *Stratêgikon* of the Emperor Maurice dealt in detail with 4 such peoples: the Persians, the 'Scythians' (Avars, Turks and other Hunnish peoples), the 'light-haired peoples' (Franks, Lombards and others) and the 'Slavs and Antes'. In each case, a caricature of the cultural make up of the people or peoples in question opens the chapter and, accompanied by a series of explanations for their behaviour and moral constitution, precedes the details of their tactical arrangements and usual battle formation. Each such description is accompanied by suggestions for the best ways with which to counter and defeat the enemy formation, and in both the *Stratêgikon* and in Leo's *Tactica*,

---

[47] Much discussion has been devoted to the system of fire-signals. The most sensible accounts remain Pattenden (1983), with Zuckerman (1994) 361–66. For the signal stations and further literature, see Const. Porph. *Three Treatises* (C) 614–46 and commentary, 254–55.

[48] See *Skirmishing* 2.3–10; 6.12–.13, with Pattenden (1983) 266 and n. 13. Dagron and Mihaescu (1986) 246–47 with n. 32, prefer to derive the element *kamino* from late *Lat. caminus* (cf. Fr. chemin), whereas Zuckerman (1994) 364 n. 18 follows Pattenden, correctly in my view.

[49] See Koutrakou (1995) for detailed discussion.

however much the latter depends upon its 6th c. exemplar, the need to know and to understand one's enemy, and especially not to underestimate him, is quite clearly expressed.

Although not the first treatise to note that the Romans should be familiar with the tactics and mores of their enemies, the *Stratêgikon* is nevertheless the first to go into such detail; and this reflects in part the fact that the fighting methods in question had already become part of the Late Roman tradition, and in part the fact that they reflected, so to speak, the two or three "models" of tactical and battlefield organisation which the commander of a Roman army could opt to employ.[50] The anonymous treatise 'On strategy', now thought to date to the middle or later 9th c. rather than, as traditionally assumed, the 6th c, includes details on how to conduct a campaign and in particular how to collect information and evaluate it, and although it mentions the Arabs, gives no details of their mode of warfare other than remarking that, like the Romans, 'many other peoples' make use of ambushes.[51] The Emperor Leo VI's *Tactica* repeats much of what the *Strategikon* has to say, but now includes details of the Arabs, and especially of the Tarsiots, who were a serious problem along the frontier in the later 9th c. Thereafter, it is the treatise on guerrilla strategy and tactics which provides the most detailed account of how to deal with the enemy along the eastern front, and another later 10th c. manual on campaign organisation describes warfare in the Balkans, although in this case enemy tactics are only discussed in terms of generalisations about not falling into ambushes and related topics.[52]

As well as being useful, of course, information was also potentially dangerous. The fear of false information and rumours which might upset or demoralise or panic the troops is clear in all the military treatises, and there are several stories in the histories of the period which bear this out. Leo's *Tactica* advises generals to beware of the misinterpretation of signs and portents among the soldiery, and to make sure that they spread

---

[50] For the Persians: *Strategikon* 11.1 (with variations on the Arabs, Leo, *Taktika*, 18.23–24, 104–34); for the Scythians (Turks): *Strategikon* 11.2; Leo, *Taktika* 18.40–72; on the Franks, Lombards and western peoples: *Strategikon* 11.3; Leo, *Taktika* 18.76–92; and on the Slavs: *Strategikon* 11.4; Leo, *Taktika* 18.93–101. For the tactical models implicit in the *Stratêgikon*, see the discussion of Dagron (1993).

[51] *Strategy* 8, 20, 62, 63.

[52] Byzantine descriptions of their enemies, along with the cultural knowledge and assumptions which such descriptions reflect, are discussed in detail in Wiita (1977). See also the discussion of Dagron (1987); and the commentary to Constitution 18 of Leo's *Taktika* in Haldon (2013).

favourable predictions to avoid demoralising the soldiers. On imperial expeditions, emperors were advised to take along not just military handbooks and literature relevant to the practice of war, but also astrological and horoscopic books which would assist them in foretelling the outcome. The emperor should take

> an oneirocritical book; a book of chances and occurrences; a book dealing with good and bad weather and storms, rain and lightning and thunder and the vehemence of the winds; and in addition to these, a treatise on thunder and a treatise on earthquakes, and other books, such as those to which sailors are wont to refer. (*Const. Porph., Three Treatises*, (C) 199–202).[53]

One or two examples of this tradition occur in the narrative sources, as when the Emperor Constantine VI was told by the court astrologer that if he attacked the Bulgar army facing him at Markellai in Thrace he would win, although several of the generals, who considered their tactical situation unsound, advised against this. Constantine duly attacked, and his army suffered a serious defeat. In spite of the powerful influence of Christian theology and dogma, pre-Christian traditions of this sort continued to have a certain influence. Alexios I reached a decision by writing down two possible courses of action on separate bits of paper, leaving them on the altar of a church during a night of prayer, and waiting to see which one God's will directed the priest to pick up first on entering the building the next morning. The Emperor Manuel I reportedly placed considerable emphasis on astrology and its predictive potential in such contexts, with similar unfortunate consequences.[54]

Both the physical structures through which information was gathered and deployed—roads, forts and fortresses, watchtowers and so forth—and the types of information that were deployed, were crucial means through which the medieval East Roman State secured its frontiers and assured its survival. While they were in themselves only one element of a complex set of practices and assumptions, they nevertheless illustrate the relative sophistication of Middle Byzantine defence.

---

[53] The books used by sailors for 'reading the weather' were not simply navigational aids, some were compiled specifically with naval warfare in mind, and included substantial horoscopic elements, and determined, in addition, on what days of the week naval warfare should be undertaken or avoided. See Dagron (1990).

[54] For Constantine VI: see Theophanes 467–68 (Mango and Scott (1997) 643). On astrology in Byzantium, see Kazhdan *et al.* (1991) art. 'Astrology', 214–16; art. 'Horoscope', 947–48. For Alexios I: Anna Comnena, 15.4 (Sewter (1969) 481–82); for Manuel I: Niketas Choniates, 95–96.

ACKNOWLEDGEMENTS

My sincere thanks to the anonymous readers of this contribution for their
very helpful remarks and suggestions.

BIBLIOGRAPHY

Primary Sources

Anna Comnena = Reinsch D. R. and Kambylis A. (2001) edd. *Annae Comnenae Alexias*
  (CFHB 50/1) (Berlin and New York 2001).
Attaleiates = Bekker I. (1853) ed. *Michaelis Attaliotae Historia* (Bonn 1853).
Basilika = Scheltema H. J. and Van Der Wal N. (1955) edd. *Basilika Basilicorum libri LX*, ser.
  A, 8 vols. (Groningen 1955).
Bryennios = Gautier P. (1975) ed. *Nicephori Bryennii Historiarum libri quattuor* (*Corpus Fon-
  tium Historiae Byzantinae* 9) (Brussels 1975).
Campaign Organisation and *Tactics* = Dennis G. T. (1985) text, trans. and notes. *Three
  Byzantine Military Treatises* (Corpus fontium historiae 25, Dumbarton Oaks Texts 9)
  (Washington D.C. 1985) 246–335.
Cod. Iust. and *Nov. Iust.* = Krüger P. (1892–95) ed. *Corpus Juris Civilis* I: *Institutiones*; Mom-
  msen Th. (1892–95) ed. *Corpus Juris Civilis* II: *Digesta*; Krüger P. (1892–95) ed. *Corpus
  Juris Civilis* III: *Codex Iustinianus*; Schöll R. and Kroll W. (1982–95) edd. *Corpus Juris
  Civilis* III: *Novellae* (Berlin 1892–95, repr. 1945–1963).
Cod. Theod. = Mommsen Th., Meyer P. *et al.* (1905) edd. *Theodosiani libri xvi cum constitu-
  tionibus Sirmondianis* (Berlin 1905).
Const. Porph. *Three Treatises* = Haldon J. F. (1990) ed. trans. and comm. Constantine
  Porphyrogenitus, *Three Treatises on Imperial Military Expeditions* (CFHB 28) (Vienna
  1990).
Const. Porph. *DAI* = Jenkins R. J. H. (1962) trans. and comm. Constantine Porphyrogenitus,
  De Administrando Imperio II (London 1962) and Moravcsik Gy. (1967) Greek ed. Con-
  stantine Porphyrogenitus, *De Administrando Imperio* I (Washington D.C. 1967).
Leo, *Taktika* = Dennis G. T. (2010) ed. trans. and comm. *The Taktika of Leo VI: Text, Transla-
  tion and Commentary* (*Corpus fontium historiae Byzantinae* 49, Dumbarton Oaks Texts
  12) (Washington, DC 2010).
Joh. Lydus, *Mag.* = Wünsch R. (1903) ed. *De magistratibus Ioannis Laurentii Lydi De magis-
  tratibus populi Romani libri tres* (Leipzig 1903).
Malchus = Müller C. and Th. (1874–85) *Fragmenta Historicorum Graecorum* 5 vols. (Paris
  1874–85).
Niketas Choniates = *Nicetae Choniatae Historia*, ed. J.A. Van Dieten, 2 vols. (CFHB 11/1–2)
  (Berlin, New York 1975).
Nikephoros Ouranos, *Tactica* = McGeer E. (1995) ed. and notes. *Sowing the Dragon's Teeth:
  Byzantine Warfare in the Tenth Century* (*DOS* XXXIII, Washington D.C. 1995) 88–167.
Procop. *Anec.* = Haury J. (1905–13) ed. Procopius, *Historia arcana*, in *Procopii Caesariensis
  Opera Omnia* 3 vols. (Leipzig 1905–13; revised ed. with corr. and addns. G. Wirth, Leipzig
  1962–64, 4 vols.).
Procop. *Aed.* = Haury J. (1905–13) ed. *Procopii Caesariensis Opera Omnia* 3 vols. (Leipzig
  1905–13; revised ed. with corr. and addns. G. Wirth, Leipzig 1962–64, 4 vols.).
Skirmishing = Dennis G. T. (1985) text, trans. and notes. *Three Byzantine Military Treatises* (Corpus fontium historiae 25, Dumbarton Oaks Texts 9) (Washington D.C. 1985)
  137–239.

Strategikon = Dennis G. T. (1984) ed. *Maurice's Strategikon. Handbook of Byzantine Military Strategy* (Philadelphia 1984) and Dennis G. T. ed. and Gamillscheg E. trans. (1981) *Das Strategikon des Maurikios* (CFHB 17) (Vienna 1981).

Strategy = *The Anonymous Byzantine Treatise on Strategy*, in Dennis G. T. (1985) text, trans. and notes. *Three Byzantine Military Treatises* (Corpus fontium historiae 25, Dumbarton Oaks Texts 9) (Washington D.C. 1985) 1–136.

Theophanes = de Boor C. (1883, 1885) ed. *Theophanis Chronographia* 2 vols. (Leipzig 1883, 1885).

Theoph. *cont.* = Bekker I. (1825) ed. *Theophanes Continuatus, Ioannes Caminiata, Symeon Magister, Georgius Monachus Continuatus* (Bonn 1825) 1–481.

Theoph. Sim. = de Boor C. (1887) *Theophylacti Simocattae Historia* (Leipzig 1887; rev. and amended ed. P. Wirth, Stuttgart 1972).

Secondary Works

Anderson J. G. C. (1896) "The campaign of Basil I against the Paulicians in 872", *CR* 10 (1896) 138–39.

Belke K. (1996) *Paphlagonien und Honorias* (Tabula Imperii Byzantini 9; Denkschr. d. Österr. Akad. d Wiss., phil.-hist. Kl. 249) (Vienna 1996).

—— (2008) "Communications: roads and bridges", in *The Oxford Handbook of Byzantine Studies*, edd. E. Jeffreys, J. F. Haldon and R. Cormack (Oxford 2008) 295–308.

—— (2010) "Verkehrsmittel und Reise- bzw. Transportgeschwindigkeit zu Lande im byzantinischen Reich", in *Handelsgüter und Verkehrswege. Aspekte der Warenversorgung im östlichen Mittelmeerraum (4. bis 15. Jahrhundert)*, edd. E. Kislinger, J. Koder, and A. Külzer (Vienna 2010) 45–58.

Belke K. and Mersich N. (1990) *Phrygien und Pisidien* (Tabula Imperii Byzantini 7; Denkschr. d. Österr. Akad. d Wiss., phil.-hist. Kl. 211) (Vienna 1990).

Belke K. with Restle M. (1984) *Galatien und Lykaonien* (Tabula Imperii Byzantini 4; Denkschr. d. Österr. Akad. d Wiss., phil.-hist. Kl. 172) (Vienna 1984).

Beševliev V. (1964) *Spätgriechische und spätlateinische Inschriften aus Bulgarien* (Berliner Byzantinistische Arbeiten 30) (Berlin 1964).

Brandes W. (1999) "Byzantine towns in the seventh and eighth century—different sources, different histories?", in *The Idea and Ideal of the Town between Late Antiquity and the Early Middle Ages*, edd. G. P. Brogiolo and B. Ward-Perkins (The Transformation of the Roman World 4) (Leiden, Boston and Köln 1999) 25–57.

Brogiolo G. P. and Ward-Perkins B. (1999) edd. *The Idea and Ideal of the Town between Late Antiquity and the Early Middle Ages* (The Transformation of the Roman World 4) (Leiden, Boston and Köln 1999).

Calder W. M., Bean G. E. and J. G. C. Anderson (1958) *A Classical Map of Asia Minor* (London 1958).

Chevedden P. E. (1995) "Artillery in Late Antiquity: prelude to the Middle Ages", in *The Medieval City under Siege*, edd. I. A. Corfis and M. Wolfe (Woodbridge 1995) 131–73.

Cosentino S. (2000) "The Syrianos' 'Strategikon': a ninth-century source?" *Byzantinistica* 184 (2000) 243–80.

Dagron G. (1987) "Ceux d'en face: les peuples étrangers dans les traités militaires byzantins", *TravMém* 10 (1987) 207–32.

—— (1990) "Das Firmament soll christlich werden. Zu zwei Seefahrtskalendern des 10. Jahrhunderts", in *Fest und Alltag in Byzanz*, edd. G. Prinzing, D. Simon and H.-G. Beck (Munich 1990) 145–56, 210–15.

—— (1993) "Modèles de combattants et technologie militaire dans the *Stratègikon* de Maurice", in *L'armée romaine et les barbares du IIIe au VIIe siècle*, edd. F. Vallet and M. Kazanski (Mémoires de l'Association française d'archéologie mérovingienne 5) (Paris 1993) 279–84.

Dagron G. and Mihaescu H. (1986) *Le traité sur la Guérilla* (*De velitatione*) *de l'empereur Nicéphore Phocas* (*963–969*). Texte établi par Gilbert Dagron et Haralambie Mihaescu, trad. et comm. par G. Dagron (Paris 1986).

Dennis G. T. (1984) trans. *Maurice's Strategikon: Handbook of Byzantine Military Strategy* (Philadelphia 1984).

—— (1985) Text, trans. and notes *Three Byzantine Military Treatises* (Corpus fontium historiae 25, Dumbarton Oaks Texts 9) (Washington D.C. 1985).

Eadie J. (1996) "The transformation of the eastern frontier, 260–305", in *Shifting frontiers in late Antiquity*, edd. R. W. Mathisen and H. S. Sivan (Aldershot 1996) 72–82.

Greatrex G. (1994) "The dates of Procopius' works", *BMGS* 18 (1994) 101–14.

Grégoire H. (1908) "Note sur une inscription gréco-araméenne trouvée à Farasa", *CRAI* (Paris 1908) 434.

Haldon J. F. (1997) *Byzantium in the Seventh Century: the Transformation of a Culture* (Cambridge 1997).

—— (1999a) *Warfare, State and Society in the Byzantine World, 565–1204* (London 1999).

—— (1999b) "The idea of the town in the Byzantine Empire", in *The Idea and Ideal of the Town between Late Antiquity and the Early Middle Ages*, edd. G. P. Brogiolo and B. Ward-Perkins (The Transformation of the Roman World 4) (Leiden, Boston and Köln 1999) 1–24.

—— (2013) *The Taktika of Leo the Wise: Critical Commentary* (Washington D.C. 2013).

Hendy M. F. (1985) *Studies in the Byzantine Monetary Economy c. 300–1450* (Cambridge 1985).

Hild F. (2010) "Verkehrswege zu Lande: die Wege der Kreuzfahrer des ersten und zweiten Kreuzzuges in Kleinasien", in *Handelsgüter und Verkehrswege. Aspekte der Warenversorgung im östlichen Mittelmeerraum* (*4. bis 15. Jahrhundert*), edd. E. Kislinger, J. Koder, and A. Külzer (Vienna 2010) 105–25.

Hild F. and Restlé M. (1981) *Tabula Imperii Byzantini* 2: *Kappadokien* (*Kappadokia, Charsianon, Sebasteia und Lykandos*) (Denkschr. d. Österr. Akad. d Wiss., phil.-hist. Kl. 149) (Vienna 1981).

Kaplony A. (1996) *Konstantinopel und Damaskos. Gesandtschaften und Verträge zwischen Kaisern und Kalifen 639–750. Untersuchungen zum Gewohnheits-Völkerrecht und zur interkulturellen Diplomatie* (Islamkundliche Untersuchungen 208) (Berlin 1996).

Kazhdan A. P., Talbot A.-M., Cutler A., Gregory T. E. and Ševčenko N. P. (1991) edd. *The Oxford Dictionary of Byzantium* (Oxford and New York 1991).

Khouri al-Odetallah R. A. (1991) "Unofficial exchanges, purchases and emancipations of Byzantine and Arab war captives", *Graeco-Arabica* 4 (1991) 109–13.

Kislinger E., Koder J. and Külzer A. (2010) edd. *Handelsgüter und Verkehrswege. Aspekte der Warenversorgung im östlichen Mittelmeerraum* (*4. bis 15. Jahrhundert*) (Vienna 2010).

Koder J. (2012) "Regional networks in Byzantine Asia Minor during the middle Byzantine period. An approach", in *Trade and Markets in Byzantium*, ed. C. Morrisson (Washington D.C. 2012) 147–75.

Koutrakou N. (1995) "Diplomacy and espionage: their role in Byzantine foreign relations, 8th-10th centuries", *Graeco-Arabica* 6 (1995) 125–44.

—— (1999–2000) "'Spies of towns'. Some remarks on espionage in the context of Byzantine-Arab relations (VIIth-Xth centuries)", *Graeco-Arabica* 7–8 (1999–2000) 243–66.

Laurent V. (1981) *Le Corpus des sceaux de l'empire byzantin, II: l'administration centrale* (Paris 1981).

Lee A. D. (1993) *Information and Frontiers: Roman Foreign Relations in Late Antiquity* (Cambridge 1993).

Mango C. and Scott R. with Greatrex G. (1997) trans. with intro. and comm. *The Chronicle of Theophanes Confessor: Byzantine and Near Eastern History, A.D. 284–813* (Oxford 1997).

Nicolle D. (1996) *Medieval Warfare Source Book I: Warfare in Western Christendom* (London 1996).

Patoura S. (1994) *Oi aichmalotoi hos paragontes epikoinonias plerophoreses* (Greek=*Prisoners of War as Agents of Communication and Information*) (Athens 1994).

Pattenden P. (1983) "The Byzantine early warning system", *Byzantion* 53 (1983) 258–99.

Philippidis-Braat A. (1985) "Inscriptions du IXe au XVe siècle", in Feissel D. and Philippidis-Braat A., "Inventaires en vue d'un recueil des inscriptions historiques de Byzance. III. Inscriptions du Péloponnèse (à l'exception de Mistra), II", *TravMém* 9 (1985) 267–395.

Ramsay W. M. and Bell G. (1909) *The Thousand and One Churches* (London 1909).

Rance P. (2007) "The date of the military compendium of Syrianus Magister (formerly the sixth-century Anonymus Byzantinus)", *BZ* 100 (2007) 701–37.

Rochow I. (2001) "Zu den diplomatischen Beziehungen zwischen Byzanz und dem Kalifat in der Zeit der syrischen Dynastie (717–802)", in *Novum Millennium: Studies on Byzantine history and culture dedicated to Paul Speck 19 December 1999*, edd. C. Sode and S. A. Takács (Aldershot 2001) 305–25.

Sewter E. R. A. (1969) *The Alexiad of the Princess Anna Comnena* (Harmondsworth 1969).

Shepard J. (1985) "Information, disinformation and delay in Byzantine diplomacy", *Byzantinische Forschungen* 10 (1985) 233–93.

Vallet F. and Kazanski M. (1993) edd. *L'armée romaine et les barbares du IIIe au VIIe siècle* (Mémoires de l'Association française d'archéologie mérovingienne 5) (Paris 1993).

Whitby M. (1985) "Justinian's bridge over the Sangarios and the date of the De Aedificiis", *JHS* 105 (1985) 129–48.

Whitby M. and Whitby Mary (1986) *The History of Theophylact Simocatta: an English Translation with Introduction and Notes* (Oxford 1986).

Wiita J. (1977) *The Ethnika in Byzantine Military Treatises* (Ph.D. diss., Univ. of Minnesota 1977).

Zuckerman C. (1990) "The military compendium of Syrianus Magister", *JöB* 40 (1990) 209–24.

—— (1994) "Chapitres peu connus de l'*Apparatus bellicis*", *TravMém* 12 (1994) 359–89.

LIST OF FIGURE

FORTIFICATIONS AND SIEGE WARFARE

FORTIFICATION AND THE LATE ROMAN EAST: FROM URBAN WALLS TO LONG WALLS

James Crow

Abstract

Fortifications are major surviving structures from the late antique world. This article demonstrates the great range of defences constructed across the East Roman Empire, beginning with a case study of the walls of Antioch based on late 18th c. engravings and revealing the scale of a major imperial 5th c. project now largely lost. The survey then reviews evidence from Asia Minor, where there is more limited evidence for new defences. On the eastern frontier, the great fortress cities are well known, but attention is drawn to fortified settlements within the frontier zone in both Roman Mesopotamia and the Balkan provinces. In the Balkan regions, however, a more elaborate response to security was the construction of a number of internal barrier walls, including the Anastasian Wall in Thrace and the newly discovered Haemus Gates. The conclusion assesses the role of fortification in the late antique world and considers the importance of providing multivocal interpretations across the frontiers of the East Roman Empire, engaging both the rich archaeological and textual sources.

INTRODUCTION

For it is not the pyramids we are about to describe, those celebrated monuments of the rulers of Egypt, on which labour was expended for useless show, but rather all the fortifications whereby this emperor preserved the empire, walling it about and frustrating the attacks of the barbarians on the Romans. And it seems to me not amiss to start from the Persian frontier. (Procop. *Aed.* 2.1.3).

At first sight, warfare and fortifications would seem to be responses to human conflicts involving communities larger than tribes, while the active engagement in warfare is a process, a series of decisions, actions and events often catastrophic for one side or the other, demanding huge resources, but sometimes resulting in vast gains of booty or territory. On the other hand fortifications and defences are the material legacy of either state or communal concerns and a consequence of capital expenditure for security or an active element in the conduct of war. Warfare in literate societies

A. Sarantis, N. Christie (edd.) *War and Warfare in Late Antiquity: Current Perspectives*
(Late Antique Archaeology 8.1–8.2 – 2010–11) (Leiden 2013), pp. 397–432

has been memorialised in popular and elite narrative and poetry from which later history is written. Work on fortifications can be recorded in texts, as in the quotation above, and in inscriptions, but more importantly can also survive as the physical setting and relics of campaigns and as a reflection of the social and political needs for both protection and display from all periods.[1] Although the discipline of Battlefield Archaeology is gaining significance for the understanding of warfare in ancient and modern periods, it is reasonable to claim that the archaeological study of fortifications still has much to offer for a proper understanding of society and warfare in late antique and Early Medieval Europe and the Near East.

This paper aims to provide a short overview of the significance of fortifications throughout the East Roman Empire in peace and war, considering certain aspects of the design and maintenance of military and urban fortifications across the 5th–7th c. A.D., with particular reference to the eastern Balkans, Asia Minor and Roman Mesopotamia. Fortifications had an important role in the conduct of warfare, especially as the eastern provinces came under increasingly frequent attacks across the Lower Danube and in Mesopotamia, where fortified cities were the focus for major campaigns and diplomatic negotiations between Rome and the Sassanians for over two centuries. This latter zone of conflict between the two great super-powers of Late Antiquity features some of the best documented sieges known from the ancient world.[2]

By way of contrast, throughout the southern Balkans, and especially well documented in modern Bulgaria and Macedonia (FYROM), there is extensive evidence for a myriad of fortified hilltop settlements and townships.[3] Founded and constructed in response to greater insecurity and the repeated failure of the river frontiers to withstand external invasions from the later 4th c. onwards, the Balkan defences describe a fortified landscape at variance with the contemporary rhetorical claims of 6th c. writers such as Procopius.[4] Through the study of the archaeological evidence for these

---

[1] Recent publications relating to the significance of fortifications in prehistory: Parkinson *et al.* (2007); and a return to typological approaches of defensive features: Keeley *et al.* (2007). For the Balkans, see the welcome publication of Ćurčić's (2010) new survey of ecclesiastical, military and urban architecture from the Tetrarchs to the Ottomans.

[2] See recently Crow (2007b) with references. Gregory's study (1995) of these fortresses often lacks personal observation. For an historian's view on fortifications as part of the infrastructure of war, see Lee (2007) 98–100.

[3] For Macedonia, see Mikulčić (2002); and review by Ćurčić (2007). For Bulgaria, see Poulter (2007); and Dinchev (2006) and (2007).

[4] 'Wishing as he did to make the Danube the strongest possible line of first defence before them and before the whole of Europe, he distributed numerous fortifications along the

frontiers and for extensive constructions throughout the eastern provinces, it will become apparent that the eastern Roman state responded in
different regions in quite distinct ways and at different times.

GREAT CITIES: CONSTANTINOPLE TO ANTIOCH

Under Augustus, almost uniquely amongst the great city-states of Antiquity, the city of Rome became an 'open city': it no longer relied on walls
and fortifications for its security,[5] and instead it came to define a new
urban topography unrestrained by walls, protected by the strength of the
potential force of its imperial armies—a pattern followed by new Roman
foundations in the Mediterranean provinces of the empire, such as Aphrodisias and Hierapolis in Asia.[6] Nothing so clearly defines the transformed
physical world of Late Antiquity from that of the High Empire as the great
defences created for Constantinople, the new Rome on the Bosporus.
First, under its founder Constantine and then, less than a century later,
to accommodate urban expansion under Theodosius II, the landward
defences of the city define fortifications as an example of urban display
not apparent in classical urbanism since the great circuits of Hellenistic Asia Minor.[7] But the Constantinopolitan land walls were not merely
for show: their scale and extent were unprecedented in the ancient and
Medieval eras, and the new fortifications demonstrated the effectiveness
of passive strength to deter the city's attackers.[8] Constantinople was not
alone among the great cities of the eastern empire, and major new circuits

---

bank of the river . . . and he placed garrisons of troops everywhere along the bank, in order
to check the crossings of the barbarians'—Procop. *Aed.* 4.1.33. Note the emphasis in this
passage on imperial concern for the *ripa* or river frontier. See Zuckerman (1998) 123–24.

[5] Haselberger (2007) 220–37.

[6] See De Staebler (2008) for a review of the evidence from Aphrodisias. Although walled
cities continued to be constructed in the north-west provinces of the empire, the extent to
which the earlier Hellenstic circuits of the cities of Asia (e.g. Assos) remained intact has
not been properly assessed. See now the important discussion in Niewöhner (2011).

[7] McNicoll (1997). Virtually nothing is known of the Constantinian walls— for references see Crow (2001) 91–92.

[8] Foss and Winfield (1986) 42–47 provide a concise introduction. For recent discussion, see Crow (2001) for a review of the evidence, and see now Crow (2007a) 262–68,
plus Asutay-Effenberger (2007). Theophanes AM 6305 records how, in A.D. 813, the Krum,
Bulgar khan, having defeated Byzantine armies throughout Thrace, reached the city and,
'Having admired the walls of the city and the emperor's well-ordered array, and giving up
hope of the siege he had contemplated, he had course for negotiation and made some
tentative proposals for peace' (Mango and Scott (1997) 686).

were constructed at Thessalonica[9] in the middle of the 5th c. and at Antioch under Theodosius II.

The circuit walls of the Syrian metropolis have received less attention than they deserve since huge sections were demolished in the mid-19th c.

The main surviving lengths of wall are known to survive from around the heights of Mt Silpius and are clearly visible from Google Earth images of the site.[10] However, the prominence of the walls for ancient Antioch is reflected in a set of six detailed folio engravings, executed by Louis-François Cassas in 1784–85 as part of the publication of his journey to record monuments in Syria and Egypt (*Voyage pittoresque de la Syrie, de la Palestine, et de la Basse-Egypte*).[11] These provide a remarkable record of the walls, comparable in many respects with the near contemporary land

Fig. 1   The south curtain of the Antioch wall from within the city
(Cassas (1799) pl. 7).[12]

---

[9] Speiser (1999); Velenis (1998); Bakirtzis and Oreopoulos (2001); Crow (2001) 93–98. Velenis prefers a date of *ca.* 400 for the main reconstruction with extensive use of brick facings and projecting towers, whereas other commentators prefer to associate the Hormisdas inscription with the mid-5th c., see now Rizos (2011).

[10] See Appendix.

[11] Auzépy and Grélois (2001) 122–23.

[12] See now the study of the walls of Mt Silpius following a recent survey in Brasse (2010).

walls of Constantinople. The engravings have been often reproduced,[13] although to my knowledge there has been little attempt to interpret how they can inform the defences' structural history and consequently the city's urban history.[14] This discussion is intended to provide a commentary on this important visual record and to draw some wider architectural and historical observations about the defences of what was the most important city in the Roman East (see figs. 1 and 2).

Comparison of selected Cassas images with later archival photographs indicates that the late 18th c. views of the city and its monumental walls can be used with some confidence. Thus Cassas' view of the Iron Gate located in the gorge north of the citadel compares favourably with two photographs reproduced in Förster's study,[15] with the slightly later photograph in the Gertrude Bell archive, and with a more detailed photograph published by Dussaud.[16] Cassas shows a pathway to the left which is clear on the Bell photograph of 1905, but not apparent from the Antioch Excavation Committee photograph of 1934. Förster's two photographs show greater detail, confirming the two central upper arched openings seen in the Cassas view, but contradicting the buttress to the right and the lower arched opening, both apparent from an 18th c. engraving. What is most clearly exaggerated is not the structural detail—which is rendered with attention and limited embellishment—but the wild pinnacles and rocks of the Bab el-Hadid gorge, which have been elevated for due romantic effect. Another Cassas view (seen from south of the citadel) shows walls and towers along the top of Mount Silpius and descending towards the south; in the foreground and to the left of a tree, part of a tower and clearly differing masonry types are illustrated.

---

[13] A Cassas view is reproduced as the cover for Foss and Winfield's *Byzantine Fortifications* (1986) and also fig. 27. The clearest reproductions are in Downey (1963) figs. 6–11; see also Kondoleon (2000); a number are reproduced by Förster (1897), who also includes some views of Antioch from Bartlett—see Downey (1961) 671. The plates reproduced here are from the copy of Cassas' portfolios in the Special Collections in Edinburgh University Library.

[14] Foss and Winfield (1986) 30 draw attention to the great prow-shaped tower on the south curtain seen in the Cassas view. Note that the map of Antioch in Foss and Winfield (1986) fig. 31 derives from Rey's map of Antioch (1871), where the cardinal point faces west, not north. Förster (1897) made the same error with important consequences in following Rey's account of the walls. Deichmann (1979) 481 draws comparison with the Theodosian walls of Constantinople.

[15] Förster (1897) figs. 9, 10.

[16] See the Cassas view in Downey (1963) fig. 9. For early photographs after Förster: Bell Website Archive C067; Dussaud (1931). For the Antioch Excavation Committee 1934 view, see Downey (1961) 17.

Fig. 2   Detail of Cassas' view across the south-east slopes of Mount Silpius
(Cassas (1799) pl 4). Note the blind arcading which may represent the same view
as fig. 3, but reversed.

In the centre of the image there is a high standing tower, partly within the
circuit, with four wide arched openings in the upper storey facing north.
This corresponds to the large tower east of the southern summit of Mount
Silpius. From the Cassas view, as the wall and towers descend towards the
South, on part of the inner face of the curtain wall, 9 arcades are depicted.
Arcades similar to this are shown in a drawing and plan of the walls of
Antioch published by Rey,[17] although this drawing, which also shows a
multi-angular pointed tower, indicates the wall climbing from the left, not
as shown by Cassas.

It is either not the same place or was erroneously inverted by Rey's
draftsman (the latter explanation is the more likely). The main tower represented by Cassas can be identified with the large tower seen east of
the southern summit of the mountain. A photograph taken in 1974 shows

---

[17] Rey (1871) fig. 51.

Fig. 3   The inner face of the curtain on Mount Silpius. Possibly a similar view to fig. 2—see Rey (1871) fig 48.

Fig. 4   Detail of a rectangular tower south of the citadel on Mount Silpius.
(Photo by Crow in 1974.)

details of this tower constructed with alternate courses of large block-work, 10 rows of brick-work and upper ones of small blocks (or *petit appareil*). The upper arcaded section does not survive, although large openings and casemates are not uncommon from other late antique towers, such as Heraclea-Perinthus in eastern Thrace, and Tocra in Libya.[18]

The descent of the curtain and towers towards the plain south of the city is clearly shown in another Cassas plate (fig. 1). Whilst significant traces of the curtain still survive on Mount Silpius, on the lower sector, the walls were almost entirely demolished in the mid-19th c.[19] This Cassas view presents the south walls in monumental grandeur comparable only to the land walls of Constantinople: tall rectangular and polygonal interval towers project in front of a high upstanding curtain built of alternating brick and stone blocks. Views by Bartlett in the early 19th c. are partly derivative, but also show how, unlike the alternating rectangular and U-shaped towers from Constantinople, many of the towers in Antioch's

---

[18] Crow and Ricci (1997); Smith and Crow (1998) 46–48.

[19] See fragments of the wall shown in the Gertrude Bell photograph taken in April 1905—Archive Co68. Förster (1897) 129 reports that the walls were demolished to construct barracks.

lower curtain have prow-shaped fronts. These majestic projecting towers were, therefore, either pentagonal or heptagonal in form, a tower shape adopted by military architects from the 5th c. on both the Lower Danube and Mesopotamian frontiers; a variation of this, the triangular tower, or redans, is found at Thessalonica from the mid-5th c.[20]

A distinctive feature is the use of brick relieving arches around the windows in the upper face of the walls; these show very close resemblance to the 5th c. land walls of Constantinople, constructed from the time of Arcadius onwards.[21] One feature quite different from Constantinople is the evidence for enclosed staircases constructed on the inner face of the two lower towers. Enclosed staircases provided greater security for the wall walk and towers and are a common feature of many late antique defences, such as Zenobia Halibiye; elsewhere, it was common to provide open access, as at Resafa and Constantinople itself.[22] On sections of the curtain, Cassas also indicates a cornice at the top of the inner face suggesting a wall walk; but the only indication for a parapet is shown in the distant view, and this appears too regular to be relied upon. There is no evidence for a galleried parapet as is known from Dara under Anastasius and also found at Constantinople and elsewhere in the eastern provinces.[23]

The textual history of Antioch's walls is discussed at some length as part of Downey's *A History of Antioch* and especially his Topographical Excursus on the city.[24] He describes how the south wall of the city was extended to incorporate an outer suburb and a new Daphne Gate known as the Golden Gate. He argues that these date from the reign of Theodosius II and in particular can be associated with the visit of the Empress Eudocia on her journey to Jerusalem in 433. In the context of elite female benefaction, this would be a rare involvement in major fortifications, a field of patronage normally involving emperors, generals, city prefects

[20] Smith and Crow (1997) 70–71, fig. 25; Crow (2001) 97–103; Foss and Winfield (1986) 30. Poly-angular towers of this type are also found on the Anastasian Wall in Thrace—see Crow and Ricci (1997). See Rizos (2011), and for the use of brick stamps to date the walls, Theocridou (2004).

[21] For the chronology, see Bardill (2004) 122–23, and pl. 3 showing tower 7 from the land walls; see now the detailed discussion of the chronology in Asutay-Effenberger (2007) 35–53.

[22] For the towers of Zenobia, see Lauffray (1983) figs. 38, 41, 42; for Resafa, see Karnapp (1976).

[23] Crow (2007a) 266–67.

[24] Downey (1961) *Excursus* 10, 612–21.

and bishops.[25] Downey shows some awareness of the differing construction methods seen from the remains at Antioch since, in his discussion of Procopius' account of the measures taken to control the winter torrent through the Iron Gates (Bab el-Hadid), he notes that the 1934 photograph shows "masonry characteristic of Justinian's time".[26] Earlier illustrations of this dam from Cassas onwards (noted above) reveal at least two main phases and show lower work, wider, and set forward towards the city, constructed, as Cassas' view of the south curtain wall shows, with alternate stone and brick bonding courses succeeded by regular stone blockwork.

In his caption to Cassas' view of the south curtain, Downey describes how "the masonry of the towers is characteristic of the period of Justinian"[27]— clearly it is the banded work that he considered to be Justinianic. The basis of his statement is unclear, since the predominant construction techniques and material for the great majority of 6th c. fortresses in Syria and Mesopotamia comprised cut-stone blocks, and the employment of brick bonding courses and vaults is an unusual form of construction over much of eastern Anatolia and Syria.[28] A notable exception is the palace and church at Qasr-ibn-Wardan, dated to 564, which included brick bands and vaulting.[29] Rather than being of Justinianic date, the south curtain at Antioch is a major work of fortification dating from the early 5th c.

Another pair of Cassas views of the North Gate (both external and internal) at Antioch leading to Beroea show construction in stone block-work quite distinct from brick and stone courses seen from the south curtain. From the exterior, this appears a single portal gate flanked by two large rectangular towers (see fig. 5). There is an outer wall (*proteichisma*) with a wide arch, flanked to the left (east) by the remains of a tower. The inner gate can be seen to comprise two entrances, the outer comprising a lower wall pierced by a gateway with a lintel formed by a flat arch. From the outside, it is clear there is a well-defined cornice along the top of this wall. Behind is a second gateway, in line with the rear face of the flanking towers,

---

[25] Eudocia's visits, see Downey (1961) 450–52. A main source is Evagr. 1.20 (Whitby (2000) 48–49, n. 176). Evagrius reports that Eudocia was also responsible for commissioning re-building of the walls of Jerusalem amongst other works in the city: 1.22—see Whitby (2000) 52; and James (2004) 53–54 for the contemporary work of female patrons in Constantinople, none of whom were linked to major programmes of fortification.

[26] Downey (1961) 551, fig. 17.

[27] Downey (1963) fig. 7.

[28] The walls and gate of Chalcis can be dated to 550–51: see Foudrin (1994). For a more general discussion of construction methods in late antique Syria and the specific use of brick, see Deichmann (1979).

[29] Krautheimer (1965) pls. 94, 95.

Fig. 5   Exterior of the Beroea Gate, Antioch (Cassas (1799) pl. 5).

with a high curtain and vaulted arch. The internal view of the gate shows clearly that there is a sequence of three entrances leading in from the *pro-teichisma* to the outer lower main gate in the gate passage and the inner, higher-arched gateway.

The inside of the inner gateway features an ornamental moulding with well-defined brackets at the springing of the arch. Two parallel walls continue the line of the gate passage within the city, but while there is no clear indication of yet another inner gate, it is apparent that these inner walls are not carried to the full height of the main curtain. The flanking towers were entered by lower entrances with a well-defined relieving arch and flat arch lintel. In the left entrance, this does not survive, which could suggest that a similar lintel for the main inner entrance has collapsed. A difficulty in using archival material for a structure that no longer survives is how to define differing phases of building, especially at Antioch, where it is known that the Late Roman walls continued to function for another six or seven centuries (there is clear repair work shown at the right corner of the right/west projecting tower). Despite this reservation, it is reasonable to assume that the majority of the work shown at the Beroea Gate belongs to Late Antiquity. All of the surviving archways show the use of the flat arch lintel, an unusual feature, better documented in Rome and Ostia, but known also from late antique Cilicia.[30]

---

[30] For a recent review of Islamic fortifications, see Northedge (2008), esp. fig. 5 for a view of the Hamdanid Gate from Anavarza in Cilicia.

The illustrations of the Beroea Gate thus provide vital evidence for late antique Antioch, revealing the importance of monumental gateways both as places of defence and display. Defence is demonstrated by the massive flanking towers, the outer wall and gate, and the two inner gates; one through a fore-wall, and the second through the main inner gate curtain between them. The latter was a forecourt, similar in function to the medieval barbican. In other Late Roman gateways there is often a courtyard behind, termed a vantage court, but the arrangement at Antioch is rare and can be best paralleled at the North Gate of Resafa, where a fore-wall shields the elaborate gate facing towards Raqqa. The complex architectural decoration of the North Gate at Resafa[31] is unmatched elsewhere, but the South or Golden Gate at Antioch (leading towards Daphne) may have rivalled it in elaboration and grandeur, the appropriate setting for the *adventus* of an emperor.[32] Recent epigraphic research has drawn attention to the continuing practice in selected cities of Asia Minor of memorialising the acclamations of city processions,[33] but in Syria and Mesopotamia, acclamations are specifically known from gateways. At Amida, inscriptions celebrated the *stratelates* Theodore and offer 'long life to the walls', and at Kyrrhos, a decorated keystone from the upper citadel has an acclamation to Justinian and Theodora.[34] Walls continued to act as epigraphic billboards, and at Mayyāfāriqīn (modern Silvan) in Roman Mesopotamia, Mango has suggested that a Greek inscription was set up on the walls by Chosroes II between A.D. 591 and 593, during a period of peace between Rome and Persia.[35]

FRONTIER REGIONS

Fortifications such as Antioch were amongst the greatest construction enterprises in the 5th and 6th c. But, even at a lesser scale, the efforts of fortification multiplied across the cities and defended settlements of the eastern empire remain a remarkable legacy, even if they too often fail to inspire like the public buildings and churches of Late Antiquity do. A full

---

[31] Crow (2007b) 440–43.
[32] Downey (1961) 615–16.
[33] Roueché (1999).
[34] Mango and Mango (1991); note also Justinianic acclamations from Hierapolis and Ma'an—see Feissel (2000) 98.
[35] Mango (1985) 101–103, fig. 9.

review is beyond the scope of this paper, but the great imperial works of Antioch and Constantinople shared proximity to potential and real threats from across the frontiers to the East.[36] In contrast, the early imperial cities of the western provinces of Asia Minor had followed the pattern of Rome by neglecting defences, and it is only in the later 4th c. that it is possible to see concern for urban defences, especially amongst some of the new provincial capitals such as Aphrodisias.[37] In certain specific instances, urban fortifications had begun before that time: at Nicaea and Nicomedia, the main defences provide evidence for imperially-derived works from the later 3rd c.[38] Fortifications in western Asia Minor are less well-documented in the 6th c., and few merit inclusion in Book 5 of Procopius' *The Buildings*.[39] Significantly, the reduction of the defences of the city of Miletus to around the theatre has now been attributed to an action of the 7th–8th c., rather than the 6th, as previously argued, and it is doubtful if extensive programmes of urban refortification can be demonstrated in western Asia Minor before the late 6th c.[40]

Urban fortification can often be seen to be part of the continuing process of imperial patronage, although in the case of two cities in central and northern Anatolia, Amorion and Euchaita, it remains unclear why these particular cities were selected. For the former, a later chronicler suggests the walls were constructed under Zeno, and a later 5th c. date is confirmed by archaeological evidence.[41] At Euchaita, which was a

---

[36] See Libanius' comments on Antioch as the great eastern campaign base against the Sassanians—Lib. *Or.* 11.177–80; Norman (2000) 42–43. The walls themselves are barely noted in the oration dated to 356.

[37] See now De Staebler (2008) for a study of the walls of Aphrodisias, arguing for the active role of the new governors. See, however, the comments of Ward-Perkins (1984) 192–94 for northern Italy between the 4th and 5th c., noting the epigraphic evidence for many of the Asia Minor cities. This has recently been collected in Lewin (1991), esp. 86–90. Note also important discussions by Niewöhner (2007), esp. 122–25 and (2010), on Anatolia. See also the new collection of studies on late antique Asia Minor, which considers a number of fortified cities, although it does not consider these in a wider context and excludes, for example, any mention of Nicaea (Dally and Ratté (2011)).

[38] For Nicaea: Crow (2001) 90–91; Nicomedia: Foss (1996).

[39] In part, this is due to Procopius' decision to prioritise specific themes in certain books. Thus, his Book 5 is primarily concerned with churches, bridges and communications, whilst defences are the dominant feature of Books 2 and 3, concerned with the eastern provinces, and of Book 4 for the Balkans.

[40] Niewöhner (2008). See the rural fortifications at Alacaoluk and Asartepe in the eastern hinterland of Troy, south of the sea of Marmara (Rose (2011)). For Cyprus at this period, see Balandier (2004).

[41] Crow (2001) 99–100. For recent excavations here, see Ivison (2007) 35–37.

developing major pilgrimage centre dedicated to St. Theodore the Recruit, two major inscriptions of Anastasius record the building of the walls and the foundation of the new bishopric.[42] Although these epigraphic texts may be recognised as chance survivals, one inscription attested the physical presence of the city and the other its sacred and regional significance. The provision of new city walls at both Amorion and Euchaita at the end of the 5th c. distinguishes these cities as part of a specific imperial investment; significantly, these strong circuits were also to provide a crucial and contingent asset later on, in the period of the long-term invasions and crises which afflicted the heartlands of Anatolia and western Asia Minor from the beginning of the 7th c.[43] In other parts of southern and central Asia Minor, new city walls were constructed, and although precise chronologies remain insecure, many are as likely to be a response to increasing problems of banditry and local insurrection, especially from Isauria and its neighbouring provinces, as from any major threat from beyond the frontiers.[44]

As we move our perspective eastward, towards the frontier lands of the Euphrates and Tigris, the presence of Late Roman fortifications becomes more common. Procopius records work on the city of Caesarea in Cappadocia, although the surviving walls are largely Seljuk in date.[45] According to Malalas, attacks by Hunnic tribes across the Caucasus into eastern Anatolia in 516 prompted Anastasius to construct defences for villages (*komai*).[46] Such village fortifications are more difficult to identify, and the subject has received little attention outside the frontier regions[47] and for the former western provinces and North Africa, where Bryan Ward-Perkins has observed that: "The pattern of rural defence in our period is perhaps best understood in terms of the emergence of selected strongholds, leaving most settlements undefended, rather than as a widespread

---

[42] Mango and Ševčenko (1972); also Haarer (2006) 71. For the ongoing Avkat survey project, see http://www.princeton.edu/avkat/reports/.

[43] Lightfoot (2007) 105 notes that in the building of the monumental South Gate at Amorium, all the stonework was newly quarried, not the ubiquitous *spolia* normal in the late urban circuits in Asia Minor.

[44] For Sagalassos, see Vanhaverbeke *et al.* (2007). The Isaurian problem continued into Anastasius' reign: Haarer (2006) ch.2; but the use of defended cities in civil conflict is best attested by the siege of Cremna in A.D. 278: Mitchell (1995).

[45] Gabriel (1931). An unpublished survey by the late Michael Balance provides the clearest study of the 6th c. fortifications at Kayseri, which incorporated two tiers of blind arcade behind the curtain.

[46] Haarer (2006) 70.

[47] See, however, the discussion in Decker (2009) 61–65 of fortified estates, farms and towers in Syria, Palestine and Arabia.

attempt to fortify every rural dwelling or to move people into enclosed defensible sites".[48] Eastern Cappadocia was notoriously poorly urbanised and it is likely that larger villages will have received walls without achieving the status of a city. One possible example is the large rectangular walled enclosure at Viranşehir, close to the modern road from Kayseri to Malatya.[49]

Roman Mesopotamia

Within the main frontier zone of Roman Mesopotamia and northern Syria, the major cities were subject to imperial programmes of construction and renovation from the 4th c. onwards. Despite their location on the contested border lands between Rome and Persia,[50] some of these fortified urban foundations were to become flourishing new cities, comparable in size to the late provincial capitals of Asia Minor, like Aphrodisias in Caria. These new imperial strongholds also became established as centres for Syriac culture and Christianity, many surviving into medieval and modern times. The scale of defences is comparable to the eastern empire's greatest cities and can be best documented at Halibiye-Zenobia, Resafa, Dara and Diyarbekir-Amida, all new foundations in this period. These fortified circuits are characterised by massive stone built curtains, great U-shaped or rectangular projecting towers, outer-walls, and arsenals of torsion artillery.[51] Significantly, none of the new circuits from Roman Mesopotamia or North Syria match the new 5th c. fortifications of Antioch, whose multi-angular towers and distinctive brickwork are representative of the contemporary works from Thessalonica and Constantinople, defining a more direct metropolitan engagement in specific urban fortification.

As this essay's introductory quotation suggested, Book 2 of Procopius' *The Buildings* was concerned to celebrate Justinian's role as defender of the empire's frontiers. The showcase for these achievements was Dara, but in addition to the fortress cities, Procopius notes a number of *phrouria*.[52] Described as places of refuge for the local population, they are specifically not strung out along a frontier road, although some lie closer to Persian

---

[48] Ward-Perkins (2000) 336.
[49] Restle (1975). The village name has now changed to Şerefiye. The rectilinear enclosure may be viewed on Google Earth 38°56'30.20"; N 36°40'41.90"E.
[50] Isaac (1998).
[51] Crow (2007b); Zanini (2007).
[52] Procop. *Aed.* 2.4.14–21.

territory than others.[53] These smaller fortified places in Roman Mesopotamia have seen limited study,[54] although a recent consideration of the
region's church architecture has shown how Google Earth images provide
detailed views of at least two smaller fortified settlements at Zerzevan
kalesi and Hisarkaya.[55] The view of the former is much clearer than the
plan published by Deichmann and Peschlow and shows a boat-shaped
hilltop, 340 m long and 50 m across, filled by ruined streets and houses. In
plan, these Mesopotamian *phrouria* resemble much more closely the fortified settlements of the inner Balkans than the 'standard' *quadriburgium*
type of forts, constructed from the late 3rd c. onwards along the *Strata
Diocletiana* and elsewhere in the Syrian and Arabian provinces.[56] The
appearance of these former sites draws attention to the rich corpus of
late antique fortifications from the Balkan provinces.

The Balkan Provinces

Historians and archaeologists have long been perplexed by the large number of places reported by Procopius in Book 4 of *The Buildings*. Scores of
names are attested, but few can be identified, and their numbers in fact
far exceed the recorded works from the eastern frontier. How far the vast
numbers of fortified hilltop sites which extend across the prefectures of
Illyricum and Oriens from the Adriatic to the Black Sea[57] correspond to
these lists remains a major challenge. The most intensive research, combining excavation and field survey, has been conducted in the region of
Nicopolis ad Istrum, north of the Haemus Mountains (Stara Planina). Here,
an extensive landscape occupied by villas and farmsteads had become
largely denuded by the later 4th or earlier 5th c.[58]

The key question is whether the new defended settlements set back
in the foothills of the mountain ranges, away from the more fertile river

---

[53] For the topography of this region, see Dillemann (1962).

[54] Deichmann and Peschlow (1977); Weissner (1980).

[55] Keyser-Kayaalp (2009). Zerzevan kalesi 37°36'30.90N; 40°29'57.04"E; Hisarkaya 37°38'38.39"N; 40°54'32.60"E.

[56] Kennedy and Riley (1990) 172–83; See, however, rectangular forts south of Dara at Qasr Curuk, Poidebard (1934) 145, pl. 132.2.

[57] See n. 3 above; the lists do not clearly differentiate between cities and other settlements, see Sodini (2007) 314–15. For a recent survey, see Rizos (2010).

[58] Poulter (2007) esp. 46–48; Curta (2001). See also the discussion on northern Greece by Dunn (2004), although his association of defended sites with a military presence is not fully demonstrated.

valleys, represent a new form of nucleated and defended rural settlement, or whether these places are part of wider, planned imperial initiative in response to the greater threats from across the Danube posed by Goths, Huns, and other invaders. Some scholars see these defended sites as essentially a new form of village, and Ward-Perkins, contrasting the evidence from the Balkans with North Africa and the former western provinces, wrote that these (in Illyricum) "may be evidence of a different policy—of helping to provide or enhance defences for large numbers of villages and other settlements".[59] By contrast, other scholars, taking their lead from Procopius, prefer a military explanation indicative of imperial direction and provision.[60]

There has been little attempt to analyse the extensive archaeological remains from these regions, and all too often the defended settlements are merely seen to complement or illustrate the textual evidence. However, the recent publication of a number of articles and short monographs by Ventislav Dinchev provides an opportunity to review the diversity and scale of these settlements.[61] While the chronology of many sites remains insecure and further excavations are required, it is evident that mono-causal explanations are unlikely to satisfy the complexity of fortified settlements which are known throughout modern Bulgaria and elsewhere. The range of defended forts and settlements describes a broad variety of tower forms—semi-circular, pentagonal and triangular,[62] with extensive occurrence of outer-walls, often associated with quite modest hilltop defended sites. Co-ordinated military architecture from the age of Justinian is well known from the re-conquered provinces of North Africa,[63] but little or nothing from the Moesian or Thracian material reveals any close

---

[59] Ward-Perkins (2000) 336, n. 39.

[60] "Instead (of campaigning north of the Danube) Justinian began an impressive plan of fortification, of size and quality the Balkans had never witnessed before"—Curta (2005) 181; see also Curta (2001). The comparative epigraphic record of Anastasius and later emperors in the Balkan provinces is discussed in Crow (2007c); and Haarer (2006). The only secure Justinianic text from the eastern Balkans notes a defended place called *Théodórias* in the region of Varna: Feissel (2000) 93.

[61] Dinchev (1990), (2006) and (2007).

[62] At Durostorum (Silistra), excavations of the Late Roman fortress have revealed a possible polygonal fortress with pentagonal angle towers—Angelova and Buchvarov (2007) 68, figs 3, 5.1, 5.2; comparable angle towers are known from the rectangular camp at Tell Brak in north-east Syria—see Kennedy and Riley (1990) 187–88, figs. 132–34.

[63] Pringle (1981); the epigraphic record from Africa is quite different from the surviving evidence from either the eastern frontier provinces or the Balkans with 16 surviving texts, see Feissel (2000) 101.

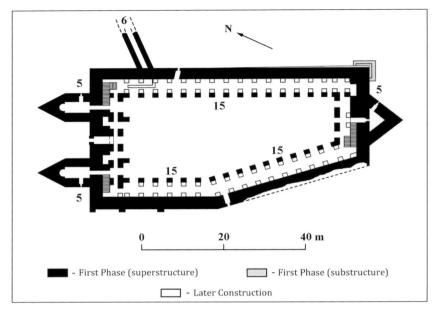

Fig. 6   The 6th c. fort at Markova Mehana in the Trajan's Gates, between Serdica
and Philippopolis (Dinchev (2007) fig. 46).

comparisons. Some forts like Markova Mehana in the Trajan's Gates are
certainly exemplars of advanced military engineering and design.

The fort is located at a point of strategic importance controlling communications on the great military road between Serdica (Sofia) and
Philippoplis (Plovdiv) leading on to Constantinople. Others are more
modest in execution and ingenuity of design, but the vast majority are
located on hilltops, indicating a desire for security away from the more
fertile open plains.

THE ANASTASIAN WALL AND THE HAEMUS GATES

A more elaborate response to the need for regional security is witnessed by
the construction of barrier walls within the Balkan provinces of Illyricum
and Oriens. Constantinople, the Thracian hinterland of the city, and the
Lower Danube provinces faced increasing barbarian invasions throughout
the 5th and 6th c.,[64] and a sequence of barrier walls was established to

---

[64] Lemerle (1954).

control movement at passes and defiles. The earliest of these were the defences of the Julian Alps, constructed in the early 4th c. to control the routes into north-eastern Italy.[65] This strategy was followed in the 5th c. by the construction of barrier walls in Greece at the Isthmus of Corinth, Thermopylae and Cassandreia, but also elsewhere in the Balkan passes and closer to Constantinople, at the Gallipoli peninsula.[66] From the historical accounts, it is clear that when these barrier walls were adequately manned, they could effectively deter barbarian invasions and raids. The technical term in Greek for these barrier walls was *to makron teichos*, 'the long wall', and significantly this phrase was also used by Procopius in his description of the remote island of Britain, in what is presumably the last classical reference to Hadrian's Wall.[67]

The most celebrated building achievement of Anastasius was the last and most monumental Roman barrier wall in Europe known as the Anastasian Wall or 'the Long Wall of Thrace'.[68] It was constructed 74 km west of Constantinople at the beginning of the 6th c A.D., probably in response to the increasing threat of new steppe invaders, the Bulgars.[69] Some doubt about an Anastasian date for the Long Wall continues to be expressed, but field survey in its southern zone has consistently recovered brick stamps which support an Anastasian rather than earlier date.[70] The wall stretches 58 km from the coast of the Black Sea in the north to the Sea of Marmara. A contemporary panegyric, praising the emperor's achievements, claimed that

> What was the grandest and passes all imagination was to raise a high and powerful wall crossing all of Thrace. It passes from sea to sea, barring the route of barbarians, an obstacle to enemy aggression. The wall of Themistocles in Athens was smaller by report. (Procopius of Gaza, 21).[71]

Survey over the past 15 years has been able to map the line of the Long Wall and identify and plan small forts, towers, and lengths of curtain surviving in the dense forest to the north.[72] Strikingly little survives for these

[65] Napoli (1997); Christie (1991).
[66] Dinchev (2008); Crow (1986); Gregory (1992), (1993) and (2000) 109–13; Crow (1995); Pazara (1987); Bakirtzis and Oreopoulos (2001) 44–45.
[67] Crow (2004).
[68] Crow (1995); Napoli (1997) 280–96; Crow (2007c); Maktav *et al.* (2009).
[69] Croke (1982) 72–74.
[70] Whitby (1985) and (2000) 183, n. 143; Haarer (2006) 106–109; but, see Bardill (2005) 124, n. 35.
[71] Chauvot (1986).
[72] See http://www.shc.ed.ac.uk/projects/longwalls/ for plans and full references to interim reports.

first 20 km apart from a scatter of stone and brick in the ploughed soil, though in places, it is possible to identify towers and the low mound of the wall itself. At the sea's edge, there is no trace of the wall, but within a few metres, it is possible to discern the dark shadow of a long mole, less than 2 m below the water, representing a long *probalos* or defence work, constructed to prevent the wall from being outflanked along the shore, similar to that described from the Chersonese Wall in the Gallipoli Peninsula.[73] From the construction debris and from trial excavations, it would appear that the wall in the southern sector may have been constructed of alternating stone and brick courses, similar in construction to many late antique city walls. The hills north of the Istanbul-Sofia railway as far as the Black Sea coast are densely forested with oak and beech, making an approach by an army difficult at any period.[74]

Where it survives best, the wall shows construction in large limestone and sandstone blocks, with a core of limestone or in some places, metamorphic rocks. The blocks and core are bonded with hard lime mortar with brick inclusions. The curtain wall is 3.2 m wide and the highest sections survive to a height of 4.5 m. In places, sections of the curtain were narrowed to 1.8 m with a series of internal arcades. Where foundations are visible, as a result of treasure hunters' activities and road building, they are 1.5–2.5 m deep. The original wall height could have reached up to 10 m; recovery of triangular-section merlon-cap stones provides the clearest evidence for a parapet and, hence, a wall-walk on the curtain. Except where the ground to the west fell away steeply, there is evidence along the entire length of a ditch, 15 m wide, located 23 m in front of the wall. This is clearly defined in satellite images of the wall and can observed on Google Earth.[75] At the small attached fort called Büyük Bedesten, a ditched outwork extends up to 80 m in front of the fort and wall. This is probably a later defensive feature associated with invasions in the later 6th or 7th c.

The curtain wall will have provided a formidable barrier, and along its length was a system of towers. At points where the line of the wall changes direction, the towers were polygonal in shape, normally pentagonal, but sometimes hexagonal. These are massive structures, projecting over 11.5 m, comparable to the largest towers from the ancient world.[76] These were clearly intended to provide platforms for torsion artillery and

---

[73] Crow and Ricci (1997).

[74] Crow (1995) 116–17.

[75] See Appendix.

[76] Crow and Ricci (1997) 239, fig. 2; see the discussion of the walls of Antioch above.

support Agathias' sarcastic account of a successful attack led by Zabergan in 558/59 which specifically mentions the absence of artillerymen:

> There was nothing to stop them, no sentries, no engines of defence, nobody to man them. There was not even the sound of a dog barking, as at least would have been the case with a pig-sty or sheep-pen. (Agathias, *Histories* 5.13.5–6).

Between these great bastions were located numerous rectangular towers, unusual for most late antique fortifications since they were 11 m wide, but in some instances projected only 2 m to the exterior; one tower extensively cleared by stone robbers revealed traces of double internal stairs and vaults.[77] The purpose of these towers may have been to provide accommodation and controlled access to the curtain wall; no external stairs have been observed. As the towers were located at distances of 80–120 m apart, a gross estimate suggests at least 340 towers along the Wall's total length.

To supplement the system of towers, there were also small forts, called in Turkish, *bedestens*. Six are documented and two have been planned in detail: the Küçük (small) and Büyük (large) *bedestens*. They are located at intervals of approximately 3.5 km apart and provided the main access points through the wall. From the two planned examples, these forts were constructed on the inner face of the wall, measuring 32 m behind the wall face and 64 m parallel to the curtain (overall dimensions of the two forts are similar; the differences in size refer to the surviving height of the walls). There were projecting rectangular towers at each of the angles. Midway along the two long axes, a gateway provided access into the fort and through the wall beyond. A micro-topographic survey of the Büyük *bedesten* shows the surviving walls, gates, and towers of the fort set in the wider topographic context.[78] There is little evidence for structures within the enclosures, and there are only very limited traces of contemporary pottery in pits dug out by stone robbers. With only limited crossing places, and with a barrier probably 10 m high, the Long Wall will have impacted strongly on movement for friend and enemy alike. In addition to the gateways at the *bedestens*, there are likely to have been major defended gateways where key West-East roads crossed the line of the wall; none of these have yet been confirmed.

---

[77] Crow and Ricci (1997) 249, fig. 8.
[78] Bayliss (2003) 288–89, fig. 6.

An inscription from the north end of the barrier wall records that it was renewed by the Emperor Heraclius and the patrician Smaragdus, indicating reconstruction probably soon after 610. However, it seems likely that the defensive line was abandoned before the Avar siege of Constantinople in 626, as Byzantium faced war on two fronts. There are no further references for active use and it subsequently fell into decay. A future monograph will discuss more fully the role, function and garrisons of the Long Wall.[79] In certain respects, the construction of such a monumental linear barrier, more an extended or advance city wall than a frontier defence, signals the inability of the East Roman State to sustain the security of the river frontiers and the Balkan passes. The presence of the Thracian wall and other linear barriers, however, marks a practical and pragmatic solution to increasing insecurity. As a measure of its success for the inhabitants of the capital, the chronicler Malalas[80] refers to it as *the Wall* of Constantinople, distinguishing it from the city's walls, which he specifically identifies as the walls of Theodosius and Constantine. A further measure of the importance of the Long Wall was that after the invasion of 558, historical accounts describe how the aged Justinian personally oversaw its restorations in a remarkable display of direct intervention outside the capital.[81]

The Haemus Gates

Recent fieldwork[82] in eastern Bulgaria, north of Messembria, has provided greater detail concerning the linear defences located in the most easterly spurs of the Balkan Mountains (*Stara Planina*), inland from the Black Sea coast, a little north of the coastal town of Obzor.

The total known length is 41 km and it comprises a series of linear barriers and forts, situated on the northern ridges of the Eminska range to the south of Dvoynitsa river and extending as far west as the Eleshnitza river. Recent excavations have been focused on the fort of Harmana, near

---

[79] See Crow (2007c); the inscription is currently under study in the Istanbul Archaeological Museum, but we are grateful to Prof. Cyril Mango for a preliminary reading.

[80] Malalas 18.129 and 18.124.

[81] Croke (1982) 69.

[82] Dinchev (2008). The unusual shape of these defences recalls the reference in Procopius concerning the circular fort at Strongylon west of Constantinople (Procop. *Aed.* 4.8; *Chron. Pasch.* 150).

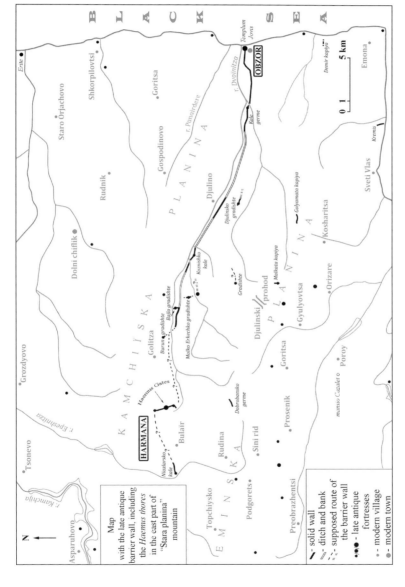

Fig. 7   Map showing the location of barrier walls at the eastern end of the Balkan Mountains. The Black Sea coast is at the extreme right. The cities of Odessos and Marcianopolis lie to the north and Anchialos and Messembria to the south of the coastal ranges (after Dinchev *et al.* (2007) fig. 70).

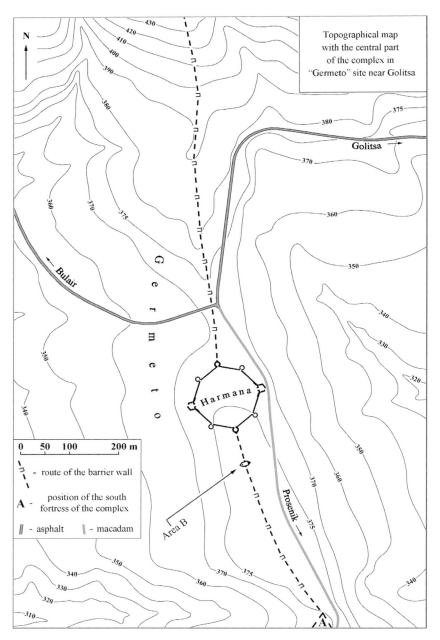

Fig. 8   Plan showing the line of the barrier wall across Germeto and the fort at
Harmana (after Dinchev *et al.* (2008) fig. 1).

Golitsa village,[83] where the line of the wall turns to run approximately North-South. This is an unusual octagonal fort, 140 m in diameter, set astride the wall, with 6 circular towers and two large pentagonal towers providing access through the line of the wall.

Dinchev identifies this as the site of the 'Haemus Gates', known from the historian Malchus as the meeting place in 478 of Theodoric Amal, leader of the Goths, and Theodoric Strabo, former *magister praesentalis*.[84] There is, however, no other specific reference in the historic accounts to the construction or active employment of this 'long wall', being only known from archaeological studies. Coin evidence from the excavations supports a 5th c. date, although earlier coins suggest activity here from the early 4th c. The overall area is very large, although soundings in the interior are as yet limited, and we lack clear evidence of how far the interior was built over. Equally intriguing is the plan of one of the excavated interval towers south of the fort, set astride the wall, with prow-shaped form to both exterior and interior.

The Abhazian Wall

At the eastern end of the Black Sea, another linear barrier is attested. In an analogous situation, between the coast and the foothills of the Abhazian Caucasus, a long wall runs 58 km inland from the mouth of the K'elasuri river, 5 km south-east of Sochumi, in a situation very similar to the Haemus Wall. The wall is noted in 6th c. Georgian sources, but it remains uncertain whether it is of Byzantine or Sassanian construction.[85] Long walls are also known from the Sassanian world, on the west and south-east sides of the Caspian Sea, at Derbent and at Gorgan. The latter wall can be dated to the later 5th or 6th c., and it is intriguing to reflect on the similar responses to the pressures exerted by the barbarian/steppe peoples from both of the two major settled empires of Late Antiquity.[86]

---

[83] Dinchev *et al.* (2007) figs. 46, 47 and (2008).
[84] Malchus, *ex. gent.* 18. 2. 14; Blockley (1983) 429.
[85] Aleksidzé (2000); the name clearly recalls the term Greek *kleisura*.
[86] Omrani Rekavandi *et al.* (2008).

Conclusion

Archaeologists and historians have become increasingly alert to the perils of using modern analogies to illuminate our understanding of past societies—'the past as foreign country' has become an overused and tired cliché, but so also has the frequent and repetitive use of 'the Maginot line' as an implied criticism of ancient linear fortifications. Enver Hoxha's pillboxes might reflect the paranoia of a 20th c. Balkan dictator, but can they really inform the workings and concerns of late antique emperors and provincial governors? If we are to accept the notion of modernity, analogies from the last century need to be applied with extreme caution to illustrate lives and policies of one and a half millennia ago. Part of the problem is the often unfavourable comparison between the Late Roman military and the armies of Caesar or Trajan. The relative uniformity of military constructions, certainly to be recognised across the camps and fortresses of the European *limites* of the Principate, was no longer apparent from the later 3rd c. onwards, although why this should be so has never been satisfactorily explained. It becomes increasingly difficult to compare 'like with like' across the empire and diachronically, and it becomes equally difficult to reconcile the claims of writers such as Procopius with the archaeological evidence for construction and defence.

In this essay, I have attempted to review a selected variety of fortified contexts ranging from the greatest cities to the unique contribution of internal linear barriers and the wide diversity of fortified settlements. By taking this intentionally broad perspective, I have aimed to demonstrate the ubiquity of fortifications throughout much of late antique society. The world view had changed: cities and settlements could no longer remain unencumbered by circuit walls and needed to revert to the closed *astē* of earlier Antiquity. But there was greater complexity than the early Greek city state, and the motivations for fortification varied according to circumstance and situation.

In reviewing the evidence as part of the built landscape of Late Antiquity, one is surprised how rarely fortifications and defences figure in recent general surveys. This attitude and prejudice does not pertain to other historic periods and cultures. Historians and art historians of the Renaissance are happy to consider the role and importance of fortifications and siege warfare as part of the primary studies of their age,[87] and a similar view applies to reviews of ancient Greek architecture and urbanism. This attitude is not reflected in a recent, valuable survey of late antique secular architecture which states: "Leaving aside works of engineering (defensive works, aqueducts and harbours)".[88] But defences and fortifications are not merely an aspect of the military affairs of the Late Empire, fit only for military historians and war gamers. Walls and gates were part of the patterns of daily life intrinsic to the settlements and cities they served; they served to protect but also to control and restrict entry and flight, and, as we have seen, gateways were places for architectural display and epigraphic announcement, integral to the public streets, stoas, and piazzas of the urban environment.

In the frontier lands beyond the urbanised core provinces of Asia Minor and the Levant, the disproportionate increase of defended places is apparent from both literary accounts and archaeological enquiry. The task of reconciling these differing sources has often provoked partisan and extreme views, hardly surprising since *The Buildings* is closer to being a spin doctor's travel brochure than the worthy guidebook it was once credited to be.[89] These diverging perspectives may defy compromise; indeed, concessions could diminish the evidential base of both the textual and material evidence. However, a wider reading of the text can allow a fuller understanding of both text and field evidence.

One example can serve in conclusion. The opposed standpoints and interpretations for the Balkan provinces have already been noted. In Book 4, Procopius presents a perplexing account of the emperor's achievements, part panegyrical eulogy as the opening quotation proclaims, but descending into bare lists of toponyms.[90] Beside this, we are aware, as already noted, of the rich corpus of archaeological evidence of fortified places. Some scholars have interpreted this as part of clear imperial defensive strategy and others have recognised both the archaeological corpus of defended settlements and the textual description as demonstrating a continued imperial involvement and support for local defence.[91] It is axiomatic that the key question is *who* resided in these fortified settlements

---

[87] See, for example, Hale (1977); Duffy (1979); Pollack (2010).

[88] Mango (2000) 924.

[89] For a recent literary perspective, see Kaldellis (2004) 55; contrast Mortimer Wheeler's grand claims (1952) 124: "they [*The Aed.*] form a datum-line from which, as archaeologists, we can work backwards towards Diocletian and Severus".

[90] See recent observations by Liebeschuetz (2007) 105–10.

[91] See n. 57 and n. 58 above.

and *who* financed their construction. Were they part of the wider pattern of large and small villages evident in the eastern provinces of the empire or were they garrisons of imperially-funded soldiers?

In comparing the defended settlements of the eastern Balkans with Roman Mesopotamia, whilst there is an obvious discrepancy between the scale of the major Mesopotamian fortress-cities and those urban survivals in the Balkans, there are very close similarities between the lesser, more numerous fortified settlements. Dinchev's studies provide a convenient collection of such fortified enclosures, including Hisarluk near Shoumen, or Gradisheto near Gabrovo. They have significant defensive circuits and the latter has clear evidence for a double defensive wall.[92] Within the enclosure walls is a dense cluster of housing with one or two churches. In appearance, their domestic dwellings and churches are not dissimilar to standing open villages known from North Syria and Rough Cilicia.

From Roman Mesopotamia, fewer sites are known or have been planned. In Book 2 of *The Buildings*, following the detailed and lengthy accounts of the emperor's works at the major fortress cities, Procopius continues to recount the renovations and new works amongst the forts (*phrouria*) of Mesopotamia located between Dara and Amida. The location of some is known, but many remain unidentified, whilst some defended sites such as Zerzevan and Hisarkaya[93] cannot readily be connected with ancient place names. However, if we can accept that these known defended sites are contemporary with the 6th c. frontier cities such as Dara, then some at least must conform to Procopius' *phrouria*. Hisarkaya is largely built over by a modern village, but Zerzevan kalesi presents a plan known from the Google Earth satellite imagery that is altogether comparable with the Balkan examples, such as Hisarlak near Shoumen, which has a walled hilltop including a dense pattern of houses and narrow streets. This is a strong candidate for being one of the forts restored by the emperor which, as Procopius describes with a rhetorical flourish, were thus made 'impregnable, so that actually they are thrown out as a mighty bulwark to shield the land of the Romans.'[94] But the text immediately continues to describe a particular project in the same district, the mountain stronghold of Basileōn, which became a secure store and a refuge for the numerous neighbouring lowland villages at times of invasion. Here, while drawing attention to the

---

[92] Dincev (2007) figs. 8, 10.
[93] See n. 53–55 above. A Justinianic inscription is known from *Bismideôn*—Feissel (2000) 97, but no remains are reported.
[94] Procop. *Aed.* 2.4.14–15.

important practical role of regional fortified places, Procopius is contrasting directly the realities of frontier life with the bombastic assertions of imperial security apparent in the phrase 'a mighty bulwark to shield the land of the Romans' directly following on from the long accounts of the reconstruction of Dara.

The written description of the fort of Basileōn and the physical remains from Zerzevan Kalesi have immediate resonances with the known forts and defended settlements of the Balkans. In this instance, the text of *The Buildings* provides two consecutive almost layered meanings, one rhetorical and the other pragmatic. What mattered for the Constantinopolitan audience were the grand strategic gestures, rhetoric which extended also to many of the epigraphic texts of the period.[95] But, what is significant for our interpretation of the extensive archaeological remains is the clear description of these defended sites as places of local security and refuge. This essay has intended to show the great diversity of fortifications throughout the eastern Roman world, from the great imperial defences at Antioch and Constantinople, vital for the maintenance of the mega-cities of Late Antiquity, to the fortified new urban centres on the eastern frontier, and to demonstrate how this variety reflects a broad range of functions and roles in contemporary society. In every instance, a monocausal explanation is not enough to do justice to the richness of the surviving archaeological and textual sources. The principal agent for these structural and settlement changes was the increasing frequency of warfare from the 5th c. onwards, although these changes reflect a broad range of state and communal responses across the provinces from the Danube to the Tigris.

APPENDIX: A NOTE ON VIEWING LATE ANTIQUE FORTRESSES ON GOOGLE EARTH

The improving resolution of many of the satellite images available through Google Earth provides the opportunity to view major cities and fortified places. Some coordinates are provided within the text, but especially clear examples may be viewed at the following sites: Antioch, the citadel on

---

[95] See Feissel (2000) for an excellent catalogue of the Justinianic building inscriptions. Note the texts from Isthmia and Byllis (92) where the scale of the works may not match the verbosity of the texts.

Mount Silpius, can be seen at 36°12'15.33"N/ 36°10'55.27"E, and the curtain with towers can be traced to the north and south along the ridge and turning south-west towards the river and the modern city.

For the Anastasian Wall, the southern end in the Sea of Marmara may be seen at 41°04'20.57"N/ 28°11'18.34". The central section of the wall frequently runs west of the forest road. This can followed north and south of the junction with the *Do20* main road at 41°18'26.59"N/ 28°19'24.47"E. The best preserved fort—the Büyük Bedesten—can be seen at 41°20'33.52"N/ 28°20'48.59"E, and the wall traced north towards the coast of the Black Sea at Evcik. The wall and wall ditch are clearly defined south of Büyük Bedesten, and an earthwork outside the fort is also visible.

ACKNOWLEDGEMENTS

I would like to thank the organisers of the Oxford conference on warfare for their invitation and hospitality, and to the editors for their patience and forbearance, especially to Neil Christie and the anonymous reviewers. I am particularly grateful to Dr. Ventzislav Dinchev for discussions about the Haemus Gates and for his permission to publish the plans and maps of these important new discoveries. I would also like to thank Riley Snyder for his assistance in re-labeling these plans in Latin characters. All other errors remain my own.

BIBLIOGRAPHY

Primary Sources

Evagr. = Whitby M. (2000) trans. and ed. *The Ecclesiastical History of Evagrius Scholasticus* (Liverpool 2000); Bidez J. and Parmentier L. (1898) edd. *The Ecclesiastical History of Evagrius with the Scholia, ed. with intr., critical notes and indices by J. Bidez and L. Parmentier* (London 1898).

Lib. *Or.* = Norman A. F. (1969–77) ed. and trans. Libanius, *Selected Works* (Cambridge, Mass 1969–77).

Malalas = Thurn I. (2000) ed. *Ionnis Malalae Chronographia* (Berlin 2000); Jeffreys E., Jeffreys M. and Scott R. (1986) trans. *The Chronicle of John Malalas* (Byzantina Australiensia 4) (Melbourne and Sydney 1986).

Malchus = Blockley R. C. (1983) ed., trans. and notes. *The Fragmentary Classicising Historians of the Later Roman Empire: Eunapius, Olympiodorus, Priscus and Malchus Vol. 2* (Liverpool and Cairns 1983).

Procop. *Aed.* = Haury J. (1905–13) ed. *Procopii Caesariensis Opera Omnia* 3 vols. (Leipzig 1905–13; revised ed. with corr. and addns. G. Wirth, Leipzig 1962–64, 4 vols.); Dewing H. B. (1940) ed. and trans. Procopius, *The Buildings* (Cambridge, Mass. and London 1940).

Theophanes = Mango C. A. and Scott C. (1997) edd. *The Chronicle of Theophanes Confessor: Byzantine and Near Eastern History, A.D. 284–813* (Oxford 1997); de Boor C. (1883, 1885) ed. *Theophanis Chronographia* 2 vols. (Leipzig 1883, 1885).

Chron. Pasch. = Dindorf L. A. (1832) ed. *Chronicon Paschale* (Bonn 1832); Whitby M. and M. (1989) trans., intr. and notes. *Chronicon Paschale 284–628 AD* (Liverpool 1989).

Secondary Works

Aleksidzé Z. (2000) "La construction de la Κλεισούρα d'après le nouveau manuscript Sinaï-tique n° 50," *TravMém* 13 (2000) 673–81.

Angelova S. and Buchvarov B. (2007) "Durostorum in Late Antiquity (fourth to seventh centuries)," in *Post-Roman Towns, Trade and Settlement in Europe and Byzantium: Vol. 2 Byzantium, Pliska, and the Balkans*, ed. J. Henning (Berlin 2007) 61–87.

Asutay-Effenberger N. (2007) *Landmauer von Konstantinopel-İstanbul historisch-topographische und baugeschichtliche Untersuchungen* (Millennium Studies 18) (Berlin 2007).

Auzépy M.-F. and Grélois J.-P. (2001) *Byzance retrouvée, érudits et voyageurs français (XVI–XVIII siècles)* (Paris 2001).

Bakirtzis N. and Oreopoulos P. (2001) *An Essay on Byzantine Fortification, Northern Greece 4th–15th c.* (Athens 2001).

Balandier C. (2004) "The defensive works of Cyprus during the late Roman and early Byz-antine periods 4th–7th c.", *Report of the Department of Antiquities, Cyprus 2003* (2004) 261–74.

Bardill J. (2005) *Brick Stamps of Constantinople* (Oxford 2005).

Bayliss R. (2003) "Archaeological survey and visualisation: the view from Byzantium", in *Theory and Practice in Late Antique Archaeology*, edd. L. Lavan and W. Bowden (Late Antique Archaeology 1) (Leiden 2003) 288–313.

Blockley R. C. (1983) *The Fragmentary Classicising Historians of the Later Roman Empire: Eunapius, Olympiodorus, Priscus and Malchus* Vol. 2, text, trans. and notes. (Liverpool and Cairns 1983).

Brasse C. "Von der stadtmauer zur Stadtgeschichte. Das Befestigungssystem von Antiocheia am Orontes," in *Neue Forschungen zu antiken Stadtbefestigungen im östlichen Mittelmeer-raum und im Vorderen Orient, Konstruktion–Funktion–Semantik*, edd. C. Wawruschka, A. Wirsching and T. Zimmer (Byzas 10) (Istanbul 2010) 261–82.

Cameron A. and Garnsey P. (1998) edd. *Cambridge Ancient History. Volume 13: The Later Empire, A.D. 337–425* (Cambridge 1998).

Cameron A., Ward-Perkins B. and Whitby M. (2000) edd. *Cambridge Ancient History. Vol-ume 14: Late Antiquity: Empire and Successors, A.D. 425–600* (Cambridge 2000).

Cassas L.-F. (1799) *Voyage pittoresque de la Syrie, de la Palestine, et de la Basse-Egypte, avec texte par Laporte-Dutheil et Langlès* (Paris 1799).

Chauvot A. (1986) *Procope de Gaza, Priscien de Cesarée, Panegyriques de l'empereur Anastase Ier* (Bonn 1986).

Christie N. (1991) "The Alps as a frontier, A.D. 168–774", *JRA* 4 (1991) 410–30.

Croke B. (1982) "The date of the Anastasian Long Wall", *GRBS* 20 (1982) 59–78.

Crow J. (2001) "Fortifications and urbanism in late antiquity: Thessaloniki and other east-ern cities", in *Recent Research on Late Antique Urbanism*, ed. L. Lavan (JRA Supplemen-tary Series 21) (Portsmouth, RI 2001) 91–107.

Crow J. (2002) "Late antique cities in eastern Thrace (Europa)", in *The Roman and Late Roman City, Proceedings of the Conference on Classical and Late Antique Urbanism, Veliko Turnovo 2000*, edd. L. Ruseva-Slokoska, R. T. Ivanov and V. Dinchev (Sofia 2002) 342–51.

—— (2004) "The northern frontier of Britain from Trajan to Antoninus Pius: Roman build-ers and native Britons", in *A Companion to Roman Britain*, ed. M. Todd (Oxford 2004) 114–35.

428   JAMES CROW

—— (2007a) "The infrastructures of a Great City: earth, walls and water in late antique Constantinople", in *Technology in Transition: A.D. 300–650*, edd. L. Lavan, E. Zanini and A. Sarantis (Late Antique Archaeology 4) (Leiden and Boston 2007) 251–85.

—— (2007b) "Amida and Tropeum Traiani, a comparison of two late antique frontier cities", in *The Transition to Late Antiquity on the Danube and Beyond*, ed. A. G. Poulter (Proceedings of the British Academy 141) (London 2007) 435–55.

—— (2007c) "The Anastasian Wall and the Danube frontier in the sixth century", in *The Lower Danube in Antiquity (The Fifth Century BC—the Beginning of the Seventh Century AD)*, ed. L. Vagalinski (Tutrakan 2007) 397–401.

Crow J. and Ricci A (1997) "Investigating the hinterland of Constantinople: interim report on the Anastasian Long Wall," *JRA* 10 (1997) 109–24.

Ćurčić S. (2007) "Topography of anxiety: 'North Macedonia' and its fortifications from the 4th to the 6th c. A.D" *JRA* 20 (2007) 670–73.

—— (2010) *Architecture in the Balkans from Diocletian to Süleyman the Magnificant* (New Haven 2010).

Curta F. (2001) "Peasants as 'makeshift soldiers for the occasion': sixth-century settlement patterns in the Balkans", in *Urban Centers and Rural Contexts in Late Antiquity*, edd. T. S. Burns and J. W. Eadie (East Lansing 2001) 199–217.

—— (2005a) ed. *Borders, Barriers and Ethnogenesis, Frontiers in Late Antiquity and the Middle Ages* (Studies in the Early Middle Ages 12) (Turnhout 2005).

—— (2005b) "Frontier ethnogenesis in Late Antiquity: the Danube, the Tervingi, and the Slavs," in *Borders, Barriers and Ethnogenesis, Frontiers in Late Antiquity and the Middle Ages*, ed. F. Curta (Studies in the Early Middle Ages 12) (Turnhout 2005) 173–204.

Deichmann F. W. (1979) "Westliche Bautechnik im römischen und rhomäischen osten", *MdI* 86 (1979) 473–543.

Deichmann F. W. and Peschlow U. (1977) *Zwie spätantike Ruinstattenin in Nordmesopotamien* (Munich 1977).

De Staebler P. D. (2008) "The city wall and the making of a late-antique provincial capital", in *Aphrodisias Papers 4, New Research on the City and its Monuments*, edd. C. Ratté and R. R. R. Smith (JRA Supplementary Series 70) (Portsmouth, RI 2008) 284–318.

Decker M. (2009) *Tilling the Hateful Earth, Agricultural Production and Trade in the Late Antique East* (Oxford 2009).

Dillemann L. (1962) *Haute Mésopotamie orientale et pays adjacents: contribution à la géographie historique de la région, du Ve s. avant l'ère chrétienne au VIe s. de cette ère* (Paris 1962).

Dinchev V. (1999) "Classification of the late antique cities in the Dioceses of *Thracia* and *Dacia*", *Archaeologia Bulgarica* 3 (1999) 39–73.

—— (2006) *Rannovizantinskiite kreposti v Bulgaria i sus nite zemi (v diotsezite thraciai Dacia)* (Razkopki I Proouchvaniya 35) (Sofia 2006).

—— (2007) "The fortresses of Thrace and Moesia in the early Byzantine period", in *The Transition to Late Antiquity on the Danube and Beyond*, ed. A. G. Poulter (Proceedings of the British Academy 141) (London 2007) 479–547.

—— (2008a) "Razkopki v Kompleks na Chemskite Porti pri c. Golitza, obshtina Dolni Chiftlik", in *HAIM- BAN Archeologicheski Otkritiya i Razkopki prez 2007*, edd. D. Gergova, P. Dimitrov, A. Cholakova, T. Christova, A. Aladjov and V. Petrova (Sofia 2008) 440–43.

—— (2008b) *Arheologicheskoto proouchvane na Haemus Thores* (Razkopki I Proouchvaniya 37) (Sofia 2008).

Dinchev V., Boshkova B., Katzarova V., Yolakova A. and Christov M. (2007) *Arheologicheskoto proouchvane na Hemskite Porti (vm. Germeto pri c. Golitza, Varnenski oblast) prez 2005 g.* (Razkopki I Proouchvaniya 37) (Sofia 2007) (with English summary 135–51).

Downey G. (1961) *A History of Antioch in Syria from Seleucus to the Arab Conquest* (Princeton 1961).

—— (1963) *Ancient Antioch* (Princeton 1963).

Dufy C. (1979) *Siege Warfare, the Fortress in the Early Modern World* (London 1979).

Dunn A. (2004) "Continuity and change in the Macedonian countryside, from Gallineus to Justinian", in *Recent Research on the Late Antique Countryside*, edd. W. Bowden, L. Lavan and C. Machado (Late Antique Archaeology 2) (Leiden and Boston 2004) 534–86.

Dussaud R. P., Deschamps P. and Seyrig H. (1931) *La Syrie antique et médiéval illustrée* (Paris 1931).

Feissel D. (2000) "Les édifices de Justinien au témoignage de Procope et de l'épigraphie", *Antiquité Tardive* 8 (2000) 81–104.

Förster R. (1897) "Antiochia am Orontes", *Jdl* 12 (1897) 103–49.

Foss C. (1996) *Survey of Medieval Castles in Asia Minor, II: Nicomedia* (British Institute of Archaeology at Ankara Monograph 21) (Oxford 1996).

—— (1997) "Syria in transition, AD 550–750: an archaeological approach", *DOP* 51 (1997) 189–268.

Foss C. and Winfield D. (1986) *Byzantine Fortifications. An Introduction* (Pretoria 1986).

Foudrin J.-P. (1994) "Une porte urbaine construite à Chalchis de Syrie par Isidore de Milet le Jeune (550–51), (avec appendice épigraphique par D. Feissel)", *TravMém* 12 (1994) 299–307.

Gabriel A. (1931) *Monuments turcs d'Anatolie, I Kayseri-Niğde* (Paris 1931).

Greenhalgh M. (1999) "Spolia in fortifications: Turkey, Syria and North Africa", in *Ideologie e pratiche del reimpiego nell'alto medioevo* (Setimane di studio del Centro Italiano di Studi sull'Alto Medioevo 46) (Spoleto 1999) 785–934.

Gregory S. (1995) *Roman Military Architecture on the Eastern Frontier* (Amsterdam 1995–97).

Gregory T. E. (1992) "Kastro and Diatiechisma as a response to early Byzantine frontier collapse" *Byzantion* 62 (1992) 235–53.

—— (1993) *Isthmia, Vol. 5, The Hexamilion and the Fortress* (Princeton 1993).

—— (2000) "Procopius on Greece", *Antiquité Tardive* 8 (2000) 105–14.

Hale J. R. (1977) *Renaissance Fortification: Art or Engineering?* (London 1977).

Haarer F. (2006) *Anastasius I, Politics and Empire in the Late Roman World* (Cambridge 2006).

Haselberger L. (2007) *Urbem Adornare: die Stadt Rom und ihre Gestaltunwandlung unter Augustus* (JRA Supplementary Series 64) (Portsmouth, RI 2007).

Henning J. (2007) ed. *Post-Roman Towns, Trade and Settlement in Europe and Byzantium, Vol. 2 Byzantium, Pliska and the Balkans* (Berlin 2007).

Isaac B. (1998) "The Eastern frontier", in *Cambridge Ancient History. Volume 13: The Later Empire, A.D. 337–425*, edd. A. Cameron and P. Garnsey (Cambridge 1998) 437–60.

Ivison E. (2007) "Amorium in the Byzantine Dark Age", in *Post-Roman Towns, Trade and Settlement in Europe and Byzantium, Vol. 2 Byzantium, Pliska and the Balkans*, ed. J. Henning (Berlin 2007) 25–60.

James E. (2004) "Building and rebuilding: imperial women and religious foundations in Constantinople in the fourth to eighth centuries", *Basilissa* 1 (2004) 50–64.

Karnapp W. (1976) *Die Stadtmauer von Resafa in Syrien* (Berlin 1976).

Kaldellis A. (2004) *Procopius of Caesarea, Tyranny, History, and Philosophy at the End of Antiquity* (Philadelphia 2004).

Keeley L. H., Fontana M. and Quick R. (2007) "Baffles and bastions: the universal features of fortifications", *Journal of Archaeological Research* 15 (2007) 55–95.

Kennedy D. L. and Riley D. N. (1990) *Rome's Desert Frontier: from the Air* (London 1990).

Keyser-Kayaalp E. (2009) *Church Architecture of Northern Mesopotamia* (D.Phil diss., Univ. of Oxford 2009).

Kondoleon C. (2000) *Antioch: The Lost Ancient City* (Princeton 2000).

Krautheimer R. (1965) *Early Christian and Byzantine Architecture* (Harmondsworth 1965).

Lauffray J. (1983) *Halabiyya-Zenobia, place forte du limes oriental et la haute-Mésoptamie au VIᵉ siècle. I* (Paris 1983).

Lavan L., Zanini E., and Sarantis A. (2007) edd. *Technology in Transition: A.D. 300–650* (Late Antique Archaeology 4) (Leiden and Boston 2007).

Lee A. D. (2007). *War in Late Antiquity: A Social History* (Oxford 2007).

Lemerle P. (1954) "Invasions et migrations dans les Balkans depuis la fin de l'époque romaine jusqu'au VIIIe siècle", *RHist* 211 (1954) 265–308.

Lewin A. (1991) *Studi sulla città imperiale romana nell'Oriente tardoantico* (Bibl. Athen. 17) (Rome 1991).

Liebeschuetz J. H. W. G. (2007) "The Lower Danube under pressure: from Valens to Heraclius", in *The Transition to Late Antiquity on the Danube and Beyond*, ed. A. G. Poulter (Proceedings of the British Academy 141) (London 2007) 101–34.

Lightfoot C. S. and Lightfoot M. (2007) *Amorium: A Byzantine City in Anatolia* (Homer Archaeological Guides 5) (Istanbul 2007).

Mango C. A. (1985) "Deux études sur Byzance et la Perse Sassanide", *TravMém* 9 (1985) 91–118.

—— (1990) *Nikephoros, Saint, Patriarch of Constantinople* (Washington, D.C. 1990).

Mango C. A. and Mango M. M. (1991) "Inscriptions de la Mésopotamie du nord", *TravMém* 11 (1991) 467–71.

Mango C. A. and Scott C. (1997) *The Chronicle of Theophanes Confessor: Byzantine and Near Eastern History, A.D. 284–813* (Oxford 1997).

Mango C. A. and Ševčenko I. (1972) "Three inscriptions of the reigns of Anastasius I and Constantine V", *ByzZeit* 65 (1972) 379–93.

Mango M. M. (2000) "Building and architecture", in *Cambridge Ancient History. Volume 14: Late Antiquity: Empire and Successors, A.D. 425–600*, edd. A. Cameron, B. Ward-Perkins and M. Whitby (Cambridge 2000) 918–72.

McNicoll A. W. (1997) *Hellenistic Fortifications from the Aegean to the Euphrates* (Oxford 1997).

Mikulčić I. (2002) (ed. M. Konrad) *Spätantike und frühbyzantinische befestigugungen in Nordmakedonien. Städt- Vici- Refugien- Kastelle* (Munich 2002).

Mitchell S. (1995) *Cremna in Pisidia. An Ancient City in Peace and War* (Cardiff 1995).

Napoli J. (1997) *Recherches sur les fortifications linéaires Romaines* (Collection de l'École Française de Rome 229) (Rome 1997).

Niewöhner P. (2007) "Archäologie und die 'Dunklen Jahrhunderte' im byzantinische Anatolien", in *Post-Roman Towns, Trade and Settlement in Europe and Byzantium, Vol. 2 Byzantium, Pliska and the Balkans*, ed. J. Henning (Berlin 2007) 119–57.

—— (2008) "Sind die Mauern die Stadt? Vorbericht über die siedlungsgeschichtlichen Ergebnisse neuer Grabungen im spätantiken und byzantinischen Milet", *AA* 2008/1 (2008) 181–201.

—— (2010) "Byzantinische Stadtmauern in Anatolien. Vom Statussymbol zum Bollwerk gegen die Araber", in *Neue Forschungen zu antiken Stadtbefestigungen im östlichen Mittelmeerraum und im Vorderen Orient, Konstruktion–Funktion–Semantik*, edd. C. Wawruschka, A. Wirsching and T. Zimmer (Byzas 10) (Istanbul 2010) 239–60.

—— (2011) "The riddle of the Market Gate: Miletus and the character and date of earlier Byzantine fortifications in Anatolia", in *Archaeology and the Cites of Asia Minor in Late Antiquity*, edd. O. Dally and C. Ratté (Kelsey Museum Publication 6) (Michigan 2011) 103–122.

Norman A. F. (2000) *Antioch as a Centre of Hellenic Culture as Observed by Libanius* (Liverpool 2000).

Northedge A. (2008) "Umayyad and Abbasid urban fortifications in the Near East", in *Der Grenzen der Welt, Arabica et Iranica ad honorem Heinz Gaube*, edd. L. Korn, E. Orthmann and F. Schwarz (Wiesbaden 2008) 39–64.

Omrani Rekavandi H., Sauer E., Wilkinson T., Abbasi G. A., Priestman S., Safari Tamak E., Ainslie R., Mahmoudi M., Galiatsatos N., Roustai K., Jansen Van Rensburg J., Ershadi M., MacDonald E., Fattahi M., Oatley C., Shabani B., Ratcliffe J. and Usher-Wilson L. S.

(2008) "Sasanian walls, hinterland fortresses and abandoned ancient irrigated landscapes: the 2007 season on the Great Wall of Gorgan and the Wall of Tammishe', *Iran* 46 (2008) 151–78.

Pazara T. (1987) *To 'Diateichisma' tis Kassandreias: Praktika tou Protou Panellenikou Symposiou Istorias kai Archaiologias tis Chalkidikis* (Thessalonica 1987).

Parkinson W. A. and Duffy P. R. (2007) "Fortifications and enclosures in European Prehistory: a cross cultural perspective", *Journal of Archaeological Research* 15 (2007) 97–141.

Pollack M. (2010) *Cities at War in Early Modern Europe* (Cambridge 2010).

Poidebard A. (1934) *La trace de Rome dans le desert de Syrie* (Paris 1934).

Poulter A. G. (2007) ed. *The Transition to Late Antiquity on the Danube and Beyond* (Proceedings of the British Academy 141) (London 2007).

Pringle D. (1981) *The Defence of Byzantine Africa from Justinian to the Arab Conquest: An Account of the Military History and Archaeology of the African Provinces in the Sixth and Seventh Centuries* (BAR International Series 99) (Oxford 1981).

Restle M. (1975) "Viranşehir-Kaleköy, ein befestiger Platz in Kappadokien", *Jahrbuch der Österreichische Byzantinistik* 24 (1975) 196–207.

Rey E. G. (1871) *Étude sur les monuments de l'architecture militaire des Croisés en Syrie et dans l'île de Chypre* (Paris 1871).

Rose C. B. (2011) "Troy and the Troad in Late Antiquity", in *Archaeology and the Cities of Asia Minor in Late Antiquity*, edd. O. Dally and C. Ratté (Kelsey Museum Publication 6) (Michigan 2011) 151–71.

Roueché C. (1999) "Looking for late antique ceremonial: Ephesos and Aphrodisias", in *100 Jahre Österreichische Forschungen in Ephesos*, vol.1, edd. H. Friesinger and R. Krinzinger (Vienna 1999) 161–68.

Rizos E. (2010) *Cities, Architecture and Society in the Eastern and Central Balkans during Late Antiquity (ca. AD 250–600)* (D.Phil. diss., Univ. of Oxford 2010).

—— (2011) "The late antique walls of Thessalonica and their place in the development of eastern military architecture", *JRA* 24 (2011) 450–69.

Škorpil K. (1930) "Constructions militaire stratégiques dans la région de la Mer Noire (Peninsule des Balkans)", *Byzantinoslavica* 2 (1930) 197–230.

—— (1931) "Constructions militaire stratégiques dans la région de la Mer Noire (Peninsule des Balkans)", *Byzantinoslavica* 3 (1931) 11–32.

Smith D. J. and Crow J. (1998) "The Hellenistic and Byzantine defence of Tocra (Teuchira)", *LibSt* 29 (1998) 35–82.

Sodini J.-P. (2007) "The transformation of cities", in *The Transition to Late Antiquity on the Danube and Beyond*, ed. A. G. Poulter (Proceedings of the British Academy 141) (London 2007) 311–36.

Speiser J. P. (1999) "Les ramparts de Thessalonique, a propos d'un livre recent", *Byzantinoslavica* 60 (1999) 557–74.

Squatriti P. (2005) "Moving earth and making difference: dikes and frontiers in early medieval Bulgaria", in *Borders, Barriers and Ethnogenesis, Frontiers in Late Antiquity and the Middle Ages*, ed. F. Curta (Studies in the Early Middle Ages 12) (Brepols 2005) 59–90.

Theocharidou K. (2004) "The walls of Thessaloniki: evidence from brickstamps", *Sanat Tarihi Defterleri* 8 (2004) 221–35.

Vanhaverbeke H., Mertens F. and Waelkens M. (2007) "Another view on Late Antiquity: Sagalassos (SW Anatolia, its suburbium and its countryside in Late Antiquity", in *The Transition to Late Antiquity on the Danube and Beyond*, ed. A. G. Poulter (Proceedings of the British Academy 141) (London 2007) 611–48.

Ward-Perkins B. (1984) *From Classical Antiquity to the Middle Ages: Urban Public Buildings in Northern and Central Italy AD 300–850* (Oxford 1984).

—— (2000) "Land, labour and settlement," in *Cambridge Ancient History. Volume 14: Late Antiquity: Empire and Successors, A.D. 425–600*, edd. A. Cameron, B. Ward-Perkins and M. Whitby (Cambridge 2000) 315–45.

Weissner G. (1980) *Nordmesopotamische Ruinenstätte* (Wiesbaden 1980).

Wheeler R. E. M. (1952) "The Roman frontier in Mesopotamia", in *The Congress of Roman Frontier Studies 1949*, ed. E. Birley (Newcastle upon Tyne 1952) 112–29.

Whitby M. (2000) trans. and ed. *The Ecclesiastical History of Evagrius Scholasticus* (Liverpool 2000).

Velenis G. M. (1998) *Ta teiche tes Thessalonikes apo ton Kassandro hos ton Herakleio* (Greek=*The Walls of Thessalonike from Cassander to Heraclius*) (Thessaloniki 1998).

Zanini E. (2007) "Technology and ideas: architecture and masterbuilders in the Early Byzantine world", in *Technology in Transition: A.D. 300–650*, edd. L. Lavan, E. Zanini and A. Sarantis (Late Antique Archaeology 4) (Leiden and Boston 2007) 381–406.

Zuckerman C. (1998) "Sur le dispositif frontalier en Arménie, le "limes" et son évolution, sous le Bas-Empire", *Historia: Zeitschrift für Alte Geschichte* 47 (1998) 108–28.

Websites

Bell Archive: http://gertrudebell.ncl.ac.uk/photos.php/
Anastasian Wall: http://www.shc.ed.ac.uk/projects/longwalls/

LIST OF FIGURES

SIEGE WARFARE AND COUNTER-SIEGE TACTICS IN LATE ANTIQUITY
(*ca.* 250–640)

Michael Whitby

Abstract

Although there are numerous remains of Late Roman walls and other defensive works, these offer little insight into how individual sieges progressed, and most of our knowledge about siege operations in Late Antiquity comes from literary sources, which, for different reasons, provide a wealth of information. Tactics and techniques were substantially the same as in earlier Roman and Hellenistic times, so that comparative evidence is relevant, and the main issue for debate is the switch from torsion-powered to traction artillery and who was responsible for this development.

INTRODUCTION

The archaeology of the siege in action is a substantially more challenging topic than the archaeology of defensive structures, since the inevitably transient operations of a siege, however protracted and bitter they will have been for all those involved, may not have left enduring marks in the material record, or at least marks which can be associated with one particular event rather than another. As a result, our knowledge about the mechanics of sieges is largely derived from literary sources. I will, therefore, first review this information, before returning to the question of how archaeology contributes to this picture.

LITERARY SOURCES

Fortunately, our literary sources provide a substantial quantity of information about sieges of both cities and fortresses. In part, this reflects how warfare was the prime component in secular historiography, and how within late antique warfare there genuinely were numerous sieges. Indeed, in some conflicts, sieges formed the dominant form of military activity: thus, in the war against Persia which occupied the whole of Constantius

A. Sarantis, N. Christie (edd.) *War and Warfare in Late Antiquity: Current Perspectives*
(Late Antique Archaeology 8.1–8.2 – 2010–11) (Leiden 2013), pp. 433–459

II's reign, there was only one pitched battle (the indecisive encounter at Singara in 344), but three sieges of Nisibis, where the repeated Persian failures dented the prestige of King Shapur.[1] Two centuries later, the Justinianic re-conquest of Italy largely revolved around the control of fortresses and cities, at least until the General Narses arrived.[2] The predominance of sieges reflected the fact that commanders were reluctant to risk precious manpower in open battle unless they had a clear advantage, while secure control of territory depended on possession of key fortified cities which attackers had to capture in order to weaken the enemy and obtain significant booty, whereas defenders had to retain them as the basis for long-term authority in a particular area.

Sieges could also provide exciting material for narration, and were sanctioned by historiographical precedent which stretched back to Thucydides' account of the siege of Plataea,[3] and more generally to the Homeric cycle of epics (especially the *Iliad* and the *Iliou Persis*). These were occasions of high drama with opportunities for a rich narrative of the ingenuity of assailants and defenders, for descriptions of a site or aspect of a site, or of a machine, and for emotive descriptions of the consequences of capture. The authors of our two most substantial secular narratives, Ammianus Marcellinus in the 4th c. and Procopius in the 6th c., each had personal experience of siege warfare, both on the defensive side—at Amida (359) and Rome (537–38)—and on the offensive—at Maiozamalcha (363) and Naples (536).[4] But, because sieges increasingly impinged on the civilian population of the empire and became intertwined, as we shall see, with religious beliefs and the reputations of particular cults or objects of devotion, we have detailed eye-witness accounts of threats to their cities by civilian observers such as Bishop John of Thessalonica in the *Miracles of St Demetrius*, or the authors of the anonymous accounts in the *Chronicle* of Pseudo-Joshua the Stylite of Kavadh's attack on Edessa in 503, and in the *Chronicon Paschale* of the 626 siege of Constantinople. Stories of apparently miraculous survival were presented to enhance the reputation of the agent, whether that was a saintly figure, as Genevieve at Paris, a bishop, as Anianus at Orleans (both during Attila's incursion in 451), or an object such as the *acheiropoietos* image of Christ at Edessa in

---

[1] For the centrality of fortified cities to warfare in the East, see Isaac (1990) 252–60.

[2] For a list of sieges in the 6th and 7th c., see Syvänne (2004) 502–505.

[3] Thuc. 2.71–77; 3.20–24.

[4] But, as Matthews (1989) 288 notes, the benefits of personal experience may be sacrificed to the rhetorical expectations of the literary tradition.

544. Thus we possess a wealth of textual information, although it must be remembered when analysing this material that many of the authors will have had reason to embellish their texts, either to create a more exciting or emotive narrative or to enhance the reputation of an honorand.

A Typology of Sieges

The simplest categorisation of sieges is in terms of length: quick, medium-length, and protracted.[5] The benefits of a quick, or relatively bloodless siege are clear, in terms of the cost to the besiegers as well as in the on-going quality of the asset which they would be acquiring: a successful but protracted siege, such as Amida in 359 and 502/503 or Dara in 573 could have a substantial impact on the attacker in terms of the opportunity cost and the investment needed to retain control of a degraded site, quite apart from the physical losses of men and equipment. As a result, surprise and treachery were sensible options. This was particularly the case for groups with a limited capacity for siege warfare: thus in 378, the Goths attempted to infiltrate traitors into Adrianople to avoid the risks and losses of a siege; in 479, Theoderic the Amal deceived the defenders of Epidamnus into abandoning their city; while Moors tricked their way into Hadrumetum in 544.[6] But rapid capture was equally beneficial to those with greater capacity at sieges: Khusro secured entry into Sura after one day's fighting by duping the bishop, while in 550, the Romans charged into the Abasgian citadel of Trachea along with the fleeing enemy.[7]

Intimidation was well worth attempting—the 'Joshua-at-Jericho' approach—especially in the early stages of a siege.[8] Thus we find Shapur at Amida in 359, Kavad at Edessa in 503, Khusro at Edessa in 544, and the Avar Chagan at Constantinople in 626 trying to overawe defenders into striking a deal, which might involve full surrender and evacuation or just the payment of a ransom. Such intimidation was usually attempted when rulers were campaigning in person. Their presence demonstrated the gravity of the threat to the besieged, who could not expect a king to withdraw

---

[5] Veg. *Mil.* (4.7) proposed a two-fold division: the blockade to starve the enemy into submission, as opposed to constant attacks using siege engines. For discussion of 'offensive' sieges in the 6th c., see Syvänne (2004) 303–309.

[6] Amm. Marc. 31.15.7–9; Malchus 20.64–88; Procop. *Vand.* 4.23.10–16.

[7] Procop. *Pers.* 2.5.17–25; 8.9.24–7.

[8] Compare Veg. *Mil.* 4.12.

unsuccessfully, though it might result in personal danger: Shapur came within range of missiles from the walls of Amida and Bezabde. Lesser leaders could not hope for the same impact, but might attempt to exploit rhetoric, as Belisarius did unsuccessfully at Naples, or psychological pressure, as Narses applied at Lucca with limited success through the fake execution of hostages.[9]

If these tactics failed, then the normal first phase of assault was a rush at the walls with ladders and bundles of osiers to fill in ditches; casualties were likely to be heavy, as the Persians experienced at Bezabde, but could succeed if attackers did not take much notice of the human cost, as when the Avar Chagan drove forward waves of unprotected subject Slavs on the first day of the Constantinople siege in 626. These efforts might offer a chance of success before the nerves of defenders had settled.[10] Even so, such rush tactics required preparation to gather the material for the bundles, assemble ladders and construct protective mantlets: at Naples, Belisarius found that an embarrassing miscalculation had been made in the off-site construction of his ladders; when attempting to force his way up the Tiber in 546, he took greater trouble with his measurements.[11]

Thereafter, sieges moved into the medium term, with defenders gaining some confidence from surviving the initial exchanges,[12] and attackers bringing up, or constructing more complex siege engines, and preparing the approach to sections of the defences which were not immediately accessible—a phase which began after a few days and might extend to several months. Particular opportunities would be exploited, as at Amida in January 503, when the Persians discovered an insecurely-blocked tunnel into the city,[13] but their main focus of energies was on the reduction of defences, using rams to batter away at gates or other weak areas, attempting to lever out stones with crow bars, destroying the upper parts of fortifications with artillery, and advancing siege towers. Obvious weak points in the defences would be assailed with force: at Singara in 360, the Persians used a mighty ram against the tower which had been destroyed in a siege a dozen years earlier; later that year at Bezabde, they also

---

[9] Amm. Marc. 19.1.3–6; 20.7.2; Procop. *Goth.* 5.8.12–18, 9.23–28; Agath. 1.12–13.

[10] Amm. Marc. 20.7.6; *Chron. Pasch.* 719.

[11] Procop. *Goth.* 5.10.22–23; 7.19.4; contrast Veg. *Mil.* 4.30 for advice on how to get it right.

[12] Veg. *Mil.* 4.12.

[13] Procop. *Pers.* 1.7.20–24, perhaps the same tunnel as exploited in 359—see Amm. Marc. 19.5.4.

managed to identify the defences' weak points, though on this occasion the local bishop was suspected of divulging the information.[14]

Progress was easier if the attackers could control the skies, whether to permit their men to operate in close proximity to the defences without constant interruption from the defenders above, or to advance their own engines to the optimum locations. In this respect, the defenders had a considerable advantage, since they almost invariably occupied higher ground than the attackers, and this was compounded by the height of their defences: they had a better view of proceedings, at least until attackers had reached the very base of the walls, and their missiles had a longer range. To have a significant impact, a besieger's stone-throwers had to be positioned no more than about 150–70 m from the defence they were trying to reduce,[15] though they would have had some effect on battlements at a greater distance. They would then, however, be well within range of the defensive artillery on the towers, both the arrow firers (whose range was naturally greater than that of stone-throwers), but also lighter-weight anti-personnel stone-throwers (sufficient to damage machines or incommode their operators). Even the defenders' heaviest machines would outreach those of the attackers, since their missiles would remain effective during their downward trajectory, causing maximum damage to their opponents' machines and men as they crashed back to earth, whereas the assailants' engines had to be set up so that their missiles would strike the walls much closer to the apex of their trajectory.

As a result, a contest began to establish domination in the exchanges of missiles. It was important for the attackers to gain extra height for their equipment by deploying mobile siege towers or by erecting mounds.[16] The Persians also occasionally used elephants to overtop (presumably fairly low) defences, but these beasts may have been expected to bring greater psychological rewards than military impact, since in any actual fighting, catapults, fire arrows, and even a squealing pig rendered them an uncertain asset.[17] At Panormus, Belisarius exploited his command of the sea by hoisting boats full of archers up to the mast-heads of his large ships and

---

[14] Amm. Marc. 20.6.5–7, 7.9; but note that he shared the deportation of the other captives, which might exonerate him.

[15] Marsden (1969) ch.4, esp. 90–91 for discussion of the effective range of machines.

[16] Mitchell (1995) 182 for evidence for the consequences.

[17] Amm. Marc. 198.2.3, 7.6; Procop. *Goth.* 8.14.10, 35f: Archeopolis.

thus overtopping the defences; his attempt in 546 to force his way up the Tiber relied on a similar tactic.[18]

War above ground would be complemented, where appropriate, by subterranean approaches, either to undermine a tower or section of wall, or to introduce a party right inside the defences. It was important to prevent defenders from learning of such attempts, for example, by concealing the spoil heaps, since countermining would invalidate the considerable effort involved. At Maiozamalcha, Julian launched a night attack to conceal the noise of his sappers who were close to breaking into the defences, while at Naples, some Isaurians carefully chiselled their way past an obstruction in an aqueduct, eschewing the normal picks and mattocks so as to avoid giving notice to the defenders of their actions.[19]

But even if these actions resulted in the attackers destroying or occupying part of the defences, that did not necessarily end proceedings. At Amida in January 503, and Dara in December 573, it is noticeable that the attackers proceeded very cautiously after securing part of the defences. This was a critical time when desperate defenders might turn the tide, as occurred at Amida in 359, when concerted missile fire drove the Persians back from the single tower they had briefly occupied. Similarly, fierce resistance inflicted heavy losses on the Persians at Bezabde after their ram had battered down a tower, and the same perhaps happened at Antioch in 540, where, even though the Persians gave the defending soldiers time to flee the city, elements of the civilian population put up a stiff resistance.[20] There was method in the steady consolidation of success, and in terms of booty, it would not matter too much if some defenders availed themselves of the opportunity to escape rather than remain to resist:[21] indeed, a reduction in resistance might be beneficial, since desperate defenders might set fire to their surroundings in a last-ditch effort to thwart their attackers, increasing casualties all round and destroying potential booty.[22] After the Persians had occupied part of the walls of Dara in 573, the commanders of the defence hid the keys to the gates to prevent the flight of their troops, so forcing them to fight to the end.[23]

---

[18] Procop. *Goth.* 5.5.15–16 and 7.19.18.

[19] Amm. Marc. 24.4.22–23; Procop. *Goth.* 5.9.19–21.

[20] Zach. Myt. *Chron.* 7.4; Joh. Eph. *HE* 6.5; Amm. Marc. 19.6.10 and 20.7.14–15; Procop. *Pers.* 2.8.27–29.

[21] Ammianus' escape from Amida (19.8.5) is an example—and the criticism which is sometimes levelled at him for failing to provide details is, I think, unjustified.

[22] Veg. *Mil.* 4.26 is relatively optimistic about the chances of destroying an enemy who had entered a city.

[23] Joh. Eph. *HE* 6.5.

If this phase ended in stalemate, with the attackers lacking the resources or determination to push matters to a conclusion, or the defences just being too strong, then matters reverted to blockade. However, the challenge of sustaining an effective blockade was considerable, and the Romans found this beyond their reach at Amida in 503/504 or Martyropolis in 589/90, when a Persian relief force managed to fight its way into the city. Thus a blockade was, in some ways, a pause for breath while the assailants considered their options, and surprise and trickery would still be exploited if the opportunity presented: for instance, at Rome in 536, towards the end of their year-long siege, the Goths launched one straight assault during a lunch break in the hope of catching the Roman garrison off guard, and then attempted to drug some of the guards.[24]

The Defenders' Perspective[25]

Preparations in advance of an attack were obviously vital, with the stock-piling of food, water, and other supplies for an extended struggle. Denuding the surrounding countryside would make life more awkward for the attackers as well as provide for the defenders, and this might involve last-minute activity, as at Constantinople in A.D. 626, when civilians harvesting crops a few miles from the walls were attacked by the Avar advance guard.[26] In 479, Theoderic the Amal could not pursue the siege of Lychnidus because the grain had already been gathered inside the walls; he had previously failed to extract supplies from Heraclea Lyncestis.[27] Some places were better prepared in this respect than others: Dara was well-equipped with storage facilities, and indeed this had been one of the main reasons for its construction, whereas in 540, Beroea, located much further back from the frontier, was in a poor state of readiness; when the Romans finally recaptured Phasis in 551, they were impressed by the excellence of Persian preparations, which included a complex three-layered water conduit, whose lowest channel they had failed to detect, and massive quantities of grain, cured meats and beans.[28]

There was often last-minute work to be done: thus at Sirmium in 374, Probus had to clear accumulated rubbish from defensive ditches and

---

[24] Theoph. Sim. 3.5.14–16; Procop. *Goth.* 6.9.12 and 16–23.
[25] For discussion of defensive sieges in the 6th c., see Syvänne (2004) 299–303.
[26] *Chron. Pasch.* 717; compare Veg. *Mil.* 4.7.
[27] Malchus fr. 20. 94–100, 116–17; compare Vitigis at Rimini: Procop. *Goth.* 6.12.25.
[28] Zach. Myt. *Chron.* 7.6; Procop. *Pers.* 2.7.6–13; Procop. *Goth.* 8.12.18–27.

belatedly complete improvements to walls and towers, while after the
first day of fighting at Adrianople in 378, the defenders blocked up the
city gates with large stones, patched up weak sections of the defences,
positioned their artillery, and stored water close to the walls, since thirst
had been a problem on the previous day.[29] When Nu'man approached
Edessa in 503:

> trenches were dug, the wall put in order and the gates of the city blocked
> with hewn stones, because they were worn out. They had been meaning to
> renew them, and to make bolts for the sluices of the river, so that no-one
> might enter by them. Sufficient iron, however, could not be found for the
> work, so an order was given that every household in Edessa should provide
> 10 pounds of iron, and when this had been done, the work was completed.
> (Josh. Styl. 52, p. 58.).

When Kavadh threatened the city the following year, there was still more
to be done, with extra-mural buildings levelled and hedges and orchards
felled.[30] Aqueducts, too, might be cut or blocked, since more than once
they provided a means of entry, as at Amida in 503 and Naples in 536,
though the attackers often then had difficulty in descending from the
elevated channel.[31] Matters could be left too late: at Antioch in 540, the
defences were compromised by the fact that at one point on the mountain
section, the walls were almost overtopped by a substantial rock beyond
the walls; Germanus wanted to attempt to neutralise this, either by creating a moat between the rock and the wall, or by occupying the rock with
a tower—but he was dissuaded by local building experts, who warned
that nothing could be achieved in time and unfinished work would merely
draw the Persians' attention to the weak point.[32] In the event, of course,
the Persians needed no assistance in identifying this opportunity. But the
building experts also had a point: Shapur captured Singara in 360 by focusing his machines on a recently reconstructed stretch of wall, whose new
masonry would have been as evident to the attackers as different masonry
phases are to modern archaeologists, and Khusro took Callinicum in 542
during repairs to its circuit.[33]

---

[29] Amm. Marc. 29.6.11; 31.15.6.
[30] Josh. Styl. 59, p. 75.
[31] Zach. Myt. *Chron.* 7.6; Procop. *Goth.* 5.9.11, compare 5.19.18 for Belisarius' careful
preparations at Rome in 537.
[32] Procop. *Pers.* 2.6.10–13.
[33] Amm. Marc. 20.6.6; Procop. *Pers.* 2.21.30.

Thereafter, the defenders had two main objectives: to keep attackers as far from their defences as possible, and to sustain morale through the inevitable tensions and panics of the crisis. The morale of the civilian inhabitants was just as important as that of the garrison, since the civilians provided, at the least, essential logistical and physical support and, on occasions such as Edessa in 503, contributed significantly to the fighting. Most major sets of fortifications included a *proteichisma*, one of whose functions was to keep the enemy at a distance and increase the length of any mine they attempted to dig and so raise the chances of its discovery; but the extra space within the outer wall might also be put to good use, as at Dara, where the inhabitants used it for their animals.[34] Ditches were another hindrance since, although they might be quickly filled in with bundles of faggots, these might not sustain the weight of advancing siege engines, as Vitigis discovered at Rimini in 537.[35] Vegetius had recommended the use of a water-filled moat as a warning device against attempted mining, and the Persians dug water-filled trenches inside the walls at Amida in 503 to thwart the Romans.[36]

Defensive siege machinery was vital in pinning the attackers back and disrupting attempts to advance substantial machines. Few attackers were as obliging as the Goths at Rome in 537, who attempted to use draught oxen to drag towers into place,[37] but accurate fire could make more sensible attempts difficult; ideally stone throwers would damage the protective coverings of the attacking machines, after which fire arrows could set them alight. To sustain this defensive fire, it was vital for battlements to be protected, since they were inevitably weaker than a solid wall and without them defenders would be fully exposed. Belisarius attempted to increase security at Rome by adding small return walls to the left of each battlement, thereby reducing the exposure of right-handed soldiers.[38] Haircloth or bolsters of rushes might be used to break the force of missiles,[39] or simply to conceal the defenders from view.[40] An inventive, or desperate,

---

[34] Procop. *Pers.* 2.13.18, and contrast 2.7.13 for the problems animals might cause within the defences.

[35] Procop. *Goth.* 6.12.6; for the principle, compare Aen. Tact. 32.8.

[36] Veg. *Mil.* 4.5; Josh. Styl. 71, p.89.

[37] Procop. *Goth.* 5.21.1–13.

[38] Procop. *Goth.* 5.14.15; Richmond (1930) 89, 265.

[39] Pirasabora: Amm. Marc. 24.2.10; Amida: Zach. Myt. *Chron.* 7.3; Onoguris: Agath. 3.6.11; Veg. *Mil.* 4.6.

[40] Bezabde: Amm. Marc. 20.11.8.

variant on this was the deployment of the children of prisoners along the rampart at Noviodunum by the Hun, Valips, in the 430s.[41]

If attackers came close enough, they reached the shadow of the walls, dead ground where wall-based missiles could not reach because of the angle of depression. They were, however, vulnerable here to material dropped directly from the rampart: at Bezabde, column drums, millstones and other heavy stones were discharged, while at Rome, even the statues on Hadrian's tomb were rolled directly down onto the attackers.[42] At Martyropolis, the Romans built a counter-tower to overtop a Persian siege tower which had reached the walls, and used a crane to drop a column which demolished the attackers' structure.[43] Boiling oil or pitch was an uncomfortable alternative which might be poured straight from basins, or distributed more widely by being flicked from the basins with a whisk.[44]

Ultimately, if attackers could not be dislodged by such methods and their destruction of the defences was proceeding, then a sally might be risked to disrupt attacks, burn machines and drive assailants back.[45] If the attackers could be caught unawares, so much the better, as at Artogerassa, where the Persians were tricked into believing that the fort was preparing to surrender.[46] The confused reception of troops withdrawing from an unsuccessful sally almost led to the capture of Ancona, and the unauthorised activities of Kutrigo at Amida revealed to the Persians a way into the city in 503.[47] As a result, commanders attempted to control such activity, but not always successfully; at Amida in 359, it proved very difficult to prevent the belligerent Gauls from launching self-satisfying but unproductive attacks.[48] Maurice's *Strategikon* categorically recommended against the practice to avoid the loss of the best soldiers.[49]

In the fiercest sieges, there came a time when a particular section of wall was under critical threat, either because battering or undermining had shaken its strength, or because a siege mound was approaching dangerously close. Construction of an inner wall could nullify the attackers'

---

[41] Priscus fr. 5.

[42] Amm. Marc. 20.11.10; Procop. *Goth.* 5.22.21.

[43] Malalas 18.66.

[44] Bezabde: Amm. Marc. 20.11.15; Topirus: Procop. *Goth.* 7.38.16; Edessa: Procop. *Pers.* 2.27.36.

[45] Aquileia: Amm. Marc. 21.12.13; Rome: Procop. *Goth.* 5.23.21, 24; Thessalonica: *Miracles of St Demetrius* 147.

[46] Amm. Marc. 27.12.6–8.

[47] Procop. *Goth.* 6.13.12–15; Zach. Myt. *Chron.* 7.4.

[48] Agath. 3.22.3–8; Amm. Marc. 19.6.3–5.

[49] *Strategikon* 10.3.36–42.

apparent success and force them to restart their efforts in a space where they might come under heavy raking fire. At Petra, existing buildings served this purpose and thwarted the Romans, who were initially exultant at collapsing a section of wall.[50] Alternatively, the defenders could attempt to increase the height of their own walls to match that of an approaching mound,[51] but here the advantage would always lie with the attackers, who had more space to construct a solid structure. At Amida in 359, the collapse of a counter-mound actually helped the Persians reach the circuit wall, while in 502, the Persians easily knocked down additions hastily built by the defence force.[52] In 540, Antioch was captured after the sudden collapse of what sounds like a scaffolded platform at a weak point in the walls, while at Edessa, the defenders simply gave up the race to surpass the attackers' great mound.[53] Countermining was a better and safer option, being used effectively at Amida in 502, where the defenders actually tunnelled through their own wall to gain access to the Persian mound, and, most famously, at Edessa in 544, where the miraculous icon of Christ was used to ignite the combustion chamber and burn through the mound.[54]

Peculiarly there are also a certain number of stories about city gates being left open, but with attackers not being tempted to approach.[55] In each case, the story is presented as a miraculous escape for the defenders, but there may also be a more human explanation, since the attackers might have suspected a trap had been formulated to lure them within range of the walls so that significant casualties could be inflicted during an over-confident approach, as John achieved against the Persians at the start of the siege of Petra. The actual gateways could be protected by caltrops, or might be prepared for rapid closure as recommended by Vegetius.[56] In certain circumstances, the defences might become the springboard for aggressive action: at Rome in 537, Belisarius dispatched sallying parties to skirmish on favourable terms or lure the Goths within range of missiles

---

[50] Procop. *Pers.* 2.29.34–43.

[51] Compare Veg. *Mil.* 4.19.

[52] Amm. Marc. 19.8.2–4; Josh. Styl. 49 p.54.

[53] Procop. *Pers.* 2.8.15–16 and 2.26.44.

[54] Zach. Myt. *Chron.* 7.3; Procop. *Pers.* 2.27.1–17; Evagr. 4.27.

[55] Edessa: Josh. Styl. 60, p. 78; 62, p. 80; Drizipera: Theoph. Sim. 6.5.4–7; jammed portcullis at Thessalonica: *Miracles of St Demetrius* 149.

[56] Procop. *Pers.* 2.17.5–10 and 7.24.16; Veg. *Mil.* 4.4.

from the walls, while at Alexandria in 610, Nicetas overcame the superior army of Bonosus once it had been demoralised by defensive firepower.[57]

Morale was the second major need for the besieged, since sustained defence depended upon confident leadership and inspiration. This might come from the military commander, as Belisarius provided at Rome in 537 with his exaggerated behaviour to show his contempt for the Ostrogothic efforts, or as Martin effected at Phasis with a fake letter about the approach of a relief army.[58] More often, however, spirits were raised by a local religious figure, usually the bishop. The most famous occasions include the Patriarch Sergius in the defence of Constantinople against the Avar siege in 626, when he was supported by the capital's collection of relics of the Virgin;[59] and the actions at Thessalonica of Archbishop John, notably the composition of the morale-boosting first book of the *Miracles of Saint Demetrius*.[60] The Persian invasions of the 540s produced various miraculous rescue stories: at Sergiopolis/Resafa in 542, a heavenly army was seen on the battlements, presumably in deference to the local patron saint, Sergius; Edessa in 544 was protected both by Christ's promise to Abgar and the *acheiropoietos* image.[61] We hear far less about occasions when these methods failed: the martyr Alexander may have saved Drizipera in 589, but the Avars captured the city a decade later and sacked Alexander's shrine—though a subsequent plague was interpreted as divine vengeance.[62] And Bishop Thomas of Apamea's display of the relic of the Holy Cross[63] failed to prevent Khusro from occupying the city—this perhaps in contravention of an agreement with the bishop—and removing all its gold and silver. At the same time, however, as morale had to be maintained, it was essential to ward against over-confidence: this may have contributed to the fall of Amida in 503, and it is possible that the recent death of the frank-spoken Bishop John had removed a factor critical to maintaining an appropriate balance in the defenders' emotions.[64]

---

[57] Procop. *Pers.*5.27.5–14; John of Nikiu 107.46–108.14.

[58] Procop. *Pers.* 5.18.42 and 5.27.25–29; Agath. 3.23–26.

[59] Theodore Syncellus 303.14–32 and 304.4–16. The bibliography is extensive: see, in particular, Baynes (1955); Cameron (1979) and (1978); Howard-Johnston (1995). For further references to ancient sources, see Whitby and Whitby (1989) 180 n. 476.

[60] *Miracles of St. Demetrius* 201–206; Lemerle (1979); Cormack (1985); Whitby (1998).

[61] Evagrius 4.26–8; Theod. *HE* 2.30; Whitby (2000b) 224–29, 323–26; Peeters (1920).

[62] Theoph. Sim. 6.5.4–7 and 7.14.11–15.3.

[63] Procop. *Pers.* 2.11.14–27; Evagrius 4.26.

[64] Josh. Styl. 53, p.60; Zach. Myt. *Chron.* 7.3.

Capacity for Sieges

Germans and Goths had the reputation for not being good at storming walls: Ammianus provides *bon mots* about the Alamanni regarding towns as tombs surrounded by nets and the Gothic leader Fritigern stating that he kept peace with walls after an unsuccessful attempt on Adrianople.[65] However, such realism did not stop these groups from attempts which sometimes succeeded: thus, the Alamanni captured Cologne after a long siege, and Mainz was taken by surprise during a Christian festival.[66] In due course, these groups naturally acquired greater skills, either learnt from the Romans or available through the employment of former Roman personnel: thus, at Cumae in 552, the Ostrogothic leader Aligern exploited the city's machines to resist Narses, though the Ostrogoths did not like being cooped up within a besieged city—recalling the frustration of the Gallic legions in Amida in 359. Even the Slavs, the least organised of Roman opponents, captured Topirus after luring its defenders outside the walls into a trap.[67]

Two European groups stand out as different: Attila's Huns in the 440s (but not really before that decade or after Attila's death) and the Avars during the 580s and again in the early 7th c. In each case, the key factor was an enormous supply of expendable manpower, subject groups who could be driven forwards in human waves which would ultimately overcome all but the most substantial defences and resolute defenders. Both groups had some knowledge of siege equipment, which they would use after the initial human assault.[68] At Naissus, the Huns are described as using a swinging beam, protected by screens of willow covered with hides, which was advanced on wheels and which permitted them to fire at the battlements in safety;[69] eventually, the Huns entered the city, in part through breaches made by the rams, and in part by scaling ladders. The Avars possessed intimidating siege engines, although we do not have

---

[65] Amm. Marc. 16.2.12 and 31.6.3–4. Although these comments are normally accepted as fact, some qualification might be in order since they saved the face of particular leaders after a reverse.

[66] Amm. Marc. 15.8.19 and 27.10.1–2; compare Libanius 18.43.

[67] Agath. 1.9.2 and 2.13.6; Amm. Marc. 19.5.2–3; Procop. *Goth.* 7.38.

[68] E.g. *Chron. Pasch.* 719.

[69] The identity of this device is uncertain, but it was probably a version of the *tolleno* described by Veg. *Mil.* (4.21), though the latter device was stationary, designed to swing a group of men around and place them on the battlements.

specific evidence for their machines repeatedly battering their way into cities as opposed to intimidating defenders into abandoning the struggle.[70] One weakness in Avar assaults, and quite possibly also in Hunnic, was being able to sustain a large attacking force at a particular place for more than about a week—a reminder of the considerable logistical challenges in prosecuting a successful siege; the most obvious exception, the long blockade of Sirmium in 581–82, was at a site located close to the Avar homeland.

The Persians had a good track record, being able to bring protracted sieges at Amida in A.D. 359 and 502/503, or Dara in 573 and 604, to a conclusion, as well as capturing rather less-prepared places like Beroea or Antioch in the late 250s and again in 540, on the former occasion after an extraordinary tactical surprise.[71] They also experienced failure—e.g. at Nisibis repeatedly in the 4th c. and at Edessa in the 6th—but even these reverses display Persian inventiveness and determination in the combination of mines, machines, intimidation and blockade. They were particularly effective at constructing siege mounds, indeed building two against Dara in 573,[72] and they seem to have been rapid miners. Their engineering works extended to damming the river which ran through Nisibis and then releasing the water in order to undermine the walls in 350,[73] and cutting through a hill to divert Dara's water supply in 573.[74] The main machine they used was the ram,[75] along with picks and crowbars to lever stones out of walls, but references to projectile machines are rare:[76] when Khusro I exploited *ballistae* at Dara in 573, they are said to have been the machines which the Romans had recently abandoned after their failed attempt on Nisibis.[77] Given that there were numerous Roman captives settled in Persia, and the necessary expertise could have been purchased, it was perhaps

---

[70] Priscus fragment 6.2; *Miracles of Saint Demetrius* 200; *Chron. Pasc* 719.

[71] Amm. Marc. 23.5.3.

[72] Joh. Eph. *HE* 6.5.

[73] This version of the attack (Julian. *Ep.* 1.28.c-d) is more plausible (even if some details were borrowed from Heliodorus' *Aethipica* 9.3ff), than the more extravagant alternative in the later speech to Constantius (Julian. *Ep* 2.62c–63a), according to which Shapur created a lake around the city and then attempted to overcome the defences with ships carrying artillery.

[74] *Chron. Pasch.* 537; Joh. Eph. *HE* 6.5.

[75] E.g. Procop. *Pers.* 1.7.12 and 2.17.9.

[76] E.g. Amm. Marc. 19.7.5, against Amida in 359; Theoph. Sim. 2.18.11, defending Beiudaes in 587. Note too the rare mention of a siege tower at Martyropolis in 531 (Malalas 18.66); the Persians are also said to have made a 'mule' against the city (Zach. Myt. *Chron.* 9.6)—potentially a siege engine but more likely a siege mound.

[77] Joh. Eph. *HE* 6.5.

that the traditional Persian strength in archery, when combined with the effectiveness of their current tactics, reduced the apparent benefits of the more complex Roman torsion equipment. The frequent presence of the Persian king made a difference to the determination with which attacks progressed, and punishment for failure was swift.[78]

Arguably, the Romans were rather less successful overall: thus, attempts to recapture Bezabde in 360, Amida in 503/504, Martyropolis in 589, immediately after their respective loss to the Persians, could not be pursued to completion.[79] Other tasks took precedence; a blockade could not be maintained; opportunities were not ruthlessly exploited; or bad weather hampered efforts.[80] There were successes, such as Naples in 536, Sisauranon in 541, and Petra in 551, but more often, surrender came after a protracted blockade, as at Auximum in 539. There is, however, no evidence that the Romans' siege equipment was defective: their engines worked well defensively, which indicates a capacity to construct the machines as well as the presence of a supply of competent operators. One could speculate that cities would have been reluctant to see specialist personnel, on whom their safety might depend, being annexed by the mobile army, but the experts could have trained others. Part of the explanation might have been psychological: a successful assault required exceptional bravery, even foolhardiness,[81] which men might be most inclined to demonstrate if the emperor was present to notice and reward their efforts,[82] yet emperors oversaw sieges much less often than their Persian counterparts. Reluctance to lose valuable manpower may also have been a factor, since Roman commanders were more cautious with their soldiers' lives than the Persian king, and much more so than the Hun or Avar leaders.

SIEGE ENGINES

We are reasonably well informed about the siege machinery of the High Roman Empire, thanks to the survival of various Hellenistic technical

---

[78] E.g. Procop. *Pers.* 1.7.28 and 2.17.11–12.

[79] This probably underlies the assessment in Maurice's *Strategikon* that 'the Persians are fearsome at besieging, but more fearsome at being besieged' (11.1.9–10).

[80] Amm. Marc. 20.11.24. It appears that the Romans did not use circumvallation, or not as regularly as in the Early Empire.

[81] E.g. Theoph. Sim. 2.18.15–25.

[82] Amm. Marc. 20.11.12 for Constantius at Bezabde, though the attack failed.

treatises, which have been well edited and investigated by Eric Marsden,[83] and to limited archaeological evidence. Siege engines had an attraction for literary writers, and there are descriptions of different items in Ammianus, Procopius and Agathias. A base line is provided by the description in Ammianus of the main types of equipment: the arrow-firing *ballista*, stone-throwing *scorpio* or *onager*, ram, *helepolis* or siege tower, and fire dart, though there is also considerable information scattered through his narrative.[84] Ammianus knew these machines at first hand, having personally witnessed at Amida their noise, their accuracy in killing the son of Grumbates, and the challenge of moving even the smaller machines in response to a Persian success; at Maiozamalcha, he witnessed the unpleasant consequences of an accident involving a *scorpio*.[85] However, close examination of his description reveals that the contents were probably lifted from a written source, and some of the actual descriptions, for example, of the *helepolis*, are hard to understand.[86] Procopius, too, had similar field experience, especially from the siege of Rome, where he describes the poorly-designed Gothic siege towers, and notes the power of a catapult missile, which could pin a man to a tree.[87] *Ballistae, onagers*, mantlets, rams and mines are all part of the siege repertoire and are duly described;[88] Procopius' account of the *ballista* is somewhat clearer than that of Ammianus.[89] Agathias, though lacking comparable personal experience, is surprisingly informative, with descriptions in particular of the Roman mine at Cumae (provided perhaps as an excuse to talk about the Sybil's cave) and mantlets at Onoguris.[90]

There is some evidence for innovations in equipment in Late Antiquity: the Sabir Huns are said by Procopius to have devised a new form of ram at Petra, and the beam contraptions deployed by the Huns at Naissus might also be a variant of a Roman device.[91] The most significant change, as well as topic for debate, relates to the switch from the torsion stone-throwing artillery of the High Empire to machines based on the principle of a beam

---

[83]   Marsden (1969) and (1971); outlined in Southern and Dixon (1996) 152–60.

[84]   Amm. Marc. 23.4, compare also 20.11.11–15 on the rams at Bezabde. Matthews (1989) 291–94.

[85]   Amm. Marc. 18.8.13, 19.1.7, 19.5.6, 19.6.10 and 24.4.28.

[86]   Matthews (1989) 293; den Hengst (1999).

[87]   Procop. *Goth.* 5.22.1–10 and 5.23.9–12.

[88]   E.g. Procop. *Goth.* 5.21.

[89]   Den Hengst (1999) 30–31.

[90]   Agath. 1.10 and 3.5.9–11.

[91]   Procop. *Goth.* 8.11.28–34; Priscus fr. 11.2.

pivoting around an axle, which it is convenient to refer to as trebuchets. These machines were already in use in China, but the earliest western literary evidence for a traction trebuchet, namely one in which the motive power was provided by pulling on ropes, is the account in the *Miracles of St Demetrius* of the first Avar-Slav siege of Thessalonica. The siege most probably occurred in 586, but the description was written about three decades later, when the city was again coming under severe pressure and it was useful for the author, Bishop John, to demonstrate the efficacy of their patron saint's protection. John may have described a contemporary machine which his audience could see outside their walls, but it is possible, though beyond proof, that similar engines had also been used in the earlier siege:

> They are very substantial four-square constructions, tapering as the height increases; substantial iron-tipped axles are attached, to which are fastened massive timbers, suitable for house-building, which had slings fitted to the back end while at the front there were strong ropes which are pulled down in order to project the sling upwards into the air with a loud crash—the noise being produced by the projecting arm smashing into a buffer at the front of the machine. (*Miracles of St. Demetrius* 1.151).

This passage clearly describes something different from the traditional Roman machine whose continued use is attested in Procopius,[92] and the development has recently been discussed by Paul Chevedden in a long article about the development of the more powerful counter-weight trebuchets in the 11th and 12th c.[93] Potentially, the Avars had brought knowledge about its construction and operation with them from the East:[94] some of their equipment and tactics were certainly regarded as superior by the Romans,[95] and so they may have possessed other new resources. Chevedden, by contrast, asserts that the Avars acquired their knowledge about this machine from the Romans, on the basis of a short passage in Theophylact relating to the Avar capture of Appiaria in 587,[96]

---

[92] Syvänne (2004) 299, suggests that the trebuchet was introduced into the Roman world considerably earlier, possibly during the 5th c. In view of the complete absence of evidence, it is impossible to disprove this, but the failure of Procopius to describe this different machine makes me doubt that the Romans had already acquired it.

[93] Chevedden (2000); see also McCotter (2003), although this does not respond to Chevedden's arguments.

[94] Howard-Johnston (1984) 193.

[95] *Strategikon* 1.2; 2.1.

[96] Theoph. Sim. 2.15.13–16.11. For discussion of the military context and this anecdote, see Whitby (1988) 149–50, 181.

when a Roman soldier called Busas transmits his knowledge of siege technology in exchange for his life after his fellow townsmen have declined to
pay a ransom for him:

> Next Busas taught the Avars to construct a sort of besieging machine, since
> they had as yet no knowledge of such implements, and he prepared the siege
> engine (*helepolis*) for a long-range assault (*akrobolizein*). Shortly afterwards
> the fort was overthrown and Busas exacted punishment for inhumanity
> by giving the barbarians skilled instruction in the technology of siegecraft.
> (Theoph. Sim. 2.16.10–11)

One problem with this argument is the chronology. Chevedden accepts
the late dating of 597 for the Siege of Thessalonica without any consideration for the broader issues this raises, since his argument about the origin
of the Avar technology would otherwise be immediately negated.[97] There
are also problems with Chevedden's translation of the Theophylact passage, since he imposes precise language onto Theophylact's typically vague
rhetoric by introducing the specific word 'trebuchet' to render *helepolis*,[98]
which literally means 'city-taker', but had become the standard, almost
technical, term for a siege tower. Theophylact was not being technical,
since he was certainly referring to a machine that could deliver an assault
from a distance, *akrobolizein*, and it is reasonable to assume that it was
some sort of stone-thrower, since the fort was then 'cast down' or 'over-
thrown' (*katebebleto*).[99] There are also issues concerning the reliability
of Theophylact's report. It is certainly true that Rome's neighbours did
benefit from her technological expertise. For example, the Avars are said
to have demanded skilled builders from the Romans for works such as a
palace and bath house, but then coerced them into constructing a bridge
over the River Sava for the blockade of Sirmium.[100] In military matters,

---

[97] Chevedden (2000) 75 n.8, following Vryonis (1981); *contra* Lemerle (1979) 2.50–61;
Whitby (1988) 117–19; Yannopoulos (1980). Syvänne (2004) 306 accepts the date of 586 for
the Thessaloniki siege, but also finds the story of Busas entirely plausible. The date of the
siege is fixed by the announcement of the attack inside the city on Sunday 22 September,
since during Maurice's reign, the day and date only coincide in 586 and 597.

[98] Chevedden (2000) 75 n. 9, where he alters the translation of Vryonis without
justification.

[99] Chevedden (2000), following Vryonis (1981), renders this as 'levelled', which suggests
more extensive destruction than need have been the case.

[100] Joh. Eph. *HE* 6.24. Compare two later stories for the transfer of siege technology to
the Bulgars in the early 9th c. by individuals snubbed by the Emperor Nicephorus: Theoph.
chron. AM6301, p. 485, AM6305, p. 498. In 663/64, a Paphlagonian carpenter built a *man-
ganike* for the Arabs, perhaps a ram since it was to be used at close quarters against a gate,
but the defenders crushed it with a large rock (*Maronite Chronicle AG* 975).

however, as noted above, they were superior to the Romans in certain respects; while a trebuchet is somewhat more complex than a bow or type of tent, there is no reason why they could not have acquired knowledge of it in the East and carried this with them during the moves towards Europe.

The thesis that the Avars derived their machine from the Romans in 587 presupposes that the latter had been prompted to change a long-standing and effective item of siege machinery, the *onager*, at some point in the preceding generation. It is unclear, however, what reasons there might have been for such a significant change. Greater power might be one. In terms of projectile capacity the most powerful Chinese traction trebuchet, with a pulling cohort of 250 men, was capable of throwing a stone of about 60 kilos a distance of more than 75 m,[101] whereas the standard Roman heavy *onager* projected a one talent missile, i.e. 25 kilos, with maximum impact at distances up to 150–70 m;[102] the Romans had some more powerful machines with a capacity of 1.5 talents, i.e. 38 kilos, though these are still far short of the Chinese weight. At the defence of Amida in 502, the defenders devised an extraordinary engine, dubbed 'The Striker' by the attacking Persians, which was capable of projecting stones of almost 100 kilos, and it is possible that for defensive purposes, great weights could be delivered to effect.[103] Disregarding such an exceptional engine, a trebuchet with significantly greater striking force than an *onager* could certainly have been developed in due course, though with a reduced range.[104] It seems unlikely, however, that the Romans could immediately have created a traction machine with the power of the best Chinese engines. The traction trebuchet would also have been less precise: this depended on the human pulling team delivering the same momentum on repeated occasions, so that the shots might be scattered quite widely,

---

[101] Chevedden (2000) 74.

[102] Marsden (1969) ch. 4.

[103] Josh. Styl. ch.53, p.59. At Cremna, two stone balls were discovered outside the defences, weighing 102 and 135 kilos. Mitchell (1995) 184–86 concluded that these must have been dropped, or rolled down, by the besieged because they were so far beyond the capacity of the normal Roman engines, but it is possible that the defenders constructed a machine like 'The Striker', since they were said to have had a talented artilleryman (Zos. 1.70). Julian, *Or.* 2.63a, refers to stones weighing 7 Attic talents, i.e. 180 kilos, being hurled by the Persians at Nisibis in 350, but this is in the context of a very fanciful account of the attack and so cannot be trusted.

[104] Syvänne, who believes the Romans had possessed the trebuchet since the early 5th c., asserts that there would have been little difference in capacity: (2004) 299 n. 3.

whereas Roman torsion machines could be adjusted as appropriate and had a good reputation for accuracy.[105]

Ease and speed of use favoured the trebuchet: torsion equipment required considerable technical skill to construct, maintain and use;[106] it would be affected by bad weather whereas the simpler trebuchet was more robust, and the re-tensioning of springs would take longer than the re-setting of the trebuchet's main beam, so a change to a less accurate engine with a reduced range might have been made on grounds of usability. Marsden believed that the skills base of the Roman Army had already declined during the 4th c., since it was composed of soldiers "who were not sufficiently amenable to discipline, and not intelligent enough to understand the benefits that artillery support could afford them".[107] These comments arise from the negative view of a progressively de-Romanised or barbarised army, which was the standard scholarly view a generation ago, but is no longer accepted.[108] With regard to the skills to operate machines, the armies whose actions are recorded by Procopius and Agathias in the 540s and 550s could still manage torsion equipment effectively, and so it would be necessary to postulate a rapid and catastrophic decline in skills, as well as the invention of a new machine within the space of a single generation, which seems unlikely. Even if it were conceded that soldiers in the mobile army came to appreciate the benefits of a somewhat rough and ready machine which they could use quickly at a particular spot, nevertheless, the defenders of a city such as Appiaria, which is where Busas derived his expertise, would still have stuck with their superior torsion equipment. The accuracy credited to the defenders of Thessalonica, who could pick off the operators of the machines,[109] suggests that they were still using torsion equipment, even if the machines in question were firing arrows.

---

[105] *Miracles of St Demetrius* 153–54; Zos. 1.70. McCotter (2003) suggests that the account in Theoph. Sim. (2.18.1–6) of the siege of a stronghold in Arzanene, in which some Roman missiles flew right over the fort, might reflect the problems caused by the recent introduction into the Roman army of the more powerful but less accurate trebuchet. In the complete absence of other evidence, this remains no more than a remote possibility, since there are other obvious explanations for the uncharacteristic inaccuracy, for example the difficulties of the elevated target.

[106] Veg. *Mil.* 4.22, 29.

[107] Marsden (1969) 195, was in fact discussing the introduction of the *onager*, probably during the 3rd c., to replace the *ballista*, which he regarded as more complicated to construct; but the assertion could be applied with equal logic to the 6th c. developments.

[108] E.g. Lee (2007); Whitby (2000a) and (2007).

[109] *Miracles of St. Demetrius* 1.153.

Finally, if the Avars did acquire a significant boost to their siege techniques in 587, we might expect improvements in Avar capacity to take cities thereafter. Although Theophylact asserts that the Avars went on to capture many other cities without difficulty, the next three attacks which he mentions, on Diocletianopolis, Philippopolis and Adrianople,[110] all failed in the face of stern resistance from the defenders; at Diocletianopolis, it was the defenders' catapults which kept the Avars at bay.[111] One year later, the Avar chagan failed again at Singidunum and Drizipera, though at the latter, he is specifically said to have constructed siege engines which intimidated the defenders.[112] By contrast, the Avar record before 587 is not bad. True, they had to resort to a long blockade at Sirmium in 581–82, but Singidunum, Viminacium and Augustae all fell swiftly in 583, even though the means of the Avars' victory is not known. Apart from the capture of Appiaria itself, it is difficult to identify any particular consequences from the supposed lessons of Busas. As a result, the anecdote of Busas should be seen for what it is, namely a story intended to explain how the supposedly barbarian Avars were capable of deploying some of the technology associated with an advanced nation and battering down city walls; the Romans knew that the Avars lacked the capacity to build substantial bridges, but would not have known that they had once had access to a tradition of military technology that was at least as rich as that of the Romans.

ARCHAEOLOGICAL EVIDENCE

How much more can archaeology contribute to the picture delineated above? If this question is restricted to Late Antiquity, the simple answer is that the great documented sieges have left so little material evidence for their actions that it is impossible to say much: we have the walls, and so can discuss how people prepared for sieges through the design of fortifications;[113] and repairs to walls can sometimes be identified, and these may indicate how people responded to some of the impacts of sieges. For example, at Rome, there is limited evidence in the surviving walls to

---

[110] Theoph. Sim. 2.16.11, 16.12–17.3.
[111] Theoph. Sim. 2.17.1.
[112] Theoph. Sim. 6.5.4.
[113] Or through clearing buildings which might obstruct fields of fire or give useful shelter to attackers: at Merida an extramural quarter to the south of the city was levelled prior to the Arab attack in the 8th c.: Alba Calzado (1997)—a reference I owe to Luke Lavan.

support Procopius' information about the preparations of Belisarius for the siege of 537, which included a particular design of merlon, and his repairs to the wall facing after recapturing the city in 547;[114] there is also evidence for hasty blocking of the Aqua Traiana, perhaps in anticipation of the siege.[115] But the bit in between preparations and repairs, the action of the siege, is largely blank. We have parts of the metal frames from four light arrow-shooting engines from late 4th c. forts at Gornea and Orsova in Romania, *ballista* bolts and a fire arrow from Dura Europos, metal fittings from an early 3rd c. stone-thrower from Hatra,[116] and diverse missiles from Cremna, including the standard 25-kilo *onager* missile, as well as two massive balls of over 100 kilos,[117] but these illustrate what we already know from the literary texts.

At this point it is worth looking more broadly at which sieges from the ancient world have in fact generated significant archaeological evidence, an approach which is legitimate, since, with the exception of the introduction in the 4th c. B.C. of projectile machines, and their subsequent evolution, there is considerable continuity in the practice of siege warfare: the main siege techniques are evident in Assyrian relief panels from the palace at Nimrud now located in the British Museum.[118] Sites such as Old Smyrna (*ca.* 600 B.C.), Phocaea (*ca.* 546 B.C.), and Old Paphos (494 B.C.) have substantial remains of Lydian and Persian siege mounds; at Tyre (332 B.C.), the causeway which Alexander constructed to approach the fortified island still connects this part of the city to the mainland; at Avaricum (52 B.C.), there are the remains of Caesar's base camps, double circumvallation, and extra measures to prevent the escape of the defenders; Maiden Castle and Hod Hill in Dorset (A.D. 40s) provide evidence of Vespasian's violent attack, with numerous catapult missiles and bones attesting the force of their impact; at Masada (A.D. 73), the Roman base camps and part of the circumvallation survive, as at Avaricum, but also the massive ramp that permitted siege engines to approach the walls, and from the same revolt, a siege mound survives at Herodion; at Dura Europus (*ca.* A.D. 256), there survive the defenders' last-minute strengthening of the

[114] Procop. *Goth.* 5.14.15 and 7.24.3–6. Richmond (1930) 72, 89, 264–67.

[115] http://users.ox.ac.uk/~corp0057/blocking.html—a reference I owe to Luke Lavan.

[116] Discussion, illustrations and references in Southern and Dixon (1996) 153–57.

[117] Mitchell (1995) 183–86.

[118] Matthews (1989) 289, 292 notes the continuity between Assyrian warfare and Late Antiquity; for an overview of ancient sieges and the material evidence for them, see the clear discussion in Coulston (2001) 31–42. For substantial continuity into the Middle Byzantine period, see Haldon (1999) 183–89.

walls with mud-brick cladding on the outside and a reinforcing bank on the inside,[119] the Persian mines and Roman counter-mines, including the skeletons of those killed in underground fighting, and the Persian siege mound sited to take advantage of a tower collapsed by earlier mining; finally, at Cremna in Pisidia (probably A.D. 278), there is a siege mound with a modest response inside the walls, the attackers' countervallations, and considerable evidence for the impact on the walls of heavy artillery.[120]

One thing the majority of these sites have in common is consequent abandonment and desertion. The exceptions are Old Smyrna and Old Paphos, where the siege mounds were incorporated into the restructured defences (though both settlements moved to new sites before long); Tyre, where the causeway came to serve a useful function within the much expanded Hellenistic city; Herodion, where re-occupation was brief; and perhaps Cremna.[121] The difficulties in finding evidence at places where occupation has been continuous are obvious: after a siege, those in charge of the fortification would remove all traces of siege mounds etc. which might threaten the on-going security of their defences, patch up damaged walls and towers, or build new sections. Thus at Amida, the evidence for the 4th c. siege would have been obliterated by the subsequent rebuilding and expansion of the city. The machines used in assaults would have been removed by the besiegers, or at least the key components, which could not readily be devised from materials on site.[122] Strikingly, the late antique sieges best attested in the literary record were all at cities with a continuing history of habitation.

Another complication with regard to Late Antiquity is the fact that many of the sites of great sieges, Amida, Edessa, Dara, Constantinople, Thessalonica, were subjected to repeated attacks over the centuries, so that the remains of one particular siege will be extremely difficult to disentangle.

---

[119] Veg. *Mil.* 4.3.

[120] Cremna is the one case where a reasonable account in a literary source (Zos. 1.69–70) can be assessed alongside the archaeological evidence; for detailed consideration see Mitchell (1995) ch. 6.

[121] The existence of 7 churches inside the walls and a further one just outside indicate that there continued to be a considerable level of population at Cremna, but no attempt was made to restore the shattered defences or remove the mound. This is a puzzle and one must assume that, for whatever reasons, the inhabitants did not feel sufficiently threatened to embark on these considerable labours.

[122] See Joh. Eph. *HE* 6.5 for the consequences of not doing so: the machines which the Romans had abandoned when they fled in panic from Nisibis were promptly used against Dara. Ammianus records that in 360 the Romans re-used against Bezabde a huge battering ram abandoned by the Persians at Carrhae, perhaps a century earlier (20.11.11).

Urban expansion over the past two centuries is also relevant, with the
Late Roman walls of Antioch being blown up, at least in the lower city,
and a comparable attempt being made in the 1930s on the more durable
defences of Amida (though these are largely medieval). Modern development might reveal hidden evidence (e.g. the siege mound at Phocaea), but
more usually will obscure and destroy it. Unexpected discoveries are not
impossible, as the finding of the mine and counter-mine from the 1546
French siege of St Andrew's castle illustrate; these had been obliterated
for over 300 years—an example of the normal tidying-up process after the
end of the siege—but excavation of the foundations for a tall house on the
corner of North Castle Street and the Scores broke into the very spacious
French mine, and the uncovering of that led to the desperate twists and
turns of the third counter-mine, which John Knox and his fellow defenders had hacked out as they homed in on the French approach.[123]

Is there scope for such lucky finds for Late Antiquity? At Amida and
Edessa, the defenders tunnelled under the 6th c. Persian siege mounds in
order to set them on fire; potentially, substantial investment of resources
to probe around the whole of the respective circuits might identify the
locations of this activity, although the benefits in terms of extra knowledge would not justify the allocation of time and money: we could pin
down the point of the city walls which the Persians chose to assault, and
perhaps also discover equipment and skeletons, but this would not add
significantly to our understanding of the attack on the individual city or
of siege warfare in general.[124] It is possible that investigations at sites
such as Sirmium or Justiniana Prima might produce clearer evidence for
their capture by the Avars, although Sirmium succumbed to a long blockade. At Justiniana Prima, there is also evidence that suggests a period of
co-existence between the urban Romans and tribal incomers, although
the presence of numerous arrow heads, including distinctive Avaro-Slav
heads, around the gates and in the streets, indicates (predictably) some
intense fighting. At some point, the city was destroyed by fire, possibly
during this assault, although the capture of the city might also have been

---

[123] Kirk (1954) 105.
[124] Thus the discovery of 14 bodies thrown down a well at Huntcliff, or a partially dismembered skeleton at Dichin which had lain unburied since its lower bones had been
chewed, perhaps by wolves (see Poulter (2007) 86), remind us that the victims of a successful attack could not expect their remains to be treated with respect and corroborate
literary evidence such as Priscus fr. 11.2.54–5, but they do not illuminate the process of the
capture of these places.

followed by a period of cohabitation with Roman survivors living under Avaro-Slav control.[125]

Sirmium's last period under Roman control generated a graffito: 'Lord Christ, help the city and smite the Avars and watch over Romania and the writer. Amen'.[126] It is perhaps ironic that the most informative material evidence relating to sieges in Late Antiquity concerns the apparently intangible issue of the morale of defenders, in particular the role of Christianity. One example is the Shroud of Turin: even if this is most unlikely to be the wonder-working icon invented at Edessa in 544 to thwart the Persian attack, it represents the sort of object that might have been used by panicking citizens.[127] The fragmentary mosaics and other evidence for the shrine of Demetrius at Thessalonica illustrate the appearance of the focal point for civilian morale in the city.[128] City walls and gates were decorated with, or reinforced by, crosses at Ephesus, Ankara, Sardis, Aphrodisias, and numerous other places, while Christ's special guarantee to Edessa was displayed over one of the gates. These are an essential reminder that, from a late antique perspective, survival would be ensured just as much by the blessings or curses of the local bishop, and by whatever other divine resources could be summoned, as by the physical structures and the individuals who manned them.

Bibliography

Primary Sources

Aen. Tact. = Whitehead D. (2001) trans. intro. and comm. *Aineias the Tactician: How to Survive under Siege: a Historical Commentary with Translation and Introduction* (2nd ed., London 2001).

Agath. = Keydell R. (1967) ed. *Agathiae Myrinaei Historiarum libri quinque* (Berlin 1967).

Amm. Marc. = Rolfe J. C. (1963) ed. and trans. *Res Gestae* (London 1963).

Chron. Pasch. = Dindorf L. A. (1832) ed. *Chronicon Paschale* (Bonn 1832); Whitby M. and M. (1989) trans., intr. and notes. *Chronicon Paschale 284–628 AD* (Liverpool 1989).

Evagr. = Whitby M. (2000) trans. and ed. *The Ecclesiastical History of Evagrius Scholasticus* (Liverpool 2000).

Joh. Eph. *HE* = Brooks E. W. (1935–36) ed. and Latin trans. *Iohannis Ephesini Historiae ecclesiasticae pars tertia* (Corpus scriptorium Christianorum Orientalium 105–106; Scriptores Stri 54–55) (Paris and Louvain 1935–36).

---

[125] Kondic and Popovic (1977) 383.
[126] Brunsmid (1893).
[127] Cameron (1981a) ch. 5, (1998).
[128] Cormack (1985) ch. 2, e.g. 52 pl. 14.

Josh. Styl. = Trombley F. R. and Watt J. W. (2000) trans. *The Chronicle of Pseudo-Joshua the Stylite* (Translated Texts for Historians 32) (Liverpool 2000).

Julian. *Ep.* = Wright W. C. F. (1913–23) ed. and trans. *The Works of the Emperor Julian* (London and Cambridge, Mass. 1913–23).

Malalas = Thurn I. (2000) ed. *Ionnis Malalae Chronographia* (Berlin 2000).

Malchus = Blockley R. C. (1983) ed., trans. and notes. *The Fragmentary Classicising Historians of the Later Roman Empire: Eunapius, Olympiodorus, Priscus and Malchus Vol.2* (Liverpool and Cairns 1983).

Maronite Chronicle = Palmer P., Brock S. P. and Hoyland R. G. (1993) trans. and intro. *The Seventh Century in the West-Syrian Chronicles* (Translated Texts for Historians 15) (Liverpool 1993).

Miracles of St. Demetrius = Lemerle P. (1979–81) *Les plus anciens recueils des miracles de Saint Démétrius et la pénétration des Slaves dans les Balkans* (Paris 1979–81).

Priscus = Blockley R. C. (1983) ed., trans. and notes. *The Fragmentary Classicising Historians of the Later Roman Empire: Eunapius, Olympiodorus, Priscus and Malchus Vol.2* (Liverpool and Cairns 1983).

Procop. *Goth.*, Procop. *Vand.*, Procop. *Pers.* = Dewing H. B. (1914–54) ed. and trans. Procopius, *History of the Wars* (London 1914–54).

Strategikon = Dennis G. T. (1984) ed. *Maurice's Strategikon. Handbook of Byzantine Military Strategy* (Philadelphia 1984); Dennis G. T. ed. and Gamillscheg E. trans. (1981) *Das Strategikon des Maurikios* (CFHB 17) (Vienna 1981).

Theodore Syncellus = Sternbach L. (1900) ed. *Analecta Avarica* (Cracow 2000).

Theod. *HE* = Parmentier L. and Hansen G. C. (1998) edd. Theodoret, Bishop of Cyrrhus, *Kirchengeschichte* (Berlin 1998); anon. trans. in Bohn's *Ecclesiastical Library* (London 1854).

Theoph. Sim. = de Boor C. (1887) *Theophylacti Simocattae Historia* (Leipzig 1887; rev. and amended ed. P. Wirth, Stuttgart 1972); Whitby M. and Whitby M. (1986) trans. *The History of Theophylact Simocatta: an English Translation with Introduction and Notes* (Oxford 1986).

Thuc. = Powell J. E. (1942) ed. *Thucydidis Historiae* (Oxford 1942).

Veg. *Mil.* = Milner N. P. (1996) trans. *Epitome of Military Science* (2nd ed., Liverpool 1996).

Zach. Myt. *Chron.* = Greatrex G., Phenix R. R., Horn C. B. and Brock S. P. (2010) edd. and trans. *The Chronicle of Pseudo-Zachariah Rhetor: Church and War in Late Antiquity* (Liverpool 2010).

Zos. = Ridley R. T. (1982) trans. Zosimus, *New History* (Canberra 1982).

Secondary Works

Alba Calzado M. (1997) "Ocupación diacrónica del área arqueológica de Morería", in *Mérida. Excavaciones arqueológicas 1994–95. Memoria* (Consorcio Ciudad Monumental Histórico-Artística y Arqueológica de Mérida) (Mérida 1997) 285–316.

Baynes N. H. (1955) "The supernatural defenders of Constantinople", in N. H. Baynes, *Byzantine Studies and Other Essays* (London 1955) 248–60.

Brunsmid J. (1893) "Eine griechische Ziegelinschrift aus Sirmium", *Eranos Vindobonensis* (Vienna 1893) 432–33.

Cameron A. (1978) "The Theotokos in sixth-century Constantinople", *JTS* 29 (1978) 79–108; reprinted in A. Cameron, *Continuity and Change in Sixth Century Byzantium* (London 1981), chapter 14.

—— (1979) "The Virgin's Robe: an episode in the history of early-seventh century Constantinople", *Byzantion* 49 (1979) 42–56; reprinted in A. Cameron, *Continuity and Change in Sixth Century Byzantium* (London 1981), chapter 17.

—— (1981a) *Continuity and Change in Sixth Century Byzantium* (London 1981).

—— (1981b) "The sceptic and the shroud", in A. Cameron, *Continuity and Change in Sixth Century Byzantium* (London 1981) chapter 5.

—— (1998) "The Mandylion and Byzantine iconoclasm", in *The Holy Face and the Paradox of Representation. Papers from a Colloquium held at the Biobliotheca Hertziana, Rome and the Villa Spelman, Florence*, edd. H. L. Kessler and G. Wolf (Villa Spelman Colloquia 6) (Bologna 1998) 33–54.

Chevedden P. (2000) "The invention of the counterweight trebuchet: a study in cultural diffusion", *DOP* 54 (2000) 71–116.

Coulston J. C. N. (2001) "The archaeology of Roman conflict", in *Fields of Conflict: Progress and Prospect in Battlefield Archaeology: Proceedings of a Conference held in the Department of Archaeology, University of Glasgow, April 2000*, edd. P. W. M. Freeman and A. J. Pollard (BAR International Series 958) (Oxford 2001) 23–49.

Cormack R. (1985) *Writing in Gold. Byzantine Society and its Icons* (London 1985).

den Hengst D. (1999) "Preparing the reader for war. Ammianus' digression on siege engines", in *The Late Roman World and its Historian: Interpreting Ammianus Marcellinus*, edd. J. W. Drijvers and D. Hunt (London 1999) 29–39.

Haldon J. F. (1999) *Warfare, State and Society in the Byzantine World 565–1204* (London 1999).

Howard-Johnston J. D. (1984) "Thema", in *Maïstor: Classical, Byzantine and Renaissance Studies for Robert Browning*, ed A. Moffatt (Canberra 1984) 189–97.

—— (1995) "The Siege of Constantinople in 626", in *Constantinople and its Hinterland: Papers from the Twenty-Seventh Spring Symposium of Byzantine Studies, Oxford, April 1993*, edd. C. A. Mango and G. Dagron (Society for the Promotion of Byzantine Studies 3) (Aldershot 1995) 131–42.

Isaac B. H. (1990) *The Limits of Empire: the Roman Army in the East* (Oxford 1990).

Kirk R. (1954) *St Andrews* (London 1954).

Kondić V. and Popović V. (1975) *Caričin Grad: Site fortifié dans l'Illyricum byzantine* (Galerie de l'Académie Serbe des sciences et des arts 33) (Belgrade 1975).

Lee A. D. (2007) *War in Late Antiquity: a Social History* (Oxford 2007).

Lemerle P. (1979) *Les plus anciens recueils des Miracles de Saint Démétrius* I (Paris 1979).

Marsden E. W. (1969) *Greek and Roman Artillery: Historical Development* (Oxford 1969).

—— (1971) *Greek and Roman Artillery: Technical Treatises* (Oxford 1971).

Matthews J. (1989) *The Roman Empire of Ammianus* (London 1989).

McCotter S. (2003) "Byzantines, Avars and the use of the trebuchet", www.deremilitari. org (2003).

Mitchell S. (1995) *Cremna in Pisidia: an Ancient City in Peace and War* (London 1995).

Peeters P. (1920) "Le légende de Saint Jacques de Nisibie", *AnalBoll* 38 (1920) 285–373.

Poulter A. G. (2007) "The transition to Late Antiquity on the Lower Danube: the city, a fort and the countryside", in *The Transition to Late Antiquity: on the Danube and Beyond*, ed. A. G. Poulter (Proceedings of the British Academy 141) (Oxford 2007) 51–97.

Richmond I. A. (1930) *The City Wall of Imperial Rome* (Oxford 1930).

Southern P. and Dixon K. R. (1996) *The Late Roman Army* (London 1996).

Syvänne I. (2004) *The Age of the Hippotoxotai. Art of War in Roman Military Revival and Disaster (491–636)* (Tampere 2004).

Vryonis S. (1981) "The evolution of Slavic society and the Slavic invasions in Greece: the first major Slavic attack on Thessaloniki, A.D. 597", *Hesperia* 50 (1981) 378–90.

Whitby M. (1988) *The Emperor Maurice and his Historian: Theophylact Simocatta on Persian and Balkan Warfare* (Oxford 1988).

—— (1998) "*Deus nobiscum*: Christianity, warfare and morale in Late Antiquity", in *Modus Operandi, Essays in Honour of Geoffrey Rickman*, edd. M. M. Austin, J. D. Harries and C. J. Smith (London 1998) 191–208.

—— (2000a) "The army, c. 420–602", in *The Cambridge Ancient History. Volume 14, Late Antiquity: Empire and Successors, A.D. 425–600*, edd. A. Cameron, B. Ward-Perkins and M. Whitby (Cambridge 2000) 86–111.

—— (2000b) *The Ecclesiastical History of Evagrius Scholasticus* (Liverpool 2000).

—— (2007) "Army and society in the Late Roman world: a context for decline?", in *Companion to the Roman Army*, ed. P. Erdkamp (Oxford 2007) 515–31.

Whitby M. and M. (1989) *Chronicon Paschale 284–628 AD* (Liverpool 1989).

Yannopoulos P. A. (1980) "Le pénétration slave en Argolide", *Études Argiennes, BCH Suppl.* 6 (1980) 323–71.

WEAPONRY AND EQUIPMENT

LATE ROMAN MILITARY EQUIPMENT CULTURE

J. C. N. Coulston

Abstract

The paper explores the cultural components of Late Roman military equipment through the examination of specific categories: waist belts, helmets, shields and weaponry. Hellenistic, Roman, Iron Age European, Mesopotamian-Iranian and Asiatic steppe nomad elements all played a part. The conclusion is that the whole history of Roman military equipment involved cultural inclusivity, and specifically that Late Roman equipment development was not some new form of 'degeneration' or 'barbarisation', but a positive acculturation.

INTRODUCTION

In recent years, what might be characterised as the 'Romanisation' debate has been dynamic and far-reaching, and it has forced scholars to take a hard look at what they mean by the definition 'Roman', and at how the cultures within and without the Roman Empire interacted.[1] In the field of Roman army studies, it has long been recognised that the term 'Roman' is useful as a geographical and temporal designator, and one which may be loosely applied to the evolving institutional development of Roman armies. Within an overarching framework of appointments and other elements of central administration, there were regional variations in organisation, language and material culture (such as frontier fortifications, installational architecture, ceramics and diet).[2] Thus it is unsurprising that military equipment, the arms, armour, and other items required for warriors and soldiers to engage in conflict, was likewise subtle in its makeup, development and cultural interplay.

---

[1] Woolf (1998) 1–23; Mattingly (2004); Hingley (2005); Schörner (2005); Janniard and Traina (2006); Gardner (2007) 24–34; Revell (2009).

[2] For discussions of diversity within the army, see Goldsworthy and Haynes (1999); James (1999), (2004) 246–54 and (2006); Coulston (2004).

A. Sarantis, N. Christie (edd.) *War and Warfare in Late Antiquity: Current Perspectives* (Late Antique Archaeology 8.1–8.2 – 2010–11) (Leiden 2013), pp. 463–492

In order to study military equipment produced by any pre-industrial society, it is necessary to put aside potentially anachronistic assumptions about centralised design, uniformity and mass production based on the practices of more modern armies. However, examination of the cultural traits and components of the Late Roman army involves an additional complication. Here, the over-burden of what might be termed 'Decline-and-Fall' studies has caused military equipment to be linked with certain pre-suppositions of declining efficiency and technological capacity, some-times backed by a selective reading of ancient authors, with an assumption that the army's 'traditional' discipline was sapped, its culture 'barbarised' through an influx of mainly 'Germanic' personnel, and its equipment poorly supplied and maintained in comparison with previous provision.

Clearly an 'episodic' examination of equipment developments will yield a jerky picture of change, and if reconstructions of, for example, *legionarii* of the 1st, 3rd and 4th c. A.D. are presented alongside each other, then they appear to represent radically different worlds, moving from the com-fortingly familiar Trajan's Column-based figure to seemingly alien pros-pects. However, the contrast is enhanced by viewing in isolation what are points on a continuum. This is precisely why the finds from Dura-Europos in Syria, predominantly dating to the mid-3rd c. A.D., are so pivotal for any examination of 4th c. developments. Not only is the extensive Dura assemblage well preserved in arid climatic conditions, but it forms a bridge between the 2nd c. and the Tetrarchy, and it is backed up by plen-tiful parallel material from wet Scandinavian contexts, and by a rich 3rd c. corpus of funerary military iconography.[3]

There are also problems peculiar to the Late Roman archaeological record which both hamper and facilitate equipment studies. Neat site abandonment deposits with their troves of unfinished, damaged and awaiting-repair artefacts, so characteristic of 1st to 3rd c. military installa-tion on dynamic frontiers, are largely absent from contexts where occu-pation shaded into the Early Middle Ages.[4] Figural military gravestones, so numerous in the first half of the 3rd c. A.D., decline to a few isolated

---

[3] In general, see Bishop and Coulston (2006) 10–14, 31–32, 149, 199. For Dura: James (2004). Scandinavia: Jørgensen *et al.* (2003); Coulston (2008); Grane (2007). Iconography: Coulston (2007).

[4] Although there are signal exceptions, as with the *Depothort* finds of helmets—see Klumbach (1973) 103–105; Miks (2008)—and artillery fittings—see Gudea and Baatz (1974).

groups in the Tetrarchic period, and to a trickle thereafter.[5] On the other hand, soldiers burst into glorious polychromy from the Tetrarchy onwards, appearing much more frequently than before in wall-painting and mosaics. Representations of soldiers, particularly imperial bodyguards, are also relatively frequent in state artworks such as stone sculptures, glassware, coins and other metalwork.[6] Funerary depositions of military equipment, always present in small numbers in previous periods, really come into their own in the 4th c., not least because of the practices of non-Roman groups outside or moving within the empire.[7]

Traditional emphasis has been placed on declining discipline leading to less wearing of bothersome armour, based almost solely on an aside made by Vegetius in his *Epitoma rei militaris*. Much has also been made of the 'foreign' nature of particular features of clothing and equipment in connection with barbarisation. The supposed decline in the use of armour by infantry has been discussed at length elsewhere, but it would seem that there was no real diminution of provision, rather the reverse, with more attention paid in the 4th c. to physical coverage.[8] There was no real change in the tactical environment on the eastern frontier in particular, and the archery of prominent enemies, such as the Goths and Sassanian Persians, would have placed even greater emphasis on defending Roman troops from missiles.[9] There does seem to have been increased emphasis on heavily armoured cavalry under both Sarmatian and Sassanian Persian influence.[10]

The evolution of textile fashions can be traced through the 3rd–5th c. A.D., and some forms of cloak characteristic of the 1st c. A.D. army, notably the circular *paenula*, ceased to be worn by the later 2nd c., being replaced by the rectangular *sagum* which became ubiquitous thereafter. Coincidentally, by the later 2nd c. A.D., and certainly by the 3rd c., long-sleeved tunics and tight, long trousers came to dominate. Covering the

---

[5] Espérandieu (1907–66) nos. 1780, 3940–43, 5496; Franzoni (1987) nos. 12–17, 20–23; Speidel (1984); Boppert (1992) no. 18; Mennella (2004); Bishop and Coulston (2006) 12, fig. 133; Coulston (2007) 542; Aillagon (2008) nos. II.11–12.

[6] Rinaldi (1964–65); Bishop and Coulston (2006) 17–18; Sumner (2009).

[7] Böhner (1963); Sommer (1984) 88–93; Schultze-Dörlamm (1985); Vallet and Kazanski (1993) 109–23, 157–86, 355–65; Wamser (2000) 219–25; Swift (2000) 50–52 and (2006) 105–106; Nagy (2005); Theuws (2009).

[8] Veg. *Mil.* 1.20; Coulston (1990) and (2002) 8–9; Elton (1996) 110–14; Glad (2009).

[9] Veg. *Mil.* 1.20; *Strategikon* 11.1. For German archery, see Pauli-Jensen (2007).

[10] Coulston (1986); Mielcsarek (1993); Harl (1996); Elton (1996) 105–107; Negin (1998); Richardot (2005) 271–86.

limbs was perhaps more practical in a military context, both for engagement in robust tasks and for operating in varied climatic environments.
Trousers (and hairstyles) may have been synonymous with barbarians in
the context of the city of Rome in the late 4th c., as suggested by the *Codex
Theodosianus*,[11] but wider societal trends in clothing fashions were also
being reflected within narrower military contexts. Campaigning along and
beyond the northern frontiers, coupled with the recruitment of northern
people into dominant army groups, spread styles from temperate Europe
around the imperial armies. Coincidentally, the long sleeved tunics of the
Mesopotamian-Iranian cultural zone also spread westwards.[12] This was
not entirely dissimilar to the reflection of civilian clothing styles in the
military contexts of later historical periods, although involving less rapid
and nuanced evolution than that seen in the armies of Early Modern, late
pre-industrial, and industrial 16th to 19th c. Europe.[13]

It is unclear which region of the Roman Empire was more influential
in this clothing transition, whether the northern frontier provinces (the
Danubian being more dominant in the 2nd c. than the Rhenish), or the
Levant. This dichotomy will be met with again, but whether one region
or both played significant parts, the cultural traits were as much securely
grounded within provincial societies as they were features of external,
'barbarian' cultures. The main discernable change over the 3rd–4th c. in
Roman military contexts was the increasing prominence of embroidered
tapestry appliqués (*orbiculi*) on tunics and cloaks, as is well substantiated
both in the archaeological textile record and in contemporary iconography.[14] However, the overall schemes of decorated hems, lower sleeves,
neck-openings, and skirts with coloured thread woven into the garment,
had evolved from decoration of 1st to 3rd c. garments.[15]

Another item which might be brought in as a clear-cut candidate for
external import into the equipment of the Late Roman army is the '*draco*'
standard. Late writers gave the *draco* prominence, and the epigraphic

---

[11] *Cod. Theod.* 14.10.2–4.
[12] Although with less prominence of the long, baggy trousers and felt calf-boots of the
eastern equestrian tradition—Colledge (1976) 98–104 and (1977) 133–34; Downey (2006)
233–36. For changes in 2nd–4th c., see Bishop and Coulston (2006) 144, 184; James (2004)
246–51 and (2006) 361–64; Sumner (2009).
[13] For example, the evolution of brimmed headwear in the later 17th to later 18th c., or
the cut of uniform coats over the same period.
[14] Rinaldi (1964–65); Deckers (1973); Bishop and Coulston (2006) 224–25; Sumner (2009)
52–70, figs. 44–47, 49, 54, 56–57, 75–8, pls. 29–30.
[15] E.g. Sumner (2009) figs. 32, 41, 98, pls. 19, 21.

record indicates the presence of *draconarii* within the rank structure of Late Roman regiments.[16] Snake-standards are also well known from the state iconography of the Tetrarchic period, appearing on the Arch of Galerius in Thessalonica (Greece) and the Arch of Constantine in Rome, and on smaller artworks such as the Ságvár (Hungary) bronze plaques.[17] However, whilst the use of wolf-headed standards by Dacians on Trajan's Column and their appearance amongst barbarian *spolia* in Flavian and later *congeries armorum* reliefs is well-known,[18] related snake-headed standards were already in use amongst Roman cavalry from the Hadrianic period onwards as evidenced in literature (Arrian) and iconography (Antonine Portonaccio Sarcophagus, Rome).[19] This is not to say that the *draco* was anything but an import from the Central Asiatic tradition of animal-headed standards with wind-sock bodies, but its adoption and development by Roman forces was a much longer term and more subtle process.

Some of the more obvious 'stalking horses' of imported cultural traits thus may prove to be more complicated in terms of the period and nature of physical transfer. The present paper will consider the development of military equipment into the 4th c. and beyond as a continuing process, rather than as some form of departure made under the influence of 'new', Late Roman factors, such as 'decline' or 'barbarisation'. It is certainly not the purpose here to revisit the 'barbarisation' debate,[20] but its parameters will be touched upon through necessity. Rather, an attempt will then be made to characterise Late Roman equipment culture through an examination of several specific classes of equipment, namely waist belts, helmets, shields and weaponry.[21]

---

[16] Amm. Marc. 15.5.16, 16.10.7, 16.12.39 and 20.4.18; Veg. *Mil.* 2.7, 13; SHA *Aurel.* 31.7; Zos. 3.19. See Speidel (1985).

[17] Coulston (1991) figs. 9–11. *Dracones* were in use by Early Medieval European armies, perhaps reinforced by Avar and Magyar contacts, and one seems to be depicted on the decorated brow band of a *Spangenhelm* from Chalon-sur-Saône in France—Böhner (1994) fig. 17; Vogt (2006) fig. 49.

[18] Coulston (1991) 101–102, figs. 1–4 and (2003) 430, pl. 10; Polito (1998) figs. 129, 146.

[19] Arr. *Tact.* 35. This evidence is fully presented in Coulston (1991).

[20] For the more recent discussions: Liebeschuetz (1991) 7–25; Southern and Dixon (1996) 46–55; Elton (1996) 136–52; Nicasie (1998) 97–116; Richardot (2001) 293–320; Janniard (2001) 356–61; Whitby (2004) 164–69; Lee (2007) 83–85; Aillagon (2008) 206–11.

[21] Saddlery and other horse-harnesses will not be examined here, but see Coulston (1986); Herrmann (1989); Bishop and Coulston (2006) 227.

WAIST BELTS

Traditionally, fittings from waist belts have played a central part in discussions of culture-change within the Late Roman army. A series of erroneous assumptions have been made based on the artefactual record. First, that the decorative style of chip-carving (*Kerbschnitt*) was seen as a Germanic form, and thus that the types of fittings themselves were Germanic. Finds of such fittings, especially in graves, were equated with the presence of German *laeti* or *foederati*, and the widespread use of such fittings was taken to indicate Germanic 'barbarisation' of the Roman army. However, analysis of the decorative elements suggests that, as with the helmet ornament discussed below, motifs were part of the Late Roman repertoire, not derivations from other artistic traditions. They formed close visual links with the decorative elements of military tunic and cloak textiles.[22] Moreover, the fittings belonged to forms of belts which were part of a typology of development going back at least to the later 2nd c. A.D. While the metalwork exhibited new combinations of decoration, and the belts bore new plate and buckle forms, the belts themselves were essentially the broad 3rd c. type with a frontal buckle, narrow strap pull-through tucked up on the wearer's right hip, and a pendent strap-end.[23] They were a central and essential part in the visual identification of military service, which spilled over into broader Roman society from the Tetrarchic period onwards with the militarisation of state administration and service professions.[24]

Major finds of belt-fittings have been made in burials associated with army installations, as in the cemetery at Oudenburg (Belgium), and also in *Waffengräber* cemeteries in northern France and the Benelux countries.[25] Certainly, some of the latter do represent the burial practices of intrusive, Germanic populations, and ceramics indicate that whole communities were moved into the empire, women and children as well as warriors, as is amply attested in the literary sources,[26] but there were pre-

---

[22] For 4th c. fittings in general, see Bullinger (1969); Sommer (1984); Bishop and Coulston (2006) 218–24.

[23] Bishop and Coulston (2006) 182–84, figs. 94, 101, 138, 141–42; Hunter (2013) figs. 7.21–22, 12.1–3, 15.3, 15.14.

[24] SHA *Gallieni duo* 30.3–5; SHA *divus Claudius* 14.5; SHA *Carus et Carinus et Numerianus* 17.1; Amm. Marc. 22.10.5; Zos. 3.19, 5.46; *Cod. Theod.* 14.10.1; *N.Val.* 20.1, 36.5. See Jones (1964) 566; MacMullen (1963) 49–76; Sommer (1984) 87–101; Gardner (2007) 209–29; Swift (2009) 169–79.

[25] Mertens and Van Impe (1971) 54–56, fig. 24–26, Pl. II, LXXXIII (Oudenburg); Bullinger (1969); Sommer (1984); Böhme (1986).

[26] Böhner (1963); Böhme (1986); Liebeschuetz (1986), (1991) 7–47 and (1993); MacMullen (1988) 199–204; Vallet and Kazanski (1993); Elton (1996) 91–94, 272–77; Nicasie (1998)

existing Roman provincial traditions of inhumation with weapons and/ or with belts and boots.[27] The geographical distribution pattern of chip-carved belt-fittings can be made to look like importation from Free Germany (where there was also a broad belt tradition).[28] Problems with this arise from the incompleteness of distribution studies within the Roman provinces, notably in the Lower Danubian, Levantine and North African regions.[29] The artificially reversed polarity of finds of Cernjachov Culture material across the Lower Danube may be cited as a close parallel to this distributional phenomenon.[30] To some extent the weapons-graves over-shadow the numerous 'Roman' burials with 3rd and 4th c. belt-fittings, often accompanied by a knife, sometimes by a sword, but not other arms.[31]

Finds of chip-carved belt sets thus may be seen as a reflection of the distribution of both provincial and extra-imperial burial practices. Overall, Late Roman belts represent continuity of development from 3rd c. designs, plus evolution of decoration and metalwork forms. Undoubtedly, such belts were supplied to Germanic troops both in regular Roman army units and in formations that were more tribal and *ad hoc*. The very personal importance of belts as indicators of military status, and their use through patronage to reward service, led to their interment with deceased soldiers perhaps as a related but not specifically Germanic rite—although separating out the two may have been problematic even at the time of burial. Precious metal sets are predictably rare in the archaeological record, as compared with tinned or silvered copper alloy fittings, and are represented more in bullion hoard contexts than in cemeteries.[32] Even in copper alloy, the finest chip-carved sets may be associated with higher class field army troops, and with Germanic formations directly equipped

---

97–114; Fischer *et al.* (1999); Lee (2007) 81–85; Leahy (2007). While the numbers of Germans within the empire increased in the 4th c., this was a continuing process throughout the Roman imperial period: Grane (2007b); Rushworth (2009).

[27] Bishop and Coulston (2006) 33. The Sixteenth Roman Military Equipment Conference (*RoMEC XVI*, Zagreb, 2010) took as its theme: 'Roman Military Equipment from Funerary Contexts' (proceedings forthcoming).

[28] Sommer (1984) maps 4–6; Böhme (1986) fig. 3; Bishop and Coulston (2006) fig. 140.

[29] Although see Nagy (2005).

[30] Heather and Matthews (1991) map 2.

[31] For example, Ivanovski (1987); Fischer (1990) 77–80, pls. 92, 108, 110, 126, 144; Petculescu (1995); Kazanski (1995b); Aouni (1998); Buora (2002); Nagy (2005).

[32] An exceptional gilded silver set has recently been discovered in excavation of the Crypta Balbi in Rome: Manacorda *et al.* (2000) 52. For belt fittings with the 4th c. Berkasovo helmets and in the 5th c. Traprain Horde (Scotland), see Klumbach (1973) pl. 10; Nagy (2005) fig. 27.1.

and patronised by central government.[33] The socio-political importance of Roman military belts also led to their residual regard and retention as insignia of power and/or legitimacy in sub-Roman contexts.[34]

Helmets

There appears to have been a typological break in helmet design in the late 3rd c. A.D., moving from a one-piece bowl with integral neck flange to more simple, multi-part bowls with separate neck defences.[35] These helmets are characterised by a prominent ridged strip or crest, running fore-and-aft, which dominates a two-, four- or six-piece riveted bowl.[36] Neck guards are narrow and tongue-shaped. When cheek pieces survive, they are either of the 'Berkasovo' type, broad and trapezoidal (for cavalry?), or of the 'Intercisa' type, with narrow, triangular cheek pieces (for infantry?). The parts were made of iron, with cheek pieces attached indirectly to the bowl by being laced to an integral textile or leather lining, and neck pieces held by buckled straps. Only a minority of helmets display direct hinge attachment of the articulated elements. Helmets with trapezoidal cheek pieces sometimes also feature a T-shaped nasal piece riveted to the front of the bowl. Many extant examples were additionally covered in a sheathing of gilded silver. This may survive forcible removal by leaving fragments under the heads of attachment rivets, or parts or the whole of the sheath may survive separate from the lost iron helmet. In the latter case, the inherent value of the sheathing material dictated retention and deposit as a bullion hoard, as with examples from Berkasovo (Serbia) and Alsóhetény (Hungary).[37]

---

[33] In 4th c. Britain, this includes a small number of burials at such sites as London and Winchester (Coulston, forthcoming). Locally recruited militias may account for regional variations in forms of British fittings: Hawkes and Dunning (1961); Hawkes (1974); Simpson (1976); Laycock (2008) 118–34.

[34] For example, in the Anglo-Saxon cemetery at Dorchester-on-Thames: Bullinger (1969) pl. LVIII; Esmonde Cleary (1989) 55–56. See also Oldenstein (1979).

[35] In general, see Alföldi (1934); Klumbach (1973); James (1986); Driel-Murray (2000); Lusuardi Siena *et al.* (2002); Born (2003); Bishop and Coulston (2006) 210–16; Miks (2008); Glad (2009) 39, 42–43, 59–60, 97–102.

[36] The term 'Guard' helmet (*Gardehelm*) has been coined for this type because the bullion sheathing and degree of decoration seemed to indicate the highest status of the owner: see Klumbach (1973) 9. Miks employed the term 'Comb' helmet (*Kammhelm*) as more descriptive of the most characteristic feature: (2008) 4–5. Similarly, 'Ridge' helmet has become current in the English literature.

[37] Klumbach (1973) 15–38; Kocsis (2003).

The corpus of ridge helmets collected for publication in 1973 by Klumbach[38] has been substantially increased in recent years by new finds and the publication of old discoveries, which have clarified constructional methods and provided additional dating evidence.[39] For example, one of two reconstructable iron helmets from a late 4th to early 5th c. context at Iatrus (Bulgaria) has a two-part bowl, a surviving neck-guard, and a 'Berkasovo' cheek-piece. Unusually it was sheathed in gilded copper.[40] A two-part iron helmet from a grave at El-Haditha (Jordan) was found in association with ceramics dating to *ca.* A.D. 350–420.[41] A near complete gilded silver sheath was found, having been folded up and inserted into the wall of the Late Roman fort at Alsóhetény.[42] A collection of iron helmet fragments found in 1988 at Koblenz (Germany) has recently been published and displays new features of copper alloy edging strips and embossed cheek piece decoration.[43] This appears to be a *Depotfund* dating to the middle third of the 4th c., based on context, coin finds, ceramics, and decorative details related to specific coin issues. It is similar to the group of at least 15 helmets found at Intercisa (Hungary) in 1909,[44] but a greater range of helmet forms seems to be present, including Intercisa and Berkasovo ridge helmets and *Spangenhelme* (see below).

The simplification of helmet design and construction represented by the ridge type may have been connected with the expansion of Roman armies under the Tetrarchy, and linked to equipment production in the centralised *fabricae* attested later in the *Notitia Dignitatum*.[45] Inspiration for this undoubted break from 1st to 3rd c. infantry and cavalry helmet forms may have come from the Partho-Sassanian sphere. The Persian helmet from the Tower 19 siege-mine at Dura-Europos (Syria), dating to the mid 250s

---

[38] Klumbach (1973): 14 helmets published in detail, 25 known including the mass of fragments from Intercisa (Hungary).

[39] Bishop and Coulston (2006) 210, 214; Miks (2008); Glad (2009) 97–102. Miks (2008) fig. 22 collected approximately 57 helmets. There are also fragments of one or more iron helmets from Osijek in Croatia (Radman-Livaja (2010) 235–38), two incomplete gilded silver sheaths of helmets in a private collection, and one helmet found in 2006 near Sremska Mitrovica (Serbia, now on display in the Vojvodina Museum with the Berkasovo helmets). All three have 'Berkasovo' type cheek-pieces. Thus there are now more than 60 known Late Roman helmets.

[40] Born (1999); Miks (2008) figs. 62, 68.

[41] Parker (1994a) and (1994b).

[42] Kocsis (2003).

[43] Miks (2008).

[44] Klumbach (1973) 103–105.

[45] *Not. Dign. or.* IX.18–39 and *occ.* XI.16–39. See James (1988); Bishop and Coulston (2006) 238–40.

A.D., has a two-part conical bowl with a ridge strip, and a T-shaped nasal piece. It substitutes a mail aventail, attached around the rim of the bowl, for cheek pieces and neck guard.[46] This helmet lies within a Mesopotamian tradition, but the features of bowl construction were adopted for Roman use by the late 3rd c., much as ring-mail armour earlier passed from west to east into Sassanian use.[47] Alternatively, there is one helmet amongst the 33 depicted on the pedestal reliefs of Trajan's Column which may be classified as a ridge helmet;[48] this suggests a Danubian route by which Roman armourers may also have experienced the ridge form, but there is as yet no indication that it was in any manner directly influential on Roman construction designs at this early date.

The decoration of ridge helmet sheaths is largely Late Roman in style, including bands of crosses, crescents, crest forms and strigilation, anchors, and classicising figural motifs.[49] Stamped motifs correspond with imperial marks found on silver ingots, and a cheek-piece from Koblenz bears a Victory holding up two wreaths in the style of coins of the house of Constantine.[50] An embossed *chi-rho* appears on the helmet sheath from Alsóhetény, and *chi-rho* 'badges' adorned the front of upstanding helmet crests.[51] The helmet of Valentinian I which was lost in a marsh along with the emperor's *primicerius* was described by Ammianus as decorated with gold and precious stones, and such 'high-end' helmets were depicted in imperial numismatic portraiture.[52]

However, a helmet from Aquincum-Budapest (Hungary), and one of the two helmets from Berkasovo (Serbia) exceptionally incorporate rectangular, lozenge, and ovoid polychrome paste settings, representing semiprecious stones such as onyx, chalcedony and emerald.[53] These form a pair of 'eyes' on the front of the bowl, a feature seen with other apotropaic signs on the iron helmets from Intercisa[54] and in Late Roman iconogra-

---

[46] James (1986) and (2004) 104, figs. 47–48.

[47] As seen on the Firuzabad (Iran) reliefs dating to the reign of Ardashir I at the very beginning of the Sassanian period: Gall (1990) pls. 6–8.

[48] South-west side, top left corner—see Coulston (2008) 319.

[49] Klumbach (1973) 26–27, 32–33, 43–45, 60, 87–89, 93, 96–98, 100–101; Miks (2008) 33–24. Distinguishable from the motifs found on later *Spangenhelme*—as Böhner (1994); Vogt (2006).

[50] Miks (2008) figs.82–83.

[51] Lyne (1994); Prins (2000); Mackensen (2007); Miks (2008) 52–54.

[52] Amm. Marc.27.10.11 (*auro lapillisque distinctam*). Compare SHA *Maximini duo* 29.9 (*fecit et galeas gemmatas, fecit et bucculas*); *Cod. Theod.* 10.22.1. Numismatics: Alföldi (1932) and (1934) 99–103; Klumbach (1973) pl. 65; Overbeck (1974); Miks (2008) fig. 113.

[53] Klumbach (1973) 18–20, 33, 43–44, pls. 1–5, 12–16, 18; Miks (2008) figs. 13, 16.

[54] Klumbach (1973) fig. 24–27, pl. 57.

phy.[55] Significantly, these examples were found in the Danubian region, and the settings may be linked stylistically to actual semi-precious stone ornament on Sarmatian metalwork.[56] There is some direct evidence for gem-setting 'eyes' on Sarmatian helmets, and this suggests the direct transference of a barbarian trait into a Roman cultural context.[57]

A second form of helmet which existed right through from at least the 1st c. A.D. outside Roman use, but which is far less prominent than the ridge helmet in the Late Roman record, was the segmental *Spangenhelm*. More conical in profile and lacking the dominant fore-and-aft ridge, this helmet first appears artefactually in Roman use in the 6th c., but is already depicted worn by Roman troops on the Tetrarchic Arch of Galerius at Thessalonica (Greece).[58] The decoration on a *Spangenhelm* from Hera-clea Lynkestis (Macedonia) identifies it as of Roman manufacture, and is related to numismatic designs and Christian iconography dating to as late as the 520s.[59] The helmet is related to the 'Baldenheim' type of *Spangen-helm*, contemporaneously common in the barbarian successor kingdoms of the West, and in Roman use in the Balkans and North Africa.[60] The design shared with ridge helmets such features as holes around the bowl rim, cheek piece edges for lace-attachment of a leather or fabric lining, and the T-shaped nasal plate. Generally, they lacked a solid neck guard, but a curtain of mail, scale, leather or textile was attached to the rear rim.

This helmet form is first encountered in 1st and 2nd c. A.D. Roman, Sarmatian and Sarmaticising iconography, notably on frescoes in tombs at Kerch (Ukraine), on Crimean gravestones, and on the reliefs of Tra-jan's Column.[61] Prominent in the Early Medieval period, it persisted in European armour design, without the cheek-pieces, but with a nasal and

---

[55] Bishop and Coulston (2006) fig. 133.2, pl. 6c.

[56] Klumbach (1973) 46; *Sarmates* (1995) nos. 86, 98, 100–102. Siepell (1999) 120, 126, no. 45.

[57] Kazanski (1995a) fig. 4.1; Simonenko (2001) fig. 38.4; Lebedynsky (2002) 136.

[58] Laubscher (1975) pls. 12.2, 31–32, 65.2.

[59] Maneva (1987); Werner (1989) 424–26, fig. 2; Böhner (1994) fig. 33; Vogt (2006) 196–98, fig. 66.

[60] For the helmet form in general, see Werner (1949–50) and (1989); Post (1951–53); Böhner (1994); Born (2003); Vogt (2006); Glad (2009) 45–51, 60–62, 104–14. Roman use in North Africa is suggested by an example from Lepcis Magna in Libya: Pirling (1974); Böh-ner (1994) fig. 34; Vogt (2006) pl. 19; and one from Dar al-Madinah, Egypt: Ebert (1909); Dittmann (1940); Vogt (2006) 77, pls. 40–41.

[61] Iconography: Kieseritzky and Watzinger (1909) nos. 606, 619, 650; Gamber (1964) figs. 4–5, 17; Lebedynsky (2002) 165, 241; Coulston (2003) pls. 4, 6–8. Trajan's Column: Cichorius (1896–1900) Scene LXXVIII. For Sarmatian helmets in general, see Brentjes (2000); Simo-nenko (2001) 263–67; Lebedynsky (2002) 112, 165–71; Vogt (2006) 101–107.

a mail or scale aventail, or worn over a mail coif, until at least the 12th c.[62] Similar helmets bearing 5th and 6th c. style decoration were used within the Sassanian Empire, and contributed to a continuous currency of conical cavalry helmets across Africa, the Levant, Persia and India up to the 19th c.[63]

Taking the surviving Roman artefactual evidence at face value, it would appear that *Spangenhelme* were the exclusive design of the future, and that ridge helmets did not outlast the early 5th c. On the contrary, it may confidently be expected that more ridge helmets will be found in future that will take the type forward chronologically within the Roman context. This is a safe assertion because 6th to 8th c. helmets from Britain and Scandinavia were related to Roman ridge designs. The Sutton Hoo (UK) helmet had a fore-and-aft ridge, a nasal-guard and 'Berkasovo' cheek-pieces. Quite extraordinarily, it also had a one-piece bowl and a separate, broad-flaring neck guard. It seems to have been old when deposited in the 7th c., and may have been made in the first or second half of the 6th c.[64] Closely-related in terms of ridge and 'T' nasal were Scandinavian Vendel period helmets. Examples from Vendel, Ulltuna, and Vallsgårde (Sweden), and from York (UK), also date to the second half of the 6th c. and extend into the 8th. They informed even later helmet designs in use alongside *Spangenhelme* in Viking period evidence.[65] Originally, they derived their bowl features from Late Roman ridge helmets, combined with forms of neck and cheek protection in the *Spangenhelm* tradition. Interestingly, distributions of 'Baldenheim' *Spangenhelme* and Vendel ridge helmets hardly overlap on distribution maps.[66] Thus it would appear likely that vagaries of survival have conspired to create a spatial and temporal gap between Late Roman and Scandinavian developments which obscures the true picture.

Use and adaptation of non-Roman helmet models was not a Tetrarchic innovation. At least 4 iron or copper-alloy, conical, one-piece bowls with hinged cheek-pieces and separate neck-curtains have been recovered in

---

[62] Edge and Paddock (1988) 13–26, 31, 34–35, 38–41, 44–49.

[63] Werner (1949–50) 184–88; Grancsay (1963); Gamber (1964) and (1968); Overlaet (1982); Vogt (2006) 96–101, 287–92, pls. 48–55; Miks (2008) 5; Glad (2009) 104–106.

[64] Bruce-Mitford (1978) 138–231; Tweddle (1992) 1090–95, figs. 530–32.

[65] Werner (1949–50) 192–93; Gamber (1968) 35–42; Klumbach (1973) 14; Bruce-Mitford (1978) 220–23; Tweddle (1992) 1087–90, figs. 537–40, 543–55; Böhner (1994) 533–47, figs. 38, 42–43; Halsall (2003) 170–71; Miks (2008) 14. Dating following Arrhenius (1983).

[66] Werner (1989) fig. 1; Tweddle (1992) figs. 523, 525; Böhner (1994) maps 1–6; Vogt (2006) fig. 38.

the Danubian region.[67] These 1st to 2nd c. helmets might be considered a reflection of Sarmatian *Spangenhelme*, 'translated' through traditional Roman bowl construction, and given embossed classicising figural decoration; alternatively, they may have been the equipment of Levantine *sagittarii* stationed along the Roman Danubian frontier, and thus represent an offshoot of non-Roman helmet designs going back to the earlier Iron Age Mesopotamian-Levantine tradition.[68] In either case, they seem to have been a developmental *cul-de-sac* leading nowhere in terms of later developments.

SHIELDS

The iconography of Late Roman shields suggests that they were generally large and oval, continuing the type which was current throughout the 3rd c.[69] Boards found at Dura-Europos were constructed of glued vertical planks, oval in shape, slightly dished to brace their structure, and rim-bound with stitched rawhide. A horizontal iron bar was riveted across the middle of the back of the shield, and a circular metal boss was attached to the front, over a cutting made in the centre to accommodate the owner's hand.[70] This was presumably the type of shield which Ammianus described falling to pieces in Julian's hand when the emperor was training.[71]

There is little evidence that the traditional rectangular shield continued in use much after the mid-3rd c., but circular shields do appear on 3rd and 4th c. gravestones, and on Tetrarchic, Constantinian and Theodosian triumphal monuments.[72] The circular shield blazons represented in manuscripts of the *Notitia Dignitatum* may represent no more than convenience to the copyist of using a compass to draw numerous circles of uniform diameter.[73] Nevertheless, circular boards may have been an

---

[67] Mansel (1938); Radulescu (1963); Robinson (1975) 85, pl. 237; Petculescu and Gheorghe (1979); Szabó (1986); Velkov (1928–29) pls. III–IV.

[68] Bottini *et al.* (1988) 22–41; Collins (2008) 36–38, 40, 45–51, 74, 78, 90–94, 101, 108–109.

[69] For 4th c. shields in general, see Bishop and Coulston (2006) 216–18.

[70] Dura-Europos: James (2004) 159–62, 176–82.

[71] Amm. Marc. 21.2.1.

[72] Gravestones: Ésperandieu (1907–66) no. 4300; Barkóczi (1944) pl. XII.2; Boppert (1992) no. 18. Triumphal monuments: Laubscher (1975) pls. 30–34, 36, 65; l'Orange and Gerkan (1939) pls. 8–9; Becatti (1960) pls. 51–54, 73b; Coulston (1990) fig. 4. Curved, rectangular shields continued in the context of 4th c. gladiatorial games.

[73] Berger (1981) 43–57; Grigg (1983); Bishop and Coulston (2006) 217–18.

import of Germanic design, the best parallels for which being the well-preserved plank boards from 3rd and 4th c. Scandinavian votive deposits.[74] Other aspects of Germanic shield usage certainly were influential on the 4th c. Roman army, including the raising of newly-acclaimed emperors on shields in barbarian fashion,[75] and the spread to Roman troops of the German war-cry (*barritus*) which used the shield as a sounding board.[76]

Some pieces of leather from Egypt, now in the Original-Abgusssammlung, University of Trier (Germany), have been convincingly identified as shield facings with painted blazons.[77] One depicts Romans and North African natives in combat. Another is richly decorated in purely geometric fashion. A third depicts a hunting scene and a full-length soldier (or emperor, or Mars?) below the boss, wearing a white tunic and a brown cloak, fastened with a prominent 4th c. crossbow brooch. He holds a spear and rests on a shield, which in turn bears a running lion blazon. All these elements are very reminiscent of 3rd c. shields from Dura-Europos, particularly those oval ones with *Amazonomachia* and Mars designs, and the lion blazon on one rectangular shield.[78] The Egyptian 'soldier' motif also brings to mind the Minerva figure on a Hadrianic shield-cover from the *legio I Minervia* fortress at Bonn (Germany), and the Hercules blazon seen on the Arch of Galerius.[79]

It is interesting that the Christian *chi-rho* motifs seen as shield blazons on Theodosian and later monuments[80] are rare in the *Notitia*.[81] The manuscript included many plain or simple geometric designs, and when these correlate with other sources to seemingly identify a specific regiment, this may be simple generic coincidence.[82] In any case, the original document

---

[74] Sternquist (1955) 119; Raddatz (1987) nos. 391–93, pls. 84–85; Jørgensen *et al.* (2003) 268, 313. For German shields in general, see Raddatz (1985) 313–15, 322; Zieling (1989); Dickinson and Härke (1992) 43–54.

[75] Notably Julian by his troops: Amm. Marc. 20.4.17; Zos. 3.9.4; Ensslin (1942); Rummel (2005) 120–23. See Tac. *Hist.* 4.15 for a German precedent. The practice was revived in 9th c. Byzantium: Walter (1975).

[76] Veg. *Mil.* 3.18. Compare Tac. *Germ.* 3; Amm. Marc. 16.12.43, 26.7.17, 31.7.11. For German tactical influences, or lack of them, see Rance (2004) 288–95.

[77] Goethert (1996).

[78] James (2004) 176–79, 182–86, pls. 6–10; compare Laubscher (1975) pl. 35.

[79] Driel-Murray and Gechter (1983) 35–36; Bishop and Coulston (2006) fig. 20.2; Laubscher (1975) pls. 34, 38.1.

[80] Becatti (1960) pls. 50b, 51a, 73b; Kent and Painter (1977) no. 11; Paolucci (1971) 46; Browning (1987) pl. 22.

[81] There are no definitive examples, but some which might be garbled Christian symbols, for example *Not. Dign. or.* 5.7–9, 22, 7.8, 21.

[82] See Alföldi (1935) and (1959); Berger (1981) 145–48; Speidel (1990); Woods (1996) and (1998) 32–34.

from which the surviving copies were derived may itself have been a copy of an official, un-illuminated working text, which was only subsequently and imaginatively illustrated as a deluxe presentation edition. It is most unlikely that the *Notitia* was ever intended to have been a 'spotter' book of Late Roman regiments. In any case, its blazons were greatly simplified, and are seen darkly in transmission through the Carolingian and later medieval manuscript tradition.[83] With no Germanic blazons surviving in reliable iconography or in the artefactual record, it cannot be determined whether there was specific barbarian influence on the decoration of Late Roman shields.[84]

WEAPONRY

Some forms of weaponry which appear in Roman contexts have been identified as 'Germanic' in origin. A few barbed spearheads with long, socketed iron shanks have been recovered from forts along Hadrian's Wall,[85] and these are best paralleled by spear types found in Scandinavia.[86] Together with inscriptions and ceramics, these do suggest the presence of Germanic formations on the northern British frontier, principally in the 3rd c.[87] A small number of axe-heads with the curved profile characteristic of 'Frankish' *franciscae* have also been found in Britain and in northern Gallic cemeteries.[88] However, it is not entirely clear that these weapons were restricted to use by German warriors in general, and by Franks in particular during the 4th–early 5th c.[89]

To these specifically identifiable influences might be added the evidence for the longevity of light 'Moorish' javelins in Roman use. These were the prime armament of North African light cavalry directly impinging on

---

[83] The manuscript tradition was discussed by Alexander (1976).

[84] German shields were certainly painted, but figural motifs have not survived: Tac. *Germ.* 6; Sternquist (1955) 118; Jørgensen *et al.* (2003) 268.

[85] Richmond (1940); Cowan (1948); Swanton (1973) 22–23, figs. 3–5; Manning (1976) nos. 21–23; Scott (1980) 339, fig. 24.4; Allason-Jones and Miket (1984) no. 5.90; Mould *et al.* (2002) 82, figs. 270.9–10.

[86] Notably, Illerup Ådel Types 5–8: Ilkjær (1990) pls. 154–217. See also Bushe-Fox (1949) pls. LVIII.284, LIX.289; Ilkjær (1990) pls. 220–31. Some of these may have been precursors to the fully developed *ango*, which, like the *francisca*, became associated with the Franks: Schnurbein (1974).

[87] Collingwood and Wright (1995) nos. 1576, 1593–94; Jobie (1979).

[88] Dahlmos (1977); Kieferling (1994); Rummel (2005) 174–79. Bushe-Fox (1949) pls. LXI.341–42.

[89] Swift (2006) 105–106.

Roman warfare from the Punic Wars onwards. *Mauri* were deployed away from North Africa for their particular missile skills under the empire, coming into particular prominence with the proliferation of light cavalry formations in the 3rd c. A.D.[90] They could be drawn upon until the western African provinces were lost to the Vandals, then again from this region's recovery by Justinian's armies through to the Arab conquest.[91] The ethnonym for light javelins continued to be applied in Maurikios' late 6th c. *Strategikon*.[92]

The sword worn by the overwhelming majority of Late Roman soldiers was the long *spatha*. It superseded the traditional infantry short sword from the Antonine period. The 3rd c. representations of soldiers almost exclusively depict *spathae*, and the development of blade forms can be traced in the artefactual record through into the 5th c.[93] What is unclear is why there was this shift in infantry armament. The suggestion that long swords were in some way more suited to a 'defensive' Late Roman Empire hopelessly muddles tactical with strategic considerations.[94] Nor can the transition be interpreted as the spread of cavalry swords to the infantry, because there is no indication that mounted fighting styles were so dominant before the 5th c. The change cannot be attributed to a radical shift in the tactical environment which might have influenced infantry weaponry. Legionary and auxiliary infantry might have required a longer reach when facing mounted opponents along the Danube and in the East, and it might be contended that the wars of Marcus Aurelius on both fronts were a catalyst of equipment change, but horsed enemies had been faced since the 1st c. B.C. in the Levant and the 1st c. A.D. in eastern Europe.

Perhaps the increasing political and cultural domination by the Danubian army group from the Antonine period onwards played a part in equipment change. Alongside a renaissance in 'Celtic' ornament on later 2nd c. military artefacts, Illyrian soldiers maye have developed a predilec-

---

[90] As depicted on Trajan's Column—see Cichorius (1896–1900) Scene LXIV. See SHA *Maximini duo* 11.7; Hdn. 3.3.4, 6.7.8, 7.2.1; Zos. 1.15, 20, 52, 4.35; *Not. Dign. or.* 31.23, 32.18, 33.26, 34.21, 35.16, 37.17, *occ.* 6.15, 18, 33.31, 34.23 (although some of these units were also styled '*Illyriciani*'). In general: Speidel (1975).

[91] Procop. *Goth.* 5.5.4, 5.25.9, 5.29.22.

[92] *Strategikon* 11.2.20.

[93] Bishop and Coulston (2006) 154–57, 202–204; Miks (2007) 77–105, pls. 54–150.

[94] Webster (1956) 25 "The short sword was characteristic of the confident, attacking soldier. When the empire went over to the defensive, the long sword (*spatha*) became more widely used. This was a weapon more adapted to keep the enemy at bay or to reach him from a defensive position."—a problem also puzzled over by Lendon (2005) 263–68.

tion for northern European sword forms.[95] This was clearly the case with the 2nd c. A.D. adoption by some Roman infantry of the short Sarmatian ring-pommel sword (*Ringknaufschwert*) at the same time as this type was circulating in Free Germany. The characteristic iron pommel is found at Roman frontier sites, and is depicted on a gravestone from Aquincum (Hungary) which is unlikely to date much later than the reign of Antoninus Pius.[96]

More controversial is the development of the method of sword suspension into the Late Roman period. Waist belt (*balteus*) carriage seems to have become predominant in the 4th c. There is some evidence for baldric suspension, but by a narrow belt rather than the broad baldric characteristic of the 3rd c.[97] Attachment of scabbard to belt using a copper-alloy, iron, bone or antler scabbard slide developed around the same time as adoption of long swords by infantry; the two may have been linked, but they were not synonymous, as is indicated by another 2nd c. Aquincum gravestone, which shows the scabbard of a traditional short sword bearing a slide.[98] Whilst the evidence suggests that this was a Danubian development which spread out to other army groups around the empire, James has suggested that the slide was adopted through Partho-Sassanian contacts in the East.[99] Scabbard slides are prominent in 3rd c. Sassanian rock reliefs. In Palmyrene sculpture, slides supersede four-ring scabbard suspension, just as they do in Roman representations, but the earliest instance is dated by inscription to A.D. 191, so not earlier than the Aquincum slide gravestone.[100] On the other hand, James drew attention to instances in Hatrene sculpture which appear to be even earlier.[101] In origin a Chinese or Central Asian development, slides spread through Asia, and into India, Iran and Europe, with steppe nomad movements.[102] In the Roman context, it is not possible at present to make a distinction between Levantine or Danubian 'first contact', and, indeed, the two avenues of development were unlikely to have been exclusive given the direct, often simultaneous,

---

[95] Bishop and Coulston (2006) 128.
[96] Gravestone: Bishop and Coulston (2006) fig. 79.2. Finds: Hundt (1953); Kellner (1966); Biborski (1994); Bishop and Coulston (2006) fig. 77.1–2; Miks (2007) 177–87, pls. 33, 36–37, 39–40, 44, 46–52, 58 and (2009). Raddatz (1960); Jørgensen *et al.* (2003) 229, 323.
[97] Bishop and Coulston (2006) 204, figs. 130, 133.2.
[98] Bishop and Coulston (2006) fig. 79.1.
[99] James (2006).
[100] Colledge (1976) 51, pl. 44 (and pers. obs.).
[101] James (2006) 369–70.
[102] The central thesis of Trousdale (1975).

impact of nomad groups on both the Roman and the Partho-Sassanian spheres.[103]

Roman archery equipment was dominated by the Levantine tradition in terms of bow construction, arrow-head forms, bow-cases and quivers. Curiously, this entirely overshadowed any influence from steppe nomad archers contacted along the Danube until the appearance of the Huns in the 4th c.[104] Then, new bows were introduced alongside new saddle types with a heightened emphasis on the skills of mounted archery. During the 4th-5th c., this new prevalence shifted the tactical balance away from the infantry main battle line (with cavalry wings) towards lines of armoured horse archer formations supported by infantry. Further reinforcement of the process came with the advent of the Avars in the 6th c.[105] The development of mounted bowmen as the tactically decisive troops meant that some of the more energetic emperors and generals were lauded for their archery skills,[106] and even occasionally depicted as horse-archers.[107]

In a discussion of the cultural make-up of Roman military equipment, it is easy to overlook the continuity of Hellenising elements. These were present throughout in the decoration of artefacts, notably in peltaform motifs, but more functionally in the continuous development and improvement of artillery. Design theory could only really be expressed through Greek mathematics, and there was a continuous Greek literary tradition.[108] However, within the Roman imperial army, empirical design appears to have been paramount, leading to great improvement in construction, mobility and performance, and to the development of new weapon forms, such as *onagri* and iron-frame *ballistae*.[109] New emphasis on the mural defence of cities in the 3rd–4th c. might be represented as a return to Hellenistic period design, but, like the artillery, it actually represented a new stage of application and enhancement.[110]

---

[103] Although direct contacts between East Asia and the Roman Danube are further emphasised by the finds of Chinese artefacts in Thracian tombs: see Bujukliev (1986) 72, pl. 10; Werner (1994).

[104] Coulston (1985) and (2003) 426.

[105] Bivar (1972) 281–86; Haldon (1975) 11–13, 20–21 and (1999) 215–17; Coulston (1985) 242–44, 273–75, 286; Ravegnani (1988) 45, 49–51; Syvänne (2004) 38–41; Rance (2005); Greatrex *et al.* (2005); Luttwak (2009) 4–61, 78–81.

[106] Sid. Apoll. *Carm.* 23; Gregory of Tours *Hist.* 2.8; Procop. *Goth.* 5.22.5–6.

[107] Aillagon (2008) no. 1.41 (Constantius II).

[108] Marsden (1971). The discussion of artillery in Latin in Vitr. *De arch.* 10.10–12 was a not particularly successful literary exercise.

[109] Marsden (1969) 195–98; Gudea and Baatz (1974); Chevedden (1995); Bishop and Coulston (2006) 206–208; Rihll (2007) 232–68.

[110] Johnson (1983); Lendon (2005) 286–87.

Discussion

Roman military equipment was never just the sum of its parts, and an evolving element which distinguished the Late Roman period from what went before was the form of display culture which developed. Roman soldiers had always worn waist belts and decorated their equipment, thus advertising rank, formation identity and status as *milites* in society. Individual 'warrior' display played an important part. However, equipment in the 1st to 3rd c. corpus is dominated by copper-alloy (*orichalcum*) and tinning, with some enamel and niello inlay. The artefactual record for the 'long' 4th c. contains a far larger element of gold, silver and gilded silver items, some with gem settings. Hierarchies within classes of equipment can be posited. Thus crossbow brooches occur in iron, copper-alloy, silver, and gold with additional settings, some with official imperial inscriptions.[111] Gilded silver sheaths to helmets and shield-bosses occur with mint marks, but the paste 'gems' mark surviving examples as belonging to a rung below the very finest items in use by high officers and emperors.[112] Gilded silver *balteus* fittings, although rare, do appear in bullion hoards, sometimes along with helmet sheaths, otherwise with the *disiecta* of *Hacksilber* collections. Spearheads were inlaid with portrait busts in the Late Roman period, notably examples from Trier, and standards were encrusted with gems in the manner of known brooches, shield bosses and helmets.[113] The bullion metal collar (*torques*), with a frontal medallion or gem-setting, was an insignia of rank, and had evolved from the *dona militaria* of earlier centuries.[114] It was worn especially by *protectores* until at least the 6th c.[115]

These classes of metalwork shared a decorative repertoire with textile ornament and painted shield blazoning to form a distinctive Late Roman military style. They perhaps represent the shift away from monetary *stipendia* towards a system of rewarding soldiers through high denomination *donativa*. This would have reflected the preference for bullion display which seems to have been a characteristic of the wider Late Roman elite.

---

[111] Keller (1971); Kent and Painter (1977) nos. 19–21; Pröttel (1988); Snape (1993) 20–23, 52–55; Siepell (1999) 121–37; Swift (2000) 42–50, pl. 17 and (2009) 159–69; Wamser (2000) no. 148; *Imperium* (2005) no. 107.

[112] Klumbach (1973) 33; Miks (2008) 32. See Amm. Marc. 13.10.4, 16.10.8.

[113] Aillagon (2008) no. 2.13. See Amm. Marc. 16.10.7.

[114] Maxfield (1981) 86–88.

[115] Amm. Marc. 20.4.18; Becatti (1960) pl. 50a; Paolucci (1971) 46; Cormack and Vassilaki (2008) no. 313. See Ensslin (1942); Speidel (1996); Siepell (1999) 115–18; Walter (2001); Rummel (2005) 120–43, 213–31.

The artefacts reviewed in this paper, so often referred to in the *Historia Augusta* in the context of imperial gifts,[116] should be viewed in this evolving context, rather than in one of 'barbarisation' and 'decline'.

The foregoing assessment of military equipment has revealed a culturally diverse and developmentally dynamic assemblage in the employ of the Late Roman army. There were Free German (shields, shafted weapons), Transdanubian (helmet design and decoration, scabbard slides), Mesopotamian-Iranian (helmet design) and North African (shafted weapons) elements. However, none of these identifiable components were overwhelmingly dominant, and certainly the Late Roman army's arms and armour cannot be said to have been 'Germanised'. German peoples did not substantially acculturate the Roman army and did not 'weaken' Roman imperial defence. On the contrary, their contribution of military manpower and leadership was immensely valuable and strengthened the empire, in both the East and the West.

Did the sum of extraneous German, steppe and Mesopotamian-Iranian elements represent 'barbarisation' of Roman equipment culture? Again the conclusion must be a qualified negative, because the whole history of Roman equipment development involved cultural inclusivity. Italic shield and shafted weapon forms were joined by 'Celtic' mail, helmets, swords, daggers, saddlery and horseman's dress from the 4th c. B.C. onwards. Archery equipment was entirely dominated by Levantine traditions until the advent of the Huns. Hellenistic artillery and siege technology was adapted and independently developed from the 3rd c. B.C. onwards. Many aspects of Hellenistic military culture, such as fortification design and the literary genre of technical treatises, were made 'Roman' and continued developing into the 6th c. A.D. and beyond. It could indeed be opined that the very cultural mélange and continuous development within one military organisation (with all the caveats of regional, army group variation) was what made equipment 'Roman' beyond a mere chronological and political epithet.

---

[116] One of many ways by which the work betrays its 4th c. composition; even in early lives, the details best suit a Late Roman context (SHA *Hadrianus* 10.5, 17.2; SHA *Maximini duo* 3.5, 29.8–9; SHA *divus Claudius* 14.2–15, 17.4–7; SHA *Carus et Carinus et Numerianus* 17.1). For the political, economic and cultural *milieu*, see Jones (1964) 623–26; Kent and Painter (1977); Bastien (1988); Mundell Mango (1995); Casey (2000); Leader-Newby (2004); Guggisberg (2013).

Acknowledgements

The writer would like to gratefully acknowledge the kind help given during the writing of this paper by Mike Bishop, Alexandra Busch, Hazel Dodge, Simon James, Luke Lavan and Greg Woolf, and by two anonymous readers who made some very valuable suggestions for textual improvement and additional literature.

Bibliography

Primary Sources

Amm. Marc. = Rolfe J. C. (1963) ed. and trans. *Res Gestae* (London 1963).
Arr. *Tact.* = DeVoto, J.G. (1993) ed. and trans. *Techne taktika: Ektaxis kata Alanon* (Chicago 1993).
Cod. Theod. = Mommsen Th., Meyer P. *et al.* (1905) edd. *Theodosiani libri xvi cum constitutionibus Sirmondianis* (Berlin 1905).
Gregory of Tours *Hist.* = Krusch B. and Levison W. (1942–51) edd. *Gregori Episcopi Turonensis libri historiarum X* (Hanover 1942–51).
Hdn. = Whittaker C. R. (1969–70) ed. and trans. *Herodian* (London 1969–70).
Not. Dign. occ. and *or.* = Seeck O. (1962) ed. *Notitia dignitatum: accedunt notitia urbes Constinopolitanae et latercula provinciarum* (Frankfurt am Main 1962).
Procop. *Goth.* = Dewing H. B. (1914–54) ed. and trans. Procopius, *History of the Wars* (London 1914–54).
SHA = Magie D. (1953) ed. and trans. *The Scriptores Historiae Augustae* (London 1953).
Sid. Apoll. *Carm.* = Anderson W. B. (1936–65) ed. and trans. Sidonius, *Poems and Letters* (London 1936–65).
Strategikon = Dennis G. T. (1984) ed. *Maurice's Strategikon. Handbook of Byzantine Military Strategy* (Philadelphia 1984) and Dennis G. T. ed. and Gamillscheg E. trans. (1981) *Das Strategikon des Maurikios* (CFHB 17) (Vienna 1981).
Tac. *Hist.* = Moore C. H. and Jackson J. (1989) edd. and trans. Tacitus, *The Histories Books IV–V, The Annals, Books I–III* (London 1989).
Tac. *Germ.* = Hutton M. and Ogilvie R. M. (1970) edd. and trans. Tacitus, *Agricola. Germania. Dialogus* (Cambridge 1970).
Veg. *Mil.* = Önnerfors A. (1995) ed. *P. Flavii Vegeti Renati epitoma rei militaris* (Leipzig 1995).
Vitr. *De arch.* = Granger F. (1989) ed. and trans. Vitruvius, *The Ten Books on Architecture* (London 1989).
Zos. = Ridley R. T. (1982) trans. Zosimus, *New History* (Sidney 1982).

Secondary Works

Aillagon J.-J. (2008) ed. *Rome and the Barbarians: the Birth of a New World* (Milan 2008).
Alexander J. J. G. (1976) "The illustrated manuscripts of the *Notitia Dignitatum*", in *Aspects of the* Notitia Dignitatum*: Papers Presented to the Conference in Oxford, December 13 to 14, 1974* (BAR International Series 15), edd. J. C. Mann, R. Goodburn and P. Bartholemew (Oxford 1976) 11–50.
Alföldi A. (1959) "Cornuti: a Teutonic contingent in the service of Constantine the Great and its decisive role in the battle at the Milvian Bridge", *DOP* 13 (1959) 169–83.

—— (1935) "Ein spätromisches Schildzeichen keltischer oder germanischer Herkunft", *Germania* 19 (1935) 324–28.

—— (1934) "Ein spätromische Helmform und ihre Schicksale im germanisch-romanischen Mittelalter", *ActaArch* 5 (1934) 99–144.

—— (1932) "The helmet of Constantine with the Christian monogram", *JRS* 22 (1932) 9–23.

Allason-Jones L. and Miket R. (1984) *The Catalogue of Small Finds from South Shields Roman Fort* (Newcastle-upon-Tyne 1984).

Aouni H. (1998) "Das spätantike-frühmittelalterliche Gräberfeld von Jülich—die 'einfachen Gürtelgarnituren'", *Acta Praehistorica et Archeologica* 39 (1998) 19–37.

Arrhenius B. (1983) "The chronology of the Vendel graves", in *Vendel Period Studies: Transactions of the Boat-Grave Symposium in Stockholn, February 2–3, 1981*, edd. J. P. Lamm and H.-Å. Nordstöm (Stockholn 1983) 39–70.

Barkóczi L. (1944) *Brigetio* (Budapest 1944).

Bastien P. (1988) *Monnaie et* donativa *au Bas-Empire* (Wetteren 1988).

Becatti G. (1960) *La Colonna Coclide Istoriata* (Rome 1960).

Berger P. C. (1981) *The Insignia of the Notitia Dignitatum* (New York and London 1981).

Biborski M. (1994) "Typologie und Chronologie der Ringknaufschwerter", in *Markomannenkriege: Ursachen und Wirkungen*, edd. H. Friesinger, J. Tejral and H. Stuppner (Brno 1994) 85–97.

Bishop M. C. and Coulston J. C. N. (2006) *Roman Military Equipment from the Punic Wars to the Fall of Rome*, (2nd ed. Oxford 2006).

Bivar A. D. H. (1972) "Cavalry tactics and equipment on the Euphrates", *DOP* 26 (1972) 273–91.

Böhme H. W. (1986) "Das Ende der Romerherrschaft in Britannien und die angelsächsische Besiedlung Englands im 5. Jahrhundert", *JRGZM* 33 (1986) 469–574.

Böhner K. (1994) "Die frühmittelalterlichen Spangenhelme und die nordischen Helme der Vendelzeit", *JRGZM* 41 (1994) 471–549.

—— (1963) "Zur historischen Interpretation der sogenannten Laetengräber", *JRGZM* 10 (1963) 139–67.

Boppert W. (1992) *Corpus Signorum Imperii Romani, Deutschland* II.5: *Militärische Grabdenkmäler aus Mainz und Umgebung* (Mainz 1992).

Born H. (2003) "Projectvorschlag zur technologischen Untersuchung spätrömischer Kamm- und frühmittelalterlicher Spangenhelme", *Acta Praehistorica et Archaeologica* 35 (2003) 79–89.

—— (1999) "Reiterhelme aus Iatrus/Krivina, Bulgarien—zur Technik spätrömischer Eisenhelme mit vergoldeten Silber- und Kupferblechüberzügen", *Acta Praehistorica et Archaeologica* 31 (1999) 217–38.

Bottini A., Egg M., Hase F. W. von, Pflug H., Schaaf U., Schauer P. and Waurick G. (1988) *Antike Helme: Sammlung Lipperheide und andere Bestände des Antikenmuseums Berlin* (Mainz 1988).

Brentjes B. (2000) "Cascos utilizados por los pueblos de las estepas Euroasiáticas en la época de los Escitas y de los Sármatas", *Gladius* 20 (2000) 51–73.

Browning R. (1987) *Justinian and Theodora* (London 1987).

Bruce-Mitford R. (1978) *The Sutton Hoo Ship Burial*, 2: *Arms, Armour and Regalia* (London 1978).

Bujukliev H. (1986) *Le Necropole Tumulaire de Catalka, Region de Stara Zagora* (Sofia 1986).

Bullinger H. (1969) *Spätantike Gürtelbeschläge: Typen, Herstellung, Tragweise und Datierung* (Brugge 1969).

Buora M. (2002) ed. *Miles Romanus dal Po al Danubio nel Tardoantico: atti del Convegno internazionale, Pordenone-Concordia Sagittaria, 17–19 marzo 2000* (Pordenone 2002).

Bushe-Fox J. P. (1949) *Fourth Report on the Excavations of the Roman Fort at Richborough, Kent* (Oxford 1949).

Casey P. J. (2000) "LIBERALITAS AVGVSTI: imperial military donatives and the Arras Hoard", in *Kaiser, Heer und Gesellschaft in römischen Kaiserzeit: Gedenkschrift für Eric Birley* (Heidelberger althistorische Beiträge und epigraphische Studien 31), edd. G. Alföldi, B. Dobson and W. Eck (Stuttgart 2000) 446–58.

Chevedden, P. E. (1995) "Artillery in Late Antiquity: prelude to the Middle Ages", in *The Medieval City under Siege*, edd. I. A. Corfis and M. Wolfe (Woodbridge 1995) 131–73.

Cichorius C. (1896–1900) *Die Reliefs der Traianssäule* (Berlin 1896–1900).

Colledge M. A. R. (1977) *Parthian Art* (London 1977).

—— (1976) *The Art of Palmyra* (London 1976).

Collingwood R. G. and Wright R. P. (1995) *The Roman Inscriptions of Britain, I, Inscriptions on Stone* (2nd ed. Stroud 1995).

Collins P. (2008) *Assyrian Palace Sculptures* (London 2008).

Cormack R. and Vassilaki M. (2008) edd. *Byzantium 330–1453* (London 2008).

Coulston J. C. N. (2010) "Military equipment during the 'Long' 4th century", in *Finds from the Frontier: Material Culture in the 4th-5th Centuries*, edd. R. Collins and L. Allason-Jones (York 2010) 50–63.

—— (2008) "Immortalising victory: votive weapons depositions in northern Europe and the Roman empire", in *Aktuelle Forschungen zu Kriegsbeuteopfern und Fürstengräbern im Barbaricum*, edd. A. Abegg-Wegg and A. Rau (Neumünster 2008) 307–30.

—— (2007) "Art, culture and service: the depiction of soldiers on 3rd century AD military gravestones", in *The Impact of the Roman Army (200 BC-AD 476): Economic, Social, Political, Religious and Cultural Aspects* (Impact of Empire 6), edd. L. de Blois, E. Lo Cascio, O. Hekster and G. de Kleijn (Leiden and Boston 2007) 529–61.

—— (2004) "Military identity and personal self-identity in the Roman army", in *Roman Rule and Civic Life: Local and Regional Perspectives* (Impact of Empire 4), edd. L. de Licht, E. A. Hemelrijk and H. W. Singor (Amsterdam 2004) 133–52.

—— (2003) "Tacitus, *Historiae* I.79 and the impact of Sarmatian warfare on the Roman empire", in *Kontakt–Kooperation–Konflikt: Germanen und Sarmaten zwischen dem 1. und 4. Jahrh. n. Chr.*, ed. C. von Carnap-Bornheim (Neumünster 2003) 415–33.

—— (2002) "Arms and armour of the Late Roman Army", in *A Companion to Medieval Arms and Armour*, ed. D Nicole (Woodbridge 2002) 3–24.

—— (1991) "The *'draco'* standard", *Journal of Roman Military Equipment Studies* 2 (1991) 101–14.

—— (1990) "Later Roman armour, 3rd–6th centuries AD", *Journal of Roman Military Equipment Studies* 1 (1990) 139–60.

—— (1986) "Roman, Parthian and Sassanian tactical developments", in *The Defence of the Roman and Byzantine East: Proceedings of a Colloquium held at the University of Sheffield in April 1986* (BAR Archaeological Reports, Supplementary Series 297), edd. P. Freeman and D. L. Kennedy (Oxford 1986) 59–75.

—— (1985) "Roman archery equipment", in *The Production and Distribution of Roman Military Equipment: Proceedings of the Second Roman Military Equipment Seminar* (BAR International Series 275), ed. M. C. Bishop (Oxford 1985) 220–366.

Cowan J. D. (1948) "The Carvoran spear-head again", *Archaeologia Aeliana* ser. 4, 26 (1948) 142–44.

Dahlmos U. (1977) "Francisca-bipennis-securis. Bemerkungen zu archäologischen Befund und schriftlicher Uberlieferung", *Germania* 55 (1977) 141–65.

Deckers J. G. (1973) "Die Wandmalerei des tetrarchischen Lagerheiligtums im Ammon-Tempel von Luxor", *RömQSchr* 68 (1973) 1–34.

Dickinson T. and Härke H. (1992) *Early Anglo-Saxon Shields* (London 1992).

Dittmann K. (1940) "Ein eiserner Spangenhelm in Kairo", *Germania* 24 (1940) 54–58.

Downey S. B. (2006) "Arms and armour as social coding in Palmyra, the Palmyrene, and Dura-Europos", in *Arms and Armour as Indicators of Cultural Transfer: the Steppes and the Ancient World from Hellenistic Times to the Early Middle Ages* (Nomaden und Sesshafte 4), edd. M. Mode and J. Tubach (Wiesbaden 2006) 321–55.

Driel-Murray C. van (2000) "A late Roman assemblage from Deurne (Netherlands)", *BJb* 200 (2000) 293–308.

Driel-Murray C. van and Gechter M. (1984) "Funde aus der fabrika der Legio I Minervia aus Bonner Berg", *Rheinische Ausgrabungen 23, Beiträge zur Archäologie des römischen Rheinlands* 4 (1984) 1–83.

Ebert M. (1909) "Ein Spangenhelm aus Aegypten", *PZ* 1 (1909) 163–70.

Edge D. E. and Paddock, J. M. (1988) *Arms and Armour of the Medieval Knight* (London 1988).

Elton H. E. (1996) *Warfare in Roman Europe, AD 350–425* (Oxford 1996).

Ensslin W. (1942) "Zur Torqueskrönung und Schilderhebung bei der Kaiserwahl", *Klio* 35 (1942) 268–98.

Esmonde Cleary A. S. (1989) *The Ending of Roman Britain* (London 1989).

Éspérandieu E. (1907–66) *Recueil general des bas-reliefs, statues et bustes de la Gaule romaine* (Paris 1907–66).

Fischer T. (1990) *Das Umland römischen Regensburg* (Münchner Beiträge zur Vor- und Frühgeschichte 42) (Munich 1990).

Fischer T., Precht G. and Tejral J. (1999) edd. *Germanen beiderseits des spätantiken Limes* (Cologne and Brno 1999).

Franzoni C. (1987) Habitus atque habitudo militis. *Monumenti funerari di militari nella Cisalpina Romana* (Rome 1987).

Gall H. von (1990) *Das Reiterkampfbild in der iranischen und iranisch beeinflussten Kunst parthischer und sasanidischer Zeit* (Berlin 1990).

Gamber O. (1964) "Dakische und sarmatische Waffen auf der Traianssäule", *Jahrbuch der Kunsthistorischen Sammlung in Wien* 60 (1964) 7–34.

Gamber O. (1968) "Kataphrakten, Clibanarier, Normannenreiter", *JKSW* 64 (1968) 7–44.

Gardner A. (2007) *An Archaeology of Identity: Soldiers and Society in Late Roman Britain* (Walnut Creek 2007).

Glad D. (2009) *Origine et diffusion de l'équipement défensif corporel en Méditerranée orientale (IVᵉ–VIIIᵉ s.): Contribution à l'étude historique et archéologique des armées antiques et médiévales* (BAR International Series 1921) (Oxford 2009).

Goethert K. P. (1996) "Neue römische Prunkschilde", in *Reiter wie Statuen aus Erz*, ed. M. Junkelmann (Mainz 1996) 115–26.

Goldsworthy A. K., Haynes I. P. and Adams C. E. P. (1999) edd. *The Roman Army as a Community: Including Papers of a Conference held at Birkbeck College, University of London on 11–12 January, 1997* (JRA Supplementary Series 34) (Portsmouth, RI 1999).

Grancsay S. V. (1963) "A Sassanian chieftain's helmet", *BMMA* 21 (1963) 253–62.

Grane T. (2007a) ed. *Beyond the Roman Frontier: Roman Influences on the Northern Barbaricum* (Rome 2007).

—— (2007b) "Southern Scandinavian *foederati* and *auxiliarii*?", in *Beyond the Roman Frontier: Roman Influences on the Northern Barbaricum*, ed. T. Grane (2007a) 83–104.

Greatrex G., Elton H. E. and Burgess R. (2005) "Urbicius' *Epitedeuma*: an edition, translation and commentary", *ByzZeit* 98 (2005) 35–74.

Grigg R. (1983) "Inconsistency and lassitude: the shield emblems of the *Notitia Dignitatum*", *JRS* 73 (1983) 132–42.

Gudea N. and Baatz D. (1974) "Teile spätrömischer Ballisten aus Gornea und Orsova (Rumänien)", *SaalbJb* 31 (1974) 50–72.

Guggisberg M.A. (2013) "Silver and donatives: non-coin exchange within and outside the Roman Empire", in *Late Roman Silver: the Traprain Treasure in Context*, edd. F. Hunter and K. S. Painter (Edinburgh 2013) 193–212.

Haldon J. F. (1999) *Warfare, State and Society in the Byzantine World, 565–1204* (London 1999).

—— (1975) "Some aspects of Byzantine military technology from the sixth to the tenth centuries", *BMGS* 1 (1975) 11–47.

Halsall G. (2003) *Warfare and Society in the Barbarian West, 450–900* (London 2003).

Harl O. (1996) "Die Kataphraktarier im römischen Heer—Panegyrik und Realität", *JRGZM* 43 (1996) 601–27.

Hawkes S. (1974) "Some recent finds of late Roman buckles", *Britannia* 5 (1974) 386–93.
Hawkes S. and Dunning G. C. (1961) "Soldiers and settlers in Britain, fourth to fifth century", *Medieval Archaeology* 5 (1961) 1–70.
Heather P. J. and Matthews J. F. (1991) *The Goths in the Fourth Century* (Liverpool 1991).
Herrmann G. (1989) "Parthian and Sasanian saddler", in *Archaologia Iranica et Orientalis: Miscellanea in honorem Louis Vanden Berghe* II, edd. L. de Mayer and E. Haerinck (Gent 1989) 757–809.
Hingley R. (2005) *Globalizing Roman Culture: Unity, Diversity and Empire* (London 2005).
Hundt H. J. (1955) "Nachträge zu den römischen Ringknaufschwertern, Dosenortbändern und Miniaturschwertanhängern", *SaalbJb* 14 (1955) 50–59.
Hunter F. and Painter K. S. (2013) edd. *Late Roman Silver: the Traprain Treasure in Context* (Edinburgh 2013).
Ilkjær J. (1990) *Illerup Ådel 2: Die Lanzen und Speere* (Jutland Archaeological Society Publications 25.2) (Aarhus 1990).
Imperium (2005) *Imperium Romanum: Römer, Christen, Alamannen. Die Spätantike am Oberrhein* (Stuttgart 2005).
Ivanovski M. (1987) "The grave of a warrior from the period of Licinius I found at Taranes", *ArchIug* 24 (1987) 81–90.
James S. (2006) "The impact of steppe peoples and the Partho-Sasanian world on the development of Roman military equipment and dress', 1st to 3rd centuries AD", in *Arms and Armour as Indicators of Cultural Transfer: The Steppes and the Ancient World from Hellenistic Times to the Early Middle Ages*, edd. M. Mode and J. Tubach (Wiesbaden 2006) 357–92.
—— (2004) *The Excavations at Dura-Europos conducted by Yale University and the French Academy of Inscriptions and Letters, 1928 to 1937: Final Report VII: The Arms and Armour and other Military Equipment* (London 2004).
—— (1999) "The community of the soldiers: a major identity and centre of power in the Roman empire", in *TRAC 98. Proceedings of the Eighth Annual Theoretical Roman Archaeology Conference, Leicester, 1998*, edd. P. Baker, S. Jundi and R. Witcher (Oxford 1999) 14–25.
—— (1988) "The *fabricae*: state arms factories of the Later Roman empire", in *Military Equipment and the Identity of Roman Soldiers: Proceedings of the Fourth Roman Military Equipment Conference* (BAR International Series 394), ed. J. C. N. Coulston (Oxford 1988) 257–331.
—— (1986) "Evidence from Dura-Europos for the origins of Late Roman helmets", *Syria* 63 (1986) 107–34.
Janniard S. (2001) "L'armée romaine tardive dans quelques travaux récents. 2ᵉ partie: strategies et techniques militaries", *Antiquité Tardive* 9 (2001) 351–61.
Janniard S. and Traina G. (2006) "Sous le concept de 'romanisation'. Paradigmes historiographiques et perspectives de recherché", *MÉFRA* 118.1 (2006) 71–166.
Jobie I. (1979) "Housesteads ware—a Frisian tradition on Hadrian's Wall", *Archaeologia Aeliana* ser. 5, 7 (1979) 127–43.
Johnson S. (1983) *Late Roman Fortifications* (London 1983).
Jones A. H. M. (1964) *The Later Roman Empire, 284–602: a Social, Economic and Administrative Survey* (Oxford 1964).
Jørgensen L., Storgaard B. and Thomsen L. G. (2003) edd. *The Spoils of Victory: the North in the Shadow of the Roman Empire* (Copenhagen 2003).
Kazanski M. (1995a) "Les tombes des chefs Alano-Sarmates au IVᵉ siècle dans les steppes pontiques", in *La noblesse romaine et les chefs barbares du IIIᵉ au VIIᵉ siècle*, edd. F. Vallet and M. Kazanski (St Germaine-en-Laye 1995) 189–205.
—— (1995b) "L'équipement et la matériel militaires au Bas-Empire en Gaule du Nord et de l'Est", *Revue du Nord-Archéologie* 77 (1995) 37–54.
Keller E. (1971) *Die spätrömische Grabfunde von Sudbayern* (Münchner Beitrage zur Vor- und Frühgeschichte 14) (München 1971).

Kellner H. J. (1966) "Zu den römischen Ringknaufschwertern und Dosenortbändern in Bayern", *JRGZM* 13 (1966) 190–201.

Kent J. P. C. and Painter K. S. (1977) *Wealth of the Roman World: Gold and Silver, AD 300–700* (London 1977).

Kieferling G. (1994) "Bemerkungen zu Äxten der römischen Kaiserzeit und der frühen Völkerwanderungszeit im mitteleuropäischen Barbaricum", in *Beiträge zu römischer und barbarischer Bewaffnung in den ersten vier nachchristlichen Jahrhunderten*, ed. C. von Carnap-Bornheim (Lublin and Marburg 1994) 335–56.

Kieseritzky G. von and Watzinger C. (1909) *Griechische Grabreliefs aus Südrussland* (Berlin 1909).

Klumbach H. (1973) ed. *Spätrömische Gardehelme* (München 1973).

Kocsis L. (2003) "A new Late Roman helmet from Hetény in the Hungarian National Museum", in *Pannonica Provincialia et Archaeologia: Studia Sollemnia Auctorum Hungarorum Eugenio Fitz Octogenario Dedicata*, (Libelli Archaeologici 1) (Budapest 2003) 521–52.

Kossack G. and Ulbert G. (1974) edd. *Studien zur Vor- und Frühgeschichtlichen Archäologie. Festschrift für Joachim Werner zum 65. Geburtstag* (München 1974).

Laubscher H. P. (1975) *Der Reliefschmuck des Galeriusbogens in Thessaloniki* (Berlin 1975).

Laycock S. (2008) *Britannia the Failed State: Tribal Conflicts and the End of Roman Britain* (Stroud 2008).

Leahy K, (2007) "Soldiers and settlers in Britain, fourth and fifth centuries—revisited", in *Collectanea Antiqua: Essays in Memory of Sonia Chadwick Hawkes* (BAR International Series 1673), edd. M. Henig and T. J. Smith (Oxford 2007) 133–43.

Leader-Newby R. E. (2004) *Silver and Society in Late Antiquity: Functions and Meanings of Silver Plate in the Fourth to Seventh Centuries* (Aldershot 2004).

Lebedynsky I. (2002) *Les Sarmates: Amazones et lanciers cuirassés entre Oural et Danube, VIIᵉ siècle av. J. c.–VIᵉ siècle apr. J. c.* (Paris 2002).

Lee A. D. (2007) *War in Late Antiquity: a Social History* (Oxford 2007).

Lendon J. E. (2007) *Soldiers and Ghosts: a History of Battle in Classical Antiquity* (New Haven 2007).

Liebeschuetz W. H. W. G. (1993) "The end of the Roman army in the western empire", in *War and Society in the Roman World*, edd. J. Rich and G. Shipley, (London 1993) 265–76.

—— (1991) *Barbarians and Bishops: Army, Church and State in the Age of Arcadius and Chrysostom* (Oxford 1991).

—— (1986) "Generals, federates and *bucellarii* in Roman armies around AD 400", in *The Defence of the Roman and Byzantine East: Proceedings of a Colloquium held at the University of Sheffield in April 1986* (BAR Archaeological Reports, International Series 297), edd. P. Freeman and D. L. Kennedy (Oxford 1986) 463–74.

Luttwak E. N. (2009) *The Grand Strategy of the Byzantine Empire* (Cambridge, Mass 2009).

Lyne M. (1994) "Late Roman helmet fragments from Richborough", *Journal of Roman Military Equipment Studies* 5 (1994) 97–105.

Lusuardi Siena S., Perassi C., Facchinetti G. and Bianchi B. (2002) "Gli elmi tardoantichi (IV–VI sec.) alla luce delle fonti letterarie, numismatiche e archeologiche: alcune considerazioni", in *Miles Romanus dal Po al Danubio nel Tardoantico*, ed. M. Buora (Pordenone 2002) 21–62.

Mackensen M. (2007) "Vergoldete Bronzebeschläge mit Christogramm von spätrömischen Kammhelmen aus dem mittleren und unteren Donauraum", *Bayerische Vorgeschichtsblätter* 72 (2007) 355–65.

MacMullen R. (1988) *Corruption and the Decline of Rome* (New Haven 1988).

—— (1963) *Soldier and Civilian in the Later Roman Empire* (Cambridge 1963).

Manacorda D. *et al.* (2000) ed. *Crypta Balbi* (Milan 2000).

Maneva E. (1987) "Casque à fermoir d'Heraclée", *ArchIug* 24 (1987) 101–11.

Mango M. M. (1995) "Silver plate among the Romans and among the barbarians", in *La noblesse romaine et les chefs barbares du IIIᵉ au VIIᵉ siècle*, edd. F. Vallet and M. Kazanski (St Germaine-en-Laye 1995) 77–88.

Manning W. H. (1976) *Catalogue of Romano-British Ironwork in the Museum of Antiquities, Newcastle upon Tyne* (Newcastle-upon-Tyne 1976).

Mansel A. M. (1938) "Grabhügelforschung in Ostthrakien", *Bulletin de l'Institute d'Archeologie Bulgare* XII (1938) 154–89.

Marsden E. W. (1971) *Greek and Roman Artillery: Technical Treatises* (Oxford 1971).

—— (1969) *Greek and Roman Artillery: Historical Development* (Oxford 1969).

Mattingly D. (2004) "Being Roman: expressing identity in a provincial setting', *JRA* 17 (2004) 5–25.

Maxfield V. A. (1981) *The Military Decorations of the Roman Army* (London 1981).

Mennella G. (2004) "La campagna di Costantino nell'Italia nord-occidentale: la documentazione epigrafica", in *L'armée romaine de Dioclétien à Valentinien Ier*, edd. Y. Le Bohec and C. Wolff, (Lyon 2004) 359–69.

Mertens J. and van Impe L. (1971) *Het Laat-Romeins Grafveld van Oudenburg* (Archaeologica Belgica 135) (Brussels 1971).

Mielczarek M. (1993) *Cataphracti and Clibanarii. Studies on the Heavy Armoured Cavalry of the Ancient World* (Lodz 1993).

Miks C. (2009) "Ein römisches Schwert mit Ringknaufgriff aus dem Rhein bei Mainz", *Mainzer Archäologische Zeitschrift* 8 (2009) 129–65.

—— (2008) *Vom Prunkstück zum Altmetall. Ein Depot spätrömischer Helmteile aus Koblenz* (Mainz 2008).

—— (2007) *Studien zur römischen Schwertbewaffnung in der Kaiserzeit* (Kölner Studien zur Archäologie und römischen Provinzen 8) (Rahden 2007).

Mode M. and Tubach J. (2006) *Arms and Armour as Indicators of Cultural Transfer: The Steppes and the Ancient World from Hellenistic Times to the Early Middle Ages* (Wiesbaden 2006).

Nagy M. (2005) "Zwei spätrömerzeitlicher Waffengräber am Westrand der Canabae von Aquincum", *ActaArchHung* 56 (2005) 403–86.

Nicasie M. J. (1998) *The Twilight of Empire: the Roman Army from the Reign of Diocletian until the Battle of Adrianople* (Amsterdam 1998).

Negin A. E. (1998) "Sarmatian cataphracts as prototypes for Roman *equites cataphractarii*", *Journal of Roman Military Equipment Studies* 9 (1998) 65–75.

Oldenstein J. (1979) "Ein Numerum-Omnium-Beschlag aus Kreuzweingarten", *BJb* 179 (1979) 543–52.

l'Orange H. P. and Gerkan A. (1939) *Der spätantike Bildschmuk des Konstantinsbogens* (Berlin 1939).

Overbeck B. (1974) "Numismatische Zeugnisse zu den spätrömischen Gardehelmen", in *Studien zur Vor- und Frühgeschichtlichen Archäologie. Festschrift für Joachim Werner zum 65. Geburtstag*, edd. G. Kossack and G. Ulbert (München 1974) I, 217–25.

Overlaet B. J. (1982) "Contribution to Sasanian armament in connection with a decorated helmet", *IrAnt* 17 (1982) 189–206.

Parker S. T. (1994a) "El-Haditha", *AJA* 98 (1994) 549.

—— (1994b) "A Late Roman soldier's grave by the Dead Sea", *ADAJ* 38 (1994) 391–93.

Pauli-Jensen X. (2007) "The use of archers in the northern Germanic armies. Evidence from the Danish war booty sacrifices", in *Beyond the Roman Frontier: Roman Influences on the Northern Barbaricum*, ed. T. Grane (Rome 2007) 143–51.

Paolucci A. (1971) *Ravenna: Una guida d'arte* (Ravenna 1971).

Petculescu L. (1995) "Roman equipment graves in Roman Dacia", *Journal of Roman Military Equipment Studies* 6 (1995) 105–45.

Petculescu L. and Gheorghe P. (1979) "Coiful roman de la Bubesti", *Studii si Cercetari de Istorie Veche Arheologie* 30 (1979) 603–606.

Pirling R. (1974) "Ein Spangenhelm des Typs Baldenheim aus Leptis Magna in Libyen", in *Studien zur Vor- und Frühgeschichtlichen Archäologie. Festschrift für Joachim Werner zum 65. Geburtstag*, edd. G. Kossack and G. Ulbert (München 1974) II, 471–82.

Polito E. (1998) *Fulgentibus Armis: Introduzione allo studio dei fregi d'armi antichi* (Rome 1998).

Post P. (1951–53) "Der kupferne Spangenhelm. Ein Beitrag zur Stilgeschichte der Völker-wanderungszeit auf waffentechnischer Grundlage", *BerRGK* 34 (1951–53) 115–50.

Prins J. (2000) "The 'fortune' of a late Roman officer. A hoard from the Meuse valley (Neth-erlands) with helmet and gold coins", *BJb* 200 (2000) 310–28.

Pröttel P. (1988) "Zur Chronologie der Zweibelknopffibeln", *JRGZM* 35 (1988) 347–72.

Raddatz K. (1987) *Der Thorsberger Moorfund Katalog, Teile von Waffen und Pferdegeschirr, sonstige Fundstücke aus Metall und Glas, Ton- und Holzgefäße, Steingeräte* (Neumünster 1987).

—— (1985) "Die Bewaffnung der Germanen vom letzten Jahrhundert vor Chr. bis zur Völk-erwanderungszeit", *Aufstieg und Niedergang der römischen Welt* II, *Principat* 12.3, *Künste* (Berlin 1985) 281–361.

—— (1960) "Ringknaufschwerter aus germanischen Kriegergräbern", *Offa* 17–18 (2000) 26–55.

Radman-Livaja I. (2010) ed. *Finds of the Roman Military Equipment in Croatia* (Zagreb 2010).

Radulescu A. (1963) "Elmi bronzei di Ostrov", *Dacia* 7 (1963) 543–51.

Rance P. (2005) "Narses and the battle of Taginae (Busta Gallorum) 552: Procopius and sixth-century warfare", *Historia* 54 (2005) 424–72.

—— (2004) "The *fulcum*, the Late Roman and Byzantine *testudo*: the Germanization of Late Roman tactics?", *GRBS* 44 (2004) 265–326.

Ravegnani G. (1988) *Soldati di Bisanzio in età Giustinianea* (Rome 1988).

Revell L. (2009) *Roman Imperialism and Local Identities* (Cambridge 2009).

Richardot P. (2005) *Le fin de l'armée romaine (284–476)* (Paris 2005).

Richmond I. A. (1940) "The barbaric spear from Carvoran", *Proceedings of the Society of Antiquaries of Newcastle* ser. 4 (1940) 136–38.

Rihll T. (2007) *The Catapult: a History* (Yardley 2007).

Rinaldi M. L. (1964–65) "Il costume romano e i mosaici di Piazza Armerina", *RivIstArch* n.s.13–14 (1964–65) 200–68.

Robinson H. R. (1975) *The Armour of Imperial Rome* (London 1975).

Rummel P. von (2005) *Habitus Barbarus. Kleidung und Repräsentation spätantiker Eliten im 4. und 5. Jahrhundert* (Berlin 2005).

Rushworth A. (2009) "Franks, Frisians and Tungrians: garrisons at Housesteads in the 3rd century AD", in *Limes XX: Estudios sobre la frontera romana*, III, edd. A. Morillo, N. Hanel and E. Martín (Madrid 2009) 1147–56.

Sarmates (1995) *Entre Asie et Europe: l'or des Sarmates: Nomades des steppes dans l'Antiquité* (Doualas 1995).

Schnurbein S von. (1974) "Zum ango", in *Studien zur Vor- und Frühgeschichtlichen Archäol-ogie. Festschrift für Joachim Werner zum 65. Geburtstag*, edd. G. Kossack and G. Ulbert (München 1974) 411–33.

Schörner G. (2005) ed. *Romanisierung–Romanisation: Theoretische Modelle und Praktische Fallbeispiele* (BAR International Series 1427) (Oxford 1982).

Schulze-Dörlamm M. (1985) "Germanische Kriegergräber mit Schwertbeigabe in Mitteleu-ropa aus dem späten 3. Jahrhundert und der ersten Hälfte des 4. Jahhunderts n. Chr.", *JRGZM* 32 (1985) 509–69.

Scott I. R. (1980) "Spearheads on the British *limes*", in *Roman Frontier Studies 1979: Papers Presented to the 12th International Congress of Roman Frontier Studies* (BAR International Series 71), edd. W. S. Hanson and L. J. F. Keppie (Oxford 1980) 333–43.

Siepell W. (1999) ed. *Barbarenschmuck und Römergold: Der Schatz von Szilágysomlyó* (Milan 1999).

Simonenko A. V. (2001) "Bewaffnung und Kriegswesen der Sarmaten und späten Skythen im nördlichen Schwarzmeergebiet", *Eurasia Antiqua* 7 (2001) 187–327.

Simpson C. J. (1976) "Belt-buckles and strap-ends of the later Roman Empire: a preliminary survey of several new groups", *Britannia* 7 (1976) 192–223.

Snape M. E. (1993) *Roman Brooches from North Britain: A Classification and a Catalogue of Brooches from Sites on the Stanegate* (BAR British Series 235) (Oxford 1993).

Sommer M. (1984) *Die Gürtel und Gürtelbeschläge des 4. und 5. Jahrhunderts im römischen Reich* (Bonner Hefte zur Vorgeschichte 22) (Bonn 1984).

Southern P. and Dixon K. R. (1996) *The Late Roman Army* (London 1996).

Speidel M. P. (1996) "Late Roman military decorations I: neck- and wristbands", *Antiquité Tardive* 4 (1996) 235–43.

—— (1990) "The army at Aquileia, the Moesiaci legion, and the shield emblems of the *Notitia Dignitatum*", *SaalbJb* 46 (1990) 68–72.

—— (1985) "The master of the dragon standards and the golden torc: an inscription from Prusias and Prudentius' *Peristephanon*", *TAPA* 115 (1985) 283–87.

—— (1984) "*Cataphractarii, clibanarii* and the rise of the Later Roman mailed cavalry: a gravestone from Claudiopolis in Bithynia", *EpigAnat* 4 (1984) 151–56.

—— (1975) "The rise of ethnic units in the Roman imperial army", *ANRW* II.3 (Berlin 1975) 202–31.

Sternquist B. (1955) *Simris: On Cultural Connections of Scania in the Roman Iron Age* (Lund 1955).

Sumner G. (2009) *Roman Military Dress* (Stroud 2009).

Swanton M. J. (1973) *The Spear-heads of the Anglo-Saxon Settlements* (Leeds 1973).

Swift E. (2009) *Style and Function in Roman Decoration: Living with Objects and Interiors* (Aldershot 2009).

—— (2006) "Constructing Roman identities in Late Antiquity? Material culture on the western frontier", in *Social and Political Life in Late Antiquity* (Late Antique Archaeology 3.1), edd. W. Bowden, A. Gutteridge and C. Machado (Leiden 2006) 97–111.

—— (2000) *The End of the Western Roman Empire: an Archaeological Investigation* (Oxford 2000).

Syvänne I. (2004) *The Age of Hippotoxotai: Art of War in Roman Military Revival and Disaster (491–636)* (Tampere 2004).

Szabó K. (1986) "Le casque romain d'Intercisa—recente trouvaille du Danube", in *Studien zu den Militärgrenzen Roms III: 13. Internationaler Limeskongress, Aalen 1983*, ed. C. Unz (Stuttgart 1986) 421–25.

Theuws F. (2009) "Grave goods, ethnicity and the rhetoric of burial rites in Late Antique Northern Gaul", in *Ethnic Constructs in Antiquity: the Role of Power and Tradition*, edd. T. Derks and N. Roymans (Amsterdam 2009) 283–319.

Trousdale W. (1975) *The Long Sword and Scabbard Slide in Asia* (Washington 1975).

Tweddle D. (1992) *The Anglian Helmet from 16–22 Coppergate* (Archaeology of York 17) (London 1992).

Vallet F. and Kazanski,M. (1995) edd. *La noblesse romaine et les chefs barbares du IIIᵉ au VIIᵉ siècle* (St Germaine-en-Laye 1995).

—— (1993) edd. *L'armée romaine et les barbares du IIIᵉ au VIIᵉ siècle* (St Germaine-en-Laye 1993).

Velkov I. (1928–29) "Neue Grabhügel aus Bulgarien", *Bulletin de l'Institut d'Archéologie Bulgare* 5 (1928–29) 13–55.

Vogt M. (2006) *Spangenhelme: Baldenheim und verwandte Typen* (Kataloge Vor- und Frühgeschichtlicher Altertümer 39) (Mainz 2006).

Walter C. (2001) "The *maniakon* or torc in Byzantine tradition", *RÉByz* 59 (2001) 179–92.

—— (1975) "Raising on a shield in Byzantine iconography", *RÉByz* 33 (1975) 133–75.

Wamser L. (2000) ed. *Die Römer zwischen Alpen und Nordsee: Zivilisatorisches Erbe einer europäischen Militärmacht* (Mainz 2000).

Webster G. (1956) *The Roman Army* (Chester 1956).

Werner J. (1994) "Chinesischer Schwerttragbügel der Han-Zeit aus einem thrakischen Häuptlingsgrab von Catalka (Bulgarien)", *Germania* 72 (1994) 269–82.

—— (1989) "Nuovi dati sull'origine degli "Spangenhelme" altomedioevali del tipo Baldenheim", *XXXVI Corso di cultura sull'arte Ravennate e Bizantina, Seminario Internazionale di Studi sul tema 'Ravenna e l'Italia fra Goti e Longobardi', Ravenna, 14–22 Aprile 1989* (Ravenna 1989) 419–30.

—— (1949–50) "Zur Herkunft der frühmittelalterliche Spangenhelme", *PZ* 34–35 (1949–50) 178–93.

Whitby M. (2004) "Emperors and armies, AD 235–395", in *Approaching Late Antiquity: the Transformation from Early to Late Empire*, edd. S. Swain and M. Edwards (Oxford 2004) 156–86.

Woods D. (1996) "The *scholae palatinae* and the *Notitia Dignitatum*", *Journal of Roman Military Equipment Studies* 7 (1996) 37–50.

—— (1998) "Two notes on Late Roman military equipment", *Journal of Roman Military Equipment Studies* 9 (1998) 31–35.

Woolf G. (1998) *Becoming Roman: the Origins of Provincial Civilisation in Gaul* (Cambridge 1998).

Zieling N. (1989) *Studien zu germanischen Schilden der Spätlatène- und der römischen Kaiserzeit im freien Germanien* (Oxford 1989).

BARBARIAN MILITARY EQUIPMENT AND ITS EVOLUTION IN THE LATE ROMAN AND GREAT MIGRATION PERIODS (3RD–5TH C. A.D.)

Michel Kazanski

Abstract

Military equipment and, as a consequence, types of combat underwent significant changes between the 3rd and 6th c. A.D. The Germanic peoples' and their neighbours' weapons became more appropriate to rapid and close tactical manoeuvres in dispersed ranks. The spread of Germanic weapons within Roman territory and in the Pontic region indicates that the same tactics were employed by the Roman army's barbarian troops and federates. A similar evolution occurred within the armies of the steppe peoples, including those fighting for the empire. The Early Roman armoured cavalry was first replaced by a lighter Alanic cavalry, and then by Hunnic mounted archers. Finally, the light Slavic infantry, with its 'irregular' guerrilla tactics, defeated the East Roman armies and conquered the Balkan Peninsula.

During the Late Roman period, the Roman Empire faced two main groups of barbarian peoples across its European borders. The sedentary Germans in western and central Europe inhabited the region named 'Germania' by Roman authors. As well as Germanic peoples, this area included the Celts of the British and Thracian Isles, namely the Carpi. Meanwhile, the Iranian-speaking nomadic people of eastern and central Europe lived in an area named 'Scythia' or 'Sarmatia' by the ancient sources. The Sarmatians lived on the Hungarian plains, while the Alans inhabited the Ponto-Caucasian steppes. All the nomads living between the Danube and the Caucasus around the 4th c. A.D. were referred to as Alans. Lastly, during the reign of Justinian (*ca.* 527–65), the empire was forced to confront a third civilisation: an eastern European forest-dwelling people named the Slavs.

These three groups had clearly distinctive fighting styles and military equipment. The peoples of Germania were infantrymen, armed predominantly with spears and shields (figs. 1–3).[1] The geographical distribution of shields with bosses, and spurs, is particularly significant. These two

---

[1] Raddatz (1985).

A. Sarantis, N. Christie (edd.) *War and Warfare in Late Antiquity: Current Perspectives* (Late Antique Archaeology 8.1–8.2 – 2010–11) (Leiden 2013), pp. 493–521

features were characteristic of the Germanic and Celtic peoples of western and central Europe, before spreading into the West during the Roman
period. The latter development only affected populations undergoing
western military influence, such as the Balts (fig. 4) and the Baltic Finns.[2]
The steppe people, on the other hand, were exclusively horsemen. They
did not carry shields, but were often armoured, at least during the first
two centuries of our era.[3] As for the Slavs, they mostly employed a light
infantry, armed with javelins and bows. They clearly preferred guerrilla
tactics to all other forms of combat.[4] Ancient authors used such military
fighting styles as ethnographic markers. It was on this basis that Tacitus,
in the 1st c. A.D., classified the Veneti (the Slavs' ancestors living on Germania's eastern border) as a Germanic people. The Veneti were swift like
the Sarmatians and yet fought on foot with shields like the Germans.[5]

THE GERMANIC ZONE

It is possible to distinguish three zones of barbarian weapon distribution
during the Late Roman period from the archaeological evidence. The first
zone comprises Germania, with the Baltic territories of the Baltic and
Finnish peoples, and the Black Sea's northern and eastern coastal areas
which were populated by sedentary barbarians. Weapon finds in male
tombs demonstrate these barbarians' high level of militarisation. These
weapons can regularly be associated with the Przeworsk culture in Poland
(see figs. 1 and 2), and with Scandinavian peoples during the Late Roman
period.[6]

　　There are exceptions to the rule, however: Černjahov tombs north of
the Danube and the Black Sea, which belonged to the Goths and their
allies, only rarely contain weapons (e.g. fig. 3).[7] This is despite the fact
that the Goths, one of the main groups living in these regions, were the
empire's most belligerent neighbours. The importance of war for these
barbarian peoples is nevertheless confirmed by the discovery in northern

---

[2] Shchukin (1994).
[3] Hazanov (1971); Nefedkin (2004).
[4] Kazanski (1999).
[5] Tac. *Germ.* 66.
[6] Raddatz (1985); Godlowski (1992) and (1994); Ilkjaer (1990).
[7] See Kokowski (1993); Shchukin *et al.* (2006) 38–51.

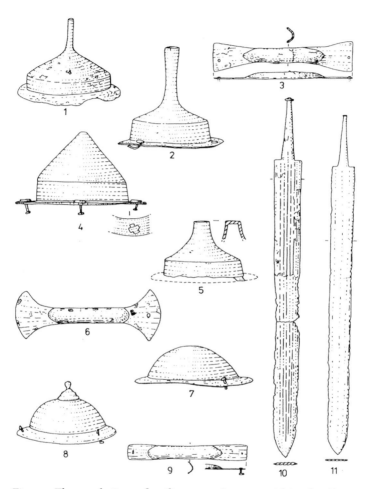

Fig. 1 The evolution of military equipment within the Przeworsk culture, periods C1a-C1b (160/80–250/70 A.D.). 1: Czarno-
cin; 2,3: Dziedzice; 4,11: Opatów; 5–8: Chorula; 9: Specymierz;
10: Cząstkowice. (Godlowski 1992).

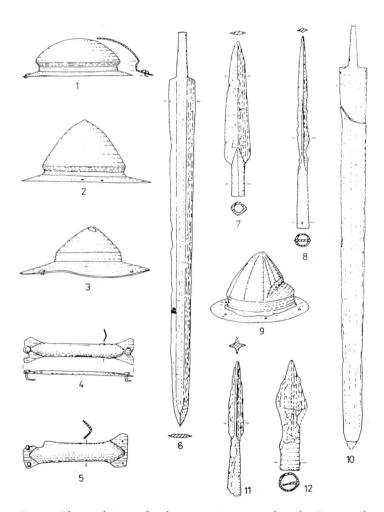

Fig. 2   The evolution of military equipment within the Przeworsk culture, periods C2–D1 (250/60–400/410 A.D.). 1: Specymierz; 2,7: Opatów; 3–5: Żabieniec; 6: Komorów; 8: Korzeń; 9,10,12: Dobordzień; 11: Nowa Wieś Legnicka. (Godlowski 1992).

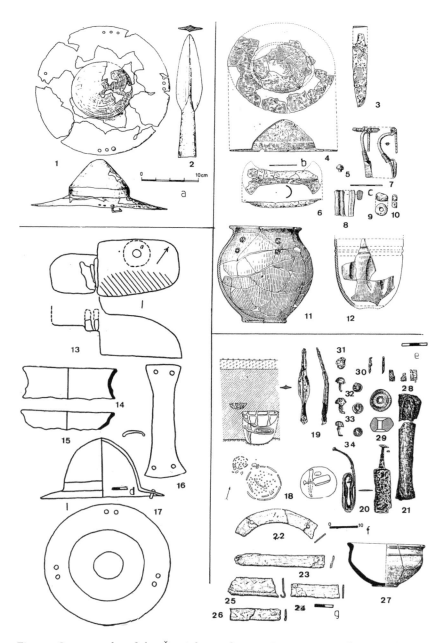

Fig. 3 Some tombs of the Černjahov culture. 1: Mogoşani, tomb 15; 2: Tîrgşor, tomb 147; 3: Belen'koe, tomb 6; 4: Oselivka, tomb 70. Scales—a: 1,2; b: 3,4,6,8,11,12; c: 5–7,9,10; d: 14–17; e: 28–34; f: 19–21; g: 22–27. (Shchukin *et al.* 2006).

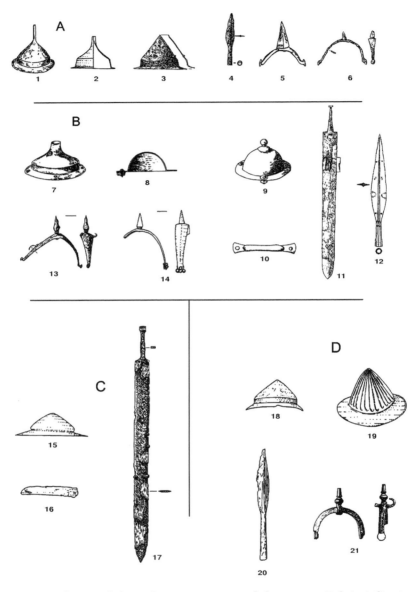

Fig. 4   Evolution of the military equipment of the eastern Balts' civilisation.
A: period C1a (160/80–210/30 A.D.); B: periods C1a late–C1b (200–250/70 A.D.);
C: periods C1b–C3 (220/30–350/70 A.D.); D: periods C3–D1 (300/320–400/410 A.D.).
(Godlowski 1994).

Europe of the sacrificial deposition of weapons in peat bogs, including Illerup, Thorsberg (e.g. figs. 5 and 6) and Ejsbøl.[8]

Archaeological funerary evidence, confirming information provided by written sources, shows that the majority of Germanic infantrymen carried spears and shields during the Late Roman and earlier periods. In fact, barbarian infantrymen during the Roman period resemble those of even earlier periods (the La Tène period, during the last centuries B.C.), but with lighter equipment. Their spears, numerous of which have been found in funerary and sacrificial contexts, are generally "en feuille" (leaf-shaped) (e.g. figs. 3.2, 19).[9] For instance, a series of relatively narrow leaf-shaped spearheads

Fig. 5   Shields from Thorsberg. (Raddatz 1987).

---

[8] Von Carnap-Bornheim and Ilkjær (1990–1996); Raddatz (1987); Ørsnes (1988).
[9] For example, Kaczaowski (1995); Ilkjaer (1990).

Fig. 6   Coat of mail from Thorsberg. (Raddatz 1987).

have been identified in areas occupied by the Balts[10] (fig. 2.7).[11] Slender spears—effectively pikes—also appear (fig. 2.8) in Late Roman Scandinavia and central Europe.[12] These spearheads mostly have two brackets, but in a minority of cases only possess one.

The shields of 'Germanic' groups were circular and made of wood (fig. 5). They were smaller than those dating from the La Tène period and had a metallic boss with a circular cap (see examples figs. 1–5).[13] Older bosses with semi-circular caps, dating back to the Early Roman Empire (figs. 1.7, 4.8), are reminiscent of Roman shield bosses which were used to deflect missile weapons. These declined in number during the 3rd c. A.D. Instead, conical and pointed bosses, which already existed during the Early Roman period, became more prevalent during the Late Roman period.[14] Some bosses possessed a needle (figs. 1.1,2, 4.1,2) which was designed for use during hand-to-hand fighting, when the sufficiently light and easily manageable shield could be used to push away or strike an enemy. Shield handles were made of iron, with fan-shaped ends (figs. 1.3,6,9, 2.4,5, 3.6,16).

Asymmetrical axes with narrow bodies and simple edges were particularly common during the Late Roman period. Numerous axes have been found in the tombs of Germanic groups in western 'Germania' and further east in the Elbe region. They have also been attested elsewhere, in eastern and northern Germanic contexts.[15] West German axes were sometimes slightly curved, prefiguring the Merovingian 'francisca', while east German axes were mostly straight-bodied. It may thus be concluded that in this period, axes, along with spears and shields, made up the kit of the average Germanic infantry warrior.

Third to 5th c. A.D. swords were longer than those of the Early Roman Empire (figs. 1.10,11, 2.6,10, 3.20, 4.11,17)[16] and have more in common with those used during the La Tène period. A considerable proportion of sword finds are of Roman origin, something shown, for instance, by peat bog discoveries. The distribution of long swords indicates that they were used during dispersed combat rather than in tightly-formed ranks. During the 5th c., swords with solid iron hilts which derived from eastern Europe

---

[10] For example, Engelhardt (1867) pl. 2.5.
[11] Compare this with Kazakevičius (1988) 41.
[12] Notably Ilkjaer (1990) 79–85, 167–69.
[13] Zieling (1989).
[14] For the chronology, see: Godlowski (1992) and (1994); Ilkjaer (1990) 257–333.
[15] Kieferling (1994).
[16] Biborski (1978).

became prominent among Germanic groups in the Danube area, and in smaller quantities in the West.[17] Some swords designed for ceremonial use with rich cloisonné decoration and dating to the same century have been found in barbarian contexts (Beja).[18]

It is also interesting to note that swords, finds of which are fairly widespread in Germanic areas, are comparatively rare in the Balto-Finnish and Baltic zones (however, see figs. 4.11,17),[19] even though other elements of 'Germanic' infantry kit have been found there.[20] Archaeologists have tended to think that this is reflective of reality given that swords are also completely absent from non funerary contexts in the Balto-Finnish area. Daggers with relatively long single-edged blades were also an important part of Germanic military equipment, especially among Scandinavian Germans (e.g. Ejsbøl).[21] By contrast, large cutlasses, typical of Germanic equipment during the Early Roman period, disappeared in around the 2nd c. Comparable daggers appeared among the Balts during the Great Migration period.[22]

Archery equipment was also used by the Germans during the Late Roman period, even though only arrow heads have been found in funerary contexts. The reinforced bow with bone plaques was used by the Roman army, but remains archaeologically unknown among finds of sedentary barbarian groups prior to the 5th c. However, a series of discoveries in the tombs of military chiefs (Blučina, Esslingen-Rüdern, Singidumnum IV)[23] demonstrate the diffusion of reinforced bows in Germanic contexts during the 5th c. Numerous types of double-hooked barbed arrows typically used by Germanic groups were common. From the era of the Great Migrations onwards, nomadic arrows, which were large and had three fins, appeared in barbarian archers' kits in Europe.[24]

Other types of weapon appear in funerary contexts, but are rarer. Seaxes and broadswords, in other words, oriental, single-edged weapons with short or long blades, which were, in my view, Byzantine, initially show up in 'princely' contexts in Germanic tombs dating to the Great Migration period. Examples include discoveries in the western tombs of

---

[17] Menghin (1994–95) 165–75.
[18] Menghin (1983) fig. 47; Kazanski (2001) fig. 4.7–12.
[19] Nowakowski (1994).
[20] See, in particular, Kazakevičius (1988).
[21] Ørsnes (1988) pl. 109.
[22] Kazakevičius (1988) 99–114.
[23] Tihelka (1963) 488–89; Christlein (1972) 261–62.
[24] Kazanski (1991) 135–36; Tejral (2003) 506–507.

Altlussheim, Tournai (the Tomb of Childeric) and Pouan.[25] These weapons were common among Germanic peoples living in the Danube area in the Hunnic period.[26] Changes in the shape of shield bosses and swords and the distribution of axes and seaxes demonstrate the growing role of hand-to-hand combat during the Late Roman and Great Migration period. The appearance of fortified bows and 'nomadic' arrowheads is undoubtedly tied to the military influence of nomadic steppe peoples.

Defensive equipment, with the exception of shields, was rare, and undoubtedly reserved for the ruling classes. This equipment, fragments of which were discovered in tombs, consisted of scale and lamellar armour and chain mail. The best preserved examples of Late Roman chain mail come from sacrificial contexts in Scandinavian or southern peat bogs (fig. 6). Helmets of Roman origin are exceptional discoveries. Of interest here are helmets from Scandinavian sacrificial sites,[27] as well as a helmet of Roman origin, dating to the beginning of the 5th c., from the tomb of a chief, probably a Goth, at Conceşti in Romania.[28]

There were no major changes in cavalry equipment among Germanic groups in the Late Roman period. Spurs, which initially consisted of a short plaque with a large needle (e.g. fig. 4.5), became progressively more arched with a smaller needle (e.g. figs. 4.13,14,21).[29] Horse bits comprised a jointed mouthpiece with two rings, or stems, for fixing the bridle. Cavalry was, in fact, relatively unimportant to the sedentary barbarians of Europe: only chiefs and their personal guards had horses available to them. In spite of this, mounted troops did become more common in Germanic armies across the period. The important role played by the Gothic cavalry in the Battle of Adrianople is of course well known. According to Procopius of Caesarea, in the 6th c., Gothic cavalrymen were mostly lancers, who were, incidentally, rather ineffective when faced by Byzantine mounted archers.[30] It is sometimes argued that the Alans had an important influence on the evolution of eastern Germanic cavalry, although this has never been proved conclusively.

Germanic warrior elites are only attested in funerary contexts from the 2nd c. One of the earliest examples is the exceptionally rich, 'princely'

[25] Kazanski (1991) 132–34.
[26] Tejral (2003) 503–506.
[27] Raddatz (1987) pl. 86–91.
[28] Skalon (1973).
[29] For this evolution, see: Giesler (1978); Godlowski (1995).
[30] Procop. *Pers.* 1.27.26–29.

tomb of Mušov in southern Moravia, which yielded weapons and spurs—
an indication of the militarised nature of social power among the Germans during this period. Later on, the 3rd c. tombs of the Hassleben-Leuna
chiefs contained silver arrows and spurs. In contrast, tombs of Germanic
military chiefs were rare in the 4th c. A notable exception is provided by
the high-status grave at Beroun-Závodi, modern Czech Republic, which
yielded many weapons, including a copy of a bronze sword.[31]

Finally, in the 5th c., the practice of burying military chiefs with only
their ceremonial sword became widespread among the Germans in the
Danube area. This was undoubtedly the influence of steppe peoples
(e.g. Lengyeltóti, Lébény, Neštin: fig. 7). Swords were sometimes supplemented by seaxes (Tomb 3 of Vienna-Leopoldau, Szyrmabesenyő) and
occasionally by bows and arrows (Blučina, Singidunum-IV). These tombs
also yielded belt- and scabbard-fittings of which some elements had cloisonné decoration (figs. 7.6,15,30–33), very much in fashion among 5th c.
barbarians.[32] Western and northern Germanic elite warrior tombs, such
as Childeric's, contained panoplies of arms in which the sword played a
significant role, prefiguring the funerary practices of military chiefs at the
beginning of the Merovingian period.[33] Judging from archaeological discoveries in Gaul,[34] it is worth noting that the Roman army's military equipment bore similarities to that discovered in contexts within 'Barbaricum'.
One may consequently conclude that West Roman armies, largely made
up of German soldiers, adopted the same tactics as the barbarians on the
other side of the frontier. It is difficult to understand how barbarian or
Roman soldiers, being used to a particular model of warfare, could have
changed their way of fighting as soon as they were compelled to fight
together in the Roman army. Whatever the case, military equipment
found in northern Gallic tombs is closely comparable with that found in
'Germania'.

Moving away from Europe to the Black Sea, the military equipment of
sedentary Pontic groups was strongly influenced by the martial culture
of the steppe nomads during the Roman period. Thus, in the 2nd c., the
heavy cavalry of the eastern Crimea and the Taman Peninsula (its capital at Pantikapaion, modern Kerch) made use of the Greek Cimmerian
Bosporus spearhead in the manner of Sarmatian and Alan cataphracts.

---

[31] Tejral (1999) fig. 14.
[32] Kazanski (1999a).
[33] See the examples in Bianchini (2000).
[34] Böhme (1974) 97–114; Kazanski (1995).

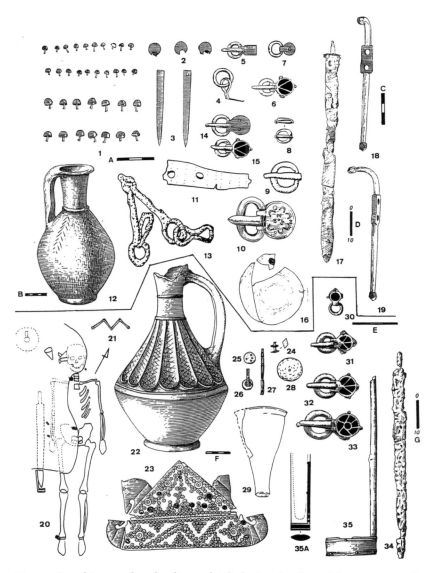

Fig. 7   Danubian tombs of military chiefs during the Great Migration period.
1–19: Lengyeltóti; 20–34: Lébény. Scales—a: 1–9; 13–16, 35; b: 2; c: 18; d: 17; 17;
e: 21–23, 30,33; f: 22; g: 34. (Shchukin *et al.* 2006).

Second to 3rd c. depictions on tombstones or in frescoes from funerary vaults depict horsemen—often cataphracts of Sarmatian or Iranian type—who are heavily armoured with long swords, armour, conical helmets and large spears. Their combat technique was also reminiscent of Iranian peoples: the evidence depicts confrontations between groups of heavily armoured horsemen supported by infantry detachments.[35] Archaeological finds indicate that long *spathae* swords, daggers (those with notches near the handle as in fig. 10.3),[36] spears, and bows and arrows, constituted essential military equipment for peoples living north and east of the Black Sea during the Early Roman Empire. The presence in tombs of harness pieces (horse bits and harness trimmings) shows the importance of the cavalry. It should be recalled that during the Roman period, the kingdoms and peoples surrounding the Black Sea formed a network of imperial 'clients', providing, as it were, the first line of defence for the 'Pontic' frontier of the empire.[37]

From the 2nd c. onwards, however, European military equipment progressively spread into the Pontic region, in other words, into the Crimea and areas along the east coast of the Black Sea.[38] Julius Callisphenus' tomb, discovered in the necropolis at Pantikapaion, and dated by its inscriptions to the first half of the 2nd c., yielded a shield boss, which is an exceptional discovery for the pre-3rd c. Crimea.[39] Its presence in the tomb suggests a Thracian military influence which auxiliary troops from Rome, then stationed at Chersonesus, spread to regions north of the Black Sea. Indeed, shield bosses in the Pontic region dating to this period are only attested in aristocratic Thracian tombs.[40] It is, nevertheless, possible that the custom of shield deposition came from the Hellenised Roman West. In fact, a boss was found in a rich grave at Homs dating to the same period.[41]

The arrival of Germanic tribes north of the Black Sea during the migration of the Goths and their allies was marked by the diffusion of 'northern' weaponry types in the Crimea. Shield bosses and axes, and sometimes even spurs, are present in the burials of Iranian-speaking peoples living in south-west Crimea (sites of the Inkerman type), namely at Ozernoe,

---

[35] Mielczarek (1999); Gorončarovskij (2003).
[36] Soupault (1996).
[37] Kazanaski (1991a).
[38] Kazanski (1994); Soupault (1995).
[39] Shchukin *et al.* (2006) fig. 8.
[40] Kazanski (1994) 436.
[41] Kazanski (1994) fig. 6.9.

Družnoe, Nejzac, Manguš, Skalistoe III and Sovhoz-10.[42] Germanic military equipment—bossed shields, axes, spears of characteristic types—is well represented in necropolises of the Aj-Todor type on the Crimean south coast. These necropolises belonged to a Germanic group which came from the north.[43]

Bosses dating to the Late Roman and Great Migration periods are also attested in Cimmerian Bosporian necropolises: at Pantikapaion/Bosporus, particularly in aristocratic tombs, and at Starožilovo.[44] Certain tombs at Bosporus yielded panoplies of prestigious weapons, in particular, richly decorated polychrome swords and golden bosses,[45] as well as polychrome harness pieces.[46] A series of bosses and spurs came to light at Tanaïs, the Greek city at the mouth of the River Don, which was a dependent of the Cimmerian Bosporus (fig. 8). It is nevertheless possible that these weapons belonged to the barbarians who destroyed the city in the mid-3rd c.[47]

In Abkhazia, on the Caucasian coast of the Black Sea (where places such as Tsibilium, Šapka, Ačandra or Krasnaja Poljana are situated), necropolises belonging to client groups of the Roman Empire (Apsilii,

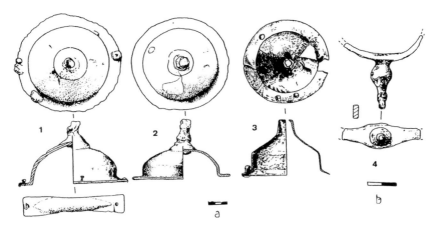

Fig. 8   Shield boss and spear from Tanaïs. Plates a: 1–3; b: 4.
(Shchukin *et al.* 2006).

---

[42] Kazanski (1994) annexe 2.
[43] Shchukin *et al.* (2006) 81–83.
[44] See, for example, Soupault (1995) pl. 4.
[45] For example, Soupault (1995) pl. 10.4.6.9.
[46] For example, Shchukin *et al.* (2006) figs. 82, 93 and 95.
[47] See the list in Kazanski (1994).

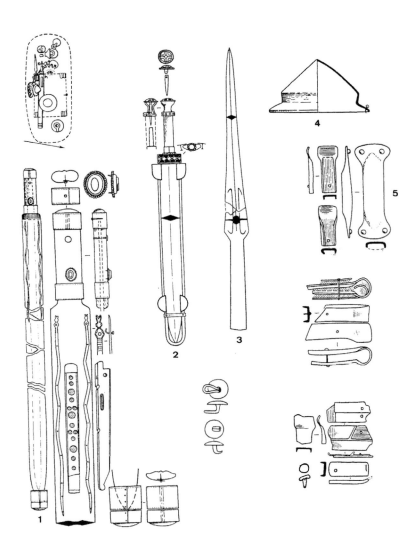

Fig. 9   Military equipment from tomb 61 at Tsibilium-1.
(Voronov and Šenkao 1982).

Abasgians, Saniges) display a similar evolution in military equipment.[48] While the spears and swords found in these graveyards were typical of the Early Roman period, from the 3rd c. onwards, characteristically Germanic shield bosses and axes started appearing in the funerary assemblages. An actual German presence in this area is extremely unlikely. It may thus be supposed that typically German weapons were diffused into these regions by 'barbarised' Roman army garrisons in the coastal fortresses of Sebastopolis (modern Soukhoumi) and Pitiunt (the modern city of Pitsunda).

The distribution of three-finned 'nomadic' arrows demonstrates the concurrent military influence of the steppe peoples. East Roman elite military fashion provided a further influence. This is demonstrated by the presence of cloisonné-decorated Byzantine swords and seaxes in 5th to 6th c. Abkhaze tombs. Tomb 61 from the Tsibilium necropolis, dated towards the end of the 4th or first half of the 5th c., is a good example of the mixture of these influences: in particular, it contains a Germanic bossed shield (fig. 9.4) and an oriental dagger (fig. 9.2) with four attachment points for a handle.

Byzantine influence also reached the sedentary barbarians of the Black Sea's north-east coast. The late 5th c. tombs of Tetraxite Gothic chieftains from the necropolis of Djurso, near the modern city of Novorossiïk, yielded ceremonial swords of Byzantine origin, as well as swords with sheet metal inlays which might indicate a Hunnic influence (see below).[49]

THE STEPPE ZONE

The second zone of weaponry distribution is the eastern part of Europe, the steppes of Scythia-Sarmatia. During the Roman period, Iranian speaking nomads—the Sarmatians and the Alans—dominated these areas. The Alans progressively imposed their name on all of the steppe tribes of the Late Roman period, only the Sarmatians of the Hungarian Plain retaining their original name. The presence of weapons in many of their tombs indicates that the Sarmatian and Alan peoples were highly militarised.[50] Cavalry equipment was the basis of steppe military paraphernalia. The frequently-attested long and pointed sword, usually with an iron

---

[48] Voronov and Senkao (1982); Soupault (1995).
[49] Kazanski (2001).
[50] Hazanov (1971); Nefedkin (2004).

hilt and a long tang for fixing the handle, is the sign of Iranian influence. Older swords dating to the 2nd c. possessed a ring-shaped pommel. These 'nomadic' swords were often accompanied by beads, which are frequently mistakenly named 'magic pendants' (as on fig. 11.2). These were in fact either belt-scabbard attachments or sword-knot endings, in other words, straps for tying the sword handle to a hand. The swords just mentioned were carried 'Iranian' style, tied to the belt, and not in the West Roman style, attached to a shoulder strap. The princely tombs of Brut (Northern Caucasus) yielded examples of ceremonial swords, probably part of an eastern tradition, which had gold sheet scabbards and were decorated in a polychrome style.[51] Byzantine swords with large hilts bearing cloisonné decoration were brought to light in the sedentary Alan sites of the central northern Caucasus (Mokraja Balka, Lermontovskaja Skala).[52]

Daggers are well-attested in funerary contexts. Most noteworthy are the ceremonial daggers from Brut (end of the 4th to first half of the 5th c.), which have iron hilts, cloisonné style decoration and gold sheet scabbards. The tombs of settled northern Caucasian Alans have also yielded daggers with gold and silver sheet scabbards decorated in scale.[53] While finds of spears (fig. 10.2) are rare, missile weapons for fighting at a distance played a dominant role in nomadic military equipment culture. Arrow heads usually had three fins, serving to increase the size of the wound they inflicted, and bows were reinforced with bone. Other types of offensive weaponry are rare.

Defensive equipment is particularly typical of the first three centuries of our era, as shown by the tombs of Kouban (Gorodskoj, Zolotoe Kladbišče). Helmets with lamellar, scale armour and chain mail were abundant, although bossed shields were extremely rare. However, this type of kit became much rarer in the 3rd to 4th c. according to tombs dating from this period. One exception is the lamellar helmet of Roman origin found in the grave of Kišpek in the northern Caucasus. This dates approximately to A.D. 300. Iconographic parallels to this helmet are depicted on the Arch of Galerius in Thessalonica, which is of A.D. 298.[54]

Cavalry equipment from tombs includes horse bits with jointed mouth-pieces, bridal rings and harness trimmings (figs. 10.5–7). Those dating to

---

[51] Gabuev (2000) and (2005) 33–42.
[52] Kazanski (2001).
[53] For example, Atabiev (2000).
[54] Kazanski (1995a) 193.

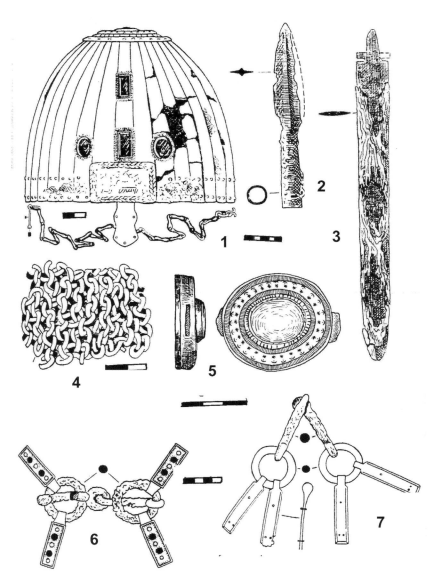

Fig. 10　Military equipment and cavalry equipment from the tomb at Kišpek. (Kazanski 1995a).

the Late Roman era present the sort of polychrome decoration typical of the period (figs. 10.5,6).[55] Spurs are completely absent from steppe contexts. Great Migration period harness trimmings bore cloisonné decoration, as shown by the finds from Brut.[56] The same tombs at Brut also yielded examples of horse whips. Finally, the Alanic tomb of the Hunnic period at Lermontovskaja Skala contained among its furnishings metal saddle fittings, proof that the Alans used hard saddles.

Funerary contexts generally impart the impression that Late Roman Alan cavalry was lighter than that of the earlier period. The cataphracts, heavy shock cavalry, which are attested in both written and archaeological sources for the two first centuries of our era, disappeared towards the 3rd c. and were replaced by faster mounted troops. For the latter, combat at a distance became increasingly characteristic and thus prefigured the appearance of the Hunnic cavalry.

High levels of political stratification in the nomadic world can be observed throughout the Roman period: 1st c. 'princely' tombs from Porogi (Ukraine) and Dači (in the Don region), and Late Roman finds at Aerodrom (the Don region) and Kišpek (North Caucasus, fig. 10), are particularly noteworthy.[57] The discovery of the 'princely' tumuli at Brut in Northern Ossetia, alongside the tombs of sedentary Alan military chieftains in the central Caucasus (Mokraja Balka, Lermontovskaja Skala, Zaragiž) provides further evidence for the elite military culture of the Hunnic period.[58]

The appearance of the Huns in Europe marks the end of Antiquity and the beginning of the Middle Ages. Swift and agile on their steppe horses, the Huns were unpredictable and formidable archers who fought within tightly organised military units. These steppe cavalrymen's mobility and superiority in numbers during decisive battles were the reasons for their military success. Only states such as China, Iran and Russia, which possessed professional armies and a developed system of fortifications, were able to withstand them. The Russians, moreover, only conquered the nomadic world in the 16th c., and this was down to the advent of fire-arms. The monstrous 'Tzar Pushka', 'the King of Canons', is today proudly commemorated at the Kremlin. This 39-tonne bronze cannon, dating to the time of Ivan the Terrible, symbolises the beginning of the nomadic world's

---

[55] Malašev (2000).
[56] Gabuev (2000) and (2005) 33–42.
[57] Kazanski (1995a).
[58] Gabuev (2000) and (2005) 33–42; Atabiev (2000).

decline. With the power of fire-arms, the Russians conquered the steppes in their vast entirety, from Kazan's ramparts on the Volga, crushed on 2nd October 1552, to the ramparts of Geok-Tepe in Turkmenistan, conquered on 12th January 1881. The Mongolian cavalry's quick-march to Beijing on 10th August 1945—admittedly flanked by the Soviet army's armoured tanks—was the last episode in the long history of the steppe warriors.

The offensive component of the Hunnic army consisted of horsemen, each of whom was supplied with two horses in accordance with steppe traditions. Their main weapons were the reinforced bow, and arrows with large heads and three fins (figs. 3, 9, 10). The shape of certain arrows was characteristic of central Asian styles (fig. 11.10). When fired from a fortified bow, this type of arrow could split a plank of wood at 30 m. In combat, a steppe warrior would have been equipped with at least one, if not two, quivers containing 20 to 30 arrows. Every arrow was precious, and Hunnic warriors would not fire them wastefully. Hunnic offensive manoeuvres were quick and numerous, enveloping enemy flanks and attacking them by surprise from behind. The Huns only ever engaged in direct hand-to-hand combat when in pursuit of a routed enemy. Indeed, without stirrups, which only appeared in the steppes in the 6th c., these horsemen would have lacked the stability for close combat. Attila's warriors thus preferred to use archery to annihilate their opponents at range. Long swords, discovered in Hunnic funerary contexts (fig. 11.9), were used to cut down enemies who had been dispersed by arrow fire. These swords sometimes possessed iron hilts (fig. 11.5). Ceremonial swords, daggers bearing polychrome decoration, and scabbards covered with gold sheeting (figs. 11.1,8), are indicative of the rich military equipment culture of the tombs of military chiefs. Defensive equipment, especially chain mail (fig. 11,7), is rare.

Harnesses and riding equipment are often found in steppe tombs from the Hunnic period.[59] They include horse bits with jointed mouthpieces, which have rings and stems for tying bridles (figs. 11.13,14). Hard wooden saddles, decorated with sheet metal appliqués have also been discovered (figs. 11.11,12). These saddles provided a stable seat for stirrup-less riders. Jordanes reports that during a difficult moment in the Battle of the Catalaunian Plain in A.D. 451, Attila decided to commit suicide. He ordered his

---

[59] Zaseckaja (1994); Anke (1998); Bona (2002); Nikonorov and Hudjakov (2004); Kazanski (2012).

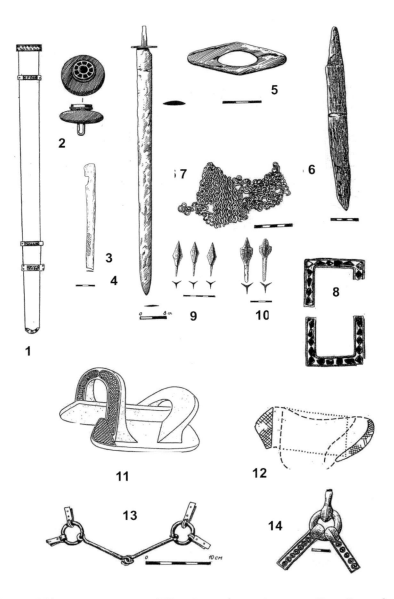

Fig. 11   Military equipment and Hunnic cavalry equipment. 1: Novo-Ivanovka;
2,4,5,8: Novogrigor'evka; 3,10: Kyzyl-Adyr; 6,14: Kubej; 7,9,13: Fedorovka;
11: Mundolsheim; 12: Pecsűszőg. (Zaseckaja 1994).

men to gather all of their saddles to form an improvised funerary pyre.[60] Even though Jordanes was writing his history at a later date, his testimony correlates archaeological evidence, which confirms that cremation was a Hunnic funerary rite. The episode reinforces what we know from the archaeological evidence: that Hunnic saddles were made of wood. Stirrups are entirely absent from Hunnic archaeological sites, as in other nomadic contexts for that matter. Aside from soldiers who were, strictly speaking, Huns, Hunnic armies comprised troops donated by subordinate allies, notably Germanic infantry and Alan cavalry. These were sometimes numerous, as on Attila's expedition to Gaul.

SLAVIC GROUPS

The third group of barbarian peoples under discussion—those of the forested areas of eastern Europe—appeared on the borders of the ancient world towards the beginning of the 6th c. They were the Slavs: the Sklaveni (who were the real Slavs) and their close kin, the Antae. The Slavs' funerary practices did not include the deposition of weapons in tombs—archaeological data is thus confined to the habitation sites of Slavic civilisations attested by the Prague (Sklaveni), Penkovka (Antae) and Koločin (unidentified group, related to those of the Penkovka civilisation) archaeological cultures. Other, more northern, forest-dwelling populations, known as the Tušemlja and the Long Kurgans, were either Slavic or Baltic or Balto-Slavonic.

According to the archaeological evidence, light weapons—spearheads, javelin points and arrows—were commonly used by Slavic groups.[61] This type of equipment suggests that they engaged in military actions that may be categorised as 'guerrilla' warfare, correlating Tacitus' testimony regarding the 1st c. A.D. ancestors of the Slavs, the Veneti.[62] Further, 6th c. authors on the Slavic military, such as Procopius and Maurice, characterised the Slavs first and foremost as light infantrymen, well-adapted to commando style actions or to combat in forested and mountainous terrain. This type of warfare was ultimately rewarded because around 600–620 A.D., the Slavs—more or less under the aegis of the Avar Khagan—became masters of the Balkans following the collapse of the Byzantine defensive system.

---

[60] Jord. *Get.* 213.
[61] Kazanski (1999).
[62] For weapons of the Veneti in Late Antiquity, see Kazanski (1997).

The role of the Avars in the conquest of the Balkans was very important and frequently decisive. They had established their domination over the Danubian Slavs during the 570s. From the early 580s, Slavic invasions of the Balkans were in most cases perpetrated in co-ordination with Avar cavalry, and were often in fact initiated by the Avar Khagan. However, Avar involvement in the Slavicisation of the Balkans should not be exaggerated. From 540 to 550, before the Avars arrived in the Balkans, the Sklaveni had succeeded in devastating the Balkan provinces on numerous occasions. Further, the Sklaveni, who started settling permanently in the Balkans from the 580s, were not entirely subordinate to the Avars. For example, in 618, the Slavic tribes living around Thessalonica proposed a military alliance to the Avar Khagan, effectively submitting to him, in order to attack Thessalonica.[63] This proves that these tribes had previously been independent of the Avars.

Returning to the Slavs' military equipment and mode of warfare, we also have written evidence for cavalrymen among the Slavs, who, according to Procopius, were incorporated by the same Byzantine troop units as the Huns, in other words, units of mounted archers.[64] The discovery of steppe-type three-finned arrows (figs. 12.1–14,16–20) and fragments of a reinforced bow (fig. 12.15) at Hitcy, in a building associated with the Penkovka culture, confirms the evidence of Byzantine authors for Slavic cavalry. Of the other pieces of material evidence suggesting steppe military influence on the Slavs, it is worth mentioning a solid iron dagger hilt from the territory of Velyki Budki (fig. 12.21), and some bone-harnessing rings characteristic of nomadic groups (figs. 12.22–24). All of this confirms, therefore, a significant steppe nomadic influence on Slavic military equipment.

Byzantine authors (Procopius and Menander) discuss the military role of Slavic chieftains. The diffusion among Slavic groups of prestigious Byzantine military belts reinforces the literary evidence for the existence of these military elites. For instance, Matynovka's 'princely' treasure contained silver belt fittings.[65] The majority of objects of this type brought to light at Slavic sites were made of bronze, however.

---

[63] Jord. *Get.* 213.
[64] Kazanski (2009).
[65] Pekarskaja and Kidd (1994) pl. 31–35. This has sometimes been wrongly attributed to steppe nomadic groups despite the fact that the treasure clearly contains no steppe-type object and is situated in the middle of the Slavic Penkova culture.

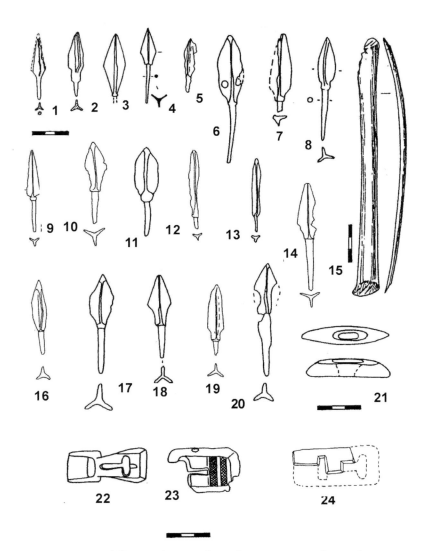

Fig. 12   Pieces of Slavic military and cavalry equipment of nomadic steppe origin (5th to 8th c.). 1: Kolodeznyj Bugor; 2: Hohlov Vir; 3: Tajamnova; 4: Pesčanoe; 5: Dem'janka; 6: Hotomeľ; 7: Raškov; 8: Dresden-Schtezsch; 9, 12: Izvoare-Bahia; 10, 14, 19: Davideni-Neamţ; 11: Sarata-Monteoru; 13: Hutor Miklaševskij; 15: Hitcy; 16: Tarancevo; 17: Novye Bratušany; 18: Ostrov Kyzlevyj; 20: Trebu-ženy; 21: Velyki Budki; 22: Vološskoe-Surskaja Zabora; 23: Klementoviči; 24: Selište. (Kazanski 1999).

Concluding Remarks

It can thus be noted that barbarian military equipment, and consequently modes of combat, underwent notable changes between the 3rd and 6th c A.D. Germanic peoples' weapons and those of their neighbours became more appropriate to rapid and close combat in dispersed ranks. The distribution of Germanic-type weapons in the Pontic region and in Roman territory demonstrates that the same tactics were adopted by the barbarised Roman army and federate, or allied, groups. A similar evolution occurred among steppe nomadic groups. The heavily-armoured lancers of the Early Roman period were replaced by first a light Alan cavalry and then by Hunnic mounted archers. Finally, the Slavic light infantry, fighting in dispersed ranks in a 'guerilla' mode of warfare, defeated the armies of the eastern Empire and conquered the Balkan Peninsula.

Bibliography

Primary Sources

Jord. *Get.* = Giunta Fr. and Grillone A. (1991) edd. *Getica: Iordaniis de origine actibusque Getarum* (Rome 1991).
Miracles of St. Demetrius = Lemerle P. (1981) *Les plus anciens recueils des Miracles de Saint-Démétrius et la pénétration des Slaves dans les Balkans* Books I and II (Paris 1981).
Procop. *Pers.* = Dewing H. B. (1914–68) ed. and trans. Procopius, *History of the Wars* (Cambridge, Mass. and London 1914–68).
Tac. *Germ.* = Perret J. (1983) ed. and trans. Tacitus, *Germania* (Paris 1983).

Secondary Works

Anke B. (1998) *Studien zur Reiternomadischen Kultur des 4. bis 5. Jahrhunderts* (Weissbach 1998).
Atabiev B. (2000) "Tombe 118. Zaragij, Naltchik", in *L'Or des princes barbares. Du Caucase à la Gaule Ve s. ap. J.-c.*, ed. M.-C. Bianchini (Paris 2000) 162–65.
Bemmann J. (1994) "Zur zeitlichen Ordnung von Waffengräbern der jüngeren römischen Kaiserzeit in Norwegien", in *Beitrage zu römischer und barbarischer Bewaffnung in der ersten vier nachchristlichen Jahrhunderten: Akten des 2. Internationalen Kolloquiums in Marburg a.d. Lahn, 20. Bis 24. Februar 1994*, ed. C. von Carnap-Bornheim (Lublin and Marburg 1994) 179–88.
Bianchini M.-C. (2000) ed. *L'Or des princes barbares. Du Caucase à la Gaule Ve s. ap. J.-c.* (Paris 2000).
Biborski M. (1978) "Miecze z okresu wpływów rzymskich na obszarze kultury przeworskiej", *Materiały Archeologiczne* 18 (1978) 53–165.
Böhme H. W. (1974) *Germanische Grabfunde des 4. bis. 5. Jahrhunderts zwischen unterer Elbe und Loire* (Munich 1974).
Bona I. (2002) *Les Huns: Le grand empire barbare d'Europe IVᵉ–Vᵉ siècles* (Paris 2002).
Christlein R. (1972) "Waffen aus dem völkerwanderungszeitlichen Grabfund von Esslingen-Rüdern", *Germania* 50 (1972) 259–63.

Engelhardt C. (1867) *Kragehul mosefund 1751–1865: et overgangsfund mellem den ældre jernalder og mellem-jernalderen* (Copenhagen 1867).

Gabuev T. A. (2000) "Mobilier d'une tombe de cavalier. Brut, Ossetie du Nord, Russie", in *L'Or des princes barbares. Du Caucase à la Gaule Ve s. ap. J.-c.*, ed. M.-C. Bianchini (Paris 2000) 138–41.

—— (2005) *Alanskii vsadnik: Sokrovishcha kniazei I–XII vekov* (Russian=*The Alan Cavalry: Treasures of the Princes 1st–13th c.*) (Moscow 2005).

Giesler U. (1978) "Jüngerkaiserzeiltiche Nietknopfsporen mit Dreipunkthalterung vom Typ Leuna", *SaalbJb* 35 (1978) 5–66.

Godlowski K. (1992) "Zmiany w uzbrojeniu ludności przęworskiej w kresie wplywów rzymskich", in *Arma et ollae* (Lódź 1992) 71–88.

—— (1994) "Die Chronologie der germanischen Waffengräber in der jüngeren und späten Kiaserzeit", in *Beitrage zu römischer und barbarischer Bewaffnung in der ersten vier nachchristlichen Jahrhunderten: Akten des 2. Internationalen Kolloquiums in Marburg a.d. Lahn, 20. bis 24. Februar 1994*, ed. C. von Carnap-Bornheim (Lublin and Marburg 1994) 169–78.

Goroncharovskii V. (2003) *Mezhdu imperii i varvarami: Voennoe delo Bospora rimskogo vremeni* (Russian=*Between the Empire and the Barbarians: the Military Art of the Cimmerian Bosporous during the Roman Era*) (Moscow and Saint Petersburg 2003).

Ilkjaer J. (1990) *Illeurp Ådal. 1: Die Lancen und Speere* (Aarhus 1990).

Kaczanowski P. (1995) *Klasyfikacija grotów broni drzewcowejnkultury przeworskiej z okresu rzymskiego* (Cracovie 1995).

Kazekevičius V. (1988) *Oruzhie baltskikh plemen II–VIII vekov na territorii Litvy* (Russian=*The Weaponry of the Baltic Tribes during the 2nd-8th c. in the Territory of Lithuania*) (Vilnius 1988).

Kazanski M. (1991) "Contribution à l'histoire de la défense de la frontière pontique au Bas-Empire", *TravMém* 11 (1991) 487–526.

—— (1991a) "A propos des armes et des éléments de harnachement 'orientaux' en Occident à l'époque des Grandes Migrations (IVe-Ve s.)", *JRA* 4 (1991) 123–39.

—— (1994) "Les éperons, les umbo, les manipules de boucliers et les haches de l'époque romaine tardive dans la région pontique: origine et diffusion", in *Beitrage zu römischer und barbarischer Bewaffnung in der ersten vier nachchristlichen Jahrhunderten: Akten des 2. Internationalen Kolloquiums in Marburg a.d. Lahn, 20. bis 24. Februar 1994*, ed. C. von Carnap-Bornheim (Lublin and Marburg 1994) 429–85.

—— (1995) "L'équipement et le matériel militaires au Bas-Empire en Gaule du Nord et de l'Est", *Revue du Nord-Archéologie* 77 (1995) 37–54.

—— (1995a) "Les tombes des chefs alano-sarmates au IVe siècle dans les steppes pontiques", in *La noblesse romaine et chefs barbares du IIIe au VIIe siècle*, edd. F. Vallet and M. Kazanski (Saint-Germain-en-Laye 1995) 189–205.

—— (1997) "Oroozhiye Kiyevskoy kool'toori" (Russian="The weaponry of the Kiev civilisation"), in *Pamyatniki starini, kontsyeptsii, otkritiya, vyersii. Pamyati Vasiliya Dmitriyevicha Byelyetskogo, 1919–1997* (Russian=*Ancient Monuments, Conceptions, Discoveries and Versions. In Memory of Vassily Dmitrievitch Beletsky, 1919–1997*) (Saint Petersburg and Pskov 1997) 262–69.

—— (1999) "L'armement slave du haut Moyen-Age (Ve–VIIe siècles). A propos des chefs militaires et des guerriers professionnels chez les anciens Slaves", *Přehled výzkumů* 39 (1999) 197–236.

—— (1999a) "Les tombes des chefs militaires de l'époque hunnique", in *Germanen beiderseits des spätantiken Limes*, edd. T. Fischer, G. Precht and J. Tejral (Cologne and Brno 1999) 293–316.

—— (2001) "Les épées 'orientales' à garde cloisonnée du Ve–VIe siècle", in *International Connections of the Barbarians in the 1st–5th Centuries A.D.*, edd. E. Istvánovits and V. Kulcsár (Aszod and Nyiregyhaza 2001) 389–418.

—— (2009) "La cavalerie slave à l'époque de Justinien", *Archaeologia Baltica* 11 (2009) 229–39.

—— (2012) "Les armes et les techniques de combat des guerriers steppiques du debut du Moyen-age. Des Huns aux Avars", in *Le cheval dans les sociétés antiques et médiévales*, ed. S. Lazaris (Turnhout 2012) 193–99, 287–96.

Khazanov A. M. (1971) *Ocherki voennogo dela sarmatov* (Russian=*Studies on the Military Art of the Sarmatians*) (Moscow 1971).

Kieferling G. (1994) "Bemerkungen zu Äxten der römischen Kaiserzeit und der frühen Völkerwanderungszeit im mitteleuropäischen Barbaricum", in *Beitrage zu römischer und barbarischer Bewaffnung in der ersten vier nachchristlichen Jahrhunderten: Akten des 2. Internationalen Kolloquiums in Marburg a.d. Lahn, 20. bis 24. Februar 1994*, ed. C. von Carnap-Bornheim (Lublin and Marburg 1994) 335–56.

Kokowski A. (1993) "L'art militaire des Goths à l'époque romaine tardive (d'après les données archéologiques)", in *L'armée romaine et les barbares du IIIe au VIIe siècle*, edd. F. Vallet and M. Kazanski (Saint-Germain-en-Laye 1993) 335–54.

Malashev V. Iu. (2000) "Periodizaciia remennyk garniture pozdnesarmatskogo vremeni" (Russian="The periodisation of belt fittings in the Late Sarmatian period"), in *Sarmaty i ikh sosedi na Donu* (Russian=*The Sarmatians and their Neighbours on the River Don*), ed. Ju. Guguev (Rostov-na-Don 2000) 194–232.

Menghin W. (1983) *Das Schwert im frühen Mittelalter* (Stuttgart 1983).

—— (1994–95) "Schwerter des Goldgriffspathenhorizonts im Museum für Vor- und Frühgeschichte, Berlin", *Acta Praehistorica et Archaeologica* 26/27 (1994–95) 140–91.

Mielczarek M. (1999) *The Army of the Bosporan Kingdom* (Lódź 1999).

Nefedkin A. K. (2004) *Pod znamenem drakona: Voennoe delo sarmatov do II v. do n. e.-V v. n. e.* (Russian=*Under the Curtain of the Dragon: the Military Art of the Sarmatians 2nd to 5th c. A.D.*) (Moscow and Saint Petersburg 2004).

Nikonorov V. P. and Khudiakov Iu. S. (2004) *'Svistialishche strely' Maoduna i 'Marsov mech' Attily* (Russian=*The 'Whizzing Arrows' of Maodun and the 'Sword of Mars' of Attila*) (Moscow and Saint Petersburg 2004).

Nowakowski V. (1994) ""Krieger ohne Schwerter" Die Bewaffnung der *Aestii* in der Römischen Kaiserzeit", in *Beitrage zu römischer und barbarischer Bewaffnung in der ersten vier nachchristlichen Jahrhunderten: Akten des 2. Internationalen Kolloquiums in Marburg a.d. Lahn, 20. bis 24. Februar 1994*, ed. C. von Carnap-Bornheim (Lublin and Marburg 1994) 379–93.

Ørsnes M. (1988) *Ejsbøl I: Waffenopferfunde des 4.–5. Jahrh. nach Chr.* (Copenhagen 1988).

Pekarskaja L. and Kidd D. (1994) *Der Silberschatz von Martynovka (Ukraine) aus dem 6. und 7. Jahrhundert* (Innsbruck 1994).

Raddatz K. (1985) "Die Bewaffnung der Germanen vom letzten Jahrhundert v. Chr. bis zur Völkerwanderungszeit", *ANRW* 2.12.3 (Berlin and New York 1985) 281–361.

—— (1987) *Der Thorsberger Moorfund: Katalog: Teile von Waffen und Pferdgeschirr* (Offa-Bücher-65) (Neumünster 1987).

Shchukin M. B. (1994) "Shields, swords and spears as evidence of Germanic-Sarmatian contacts and Barbarian-Roman relations", in *Beitrage zu römischer und barbarischer Bewaffnung in der ersten vier nachchristlichen Jahrhunderten: Akten des 2. Internationalen Kolloquiums in Marburg a.d. Lahn, 20. bis 24. Februar 1994*, ed. C. von Carnap-Bornheim (Lublin and Marburg 1994) 485–95.

Shchukin M., Kazanski M. and Sharov O. (2006) *Des Goths aux Huns: Le Nord de la Mer Noire au Bas-Empire et à l'époque des Grandes Migrations* (BAR International Series 1535) (Oxford 2006).

Skalon K. M. (1973) "Der Helm von Conceşti", in *Spätrömische Gardenhelme*, ed. H. Klumbach (Munich 1973) 91–94.

Soupault V. (1995) "Les tombes à épée au nord-est et à l'est de la mer Noire au Bas-Empire", in *La noblesse romaine et chefs barbares du IIIe au VIIe siècle*, edd. F. Vallet and M. Kazanski (Saint-Germain-en-Laye 1995) 227–57.

—— (1996) "A propos de l'origine et de la diffusion des poignards et épées à encoches (IVe–VIIe s.)", *Matyeriali po Arhyeologii, Istorii i Etnografii Tavrii* 5 (1996) 60–76.

Tejral J. (1999) "Die spätantiken militärischen Eliten beiderseits der norisch-pannonischen Grenze aus der Sicht der Grabfunde", in *Germanen beiderseits des spätantiken Limes*, edd. T. Fischer, G. Precht and J. Tejral (Cologne and Brno 1999) 218–92.

—— (2003) "Neue Erkentnisse zur Frage der donaulandisch-ostgermanischen Krieger-beziehungsweise Männergräber des 5. Jahrhunderts", *Fundberichte aus Österreich* 41 (2003) 496–524.

Tihelka K. (1963) "Knížecí hrob z období stěhování národů u Blučiny, okr; Brno-Venkov", *Památky Archeologické* 65/2 (1963) 467–98.

Von Carnap-Bornheim C. and Ilkjær J. (1990–96) *Illerup Ådal* (Aarhus 1990–96), Bd. 1–8.

Voronov Iu. N. and Šhenkao N. K. (1982) "Vooruzhenie voinov Abkhazii IV–VII vv." (Russian="The military equipment of the Abkhazian peoples during the 4th to 7th c. A.D."), in *Drevnosti epokhi velikogo pereseleniia narodov V–VIII vv.* (Russian=*Antiquities of the Era of the Great Migrations, during the 5th to 8th c.*), edd. A. K. Ambroz and I. Erdelyi (Moscow 1982) 121–64.

Zaseckaia I. P. (1994) *Kul'tura kochevnikov iuzhnorusskikh stepei v gunnskogo epokhu (konec IV–V vv.)* (Russian=*The Nomadic Civilisation of the Steppes in the South of Russia during the Hunnic era (Late 4th to 5th c.)*) (Saint Petersburg 1994).

Zielung N. (1989) *Studien zu germanischen Schilden der Spätlatène und der römischen Kaiserzeit im freien Germanien* (BAR International Series 505) (Oxford 1989).

LIST OF FIGURES

RECREATING THE LATE ROMAN ARMY

John Conyard

Abstract

This paper attempts to give some insight into the role that Roman military reconstruction archaeology can play in the understanding of Roman military equipment from Late Antiquity. It can only provide a brief introduction to some of the equipment of the Late Roman army though, and Bishop and Coulston's *Roman Military Equipment*, first published in 1993 (2nd ed., 2006), must remain the standard work.[1] This contribution will chiefly aim to examine how items of equipment were made, and more importantly, to consider how they were used.

INTRODUCTION

Experimental archaeology has a long history, which has included some notable achievements in the field of Roman military equipment. In the late 19th and early 20th c. A.D., French and Prussian officers worked on reconstructing Roman artillery. In 1969, Russell Robinson reconstructed the *lorica segmentata* found at Corbridge, and during the 1970s, assisted the 'Ermine Street Guard', one of the first Roman re-enactment groups, in equipping themselves accurately.[2] Peter Connolly, the technical illustrator of Robinson's *The Armour of Imperial Rome* (London 1975), has since published a series of books that have brought Roman military artefacts to life for another generation of students.[3]

This interest in Roman military equipment has led to a profusion of Roman re-enactment groups specialising in reconstructions of the 1st and 2nd c. A.D. The best of these groups bring to the general public's notice reconstructions of Roman military equipment that have been thoroughly researched. An excellent reproduction of an archaeological find can help the public better understand and imagine the period. It can also shed

---

[1] Bishop and Coulston (1993) and (2nd ed., 2006).
[2] Robinson (1975) 186.
[3] Robinson (1975).

A. Sarantis, N. Christie (edd.) *War and Warfare in Late Antiquity: Current Perspectives*
(Late Antique Archaeology 8.1–8.2 – 2010–11) (Leiden 2013), pp. 523–567

new light on the use of Roman weaponry, thereby placing in context the information gleaned by historians and archaeologists from literary texts and material evidence. In this way, the unhelpful differentiation between academics and enthusiasts loses its validity. Indeed, although the author of this paper is very much an enthusiast, like academics, he makes a living from reconstructing the past and treats his work in a similarly professional manner. The Late Roman period had received little attention from re-enactment groups until 2002, when the author founded *Comitatus* to recreate something of the Late Roman army that had been based in northern Britain in the 4th and early 5th c. A.D.[4]

There have been many definitions of experimental archaeology, most of them based on the different ways in which ancient artefacts can be reconstructed. In some cases, accurately recreated contemporary tools are used to construct ancient weaponry. In others, modern tools are used to reproduce less authentic Roman weapons. Ultimately though, no reconstruction can ever claim to be entirely authentic. The materials used will always differ slightly, and the modern artisan cannot escape the fact that they will approach their task from an inherently different artistic standpoint from their Roman predecessors. Nevertheless, by exploring different ways of reproducing an artefact, an experimental archaeologist can at least establish the limitations in the techniques possibly used by contemporaries in its construction.

The major interest in this process lies not so much in the reconstructed artefact itself, but in how it was used and how it functioned. However, even though the best Roman re-enactment groups may have a good deal of information to offer, as can be seen from their websites, they have contributed relatively little in terms of published research. Such groups raise funds by holding public shows that are part of the heritage industry, and few truly engage in reconstruction archaeology in an academic sense. Indeed, to the knowledge of this author, *Comitatus* is the only re-enactment group to have sponsored an archaeological conference.[5] In the field of reconstruction, Peter Connolly's work on the Romano-Celtic saddle stands out as the best example of what can be achieved.[6]

---

[4] A small group of re-enactors called the *Milites Litoris Saxoni* were active in the 1980's.

[5] The Arbeia Society, including a 3rd c. re-enactment group called *Cohors Quinta Gallorum*, have published much useful reconstruction material in the *Arbeia Journal*.

[6] Connolly (1987).

Sources

Archaeological finds will form the basis of any reconstruction. It is possible to use iconography to support the impression given by physical finds, but the hidden messages and conventions of contemporary artistic genres mean that representational evidence must be treated with great care. Period representations of soldiers must be viewed with 'period' sensibilities that are beyond the scope of this paper.

Written evidence can also be used to support reconstructions of military equipment and their use. The major relevant texts from this period include those written by Vegetius, Procopius and Maurice. Vegetius, writing sometime in the late 4th, or perhaps early 5th c. A.D., included a good deal of valuable information interspersed with his somewhat idealised interpretation of the Early Imperial army. Later, 6th c. writers also provide useful material, for instance, Procopius, who was a staff officer serving with Belisarius in Persia, Africa and Italy from A.D. 527 to around 540. In its provision of clear, practical advice on weaponry, armour and organisation, Maurice's *Strategikon* is an invaluable documentary guide. This late 6th c. A.D. military manual concentrates on the cavalry, but includes a chapter on the infantry that may derive from an earlier work.[7]

Defensive Equipment

Helmets

Mass-produced Dominate helmets consist of two types: the Ridge Helm, which, at its simplest, was composed of two halves joined by a central ridge; and the Spangenhelm, which was composed of several panels riveted into an iron frame. The ridge helms were fitted with neck-guards and cheek-pieces attached to a leather edging, or fabric lining, often without the use of metal hinges. The iron edges of the helm were not even properly finished, but left raw, and bound with leather or rawhide. They were often sheathed in gilded silver foil, and an example from Augst has three slots cut into the central ridge, perhaps to hold a crest box of feathers or hair.[8] Ridge helms are often simply categorised as either 'infantry helms'

---

[7] Dennis (1984) xviii.
[8] Bishop and Coulston (2006) 213.

with open faces and holes for ears, or as cavalry helmets with applied
nasal protection. However, there is no reason why light, simple helmets
could not have been worn by the cavalry, or why heavy, enclosed helmets
could not have been worn by the infantry.[9]

All helmets need some form of padding, which would explain Vegetius'
reference to the *pilleus Pannonicus*.[10] This 'Pannonian cap' can be identified with the hats worn by the soldiers featured on the Arch of Constantine. Shaped liked a pillbox, it is particularly suited to the shape of the
ridge helm. It is also capable of soaking up large amounts of sweat as we
have found using reconstructed versions. Such helmets must have fitted
the individual much like a modern motorcycle crash helmet, without any

Fig. 1   Cavalry ridge helms, showing a large variation in skull shape. Left: The
Deurne helmet, with hinge protectors mounted correctly (they are mounted
upside down in the Leiden Museum). Middle: A ridge helm based on the plain iron
bowl from Burgh Castle, with cheek-pieces and neck guard copied from examples
from Berkasovo. Right: The Berkasovo two-helm, with a two-part bowl.

---

[9] Bishop and Coulston (2006) 210–16.
[10] Veg. *Mil.* 1.20.

undue movement. This would have been particularly important where helmets used by horsemen were concerned. The cheek pieces needed to be padded, and the brow band may have needed individual padding because any heavy pressure on the front of the helmet would have forced it down onto the bridge of the wearer's nose.

Our experience of reconstructing helmets shows that they can fit individuals differently and place different constraints on them. For instance, the enclosed ridge helms provide excellent all round protection, but affect the wearer's hearing. Some reproductions, especially of the Deurne cavalry helmet, seem to reduce visibility and ease of movement. These must have been important considerations for horse archers.

Reconstructing helmets can help place in context archaeological finds. For example, all that remains of the so-called Deurne helmet exhibited in the Leiden Museum is the gilded sheathing that once covered the helmet. Its individual pieces were discovered in a flattened state in 1910. They were passed on to a local goldsmith who assembled and 're-inflated' them into the presumed shape of the helmet. When viewing the original in Leiden Museum, it is noticeable that its hinge protectors have been mounted upside down.

Armour

In the Dominate period, body armour consisted of copper-alloy scales, *lorica squamata*, or mail, *lorica hamata*.[11] No serious attempts have been made to reconstruct the metal or leather muscled cuirasses depicted in contemporary sculpture. These are possibly a mere artistic convention.

Reconstruction work has shown that scale armour can be either flexible or inflexible. Surviving copper alloy scales are generally smaller than iron examples, which seem to have been used principally for horse armour.[12] Robinson gives an excellent breakdown of the size, typology and nature of scale armour.[13] This flexible armour was constructed by wiring all of the scales together, and then sewing them to backing fabric. In the find from Carplow, a horizontal woollen thread was used to strengthen the stitching.[14] The armour was then given leather edging for comfort. The resulting armour must have been quick to construct and relatively light.

---

[11] Bishop and Coulston (2006) 208.
[12] James (2004) 111.
[13] Robinson (1975) 154–59.
[14] Bishop and Coulston (2006) 170–71.

Fig. 2   Top left: Flexible scale; note the lacing arrangement. Right: Inflexible or
rigid scale. Bottom left: Mail with a 6 mm internal diameter.

Reconstructions are capable of expanding to allow for heavy breathing. The same has been found with reconstructions of mail. The flexibility of such armour means that it can be used for protecting limbs and extended below the waist. Finds of loose scales, or rows, are often assumed to come from shirts, but may well have belonged to limb defences.[15] Through experimentation, we have found that this armour provides excellent protection against downward blows, horizontal strikes, and does better than one would expect when assailed with upward stabs thanks to the stitching of horizontal cord and wire.

Inflexible scale armour consisted of larger scales that were wired to each other, on top, at the bottom and on both sides. Our reconstructions have been given a linen backing and leather edging. The relative inflexibility of this design means that the rigid scale shirts that we have reproduced do not extend below the waistline. They are relatively light, but

---

[15] James (2004) 113.

their scales give excellent protection by quickly deflecting the force of a direct blow to neighbouring scales.

Although there are no finds of 4th c. A.D. mail shirts with openings, reconstructions of scale body armour are generally made with an opening on the left-hand side.[16] This is so that the fastenings are protected by the wearer's shield. Reconstructions have found that blows, or the abrasion of belts and sword hilts, often bend the scales. Repeated folding can lead to scales splitting, normally along the holes that have been drilled in them so that they can be fixed together. The constant movement of equipment on horseback quickly ages scale armour, its scales working loose and bending with time. The cavalryman's natural action of leaning forward can result in a fold in the bottom of the cuirass. This all suggests that compared to mail armour, scale armour must have required much greater maintenance in Late Antiquity.

Mail armour is made up of alternating rows of punched and riveted rings; each ring fastened to four others to form a flexible "net". The diameter of rings that have survived from the Late Roman period vary between 3 and 9 mm in size.[17] There are several such finds of Late Roman mail. For instance, a shirt was found at South Shields, dating from the late 3rd or early 4th c. A.D., the rings of which were 7 mm in diameter.[18] We have found that such armour is extremely effective at protecting individuals against slashing cuts. Mail armour requires little maintenance, but is very hard wearing on underclothing, causing deterioration and staining. At the same time, regular wear helps keep the armour rust-free by ensuring that the iron rings constantly abrade against each other.

Armour was normally worn over a padded garment, a *thoracomachus* or *subarmalis*. An anonymous late 4th or early 5th c. A.D. military manual, the *De Rebus Bellicis*, identifies the *thoracomachus* as a thick cloth garment consisting of many layers of felt, with linen or leather *pteruges* attached to protect the wearer's upper arms and legs.[19] It has been suggested that a 'Libyan' hide (probably oiled goatskin) was used on top of the *thoracomachus* to keep it dry.[20] The padding would have helped protect an individual from the effects of blunt trauma (as confirmed by our

---

[16] There are finds of chest-pieces from the 2nd and 3rd c. A.D. These can be used to open and close the neckline. This can also be done by a simple lacing system at the rear of the shirt.

[17] Robinson (1975) 164–73.

[18] Croom (2001) 55–60.

[19] Bishop and Coulston (2006) 208; Dennis (1985) 54.

[20] Sumner (2003) 37–39.

weapon tests), although what form this padding took is difficult to say, iconographic evidence providing only a few hints.[21] The *thoracomachus* and the hide covering it are depicted as T-shaped tunics in illustrations from early medieval copies of the *De Rebus Bellicis*, although later copies show them as quilted. Whether felt or linen, the fibres in the *thoracoma-chus* garment would ideally have run in different directions, making it harder to cut through and, therefore, more protective.

Segmented body armour, consisting of a series of overlapping iron or copper-alloy plates connected by leather straps, may have survived in Spain into the 4th c.[22] Indeed, artistic representations of limb defences survive from the period, in both military and gladiatorial contexts, and 3rd and 4th c. finds also confirm their continued use.[23] Reconstructed segmented body armour is surprisingly flexible and comfortable to wear, allowing one to bend one's arm while drawing a bow. Because the plates overlap from the hand to the shoulder, they ensure that a blade slides off the armour upon an upward strike, rather than landing between the lami-nated plates. The *manica* is tied to the padded *subarmalis* at the shoulder, and in our re-enactments we have lined it with felt to increase comfort and reduce staining to clothing.

The *Strategikon* mentions iron and even wooden greaves.[24] Although none have been found from the 4th c., Vegetius also advocates their use,[25] and the metal greaves illustrated in this paper are based on a 3rd c. exam-ple from Kunzing in Germany.[26] Wooden greaves were probably of 'splint construction', made up of several vertical bars held together by a leather backing. Little leather armour has been found from the period, although two mid-3rd c. cavalry leather thigh-guards, preserved by the dry condi-tions at Dura, are exceptions (fig. 3). Possibly from a non-Roman tradition, they were worn like riding chaps, although some argue that they were more likely to have been crinets for a horse.[27] They consist of overlap-ping scales attached to each other with leather lacing. Each thigh-guard is laced in a distinct fashion. Reconstruction has shown that they defended a rider against horizontal blows and strikes from above, presumably from

[21] Sumner (2003) 37–39.
[22] Aurrecoechea *et al.* (2008) 255–64.
[23] Bishop (2001) 169–70; James (2004) 114–15.
[24] *Strategikon* 12.2.4.
[25] Veg. *Mil.* 1.20.
[26] Robinson (1975) 189.
[27] Stephenson and Dixon (2003) 48.

enemy cavalrymen, and arrows. Although the armour was in fact a form of lamellar, it was constructed in the same way as scale armour. Reconstructions have shown that the lacing method and materials used result in flexible defensive armour, which fits over the knee and protects an individual from the waist to the shin. Heated wax or oil would probably have been used to treat each scale, in order to toughen and shrink it at the same time.[28] Such armour is light to wear and easy to repair. All types of armour certainly will have given soldiers greater confidence, or perhaps a false sense of security.[29]

Fig. 3   Dura lamellar thigh-guards showing one version of the lacing system. A copper alloy *manica*, mace and Germanic type 1 pattern-welded *spatha*.

---

[28] James (2004) 122–25.

[29] See Keegan (1976) 172–77 on the psychological impact of war. Polyb. 6.23: 'The effect of these (a set of long feathers) being placed on the helmet, combined with the rest of the armour, is to give the man the appearance of being twice his real height and to give him a noble aspect'. Davis-Hanson (1991) 74–78 argues that the evolution of hoplite armour was down to technological rather than tactical factors, principally the socio-economic status of the hoplites who were now able to dress the part.

Shields

Both cavalry and infantry troops would have had to train for a variety of
missions, using small or large shields as appropriate. There are few finds
of Dominate shield fittings. Iconographic evidence seems to suggest the
use of oval infantry shields of similar proportions to those of the finds
from Dura-Europos, and circular shields possibly adopted from Germanic
peoples.[30] The oval Dura shields measure 107–118 cm in length and 92–
97 cm in width. They were made from planks glued together from edge
to edge, with a thickness of 3–9 mm. The faces of these shields could be
covered in linen, leather, rawhide, parchment, or fibrous glue covered in
gesso, and edged in rawhide, which was sewn around the rim.[31] Reconstruction work makes clear that covering the face and edge of a shield
contributes to its structural stability. The painted surfaces of round Illerup
shields were covered in transparent, thin, oiled rawhide, to protect them.[32]
Fragments of preserved painted leather facings from 4th to early 6th c.
shields are on display in Trier. Found in Egypt, these seem to derive from
circular dished shields.[33] Dished shields give greater integral strength,
deflect blows, and improve the visibility of the bearer. This seems to have
been an important reason for the move away from plywood to 'planked'
shields in Late Antiquity.

It seems that laminated plywood shields could break down in wet conditions, necessitating the use of lanolin, waxed, leather shield covers.[34] It
is possible that the planked construction of Dominate shields made such
covers redundant. An iron boss, or *umbo*, protected the hand holding the
horizontal shield handle. Such shields must have been perfect for both
close order and loose order combat. The external face of the shield would
have been painted with an identifiable unit design. Fellow combatants from
the same formation could then identify one another by the personalised
colours and designs on the internal side of their shields. We have found
that such paintwork also stops wooden shields from soaking up water and
losing structural stability. Shields at Dura were mainly primed with gesso,
or a thin layer of parchment, before they were painted. The paint itself
used a tempera medium, while the yolk was mixed with strained whisked

---

[30] Bishop and Coulston (2006) 216–77.
[31] James (2004) 159–87.
[32] Jørgensen *et al.* (2003) 322.
[33] Goethert (1996) 115–26.
[34] Bishop and Coulston (2006) 94.

egg white, which had been allowed to stand.[35] A painted shield would have been visible miles away. Therefore, leather shield covers were used to both protect and camouflage the shield. Finds from Dura had a single rivet, placed in the top right-hand quarter.[36] This could have secured a leather carrying-strap, with the other end tied around the handle. Carrying straps could also be sewn on to the shield cover.

Horse-riding while carrying a large and heavy shield is difficult. Carvings, such as those on the Arch of Galerius, suggest that soldiers could carry the shield on their left arm using a series of straps to attach it. A number of modern interpreters who have followed this method have also padded out the interior face of the shield so that it rests more comfortably on the left leg. However, there are no archaeological finds to suggest that this practice was followed in Late Antiquity. Practice shows that a large oval shield can be carried by the horizontal handle. This ensures that the shield boss protects the left hand of the shield-bearer. It also means that the rider can turn the horse to the left using the reins in his left hand, or press the shield onto the horse's neck to turn to the right. The shield can be rested on the cavalryman's left foot when not actively in use. However, Maurice describes the ideal cavalryman as carrying the *kontos*,[37] the 4 m long lance, and a bow, both of which would have required the use of two hands.[38] Maurice believed that you could not draw a bow effectively while carrying a shield.[39] However, I have experimented with a small shield, 450 mm in diameter, strapped to the left forearm, and can confirm that it is still possible to hold the *kontos* in both hands and fire a bow, even with the western release method.[40] The shield boss was retained in this experiment so that I could still carry the shield in a more conventional manner. Literary evidence adds weight to my conclusion. For instance, Procopius mentions the use of small shields strapped to the upper left arm,[41] and Agathias mentions cavalrymen serving under Narses at Casilinum armed with shields, spears, and bows and arrows.[42]

---

[35] James (2004) 164.
[36] James (2004) 176–78.
[37] Bishop and Coulston (2006) 130.
[38] *Strategikon* 1.1.
[39] *Strategikon* 2.8.
[40] Coulston (1985) 281 states that this is impossible.
[41] Procop. *Pers.* 1.1.12.
[42] Agath. 2.8.8.

Missile Weapons

Self-Bows and Composite Bows

Vegetius says that one-quarter to one-third of new infantry recruits, *tirones*, should be trained as archers or s*agittarii*.[43] He mentions the use of wooden bows for training, and suggests that these were simple, self-bows that had been formed from a single piece of wood.[44] It is not possible to be sure what form these Roman self-bows took.[45] Practice tells us that up to a limited distance, and pulled back to a limited draw length, a short bow will shoot faster and further than what the Tudors called a long bow, since its limbs weigh less. However, a short bow pulled back to the same draw length as a long bow will be placed under more strain, and past a certain point, will break. At full draw, the angle between the string and the stave on the short bow will be greater than on a long bow, and will result in a slower stave. This is because the draw weight will stack up towards the end of the draw so that energy is wasted. The only ways to combat this problem are to make the limbs of the bow longer, or to re-curve its tips, like those of the composite bow.

All of this suggests that the Romans trained with long bows, similar to those found in Germanic lake deposits that were made from yew or fir.[46] Different woods and materials are capable of storing varying amounts of energy, yew being the ideal wood for a bow.[47] Some of the Germanic bows were self-nocked, with a second set of nocks cut into the stave. This has been interpreted as a way of shortening the string and increasing the power of the bow.[48] In contrast, it is more likely that the outer set of nocks operated as a stringer. Holding the bow horizontally, the archer attaches a long length of string to the two outer nocks. By standing on the stringer and raising the bow to his chest, a second man can slip the bow string over the inner nocks.

The Romans used the composite bow in combat. This was constructed around a wooden core, upon which animal sinew and horn was carefully glued to produce a re-curved shape. 'Ears' were then attached to the ends

---

[43] Veg. *Mil.* 1.15.
[44] Veg. *Mil.* 1.15.
[45] Coulston (1985) 287.
[46] Hardy (1976) 21.
[47] Hardy (1976) 223–24.
[48] Hardy (1976) 22.

of the bow. These were protected by bone or antler, and acted as levers for the flexible parts of the bow's limbs.[49] Laths on the grip stiffened the bow handle to prevent it from flexing and bucking after the string had returned to rest after release. Archaeologists have discovered these bone ear laths at several sites in Britain, Europe and Asia.[50] To stop the glue from breaking down in damp conditions, the limbs of the bow were waterproofed using bark, and coated in lacquer. Re-curved bows were produced for the West Roman Empire in *fabricae* near Pavia.[51] In the East, where such bows were more common, the army could probably have bought them on the open market. Re-curved bows are shorter than self-bows, allowing them to be fired from a kneeling position or from horseback. Our research has demonstrated how the materials used made the bow more efficient by transferring more power from the bow to the arrow.

The velocity of the arrow depends on the efficiency and power, or draw weight, of the bow (the draw distance from stave to ear normally being around 700 mm), the weight of the arrow, and the drag of the arrow through the air. Penetration depends upon the velocity, weight, and design of the arrowhead, and the composition of the target. Unlike medieval English archers, who were taught from an early age, most Roman recruits would come to the discipline relatively late in their lives, which means that they would perhaps have found it difficult to use bows with a high draw weight.[52] While some medieval self-bows seem capable of achieving up to 180 lb of pull, finds from votive lake deposits suggest that 4th c. bows would have been less powerful (based on the diameter of the stave and the type of wood used).[53] A pull of 80–100 lb would seem reasonable for a Roman 'D' section self-bow. After mastering the self-bow, the archer could move on to a recurve bow of similar power, but greater efficiency. By using horn and animal tendon, the recurve bow has a better 'cast' (is more flexible and returns to its original position more 'snappily').

The reconstruction of Roman bows cannot be an exact science. Little is known about the actual style of construction used for 4th c. Roman

---

[49] Bishop and Coulston (2006) 164.
[50] Coulston (1985) 238–45.
[51] Feugère (2002) 186.
[52] Draw weight is the peak amount of weight an archer will pull while drawing the bow, given in pounds. English archers were trained from the age of 8 (Hardy (1976)) whereas Roman soldiers were only recruited to the army between the ages of 20–25 and 19–35 from the 4th c. (Jones (1964) 614 and 616).
[53] Hardy (1976) 22.

recurved bows.[54] The length of some of the bone and antler ear laths suggests that the bows were not as heavily recurved as later Mongol examples. A Parthian bow has been reconstructed from its partial remains, which were found at Baghouz.[55] Known as the Yrzi bow after the area of the cemetery in which it was found, the reconstruction had a draw weight of approximately 60–70lb.[56] However, the Middle-Eastern tradition of bow-making would have differed from that of the Huns of Central Asia, and possibly from whatever methods were used in the imperial *fabricae.* The Central Asian influence can be seen in the 'Qum-Darya Bow', which was found in a mass grave associated with a Chinese frontier post. Dating from the 1st c. B.C. to the 3rd c. A.D., similar ear and grip laths spread west along with Hunnic political and military influence. They have been found in western Europe at sites such as Blucina and Wien-Simmering. Such bows used up to 7 ear and grip laths, compared to the mere 4 of the Yrzi bow.[57]

Modern recurve bows cannot truly mirror those of the past given the difficulty in finding materials suitable for their reconstruction. The same can be said of the powerful modern yew self-bows, which do not exactly correlate archaeological finds. The author's best 80 lb bow is made from slow-grown North American yew, *Taxus brevifolia.* Grown in Oregon, it has a close grain without knots, and is used to make an approximation of a Roman self-bow. European yew, *Taxus baccata,* would have given a better cast and been more efficient, but is rarely available today for use in high poundage bow-making.[58]

Two types of release could have been used by Late Roman bows. The eastern, or Mongolian, release may have been used in the East from the 3rd c., with the arrow shot to the right of the bow and the string drawn back by the thumb. This eastern thumb draw uses a thumb ring, whereas a western, or Mediterranean, two or three-fingered release seems to have been the general method used in Roman Europe. In this technique, arrows were shot to the left of the bow, with the nock of the arrow held between the index and middle fingers.[59]

---

[54] Coulston (1985) 248–59.
[55] Coulston (1985) 239.
[56] Coulston (1985) 240. James (2004) 191 gives a measurement of 80 lb.
[57] Coulston (1985) 242–43.
[58] Soar (2010) 43–44.
[59] Bishop and Coulston (2006) 168.

Arrows were either 'broad heads', or trilobate in design, so that they would cut as much muscle and blood vessel as possible, or narrow bodkins designed to penetrate shields and armour. Experimental archaeology shows that arrowheads can be socketed or tanged. A shaft with a tanged head will be susceptible to breakage in certain conditions. This is because the spike on the back of the arrowhead is burnt into the shaft, which is, hence, more likely to split upon impact. The weight of an arrowhead will affect the distance an arrow can be shot. Light, 40 g flight arrows can travel over 200 m from the author's 80 lb bow. This concurs approximately with Vegetius' instruction that targets should be set up at a distance of 600 Roman feet (177 m).[60] However, it is probable that an archer would carry a selection of light, medium and heavy arrows to allow them to respond to a variety of threats. For instance, the author has found that heavy 70 g arrows have their greatest velocity during the first 50 m of flight, and can be used at relatively close ranges. In contrast, an archer could pepper a target with light arrows from as far away as 200 m.

The arrows retrieved from Dura and those from Micia in Roman Dacia were made of reed and were fitted with wooden foreshafts to accommodate their arrowheads.[61] At the same time, arrows from bog depositions provide us with examples of western-style arrow construction from solid pine or ash.[62] Shafts had parallel sides, but were tapered slightly at the fletchings and widened again at the nock to prevent breakage.[63] This shaft-shape would have also ensured that arrows left the shaft cleanly. James suggested that the wooden foreshafts at Dura were not designed for holding a metal arrowhead, and that the reed arrows were primarily intended for hunting or target shooting.[64] My experimentation with reed arrows suggests that James is right and that they were too weak to be shot from high poundage bows and better suited to weaker hunting bows.

Fletchings were not 'corkscrewed' about the shaft to impart a spin, and would only have increased the drag on an arrow (fig. 4). Instead, the natural curvature and twist of the feather imparted a spin and gave increased accuracy. Surviving fletchings from Dura show that both western and eastern styles were used in the East. While arrows found in the West feature a

---

[60] Veg. *Mil.* 2.23.
[61] Bishop and Coulston (2006) 168.
[62] Jørgensen *et al.* (2003) 270.
[63] Jørgensen *et al.* (2003) 269. For the un-initiated, a nock is positioned at the ends of the bow and is where the bow string is inserted. A fletching is a feather on the end of an arrow.
[64] James (2004) 196.

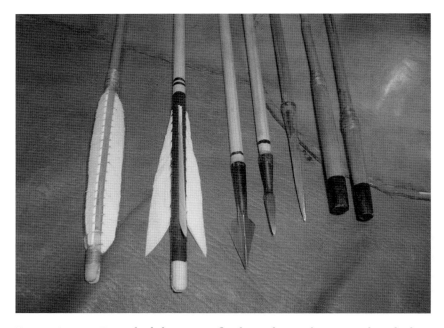

Fig. 4   Arrows. From the left: western fletchings fastened using pitch and whip-cording, tanged and socketed bodkin heads, two cane arrows with wooden fore-shafts, two iron trilobate heads, eastern style cane shafts and fletchings.

recognisable cock-feather at 90 degrees to the nock, in the East, one of the three feathers is on the axis of the nock. Western style fletchings would also stop around 25 mm from the nock to allow the archer's fingers to grip the arrow. Conversely, eastern style fletchings could be taken to the end of the nock.[65]

Through our experimentation, we have found that bow cases are an essential piece of equipment, although they weigh a lot. In earlier periods, archers seem to have carried unstrung bows. However, when on campaign, it would have made sense to carry a strung bow. Even though there is no Dominate evidence for the shape of bow cases, there are many ethnographic parallels from contemporary Sassanid and Central Asian sources from which we can build up a picture. In particular, iconography on the Orlat plaques shows a strung bow case with two tubes holding arrows

[65] James (2004) 197–98.

attached to the front.[66] For mounted displays the author has reconstructed a case that can carry a strung bow as mentioned in Maurice.[67]

The Arcuballista or Crossbow

Roman crossbows are mentioned by Vegetius[68] and possibly by Arrian, who in his section on machines, refers to their use by mounted archers.[69] My reconstruction is based on two 3rd c. carvings of hunting equipment from the Haute-Loire region of France, which seem to show crossbows in detail. In these carvings, a recurve bow of probably composite construction is mounted on a tiller, with a revolving circular bone nut forming part of the trigger mechanism.[70] A wooden handle is placed at the end of the tiller. The trigger itself is a simple 'Z-shaped' lever, which was typical of early crossbows.[71] Baatz suggested that the archer would have placed his feet on the bow, on either side of the tiller, using his hands to pull the string upwards, as with a medieval crossbow.[72] However, through experimentation, we have found that this technique could damage the bow itself, especially if the operator is wearing hobnailed boots, which we must assume that Late Roman soldiers often were.[73] Instead, we have found that when on foot, it is more natural to place one's right hand on top of the handle, forcing the bow into the ground vertically, while pulling the string back and securing it to the nut with the left hand. On horseback, the handle can be braced on the front of the saddle, while the string is pulled downwards with both hands. The handle then provides an almost pistol-like grip, allowing the crossbow to be fired one-handed. The trigger releases the circular bone nut which rolls forward to release the string. The reconstruction illustrated here has a draw weight of 45 lbs (fig. 5). However, a more powerful bow could have been used, and the lashing to

---

[66] Mode (2003). The Orlat plaques were discovered in the 1980s in Uzbekistan. They may have been used by their Central Asian creators as belt buckles. They date from the 1st c. A.D.

[67] *Strategikon* 1.1 and 1.2.

[68] Veg. *Mil.* 4.22.

[69] Arr. *Tact.* 43.2 reproduced in Hyland (1993) 76, 81 and 153.

[70] MacGregor (1985) 158–61.

[71] Paterson (1990) 59.

[72] Baatz (1991) 283–90.

[73] See D'Amato (2005) 20–21 on boots. Particular impressive are the two fragments of a leather boot discovered in the 5th c. destruction layer at Aquileia in Italy.

Fig. 5   Stringing the *arcuballista*. The right hand presses down on the handle,
while the left draws back the string. The bone nut is visible. Note the infantryman's so-called Coptic tunic and broad military belt with propeller stiffeners.

the tiller strengthened. The maximum draw weight is limited by the hand
draw to about 90 lbs.

The French carvings referred to earlier show a quiver that was long
enough to hold a normal size arrow. However, scale models of the crossbow depicted in the carvings show that its draw distance was relatively
small, only 300 mm, compared to the 700 mm of a normal bow. This
has led me to use light 25 g bolts in my reconstructions. The low kinetic
energy of these missiles allows for the use of bone rather than iron heads.
A bolt with a bone head can be as light as 10 g. The weapon can shoot
such a bolt as far as 90 m with some degree of accuracy, and within 40 m
the accuracy can be startling. Even when shot at such a low velocity,
these bolts could certainly have been used in a military context. During
sieges and sniper operations, the operator would only have had to expose
the upper portion of their head, and could easily master the weapon in
such a position. However, the crossbow must have been most effective as
a hunting weapon. The *arcuballista* takes twice as long to load as a normal
bow when on foot, but considerably longer on horseback, which surely
hampered its use on the battlefield. On the positive side, it would allow

the Roman soldier to out-range all barbarian weapons, except for bows. Although a speculative point, it seems plausible that soldiers armed with crossbows could have been cavalry as well as infantry.[74]

Sling and Staff Sling

According to Vegetius, all soldiers were given basic training with the sling.[75] While slings can be constructed from hair or plant fibres, leather, as used in the find from Vindolanda, is an easier option.[76] This sling consists of a 100 mm long pouch, with cords of around 600 mm in armpit to finger length. Experimentation shows that rocks and pebbles can be used as ammunition over shorter distances, while a longer range and greater consistency can be achieved with a specially cast lead shot, the *glandes*, which weighs 50–70 g. The lead bullets require smaller sling pouches, which in turn create less drag. A bullet can be roughly cast by simply using a thumb in-print in the ground. Finds of Late Roman sling-missiles are rare, but lead sling-bullets were found in a 4th c. context at Vindolanda.[77] It takes practice to use the weapon accurately, either by swinging the sling overhead, over-arm or under-arm. It is possible to be accurate at 40 m and to get the bullet to travel around 80 m in any given direction.

The staff sling, or *fundibulum*, would have been a much easier weapon to use, mainly because it was merely a sling mounted on a pole.[78] Our reconstructions suggest that a new recruit would quickly understand how to cast a missile along any given axis. However, judging the distance of a shot would have taken them a much longer time to master. In effect, this weapon acted as a portable artillery piece, with the power to shoot over the heads of several ranks of infantry. Vegetius suggests that the slinger should practise at a range of 600 Roman feet (177 m).[79] This is feasible with a lead bullet, although hitting a single man at this distance would have been difficult. Our experimentation has demonstrated that the sling can match the range of the bow, and deliver a missile that cannot be followed in flight by the eye, or dodged. It is also less affected by crosswinds

---

[74] Amm. Marc. 16.2.5 mentions *balistarii* and *cataphractarii* accompanying the Caesar Julian in wooded terrain on his Gallic campaign. It may be assumed that the *balistarii* were also mounted.

[75] Veg. *Mil.* 1.16.

[76] Bishop and Coulston (2006) 88.

[77] Greep (1987) 191.

[78] Veg. *Mil.* 3.14.

[79] Veg. *Mil.* 2.23.

than an arrow. The trajectory of the bullet can be altered by varying the length of the cords, and by 'forcing' the slinging motion. A forced cast will flatten the trajectory and the shot may in fact 'bounce' along the ground, hitting more than one target. An easy casting motion gives the bullet a high trajectory and greater distance.

Plumbata or Mattiobarbuli

These are lead-weighted throwing darts, with tanged or socketed iron heads averaging between 100 and 200 mm in length, and weighing around 40–180 g (see fig. 6). No organic parts of the weapon have survived, but great numbers have been reconstructed and tested, of various lengths.[80] I have tried firing darts of up to 1 m long, throwing them over-arm like javelins, both with and without thonging around the end of the dart (which provides an extra mechanical advantage). The best range can be obtained by comparatively short weapons of around 450 mm in length, and between 170 and 200 g in weight, which have to be gripped at the rear, behind the flight. There has been some debate as to whether these weapons were thrown under-arm or over-arm. In practice, both ways could have been effective. Thrown under-arm, they can clear the shields of opponents and land on their heads at a range of 80–90 m. Experiments have shown that as the target gets closer, it is best to throw the darts over-arm, with a straight arm, great power, and a flat trajectory. The speed at which the dart can be thrown from close range added to its weight makes its effectiveness on the battlefield a terrifying prospect.

Vegetius states that up to 5 of these darts could be kept attached to the inside of the shield.[81] This arrangement is generally reconstructed as a series of straps nailed to the shield, which hold the darts flat against its upper right inner face. However, this arrangement leaves the darts open to damage from blows coming through the shield board. Perhaps more importantly, the weight of the darts pulls the shield downwards and to the right, making it impractical for its bearer. Maurice mentions the use of leather buckets to carry darts,[82] and a bucket can be simply tied onto the shield grip without recourse to nails or straps. The weight of the bucket is born along the centreline of the shield, which means that it does not

---

[80] Musty and Barker (1974) 275–77; Eagle (1989) 247–53.
[81] Veg. *Mil.* 1.17.
[82] *Strategikon* 12.B.4.

interfere with the shield's balance. The shield protects the darts and the bucket can be easily discarded.

The range of such darts can be increased to over 100 m by projecting them from a staff sling, using a simple arrangement of cord. These weapons out-range javelins, and would have given heavily-armed foot soldiers the ability to out-range most light skirmishers, while still standing in close formation. Excepting the inconclusive finds from the fort at Burgh Castle,[83] garrisoned according to the *Notitia Dignitatum* by the *Equites Stablesiani Gariannoneses*, there is no evidence suggesting that horsemen used such darts in the late 4th c. It should be stated, however, that large numbers can be carried in a bucket tied to the saddle, and thrown over-arm with great force at around 20–30 m.

Javelins: Spicula and Veruta

Much confusion lies in the terminology used to refer to these hand-thrown weapons. I have followed Vegetius in considering the *spiculum* to have been developed from the old legionary *pilum*. According to Vegetius, these Late Roman javelins consisted of a long metal component, 9 Roman inches long (200 mm), attached to a shaft of 5.5 Roman feet (1,628 mm) in length.[84] When reconstructing such a weapon, it is inevitable that the size of the iron head will vary. My reconstruction of the South Shields find weighs 665 g.[85] A thin shank lies underneath its barbed head. The weapon can pierce shields, armour and flesh thanks to its weight and the narrow cross section of its head. Once the head cuts through a shield, the thin shank slides through the wood and penetrates right up to the wooden shaft. The shaft often bends upon contact with a hard surface, such as the ground. Legionaries were able to carry up to two of these weapons.

The *verutum*, or light javelin, was an inexpensive weapon designed to saturate the target area. It was a very simple weapon, made from a single triangle of iron that was formed around an anvil and socketed onto a wooden shaft (see fig. 6). It is probable that like the *speculum*, the *verutum* was not endowed with a hardened cutting edge. This is presumably because a wrought iron cutting-edge can be as sharp as that of hardened steel, but will not hold its edge as well. Since these weapons were disposable, they

---

[83] Johnson (1983).
[84] Veg. *Mil.* 2.15.
[85] Allason-Jones and Miket (1984) 297–99.

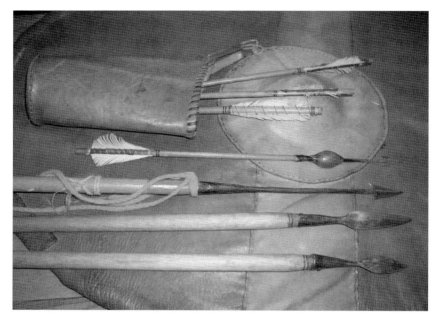

Fig. 6   From the top: a leather case or bucket of *plumbatae*, a *plumbata* based on
a Wroxeter find, a reconstructed *spiculum* from South Shields, and two *veruta*.

only had to hold their edge for a short time.[86] It is very easy to straighten
and even re-shape wrought iron javelin heads when they get damaged.
A skilled artisan can make a single head in less than 6 minutes from an
iron billet. In contrast, it takes the author three times as long. When bent,
the head can be straightened and re-sharpened in under a minute. A file
and a sharpening stone would have been important implements for an
infantryman bearing these weapons. Vegetius describes these weapons as
having an iron head of 5 Roman inches (114 mm) long, with a shaft of 3.5
Roman inches (1,030 mm).[87] Examples vary in weight from 325 to 350 g.
Finds of such weapons show that the heads also tended to vary in length.
The weight of these heads would have made even the cheap *verutum* a
powerful weapon at short range.

Both types of javelin have an average range of 20 m when thrown by
someone wearing armour and carrying a shield. However, a cavalryman
must try to use the speed and weight of their horse to magnify the range and

[86] Sim and Ridge (2002) 88–89.
[87] Veg. *Mil.* 2.15.

power of these weapons. Reconstruction work shows that it is possible to ride with a large quiver containing up to 8 javelins behind the rider's right leg. The quiver is pulled forward in front of the leg for ease of access when throwing. The javelins are kept pointing downwards in the quiver, with their sharp points resting against a disc of wood, so that the rider can speedily grab each shaft in turn without having to reverse the weapon. A simple length of linen or leather, tied around the correct point of balance of each javelin, makes the accurate throwing of the weapon much faster. Easy to produce and use, it is reasonable to assume that such javelins will have constituted the basic missile weapon in Late Antiquity.

HAND-HELD COMBAT WEAPONS AND THEIR EFFECTIVENESS

The effectiveness of hand-held combat weapons is harder to evaluate than that of projectiles, even though their shape and usage are comparatively less ambiguous. From the 3rd c., legionaries carried a spear and a sword. What little evidence exists for the length of Roman spears suggests that it remained remarkably constant through time, at somewhere between 2.4 and 2.7 m. The blade of a spear was designed to penetrate and cut, while the butt of the shaft was capped with a ferule. Re-enactment work makes clear that this allowed the soldier to stand his weapon in the earth, as well as deliver a killing blow to an opponent on the ground. Evidence suggests that the shafts were predominantly made of ash, a wood well-suited to withstanding shock.[88] The author's reconstruction is 2.4 m long with a weight of 1.5 kg. The weapon can be thrown up to 8 m, and its weight ensures great penetration.

The sword, or *gladius*, is perceived as the primary weapon of the Roman soldier. Vegetius describes in some detail the way in which the ancients trained by using wicker shields and wooden foils against wooden posts.[89] The *gladius* is now associated with the short stabbing weapon used by legionaries in earlier periods for close order fighting. The longer sword, known as the *spatha*, was originally a cavalry weapon which was used by riders to strike prone figures on the ground. However, from the 2nd c., these longer weapons became more widely used. It is possible that the

---

[88] Jørgensen *et al.* (2003) 277.
[89] Veg. *Mil.* 1.11.

move towards pattern-welded swords at the same time was more conducive to the manufacture of longer swords.

The weight and balance of the sword will have dictated its function.
Swords tend to fall into two categories based on the proportions of their
blades. With some exceptions to the general rule, long, narrow, and
slightly tapering blades are named after finds from Straubing and Nydam.
These swords are around 650–800 mm long, and 44 mm at their widest section. The shorter and wider Lauriacum, or Hromowka form has a
length of 557–655 mm, and a width of 62–75 mm, with parallel edges and
a triangular point.[90] My long *spatha* has a blade which is 720 mm long, 44
mm wide, tapering to 32 mm, and 810 g in weight. Bishop and Coulston
have proposed that the short, heavy blades were cavalry weapons, while
the longer, thinner blades would have been used by the infantry.[91] From
our experimentation work, the opposite interpretation seems more plausible. The longer and thinner blades make good cavalry weapons, giving
good reach, and when using the speed of the horse, producing powerful
cutting motions. The shorter, broader blades seem better suited to close
infantry combat. It is imperative that a wielder of these swords protects
their hardened edges, using them only to cut and not to parry blows. The
shield needs to be used for the latter purpose. This is because blows par-
ried with a sword can seriously damage its cutting edge.

There are many finds of axes from military contexts in Britain. Even
though many of them will have been used primarily for woodworking,
they also made for efficient, if unwieldy, weapons. In contrast with a
sword, the whole weight of an axe is transferred to a relatively small cutting edge. Consequently, while a sword will cut through flesh and bone,
an axe will cut through flesh and then chip and shatter bone. Axes could
also have been used to hook an enemy's shield or leg, and as a projectile.
A Dominate tombstone from Gamzigrad shows a horseman with what
could be interpreted as an axe hammer.[92] The axe hammer is generally
considered an eastern weapon, in use from the 4th c. My reconstruction
has a head that weighs 430 g. It consists of, on one side an axe blade for
cutting, and on the other, a hammerhead for crushing. The hammerhead
is especially effective when employed against armour and helmets, when
its weight is brought to bear on a relatively small surface area. During

---

[90] Bishop and Coulston (2006) 154–56, after Ulbert (1974) 197–216.
[91] Bishop and Coulston (2006) 268.
[92] Bishop and Coulston (2006) 209.

reconstruction work, riders have proved that the unhardened axe blade can cut through 2 mm of iron shield boss, while the hammer can easily penetrate 12 mm of modern plywood. However, as with all such tests, the hardness of the axe's cutting edge and the nature of its defence will not exactly mirror those of the original Roman weapon. The weapon can be attached to the front of the saddle, but care needs to be taken to ensure that its cutting edge does not injure the rider or the horse.

Possibly adopted by the Romans from the barbarians, the *francisca* was a single-blade axe, designed to be thrown at close quarters.[93] Two axe heads recovered from Burgh Castle show all the characteristics of early *franciscae*.[94] These axe heads are generally pierced at an angle in order to receive the shaft of the handle. Experimental archaeology shows that *franciscae* can be used at up to 60 m, but are accurate at 10 m or less. Writers have tried to calculate the precise distances at which the axe could kill an opponent when the axe head is uppermost in its rotation as it travels through the air.[95] However, this depends on how fast the axe is rotating and the speed it is travelling at. Whichever part of the axe struck the enemy, it will have hurt them. When used at close range, the velocity and 475 g weight of this weapon would have given infantrymen something that matched the weapons thrown with greater velocity by the cavalry, such as spears. When used over distance, an axe could potentially be thrown further than a javelin, as shown by reconstruction work.

Another weapon not usually thought of as Roman is the mace. In his *Ars Tactica*, Arrian refers to small axes with spikes, by which he presumably denotes maces.[96] Eastern examples have been found, including a copper alloy version from Dura.[97] The advantage of maces is that because they lack a cutting edge, they can easily be attached to the saddle. They were designed to crush rather than cut, and to be used against armour and helmets. They can also be used as projectiles.

Little attempt has been made to quantify the effectiveness of ancient and medieval weapon systems. What little has been achieved in this field can be traced back to W. T. Thomson's *An Approximate Theory of Armour Penetration* from 1955. However, the conclusions it reaches are at best highly questionable. P. H. Blyth attempted the same task for the

---

[93] Dahlmos (1977) 141–65.
[94] Johnson (1983) 303–12.
[95] Dahlmos (1977) 141–65; Thompson (2004) 54.
[96] Arr. *Tact.* 4.9, reproduced in Hyland (1993) 80.
[97] James (2004) 190.

Greco-Persian wars. Using a 'ballistic pendulum', and taking into account a certain amount of give in the target, he produced more plausible estimates.[98]

While some weapons may seem more impressive in their destructive capabilities than others, a whole host of variables must be taken into account when assessing their effectiveness. Projectiles with a narrow cross section, which are designed to penetrate flesh and armour, will be more efficient than those with broad cutting heads. For example, armour-piercing bodkin arrowheads can penetrate deeper than those with broad hunting heads, which are designed to cut muscle and blood vessel. The performance of arrows is further complicated by their weight, size and drag through the air. Heavier arrows with large heads produce high drag and are, therefore, more effective at close range. The performance of armour is equally difficult to quantify. The quality of metal armour varies, while the effect of soft or low-density material worn under metal armour can rob a weapon of its momentum, and reduce its impact to varying degrees. Further, as Vegetius realised, the impact of projectiles is analogous to the height from which they are fired.[99]

Experience has made me sceptical of such efforts at objectivity. Modern reconstructions of weapons and armour very rarely employ the same techniques and materials as will have been used to make original versions. Differences in the hardness and sharpness of reconstructed weapons are also prominent concerns. The varying strengths and abilities of the individuals carrying out the experiments should also be borne in mind. The same blade can be used by two individuals with greatly differing results, depending on their strength, the angle at which they cut, and the strength of the target. Rather than just hitting the target with the blade, which often causes it to bounce off, the sword edge needs to be drawn deeper into the wound with a deliberate cutting motion.

Some general points can be confirmed from experimentation, however. Targets will back away at the moment of impact, reducing the momentum of the weapon. Armour that may adequately protect the body will not cover target areas such as eye sockets, or veins and arteries in the neck. It is safe to assert that missile weapons have the greatest momentum at close range, up to 50 m in the case of arrows. Looking at the evidence for offensive weaponry and defensive armour in Late Antiquity, it is possible

[98] Blyth (1977).
[99] Veg. *Mil.* 4.28.

to deduce that, as in most periods, technological developments in both equipment/weaponry types were related, as innovations in armour, helmets and shields responded to new types of projectile and hand-wielded weaponry.

A Few Comments on Artillery

Since the 19th c., much effort has been devoted to reconstructing Roman artillery, an especially controversial subject, which has provoked numerous disagreements regarding what representational, material and textual evidence can tell us about artillery pieces. The reproductions of Roman artillery can be used to illustrate some of the general limitations of reconstruction work. The Late Romans used just two types of artillery. The onager was a large stone-thrower, primarily deployed in sieges, where it was used to strip battlements and defenders from walls. Using small stones, it was perhaps principally a close range, anti-personnel weapon. The iron-framed *ballista* was the everyday artillery piece of the army and navy, developed from less powerful wooden-framed weapons near the end of the 1st c. A.D.

Plans for such machines were discovered in the mid-19th c., and have been related to archaeological finds across Europe and the Middle East. Many working examples have been reproduced, and the *Comitatus* re-enactment group uses a portable iron-framed *ballista*, constructed by Len Morgan, and based on work by Alan Wilkins (fig. 7).[100] Coiled rope springs hold an estimated 750 lb of pull in the metal arms of the weapon. A two-handled winch system ratchets the string back, the side ratchets providing a safe system in case the winch-rope breaks. A two-man crew can achieve three shots a minute using small 85 g bolts.

The controversy mentioned above centres on certain key parts of the original design. Some reconstructions favour the traditional out-swinging arms, while others adopt a more radical approach, using in-swinging arms.[101] An additional problem is that some period materials are very difficult to reproduce. For instance, contemporary writers, including Vegetius, mention the use of sinew rope.[102] However, modern reconstructions

---

[100] Wilkins (1995) 5–59 and (2000) 77–101.
[101] Campbell (2003) 42–44.
[102] Veg. *Mil.* 4.22.

Fig. 7   An iron-framed *ballista*.

use pre-stretched modern rope, or sometimes horsehair rope, which is mentioned in contemporary accounts as a last resort. They both have a similar performance, but lack the elasticity of sinew. Wilkins suggested that Roman bolt shooters could achieve a distance of 500 m, and shoot with a flat trajectory over 250 m.[103] This would allow them to out-range archers. Modern machines are unlikely to shoot beyond 200 m, and are thus easily within range of a war bow.

However, modern reconstructions do allow us to understand many technical aspects of the machine, such as the springs, washers and trigger mechanisms. The bolts can be reconstructed based on the finds from Dura, which have iron heads with wooden shafts and flights (see fig. 8).[104] James raised the possibility that at Dura, different sizes of bolt could have been deliberately used, the finds naturally falling into bands of 290–300 mm, 330 mm, 350–65 mm, 385–400 mm and 430–35 mm long, from the tip of the tail to the beginning of the iron socket.[105] This seems very likely because

---

[103] Wilkins (2003) 52.
[104] James (2004) 209–30.
[105] James (2004) 213.

different sized bolts could have been manufactured for specific machines. Or it could mean that by using a single *ballista* at constant power, varying distances could be achieved by using bolts of differing lengths. For maximum distance, the *Comitatus ballista* shoots bolts with a shaft of 190 mm. A shaft length of 400 mm reduces the range on average by 20 m. But the greater weight of the longer bolt of 100 g insures greater penetration of the target. In effect, it seems certain that the operator of the *ballista* could have selected different bolts for different tasks.

According to modern reconstructions, the speed of the missile means that feathered flights would have flattened out and ceased to have any effect, while wooden flights would have acted as barbs by sinking into the flesh of the target. In modern recreations, the blunt end of the bolt is carefully shaped to fit the trigger mechanism, and to reduce drag when the bolt is travelling through the air. The tapering shaft is more stable through the air than a cylindrical shaft.[106] Various metal heads could be used to punch their way through targets, or even to set them on fire by delivering flames held in a small cage. The square-section bodkin heads are perfect for high velocity flight.

CAVALRY

Saddles and Tack

Peter Connolly used the surviving evidence of leather covers, their stitching, stretch and wear marks, as well as metal horn plates, to produce a working Romano-Celtic saddle. He produced a design based upon a solid wooden four-horned frame. The size of the horns is in part dictated by the surviving copper alloy horn plates, which possibly acted as stiffeners. Some plates are surprisingly thick, suggesting that they were designed to protect the horse and rider. However, these protectors, or stiffeners, do not give an absolute indication of the angle of the horns. This can be derived from sculptural evidence. Surviving pieces of harness fitting also give clues as to how the saddle was attached to the horse.[107]

Various other attempts have been made to reproduce four-horned saddles using alternatives to the solid wooden frame, in part to justify simpler

---

[106] Wilkins (2003) 54.
[107] Connolly (1987) 7–28; Bishop (1988) 105–108.

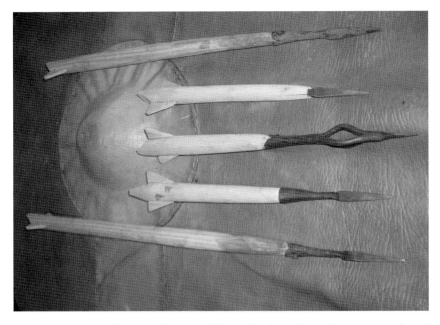

Fig. 8   Dura style bolts, with a caged head for fire, alongside one tanged and
three socketed bodkin heads.

and cheaper reconstructions. Flexible padded saddles without a wooden
frame, as used by Junkelmann for 1st–2nd c. cavalry simulations, can produce similar wear and stretch marks as found on surviving late antique
saddle covers.[108] The metal horn stiffener can be attached to the padded
horns internally or externally, or not used at all.[109] The fact that individual
names have been found scratched or punched onto the stiffeners has been
used as evidence that they were used externally.

Artefacts presented at the Carlisle Millennium Project conference in
2004 were found during excavations on the Castle Green between 1998
and 2001.[110] Two saddle covers were illustrated which both showed stretch
marks where they had been pressed down over a wooden frame. The covers were well worn, and had both been patched many times. Overall, the
stitch pattern used on each cover was the same as that found at other sites,
but these covers retained trapezoidal flaps of leather, about half as deep

---

[108] Junkelmann (1992) 34–74.
[109] Bishop (1988) 104.
[110] Winterbottom (2006) 7–11.

as they were long, the widest edges of which hung lowest from the horse. They demonstrate that rather than just being sewn up under the saddle as originally believed, leather covers could be secured over the horns and wooden frame of the saddle (fig. 9). These saddle covers simply hung down the sides of the horse, having a substantial fringed curtain of leather hanging from their lower edge. These seem to be covers from riding saddles rather than pack saddles, protecting the rider's legs against the girth and edge of the wooden frame. The girth strap, rather than being stitched into the saddle cover, as initially thought, was attached directly to the saddle frame. This will have given the rider greater stability. A piece of wood was exhibited at the Carlisle conference which conformed exactly to the curved piece of the saddle frame that crossed the withers in the Connolly reconstruction.[111] Such a design poses questions about how much padding was used in the saddle, and how it was held in place.

Many people have ridden in reconstructed Roman saddles in recreations of the cavalry of the 1st and 2nd c. For instance, Junkelmann included a reconstructed Late Roman horseman in his *Die Reiter Roms*.[112] In 2005–2006, I wanted to recreate systematically the skills and equipment of the Late Roman cavalryman. This meant that I had to learn to ride. The process I went through in part mirrored that of a Roman infantryman being inducted into the cavalry. I was used to the weapons and equipment, but not the horses. Unlike me, Roman recruits had the option of very severe bits and less humane methods of horse control. It took me a year of intensive practice to become a convincing Roman cavalryman. The lack of stirrups probably simplified the learning process, and to gain experience, I rode a variety of horses, and used several different period saddles. Spurs were not needed on all of the horses, and this suggests that not all Roman cavalrymen would have worn them.

Returning to the saddle, its purpose is to lift the weight of the rider from the horse's spine. Both the solid framed and padded styles of the four-horned saddle can meet this basic requirement, and both have been advocated by reconstructors: the wooden framed saddle by adherents of Connolly's thesis; and the 'pad' saddle by adherents of Junkelmann. Adherents of the pad saddle argue that, without the internal wooden frame, it is kinder to the horse's back, and fits a greater range of horse sizes. Indeed, the author initially suspected that the solid wooden frame

---

[111] Winterbottom (2006) 7.
[112] Junkelmann (1992) 154–55.

of a four-horned saddle would be inflexible, and potentially painful for a horse's back. Each saddletree would only be fit for use on one shape of horse, and even a saddle made to fit a specific horse would cease to fit if the horse lost condition on campaign. This would result in pressure sores, and calloused and thickened skin. But experience has altered the author's view. A solid Roman saddle with a wooden frame can be made to fit most horses, with the addition of good padding in the form of a saddlecloth or furs. The same was true of the solid wooden-framed military saddles of the 19th c., when cavalrymen were taught to fold their saddle cloths to fit their horse and saddle, especially on campaign.[113]

Moving away from the issue of the humanity of modern reconstructions, from the perspective of historical accuracy, the saddle covers from Carlisle provide fairly conclusive evidence that the Romans did use wooden-framed saddles. But, as Connolly and Van Driel Murray pointed out back in 1991, there is no reason to believe that there was just one design of Roman saddle.[114] Larger saddles, perhaps reinforced by copper alloy, may have been used by armoured riders or shock troops. While the military used wooden saddles, civilians could have used versions of the padded saddle. Indeed, price edicts do suggest cheaper saddles in use alongside more expensive military saddles.[115]

Returning to saddle design, the rear horns were particularly important in bracing the rider against powerful thrusts, and when riding uphill. The copper alloy stiffeners certainly played an important role in re-enforcing the horns, the rear stiffeners giving optimum reinforcement by stretching completely across the rear of the saddle. The author's saddle horns lack copper alloy horn stiffeners, and at different times he has broken both of the rear horns. However, the design of his saddle allows the leather cover to be lifted off, or the stitching to be cut open, and the horn replaced. Experimentation shows that this can be carried out in less than two hours. The author's saddle is a light 4.8 kg design, which is easily carried and stored, and which has very little padding for the rider's comfort. The second saddle he used was a little larger, at 5.2 kg, while Connolly's initial reconstruction weighed 6.8 kg. This variation in weight can relate to the saddle's size, the presence or absence of copper alloy stiffeners, or the amount of stuffing in the saddle.

---

[113] Congdon (1864) 101–103.
[114] Connolly and Van Driel-Murray (1991).
[115] Diocletian's *Edict on Maximum Prices* 11.4, in Graser (1940) 356.

Padded versions of these saddles that have been made without a wooden frame often have a metal bar towards the front for stability. Reconstructions are generally very heavy at 11–12 kg, and are much larger than examples based on a wooden frame. The weight of the rider forces the seat of the saddle downward and makes the horns lock around the rider's legs. While this gives a very secure seat, the rider will find it difficult to get out of the saddle if the horse falls, and so some movement in the saddle is to be preferred. The wooden frame seems by far the more usable of the two designs. It is a good design, but it is time-consuming to produce, and the horns represent intrinsic weaknesses. Initially, it feels as if the rear horns do not offer sufficient support. This can relate to the angle that the saddle sits on the horse. If the rear of the saddle is not high enough, the rider's full weight will constantly be hammering on the two rear horns. But riders soon get used to trusting the rear horns and using their legs to grip the front horns. In a short time, the rider becomes confident enough to lean well out of the saddle, instinctively riding with their legs bent and toes pointing downward, in the manner of the riders depicted on Roman monuments. Long periods of riding can be very hard on the rider's legs, and serious cramp can result in the rider having to be lifted out of the saddle. This is especially the case when riding with one's legs hooked under the horns of the saddle.

The girth and other tack can vary between reconstructions. The saddles do not fit as securely as modern saddles, and breast and breaching straps are required to hold them in place. A 'surcingle', a simple strap, wrapped round both horse and saddle, can be used to fasten the saddle more securely to the horse. However, a split girth holds the saddle in place more securely than a single girth, which results in the saddle moving around. A split girth, with two ends of the strap attached to the front and back of the saddle, provides more security. Reconstructions of tack from the 1st and 2nd c. are generally richly decorated with copper alloy fittings, and are often tinned or silvered, according to the archaeological finds on which they are based.[116] Few such fittings date from the 4th or 5th c. However, throughout the Roman period, amulets on horse tack made from the bases of shed antlers were widely used. The denticulated edge of these amulets is no more than the burr, the natural coronet of the antler, channelled and perforated by the presence of blood vessels in the velvet (the highly vascular skin covering the antler) during growth. One or more

---

[116] Bishop and Coulston (2006) 120–23.

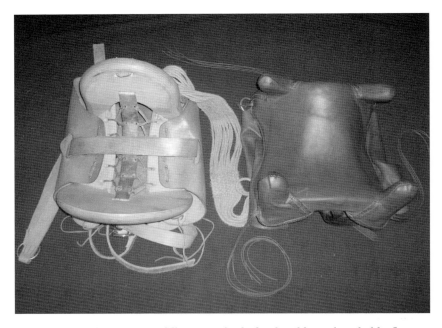

Fig. 9   Left: The steppe saddle. Note the lack of padding, detachable flaps to protect the leg, and the woven girth strap, directly attached to the robust frame. Right: A wooden-framed four-horned saddle with a Carlisle-style saddle cover with side flaps. The front of each saddle is located at the top of the picture.

holes drilled in the disc allowed for its suspension from the harness. The most common amulet design is the phallus, perhaps intended to ward off the evil eye, while the use of the antler may suggest some sort of special talismanic significance.[117] Triplet straps hanging from the front and rear of the saddle are very useful for securing equipment, and may have helped secure the leather cover to the wooden frame in Late Antiquity.

The horse is directed by weight distribution, leg pressure, verbal commands, and primarily, the bit in the horse's mouth held by the reins and bridle. Every horse needs different degrees of direction. Romans used either the snaffle bit of Celtic origin not unlike a modern bit, or the potentially severe curb bit. The Romans could also use the hackamore to increase leverage on the horse's jaw.[118] Various metal examples have been discovered, yet many more could have been made of leather or even dried grass. A simple hackamore would have no bit, and the 1st c. tombstone,

---

[117] MacGregor (1985) 107.
[118] Junkelmann (1992) 31.

found in Lancaster in 2005, seems to show a bit-less bridle.[119] This system is useful for young horses, or those with sensitive mouths, but is generally not associated with Romans. Today, metal hackamores can be covered with sheepskin for the horse's comfort, and it is possible that some Roman hackamores would have been similarly covered. The rider has to learn to neck rein, using one hand to control the horse by exerting pressure on the horse's neck with the reins, or even at times his shield.

The steppe saddle was introduced to the West by the Huns and their allies in the 4th c. (see fig. 9).[120] In time, it would develop into the medieval saddle and the modern Portuguese and Spanish saddles. It is a simple and strong design. Some steppe saddles may have been built with one piece of wood, but reconstructions are made of up to four pieces of wood, joined and shaped to transfer the weight of the rider to the horse's sides. The proportions of the pommel and cantle can only be deduced from surviving metal decoration. The earliest such fittings from Europe are a set of early 5th c. curved and triangular-shaped gold sheet mounts from Mundolsheim, Alsace.[121] These suggest a very high-fronted saddle, used to display wealth and status. Lower status riders could have used lower fronted saddles, for which rare, small and functional fittings have been found of later dates.[122]

The steppe saddle does not need integral padding and can be left just as bare wood, weighing 6.4 kg. It sits on several layers of wool or fur to protect the horse. It does not need breast or breaching straps, although they may be of use over long distances and rough terrain. Coming from a four-horned saddle, the Roman reconstruction specialist is initially concerned about sliding out of the 'side door'. They try and hook their legs under the front cantle to secure themselves in the seat, as they would under the front horns of the four-horned saddle. But the steppe saddle is not designed to be used in this way, and the rider soon becomes very uncomfortable. It is instead necessary to ride with a straight leg and a very deep seat when cornering. Such a position is relatively easy on the rider's legs, and can be maintained for long periods of time. This saddle design naturally benefits from the invention of the stirrup, which gives greater stability. Stirrups also enable a horseman to raise himself in the saddle to cushion the effect of the movement of the horse whilst they engage in

---

[119] For illustrations, see Bull (2007) 15 and 28. However, the illustration reconstructing the cavalryman shows a bridle with a bit.
[120] Evans (2004) 23–26.
[121] Schnitzler (1997) 86.
[122] Evans (2004) 23.

horse archery, important in a steppe culture. And, perhaps most useful of all, the stirrup allows the horse to be easily mounted.

The issue of just how Romans mounted their horses is unresolved. Contemporary books mention mounting from either side of the horse.[123] Fences and infantrymen are both good mounting blocks, and in armour it is just possible to mount while stationary with the assistance of a spear. Rope attached to the spear and used to carry the weapon over the shoulder can make a simple mounting step. A strong loop of rope over the front horns can also make a useful 'step' for mounting, but there is no evidence of such devices in Late Antiquity. Finally, modern re-enactment by stunt riders and enthusiasts has shown that, with considerable practice, a horse can be taught to kneel and a rider can leap directly into the saddle.

The Horse

Much has been written on the size of the Roman horse.[124] Hyland has considered the various ancient breeds potentially available to the Roman cavalry, although she shows a bias towards the Arab.[125] To generalise, there is a consensus that Roman horses in the West were around 13 to 14 hands, with some as tall as 15 hands (fig. 10).[126] Roman monuments certainly depict a small, stocky animal. Recent work on bone evidence suggests that actual military horses were what we would call ponies, robust specimens of 13.2 hands, with small regional differences.[127] It is certainly safe to assume that strong animals were needed to carry armoured riders over considerable distances, and speed would have been a secondary consideration. Junkelmann used Camargue horses for his reconstructions, while native British breeds similar to the Fell or Dartmoor pony would be best adapted to the British climate.[128] The issue of horse size is crucial in determining the speed of manoeuvre and effectiveness of Roman cavalry.

---

[123] Veg. *Mil.* 1.18.

[124] The English-speaking world measures the height of horses in hands, measured from the highest point of an animal's withers, where the neck meets the back. This is a stable point of the anatomy, unlike the head and neck, which move up and down. One hand is 4 inches (10 cm). Intermediate heights are defined by hands and inches, rounding to the lower measurement in hands, followed by a decimal point and the number of additional inches between one and three. Thus, a horse described as 14 hands is 140 cm.

[125] Hyland (1990) 11–29.

[126] Dixon and Southern (1992) 163–73.

[127] Johnstone (2004).

[128] Junkelmann (1990) 44–48.

Fig. 10   The typical Roman horse of around 14 hands, unshod, strong, with a broad back. An unstrung recurve bow is carried in a case. The bridle is a simple arrangement minimising the need for buckles as with a modern western bridle. The rider is wearing flexible armour of tinned copper alloy scales.

The Roman horseman will have needed considerable trust in his mount. Not only would he have lacked stirrups, but for some manoeuvres, he would not have been using reins. My experimentation shows that the control came from weight distribution, verbal commands and leg pressure. Back in 2005, after riding several horses including polo ponies and thoroughbreds, I settled on an Irish Cob of just over 14 hands to act the part of a Roman military horse. This breed has a reliable temperament, can easily carry a man in armour, and has strong hooves. The gelding of this horse was unshod, whereas the same was not necessarily the case for Roman horses. It took time for the horse to learn how to respond to neck reining, and to the Roman saddle, my armour and equipment. Riders have to find a way of carrying their shield, bow, arrows, lance and sometimes javelins, either hanging from the saddle or about their person. As the late 6th c. *Strategikon* states, riders had to be able to hang their lance from their shoulder while drawing the bow and placing an arrow on the string.[129]

---

[129] *Strategikon* 1.1.

They had to then develop the ability to replace the bow and ready the lance. Put simply, riders had to put in considerable practice and develop immense skill to get to a point where they were comfortable with their kit and weaponry.

The Roman-style cob showed a typical speed of 10 kph at the walk, 15–20 kph for the trot, 40 kph for the canter, and 56 kph at the gallop. Trotting without stirrups is uncomfortable for any length of time, and accuracy with missile weapons is difficult, so I carried out general manoeuvres at the canter. At this speed, the rider and horse provide a difficult target, but missile weapons can be used more precisely.

Cavalry Weapons: the Bow and the Kontos

In the late antique period, two cavalry weapons stand out: the *kontos* and the bow. The *kontos* was a 3–4 m-long lance, designed to outreach cavalry opponents (fig. 11). It could also pick out infantrymen from static formations, keeping the rider beyond the reach of spears and swords. Modern experimentation has shown that the horseman can hold the weapon with both hands, giving great power to the thrust, while controlling the horse with his legs. The *kontos* can be used either in a low guard across the horse's neck, or in a high position for downward blows. Such a long weapon is liable to flex if the diameter of the shaft is too narrow. Accuracy is easier at the walk, the canter or the gallop, while the trot can emphasise the amount of flexibility in the shaft.

Comitatus riders carry the *spatha* from a waist belt, secured by a scabbard slide. Often the bow case is tied to the same belt, or is attached to another waist belt. The bow case is secured with two ties, just in case one breaks. When carrying the bow in the bow case it is liable to bounce around, hitting the leg. Carrying the *spatha* over the case helps secure it. The case can be pulled out from behind the *spatha*, and twisted around so that the bow points forward to ease its draw. When replacing the bow, the case is twisted so that the top laths point towards the rear and the case is secured once more behind the *spatha*.

Horse archery is the hardest skill to learn, and it is possible that many second line units never used bows, or perhaps used them only from stationary positions. Reconstruction shows that the right-handed rider should be able to loose the arrow forwards to the right or left of the horse's head (see fig. 12). This means he must pull his right shoulder backwards and stretch forward with his left arm. But draw length may be limited, especially while wearing rigid scale, in turn limiting the power of the shot. Shooting to the

Fig. 11   The *kontos*, in this case a 4 m-long slender lance in two halves, joined by an iron collar. An iron ferrule is attached to the butt. Note the *manica* worn on the right arm, and the Orlatt-style bow case holding the strung bow with tubular quivers for light and heavy arrows.

rear, the famous Parthian shot, in many ways seems easier. The left arm is extended over the horse's rear, while the right holds the string to the ear. The draw length is maximised, but care must be taken to ensure that the left shoulder does not lie too far within the bow. If it does, the string may hit the left shoulder, robbing the shot of its power.

Loosing the arrow to the left when doing the Cantabrian circle is, by comparison, a basic skill. The rider starts with the arrow held under tension on the bow with the left hand. He rides, unusually, with the reins in the right hand. The rider approaches the target at approximately 40 kph and puts the horse into a right turn. When the horse is balanced, he drops the reins, relaxes, looses the arrow, finds the reins, and turns to the right

Fig. 12   Horse archery with shield at the canter, western style with the arrow to the left of the bow stave. The rider's body is restricted within a *subarmalis* and a cuirass of flexible scale, using his weight distribution, legs and voice to control the horse.

to come back to the starting point. Modern reconstruction experts, when recreating Mongolian horse archery with stirrups, shoot to the right side of the bow, using an eastern release, and are able to shoot and 'reload' on the move. They carry spare arrows in their left hand, which is resting against the stave of the bow. After release, they can use their right hand to pull a new arrow down on to the string, to the right side of the stave. The way eastern arrows are fletched means that there is no right or wrong way of placing the arrow on the string. Riders can stand in their stirrups to minimise rising and falling with the movement of the horse. Roman riders at the canter, without stirrups, shooting in a western style, and using western fletchings, take longer to nock a new arrow to the string. I have always shot using a western style and find it almost impossible to adapt to the Mongolian release.

Conclusion

This essay has examined selected items of Late Roman military equipment, and given an insight into their practical usage according to modern experimentation. Some may take the equipment described as proof of the 'barbarisation' of the Late Roman army. Nearly every piece of equipment mentioned in this paper can be traced back to a non-Roman source. But such a view would be too simplistic. The Roman army had always adopted equipment used successfully against it. In the same way, the army had a tradition of relying on allied peoples to supply them with troops skilled in differing fighting methods. This was in no way a Late Roman phenomenon, but a constant throughout the history of the Roman army, and neither was it a one-way process. The so-called 'barbarians' were also happy to adopt Roman weapons, equipment, tactics and troops.

In reconstructing these various items of equipment, I have relied primarily on archaeological evidence, occasionally using iconographic and written evidence to support my work. Vegetius, Maurice and many others can be used to recreate equipment and contribute to an understanding of how it was used. But there are good reasons not to place too much trust in written evidence, given what the ancient writers left out or assumed we would already know. There is perhaps even greater reason to doubt the objectivity of Late Roman art. The use of artistic licence, or even artistic convention, in the representational evidence is a major obstacle to the reconstruction of Roman equipment. Based solely on surviving material evidence, modern reconstructions are innately conservative, and rarely challenge the way military equipment is perceived. Indeed, re-enactors generally lack access to new research and academic journals, so reconstructions are generally based on well-known finds.

Over recent years, the quality of readily available, affordable reconstructions has increased exponentially. The fact that reconstructed helmets and armour are by their nature conservative interpretations of the evidence may come as a shock to some academics, who still believe that reconstruction archaeology is just one step away from fantasy role playing. But equally unhelpful is the contempt shown by some re-enactors, used to handling reconstructed equipment, for the academic who cannot identify a simple artefact.

While individual reconstructions may be conservative, placing together an assemblage of reconstructed artefacts to recreate a Late Roman soldier is by its very nature a speculative endeavour. Individual items may share a close resemblance to the original finds, but placing them together as a whole 'simulation' often moves beyond the available evidence into the realm of supposition.[130] Members of *Comitatus* try to recreate the look of

---

[130] James (2004) 256–59.

Late Roman soldiers in the north of Britain, but much of their equipment will be, from necessity, based on finds from elsewhere in the empire. However, by recreating or simulating the clothing and equipment of an imagined Late Roman soldier, we can begin to appreciate the various ways in which such individuals must have stood, moved and fought, and the likely constraints on these actions. An artist's impression of the same soldier would not provide the same level of understanding. In fact, those that have worked in period clothing and equipment are often the best judges of such artistic endeavours.

To understand, make and use reconstructed items in simulating the Late Roman soldier, it is of course necessary to learn the same skills as possessed by the soldier. I am in a position where I use equipment from many different historical periods, and it is enjoyable and rewarding work. While there are dangers in transferring experiences and knowledge gleaned from one period to another, there are also many advantages. For example, a thorough knowledge of Middle-Eastern and Central Asian horse archery gives a better understanding of how the Romans could have approached the discipline. Reconstructions have a powerful visual impact. They should be viewed as integral to the understanding of how artefacts were used and the people who used them.

BIBLIOGRAPHY

Primary Sources

Agath. = Keydell R. (1967) ed. *Agathiae Myrinaei Historiarum libri quinque* (Berlin 1967); Frendo J. (1975) trans. Agathias, *The Histories* (Berlin 1975).
Amm. Marc. = Rolfe J. C. (1963) ed. and trans. *Res Gestae* (London 1963).
Strategy = *The anonymous Byzantine treatise on strategy*, in Dennis G. T. (1985) ed., trans. and notes. *Three Byzantine Military Treatises* (Corpus fontium historiae 25, Dumbarton Oaks Texts 9) (Washington D.C. 1985) 1–136.
Arr. *Tact.* = Wirth G. W. (1968) trans. Arrian, *Ars Tactica* (Leipzig 1968).
Strategikon = Dennis G. T. (1984) ed. *Maurice's Strategikon. Handbook of Byzantine Military Strategy* (Philadelphia 1984); Dennis G. T. ed. and Gamillscheg E. trans. (1981) *Das Strategikon des Maurikios* (CFHB 17) (Vienna 1981).
Polyb. = Paton W. R. (1975–79) ed. and trans. Polybius, *The Histories* (Cambridge, Mass. 1975–79).
Procop. *Goth.*, Procop. *Vand.*, Procop. *Pers.* = Dewing H. B. (1914–54) ed. and trans. Procopius, *History of the Wars* (London 1914–54).
Veg. *Mil.* = Milner N. P. (1996) trans. *Epitome of Military Science* (Liverpool, 2nd ed. 1996).

Secondary Works

Allason-Jones L. and Miket R. (1984) *The Catalogue of Small Finds from South Shields Roman Fort* (The Society of Antiquaries of Newcastle-Upon-Tyne Monograph Series 2) (Gloucester 1984).

Aurrecoechea, J., Ibáñez C. F., García Marcos V. and Morillo Á. (2008) "Un protector laminado de brazo (manica) procedente del campamento de la legio VII Gemina en León", *ArchEspArq* 81 (2008) 255–64.

Baatz D. (1991) "Die römische Jagdarmbrust", *ArchKorrBl* 21.2 (1991) 283–90.

Blyth P. H. (1977) *The Effectiveness of Greek Armour Against Arrows in the Persian War 490–79 B.C: an Interdisciplinary Inquiry* (Ph.D. diss., Univ. of Reading 1977).

Bishop M. C. (1988) "Cavalry equipment of the Roman army in the first century AD", in *Military Equipment and the Identity of Roman Soldiers: Proceedings of the Fourth Roman Military Equipment Conference*, ed. J. C. N. Coulston (BAR International Series 394) (Oxford 1988) 67–195.

—— (2001) "Stainmore. The archaeology of a North Pennine pass", in *Tees Archaeology Monographs 1*, ed. B. Vyner (Hartlepool 2001) 169–70.

Bishop M. C. and Coulston J. C. N. (2006) *Roman Military Equipment from the Punic Wars to the Fall of Rome* (2nd ed., Oxford 2006).

Bull S. B. (2007) *Triumphant Rider: the Lancaster Roman Cavalry Tombstone* (Lancaster 2007).

Campbell D. B. (2003) *Greek and Roman Artillery 399 BC–AD 363* (Oxford 2003).

Congdon J. A. (1864) *Cavalry Compendium* (Philadelphia 1864).

Connolly P. (1987) "The Roman saddle", in *Roman Military Equipment: the Accoutrements of War: Proceedings of the Third Roman Military Equipment Seminar*, ed. M. Dawson (BAR International Studies 336) (Oxford 1987) 7–28.

Connolly P. and Van Driel-Murray C. (1991) "The Roman cavalry saddle", *Britannia* 22 (1991) 33–50.

Coulston J. C. N. (1985) "Roman archery equipment", in *The Production and Distribution of Roman Military Equipment: Proceedings of the Second Roman Military Equipment Seminar*, ed. M. C. Bishop (BAR International Series 275) (Oxford 1985) 220–366.

Croom A. (2001) "A ring mail shirt from South Shields Roman fort", *Arbeia Journal* 6–7 (2001) 55–60.

Dahlmos U. (1977) "Francisca-bipennis-securis. Bemerkungen zu archäologischem Befund und schriftlicher Überlieferung", *Germania* 55 (1977) 141–65.

D'Amato R. and Sumner G. (2005) *Roman Military Clothing 3 AD 400–640* (Oxford 2005).

Dixon K. R. and Southern P. (1992) *The Roman Cavalry: from the First to the Third Century AD* (London and New York 1992).

Eagle J. (1989) "Testing plumbata", in *Roman Military Equipment: the Sources of Evidence: Proceedings of the Fifth Roman Military Equipment Conference*, ed. C. van Driel-Murray (BAR International Series 476) (Oxford 1989) 247–53.

Evans C. E. (2004) "The saddle in Anglo-Saxon England and its European background", in *In the Saddle: an Exploration of the Saddle through History: a Meeting of the Archaeological Leather Group at Saddler's Hall, London, 23 October 2002*, ed. L. A. Gilmour (London 2004) 21–30.

Feugère M. (2002) *Weapons of the Romans* (Stroud 2002).

Graser E. R. (1940) "A text and translation of the Edict of Diocletian", in *An Economic Survey of Ancient Rome Volume V: Rome and Italy of the Empire*, ed. T. Frank (Baltimore 1940) 307–421.

Greep S. J. (1987) "Lead sling-shot from Windridge Farm, St Albans and the use of the sling by the Roman army in Britain", *Britannia* 18 (1987) 183–200.

Goethert K. P. (1996) "Neue romische Prunkschilde", in *Reiter wie Statuen aus Erz*, ed. M. Junkelmann (Mainz 1996) 115–26.

Hardy R. (1976) *Longbow: a Social and Military History* (Cambridge 1976).

Hyland A. (1990) *Equus: the Horse in the Roman World* (New Haven and London 1990).

—— (1993) *Training the Roman Cavalry from Arrian's Ars Tactica* (Stroud 1993).

James S. (2004) *Excavations at Dura-Europos 1928–1937: Final Report VII: the Arms and Armour and Other Military Equipment* (London 2004).

Johnstone C. L. (2004) *A Biometric Study of Equids in the Roman World* (Ph.D. diss., Univ. of York 2004).

Johnson S. (1980) "A Late Roman helmet from Burgh Castle", *Britannia* 11 (1980) 303–12.

Jones A. H. M. (1964) *The Later Roman Empire, 284–602: a Social, Economic and Administrative Survey* (Oxford 1964).

Jørgensen L., Storgaard B. and Andersen J. S. (2003) edd. *The Spoils of Victory: the North in the Shadow of the Roman Empire* (Copenhagen 2003).

Junkelmann M. (1990–92) *Die Reiter Roms I, II und III.* (Mainz 1990–92).

—— (1996) *Reiter wie Statuen aus Erz* (Mainz 1996).

Keegan J. (1976) *The Face of Battle* (New York 1976).

MacGregor A. (1985) *Bone Antler Ivory and Horn: the Technology of Skeletal Materials since the Roman Period* (Beckenham 1985).

Mode M. (2003) "Heroic fights and dying heroes—the Orlat battle plaque and the roots of Sogdian art", accessed at http://www.transoxiana.org/Eran/Articles/mode.html.

Musty J. and Barker P. A. (1974) "Three plumbatae from Wroxeter, Shropshire", *AntJ* 54 (1974) 275–77.

Paterson W. F. and Credland A. G. (1990) edd. *A Guide to the Crossbow* (London 1990).

Robinson H. R. (1975) *The Armour of Imperial Rome* (London 1975).

Schnitzler B. (1997) "A l'aube du Moyen Age, l'Alsace merovingienne", in *Les collections du Musée Archéologique* 5 (Strasbourg 1997) 86–87.

Sim D. and Ridge I. (2002) *Iron for the Eagles: the Iron Industry of Roman Britain* (Stroud 2002).

Soar H. D. H., with Stretton M. and Gibbs J. (2010) *Secrets of the English War Bow* (Pennsylvania 2010).

Stephenson I. P. and Dixon K. R. (2003) *Roman Cavalry Equipment* (Stroud 2003).

Thompson L. (2004) *Ancient Weapons in Britain* (Barnsley 2004).

Thomson W. T. (1955) "An approximate theory of armour penetration", *Journal of Applied Physics* 26 (1955) 919–20.

Wilkins A. (1994) "Reconstructing the *cheiroballistra*", in *Roman Military Equipment: Experiment and Reality: Ninth International Roman Military Equipment Conference, Leiden*, ed. C. van Driel-Murray (Leiden 1994) 5–59.

Wilkins A. (1995) "Reconstructing the *cheiroballistra*", *JRMES* 6 (1995) 5–59.

—— (2000) "*Scorpio* and *cheiroballistra*", *JRMES* 11 (2000) 77–101.

—— (2003) *Roman Artillery* (Princes Risborough 2003).

Winterbottom S. (2006) "On the fringes of empire: recent finds of saddle leather from Carlisle", *Newsletter 24 of the Archaeological Leather Group* (2006) 7–11.

List of Figures

Fig. 6   From the top: a leather case or bucket of *plumbatae*, a *plumbata* based on a Wroxeter find, a reconstructed *spiculum* from South Shields, and two *veruta*.

Fig. 7   An iron-framed *ballista*.

Fig. 8   Dura style bolts, with a caged head for fire, alongside one tanged and three socketed bodkin heads.

Fig. 9   Left: The steppe saddle. Note the lack of padding, detachable flaps to protect the leg, and the woven girth strap, directly attached to the robust frame. Right: A wooden-framed four-horned saddle with a Carlisle-style saddle cover with side flaps. The front of each saddle is located at the top of the picture.

Fig. 10   The typical Roman horse of around 14 hands, unshod, strong, with a broad back. An unstrung recurve bow is carried in a case. The bridle is a simple arrangement minimising the need for buckles as with a modern western bridle. The rider is wearing flexible armour of tinned copper alloy scales.

Fig. 11   The *kontos*, in this case a 4 m-long slender lance in two halves, joined by an iron collar. An iron ferrule is attached to the butt. Note the *manica* worn on the right arm, and the Orlatt-style bow case holding the strung bow with tubular quivers for light and heavy arrows.

Fig. 12   Horse archery with shield at the canter, western style with the arrow to the left of the bow stave. The rider's body is restricted within a *subarmalis* and a cuirass of flexible scale, using his weight distribution, legs and voice to control the horse.

LITERARY SOURCES AND TOPOGRAPHY

REPORTING BATTLES AND UNDERSTANDING CAMPAIGNS IN PROCOPIUS AND AGATHIAS: CLASSICISING HISTORIANS' USE OF ARCHIVED DOCUMENTS AS SOURCES

Ian Colvin

Abstract

This paper identifies the source material for Procopius' and Agathias' military narratives of Justinian's Lazican war, A.D. 548–57, as specific, archived documents. Their use of these archived documents explains striking characteristics of their accounts of battles and campaigns, not only in Lazica, but also in other parts of their histories. The commonly-held scholarly view that Procopius and Agathias, and perhaps other classicising historians, were largely dependent on oral sources, or in the case of Procopius on autopsy and oral sources, should therefore be modified.

INTRODUCTION: THE CONTEXTUAL SHORTCOMINGS OF PROCOPIUS' AND AGATHIAS' MILITARY NARRATIVES

This paper evolved from a talk on the literary and topographic evidence for battles in Late Antiquity that was delivered at the 2007 LAA conference in Oxford. It was thought that it might prove fruitful to try to explain any discrepancies between the topographic evidence provided by late antique literary sources like Procopius and the topographic evidence recovered from modern material evidence. It was the search for such discrepancies in the extensive and detailed material Procopius and Agathias offer for the Roman-Persian wars in Lazica that stimulated the following observation, which serves as the starting point for the paper: although Procopius and, less so, Agathias, are often praised for their extensive and detailed accounts of Justinian's wars, neither provides much detail in terms of terrain and topography, especially with regards to battles, either here or in Italy or Africa.[1]

---

[1] Cameron (1985) 184; Kouroumali (2006) 216–17.

A. Sarantis, N. Christie (edd.) *War and Warfare in Late Antiquity: Current Perspectives*
(Late Antique Archaeology 8.1–8.2 – 2010–11) (Leiden 2013), pp. 571–597

This observation must be qualified. These historians do orientate their readers with a general account of the location of Lazica, and they give impressionistic accounts of the terrain there.[2] They also mention the names of a variety of places within the theatre of campaign. In the case of sieges and battles in the vicinity of such named places, they often tell us some further information about the site, but even in these cases, the information is in truth very limited and often ambiguous.[3] By comparison, modern material evidence from mapping, satellite imaging, personal autopsy and archaeological study is extensive and precise; and other related archaeological sciences such as palaeobotany and palaeo-environmental studies can further enrich our understanding of the geographical context of late antique campaigns.

So limited is the topographical information yielded by the literary sources that a comparison of the evidence of these two very different types of source shows little by way of informative discrepancies. Late antique literary sources, though they name the sites of battles and sometimes give other nuggets that can further aid our understanding, do not and cannot compete with the rich present-day sources of geographical information. It is clear, therefore, that to fully understand the geographical context of the battles and campaigns our sources report we must rely first on the material evidence supplemented with what scraps the literary sources provide us.[4]

Geography is not the only area in which the narratives of Procopius and Agathias are of strikingly mixed quality and limited use. Their accounts are arranged year by year by campaigning season. Each campaign is centred on one or more encounters, usually written up in some detail. The amount of campaign background—that is the events and manoeuvres leading up to and subsequent to the encounter—is quite variable: in A.D. 548, 551 and 552, for example, parts at least of the campaign are described at reasonable length (though, unusually, in 552, no battle is written up in detail); in the conflict near the River Hippis later in 549, by contrast, we have a detailed battle account that sits almost, but not quite,

---

[2] Procop. *Pers.* 1.12.2, 2.29.14, 8.2–6; Agath. 2.18.4. The latter and Procop. *Pers.* 8.1.10 locate Lazica in myth as well as space, Braund (1994) ch. 1; Colvin (forthcoming) ch. 2.

[3] About 20 places in total are named by both historians, ranging in importance from a plain with a pottery market to the *polis* of Petra and the district of Mucheirisis. The great majority are fortresses of one sort or another. Interestingly, and, exceptionally, Agathias in 4 places provides precise indications of the distances between locations—see Colvin (forthcoming) ch. 2.

[4] Compare Lillington-Martin's paper in this collection.

entirely independently of any campaign context (there are a few introductory lines and one at the end that hints at wider operations). The narrative dealing with A.D. 550 sits between these extremes, with an account of Roman operations against the Abasgians and Apsilians, but with only the most perfunctory description of Roman or Persian operations in Lazica itself.[5] The wide variability in background information, in terms of both grand tactical context and topography, is a notable feature of accounts that are quite detailed in other areas.

It might be thought that the witnesses on whom these historians are supposed to have depended for their accounts would have described the country and terrain in which these battles were fought, the movements of the armies, other events leading up to the encounters, and their ultimate effects. Yet Procopius and Agathias seemingly often knew little of such context for the battles they describe. One might be tempted to conclude simply that classicising historians and their readers were uninterested in the topography and terrain of the battles about which they wrote or read, and that accounts of feats of arms performed interested them more than either the causes or the results of these battles; but such an argument runs into the problem that historians did sometimes describe terrain and topography and make efforts to provide context. In other words it is the patchiness of their information, rather than its absence, which demands explanation. Why *do* Procopius and Agathias, praised for their detail and the quality of their reportage, offer so little geographical and grand tactical context to their accounts of battles and campaigning? The answer, I suggest, lies in a dependence on specific documentary sources that were written with a more limited purpose.

Procopius' and Agathias' Military Narratives—Make-Up and Component Parts

To explain why geographical and other campaign context is so often lacking in the literary accounts of warfare, it is important first to lay out what sorts of information these accounts do contain. To that end we may divide the information contained in the battle accounts into 6 types.

---

[5] Pursuit of the 5,000—Procop. *Pers.* 2.30.43f; perfunctory account of Persian operations of 550—Procop. *Pers.* 8.9.6; on Roman operations in Abasgia and Apsilia the same year—Procop. *Pers.* 8.9 and 10; on Bessas' operations—Procop. *Pers.* 8.11.11.

Firstly, a close examination of the Lazican campaigns demonstrates that the vivid, anecdotal evidence for which Procopius is often praised largely belongs to a very specific category of information: accounts of heroic actions performed by one or more individuals. In both Procopius and Agathias, these types of actions provide the heart of the vast majority of their accounts of those battles that have received a detailed treatment; where they are lacking, the absence is very noticeable.[6]

Second is the speech or speeches made before, or sometimes after, the battle by one or more participants, usually the generals. Where present, these are almost certainly the imaginative work of the historian and not a record of what was actually said, nor even a guarantee that there was a speech. Often they serve to dramatise some detail, such as the resolve of the Persian defenders of Petra's acropolis in 551, who were burned to death after resisting a Roman soldier's exhortations to surrender; or the disagreement between the Romans and the Laz at the battle near the Hippis River in 549.[7]

A third category of information is the excursus. Both our authors frequently introduce, or interrupt, their accounts of a battle with an excursus of some sort—such as geographical and topographical excursuses, or how to repel elephant attack, or omens that occurred. Like the speeches, these were an expected element of the genre. Procopius and Agathias link them loosely to surrounding events, but these passages rarely add much detail to the battle being described. They gave an elegant and learned air to the

---

[6] Heroic anecdotes are particularly noticeable in John Gouzes and his followers' temporary penetration of the fortifications of Petra in 548: Procop. *Pers.* 2.30–3-6; several occur at the battle near the River Hippis in 549—Procop. *Pers.* 8.1.3–6, 8.8; at Telephis-Ollaria in 555—Agath. 2.20.7–21.4; at the siege of Phasis 556—Agath. 3.19.8–28.10; in Maxentius' and Theodore's raid on the Persians' Sabir allies in 556—Agath. 4.14; and at the Roman assault on the village by the fortress of Tzakher-Siderun in late 556 or early 557—Agath. 4.17–20. Heroic details (particularly named individuals) are notably absent from the encounters in 552—Procop. *Pers.* 8.17–19, even though the encounter near Archaeopolis would seem suitable to receive a much fuller treatment; heroic anecdotes are also lacking in the case of sieges the Romans lost: Ukhimereos in 551—Procop. *Pers.* 8.14.50–4, 16.1–5; Onoguris in 555—Agath. 3.5.6–8.3. For detailed discussion, see Colvin (forthcoming).

[7] Speeches or councils of war are inserted at the battle near the Hippis in 549—Procop. *Pers.* 8.8.7; after the siege of Petra in 551—Procop. *Pers.* 8.12.4–13; at the siege of Archaeopolis in 551—Procop. *Pers.* 8.14.14–21; at the siege of Onoguris 555—Agath. 3.6.1–8; and before the massacre of Sotirichus in 556—Agath. 3.16.1–4. Cameron (1985) 148 views speeches generally as the author's own compositions and "little more than formal exercises", though she accepts that they may provide characterisation and add some insights to the war. Treadgold (2007) 216 considers some of Procopius' speeches and letters genuine, and even his own compositions for Belisarius, perhaps as Belisarius' secretary. Neither Procopius nor Belisarius were present in Lazica.

work in the eyes of the original readers, even if modern readers some-times find they interrupt the action. Although they may be of consider-able interest as evidence for literary tastes, or for understanding what the author was trying to do more broadly, they are rarely of much value from the point of view of military history.[8]

Fourthly, many battles, particularly those thin on detail, are padded out with shorter or longer passages of what might be termed generalised battle description—i.e. generic descriptions of fighting that offer no evi-dence that they represent more than imaginative reconstruction. Clouds of arrows darkening the sky, clashing shields and weapons, neighing horses etc. are all likely elements of a battle. But, without further detail specific to the battle being described, it is reasonable to discount these sections as direct evidence of 'what happened'. They are just as likely to be liter-ary *topoi* of combat, and cannot therefore be considered evidence of oral accounts from eyewitnesses. In fact, Agathias often gets these boilerplate/formulaic elements wrong, to the detriment of his account: as with the suggestion that Germanus' cavalry pushed back the Persians with their shields during a mounted charge, his description of the night-time mas-sacre of the General Soterichus and his entourage by the Misimians, or the Dilimnites' abortive ambush of the Sabirs outside Archaeopolis in 556.[9]

A related, fifth type of information in Procopius' and Agathias' accounts is authorial commentary. At times, Procopius and Agathias report things that they or their sources are unlikely to have known, and which must therefore be assumed to be supposition or reconstruction (whether autho-rial or their source's). They also pass opinions on the nature of fate, or the lessons that can be drawn from the event just described. Though such comments may help our understanding of the author, they only illumi-nate the battle or campaign itself if grounded in better information than our authors and their sources have transmitted to us.[10]

---

[8] The obvious exceptions to the above statements about these adding nothing to the account of the battle are the topographical descriptions of Petra, Archaeopolis and Phasis. Procopius inserts excursuses on the best way to repulse elephant attacks and the birth of a two-headed infant at Edessa, right at the climax of his account of the siege of Archaeop-olis—Procop. *Pers.* 8.14.35.

[9] General battle prose: Agath. 3.25.1–9. Procopius' re-use of Battle of Callinicum phrasing at the Battle of Hippis—Procop. *Pers.* 1.18.45–8, 8.8.31–32; Germanus' cavalry charge—Agath. 3.25.9; Soterichus' massacre—3.16.6–8; Sabir counter-ambush of Dilim-nites—3.18.5–9. See Ites (1926); and Cameron (1970) 44–49 for criticism of Agathias' battle accounts, and Colvin (forthcoming) chapters 8 and 9 on which elements can be trusted.

[10] Agathias is particularly well-known for his insertion of moralistic comments on events, e.g. at Onoguris—Agath. 3.8.2–3; the massacre of Sotirichus—3.16–17.2; at Phasis—3.24

Lastly, if one strips out the above categories, one finds that there usually remain some bedrock facts that are not clearly part of any of the aforementioned categories. These include basic details of the battle such as: where it occurred, between which forces, the respective sizes, losses incurred or inflicted, and details of prisoners and plunder taken.

Analysing Procopius' and Agathias' accounts in the above manner clarifies two important distinctions between the categories of information they convey. Firstly, a distinction between the elements of Procopius' and Agathias' accounts that appear to transmit real knowledge of events (categories 1 and 6 above) and those that are largely authorial invention (the other categories—even if they contain germs of truth). Some of the latter were added to meet the genre expectations of readers or to fill out an otherwise patchy account; others may have been literary 'showing off'; and some may have been intended to convey a poetic rather than a literal truth. Secondly, within the categories that show real knowledge of events, there is an obvious contrast of kind between the detailed anecdotal material that focuses on the heroics of individuals and units (category 1) and the more general facts of the battles' occurrence and outcome (category 6).

It follows from the first distinction that in terms of getting at what actually happened, one must concentrate on those parts of Procopius' and Agathias' accounts that transmit knowledge of events. These seem to represent the closest we can get to the sources embedded within the literary work; the other parts, the literary 'chaff', should be accorded much less evidential weight. Indeed we shall ignore them for the purposes of the present article.

The second distinction suggests we have a hierarchy of information about the wars: at the bottom is information about the heroic actions of individuals or small groups; higher up are details of the battle itself; then information belonging to each season's campaign, a grand tactical level; and finally, the highest level of information, the political, diplomatic and strategic events. At the most detailed level, Procopius and Agathias provide lots of interesting reportage, but in the Lazican campaign, of a very specific type: the heroic anecdote. At the battle level, they also preserve good information, often embedded in a surround of literary padding; battles are at the heart of the narratives. They are much weaker at the

---

and 28; and during the Misimian campaign—4.15.6–16.1, 19.1–20.2—but Procopius also indulged in moralising and reflections on the nature of fate: e.g. Procop. *Pers.* 8.12.30. See also Cameron (1970) 44.

campaign level, not always providing detailed information. And, although I shall not discuss this in any detail in the present article, they are well-informed at the political and diplomatic level.

The questions that emerge are: how can we account for both the short-comings and the character of the information Procopius and Agathias provide? Why were detailed accounts of individual heroics transmitted to us while so much useful and relevant context, geographical and otherwise, was not? If, as is usually stated, their sources for these battles were inter-views with participants, surely those participants would have described more of the battle, its geographical and campaign circumstances, and its strategic results, rather than limiting themselves to the few moments of heroics the historians relate? If Procopius and Agathias *did* know more about the context of these events, why do they so often fail to transmit this knowledge? Did their informants *not* describe the events leading up to the battle? Did these sources conclude their accounts without relating the effects the outcome of that battle had on the wider situation in the theatre of campaign? Or have Procopius and Agathias filtered out these elements, concentrating instead on deeds in battle in relative isolation from the sur-rounding campaigning? How can we explain the wide variation from year to year in the campaign information Procopius and Agathias relate, and the unusual absence of heroic anecdotes in 552? How exactly should we envisage information passing between theatres of campaign and Constan-tinople, and in what form did it reach our authors?

PROCOPIUS' AND AGATHIAS' SOURCES

Scholarly Views of Procopius' Sources

Modern scholarship on Procopius goes back at least as far as Felix Dahn's study of 1865. While much-studied in recent years, views of Procopius' sources seem to have changed little in the century and a half since Dahn.[11] Scholars commonly assert that Procopius wrote largely of events he wit-nessed himself, and that for other information he drew on the testimony

---

[11] Dahn (1865) 58–69. Specialists now have a more sophisticated understanding of the difficulties Procopius' works present, especially with regard to their evidential value: see Cameron (1985); Tougher's (1997) review article; Roueché (2000) on the *Buildings*; Greatrex (1998); Kaldellis (2004); Kouroumali (2006); and, most recently, Treadgold (2007). Despite these and other works, Procopius' evidence continues to be widely misused.

of contemporary eyewitnesses.[12] It is generally accepted that he may have used some literary sources for his 'archaeologies', such as the unidentified 'Armenian history', or the lost history of Eustathius of Epiphania, but he is not thought to have relied heavily on literary sources. Indeed, in a recent book, Treadgold states that Procopius was surprisingly uninterested in them.[13]

Opinions are mixed on whether, and how far, Procopius drew on documents. It is commonly claimed that he must have kept a journal or other record of events as they happened.[14] And many scholars accept that he made use of military records on occasion. The nature of these and the extent of their use have not, however, been explored in any detail.[15] Most seem to think oral sources were of greater importance by far, although Greatrex argues that: "Whether such archives were employed by Procopius must remain in doubt, since he nowhere quotes any official documents *verbatim*".[16]

This last view is surprising because more than half of Procopius' history—including the great bulk of the military narrative post-540 and most events pre-540 that did not involve Belisarius—concerns events

---

[12] E.g. Stein (1949) 713–14; Greatrex (1998) 62; Cameron (1985) 15, 136; Treadgold (2007) 215 n.154, 216. Procop. *Pers.* 1.1.3 is the foundation of claims Procopius witnessed most of the events; see n.51 for instances of Procopius' genuine eyewitness.

[13] Treadgold (2007) 215–17 on his use of Herodotus and Thucydides, 189 on his annoyance at the failure of his audience to pick up on subtle allusions; Stein (1949) 713; Cameron (1985) 216–17 on the use of Arrian.

[14] As suggested by Bury (1958) 420–21, for the Vandal expedition, to explain the noticeable increase in detail from this point; Greatrex (1998) 63; Cameron (1985) 13, 148; Treadgold (2007) 179; compare with Cameron (1970) 40 doubting Agathias' use of records, and even that they existed—*contra* Vasiliev (1952) 180.

[15] Cameron (1985) 13, 136—n. 15 suggests use of army lists, but in the main text Cameron assumes most information was from 'oral sources'; 146 (she recognises that Malalas drew on official (presumably written) sources but seems to imply Procopius did not), 156 (use of written sources—perhaps documentary perhaps literary), 180 (assumes eyewitness account of African affairs, but 180–85 on African section of *Buildings* also recognises personal autopsy cannot be true of whole, and suggests use of lists from Constantinople). Treadgold (2007) 216, 221 thinks some of the speeches and letters in the *Wars* were genuine and written by Procopius as Belisarius' secretary; he suggests, 218, Procopius' use of military rolls and reports, and official records—despite his general assumption that eyewitness testimony and oral sources were the main sources. Kouroumali (2006) 212–16 expects he used written reports of events but doubts he had access to "reports from the centre of operations and decisions" on account of the implausibility of his speeches and letters. By contrast to the lack of work on Procopius' sources, compare Jeffreys (1990) on Malalas, or Croke (2001) on Marcellinus Comes.

[16] Greatrex (1998) 64; Bury (1958) 419 n. 3; see also Treadgold (2007) 216.

that few scholars believe he was a witness to.[17] He must, therefore, have obtained most of his information on these from documents, individuals, or a mixture of the two. Cameron and Treadgold both seek to identify as sources individuals who are named in the narrative, and may in this be taken as typical. The method is perfectly logical, but Cameron herself recognises that it is not entirely successful.[18]

Furthermore, probably from 540, and certainly by the time the Lazican war got under way in 548, Procopius was writing about events more or less as they occurred. One must, therefore, consider what opportunities he would have had to interview serving soldiers who were still campaigning in theatre—assuming, as is generally agreed, that Procopius was in Constantinople. One would have to imagine one or more individuals (i.e. witnesses of the campaigning) returning to Constantinople, perhaps during the winter lull, and Procopius debriefing them then. It is uncertain how common such a furlough would be. The sources are clear that the army as a whole dispersed to winter quarters in theatre. Might some, nevertheless, have returned to Constantinople?[19] Alternatively, one might speculate that Procopius' sources wrote to him from the front. Fortunately, the sources themselves provide adequate evidence for other channels of information. As we shall see below, Procopius made much greater use of the reports and letters that passed between Constantinople and the theatre of campaign than is usually recognised.[20]

---

[17] Haury's belief that Procopius accompanied Belisarius on his second trip to Italy in the mid-540s is not generally accepted today. Greatrex and others argue he may have accompanied the general to the East in 541.

[18] For example, Cameron (1985) 191 notes that even though Procopius is no longer drawing on personal experience by Procop. *Pers.* 8, he can still tell a convincing and detailed story, "though without the anecdotal element of *Gothic Wars* 1 and 2". For the main narrative of Procopius' *Gothic Wars* post-540 or 542, she considers members of Belisarius' bodyguard as the most likely candidates for his information; she presumes that military records were no longer available to him—(1985) 202–203. See also Bury (1958) 419 n. 3.

[19] Roman military concentration near Phasis as winter came on, dispersed by Persian action—Procop. *Pers.* 8.16.18; winter quarters in Lazica—Agath. 3.8.3, 4.12.1, 4.20.10. On the difficulties of the land route to Lazica, see Bryer and Winfield (1985) 17–20; the sea route was more usual (Priscus fragment 33.1; Procop. *Pers.* 8.2.19), but considered hazardous in winter.

[20] Messengers certainly did travel between Constantinople and theatre, carrying letters and reports: e.g. Procop. *Pers.* 8.2.18; Agath. 3.3.1–7 and 3.23.5–13 (the effectiveness of Martin's ruse assumes the plausibility of such a message). See arguments below for a passage of letters and reports between Constantinople and Lazica.

Scholarly Views of Agathias' Sources

Scholars' evaluations of the historical worth of Agathias' *Histories* tend to be low,[21] even if most assume that the majority of Agathias' evidence derives from interviews with eyewitness participants. An exception is Schubert, who recognised in Agathias' account of the wars in Italy, the use of military dispatches or diaries—but Schubert's views do not seem to have been generally accepted. Treadgold also assumes that Agathias derived some of his figures from archival sources, stating that he "surely had good sources for most of what he wrote about the wars in Italy and Lazica"; "He knew bureaucrats with access to military reports, and he could have met veterans and travellers returning to Constantinople; once he names a native of Campania as his source". Yet he says nothing about the form of the documents these figures came from, and he is sceptical of other figures Agathias offers.[22]

ORAL SOURCES OR DOCUMENTS?

The following discussion is limited to the military narratives of the war in Lazica and will ignore the historians' lengthy and varied excursuses, their speeches, their authorial comments, and generalised battle description. It will concentrate on the question of where Procopius and Agathias acquired the core information for their accounts.

It is an old assumption that the majority of Procopius' and Agathias' information, on battles and campaigns they were not themselves present at (there is no reason to believe Procopius or Agathias ever travelled to Lazica), was furnished by individuals—the so-called oral sources. This assumption is, however, one founded more on inference than on hard evidence. Procopius is generally thought to have witnessed the majority

---

[21] A particularly negative view of Agathias was put forward by Ites (1926), who, through wilful misunderstanding of Agathias' accounts, concluded that much of Agathias' account of the wars in Italy and Lazica was a 'fantasy'. See critique in Colvin (forthcoming) chapters 8 and 9. Stein and Cameron's use of this excessively critical analysis of Agathias' military narrative is probably responsible for its widespread acceptance: Stein (1949) 511–16 esp. 511 n. 2 and 514 n. 2; Cameron (1970) ch. 4.

[22] Schubert (1884) 99, rejected by Cameron (1970) 40, who envisages Agathias as having acquired most of his information from 'oral sources', 40–43. Treadgold (2007) 289 and (1995) 49–58, 59–63. Cesa (1993) 1179–80 suggests a Laz informant for at least some of his information.

of the events he describes in the early parts of the *Wars*—for he claims as much in his preface. If one accepts this claim, then it is not unnatural to infer that where he was not present, he drew on others' eyewitness accounts. Procopius' and Agathias' occasional use of *hos phasi* ('as they say') and similar phrases could support such an inference.[23] However, relatively few of these phrases relate directly to the sections of campaign and battle narrative; most are in 'archaeologies' or excursuses.[24] Furthermore, while such phrases might imply receipt of spoken information, they may also simply be figures of speech; it is even possible that such phrases could have originated within the written source Procopius and Agathias were using at the time.[25] At best, these phrases are ambiguous.

Although some have claimed that the existence or accessibility of written reports is unproven,[26] scholarship of the last 30 years has done much to dispel such doubts, and it is no longer possible to argue that there is no evidence for the existence, retention, or availability to late antique historians of numerous classes of documents in archives in Constantinople.[27] Indeed, as is demonstrated in the following section, Procopius' and Agathias' accounts of the wars in Lazica mention—explicitly or implicitly—two classes of document that would have been retained in Constantinopolitan archives.[28]

These authors' reliance on these mentioned documents as sources for their histories better explains the shortcomings and character of their accounts than any hypothetical oral sources. Firstly, our authors mention letters and reports, and messengers and embassies sent between Constantinople and participants in Lazica. Secondly, the existence of citations for good conduct in battle can be deduced from certain passages. Finally,

---

[23] Dahn (1865) 58–69 has been followed by many since; Treadgold (2007) 215 n. 154.

[24] For example, three of the five instances Treadgold (2007) 215 n. 154 cites.

[25] Compare with Cameron (1985) 209 who is against assuming phrases like 'it seems to me' represent an original opinion.

[26] Cameron (1970) 40, though her (1985) 156, 202 assumes Procopius would no longer have had access to them after Belisarius' recall in 540.

[27] E.g. Lee (1993) 8, 33–40; Baldwin (1978); Kelly (1997) on the archives beneath the Hippodrome. Note, however, the point about the writers of the Theodosian Code being unable to obtain central copies of many laws, and having to write to the provinces for copies, while Lydus claimed that even if originals were destroyed, there were summaries of decisions that could be relied on. Noble (1990) on papal record-keeping. Kelly (2004) 117–20; Howard-Johnston (1999) 8–14; Blockley (1985) 18–20; Jeffreys (1990) ch. 7 esp. 200–11; Croke (2001).

[28] Archives like the one under the Hippodrome: Kelly (1997). Blockley (1985) 18–20 suggests envoys' reports and treaties were retained.

the possibility of a third type of battle account might be inferred from Marcellinus Comes' repeated use of an interestingly standardised formula in reporting battles.

Letters, Reports, Messengers and Embassies

The first category of contact between Constantinople and Lazica is that of letters, reports and embassies. These can be further divided into three subcategories by reference to the correspondents. The first relate to letters, reports and embassies sent between the Emperor Justinian and the Laz King Gubaz.

1. Correspondence between Justinian and Gubaz

Procopius and Agathias quite often mention correspondence between Gubaz and Justinian. For example, here are Procopius' summaries of three exchanges of letters in A.D. 548. First:

> And Gubaz reported to the Emperor Justinian the condition in which they [the Laz] were, and begged him to grant forgiveness for what the Laz had done in the past, and to come to their defence with all his strength, since they desired to be rid of the Median rule. (Procop. *Pers.* 2.29.9).

Procopius follows this letter with Justinian's response: the despatch of 8,000 men under Dagisthaeus to Lazica; their siege of Petra; and the Sassanian despatch of a relief force. He then inserts a brief—and error-filled—geographical excursus. After this, he returns to the action with Gubaz's instructions to Dagisthaeus and then the background to a second exchange: Gubaz, he writes, had much earlier arranged an alliance with the Sabirs and Alans, according to which they would attack Iberia in return for 3 *kentenaria* (i.e. 300 lbs of gold):

> So he reported the agreement to the Emperor Justinian and besought him to send this money for the barbarians and afford the Laz some consolation in their great distress. He also stated that the treasury owed him his salary for 10 years, for though he was assigned a post among the privy counsellors in the palace, he had received no payment from it since the time when Khusro came into the land of Colchis. And the Emperor Justinian intended to fulfil this request, but some business came up to occupy his attention and he did not send the money at the proper time. (Procop. *Pers.* 2.29.30–32)·

Procopius then turns to Dagisthaeus' mishandling of the siege of Petra—some details of which very likely come from Gubaz's correspondence, as he is known to have complained to Justinian about the general's handling of the campaign; others came from Dagisthaeus' letters to Justinian.[29] The siege made slow progress because of stubborn resistance, but also, it seems, because of Dagisthaeus' own failings. Procopius' narrative switches between the relief force's advance and the progress of the siege, punctuating the former with an anecdotal account of a heroic attack on Petra's walls by a small group of Romans that nearly succeeded, but ultimately failed through lack of support. At last he recounts how Mihr-Mihroe's army forced a pass that Dagisthaeus had failed to defend adequately, that Dagisthaeus lifted the siege on news of the defeat, and, finally, how Mihr-Mihroe reinforced the garrison of Petra and subsequently withdrew from Lazica. The third letter under consideration closes this episode:

> The Emperor Justinian at this time sent to the nation of the Sabirs the money which had been agreed upon, and he rewarded Gubaz and the Laz with additional sums of money. And it happened that long before this time he had sent another considerable army also to Lazica, which had not yet arrived there. The commander of this army was Rhecithancus, from Thrace, a man of discretion and a capable warrior. (Procop. *Pers.* 2.30–28–29).

This letter is particularly interesting because of the peculiarity of the appended information about reinforcements. I am convinced that this detail belongs to the letter mentioned the line before because that is the only logical reason for Procopius to place it here. In terms of narrative, the natural point for the historian to give details of reinforcements is when they arrived in theatre, or conceivably when they were despatched. Those would also be the natural points for an oral source to report reinforcements—as indeed for most other types of document.[30] Had Procopius known those dates, he would surely have mentioned the army's despatch or arrival at the proper place in his narrative; his failure to do so, and his reporting instead of the bizarre information that reinforcements had been sent 'long before' but had not yet arrived, strongly suggests Justinian's encouraging Gubaz with news of the imminent arrival of more aid. Procopius has simply drawn this information straight from the letter before him, and, having no better information for the army's despatch or arrival, added it at the place mentioned in the correspondence. I infer that

---

[29] Procop. *Pers.* 8.9.1–4. See next section below.

[30] For example, if this information hailed from financial documents or military lists describing the raising or equipping of troops or the ships to carry them to Lazica, these would surely have been dated and Procopius could have inserted the information at a more natural point in his narrative.

he lacked either the means or the inclination to make further inquiries into the despatch, arrival and later dispositions of the reinforcements Justinian mentioned. This provides, then, both supporting evidence for Procopius' use of a register of letters and what appears to be an indication to put it no more strongly—that, for certain details at least, he relied solely upon it.[31]

That Procopius found these letters together in a register is suggested by the fact that they usually appear in pairs: information is reported to Constantinople and the emperor acts upon it. Copies of correspondence received and sent were filed together.[32] It would be perverse to suggest that he must have got these details from anywhere other than the letters themselves: Occam's razor insists we should reject the idea of an intermediate oral source.

Procopius and Agathias both drew on further material from this register. For example, Gubaz made repeated complaints to Justinian about senior Roman officers in Lazica. Both the *magister militum per Armeniam*, Dagisthaeus, and his successor Bessas were eventually sacked as a result of this lobbying. In the case of Dagisthaeus, Gubaz sent ambassadors to make his point:

> The Laz began to slander Dagisthaeus to the emperor, going to Byzantium to do so, charging him with treason and Medizing. For they declared that he had yielded to the persuasion of the Persians in refusing to establish himself inside the fallen circuit-wall of Petra, while the enemy in the interval had filled bags with sand and laid courses with them instead of stones, and thus had made secure such parts of the circuit-wall as had fallen down. And they stated that Dagisthaeus, whether impelled to do so by a bribe or through negligence, had postponed the attack to some other time, and had thus let slip for the moment the precious opportunity which, of course, he had never again been able to grasp. The emperor consequently confined him in prison and kept him under guard; he then appointed Bessas... and sent him to Lazica... (Procop. *Pers.* 8.9.1–4).

One might infer that Procopius met members of this embassy or learnt of their mission from officials who were present at their audience, but it seems much more likely he used either a letter carried by the embassy,

---

[31] A remarkably similar instance of Procopius mentioning reinforcements alongside Justinian's correspondence with Gubaz is at Procop. *Pers.* 8.9.4. The same pattern of letter to Justinian followed by mention of reinforcements already sent can be seen in the Gothic Wars at Procop. *Goth.* 5.14.1–21.

[32] See n. 27 on archives generally, and Noble (1990) in particular on Late Roman filing habits as demonstrated by the Papal registers.

minutes of their audience with Justinian, or both. It would be interesting to know whether, if minutes were the source, they were bound into the same register as the letters, or belonged to a separate archive.[33] Gubaz's complaint about Bessas, on the other hand, was seemingly contained in a letter:

> [After the Romans' flight from the Persians at Telephis in 555, Gubaz] lost no time in sending a detailed report to Justinian in which he held the gener-als responsible, laying the blame for everything that had happened on their incompetence, and singling out Bessas as the chief culprit. He also named Martin and Rusticus.... When the emperor came to hear of these further misdemeanours he remembered the earlier ones and was immediately con-vinced by the report. Accordingly, he relieved him of his command, confis-cated his property and relegated him to the country of the Abasgi, where he was to remain until the emperor's further pleasure. (Agath. 3.2.3–7)

What were the previous misdemeanours that Justinian had heard of? Agathias repeats a report Procopius provides at *Wars* 8.13.11–14: in 551, when the Sassanians took eastern Lazica and Suania, Bessas was accused of failing to secure the borders of Iberia, instead leaving for Armenia in order to levy money from the cities there. It seems entirely probable that a register of letters between Gubaz and Justinian was also Procopius' source for this complaint against Bessas, and probably Agathias' source too.[34]

2. *Correspondence with Generals in Theatre*

The second subcategory of letters, reports and embassies comprises com-munications between Constantinople and Roman commanders in the field. These are explicitly mentioned several times, and there are a great many further cases where communications not explicitly mentioned are the most probable source of information. Four examples will suffice. The first is from 548. Procopius' description of Dagisthaeus' lackadaisical prosecution of the siege of Petra, already summarised above, clearly owes

---

[33] Lee (1993) 38–40. Noble (1990) on use of registers. Presumably Agathias' account of the delegation of Laz nobles who visited Constantinople in winter 555/56 derives from a similar source: Agath. 3.14.2–4.

[34] A third exchange between the Laz and the emperor is recorded after Gubaz's death, when a deputation of Laz travelled to Constantinople to report Gubaz's murder to the emperor, and to petition him to appoint Gubaz's younger brother Tzath, who was a hostage in Constantinople, king in his place: Agath. 3.14.1–4. This provided Agathias the germ that he grew into a long debate between the Laz, setting forth the arguments of the pro-Roman and pro-Persian factions, won, of course, by the pro-Roman side: Agath. 3.8.4–14.2.

something to Gubaz's complaints. However, Procopius also mentions Dagisthaeus' letters to the emperor:

> For this reason [D's confidence that the city would soon fall] Dagisthaeus sent word to the emperor of what had come to pass, and proposed that prizes of victory should be in readiness for him, indicating what rewards the emperor should bestow upon himself and his brother; for he would capture Petra after no great time. (Procop. *Pers.* 2.29.40).

No doubt this was not the only report Dagisthaeus sent the emperor during the siege. Much of Procopius' information on operations, especially drawn-out siege operations, such as undermining walls, must have been derived from commanders' updates of this sort. Confidence and positive spin were their hallmark. No wonder that a counterweight, as Gubaz's critical reports were, was so valuable—for historian *and* emperor.

One suspects Bessas' voice in Procopius' description of a Sassanian invasion that penetrated as far as Abasgia in 551. The Persian commander in question, Nabades, 'accomplished nothing', Procopius says, immediately contradicting himself (or Bessas) by adding that during this invasion they took hostages from the Abasgian nobility and captured the former Laz queen, a Roman noblewoman, all of whom they took back to Persia (they presumably captured the queen when they seized the main fortress in Apsilia).[35] Justinian likely saw through much of this spin: 'When the Emperor Justinian heard this, he commanded Bessas to send a strong army against them [the Abasgians].'[36]

Commanders were no doubt quick to report victories; and they would send trophies, prisoners, and a percentage of the spoils back to Constantinople. These had to be carefully accounted for. Procopius refers to an exchange between Bessas and Justinian that took place immediately after the fall of Petra in early 551:

> Bessas now straightaway sent all the prisoners to the emperor and razed the circuit-wall of Petra to the ground in order that the enemy might not again make trouble for them. And the emperor praised him particularly for the valour he had displayed [in the assault] and for his wisdom in tearing down the whole wall. (Procop. *Pers.* 8.12.28).

A similar report followed Odonachus and Babas' victory over the Persian army besieging Archaeopolis later the same year:

---

[35] Procop. *Pers.* 8.10. See Colvin (forthcoming) ch. 7.
[36] Procop. *Pers.* 8.9.12.

Four thousand of the barbarians fell there, among whom, as it happened, were three of the commanders, and the Romans captured four of the Persian standards, which they immediately sent to Byzantium for the emperor. (Procop. *Pers.* 8.14.43).

In short, Procopius and Agathias seem to have derived a good deal of their information on the campaigns and battles in Lazica from exchanges such as these between Justinian and his generals.[37] There was an obvious incentive for commanders to play up their successes and play down their failures, but the emperor—and contemporary historians—were aware of this bias.[38]

3. *Other Officers*

The third and last subcategory of letters, embassies and reports between Constantinople and Lazica, mentioned by Procopius and Agathias, illustrates the emperor's efforts to monitor his generals. Agathias twice mentions the presence in Lazica of officials whose duties involved keeping the emperor informed through confidential reports. He also describes Justinian's despatch of a senator to Lazica to investigate King Gubaz's murder. Other hints in the sources support the inference that military disasters prompted inquiries into their circumstances. It is worth quoting in full Agathias' two descriptions of the roles of the aforementioned officers:

> Now Rusticus was a Galatian, and was not there as a general, or a commander, or in any military capacity, but merely as the emperor's purse-bearer. He was not in charge of the revenue resulting from the payment of tribute (that was the province of a different official), but of the payments the emperor made out of his privy purse as reward money for those soldiers who distinguished themselves at the front. Consequently, his influence was immense, and the fact that he had access to confidential reports meant that

---

[37] A similar exchange is in Malalas 18.16: a raid is reported and prompts Justinian's reaction (a letter ordering pursuit). The result of the ensuing encounter is then given. See also Belisarius' letter to Justinian from Rome: Procop. *Pers.* 5.14.1–21. The pattern of letter to Justinian followed by response, which includes mention of reinforcements already despatched, suggests that Procopius had before him a copy of the exchange of letters, presumably from archives, rather than that he wrote the letter on Belisarius' behalf, as Treadgold (2007) 182 believes.

[38] In the interests of simplicity, I have passed over an interesting sub-category, that of letters between commanders within theatre. There are only a couple of definite examples from the Lazican war (such as Procop. *Pers.* 2.29.27, 2.30.35), but there are many possibilities elsewhere in Procopius' works, e.g. Procop. *Goth.* 5.17.1–2 (and note 5.16.7, where captured commanders are sent to Belisarius rather than to the emperor). The assumption is that at least some of these letters between generals were kept, filed and then sent on to Constantinople.

official instructions seemed to carry more weight when they met with his approval. (Agath. 3.2.4–5).

When Martin realised what was happening, he dispatched with all speed to take over the supreme command a man who, though a Cappadocian by birth, had long been honoured with the rank of general. His name was John, but he was also known as Dacnas. He had been sent quite recently by the emperor to Lazica, and his duties were the same as those of Rusticus had been, namely to keep the emperor accurately informed of all that was going on, and to distribute the imperial largesse to those soldiers who distinguished themselves in the field. (Agath. 4.17.2–3).

Did Procopius and Agathias have access to the 'confidential reports' these men sent and received? Unfortunately, the one unambiguous example that Agathias gives of the confidential communications between these men and the emperor does not decide the question. The example provided is far from typical: the despatch, by Rusticus and the General Martin, of Rusticus' brother John to the emperor in Constantinople. The generals intended to persuade the emperor of King Gubaz's treachery by this secret interview. They would then, we are told, be able to 'do away with him'. The emperor, however, was not entirely convinced, and his cautious written response was later presented by Rusticus and John in their defence at their trial for Gubaz's subsequent murder. Agathias quotes their interview in direct speech, adding that the emperor 'expressed much the same view in a letter to the generals.'[39] This might suggest direct access to minutes of the meeting, to this letter, and, therefore, possibly to other confidential correspondence, were it not that the entire story probably derives indirectly from the report of senator Athanasius' investigations into Gubaz's murder and the ensuing trial.

With a case of such political moment—Roman credibility in Lazica depended on its handling and outcome—it is hard to decide what is fact and what may be cover-up. And the problem is further complicated by the way that Agathias has heavily written up the trial, which forms the centrepiece for his history. Because the classicising genre allowed and encouraged practitioners to insert apt speeches and arguments into protagonists' mouths, it is difficult to be sure that Agathias had before him a copy of the confidential letter he describes, and safer to assume that this extremely unusual example of the emperor's direct speech is Agathias' dramatic invention.

---

[39] Agath. 3.3.7.

However, Athanasius' appointment as investigating official by itself implies a report, and Agathias appears to summarise it at *Histories* 4.11.1–2:

> His finding was that there was no evidence of treasonable or seditious activity on the part of Gubaz and that his murder was unjust and absolutely illegal. The refusal to take part in the expedition against Onoguris had been the result not of pro-Persian feelings, but of anger at the conduct of the generals in losing possession of the stronghold [Telephis] through their indolence, complacency and carelessness. After he had come to this conclusion, he decided to refer the matter of Martin's alleged complicity to the emperor. With regard to those who openly admitted to the killing, he gave a written verdict to the effect that they were to be executed forthwith and that the manner of death was to be by beheading. (Agath. 4.11.1–2).

Agathias built this into one of the major set-pieces of his history: the trial scene occupies much of Book 4 while the back story to it is threaded throughout his narrative. It seems quite likely that all this derives from Athanasius' report.[40]

There is some evidence that Agathias and Procopius might have had access to other reports, generated by inquiries into military defeats. That, at least, is one possible inference from the apparent fact that in several places the historian had obtained more than one account of a defeat, and from the extra concern to explain reasons for defeats as opposed to victories. The best-known example of this in fact comes from the two distinct accounts of the Battle of Callinicum given by Procopius and Malalas.[41] However, the detail with which the defeat at Telephis-Ollaria is dissected by Agathias suggests such an inquiry; as does the similar examination of failure at Onoguris; and the murder of Soterichus in Misimia. At the very

---

[40] It is reasonable to assume that Agathias could have accessed the report in full or in summary within the archives. Other details in Agathias' account of the trial, such as the legal paraphernalia, may simply reflect familiarity with law courts and legal procedure, rather than access to detailed transcripts, and the speeches are almost certainly his own rhetorical invention, in accordance with classicising norms. Transcripts may well have been taken, as Agathias' account of the officials present implies, but there is nothing else to indicate that he made use of them: 'Accordingly Athanasius donning the garb of the highest civic magistrates, took his seat on a raised tribunal amid great pomp and splendour. Trained shorthand writers were in attendance upon him and there was the full complement of all the other grander and more impressive officials who are especially well-versed in the niceties of legal procedure. Also present were heralds, and ushers armed with whips. All these people had been selected from the various official bureaux in Constantinople. Those who were charged with that particular duty carried with them iron collars, racks and various other instruments of torture.' (Agath. 4.1.2–3).

[41] Malalas 18.60; compare with Procop. *Pers.* 1.18. See also Greatrex (1998) 194–95, 200–207.

least, it can be said that the account of the Telephis-Ollaria debacle shows traces of both excusing and blaming the commanding generals' actions, suggesting the sources Agathias used presented both points of view.[42] It is notable that Procopius had more than one account, it seems, of a similar disaster, the loss of Petra (and consequently all Lazica, Abasgia and Apsilia) in 541. And it is the need to explain the loss of Uthimereos and Suania-Skymnia that prompts Procopius' more detailed description of the plight the Romans and Laz faced in Lazica in 551.[43]

Citations

These three sources of exchanges between Lazica and Constantinople account for much—maybe nearly all—the information Procopius and Agathias provide at campaign level in Lazica, that is to say the third level in the hierarchy of information we identified above. Furthermore, a significant part of the factual skeleton of their battle accounts (the second level in our hierarchy; category 6 in the analysis above) may derive from these as well: who fought whom where; how well the generals led and with what result; how many were slain and captured; and how much booty was seized.

But general letters and reports are not the obvious source for the distinctive anecdotal element that marks many of their battle accounts (category 1, or the lowest level in the hierarchy). This is the material for which Procopius has been so highly praised, that has been thought to mark him out as a skilful 'reporter'. In fact, however, the same kinds of anecdotes are present in Agathias' accounts of battles—though he often relates them much less successfully. These detailed and self-contained sections of the battle accounts sometimes describe decisive moments in a battle; but not always, so this cannot be the basis upon which such anecdotes are included.[44] They include deeds of single combat between champions carried out between the armies, the rallying of panicked troops, and the bravery of the first man over besieged fortress walls. What they all have

---

[42] Agath. 2.19–22, 3.5.5–3.8, 3.15–17. See Colvin (forthcoming) ch. 8 for more detailed commentary.

[43] Procop. *Pers.* 2.17.11–12 and 2.8.16. See Colvin (forthcoming) chapters 6 and 7. Compare with Procopius' explanation for the loss of the Laz border forts of Skanda and Sarapanis (Skande and Shorapani) *ca.* 528: Procop. *Pers.* 1.12.15–19.

[44] Skilful reporter: Cameron (1985) 151. For example, Theodore and Maxentius' foolhardy sortie against the besieging Persians outside Phasis in 556—Agath. 3.22—though risky, was neither a turning point in the siege nor a potential one.

in common is that they describe the praiseworthy conduct of individuals (usually named) or distinct groups of soldiers in the battle. These are the 'deeds of singular importance' (*ta erga hypermegethe*), and those 'worth re-telling' (*axiaphegeta*), to which Procopius and Agathias refer in their respective introductions.[45]

I have already mentioned Agathias' descriptions of Rusticus and John Dacnas' responsibilities for keeping Justinian informed of the progress of events in Lazica. They were also responsible, he says, for distributing gifts from the Privy Purse to the bravest and best soldiers, those who gained prizes for valour.[46] It is inconceivable that this money would have been dispensed without the keeping of careful financial records; and it is improbable that such accounts would not have been accompanied by a brief, or else extended, description of the heroism that engendered the prize. The sort of heroic anecdotes that typify many of Procopius' and Agathias' battle accounts so exactly match the likely content of these citations that in my opinion they confirm the hypothesis. Procopius also mentions the awarding of military prizes. At *Wars* 7.1, he contrasts the generosity of Belisarius towards his soldiers with the meanness of Alexander the Logothete, who was sent to control expenditure after the general's recall:

> As a commander the love ever felt for him [Belisarius] both by soldiers and peasants was irresistible, seeing that, in his treatment of his soldiers on the one hand, he was surpassed by none in generosity; (for when any had met with misfortune in battle, he used to console them by large presents of money for the wounds they had received, and to those who had distinguished themselves he presented *armillae* and *torques* to wear as prizes, and when a soldier had lost in battle horse or bow or anything else whatsoever, another was straightway provided in its place by Belisarius). (Procop. *Goth.* 7.1.8).

> In the second place, he [Alexander 'Snips' (*Psalidion*) the Logothete][47] disappointed the soldiers by the niggardliness of the reckoning with which he repaid them for their wounds and dangers. Hence ... not one of the soldiers was willing any longer to undergo the dangers of war, and by wilfully refusing to fight, they caused the strength of the enemy to grow continually greater. (Procop. *Goth.* 7.1.33).

These specific instances, and the allusions in the two historians' prefaces, are convincing evidence for the continuation (or, conceivably, the revival) of the Roman military practice of making awards to soldiers for valour. As

---

[45] Procop. *Pers.* 1.1.1 compare with 1.1.6–7, 16; Agath. Praef.20, note also Praef.3.
[46] Agath. 3.2.4–5, 4.17.2–3.
[47] Martindale (1992) 43–44, *qv* Alexander 5.

importantly, they suggest that the records of these awards were available to historians in Constantinople.[48] Finally, as campaign context was *not* important to the main purpose of these citations, we have here an explanation for its comparative absence in Procopius' and Agathias' derived accounts.

Marcellinus Comes' Evidence

There is one further piece of evidence that may relate to the reporting of battles and campaigns to Constantinople. It comes, not from Procopius or Agathias, but from Marcellinus Comes, who wrote a Latin chronicle in Constantinople that concluded around 518 and was later updated to include events down to 534 and then 545. A series of entries reports battles and campaigns in the Balkans in a strikingly regular format:

> Commanding general X, with y thousand men, z number of wagons, set out against opponent P. They engaged in battle at location Q, suffered r thousand casualties; [and lastly Marcellinus' comment]. (Marcell. com 493, 499, 503, 505 and 508).

> The Master of the Illyrian Soldiery, Aristus, with 15,000 armed men and 520 wagons, weighed down with the arms necessary for fighting, set out against the Bulgars who were invading Thrace. They engaged in battle beside the river Tzurta where more than 4,000 of our men were killed, either in flight or in the collapse of the river's bank. There perished the soldiery's Illyrian gallantry with the deaths of counts Nicostratus, Innocent, Tancus and Aquilinus. (Marcell. com 499).

> Sabinianus, the son of Sabinianus Magnus, was appointed Master of the Soldiery and gathered arms against Mundo the Goth. He set out to fight, taking with him 10,000 armed recruits and wagons of arms and provisions. When battle had begun at Horreum Margi and many thousands of his men were lost in this conflict and drowned in the Margus River, and especially as the wagons had been lost at the fort called Nato, Sabinianus fled with a few men. So much of the soldiers' hope was destroyed in this unfortunate war that mortal men could never hope to make it up. (Marcell. com. 505).

---

[48] Prefaces: n.45 above. On Roman military decorations, see Maxfield (1981). Despite Procopius' evidence above, and that of the *torques* worn by the guardsman on the famous S. Vitale mosaics and other Late Roman and Byzantine depictions, she believes the old system of military decorations was replaced with financial rewards from the Severan period. She apparently was not familiar with Agathias' evidence, nor with the clear evidence of Theophylact Simocatta, e.g. Theoph. Sim. 2.6.10–12 (presentation of spoils as rewards for wounds and valour), 18.15–25 (first to mount the ramparts in assault on besieged town).

We are a long way from Lazica, but the details given are remarkably similar to those I have categorised above as the 'basic facts' about a battle (category 6 above, or level two in the hierarchy). These are what remains if one strips Procopius' and Agathias' accounts of those sections that might well be each author's own non-source-based additions, and also removes the heroic anecdotes. Add a couple of citation reports and we would have a battle description remarkably similar to any of Procopius' or Agathias'. This may be chance—after all, basic facts are, well, basic, and are likely to be included by any author describing a battle—but the regular format may well be the result of Marcellinus' use of a standardised report, which might in that case have been available to Procopius and Agathias too.

CONCLUSION

The above account lays out the argument that archived documents provided the key sources both Procopius and Agathias used to construct their military narratives for Lazica. Several classes of documents that conveyed information and orders between theatre and Constantinople are clearly attested, and one may infer that letters and reports to the emperor from the Laz king and Roman generals were kept, next to the imperial responses to them, in registers. The preservation of citations may also be inferred from the form of the heroic anecdotes that both historians supply and the fact that those making prize payments out of the Privy Purse would have been obliged to return accounts. Procopius' and Agathias' reliance on these documents better explains the wide variability observed in the quality and quantity of the different categories of information these historians relate than hypothesised oral sources do. The role accorded individuals (i.e. these oral sources) must therefore be greatly reduced—certainly for the Lazican wars.

While the above argument has centred chiefly on Lazica, it is *prima facie* improbable that these historians would have ignored similar bodies of material available for their accounts of wars in other theatres. For example, Procopius was present during Belisarius' early years in Italy to 540, and it is usually assumed that autopsy and oral sources were his primary sources, possibly supplemented by military documents to which his position as Belisarius' secretary gave him special access. Yet, although the account of the Italian war to 540 is punctuated by a relatively fuller complement of speeches and excurses than the Lazican campaign, much of the military narrative itself, the 'embedded' source information identified

above, is not qualitatively different. The campaigns—the context for the
sieges and battles that punctuate it—are described quite briefly; topography is often no better than vague.[49] In addition to these shared characteristics, there are many clear examples of the types of official documentation
identified. And the narrative appears to be constructed around them in a
broadly similar way.[50] For this reason I believe that Procopius structured
his account of the Gothic war, not by reference to a hypothetical journal,
but by reference to letters and reports that were readily available to him
in the archives and many of which he mentions in his text, exactly as he
did for the Laz war.

This is not to claim that Procopius does not make use of his own eye-
witness evidence. Not only are there a few clear instances of him drawing
directly on his own first-hand experience of events, but elsewhere, there
are distinctive touches unlikely to derive from documents.[51] Furthermore,
during the Gothic wars to 540, he seems better acquainted with Belisarius'
motives for his actions than he does for those of the Roman commanders
in Lazica. Even where he was not present, as in Lazica, he manages to
write up (i.e. expand) his documentary sources into engaging literary history, inferring things like commanders' motives—no doubt accurately in
many cases. His experience of military life helped him use the information
available well, much as it helped him write convincing generalised battle
descriptions. Agathias, by contrast, struggles at times to portray military
events convincingly and frequently misunderstands or misrepresents the

---

[49] E.g. the capture of Sicily and Belisarius' advance via Naples to Rome: Procop. *Goth.*
5.5–14. The military narrative is exceptionally brief, bulked out with speeches, omens and
background history. See Kouroumali (2006) v–vi and ch. 6 on the deficiencies of Procopius'
discussion of the Italian landscape and topography. The passage on the siege of Rome,
Procop. *Goth.* 5.17–6.10, is atypically lengthy and needs detailed treatment elsewhere.

[50] There are numerous examples of exchanges of letters: diplomatic exchanges—e.g.
Procop. *Pers.* 5.2.23, 5.3.5–9, 5.3.12–28, 5.3.29–30, 5.4.15–22, 5.7.23–4; exchanges with military commanders—5.5.1–7, 5.6.27, 5.7.26, 5.8.3, 5.24.1–21; some where the exchanges are
between Belisarius and his sub-commanders or Belisarius and Goths or Italians—5.16.1,
5.16.7, 5.17.1–2; and passages that may derive from citations for bravery or receipt of a
wound—e.g. Procop. *Pers.* 5.18.1–18, 5.27. Procop. *Pers.* 6.2.37 even suggests the availability
of a tally of encounters.

[51] E.g. Procop. *Pers.* 3.12.3, 3.15.35, 4.14.39, 6.4, 6.17.10, 6.23.23–28. At other points eye-
witness accounts may have supplemented official data: sieges of Naples (5.8.43–10.29);
commanders' reports on siege progress and capture of city; citations for Pacurius, Magnus
and Ennes, and the unnamed lead soldier who climbed out of the aqueduct; and Rome,
where many of the types of evidence are mentioned, but with many additional details—
e.g. much of Procop. *Goth.* 5.10.5–12, 5.10.22–23; 5.18.43 (Belisarius, fasting well into the
night, encouraged to take a little bread by his wife and friends).

motivations for actions, despite the fact that he probably used much the same types of source as Procopius.[52]

I submit that even when Procopius was present at events, he depended heavily on archived documents to compose his history. Imperial correspondence and officers' letters or reports that passed to and fro between theatre and Constantinople provided the skeleton and much of the meat of his narrative. He expanded generals' and officials' reports on the occurrence and outcome of battles with dramatic anecdotes which he drew from military citations sent back to Constantinople with the financial accounts of prize money awarded from the Privy Purse, and filling this material out with speeches, omens and excursuses, and generic descriptions of fighting. The whole provided material for authorial commentary.[53] Agathias constructed his military accounts in much the same way—though without the benefit of his own eyewitness experience, and with less talent for expanding his material.

Other historians very likely used comparable materials. For example, it is striking that Michael and Mary Whitby have observed a shortcoming in Theophylact Simocatta's account of the Balkan campaigns in the 590s that is highly reminiscent of the deficiencies observed above in Procopius' and Agathias' campaign level of information: his account, they say, "is inclined to disintegrate into a patchwork of detailed reports of individual incidents deprived of their strategic context".[54] Even a cursory glance through Theophylact's work brings up examples of his use of military citations similar to Procopius' and Agathias'.[55] The documents identified in this paper are visible in other late sources, such as Malalas, the *Chronicon Paschale* and Theophanes.[56] Given the importance of military citations to classicising historians' accounts, it is little wonder that these historians emphasise that their histories are concerned with 'deeds'.[57]

---

[52] See n. 21 above.

[53] One might conjecture that Procopius found archived letters a more convenient and accurate framework than relying on unaided memory. Certainly these attested sources better fit the evidence of the texts than Bury's hypothesis that Procopius drew on his own records starting from 532. This, Bury inferred from the increased scale of Procopius' account from this date: Bury (1958) 420. This increased scale might then be explained by a change in the availability of documentary records from that date. Might the Nika riots have damaged the archives? Or was there a change in administrative practice? A more careful analysis of Procopius' *Persian Wars* may guide us.

[54] Whitby and Whitby (1986) xxiii.

[55] E.g. Theoph. Sim. 2.6.10–12, 18.15–25.

[56] See n. 37; Howard-Johnston (1999) 8–14, 169–88, 438–45, 448–54.

[57] See n. 45 above.

There is, therefore, a good case for re-evaluating the relative importance of documents as opposed to oral sources for late antique historians more generally. A further study looking at the documents used by historians across Late Antiquity would, by providing many more examples, clarify the range of these documents and offer additional clues as to their form and nature. In short, it would enhance our understanding of the processes by which historians produced their narratives and provide a better basis for evaluating their evidence.

ACKNOWLEDGEMENTS

I should like to thank Geoffrey Greatrex, Jeremy Colvin and Lavonne Leong for their helpful comments on an early draft of this paper, James Howard-Johnston for his help and encouragement, and Maria Kouroumali for sending me a copy of her D.Phil. dissertation and Neil Christie for his improving edits. The opinions and remaining errors are, of course, the responsibility of the author.

BIBLIOGRAPHY

Primary Sources

Agath. = Keydell R. (1967) ed. *Agathiae Myrinae Historiarum Libri Quinque* (Berlin 1967); Frendo J. D. (1975) trans. Agathias, *The Histories* (Berlin and New York 1975).

Chron. Pasch. = Whitby M. and Whitby M. (1989) trans., intro. and notes. *Chronicon Paschale 284–628 AD: Translated with an Introduction and Notes* (Liverpool 1989).

Malalas = Jeffreys E., Jeffreys M. and Scott R. (1986) edd. *The Chronicle of John Malalas* (Melbourne 1986).

Marcell. com. = Croke B. (1995) trans. *The Chronicle of Marcellinus: a Translation and Commentary (with a Reproduction of Mommsen's edition of the Text)* (Sydney 1995).

Menander = Blockley R. C. (1985) trans. *The History of Menander the Guardsman: Introductory Essay, Text, Translation and Historiographical Notes* (Liverpool 1985).

Priscus = Blockley R. C. (1983) *The Fragmentary Classicising Historians of the Later Roman Empire. Eunapius, Olympiodorus, Priscus and Malchus 2. Text, Translation and Historiographical Notes* (Cambridge 1983).

Procop. *Goth.* and Procop. *Pers.* = Dewing H. B. (1914–54) ed. and trans. Procopius, *History of the Wars 1–5* (Cambridge, Mass. and London 1914–54).

Theophanes = Mango C. and Scott R. (1997) edd. *The Chronicle of Theophanes Confessor: Byzantine and Near Eastern History A.D. 284–813* (Oxford 1997).

Theoph. Sim. = Whitby M. and Whitby M. (1986) trans., intro. and notes. *The History of Theophylact Simocatta: an English Translation with Introduction and Notes* (Oxford 1986).

Secondary Works

Baldwin B. (1978) "Menander Protector", *DOP* 32 (1978) 101–25.

Blockley R. C. (1985) *The History of Menander the Guardsman: Introductory Essay, Text, Translation and Historiographical Notes* (Liverpool 1985).

Bury J. B. (1958) *History of the Later Roman Empire: from the Death of Theodosius I to the Death of Justinian*, vol. 2 (New York 1958).

Braund D. (1994) *Georgia in Antiquity* (Oxford 1994).

Bryer A. and Winfield D. (1985) *The Byzantine Monuments and Topography of the Pontus*, 2 vols. (Washington D.C. 1985).

Cameron A. (1970) *Agathias* (Oxford 1970).

—— (1985) *Procopius and the Sixth Century* (London 1985).

Cesa M. (1993) "Agatia Scolastico lettore di Procopio", *Studi B. Gentili:* III (Rome 1993) 1171–80.

Colvin I. (forthcoming) *Justinian's Wars in the Caucasus: Procopius and Agathias on Roman and Sassanian Rivalry in Lazica 518–565 AD* (forthcoming D.Phil. diss., Univ. of Oxford).

Croke B. (2001) *Count Marcellinus and his Chronicle* (Oxford 2001).

Dahn F. (1865) *Prokopios von Cäsarea* (Berlin 1865).

Greatrex G. (1998) *Rome and Persia at War, 502–532* (Leeds 1998).

Howard-Johnston J. (1999) "Heraclius' Persian campaigns and the revival of the East Roman Empire, 622–630", *War in History* 6 (1999) 1–44.

Ites M. (1926) "Zur Bewertung des Agathias", *ByzZeit.* 26 (1926) 273–85.

Jeffreys E., Croke B. and Scott R. (1990) edd. *Studies in John Malalas* (Byzantina Australiensia 6) (Sydney 1990).

Jeffreys E., Jeffreys M. and Scott R. (1986) *The Chronicle of John Malalas* (Melbourne 1986).

Kaldellis A. (2004) *Procopius of Caesarea: Tyranny, History, and Philosophy at the End of Antiquity* (Philadelphia 2004).

Kelly C. M. (1997) "Later Roman bureaucracy: going through the files", in *Literacy and Power in the Ancient World*, edd. A. K. Bowman and G. Woolf (Cambridge 1997) 161–76.

—— (2004) *Ruling the Later Roman Empire* (Cambridge, Mass. 2004).

Kouroumali M. (2006) *Procopius and the Gothic War* (D.Phil. diss., Univ. of Oxford 2006).

Lee A. D. (1993) *Information and Frontiers: Roman Foreign Relations in Late Antiquity* (Cambridge 1993).

Martindale J. R. (1992) ed. *The Prosopography of the Later Roman Empire* 3 (Cambridge 1992).

Maxfield V. (1981) *The Military Decorations of the Roman Army* (London 1981).

Noble T. F. X. (1990) "Literacy and the papal government in Late Antiquity and the Early Middle Ages", in *The Uses of Literacy in Early Medieval Europe*, ed. R. McKitterick (Cambridge 1990) 82–108.

Roueché C. (2000) ed. De Aedificiis: *le texte de Procope et les réalités (Antiquité Tardive* 8) (Turnhout 2000).

Schubert H. von (1884) *Die Unterwerfung der Alemannen unter die Franken* (Ph.D. diss., Univ. of Strasbourg 1884).

Stein E. (1949) *Histoire du Bas-Empire: de la disparition de l'Empire d'Occident à la mort de Justinien (476–565)* vol. 2 (Paris, Brussels and Amsterdam 1949).

Tougher S. (1997) Review of Cameron A., *Procopius and the Sixth Century* in *Histos* 1 (1997) accessed at: http://www.dur.ac.uk/Classics/histos/1997/tougher.html.

Treadgold W. T. (1995) *Byzantium and its Army 284–1081* (Stanford 1995).

—— (2007) *The Early Byzantine Historians* (New York 2007).

Vasiliev A. A. (1952) *History of the Byzantine Empire* vol. 2 (Madison 1952).

Whitby M. and Whitby M. (1986) *The History of Theophylact Simocatta: an English Translation with Introduction and Notes* (Oxford 1986).

PROCOPIUS ON THE STRUGGLE FOR DARA IN 530
AND ROME IN 537–38: RECONCILING TEXTS AND LANDSCAPES

Christopher Lillington-Martin

Abstract

This paper examines Procopius' descriptions of Roman and Persian strategies to control Dara in 530 and Roman and Gothic strategies to control Rome in 537–38 by reconciling texts with the landscapes of the areas concerned, drawing on satellite imagery, cartography and field visits. The traditional approach to this history has been to use written sources only, but, as will be shown, these are subject to multiple interpretations. Study of the landscape provides a different, complementary perspective, which is in some ways more reliable, as the physical features have not changed too significantly over the centuries, and modern technology has opened up new ways of reading them. These two case studies strongly suggest that Procopius is reliable when he is interpreted carefully, and this has implications for studies of the many other events for which he is the main source.

INTRODUCTION

This paper re-interprets Procopius' descriptions of opposing Roman, Persian and Gothic strategies to control Dara in A.D. 530 and Rome in 537–38, especially those relating to the location of temporary army camp sites and the identification of river bridges.[1] This is achieved by reconciling texts with the landscapes of the areas concerned, drawing on satellite imagery, cartography and field visits. The traditional approach to the history of this era, which has been studied by historians such as Bury, Dewing, Evans, Greatrex and Lieu, Kaldellis, Kouroumali and Whitby, has been to use textual sources only, but, as will be shown, these are subject to multiple interpretations. Study of the landscape provides a different, complementary perspective which is in some ways more reliable, as the physical features have not changed too significantly over the centuries, and mod-

---

[1] Procopius of Ceasarea was an adviser to Justinian's general Belisarius, *ca.* 505–65. He was an eye-witness to many of the events discussed, and seems to have had access to reliable official written documentation (but see now Colvin, in this volume).

A. Sarantis, N. Christie (edd.) *War and Warfare in Late Antiquity: Current Perspectives*
(Late Antique Archaeology 8.1–8.2 – 2010–11) (Leiden 2013), pp. 599–630

ern technology has opened up new possibilities of reading them. Bringing the two approaches together, therefore, provides a powerful tool for
the study of the past. Thus, by reconsidering Procopius' account in conjunction with visits to the landscapes he describes near Dara and Rome,
it will be shown that we can gain additional insights, which help us to
re-interpret military strategy and events.

It seems particularly appropriate to analyse landscapes and reconcile them with the literary description provided by Procopius as, with
Homer in mind, he himself offers reconciliation between landscape and
literature:

> Tarracina; and very near that place is Mt. Circaeum, where they say Odys-
> seus met Circe, though the story seems to me untrustworthy, for Homer
> declares that the habitation of Circe was on an island.[2] I am able to say…
> Mt. Circaeum, extending…far into the sea…has every appearance of
> being an island…for this reason, Homer perhaps called the place an island.
> (Procop. *Goth.* 5.11.2).

So, we will reconsider the strategies which culminated in three engagements: one in 530 on a site 20–24 km west-north-west of Nisibis (modern
Nusaybin, Turkey), just west of the 6th c. Roman-Persian frontier in northern Mesopotamia (near Dara, modern Oğuz, Mardin, Turkey); and two in
537–38, between the River Anio and the Aurelian Walls at Rome. Military
fortifications were related to all three engagements. Belisarius used them
as bases from which to direct field armies as part of his campaign strategy.
New interpretations will be presented which are entirely compatible with
Procopius' account, which it will be suggested has been misinterpreted by
previous Anglophone historians. We will first consider how this straightforward approach has been used to argue for a more precise location of
the battlefield of Dara, 530, with a consequent re-interpretation of camp
locations. Then we will consider the identification of an anonymous bridge
which has important implications for our understanding of the Gothic
army's strategy regarding Rome, 537–38, led by King Wittigis.

---

[2] Hom. *Od.* 10.135: 'we came to the island of Aeaea, the home of the beautiful Circe'.

The Background to the Roman-Persian Struggle for Dara in 530

The border fortress of Dara was constructed on the orders of the emperor Anastasius in ca. 505. Procopius described the location and founding of Dara thus:

> The Emperor Anastasius, after concluding the treaty with Kavad, built a city in a place called Dara, exceedingly strong and of real importance, bearing the name of the emperor himself. Now this place is distant from the city of Nisibis 100 stades lacking two, and from the boundary line which divides the Romans from the Persians about 28. (Procop. *Pers.* 1.10.14).

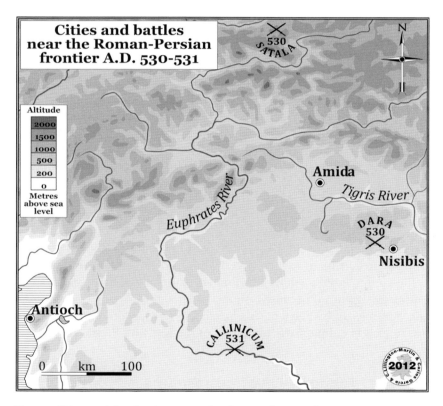

Fig. 1   Cities and battle sites near the Roman-Persian frontier, A.D. 530–531. (prepared with Carlos García).

Dara was planned as a forward post to launch potential Roman attacks eastwards towards Nisibis and to deter, or delay, potential Persian attacks north-westwards towards Diyarbakir (ancient Amida), and westwards towards Antakya (ancient Antioch). The existence of this fortress so close to the border provoked diplomatic crises and intermittent warfare, and full-scale Persian invasions in 530, 540, 544 and 573. The battlefield and settlements of Dara, Ambar (2.4 km south), Amuda in north-east Syria (ancient Ammodios), and Nisibis, are set amongst field systems and divided by the modern Turkish-Syrian border. There are sightlines from the hilltop of Ambar to Dara, Ammodios and Nisibis, but not between Nisibis and Dara because of the low hills to the south-east of Dara. There is a 2–3 km geographical gap between Ambar and the low hills.

The Battle of Dara, fought in the early summer of 530, was important because the Romans won it decisively, and it confirmed the importance of the fortress as well as the relative security of that part of the frontier (fig. 1). Another victory at Satala (Sadak, Gümüşhane, Turkey), achieved by Sittas later that summer, led to Roman advantages in Armenia. Following these setbacks, in 531, the Persians sought an alternative route of attack, ending in a Persian tactical, if not strategic, victory at the Battle of Callinicum (Ar Raqqah, Syria), and further Armenian campaigns.[3] These campaigns, combined with the death of the Persian King Kavad in 531, contributed to conditions for an 'Endless Peace' treaty in 532, between the Roman Emperor Justinian and the new Persian King Khusro I. This allowed for the redeployment of Roman troops and resources, to be led initially by Belisarius, for the conquest of Vandal Africa in 533–34, the first stage of the partial re-conquest of the West by Justinian's forces. So, along with its precursors in 527–29 (see below), and the battles of Satala and Callinicum referred to above, the Roman victory at the Battle of Dara was especially significant because Justinian ordered the assembly of one of the largest armies of his reign at this frontier to force a confrontation which was to lead to a diplomatic resolution of the war with Persia.

LOCATING THE BATTLEFIELD OF DARA, A.D. 530

The accurate identification of any battle site as precisely as evidence permits is significant for military history, potential battlefield archaeology and

---

[3] Greatrex and Lieu (2002) 91–96.

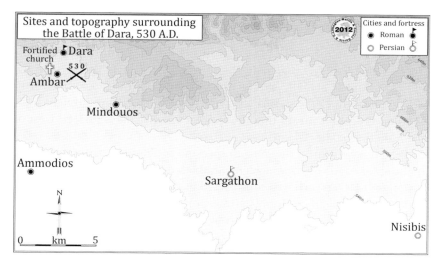

Fig. 2   Sites and topography surrounding the Battle of Dara, A.D. 530.
(prepared with Carlos García).

the interpretation of ancient sources. Here we will argue that the Battle of Dara occurred approximately 2–3 km south of Dara, east of Ambar (fig. 2), rather than immediately outside its walls, as proposed by Bury, Evans, Greatrex, Haldon and Whitby.[4] The line of reasoning by which this location has been determined takes into account Procopius' description of the topography and his record of various distances to describe sites, including the position of this battle site. These distances can be used alongside Procop. *Pers.* 1.10.14 cited above, and other internal evidence, to tentatively convert the distances Procopius provides into kilometres and to better locate the battlefield within the landscape.

However, we should bear in mind that such calculations may not be as precise as we would like. One of his measurements of distance is at Procop. *Vand.* 3.17.17, where Procopius refers 'to Decimum, 70 stades distant from Carthage'. This suggests, considering that ad Decimum was Latin for '10 mile post' (15 km), that for Procopius, one mile equated to 7 stades.[5] Classical authors such as Pliny and Strabo equated one Roman mile to 8 stades.[6] Therefore, if we divide 28 stades by 7, Procopius would locate

---

[4] Bury (1923) 82–83; Evans (2000) 117; Greatrex (1998) 172; Haldon (2001) 23–35; Lillington-Martin (2007) 302; Whitby (1986) 758–59.

[5] www.unitconversion.org.

[6] Feissel (2002) 383.

Dara 4 Roman miles (6 km) from the boundary with Persia, and by dividing 98 by seven, we can see Procopius placed it 14 Roman miles (or 21 km) from Nisibis. So Procopius' stades measure *ca.* 211 m. Turning now to modern measurement technology in the form of the Google Earth ruler, we find that Dara is actually 27 km from Nisibis, via the geographical gap mentioned above. This anomaly may be a coincidence, but it might indicate that Procopius meant that the frontier was 98 stades (21 km) west of Nisibis and 28 stades (6 km) east of Dara.

We can now turn to the Persian invasion of Roman territory with the intention of capturing Dara which culminated in the battle of 530. Procopius states that a trench was constructed by the Romans as a field defence across the battlefield near a πύλη (interpreted here as a geographical 'gap' rather than Dewing's 'gate'), to disrupt the Persian attack:

> [S]uddenly, however, someone reported to Belisarius and Hermogenes that the Persians were expected to invade the land of the Romans, being eager to capture the city of Dara. And when they heard this, they prepared for the battle as follows. Not far from the gap (πύλης) which lies opposite the city of Nisibis, about a stone's throw away, they dug a deep trench with many passages across it. Now this trench was not dug in a straight line, but in the following manner. In the middle, there was a rather short portion straight, and at either end of this, there were dug two cross trenches at right angles to the first; and starting from the extremities of the two cross trenches, they continued two straight trenches in the original direction to a very great distance. Not long afterwards, the Persians came with a great army, and all of them made camp in a place called Ammodios, at a distance of 20 stades from the city of Dara. (Procop. *Pers.* 1.13.12–14).

The translation of πύλη as 'gate' by Dewing seems to have contributed to several scholars locating the trench-line and battle within a few metres of the fortress walls. Whitby proposed that the rock-cut moat may have been part of the field fortification constructed prior to the battle, and Greatrex suggested the trenches "used in the battle may subsequently have been integrated into the defences of the city", or that "Belisarius may have adapted the trenches already under construction"; both scholars implied that the fortifications of Dara were not complete after 25 years of building, which seems unlikely to have been the case.[7] Dara's defences probably would have been finished before 530, given the attempts at building an outlying fort in 528. Belisarius is likely to have ensured that Dara was

---

[7] Dewing (1914–40) 105; Greatrex (1998) 171 and n.10 and 172; Haldon (2001); Mitchell (2007) 134; and Whitby (1986) 761.

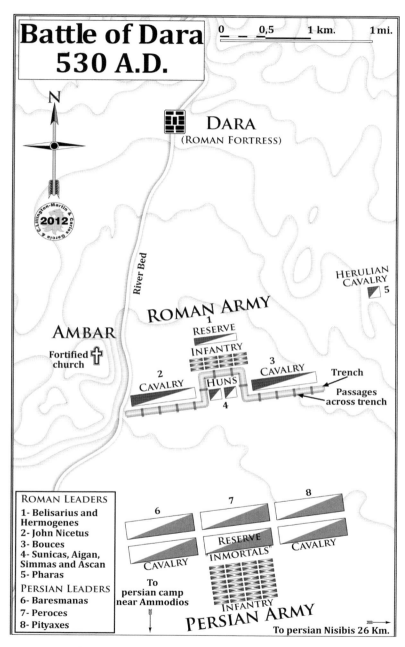

Fig. 3   The Battle of Dara: Roman and Persian army deployments.
(prepared with Carlos García).

completed before risking the movement of the workforce elsewhere.[8] Such a fort-building workforce was destroyed at Mindouos in 528 (fig. 2).[9]

Considering the space required for the deployment of the 25,000-strong Roman army, including cavalry, and analysing the landscape, it seems more likely that the trenches were constructed at a greater distance from the fortification wall. This would correlate the testimony of John Malalas (*ca.* 490–575), who states that the Roman army was encamped outside Dara.[10] Furthermore, by interpreting πύλη as gap (rather than 'gate'), we can convincingly reconcile text and landscape because there is a geographical gap 'opposite the city of Nisibis', whereas there is no gate in the eastern wall of Dara facing Nisibis.[11] Procopius may even have used πύλη to evoke the Battle of Thermopylae, 480 B.C.,[12] in his readers' minds, where a huge Persian army attacked another Greek-speaking one which was defending field fortifications in a geographical gap. Regarding distances, Procopius uses the term 'stone's throw' (οσον λίθου βολὴν) at *Pers.* 1.13.13, and during the siege of Rome, at *Goth.* 5.22.13, where the distance concerned was approximately 85 m.[13] This suggests a trench located very near the gap 2.4 km south of Dara.

At the Battle of Dara, Procopius relates Roman deployment and all tactical manoeuvres to the trench-line and a low hill on the eastern side of the plain (fig. 3). According to Procopius, the Persians were out-manoeuvred by Belisarius' tactics, including an ambush (by the Herulians) from behind low hills and internal flank attacks from the centre (made possible by the trench-line being designed with many crossing points). These attacks were executed by well-positioned and well-led cavalry units, including Hunnic mercenaries and Belisarius' reserve. The Roman victory depended on a number of factors, such as the design of, and intelligent army deployment along, the trench-line. Therefore, the most likely position of the Roman battle line is approximately 2–3 km south of Dara and 4–6 km north of Ammodios, in, or very near, the geographical gap, which is 2–3 km wide between Ambar and the low hills to the east. This is where local farmers informed me that they find arrowheads in the fields, which they leave *in situ*. One farmer drew a sketch of an arrowhead, but I did not see any.

---

8 Compare with Greatrex and Lieu (2002) 89.
9 Procop. *Pers.* 1.13.1–8.
10 Malalas 18.50.
11 Lillington-Martin (2007) 301–303.
12 Hdt. 7.138–239.
13 Lillington-Martin (2007) 302.

The gap at Ambar was ideal for the Roman army of 25,000 men to prevent access to Dara by the invading Persian army of 50,000, as the restricted space within the landscape neutralised the difference in numbers by preventing a Persian envelopment of the Roman army wings (although the Persians were able to double their lines and rotate troops to manage fatigue). The study of this battle improves our understanding of Roman military planning by providing details of deployment, and furthers our understanding of battle descriptions within historical sources. In addition to Procopius perhaps alluding to the Battle of Thermopylae, he may have intended his readers to recall the Battles of Salamis, 479 B.C.,[14] where a large Persian fleet advanced into narrow straits and was ambushed and defeated by a smaller force, or Marathon, 490 B.C.,[15] where a smaller Greek army initially defended a position before attacking and routing a larger Persian army. Procopius' Dara battle description brings to mind all three of Herodotus' famous battle descriptions.[16] So, by combining the literary evidence provided by Procopius with satellite imagery and field visit experience, it is possible to gain a better understanding of the battle of June/July 530.[17]

LOCATING THE PERSIAN AND ROMAN CAMP SITES, A.D. 530

In this section, we will analyse Procopius' text, and consider measurements of distances and relative positions of temporary field fortifications linked to Dara and Ammodios, *ca.* 8 km to the south, to re-evaluate Roman and Persian campaign strategies. Satellite imagery and evidence from field visits will be discussed, with particular reference to topographic features relating to the Battle of Dara. The relationship between textual and material evidence can be problematic, especially when there are few literary accounts to contrast with that of Procopius, whose evidence we are using in a relatively literal way.

Procopius explains that the '... Romans ... dug a deep trench .... [the] Persians ... made camp in ... Ammodios, at a distance of twenty stades ...'.[18] The location of the Persian camp in Ammodios can be calculated

---

[14] Hdt. 8.40–96.
[15] Hdt. 7.207–229.
[16] Procop. *Pers.* 1.13.9–14.
[17] Lillington-Martin (2007) 310.
[18] Procop. *Pers.* 1.13.12–14.

in a similar way to calculation of the distance between Dara and Nisibis in the previous section. Twenty stades would equate to 2.85 Roman miles (4.2 km). Whereas the distance from Dara to Ammodios was calculated as 7.7 km by Dillemann in 1962,[19] my research using the Google Earth ruler suggests that Ammodios is little more than 4.2 km (20 stades) from the geographical gap discussed above, which might indicate that Procopius meant that the Persian camp was 20 stades south of the Roman trench and battle-line, which would be consistent with the quote cited above. The discrepancy in the distances of 20 stades (4.2 km) and 7.7 km has attracted attempts at reconciliation, including Whitby's idea that Procopius' stades need to be doubled to allow for the difference, which is unnecessary.[20] Another, unexplained, hypothesis by Evans reads: "A battle was fought at Dara three and a half kilometres from the fortress".[21] Perhaps, in this latter case, Procopius' 20 stades were similarly calculated as 4.2 km then deducted from Dillemann's 7.7 km, resulting in a 3.5 km difference, and thereby placing the Persian camp at Ammodios 4.2 km away from a battlefield 3.5 km south of Dara. However, this idea was not explained and then withdrawn completely from Evans' second edition of *The Age of Justinian* (published in 2000). To overcome this problem without seeking solutions in the geography of the region, we might conclude that Procopius' knowledge of distances is inaccurate, unreliable or, perhaps, rhetorical.

Alternatively, we can consider the possibility that Procopius has been misinterpreted by modern scholars and re-examine the landscape in light of this. '[A]place called Ammodios' is likely to refer to the nearest named area to the Persian camp, where there was a good water supply. Furthermore, it would have been fundamentally sound military strategy for the Persians to camp at least part of their 50,000-strong army on the north side of Ammodios, to control the east-west road, as well as to separate this Roman outpost from Dara. Such an army would have occupied an extensive area: at 2 m² per man, 50,000 men would occupy 10 ha just by lying upon the ground. Hunter-gatherer campsites have been calculated as occupying between 5.9 and 10.2 m² per person.[22] The Persian army had myriads of horses to cater for, so its camp at Ammodios is likely to have extended across many hectares. This interpretation could situate the

[19] Greatrex (1998) 170–71, n. 9.
[20] Whitby and Whitby (1986) 136 n. 17.
[21] Evans (1996) 117.
[22] Hassan (1981) 67 citing Wiessner (1974).

Persian camp straddling an area up to a few hundred metres north of the current Turkish-Syrian border (perhaps to within 20 stades of Dara). The fact that Ammodios is little more than 20 stades and 'a stone's throw' from the geographical gap area, with its Roman trenches and battle-line, suggests that Procopius' measurement may refer, in fact, to the distance between the Roman trenches and Persian camp defences. Whichever way we view these possibilities, Procopius' numerical distances should, therefore, be considered generally accurate and reliable.

As noted above, the Roman army was encamped, according to Malalas, outside Dara, although part of it may have been partially accommodated within the fortress.[23] However, Dara could not have accommodated 25,000 Roman soldiers and their horses because, whether the defences had been completed or not, it was too small.[24] The wall is only about 2.7 km in circumference.[25] The plans of Dara's walls may not be entirely accurate, as the discovery of a possible Anastasian mosaic on the floor of a structure outside the proposed circuit may indicate that the circuit wall of Dara was slightly larger than previously thought, if the structure had been enclosed by it.[26] However, this would not significantly change the fact that "The internal area is fairly small ... and the area suitable for habitation limited by the steep, rocky ground".[27] The main Roman camp outside the city walls would have needed several hectares for the same reasons as the Persian camp at Ammodios. In any case, deploying a large army in a relatively small fortress would not have been a sensible strategy given the potential problems with supply were the fortress to come under attack before the army were deployed in the field (Procopius delivers a set piece description of the opposite, more sensible, strategy of 537–38, when Belisarius garrisoned Rome, a large fortified city, with a small army (see below)).

---

[23] Malalas 18.50.

[24] Millett (1990) 182–183, citing Hassan (1981) 66–67 on urban population estimates at between 137 and 216 people per ha.

[25] Ahunbay (1991); Croke and Crow (1983); Greatrex (1998); Haldon (2001); Sinclair (1987–90); Whitby (1986); and Zanini (1990).

[26] The discovery at Dara, by Professor Metin Ahunbay, of a 2.5 × 3.5 m floor mosaic, with a 1 × 1 m Greek, possibly Anastasian, inscription (at 37°10'37.12"N, 40°56'53.13"E, approximately 100 m west of the probable circuit wall), was announced via www.mardin .gov on 22 October 2007. ΤΟΠΟΤΗ at the end of line three of the mosaic inscription suggests τοποτηρητὴς, which has been associated with a military rank, appointed by a *dux*, associated with building projects (*SEG* 14, no.1931, page 563) and someone concerned with the building and restoration of a hostel (*SEG* 15, no. 1505, page 511).

[27] Croke and Crow (1983) 150.

Indeed, the fact that only a fraction of the Roman army could have fitted into the fortress supports the view that the Roman force was never intended as a garrison. This suggests an offensive Roman strategy at the outset of the campaign, something which would not have been lost on the Persians. Indeed, Malalas informs us that the Persians invaded when they heard that the Roman army was at Dara.[28] It is likely that the Romans had intended to invade Persian territory, but were surprised by the fact that the Persians had already gathered an even larger army in the same area, which is a credit to Persian strategic organisation. Procopius tells us that the Romans' trench-line preparation only began when: 'someone reported to Belisarius and Hermogenes that the Persians were expected to invade the land of the Romans'.[29]

The Roman political and military strategy is likely to have been to attack Nisibis, or perhaps to oblige the Persians to negotiate. As it transpired, the Persians' intelligence allowed them to pre-empt the Romans, resulting in their strategic decision to invade Roman territory, even though their tactical assault towards Dara was unsuccessful. Had the Persian commanders heavily fortified the Ammodios area they might, with patience, have blockaded the Roman army of 25,000 at Dara, compelling it to abandon its defensive field tactics or negotiate. They certainly lingered in the area to negotiate even after losing the battle, as Procopius records: 'the Persians, though defeated by Belisarius in the Battle at Dara, refused even so to retire from there'.[30] By placing this comment immediately after Pers. 1.15 (which narrates Roman success at repelling another Persian invasion, this time further north, at the Battle of Satala, weeks after that of Dara and Roman advantages gained in Armenia), and just before Kavad's supposed diplomatic speech to Rufinus,[31] Procopius may well have been implying that the defeated Persian army, which remained deployed in the area between Nisibis and Dara to pin-down Roman forces there, continued to be a serious force to be reckoned with for several months. Therefore, Persian strategy was an offensive one, and as part of it, Kavad had assembled two large armies: to attack the Romans in both northern Mesopotamia and Armenia.

To conclude this section, it seems highly likely that the Roman trenches, serving the dual purpose of protecting the troops encamped outside Dara

---

[28] Malalas 18.50.
[29] Procop. *Pers.* 1.13.12.
[30] Procop. *Pers.* 1.16.1.
[31] Procop. *Pers.* 1.16.7.

and dictating the tactical course of the battle, lay approximately 2–3 km south of Dara, while that the northern edge of the Persian camp was about 1–2 km from Ammodios. This leaves a distance of 20 stades between them and confirms the accuracy of Procopius' account, which will have been written up from official records, notes and/or eye-witness testimony several years later. This accuracy is important when interpreting his descriptions of other sites, conflicts and events, such as those in Italy.

THE ROMAN-GOTHIC STRUGGLE FOR ROME IN A.D. 537–38

Having argued for Procopius' accuracy in recording distances regarding relative army positions and camps near Dara in 530, this section will now compare his text with the landscape to appreciate the probable routes taken by the Gothic army from Ravenna to Rome in 537, and its route of retreat in 538.

These movements led to the first and last Roman-Gothic encounters at Rome, 537–38, which were fought near an anonymous river bridge.[32] The identification of this bridge has strategic implications regarding the route of the Goths' march, and, therefore, the strategies employed by both Romans and Goths. Wittigis, the king of the Goths and Italians (A.D. 536–40), approached Rome in 537 via an anonymous river bridge in order to lay siege to the Roman army under Belisarius. There has been considerable disagreement amongst scholars about the identification of this bridge, but this paper maintains that Procopius' account needs to be more carefully interpreted. It will compare his description of the initial stages, and final lifting, of the siege of Rome, with topographic evidence obtained by means of satellite imagery, field-visits and cartographic materials.[33] The results challenge conventional interpretations made by 19th and 20th c. Anglophone scholars, such as Mahon, Hodgkin and Dewing, who, following Gibbon, have suggested that the anonymous bridge was the Milvian crossing of the Tiber.[34] Their interpretation has been repeated by 21st c. scholars, such as Kaldellis and Kouroumali.[35] My results instead support Gregorovius' suggestion that this bridge was in fact the Salarian, which

---

[32] Procop. *Goth.* 5.17–18 and 6.10.
[33] *Carta Topografica dei Dintorni di Roma* and Google Earth.
[34] Mahon (1848) 193–94; Hodgkin (1896) 118–20, 194 and 250; and Dewing (1914–40) 169.
[35] Kaldellis (2004) 33; Kouroumali (2006) 187.

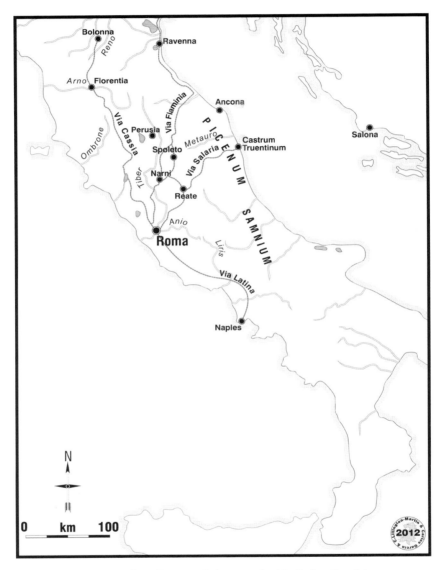

Fig. 4   Italy, A.D. 537–38. (prepared with Carlos García).

crosses the Anio, and it will be shown that this has implications for how we understand the strategies adopted by the Gothic army.

Procopius was not the only eye-witness account we can draw upon. Another textual source, the *Liber Pontificalis*, comments on some of these events leading to the Siege of Rome in 537–38, which led directly to the deposition of Pope Silverius. Davis notes "an incompetent chronological join between" the two parts of the biography of Silverius, and that the "account of that siege given in the first part suggests that the author had not yet witnessed the two worse sieges Rome was to endure in the next decade".[36] As the next siege occurred in 546, the author of the first part of Silverius' biography was a contemporary or eye-witness to the events and "it was produced no later than the 540s".[37]

Eye-witnesses' texts such as Procopius and *Liber Pontificalis* are obviously of immense value in historical research, and may be expected to provide more accurate information than accounts which have acquired their information second-hand. However, even first-hand narratives are hard to reconcile with the landscape because they omit certain details— in this case, the precise identification of rivers and bridges, the roads between them, and the gates (in the Aurelian Walls) of Rome. This not only leads us to embark upon further research in order to reach a logical reconciliation between topography and text, but raises questions about the objectives and research methods of the primary source. It may be the case that the details of interest to us were un-recorded, forgotten, or intentionally left out for the sake of simplicity (in Procopius' case, this would aid communication to an eastern audience, far from the theatre of military operations, who expected to be entertained with drama and heroism rather than be bored with specific geographic details).

The historical background to our discussion is as follows (fig. 4). In December 536, Belisarius led his army, fresh from sacking Naples, into Rome through the Asinarian Gate. Procopius dates this to the 'ninth day of the last month', while the *Lib. Pontif.* by Silverius assigns it to '10 December'.[38] At the same time, the 4,000-strong Gothic garrison left Rome (leaving behind their commander Leuderis) via the Flaminian Gate, and headed north up the *Via Flaminia*. Belisarius sent Leuderis to Constantinople, but we hear no more of him.[39] The leaderless Gothic army will have crossed the Tiber

---

[36] Davis (2000) xliii.
[37] Davis (2000) xiii and xlvi.
[38] Procop. *Goth.* 5.14.14; *Lib. Pont.* 60.4.
[39] Procop. *Goth.* 5.14.13–15, 24.1.

at the Milvian Bridge.[40] His comment that the Goths had left along the *Via Flaminia* may, in part, have led some scholars to make assumptions about their return route under King Wittigis in February or March 537.

Belisarius began preparations to withstand a siege by strengthening the fortifications of the Aurelian Walls and bringing in provisions.[41] Procopius records that, at this time, a Goth named Pitzas came to Belisarius to surrender 'half of … Samnium, which lies on the sea, as far as the river' (Biferno or Sangro), and was given 'a small number of soldiers to help him guard that territory.[42] In any case, 'the Goths who were settled on the other side of the river were neither willing to follow Pitzas nor to be subjects of the emperor'.[43] These Goths no doubt felt safer from Roman attack since they were settled further north and away from the coast, and there were doubtless links between this area and the important neighbouring Gothic settlement region 'concentrated in Picenum' to the north, as has been shown by Heather.[44] Belisarius was now in control of the southern half of Italy, from Rome, around the coast, to southern Samnium, as well as the Dalmatian coast.[45] In December 536, he sent his generals Constantinus and Bessas north to occupy numerous strategic strongholds in Tuscany: Perusia, Spoletium, Narni 'and certain other towns' (fig. 4).[46]

Wittigis responded by sending an army from Ravenna to Perusia, commanded by Unilas and Pissas, which Constantinus defeated completely. Both Gothic commanders were captured and sent to Belisarius in Rome, although they are not mentioned again.[47] Their capture may have been contrived, and perhaps in light of this and previous surrenders by Gothic commanders (Sinderith surrendered at Syracuse in 535, and Ebrimuth at Reggio di Calabria, Leuderis at Rome and Pitzas followed in 536), no further Gothic army was sent against the Romans until Wittigis led one himself.[48] So Procopius records that by December 536, several Gothic leaders either changed sides, or fell into Roman hands. This suggests a less than loyal attitude towards the Gothic kingship. When Wittigis marched his army southwards to Rome in early 537, he doubtless collected troops

---

[40] Procop. *Goth.* 5.14.14; Bury (1923) 179–80.
[41] Procop. *Goth.* 5.14.15; *Lib. Pont.* 60.4.
[42] Procop. *Goth.* 5.15.1–2; Dewing (1914–40) 148–49, n. 1.
[43] Procop. *Goth.* 5.15.2.
[44] Heather (1996) 238, Figure 8.1.
[45] Procop. *Goth.* 5.7.36.
[46] Procop. *Goth.* 5.16.3.
[47] Procop. *Goth.* 5.16.6.
[48] Jord. *Get.* 60.308–12.

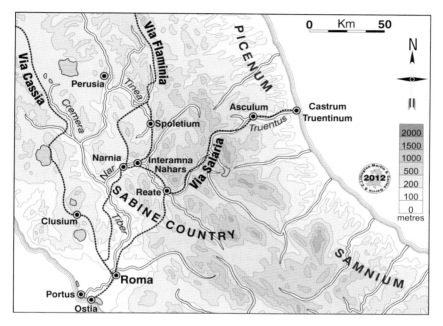

Fig. 5   Spoletium to Rome via Sabine country (Interamna Nahars and Reate) and
Rome to Narni. (prepared with Carlos García).

from his subjects in Picenum along the northern section of the *Via
Flaminia* towards the Apennines, and could have been joined by others
from northern Samnium at Reate, by way of the *Via Salaria, Via Caecilia*
and *Via Claudia Nova* (fig. 5).[49]

When Wittigis marched his army southwards, Belisarius recalled the
cavalry commanded by Constantinus and Bessas from Perusia, Spoletium
and Narni, where they had established control, and posted garrisons to
obstruct one of Wittigis' potential routes to Rome. Before leaving, however, Bessas engaged and routed Wittigis' advance guard before being
overpowered by numbers, after which he retired first to Narni and then
to Rome (foreshadowing Belisarius' first conflict outside Rome soon afterwards). Wittigis had 'made no attempt to capture Perusia and Spoletium,'
nor did he 'attempt anything' at Narni.[50] This was because, of the 'two
roads leading [to Narni, one]...is very narrow [with] precipitous rocks,

49   Talbert and Bagnall (2000) Italia, Map 42, Arretium-Asculum.
50   Procop. *Goth.* 5.17.1–9.

while the other cannot be reached except by way of the [Augustan] bridge (τὴν γέφυραν).'[51]

> [S]o Wittigis, not ... to have his time wasted there [Narni area], departed thence with all speed and went with the whole army against Rome, making the journey through Sabine territory (διὰ Σαβίνων τὴν πορείαν ποιούμενος). And when he drew near to Rome, and was not more than 14 stades away from it, he came upon a bridge over the Tiber River (Τιβέριδος τοῦ ποταμοῦ γεφὺρα). (Procop. *Goth.* 5.17.12–13).

Procopius leads us to believe that Belisarius' strategy, of seizing and garrisoning Narni, Perusia and Spoletium, culminating in the conflict at Narni, caused Wittigis to leave the *Via Flaminia* east of the Tiber at Interamna Nahars (modern Terni), 12 km east of Narni, and 'journey through Sabine territory', leading his army along the *Via Curia* until it joined the *Via Salaria* at Reate (fig. 5). This slowed Wittigis down and gave Belisarius more time to provision Rome and prepare its defences. Alternatively, Wittigis may have planned to use this itinerary so as to collect troops from Picenum and northern Samnium en route, and thence move south-west to Rome.[52] This route had been used by Alaric's Goths, who laid siege to Rome in August 410.[53] Therefore, Procopius may have presented what was a prudent Gothic strategy of advancing through Sabine country to collect troops, and thus to arrive at the more vulnerable north-east side of Rome, in such a way as to denigrate Wittigis' and improve Belisarius' reputations.

Although the Τιδέριδος τοῦ ποταμοῦ γεφὺρα is not named by Procopius, most scholars (as mentioned above in n.34 and n.35) have taken it to signify the Milvian Bridge (crossed by the *Via Flaminia*).[54] This is based largely upon the fact that the *Lib. Pontif.* states that Wittigis 'collected an enormous army of Goths and returned to attack Rome on 21 February' 537 and 'pitched camp by the Milvian Bridge'.[55] Rubin discusses whether 21 February was the date on which Wittigis left Ravenna or arrived at Rome. The *Lib. Pontif.* date and bridge-name appear to have convinced many

---

[51] Procop. *Goth.* 5.17.10–11.
[52] Talbert and Bagnall (2000) Italia, Map 42, Arretium-Asculum.
[53] Heather (2005) 227–29; Lançon (2000) 36–39.
[54] Hodgkin (1896) 118, n. 2.
[55] *Lib. Pont.* 60.1.4, trans. Davis (2000) 53; Kouroumali (2006) 187, n. 56; Rubin (1995) 105 n. 286.

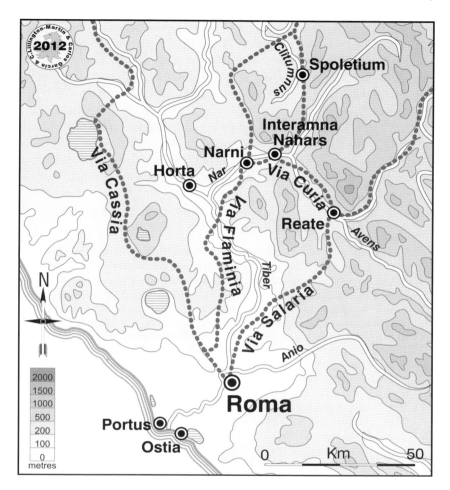

Fig. 6   *Via Flaminia, Via Curia*, Reate and the *Via Salaria* to Rome.
(prepared with Carlos García).

scholars as to the time and place of Wittigis' arrival, including Dewing, whose translation refers to both.[56]

However, there is good reason to doubt whether the Milvian Bridge could have formed any part of Wittigis' route, given that his march down the *Via Flaminia* was blocked by Narni, and that he made his 'journey

---

[56] Dewing (1914–40) 169, n. 1 and margin note, but see Veh (1966) 129–33 with notes on 1028.

through Sabine territory' (figs. 5 and 6). Hodgkin considers, but rejects, the suggestion by Gregorovius that Wittigis did not cross the river via the Milvian Bridge.[57] He prefers "to sacrifice the words διὰ Σαβίνων rather than the words Τιβέριδος τοῦ ποταμοῦ γεφύρα", which highlights the geographical incompatibility of the two phrases. Kouroumali does not deal with this incompatibility and states that: "Wittigis, ... chose a route through Sabine territory ... Belisarius had established a guard in a tower on the Milvian Bridge over the river Tiber as a means of checking the descending Gothic army".[58] This is geographically impossible because the Sabine route does not lead to the Milvian Bridge. Martindale mentions the River Anio without discussing any bridge at all, and refers to Bury,[59] who agreed with Hodgkin in 1889, but had changed his mind by 1923. His note is worth quoting in full because it explains the controversy well:

> The usual view has been that the Goths advanced by the *Via Flaminia* (regaining it somewhere presumably between Narnia and Ad Tiberim, now Magliano, where there was a bridge), and that the bridge where Belisarius placed the garrison was the *Pons Milvius*, now Ponte Molle, two miles from Rome. This view was held by Gibbon and maintained by Hodgkin. But it is certainly erroneous and inconsistent with the story. If the fighting had been at the Milvian Bridge, the Roman fugitives would have returned to the *Porta Flaminia*, not to the *Porta Salaria*. The cause of the error is that Procopius does not name the bridge, but calls it simply Τιβέριδος τοῦ ποταμοῦ γεφύρα, 'a bridge of the Tiber'. Hence, as the Milvian was the only bridge which spanned the Tiber north of the city, it was naturally supposed to be meant. But Τιβέρις is ambiguous in Procopius; it means (1) the Tiber, (2) the Anio. That it means the Anio in this passage is shown by the statement in the context that there are bridges over the river in other places (πολλαχόσε τοῦ ποταμου), meaning, of course, in the neighbourhood of Rome. This is not true of the Tiber, which had only the one bridge outside the city; but it is true of the Anio, which is crossed, near Rome, by the *Via Nomentana* and the *Via Tiburtina*, as well as by the *Via Salaria*. In two other passages (Procop. *Goth.* 7.10.23, and 24.31), Τιβέρις clearly means the Anio. This was the view of Gregorovius, *Rome in the Middle Ages*, 1.372; is accepted by Hartmann, *Gesch. Italiens*, 1.295, *n.* 19; and has been defended in a special monograph by L. Fink, *Das Verhältnis der Aniobrücken zur Mulvischen Brücke in Prokops Gothenkrieg*, 1907. Procopius knew the localities, and the ambiguous use of Τιβέρις cannot be due to ignorance. The explanation may be found in the modern name of the Anio, Teverone, and the use in Procopius be taken to

---

[57] Hodgkin (1885) vol. 4, 134, n.1 refers to Gregorovius, *Geschichte der Stadt Rom* (1859), i.349, n. 1.
[58] Kouroumali (2006) 187, n. 56.
[59] Martindale (1992) IIIA 197 cites Bury (1923) II, 182.

show that the old name had passed out of common speech before his time. (Bury (1923) II, 182, n. 1.).

This idea has Procopius keep Wittigis on the eastern side of the Tiber (from Narni) as proposed by Gregorovius (fig. 6).[60] Hodgkin accuses Gregorovius of suggesting that Procopius "here as elsewhere confused the Tiber with the Anio", but he fails to specify any other passages where Procopius undoubtedly uses the name Tiber when he means the Anio. The Tiber and Anio rivers are recorded by 19th c. cartography as the Tevere and Teverone, so it would have been understandable if they were equated or even confused if their names were equally similar in Late Antiquity.[61] Furthermore, the Salarian Bridge crosses the Anio less than 1 km from its confluence with the Tiber, so Procopius could easily have equated the rivers or merely simplified his description for his readers.

Alternatively, the confusion may have been caused by Procopius teasing his readers. On 28 October 312, the Emperor Maxentius died by drowning at the Milvian Bridge after losing a battle north of it to Constantine the Great. During the skirmish at the anonymous bridge in 537, Procopius claims that 1,000 Goths fell and 'many of the noblest' of Belisarius' household were slain, but he only names one: a certain 'Maxentius'.[62] Perhaps Procopius made this nonchalant comment for his readers to spot, alluding to the Battle of the Milvian Bridge of 312, and perhaps this is why he does not name the bridge.

At this stage, Belisarius' plan seems to have been to further delay the Goths from advancing southwards on the east of the Tiber, north of the anonymous bridge (as his garrisoning of Tuscany had prevented Gothic movements along the *Via Flaminia* on the west of the Tiber, south-west of Narni). This would have been intended to delay the Goths or force them to re-route their approach to Rome, perhaps from further east. Belisarius would thereby have gained more time to bring in additional supplies to Rome and harass the Goths from the safety of a fortified camp at a river crossing with a fortified bridge. The cavalry troops which would have been based in the intended camp would have operated to the north of the Salarian Bridge, and later, as necessary, withdrawn to Rome just as Constantinus and Bessas had withdrawn from Perusia, Spoletium and Narni.

---

[60] Hodgkin (1896) 118, n. 2.
[61] *Carta Topografica dei Dintorni di Roma* (1884).
[62] Procop. *Goth.* 5.18.14.

Landscape evidence gained from satellite imagery (confirmed by my field visit), combined with detailed analysis of internal textual data from Procopius, gives good reason for re-examining the situation, and suggests the validity of Gregorovius' proposal, which has created an opposing convention amongst German scholars, who accept the *Via Salaria* route for Wittigis' march south.[63] Belisarius had taken command of the Salarian and Pincian gates and stationed Constantinus at the Flaminian and Bessas at the Praenestine gates on their return to Rome (fig. 7). At the anonymous bridge (γεφὺρα), Procopius tells us that 'Belisarius had built a tower (πὺργον), furnished it with gates (πὺλαι) and a guard of soldiers, not because it was the only point at which the "Tiber" could be crossed by the enemy,' but to delay the advancing Goths.[64] When the Goths reached Belisarius' fortified and garrisoned anonymous bridge, Procopius continues:

> ...the Goths bivouacked there that day,...supposing that they would... storm the tower on the following day; but 22 deserters came to them, men who were barbarians by race but Roman soldiers, from the cavalry troop commanded by Innocentius. (Procop. *Goth.* 5.17.16–17).

From the Aurelian Wall to the Milvian Bridge, the *Via Flaminia* is straight and leads northwards over the River Tiber (the landscape is very flat and a tramline now operates along this section of the route). We cannot fully appreciate the lines of sight northwards today because the road is tree-lined and in a residential area. However, its straightness to the Milvian Bridge, and the flatness of the terrain to the bridge and just beyond it, can be appreciated to a sufficient extent on the ground, on maps, and via satellite imagery (fig. 7). This suggests that only Constantinus, from his position at the Flaminian Gate, had a clear view towards the Milvian Bridge, 2.7 km along the *Via Flaminia*. Belisarius' view, towards that bridge from the Pincian-Salarian Gate section of the wall, was obstructed by the hilly landscape, as was his view to the Salarian Bridge (which crosses the Anio, where it is approximately 30 m wide).

When the Goths took the anonymous bridge, Constantinus commanded a position at the Flaminian gate, and Belisarius commanded a position at the Salarian and Pincian Gates, prior to Belisarius' all-day skirmish near the anonymous bridge.[65] So Belisarius could not have seen either bridge,

---

[63] See n. 55–57.
[64] Procop. *Goth.* 5.17.14.
[65] Procop. *Goth.* 5.18.1–29.

and he could not have known of the capture of one of them by the Goths unless a message had reached him, which it evidently had not, given his subsequent actions.

It is apparent that the Goths had not encamped north of the Milvian Bridge on their arrival near Rome because had they done so, Constantinus would have seen their camp fires overnight from the Flaminian Gate, or would have been able to easily receive a signal or message from a tower had there been one on the Milvian Bridge (fig. 7). Furthermore, Procopius mentions the Goths building a seventh camp there (below) as an addition. Such information could have been conveyed to Belisarius before dawn. However, clearly no such information reached him and:

> it occurred to Belisarius to establish a camp near the Tiber River,...(to) hinder...the crossing of the enemy...But all the soldiers who, as has been stated, were keeping guard at the bridge,..., abandoned by night the tower...(as) they could not enter Rome, they marched toward Campania. (Procop. *Goth.* 5.17.18–19).

Therefore, the Goths must have been encamped north of another bridge which is out of sight of the Aurelian Walls. This concords with the suggestion that it was the Salarian Bridge, as this is completely out of sight of the city walls, from which it is obstructed by the landscape, which rises gradually from the Salarian Gate for about 2.5 km north-eastwards along the *Via Salaria*, as far as the Cemetery of Priscilla (avoiding the Villa Ada hilly area), then drops more steeply northwards out of sight of Rome for 1 km to the Salarian Bridge (fig. 7). A Roman camp would have been advantageous here.[66] This strategic point commands the view northwards. Indeed, today there are remains of an ancient tower, the *Torre Salaria*, 200 m north of the Salarian Bridge. In addition, those bridge guards who did not desert to the Goths but 'marched toward Campania' would, to have escaped out of sight of Rome, have followed the Anio east of Rome before heading south. This suggests that, in this quarter at least, the morale and communications system of Belisarius' army was buckling under the stress caused by the swift march and size of Wittigis' army, leading to Roman desertions at a critical time and in a crucial place.[67]

---

[66] See fig. 7; Talbert and Bagnall (2000) Italia, Map 43, Latium Vetus; and *Lib. Pont.* trans. Davis (2000) Map I.

[67] Liebeschuetz (1996) 230–39.

All of Procopius' next chapter, 5.18, is devoted to the skirmish, which lasted the whole of the following day: 'the Goths destroyed the gates of the tower with no trouble and made the crossing, since no one tried to oppose them'. If this crossing had taken place at the Milvian Bridge, it could not have proceeded unnoticed because it would have been in full view of Constantinus' men at the Flaminian Gate, even though it was possible that the visibility could have been reduced on a February or March morning. Even if Procopius used this episode to glorify Belisarius in what follows, this would not affect the fundamental tenets of this hypothesis. So, without any visual information or messages from the 'soldiers who . . . abandoned . . . the tower' on the anonymous bridge,

> Belisarius, who had not . . . learned what had happened to the garrison, was bringing up 1,000 horsemen to the bridge over the river, in order to look over the ground and decide where it would be best for his forces to make camp. But when they had come rather close, they met the enemy already across the river, and not at all willingly they engaged with some of them. (Procop. *Goth.* 5.18-2-3).

Thus, whilst Belisarius could have known from his control of Narni that Wittigis was not marching southwards along the *Via Flaminia*, he did not know how quickly Wittigis had marched southwards east of the Tiber. He did not believe it was yet time to prepare to receive an immediate attack on Rome. This corresponds with the idea that the landscape did not permit a clear view from Belisarius' starting point, the Salarian or Pincian Gate, to his destination, the anonymous towered bridge. Had Constantinus seen the Goths crossing at the Milvian Bridge and an engagement between them and Belisarius, he would surely have reacted by either leading reinforcements there or preparing to receive Belisarius' men. Therefore, it is reasonable to conclude that the Goths did not cross the Tiber at the Milvian Bridge, but made their crossing further east, probably across the Anio near the confluence with the Tiber, for which the only likely candidate is the Salarian Bridge.

This conclusion would correlate Procopius' comment that, after the skirmish between Bessas and the Gothic vanguard in the Narni area, Wittigis marched his army through 'Sabine territory'. This was either because the Roman garrison at Narni prevented his army's progress, or because he wanted to rendezvous with troops en route from Picenum and Samnium, perhaps in the vicinity of Reate. This route conveyed the Goths, partly by way of the *Via Salaria*, to the north-east side of Rome, where, once they crossed the Anio, via the anonymous bridge, they:

made 6 fortified camps from which they harassed the portion of the wall containing 5 gates, from the Flaminian as far as the Praenestine Gate; all these camps were made on the left bank of the Tiber River. (Procop. *Goth.* 5.19.2.).

Procopius is very clear that these 6 camps were sited east of the Tiber, south of the Anio and north and east of the Aurelian Walls. Maps confirm

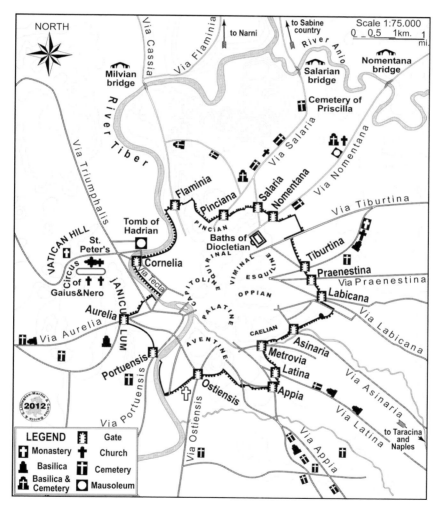

Fig. 7   Main gates, roads and bridges of Rome. (prepared with Carlos García).

that this area is reached from Ravenna by crossing the Anio after traversing Sabine territory (figs. 4 to 7 and n.55 and n.66 above).

To return to Procopius' description of the skirmish at the anonymous
bridge: 'And the battle was carried on by horsemen on both sides...the
Romans turned the enemy to flight,...the Gothic infantry...forced them
back,...cavalry reinforced the Goths,...the Romans fled at top speed
until they reached a certain hill, which they climbed, and there held their
position.'[68] Such hills are discernible via satellite and by field visit, and
fill the landscape between the rivers and walls, including along the *Via
Salaria*, especially where it drops north from the Cemetery of Priscilla (fig. 7).
Then, 'the enemy's horsemen were upon them directly, and a second cavalry battle took place...the Romans escaped, and arrived at the fortifications of Rome...the barbarians in pursuit...(to) the Salarian Gate.'[69]
Procopius' statement that the Goths pursued Belisarius to the Salarian,
and not to the Flaminian, Gate favours the hypothesis presented here.

Although Hodgkin comments on the possibility that Belisarius arrived
at the nearby Pincian Gate, which is linked to the Salarian Bridge by the
Via Salaria, we can be certain, based on the evidence above, that it was
not the Flaminian Gate.[70] 'Those inside the fortifications...were without
a general...and the battle which had begun early in the morning did not
end until night.'[71] It is reasonable to conclude that Belisarius returned to
the gate he had left that morning along the same road. Had his destination been the Milvian Bridge, he would surely have left from the Flaminian Gate, which Constantinus commanded, seen the Goths crossing, and
then retreated along the *Via Flaminia*, rather than use either the Salarian
or Pincian Gates. Furthermore, when Procopius does specifically mention
the Milvian Bridge, it is two chapters after the skirmish at the anonymous
bridge, and in the context of Gothic camp building, where, he states:

> the barbarians feared lest their enemy, by destroying the bridge which bears
> the name of Milvius, should render inaccessible to them all the land on the
> right bank of the river as far as the sea...so they fixed a seventh camp across
> the Tiber in the Plain of Nero, in order that the bridge might be between
> their two armies. (Procop. *Goth.* 5.19.3).

---

[68] Procop. *Goth.* 5.18.3–17.
[69] Procop. *Goth.* 5.18.18–19.
[70] Hodgkin (1896) 122, n. 2; and Dewing (1968) 176, n. 2.
[71] Procop. *Goth.* 5.18.25–9.

This fits the hypothesis that the anonymous bridge was on the Anio rather than the Tiber because the Milvian Bridge is only mentioned after the first six camps had already been constructed to threaten five gates of Rome, from the Flaminian (Popolo) to the Praenestine (Maggiore) Gates. In this way, Procopius provides internal evidence that the Goths built their last and not first, camp north of the Milvian Bridge, which means that the anonymous bridge that they initially crossed lay to the east. Once again, therefore, the identification of the anonymous towered bridge with the Milvian Bridge is insecure whereas the Salarian Bridge, or another on the Anio, is a much better candidate.

We can now turn to the statement in the *Lib. Pontif.* that Wittigis 'collected an enormous army of Goths and returned to attack Rome on 21 February' 537. It is unspecified whether this was the date Wittigis arrived outside Rome, or when he left Ravenna. The statement: 'he pitched camp by the Milvian Bridge'[72] probably denotes the last camp the Goths built, which Procopius refers to as the 'seventh camp across the Tiber in the Plain of Nero'.[73] It would follow that the skirmish at the anonymous bridge occurred a few days before the seventh camp was built, because Procopius records that the Goths returned to bury their dead 'on the third day, when the barbarians had made camp hard by the circuit-wall of Rome'.[74] During the building of the first six Gothic camps, the Romans evidently still had access to the Milvian Bridge via the west bank of the Tiber, because the Goths feared that the Romans could destroy it and 'render inaccessible to them all the land on the right bank of the river'.[75] So there was no Gothic camp there initially. This further supports the hypothesis that the Goths approached Rome from the east to focus their attack on the north-east section of the Aurelian Wall, where it is not protected by the Tiber. Wittigis' march on Rome was swifter than expected by Belisarius, who was surprised by the Goths' arrival at the anonymous bridge, which may justify a slightly more positive assessment of Wittigis' generalship. Overall, therefore, this re-examination of textual and topographic information provides compelling evidence that the Salarian Bridge was the Gothic point of arrival.

We can now briefly deal with the last engagement at Rome in 538. Procopius relates that 'one year...and 9 days' after the start of the siege, 'the

---

[72] *Lib. Pont.* Silverius, trans. Davis (2000) 54.
[73] Procop. *Goth.* 5.19.3.
[74] Procop. *Goth.* 5.18.31.
[75] Procop. *Goth.* 5.19.3.

Goths, having burned all their camps, set out at daybreak', and 'Belisarius . . .
when he saw that more than half of the enemy had crossed the bridge,
led the army out through the small Pincian Gate, and (to) . . . battle',
after which 'each man' of the Goths rushed 'to cross the bridge first', and
'many . . . fell off the bridge . . ., sank with all their arms, and perished'.[76]
Belisarius would have led his army from the Pincian Gate along a road
which communicated directly with the anonymous bridge (the *Via Pinci-
ana* connects with the *Via Salaria*) (fig. 7). Had the Goths been retreating
over the Milvian Bridge, Belisarius would surely have attacked the Goths
from the Flaminian Gate up the *Via Flaminia*. For Wittigis, it would have
been safer to withdraw most of the Goths from the camps over the Salarian Bridge rather than over the Milvian, given that it was further from, and
out of sight of, Rome.

Therefore, it is most likely that Wittigis retreated with most of his
forces back the way he came, over a bridge to the north-east (from which
communications led to Gothic settlements in Picenum and northern
Samnium, where many of his troops had homes and families). Furthermore, Procopius states that Ildiger and Martinus were sent by Belisarius
along 'another road', different from Wittigis' retreat route, and Procopius specifies that these Romans did use the *Via Flaminia*.[77] However,
as Wittigis sent some garrisons north, it is likely that the *Via Cassia*
was used by part of his force, perhaps troops from the seventh camp,
north of the Milvian Bridge, who could have retreated by that route, and
perhaps some of those east of, but near, the Milvian Bridge. Even though
Procopius does not name the bridge which Wittigis used, the Salarian is
the most likely candidate when we take landscape evidence into consideration alongside the textual evidence.

D'Agincourt's (*ca.* 1820) detailed plan of the Salarian Bridge, which was
restored by Narses in 565, and which survived into the 19th c., includes
two inscriptions, which serve as further evidence. Line six (*LIBERTATEVR-
BISROMAEACTOTIUSITALIAERESTITUTA*) of the ten-line-inscription pro-
claimed 'the restoration of the liberty of the city of Rome and the whole
of Italy'.[78] Lines 9 to 10 continue: 'the river bed has been cleansed'.[79] Such

---

[76] Procop. *Goth.* 6.10.13–18.
[77] Procop. *Goth.* 6.11.4 and 8 respectively.
[78] Cameron, Ward-Perkins and Whitby (2000) 534; *CIL* VI 1199; Zanini (1998) 182–83
and cover illustration.
[79] Mitchell (2007) 385.

a cleansing would have been appropriate after significant loss of life there in 537, and especially 538. Although this inscription dates from nearly 30 years later, it may be significant that this particular bridge was inscribed in this way. This supports the hypothesis that the Salarian Bridge is the most likely site of the first and last engagements in 537 and 538, confirming Procopius' testimony that Wittigis did indeed march through Sabine territory in early 537.

Conclusion

In conclusion, this paper has reconciled landscape and textual evidence to carefully re-interpret two of Procopius' battle descriptions. In the East, Procopius' accuracy is supported by topographic evidence for the precise locations of forts, camps, trench lines and battles. In the West, this paper has mapped out the lines of advance and retreat during the Gothic army's attack on Rome, 537–38, with corresponding strategic moves by Belisarius. It has been highlighted that, to a significant extent, we can trust Procopius as a sound historical source, and we can gain valuable insights by using such textual evidence in close combination with topographic evidence. Thus it has been shown that historical sources, even eye-witness accounts, leave us records which need to be carefully interpreted, and that their reconciliation with landscape, through the use of using satellite imagery or field visits, can lead to new interpretations of locations, events and strategies.

Our research raises questions about the objectives and research methods of primary sources, such as Procopius, and their attitudes to readers. Sometimes, they may have mistakenly equated, left unrecorded, forgotten or purposely left ambiguous details such as river or bridge names. Logical reconciliation of literary and landscape evidence can lead us to recover this detailed information, and so re-interpret locations and strategies. This permits a better analysis of our literary source, an improved historical interpretation of events and, therefore, an enhanced insight into the mind-set of both the decision makers in and commentators on the conflicts concerned. The results of our investigation indicate that we can usually trust the fundamental tenets of Procopius' landscape details, from which we can ascertain more precise information with the use of comparative topographical evidence and a cautious re-appraisal of translations. This vindicates the opinion of Peter Heather, who wisely suggests "reading

Procopius' gripping, first-hand account of the action" as it informs more than we might expect.[80]

ACKNOWLEDGEMENTS

I am delighted to acknowledge the support I have received from Dr Roger Palmer (Aerial Archaeology Research Group, Cambridge) and the British Institute of Archaeology at Ankara, which granted me funds to visit Turkey. Professor Metin Ahunbay showed me around Dara and discussed the site. I am very grateful for the translation skills of Dr Deniz Beyazit (Metropolitan Museum of Art, New York) which facilitated communication. The commander of the Turkish garrison at Dara, Kamil Gündüz, J. Bcvş, Oğuz J.Krk.K, expedited my visit to Dara's hinterland. Ambar and Dara farmers were most helpful in talking of their finds. Professor Wolf Liebeschuetz (Nottingham), Professor Stephen Mitchell (Exeter), Professor Enrico Zanini (Sienna) and Dr Oliver Schmitt (Martin-Luther-Universität) have helped in various ways. I should like to thank Dr Luke Lavan (Kent) and Dr Alexander Sarantis (Kent) for agreeing to publish this paper. I am very grateful to Carlos García for his map-making skills. Last, but not least, I wish to thank all of my University of Oxford tutors, especially Dr. Bryan Ward-Perkins, and the referees who provided useful feedback and comments.

BIBLIOGRAPHY

Primary Sources

CIL = Reimerum G. (1862) ed. *Corpus Inscriptionum Latinarum* (Berlin 1862).
Hdt. = de Selincourt A. (1972) trans. Herodotus, *Histories* (London 1972).
Hom. *Od.* = Rieu E. V. (2003) trans. Homer, *Odyssey* (London 2003).
Lib. Pont. = Davis R. (2000) trans. Liber Pontificalis. *The Book of Pontiffs: The Ancient Biographies of the First Ninety Roman Bishops to AD 715* (2nd ed., Liverpool 2000).
Jord. *Get.* = Mierow C. C. (1915) trans. *The Gothic History of Jordanes* (Princeton 1915).
Strategikon = Dennis G. T. (1984) ed. *Maurice's Strategikon. Handbook of Byzantine Military Strategy* (Philadelphia 1984).
Procop. *Goth.*, Procop. *Vand.*, Procop. *Pers.* = Dewing H. B. (1914–54) ed. and trans. Procopius, *History of the Wars* (London 1914–54); Veh O. (1966) trans. *Gotenkriege Prokop* (Munich 1966); Signes Codoñer J., García Romero F. A. and Flores Rubio J. A. vols. I–III (2000–2007) trans. Procopio de Cesarea, *Historia de las guerras* (Madrid 2000–2007).

---

[80] Heather (1996) 264.

Malalas = Jeffreys E., Jeffreys M. and Scott R. with B. Croke (1986) trans. *The Chronicle of John Malalas* (Melbourne and Sydney 1986).

SEG = (1993–4) Chaniotis A., Corsten T., Stroud R. S. and Tybout R. A. (1994–95) edd. *Supplementum Epigraphicum Graecum, volumes 44 and 45* (Leuven and Boston 1994–95).

Theoph. Sim. = Whitby M. and Whitby M. (1986) trans. *The History of Theophylact Simocatta: an English Translation with Introduction and Notes* (Oxford 1986).

Zach. Myt. *Chron.* = Greatrex G. Phenix R. R., Horn C. B. and Brock S. P. (2010) edd. and trans. *The Chronicle of Pseudo-Zachariah Rhetor: Church and War in Late Antiquity* (Liverpool 2010); J. F. Hamilton and E. W. Brooks (1899) trans. *Historia Ecclesiastica* (London 1899).

Secondary Sources

Ahunbay M. (1991) "Dara-Anastasiopolis 1990 Yili Çalismalari.", *Kazi Sonuçlari Toplantisi* 13.1 (1991) 197–203.

Bury J. B. (1923) *History of the Later Roman Empire from the Death of Theodosius to the Death of Justinian*, 2 vols. (London 1923).

Cameron A. Ward-Perkins B. and Whitby M. (2000) edd. *The Cambridge Ancient History Volume 14. Late Antiquity: Empire and Successors AD 425–600* (Cambridge 2000)

Croke B. and Crow J. G. (1983) "Procopius and Dara", *JRS* 73 (1983) 143–59.

Evans J. A. S. (1996) and (2000) *The Age of Justinian: The Circumstances of Imperial Power* (London 1996) (2nd ed., London 2000).

Feissel D. (2002) "Les itinéraires de Procope et la métrologie de l'Antiquité tardive", *Antiquité tardive* 10 (2002) 383–400.

Greatrex G. (1998) *Rome and Persia at War, 502–532* (Leeds 1998).

Greatrex G. and Lieu S. (2002) edd. *The Roman Eastern Frontier and the Persian Wars: a Narrative Sourcebook* (London 2002).

Hassan F. A. (1981) *Demographic Archaeology* (New York 1981).

Haldon J. F. (2001) *The Byzantine Wars: Battles and Campaign of the Byzantine Era* (Stroud 2001).

Heather P. J. (2005) *The Fall of the Roman Empire: a New History* (London 2005).

—— (1996) *The Goths* (Oxford 1996).

Hodgkin T. (1880–99) *Italy and her Invaders* (Oxford 1880–99).

Humphries M. (2000) "Italy, A.D. 425–605", in *The Cambridge Ancient History Volume 14. Late Antiquity: Empire and Successors AD 425–600*, edd. A. Cameron, B. Ward-Perkins and M. Whitby (Cambridge 2000) 525–51.

Istituto geografico militare (1884) *Carta topografica dei dintorni di Roma* (1884).

Kaldellis A. (2004) *Procopius of Caesarea: Tyranny, History, and Philosophy at the end of Antiquity* (Philadelphia 2004).

Kennedy D. L. and Riley D. (1990) *Rome's Desert Frontier from the Air* (London 1990).

Kouroumali M. (2006) *Procopius and the Gothic War* (D.Phil. diss., Univ. of Oxford 2006).

Lançon B. (2000) *Rome in Late Antiquity: Everyday Life and Urban Change, AD 312–609* (Edinburgh 2000).

Liebeschuetz J. H. W. G. (1996) "The Romans demilitarised: the evidence of Procopius", *Scripta Classica Israelica* 15 (1996) 230–39.

Lillington-Martin C. (2007) "The archaeological and literary evidence for a battle near Dara, AD 530: topography, text and trenches", in *The Late Roman Army in the East from Diocletian to the Arab Conquest: Proceedings of a Colloquium held at Potenza, Acerenza and Matera, Italy (May 2005)*, edd. A. Lewin and P. Pellegrini (BAR International Series 1717) (Oxford 2007) 299–312.

Mango M. M. (1982) "Deux eglises de Mesopotamie du Nord: Ambar et Mar Abraham de Kashkar", *Cahiers archéologiques* 30 (1982) 47–70.

Martindale J. R. (1992) *The Prosopography of the Later Roman Empire. Volumes 2 and 3* (Cambridge 1992).

Millett M. (1990) *The Romanization of Britain: an Essay in Archaeological Interpretation* (Cambridge 1990).

Mitchell S. (2007) *A History of the Later Roman Empire AD 284–641: the Transformation of the Ancient World* (Malden and Oxford 2007).

Moorhead J. (2000) "Totila the revolutionary", *Historia* 49 (2000) 382–86.

Nicholson O. (1985) "Two notes on Dara", *AJA* 89 (1985) 663–71.

Rubin B. (1995) *Das Zeitalter Iustinians* (Berlin and New York 1995).

Stanhope P. H. (1848) *The Life of Belisarius* (2nd ed., London 1848).

Talbert R. J. A. and Bagnall R. S. (2000) *Barrington Atlas of the Greek and Roman World* (Princeton and Oxford 2000).

Whitby M. (1986) "Procopius' description of Dara (Buildings II.1–3)", in *The Defence of the Roman and Byzantine East: Proceedings of a Colloquium held at the University of Sheffield in April 1986*, edd. P. Freeman and D. Kennedy (BAR International Series 297) (Oxford 1986) 737–83.

Whitby M. and Whitby M. (1986) trans. *The History of Theophylact Simocatta: an English Translation with Introduction and Notes* (Oxford 1986).

Wood G. A. (2004) "The Roman fort at Qubur al Bid, Mesopotamia", *JRA* 17 (2004) 397–405.

Zanini E. (1990) "La cinta muraria di Dara. Materiali per un'analisi stratigrafica", in *Costantinopoli e l'arte delle province orientali* (Rome 1990) 229–52.

Zanini E. (1998) *Le Italie bizantine. Territorio, insediamenti ed economia nella provincia bizantina d'Italia (VI–VIII secolo)* (Bari 1998).

Websites

Fuller M. J. http://users.stlcc.edu/mfuller/area1roman.html. (accessed 10 November 2011).

Google Earth leverages Landsat satellite imagery and Shuttle Radar Topography Mission data, http://www.google.com/.

http://www.ourpasthistory.com/roman_scotland/Imgp0696.jpg (accessed July 2007).

http://www.unitconversion.org/length/kilometers-to-miles-roman-conversion.html (accessed July 2007).

http://www.world-gazetteer.com (accessed July 2007).

LIST OF FIGURES

AMMIANUS MARCELLINUS
AND THE NISIBENE HANDOVER OF A.D. 363

Susannah Belcher

Abstract

This article focuses on the Roman Emperor Jovian's handover of Nisibis to the Persian King Shapur II in A.D. 363. This event is presented by an eyewitness, Ammianus Marcellinus, as a definitive moment in the history of the Roman State: when the empire's endurance diverges substantially from her age-old pact with *Iustitia* (which he defines as the presiding causative deity) towards deeds which contravene the historian's ideal of Rome and the responsibility of her agents to further her interests. Alongside this wider interpretation, the article considers the trauma of the handover for citizens of the strategically important city of Nisibis, and the contrasting portrait painted by Ephrem.

et principe permittente Romano, civitatem ingressus, gentis suae signum ab arce extulit summa, migrationem e patria civibus nuntians luctuosam.

With the permission of the Roman emperor, he entered the city and raised the flag of his nation on the top of the citadel, announcing to the citizens their sorrowful departure from their native place. (Amm. Marc. 25.9.1).

So Ammianus Marcellinus begins his account of the handover of the citadel of Nisibis to the Persians in A.D. 363.[1] The Roman Emperor Jovian ceded Nisibis, *Orientis firmissimum claustrum*,[2] to the Persian King Shapur II, along with Singara, some 15 other fortified sites in the Mesopotamian region, 5 satrapies along the Upper Tigris,[3] and the concession that the Romans would not intervene on behalf of their client king in Armenia. This shameful treaty[4] was extracted from the hastily-elevated Jovian *pro redemptione nostra*,[5] for the price of safe passage for Julian's defeated Roman army, of which Ammianus was a part. Significantly, this handover

---

[1] Amm. Marc. 25.9.8–11.
[2] Amm. Marc. 25.8.14.
[3] Amm. Marc. 25.7.9. The Persians had ceded this (including Nisibis) in A.D. 299. Blockley (1988) 244.
[4] Amm. Marc. 25.9.8.
[5] Amm. Marc. 25.7.9.

A. Sarantis, N. Christie (edd.) *War and Warfare in Late Antiquity: Current Perspectives* (Late Antique Archaeology 8.1–8.2 – 2010–11) (Leiden 2013), pp. 631–652

did not only include a series of key fortifications, but also the border's primary trading town and associated revenues. Said revenues were intended as compensation for the damage caused to Persian territory by the Julianic invasion. Analyses of this pivotal treaty have necessarily concentrated upon Nisibis, rather than other cities handed over to the Persians, such as Singara. This is in part down to the nature of the surviving textual evidence (both Ammianus and Ephrem focusing on Nisibis), and in part down to Nisibis' unusual position of having resisted falling to the Persians three times during the reign of Constantius II.[6] This paper will be no different in its focus.

Modern day Nusaybin retains few of its older features, at least above ground. As Lightfoot notes, the layout, position and size of the fortress is unknown due to a lack of excavation, or even survey.[7] The meagre nature of the extant remains does not help either. This is to say nothing of the problems associated with working directly on the Turkish-Syrian border, attested by the sad deaths of Metin Akyurt and Bahattin Devam in a bomb attack organised against the excavation team at Mardin, Nusaybin in 1991.[8] The city of Nusaybin's economy continues to be linked to frontier administration, in particular, trade and contact with Syria, whose counterpart, Al-Qamlishi, it faces across the Görgarbonizra River.[9] It is still situated on the upper trade routes from Mosul in Iraq (approximately 120 miles southeast), and is a stop on the Istanbul-Baghdad railway.[10] It has a population of approximately 51,000 people (1990), up from 31,000 in 1980.

The only extant antique building is the Church of Mor Ya'qub (St. Jacob), the baptistery of which appears from the epigraphic evidence to have been built by Bishop Vologaeses and the deacon Acepsimas in

---

[6] The first invasion was probably in spring A.D. 338: Theod., *HE* 2.30.2; Philostorgius 3.23; Theophanes AM5829. The second was in A.D. 346: Jer. *Chron.* ann. 346; Theophanes AM5838. The third was in A.D. 350: Ephr. 1–3, 11.14–18; 13.14–18, 10.vv.143–150, 15.vv.55–62 and 101–44.

[7] Lightfoot (1988) 109. I am much indebted to Lightfoot for a great deal of information concerning Nisibis.

[8] http://www.arkeo.hacettepe.edu.tr/en.05.library.htm. They are to be memorialised by a library.

[9] Although cross-border trade has been hampered by the recent civil war in Syria.

[10] http://lexicorient.com/e.o/nusaybin.htm; http://www.britannica.com/eb/article-905 6540/Nusaybin Nisibis' perpetual importance as a stage post is attested by Buckingham (1827) 1.415, who meets "less than two hours after our setting out" (from Mardin to Nisibis via a putative Dara) "two Tartars from Constantinople going to Bagdad, in charge of papers from the British Consul General at that capital, to the East-India Company's resident at Bagdad." For information about the railway, originally Berlin-Baghdad, see Henderson (1948). Nisibis was incorporated into the line during World War One.

A.D. 359.[11] This is probably apt, given the role of the clergy in strengthening the resistance of the citadel when confronted with Shapur II's repeated assaults.[12] There are also some Corinthian columns, standing "visible in the no-man's land of the modern Turko-Syrian frontier" that may indicate the possible location of a forum or a temple.[13] Apart from these, we have the attestation of the ruins of walls and a bridge by earlier travellers,[14] and a description of an inscribed block of marble seen by one French visitor. A certain Olivier reports seeing this stone in the region of the aforementioned columns, and being able to make out the Latin words *currus . . . victoriam stadii*, possibly suggesting that Nisibis had a circus.[15]

We can, at any rate, expect it to have had the usual variety of civic buildings as a result of its importance. In all probability, Nisibis served as a legionary base,[16] and was the headquarters of the *dux Mesopotamiae*, while frequently acting as the "forward mustering-point" for the forces of the *magister militum per Orientem*.[17] This, in and of itself, makes it likely

---

[11]   Khatcharian (1957) 407–21. See also Fiey (1977) 29–30.

[12]   See Ephr. 13.19–21 for a description of St. Jacob's aid, living and dead.

[13]   Lightfoot (1988) 110.

[14]   For example, Tavernier (1724) 1.236–37 says that "On voit sur le chemin plusieurs pans de muraille avec une grande arcade, d'où l'on peut juger qu'anciennement la Ville s'éntendoit jusqu'à la rivière." Kinneir (1818) 441–43, although deeply concerned about his companion, a M. Chavasse, suffering from a headache sustained after "going to the bath at Merdin, and exposing himself too soon afterwards to the draught of an open window", nonetheless informs us that "the substructions of the walls may yet be traced, and appear to have been carried along the edge of some eminence, defended by the Mygdonius to the N.E., and a morass to the S. I should guess their circumference to be about three miles, or probably more." Buckingham (1827) 1.443–44 notes the columns, saying "The temple, which is without the precincts of the present town, on the south, has five columns still erect, supporting an architrave, a portion, no doubt, of the original portico. It appeared to be of the Corinthian order, but small, and of ordinary execution." Buckingham was unable to get closer due to having a quantity of his clothing stolen from his back by a group of four villagers, but manages to note this of the bridge: that it "is a long and level work of masonry, thrown across the river, and supported on 12 arches of Roman work. . . . It resembles the bridge seen near Khallet el Hhearin, on the road from Antioch to Aleppo, and, like it, was no doubt originally of Roman construction, though it has undergone repairs, in later times, from Mohammedan workmen; and this portion of it is now in a still more ruined condition than the more ancient one." Interestingly, he also observes that (1.440): "In Syriac, the name, in the plural, signifies "a place of columns;" but in Hebrew, Chaldaic and Arabic, it implies, in the singular, a military post. Either of these etymologies would be sufficiently consistent with its former state and history to be adopted . . ." See also Lightfoot (1982) 118 n.118.

[15]   Olivier (1801–1807) 4.243 "C'était, peut-être là, le stade, où se faisaient les courses des chevaux."

[16]   Lightfoot (1988) 108; *Not. Dign. Or.* 36.29, *leg. I Parthica 'Nisibena'* at Constantina.

[17]   Lightfoot (1982) 93 and (1988) 107.

that the civil governor must also have used Nisibis as his headquarters.[18] In addition, Constantius seems to have spent some time there during the A.D. 340s,[19] which makes perfect sense in the context of defending the eastern frontier. Ammianus says that in A.D. 363, Jovian refused 'to enter and to take up his residence in the palace as was usual with the emperors', *ingressus palatio more succederet principum*, which in turn implies that the town was equipped for imperial visits.[20] Most likely it contained a council chamber (which Sabinus, distinguished among his citizens for his wealth and high birth, might have attended),[21] a law court (from which such characters as Silvanus, an outspoken pleader, might have issued),[22] baths and a gymnasium, temples,[23] and of course a large trading concourse, where the produce and wealth of the two empires was traded in full view of the tax collector. As Lightfoot suggests, Nisibis may well have been rather similar in appearance to Dura-Europos, the remains of which, having been abandoned in A.D. 256 after falling to the Persians, still stand comparatively unmolested.[24]

Ammianus tells us of the city's *illi ... habili situ, et moenium magnitudine*, and says that Bineses raised the flag of Persia at the top of the citadel.[25] However, most of Ammianus' evocation of the city is somewhat general. For example, there is none of the panoramic sweep and detail evidenced, for example, in his account of Constantius II's *adventus* in Rome,[26] or in his many geographic excursuses. On the other hand, this may be a good thing. When Ammianus does write in elaborate detail, the immediacy and graphic character of the narrative undoubtedly adds a great deal to the gripping nature of the narrative, with its sheen of authenticity. Nevertheless, such descriptions have unfortunately proved to be deeply questionable on occasion. Notable in this respect is his famous error regarding the geographic features of the city of Amida, to whose siege in 359 he was not

---

[18] Lightfoot (1988) 107.
[19] Lightfoot (1988) 107; also a rescript of 12th May 345 in *Cod. Theod.* 11.7.5.
[20] Amm. Marc. 25.8.17.
[21] Amm. Marc. 25.9.3.
[22] Amm. Marc. 25.9.4.
[23] Ephrem describes the destruction of pagan temples at Nisibis: Ephr. *c. J.* 2.22.
[24] There are many publications on Dura-Europos, but Lightfoot (1988) 110 suggests as particularly relevant Rostovtzeff (1983) 50–55; Perkins (1973) 23–32; Matheson (1982) 17–19, 22–24, fig.15. See also James (2004).
[25] Amm. Marc. 25.8.14.
[26] Amm. Marc. 16.10.

only an eyewitness, but an active participant.[27] Even the moments of vivid personal detail are sometimes not all that they seem. For example, Ammianus describes at 18.8.12 his night as part of the crush of people, desperately trying to reach the safety of Amida along a single narrow approach, while artillery crashed down from the battlements above them:

> *ita conferti, ut caesorum cadavera multitudine fulta, reperire ruendi spatium nusquam possent, utque miles ante me quidam, discriminato capite, quod in aequas partes ictus gladii fiderat validissimus, in stipitis modum undique coartatus haereret.*

> ...so crowded together that the bodies of the slain, held upright by the throng, could nowhere find room to fall, and that in front of me, a soldier with his head cut in two, and split into equal halves by a powerful sword stroke, was so pressed on all sides that he stood erect like a stump. (Amm. Marc. 18.8.12).

As Matthews observes, "again, one wonders a little, for men who have died in this way appear as victims of the Goths—or of Ammianus' rhetoric—on the battlefield of Ad Salices (31.7.14). How did Ammianus' companion get there in the first place?"[28]

All of which is simply to illustrate the point that Ammianus' evidence, even as an eyewitness, cannot be easily or unwarily mined for discernible historical fact. An obvious point, but the Gibbonian assessment of Ammianus as an essentially honest and reliable historian, plus the historian's status as an eyewitness to the events dealt with in this paper, continues to cast a long shadow.[29] Ammianus' description of the events at Amida has been thoroughly challenged, on the grounds of loyalty to Ursicinus distorting the picture,[30] literary aspirations (to which I would add historiographic

---

[27] Amm. Marc. 18.9.2. Lightfoot (1989) 286 tries to explain this away with a comparison of the points of the compass given by Ammianus describing the siege again at 19.2.3, but is forced to conclude: "More difficult to explain is his contention that Grumbates had approached Amida from the East, and that when the fighting began, the Chionite troops were allotted that quarter because it was there that the royal prince had fallen. The position of the fortress with its eastern walls perched on cliffs above the Tigris makes it hard to envisage how an approach, not to mention an assault, could have been made from that side." Blockley (1988) 246 deals with the problem by stating that "Ammianus emerges as a rather skilful writer who was prepared to take liberties with the truth both for artistic and for personal motives." However, such inaccuracies could simply have been down to an error of memory, due perhaps to Amida facing east to the Tigris, but being approached from the south by a bridge over the Tigris.

[28] Matthews (1989a) 552.

[29] Gibbon (1909) 3.128.

[30] Thompson (1947) 42–55.

methodology and aim),[31] and an impetus towards the aggrandisement of Amida, itself connected to the exoneration of Ursicinus.[32] Blockley summarises the technique of the historian when he says that:

> it is through literary presentation, including the organisation of the narrative, that Ammianus communicates, or rather imposes, his interpretation of events. Although, because of his diffuseness (and, I suspect, basic honesty), Ammianus does provide us with some data to support alternative interpretations, his usual approach to his material is, like that of Tacitus, authoritative. (Blockley (1988) 249).

Ammianus is a self-consciously literary and referential historian, whose constructed tableaux yield a great deal more than sole historicity. As in the case of Amida,[33] so Nisibis. Ammianus' description of the handover of Nisibis continues:

> *et vertere solum extemplo omnes praecepti, manusque tendentes fleutesque, orabant ne imponeretur sibi necessitas abscedendi, ad defendendos penates se solos sufficere sine alimentis publicis affirmantes et milite, satis confisi adfuturam iustitiam pro genitali sede dimicaturis, ut experti sunt saepe.*

> And when all were commanded to leave their homes at once, with tears and outstretched hands they begged that they might not be compelled to depart, declaring that they alone, without aid from the empire in provisions and men, were able to defend their hearths, trusting that Justice herself would, as they had often found, aid them in fighting for their ancestral dwelling-place. (Amm. Marc. 25.9.2).

The reference to *Iustitia* is book-ended by a commentary on the shameful nature of the treaty.[34] These sandwich the account of the evacuation:

> *tu hoc loco (Fortuna orbis Romani) merito incusaris, quae, difflantibus procellis rem publicam, excussa regimenta perito rei gerendae ductori, consummando iuveni porrexisti, quem nullis ante actae vitae insignibus in huius modi negotiis cognitum, nec vituperari est aequum, nec laudari. illud tamen ad medullas usque bonorum pervenit, quod dum extimescit aemulum potestatis, dumque in animo per Gallias et Illyricum versat, quosdam saepe sublimiora coeptasse, famam adventus sui praevenire festinans, indignum imperio facinus amictu periurii fugiendi, commisit, nisibi prodita, quae iam inde a Mithridatici regni temporibus, ne Oriens a Persis occuparetur, viribus restitit maximis.*

---

[31] Rosen (1970) 10–68.

[32] Sabbah (1978) 472–78. Blockley (1988) 259–60 suggests that it is loyalty to Ursicinus, as well as personal responsibility as a member of campaign staff.

[33] Blockley (1988) 244–60, esp. 247. He rightly emphasises the theatrical nature of the Amida scene and the role of Ursicinus and Shapur as its principals.

[34] Amm. Marc. 25.7.13.

You here will be justly censured, O Fortune of the Roman world! That, when storms shattered our country, you did snatch the helm from the hands of an experienced statesman and entrust it to an untried youth, who, since he was known during his previous life for no brilliant deeds in that field, cannot be justly either blamed or praised. But what grieved the heart of every patriotic citizen was this, that fearful of a rival to his power and bearing in mind that it was in Gaul and Illyricum that many men had taken the first steps to loftier power, in his haste to outstrip the report of his coming, under pretext of avoiding perjury he committed an act unworthy of an emperor, betraying Nisibis, which ever since the time of King Mithridates' reign had resisted with all its might the occupation of the Orient by the Persians. (Amm. Marc. 25.9.7–8).

The coupling of *Iustitia* with *Fortuna orbis Romani* is extremely significant. Julian (who took his first steps to higher power in Gaul and Illyricum) did not possess his own *genius*, but dreamt instead of the *Genius Publicus*.[35] The *Genius Publicus*, or spirit of the state, is necessarily ruled by the *Fortuna orbis Romani*, herself an agent of the decisions of *Themis* and *Adrastia*.[36] *Themis* acts as the advertising arm of the causative scheme, *Adrastia* as the executive, she who wields the *fata*. Rome's eternal pact with *Virtus* and *Fortuna* is a pact between the *genius* of the Roman people, and the causative scheme influencing the city's destiny.[37] *Adrastia* is:

> *ius quoddam sublime numinis efficacis, humanarum mentium opinione lunari circulo superpositum, vel ut definiunt alii, substantialis tutela generali potentia partilibus praesidens fatis, quam theologi veteres fingentes Iustitiae filiam, ex abdita quadam aeternitate tradunt omnia despectare terrena. haec ut regina causarum, et arbitra rerum ac disceptatrix, urnam sortium temperat, accidentium vices alternans, voluntatumque nostrarum exorsa interdum alio quam quo contendebant exitu terminans, multiplices actus permutando convolvit.*

the sublime jurisdiction of an efficient divine power, dwelling, as men think, above the orbit of the moon; or as others define her, an actual guardian presiding with universal sway over the destinies of individual men. The ancient theologians, regarding her and the daughter of Justice, say that from an unknown eternity, she looks down upon all the creatures of earth. She, as queen of causes and arbiter and judge of events, controls the urn with its lots and causes the changes of fortune, and sometimes she gives our plans a different result than that at which we aimed, changing and confounding many actions. (Amm. Marc. 14.11.25–26).

---

[35] See Amm. Marc. 20.5.10; Rike (1987) 22–23.
[36] Amm. Marc. 14.11.25–26.
[37] Amm. Marc. 14.6.3.

While *Themis* has this quality:

> *elementorum omnium spiritus, utpote perennium corporum praesentiendi motu semper et ubique vigens, ex his, quae per disciplinas varias affectamus, participat nobiscum munera divinandi: et substantiales potestates ritu diverso placatae, velut ex perpetuis fontium venis, vaticina mortalitati suppeditant verba, quibus numen praeesse dicitur Themidis, quam ex eo quod fixa fatali lege decreta, praescire facit in posterum, quae τεθειμένα sermo Graecus appellat, ita cognominatam, in cubili solioque Iouis, vigoris vivifici, theologi veteres collocarunt.*

> The spirit pervading all the elements, seeing that they are eternal bodies, is always and everywhere strong in the power of prescience, and as the result of the knowledge which we acquire through varied studies makes us also sharers in the gifts of divination; and the elemental powers, when propitiated by divers rites, supply mortals with words of prophecy, as if from the veins of inexhaustible founts. These prophecies are said to be under the control of the divine *Themis*, so named because she reveals in advance decrees determined for the future by the law of the fates, which the Greeks call *tetheimena*; and therefore the ancient theologians gave her a share in the bed and throne of Jupiter, the life-giving power. (Amm. Marc. 21.1.8).

Iustitia then emerges as the *Numen* of the *Res Gestae*. This is clear from the fact that it runs through everything, and is presented as both the presiding divinity and overarching textual causative structure, the starting point from which all else emanates. It therefore becomes apparent that the citizens of Nisibis, in appealing to *Iustitia*, are appealing to the destiny of the Roman people, indeed, the very fabric of empire, since it is Rome's pact with *Iustitia* that facilitates her expansion, and the security of her holdings, while her past, literary, individual and historical, provides the backdrop against which her agents rise and fall. *Iustitia* surveys the world with her *inconivus oculus*, she is *arbiter et vindex perpetuus rerum* 'the eternal witness and avenger of all things', she is *vigilavit attente*,[38] she is the very fabric of the Roman Empire, since *leges* are *fundamenta libertatis et retinacula sempiterna*, 'the everlasting foundations and moorings of liberty'.[39]

The handover of Nisibis thus appears as a particularised literary scheme, criticising the path on which the empire found itself, far beyond the immediate Jovian/Julian comparison which suggests itself. Rome's pact with *Iustitia* is particularly relevant in the case of the 'destructive and impious'

---

[38] Amm. Marc. 29.2.20.
[39] Amm. Marc. 14.6.5.

condition that 'Arsaces, our steadfast and faithful friend should never, if he asked it, be given help against the Persians', *quibus exitiale aliud accessit et impium, ne post haec ita composita, Arsaci poscenti, contra Persas ferretur auxilium, amico nobis semper et fido.*[40] This is especially relevant because the preservation of borders, or the geographic fabric of empire, which includes honourable treatment and protection of client kings such as the Armenian, Arsaces, forms a central part of the metaphorical empire that is Rome within Ammianus' *Res Gestae.*[41]

For much the same reason, the Siege of Amida is described as a result of *caeleste numen ut Romanae rei totius aerumnas intra unius regionis concluderet ambitum* 'the power of heaven, in order to compress the miseries of the whole Roman Empire within the confines of a single region'.[42] The fortunes of the Roman world are played out on the borders, and thus Nisibis becomes, for this section of the narrative, a cipher for the empire herself, the stage on which the play continues, and the scene in which its themes are revealed. The fortune of the Roman world has gone against *Iustitia*, and Julian is dead, the inevitability and logicality of which is signified by the sad sidling away of the *Genius Publicus.*[43] However, Fortune, as wielded by *Adrastia*, takes the blame for this contraction of the empire or what happens next, having placed power in the hands of this 'untried youth'.[44] It is clear that Rome's pact with *Iustitia* is gone badly awry.

Ammianus is not alone in seeing the treaty as calamitous,[45] yet most Christian authors (sensibly) locate the blame with Julian's disastrous Persian campaign. Lieu notes "the treaty of 363 with Persia was a major landmark, both from the political and human perspectives, for the history of Mesopotamia".[46] Ammianus does not blame Julian's failed campaign, since as demonstrated above, from the second Julian submits to the role of Augustus, he receives the guardianship of the *Genius Publicus.*[47] Julian's

---

[40] Amm. Marc. 25.7.12.

[41] In this context, see the treatment of Papa, client king of Armenia (30.1), which serves as the definitive parable on this point in the *Res Gestae*. Ammianus describes the death of Arsaces at the hands of Shapur at 27.12.3: *calcata fide sub Ioviano pactorum, iniectabat Armeniae manum ut eam, velut placitorum abolita firmitate, dicioni iungeret suae.* 'He laid his hand on Armenia, with the intention of bringing the country under his sway, as if all force of the agreements that had been made was at an end.' (Amm. Marc. 27.12.1).

[42] Amm. Marc. 19.1.4.

[43] Amm. Marc. 25.2.6.

[44] Amm. Marc. 25.9.7.

[45] Lib. *Or.* 1.134, 18.277–78; Agath. 4.26.6–7.

[46] Lieu (1986) 476.

[47] Amm. Marc. 20.5.10.

genius is not his own, he is wholly lacking in an individual destiny.[48] The placing of the diadem of 'Augustus' on his head leaves him with very little free will: the inexorable path to death in Persia is begun, no matter how many portents he ignores. Ammianus' complaint against Fortune thus is two-fold. The 'taking of the helm' from Julian, that 'martyr' of the *Res Gestae*, whose death is a function and precondition of his heroism, is explicable, but Ammianus nonetheless rails against it, particularly in the context of what comes next.

Ammianus' complaint against Fortune is not inconsistent: for Fortune acts in the *Res Gestae* as "no *true* part of the divine apparatus, but only a sign for that screen which separates men from the comprehension of thoroughly rational and appropriate *fata*".[49] It is important to distinguish this from the age-old problem of why bad things happen to good people, as exemplified for Ammianus by the death of Julian. *Adrastia* is not responsible for Julian's death, for (within the *Res Gestae*) he has done little to incur her wrath; merely ignoring her sister's warnings—though there is no guarantee that taking heed would have changed the outcome. As Ammianus says:

> *haec et huius modi quaedam innumerabilia ultrix facinorum impiorum, bonorumque praemiatrix, aliquotiens operatur Adrastia, (atque utinam semper!)*

> These and innumerable other instances of the kind are sometimes (and would that it was always so!) the work of Adrastia, the chastiser of evil deeds and the rewarder of good actions. (Amm. Marc. 14.11.25).

Ephrem's Julian also acts on a wider stage of divine cause and effect where the causality is the opposite:

> For [Julian] foretold and promised and wrote and sent to us
> that he would come down and trample it; Persia he would disperse.
> Singara he would rebuild. [This was] the threat of his letter.
> Nisibis was taken away by his campaign,
> but by his conjurers he cast down the power in which they believed.
> As a [sacrificial] lamb, the city saved his encampment.
> Nisibis that was captured—as a type of mirror
> [God] set it up, that we might see in it the pagan who set out to take what
>   was not his; he lost what was his.

---

[48] An example of this is the fact that Ammianus locates the rationale for the Persian invasion with Constantine (compare the Metrodorus story at 25.4.23), after which the war gains such momentum (the Persians make so many assaults upon the Roman State) that the invasion is seemingly obvious. Amm. Marc. 22.12.1, 25.4.24–26; Blockley (1988) 250.

[49] Rike (1987) 21 n.44. See Amm. Marc. 21.1.14.

> For it was the city that proclaimed to the world
> the shame of his conjurers and became his constant reproach....
> Let us seek the cause how and why
> the shield of all the cities, that city, was given up.
> The madman raged and set fire to his ships near the Tigris.
>   (Ephr. *c. J.* 2.15–16; 18).

For Ammianus, Nisibis is indeed 'a type of mirror', but rather than showing Julian getting what was coming to him, it shows the empire. The handover of Nisibis is a failure of the Roman State in its most basic aspect, namely zealous self-preservation. It is for this reason that Ammianus laments Nisibis, to a far greater extent than Adrianople, as the greatest disaster ever suffered by the state:

> *numquam enim ab urbis ortu inveniri potest annalibus replicatis (ut arbitror) terrarum pars ulla nostrarum ab imperatore vel consule hosti concessa, sed ne ob recepta quidem quae direpta sunt, verum ob amplificata regna triumphales glorias fuisse delatas. unde Publio Scipioni...Fulvio...et Opimio...triumphi sunt denegati. id etiam memoriae nos veteres docent in extremis casibus icta cum dedecore foedera, postquam partes verbis iuravere conceptis repetitione bellorum ilico dissoluta*[50]

> For never (I think) since the founding of our city can it be found by a reader of history that any part of our territory has been yielded to an enemy by an emperor or a consul; but that not even the recovery of anything that had been lost was ever enough for the honour of a triumph, but only the increase of our dominions. Hence it was that triumphs were refused to Publius Scipio...to Fulvius...to Opimius...In fact, the ancient records teach us that treaties made in extreme necessity with shameful conditions, even when both parties had taken oath in set terms, were at once annulled by a renewal of war. (Amm. Marc. 25.9.9–11).

This section sets out very clearly the rules governing the empire, that is to say the *Res Gestae*, presented by the narrative.[51] Ammianus argues at 25.7.8 that Jovian should have double-crossed the Persian envoys, and retreated to Corduene in the breathing space accorded by their return to their master. After all, *erat tamen pro nobis numen dei caelestis aeternum*, 'the eternal power of God in heaven was on our side', and the Persians

---

[50] *annalibus* and *ab urbis ortu* seem to hint at a Livian comparison at this point. There appears to be a direct Livian reference (9.6.1) at 25.9.11, when Ammianus refers to the Caudine Forks in Samnium—though he could, of course, have also derived this from Flor. 1.1.9.

[51] A number of these examples are manifestly misleading, which is consistent with the textual aims of the historian.

sue for peace first, being (or so Ammianus says) *animos ipsi quoque despondentes, quos omnibus paene proeliis pars Romana superior gravius quassabat in dies*, 'also themselves low in their minds, which the fact that the Roman side was superior in almost every battle shook more and more every day'.[52]

Perversely, the treaty results in even more Roman deaths.[53] It is evident that Ammianus is marking Nisibis as a pivotal point in his narrative. The historical temperament of *Romanitas* is altered inexorably by this very act. The Nisibene handover is highlighted by the historian because it, rather than the death of Julian, which is after all causality in action, encapsulates one of the decisive and cumulative themes of the work. This is Rome's enduring survival, but by means which are (to the author) distasteful, dubious, and which transgress his received and constructed ancestral ideal. It is instructive to recall that Nisibis (among Singara *et al.*) was taken in A.D. 114 by Trajan,[54] one of the premier *exempla* who coalesce around Julian. Ammianus makes this temporal and temperamental shift explicit with a curious story about Constantius. This most proud of emperors, a living status symbol of his own power, who did not even turn his head, nor spit,[55] whom Ammianus does not praise, was prepared to beg bread from the lowest of the low rather than concede his land. Sabinus spits out the story in impassioned plea:

> *Constantium immani crudescente bellorum materia, superatum a Persis interdum, deductumque postremo per fugam cum paucis ad Hibitam stationem intutam, panis frusto vixisse precario, ab anu quadam agresti porrecto, nihil tamen ad diem perdidisse supremum, et Iovianum inter exordia principatus, provinciarum muro cessisse, cuius obices iam inde a vetustate innoxiae permanserunt.*

> Constantius once, when the flames of a cruel war were raging, had been defeated by the Persians and finally had been driven in flight with a few followers to the unprotected post of Hibita, where he was obliged to live on a bit of bread which he begged from an old peasant woman; yet up to his last day he had lost nothing, whereas Jovian at the beginning of his Principate, had abandoned the defence of provinces whose walls had remained unshaken from the earliest times. (Amm. Marc. 25.9.3).

---

52 Amm. Marc. 25.7.5.
53 Amm. Marc. 25.8.1.
54 Lightfoot (1990) 115–26.
55 Amm. Marc. 16.10.10.

The contrast between Jovian's coinage, which celebrated the safe return of the expeditionary force as though it were a victory,[56] and this accompanying image of his predecessor living on scraps of peasant bread, but with his possessions and heritage intact, could not be stronger.

Ephrem also sees Nisibis as marking a new empire—the bier bearing the dead Julian sits before the walls, and he says:

> I knew it was a pre-arrangement, a miracle of justice
> That when the corpse of the fallen one crossed over
> the fearful standard went up....
>
>   ....and I said, 'Who will fear
> this corpse and deny the True One? (Ephr. *c. J.* 3. 2; 6).

He contextualises Julian's ruinous invasion, culminating in Persian territorial gains, as a spectacular setback for the emperor's paganism, since the empire has lost Nisibis, but been re-delivered into the hands of God by the workings of divine justice. The theologian lays the blame for the loss of Nisibis squarely at the feet of the apostate, but Ammianus argues that responsibility lies with his successor, Jovian, who is no real emperor at all. This serial escort of imperial corteges, whose power is *et cassum et umbratile (ut ministro rerum funebrium)*, 'of an empty and shadowy kind, since he was merely the director of a funeral procession',[57] is crowned inauspiciously by the first city of his empire to which he comes as *imperator*:

> cumque nihil promoveretur, iuris iurandi religionem principe destinatius praetendente, cum oblatam ei coronam aliquamdiu recusans, coactus denique suscepisset, Silvanus quidam causarum defensor, confidentius exclamavit: "ita" inquit, "imperator, a civitatibus residuis coroneris."

> But when nothing came of this, since the emperor the more stoutly maintained the sanctity of his oath; and when for a time he had refused the crown that was offered to him but was finally forced to accept it, one Silvanus, a pleader at the bar, was bold enough to say: 'Thus may you be crowned, O emperor, by the remaining cities.' (Amm. Marc. 25.9.4).

At that very moment, Jovian stands a fake emperor on foreign soil, despised by his (ex) citizens, his gold crown echoing the ration samples and courier horses earlier mistakenly shown to him.[58] The (entirely rational)

---

[56] Ehling (1996) 186–91. Legends include VICTORIA ROMANORUM and VICTORIA AUGUSTI. "His victory over the Persians could also be shown pictorially as a chained prisoner under a standard with a Chi-Rho on banner" – 191.

[57] See Amm. Marc. 21.16.21, compare with 25.10.5. Ammianus' obituary is not denigratory, but merely emphasises the emperor as a nonentity within the *Res Gestae*.

[58] Amm. Marc. 21.16.21.

entreaties of the Nisibenes fall upon deaf ears, since (Ammianus says) *imperatore (ut fingebat, alia metuens), periurii piacula declinante*, 'the emperor (as he pretended while moved by other fears) did not wish to incur the guilt of perjury.'[59] Ammianus juxtaposes the legal term with the citizens' altogether higher appeal to *Iustitia*—*periurii*, which balances *iuris iurandi*, as well as the later *amictu periurii fugiendi*[60] and *iuravere*,[61] the contravening of which is sanctioned by the *Iustitia* which holds sway over the Roman Empire, a very different Justice from that of Ephrem. That Jovian is no representative of that justice is evident; to hammer it home, Ammianus describes his rebuke by a representative of the law—Silvanus the *causarum defensor*.

Ammianus insinuates heavily that the decision to trade large swathes of Mesopotamia was based on fear of a challenge for the throne by Procopius:[62]

> *cum pugnari deciens expediret, ne horum quicquam dederetur, adulatorum globus instabat timido principi, Procopii metuendum subserens nomen, eumque affirmans, si redit cognito Iuliani interitu, cum intacto milite quem regebat, novas res nullo renitente facile moliturum. hac perniciosa verborum ille assiduitate nimia succensus, quae petebantur.*

> whereas it would have been better to fight 10 battles than give up any one of these [sites and satrapies conceded], the band of flatterers pressed upon the timid emperor, harping upon the dreaded name of Procopius, and declaring that if he returned on learning of the death of Julian, he would, with the fresh troops under his command, easily and without opposition make himself emperor. Jovian, inflamed by these dangerous hints too continually repeated, without delay surrendered all that was asked. (Amm. Marc. 25.7.10–11).

It is interesting that Ammianus here attributes one of Julian's fatal weaknesses, namely his over-reliance on his tame philosophers, his 'flatterers', to Jovian, who is controlled puppet-like by the 'too often' repetition of threats by his advisers. Jovian is a useful foil to the figure of Julian—Julian's weaknesses and errors are transposed onto Jovian, who both takes on some of his predecessor's characteristics (chiefly the negative), but also acts as everything he is not. Jovian is unjust, he is timid, he fears

---

[59] Amm. Marc. 25.9.2.
[60] Amm. Marc. 25.9.8.
[61] Amm. Marc. 25.9.11.
[62] Eutr. 10.17.3 concurs.

the Persians, he fears challenges to his throne, he is no real emperor, while Julian is the most real emperor of all.

Nonetheless, since every Ammianean portrait must have a semblance of balance, he does not ignore entirely certain concessions extracted by Jovian from Shapur. Most importantly perhaps, the treaty appears to have had a temporary character. Ammianus says it was to be in force for 30 years,[63] backed by Pseudo-Joshua Stylite, who says either 25 or 30 years (depending on interpretation), while others range from 100 to 120 years.[64] As Dignas and Winter note, this necessarily assigned it a provisional character, and meant that it cannot have been viewed as binding or definitive by either side. This is evident even much later. While Agathias called it humiliating,[65] in a counter example, Pseudo-Joshua informs us that the Sassanian King Balas (A.D. 484–88), on approaching the Emperor Zeno for a loan to fund his war against the Hepthalites, was rebuffed with the response that the taxes of Nisibis from which the Persians had benefited for many years were sufficient. In fact, Zeno demands the return of Nisibis, saying that he has wars of his own to fund.[66] Not only does this suggest that, long term, the damage was financial, it also suggests that Zeno is implying that the Persians had had Nisibene revenues on loan for some time.

We can perhaps conclude that the treaty was intended to surrender Nisibis for 30 years, the revenue from which would pay for the damage caused by the marauding Roman army, the populace would be retained initially, and that the city would eventually revert to the Romans. In essence, therefore, the treaty may have been a quasi-lease arrangement. Since histories trade in current as well as future capital, since they remark on the present as well as the past, we can perhaps detect a none-so-subtle hint from Ammianus that it was time to reclaim the lost territory. The 30 years was nearly up, after all.[67]

Ammianus acknowledges that Jovian gained this valuable concession on the part of the citizens:

---

[63] Amm. Marc. 25.7.14.

[64] Lieu (1986) 497; Josh. Styl. 7–8, 18–20; Zos. 3.31.1; Dignas and Winter (2007) 133–34; Fiey (1977) 35.

[65] Agath. 4.26.7.

[66] Dignas and Winter (2007) 133; Josh. Styl. 18, 20.

[67] Our *terminus post quem* for the *Res Gestae* is A.D. 391, based on a reference to the Serapeum as though it were still standing at Amm. Marc. 22.16.12.

difficile hoc adeptus, ut Nisibis et Singara sine incolis transirent in iura Persarum, a munimentis vero alienandis, reverti ad nostra praesidia Romani permitterentur.

with difficulty he succeeded in bringing it about that Nisibis and Singara should pass into control of the Persians without their inhabitants, and that the Romans in the fortresses that were to be taken from us should be allowed to return to our protection. (Amm. Marc. 25.7.11).

As noted by Lieu, the citizens of Nisibis 'should count themselves fortunate' that Jovian did extract this concession. Shapur had adopted a policy of populating Roman frontier cities with Persians,[68] for obvious reasons. Furthermore, the manpower shortage in the Persia Empire, coupled with the desirability of Roman citizens' skill base, was resulting in repeated deportations to sites within the Persian Empire, characterised by forced marches, construction work, followed by (for the lucky few who survived all this) the possibility of social and economic advancement.[69] For example, in the A.D. 330s, Shapur had used prisoners from the region of Nisibis, Singara and Amida to settle his new royal foundation, Karka de Ledan, in Bet Huzaie. In order to encourage a greater social mix, Shapur also relocated Persian citizens from other parts of the Eranshahr, including one Pusai, a celebrated craftsman who was to receive a royal commission, and who was himself the son of a prisoner whom Shapur, the son of Hormizd (II), had led out of the Roman Empire.[70]

From Ammianus himself, we know something of the fate of women, at least those of relatively high standing, since he tells us of how Craugasius' wife arranged his defection and reception out of love and the fear of being re-married to another.[71] Though Ammianus says that 'all' the Nisibenes were compelled to leave within three days, and Jovian ordered that *intra triduum omnes iussit excedere moenibus*,[72] it is evident that not everyone did leave behind their homes at once. The terms of the treaty did indeed stipulate that the city be handed over denuded of its inhabitants,[73] but the time limit seems to have been more flexible. This is apparent from the evidence of Ephrem, who lived out the last 10 years of his life in Edessa, going via Amida, but staying behind to witness the handover.[74] He comments

---

[68] Julian. *Or.* 1.27A/B.
[69] See Lieu (1986).
[70] Lieu (1986) 484.
[71] Amm. Marc. 19.9.3–6.
[72] Amm. Marc. 25.9.4.
[73] Malalas 13.27; compare Amm. Marc. 25.7.11.
[74] Ephr. *c.J.* 2.22–23.

on the deference that Shapur showed to his formerly indomitable enemies (and their Christian shrines). It therefore appears that Ammianus has condensed a more protracted departure into a single scene for dramatic effect.

Hence a distinction needs to be made between the actual grief of the citizens, as they are forced to leave their homes, and the grief of the citizens as constructed by Ammianus. For the two are separate, and had/have very different purposes. First of all, it is relatively easy to dissect the actual expressions of Nisibene distress from the passage. For example, at 25.8.13–14, Ammianus describes how the citizens, when rumour reached them of the treaty, became very fearful of retributions against them by Shapur, since it was their repeated and stalwart resistance which had prevented him previously from over-running the region. Incidentally, this rather exonerates Jovian—since he managed to extract the concession that the Romans could evacuate the city[75]—but naturally, Ammianus manages to undercut this, saying:

> spe . . . sustentari potuerunt exigua, hac scilicet velut suopte motu vel exoratus eorum precibus, imperator eodem statu retinebit urbem, Orientis firmissimum claustrum.

> they could sustain themselves with one slight hope, namely, that the emperor would, of his own accord or prevailed upon by their entreaties, keep the city in its present condition, as the strongest bulwark of the Orient. (Amm. Marc. 25.8.14).

The pathos of the plight of the citizens arises from their inability to defend themselves against their now master Shapur II, as they had done three times before. Ammianus in fact achieves his most intense sense of paradox from his repeated insinuation that Jovian, agent of Rome,[76] is acting for the aggressor against the city. It is Romans who are *appositis compulsoribus*, 'appointed to drive them out', and who *mortem siqui distulerit egredi minitantibus*, 'threaten with death all who hesitated to leave'.[77]

It is within this context that the most densely allusive section of the passage should be considered:

---

[75] Dignas and Winter (2007) 133 also observe that it seems as though Shapur did not gain back all the territories ceded in A.D. 298, as Sophanene and Ingilene stayed under Roman influence.

[76] Amm. Marc. 14.6.5 *ideo urbs venerabilis, post superbas efferatarum gentium cervices oppressas, latasque leges, fundamenta liberatis et retinacula sempiterna, velut frugi parens et prudens et dives, Caesaribus tamquam liberis suis regenda patrimonii iura permisit.*

[77] Amm. Marc. 25.9.5.

moenia permixta sunt lamentis et luctu, et per omnia civitatis membra una
vox cunctorum erat gementium, cum laceraret crines matrona, exsul fuganda
laribus in quibus nata erat et educata, orbataque mater liberis vel coniuge
viduata, procul ab eorum manibus pelleretur, et turba flebilis postes penatium
amplexa vel limina, lacrimabat. exin variae complentur viae, qua quisque
poterat dilabentium. properando enim multi furabantur opes proprias quas
vehi posse credebant, contempta reliqua supellectili, pretiosa et multa. hanc
enim reliquerunt penuria iumentorum.

Lamentation and grief filled the city, and in all its parts, no sound save universal wailing was to be heard; the matrons tore their hair, since they were
to be sent into exile from the homes in which they were born and reared;
mothers who had lost their children, and widows bereft of their husbands,
mourned that they were driven from the ashes of their loved ones; and the
weeping throng embraced the doors or the thresholds of their homes. Then,
the various roads were filled with people wherever each could find refuge.
In their haste, many secretly carried off such of their own property as they
thought they could take with them, disregarding the rest of their possessions, which, though many and valuable, they were obliged to leave behind
for a lack of pack animals. (Amm. Marc. 25.9.5–6).

The passage contains echoes of Vergil, Livy and Valerius Flaccus.[78] Yet the
Livian parallel is most striking. As observed by Fornara,[79] the phraseologi-
cal similarities are evident, and thematically, the similarity is obvious. Livy
describes the evacuation and razing of Alba Longa, as her citizens are subsumed into Rome, while Ammianus describes the evacuation of Nisibis as
her physical presence is subsumed into Persia. This allusion with a twist is
a common tenet of the Ammianean technique:[80] so it is that in Ammianus,
Nisibis herself takes on the role of the deported citizen. If the merger with
Alba Longa is an integral part of the creation of a dominant Rome, then
the handover of Nisibis is a tragedy, one that has never been seen since
the founding of the city, and thus strikes at the very roots of empire. Her
citizens remain Roman, but no longer Nisibene, for Nisibis ceases to exist.
By being removed from their native place, they are stripped of their civic
identity, which is one of the twin loyalties (Nisibis; Rome) that make up
their state allegiance.[81] It is interesting to note that just as "Alba continues
to survive as a religious centre, an externally "absent" city",[82] so did Nisibis, in the form of the School of 'the Persians' at Edessa.

---

[78] Valerius Flaccus 4.373; Verg., *Aen.* 2.490; Livy, *Epit.* 1.29.
[79] Fornara (1993) 433–35.
[80] See, for example, Fornara (1993) 435.
[81] Cic. *Leg.* 2.5.
[82] Feldherr (1998) 125.

To conclude, as demonstrated above, Ammianus' presentation of the handover is formed by his thematic concerns. These include a shift in the history of the empire away from a course mainly consonant with its pact with *Iustitia*, an exoneration of Julian, and a parallel depiction of Jovian as a shadowy imperial presence, a foil to his predecessor. In Ammianus' narrative scheme, the geographic boundary of empire was redrawn at the same time as the juncture in its history created by the Nisibene handover. However, Ammianus does not wholly exaggerate the shock of the treaty of A.D. 363, which was indeed immense. Nisibis was now Persian, with Persian overlords, and it was now used as a base for Persian raids into Roman territory,[83] as it had been in A.D. 299.

Raids and skirmishes between the two empires shifted further north and west, though still within the range of territory through which they had oscillated throughout the centuries. Rome fortified Edessa more heavily, and in 505, Anastasius authorised the fortification of Dara as a replacement Nisibis, on the basis of desperate military need. However, it must be acknowledged that the eastern border was a necessarily fluid entity.[84] Both empires were accustomed to shifting frontiers in this region. Amida and Singara had fallen into Persian hands before, and did so again. Amida fell to Kavadh I in A.D. 502, and was regained by the Romans in 504, while the Emperor Maurice sacked Singara in 578. Hence the citizens of border towns cannot have been unprepared for the risks their locale presented, yet they must also have been sensitive to the economic opportunities provided by that very frontier region.

As a result, Nisibis has endured. Its continued role on a border of one sort or another, and, therefore, its importance as a trading centre coupled with its military utility, has ensured both periods of prosperity and its survival throughout the centuries. Despite experiencing cycles of decline, notably following the Mongolian invasions in the 13th c., and preceding the battle of Nizib, 24th June 1839, when the Ottomans were defeated by the Egyptians,[85] such decline has been succeeded by continued investment

---

[83] Fiey (1977) 37, after which Qarpos, a bishop of Sur, appears to have been martyred in the town.

[84] See Hodgson (1989) 177–85 on the differences between the western and eastern frontiers as due to economic geography, resulting in a necessarily more porous system in the East.

[85] Both times it has recovered. Buckingham (1827) 1.441–42 describes a severely diminished Nisibis, suffering from the economic decline then endemic in the Ottoman Empire: "At the present moment, it is occupied by about 300 families of Arabs and Koords, mixed, under the government of Sheikh Farsee, who is himself a Koord horseman . . . The houses

and renewed growth. This continues to the present day. In 2004, the Turkish government announced that Nisibis was to be de-mined in the hope of oil discovery.[86] However, the recent conflict in Syria has resulted in the closure of the border at Nusaybin, as turbulent times once again visit the region.

ACKNOWLEDGMENTS

Many thanks to Dr. Neil McLynn for his kind assistance with this paper, and Dr. David Gwynn for his invaluable help with Ammianus as a whole.

BIBLIOGRAPHY

Primary Sources

Agath. = Keydell R. (1967) ed. *Agathiae Myrinaei Historiarum libri quinque* (Berlin 1967).
Amm. Marc. = Rolfe J. C. (1963) ed. and trans. *Res Gestae* (London 1963).
Cic. *Leg.* = Keyes C. W. (2000) ed. and trans. Cicero, Marcus Tullius, *De re publica; De legibus* (Cambridge, Mass. and London 2000).
Cod. *Theod.* = Mommsen Th., Meyer P. *et al.* (1905) edd. *Theodosiani libri xvi cum constitutionibus Sirmondianis* (Berlin 1905).
Ephr. = McVey K. E. (1989) trans. *Ephrem the Syrian: Hymns* (New York 1989).
Eutr. = Santini S. (1979) ed. *Eutropii Breviarium ab urbe condita* (Leipzig 1979); Bird H. W. (1993) trans. *The Breviarium ab urbe condita of Eutropius, the Right Honourable Secretary of State for General Petitions: dedicated to Lord Valen, Gothicus Maximus and Perpetual Emperor* (Translated Texts for Historians 14) (Liverpool 1993).
Flor. = Forster E. S. (1984) ed. and trans. Florus, Lucius Annaeus, *Epitome of Roman History* (London 1984).

---

of the modern town, which are found erected on the ruins, scarcely exceed a hundred habitable ones, and these are small square buildings of stone and mud, with flat roofs of straw, divided by narrow alleys—for they can scarcely be called streets—and wearing altogether an air of great poverty." Kinneir (1818) 442 concurs, calling it "this miserable village". Buckingham (1827) 1.440–42 contrasts this with the prosperity recorded by Rabbi Benjamin of Tudela in 1173 (who visited the city on a journey through Mesopotamia since it then had an assembly of 1,000 Jews) and Otter, in 1736, who notes a story by his guide that "il y avoit sur les bordes de cette rivière plus de quarante mille jardins, dans lesquels on trouvoi quantité de roses blanches; mais pas une rouge." The poverty of the town in Buckingham's time is also reflected in the exorbitant safe conduct fee demanded by Sheikh Farsee, to say nothing of the multiple thefts he endured during his stay (1.427–8, 447). Tavernier (1724) 1.235–36 concurs in earlier prosperity, describing the fertility around this "gros village". He says the majority of inhabitants then (between *ca.* 1630–66) were Nestorian and Armenian Christians, and describes the many candles offered up in prayer for healing etc. in the Church of St. Jacob.

[86] http://news.bbc.co.uk/2/hi/middle_east/3541147.stm.

Jer. *Chron.* = Donalson M. D. (1996) trans. *A Translation of Jerome's* Chronicon *with Historical Commentary* (Lewiston 1996).

Josh. Styl. = Wright W. (1882) trans. *The Chronicle of Joshua the Stylite* (Amsterdam 1968).

Julian. *Or.* = Wright W. C. F. (1913–23) ed. and trans. *The Works of the Emperor Julian* (London and Cambridge, Mass. 1913–23).

Lib. *Or.* = Norman A. F. (1969–77) ed. and trans. Libanius, *Selected Works* (Cambridge, Mass. 1969–77).

Livy, *Epit.* = Foster B. O., Moore F. G., Sage E. T. and Schlesinger A. C. (1919–59) edd. and trans. Livy, *History of Rome* (Cambridge, Mass. and London 1919–59).

Malalas = Thurn I. (2000) ed. *Ionnis Malalae Chronographia* (Berlin 2000).

Not. Dign. or. = Seeck I. (1962) ed. *Notitia Dignitatum: accedunt notitia urbis Constantinopolitananae et Laterculi provinciarum* (Frankfurt 1962).

Philostorgius = Amidon P. R. (2007) trans. *Philostorgius: Church History* (Writings from the Greco-Roman World 23) (Atlanta, GA 2007).

Theod. *HE* = Parmentier L. and Hansen G. C. (1998) edd. Theodoret, Bishop of Cyrrhus, *Kirchengeschichte* (Berlin 1998); anon. trans. in Bohn's *Ecclesiastical Library* (London 1854).

Theophanes = de Boor (1883, 1885) ed. *Theophanis Chronographia* 2 vols. (Leipzig 1883, 1885).

Valerius Flaccus = Mozley J. H. (1936) ed. and trans. *Valerius Flaccus* (Cambridge, Mass. and London 1936).

Verg. *Aen.* = Dryden J. and Keener F. M. (1997) edd. and trans. *Virgil's Aeneid* (London 1997).

Secondary Works

Blockley R. C. (1988) "Ammianus Marcellinus on the Persian invasion of 359", *Phoenix* 42.3 (1988) 244–60.

Buckingham J. S. (1827) *Travels in Mesopotamia, Including a Journey from Aleppo to Bagdad by the Route of Beer, Orfah, Diabekr, Mardin, and Mousul: with Researches on the Ruins of Nineveh, Babylon, and other Ancient Cities* vols. 1–2 (London 1827).

Dignas B. and Winter E. (2007) *Rome and Persia in Late Antiquity: Neighbours and Rivals* (Cambridge 2007).

Ehling K. (1996) "Der Ausgang de Perserfeldzuges in der Münzpropaganda des Jovian", *Klio* 78 (1996) 186–91.

Feldherr A. (1998) *Spectacle and Society in Livy's History* (Los Angeles and London 1998).

Fiey J.-M. (1977) *Nisibe: métropole syriaque orientale et ses suffragants des origines à nos jours* (Corpus Scriptorum Christianorum Orientalium vol. 338 t. 54) (Louvain 1977).

Fornara C. W. (1993) "Studies in Ammianus Marcellinus II", *Historia* 4 (1993) 420–38.

Gibbon E. (1909) *The Decline and Fall of the Roman Empire*, ed. J. B. Bury (London 1909).

Henderson W. O. (1948) "German economic penetration in the Middle East, 1870–1914", *The Economic History Review* 18 (1948) 54–64.

Hodgson N. (1989) "The East as part of the wider Roman imperial frontier policy", in *The Eastern frontier of the Roman Empire: Proceedings of a Colloquium held at Ankara in September 1988*, edd. D. H. French and C. S. Lightfoot (BAR International Series 553) (Oxford 1989) 177–85.

James. S. (2004) *Excavations at Dura-Europos 1928–1937 Final Report VII: the Arms and Armour and other Military Equipment* (London 2004).

Khatchatrian A. (1957) "Le baptistère de Nisibe", *Actes du Vème Congrès international d'archéologie chrétienne, 1954* (Paris and Rome 1957) 407–21.

Kinneir J. M. (1818) *Journey through Asia Minor, Armenia and Koordistan, in the years 1813 and 1814; with Remarks on the Marches of Alexander and Retreat of the Ten Thousand* (London 1818).

Lieu S. C. (1986) "Captives, refugees and exiles: a study of cross-frontier civilian movements and contacts between Rome and Persia from Valerian to Jovian", in *The Defence of the Roman and Byzantine East: Proceedings of a Colloquium held at the University of Sheffield in April 1986*, edd. P. Freeman and D. L. Kennedy (BAR International Series 297) (Oxford 1986) 475–505.

Lightfoot C. S. (1982) *The Eastern Frontier of the Roman Empire with Special Reference to the Reign of Constantius II* (D.Phil. diss., Univ. of Oxford 1982).

—— (1989) "Sapor before the walls of Amida", in *The Eastern frontier of the Roman Empire: Proceedings of a Colloquium held at Ankara in September 1988*, edd. D. H. French and C. S. Lightfoot (BAR International Series 553) (Oxford 1989) 285–94.

—— (1990) "Trajan's Parthian war and the fourth century perspective", *JRS* 80 (1990) 115–26.

Matheson S. B. (1982) *Dura Europos: the Ancient City and the Yale Collection* (New Haven 1982).

Matthews J. F. (1989a) "Ammianus and the eastern frontier in the fourth century: a participant's view", in *The Eastern frontier of the Roman Empire: Proceedings of a Colloquium held at Ankara in September 1988*, edd. D. H. French and C. S. Lightfoot (BAR International Series 553) (Oxford 1989) 549–64.

—— (1989b) *The Roman Empire of Ammianus* (London 1989).

Olivier G. A. (1801–1807) *Voyages dans l'empire ottoman, l'Égypte et la Perse* (Paris 1801–1807).

Perkins A. (1973) *The Art of Dura Europos* (Oxford 1973).

Rike R. L. (1987) Apex Omnium: *Religion in the* Res Gestae *of Ammianus* (California 1987).

Rosen K. (1970) *Studien zur Darstellungskunst und Glaubwürdigkeit des Ammianus Marcellinus* (Bonn 1970).

Rostovtzeff M. (1983) *Dura Europos and its Art* (Oxford 1983).

Sabbah G. (1978) *La méthode d'Ammien Marcellin: recherches sur la construction du discours historique dans les Res Gestae* (Paris 1978).

Tavernier J. B. (1724) *Les six voyages de Monsieur J. B. Tavernier, Ecuyer, Baron d'Aubonne, en Turquie, en Perse, et aux Indies* (Rouen 1724).

Thompson E. A. (1947) *The Historical Work of Ammianus Marcellinus* (Cambridge 1947).

THE WEST

IMPERIAL CAMPAIGNS BETWEEN DIOCLETIAN AND HONORIUS, A.D. 284–423: THE RHINE FRONTIER AND THE WESTERN PROVINCES

Hugh Elton

Abstract

This paper focuses on the archaeological evidence for western imperial campaigns between the reigns of Diocletian (A.D. 284–305) and Honorius (A.D. 395–423). Military campaigning is an ephemeral and rapidly changing process of human interactions. Although Roman campaigning is often well-documented, archaeological evidence is not especially well-suited to documenting events within a particular year, though it is very useful in enhancing our knowledge of resources and processes. This paper analyses the army's actions, and then discusses how the archaeological evidence contributes to our understanding. There were enormous differences between the resources available to Rome and her enemies in the 4th c. West, even if frontier culture was similar.

THE ROMAN DEFENSIVE SYSTEM

To evaluate the evidence, whether literary or archaeological, it is necessary to understand the army's objectives. The purpose of the army was to defend the Roman Empire, a task that involved keeping barbarians out and destroying any domestic enemies, such as challengers to imperial power or bandits. There were three major frontier regions to be defended, Britain, the Rhine and Upper Danube, and North Africa. There were also requirements for troops for internal security in the whole of the empire. Enemies faced in Britain included Picts, Scots (from Ireland) and Saxons, so naval resources were particularly important. On the Rhine, the Romans faced various groups of Franks and Alamanni, and on the Danube, Sarmatians and Quadi. And then there was a third long frontier region in North Africa, where the challenges came from various tribes of Numidians and Moors. Of these three regions, the Rhine-Danube was the most important in the 3rd and 4th c. A.D., but this situation changed dramatically in 429 when Africa became a critical zone following invasion by the Vandals.

A. Sarantis, N. Christie (edd.) *War and Warfare in Late Antiquity: Current Perspectives* (Late Antique Archaeology 8.1–8.2 – 2010–11) (Leiden 2013), pp. 655–681

The difficulty of demonstrating this change archaeologically is a warning of the limitations of this sort of evidence for this sort of problem. The seriousness of the threat posed on the Rhine and Danube in the 4th c. has recently been challenged, particularly for Gaul by John Drinkwater, but the seriousness of the Saxon threat has also been called into question.[1] Nonetheless, even if the Romans exaggerated the threats, centuries of exposure to Roman military methods had made the enemies faced by the empire in the 4th c. more dangerous than the barbarian groups faced by the High Empire. On the other hand, the Roman army had evolved too, and many scholars now believe it was more effective in the 4th c. than in the 1st. c. A.D., an approach followed here.

The imperial objective of keeping barbarians out of the empire was achieved by a combination of defensive and offensive measures. Defensively, preclusive security was provided by stationing troops along the borders in fortifications. In addition (and in recognition of the fact that the barbarian threat could not be eradicated permanently), the enemy were kept off balance by a combination of political activity and pre-emptive strikes into the *barbaricum* (barbarian territory). Until A.D. 395, most of these strikes were carried out by field armies and led by an emperor. After the death of Theodosius I, Honorius' age (he was only 10 when he took over the western Empire) kept him from field command, but the same system of field armies continued, though led by the senior *magister militum*, most notably Stilicho between 394 and 408, then Constantius between 411 and 421.[2]

The effectiveness of this system is hard to assess. Many contemporaries thought that too much was spent on defence (i.e. that their taxes were too high) or that the army performed poorly. In analysing practice, it is probably better to focus on what was done, not on what contemporaries felt about what should be done. Vegetius, for example, felt that the quality of Roman infantry was low, though he was more complimentary about the quality of Roman cavalry.[3] Nothing substantive can be said with confidence about the cost of defence in the 4th c., or its relationship to the finances of the Roman State. Nonetheless, the Roman Empire could not have afforded a defensive system that kept all barbarians outside at all times. And focusing on financial resources alone may be missing the point

---

[1] Drinkwater (2007) 177–79; Pearson (2005) 73–88.
[2] Lee (2007) 22–33.
[3] Veg. *Mil.* 1.20.

since, as Synesius (responsible for administering some of the defences of Cyrenaica in the early 5th c.) put it, 'for war we need hands, not a list of names'.[4]

The threats and responses in each frontier region evolved. Thus, the Rhine formed the border of Gaul until 406, but after the Vandal, Sueve and Alan crossing of 406, it continued to act as a frontier region, though the tasks of the Gallic army were now more complex, having to deal with both defence on the Rhine and internal enemies. And in addition to the problems posed by the 406 invaders, there were those posed by both rival emperors, such as Constantine III, and the arrival of Goths from Italy.[5] The defensive system thus worked well to 406 since cities continued to function in the frontier regions and the border remained in the same place. The assertion of an effective system is an imperial perspective, however, and levels of military efficiency may have appeared different to different contemporaries. Thus, Jerome's panic (from Palestine) about the 406 invaders was probably quite different from Stilicho's response since both had different expectations.[6] Similarly, taxpayers on the Rhine might be more concerned with the level of security provided, taxpayers in Spain more with the level of taxation. The impact of taxes might be shown by the dissent caused when Galerius attempted to collect taxes from the population of Italy in 307. The claims to power of Maxentius at this point show that taxation was a political issue, not surprising as it had recently been imposed by Diocletian.[7] Perceptions of the success of the system might vary over time; in 356, the Rhineland with wandering barbarian bands looked far more insecure than it did in 358 following Julian's victory at Strasbourg. Archaeological evidence, even more so than literature, is rarely precise enough to distinguish chronologically between these situations.

THE ROMAN ARMY

The defensive campaigns and cross-border strikes of the emperor (or senior *magister militum*) and his field army made up much of the empire's campaigning between Diocletian and Honorius. Closest to the emperor were

---

[4] Syn. *Ep.* 78.
[5] Elton (1992) 167–76; Kulikowski (2000a) 325–45.
[6] Jer. *Ep.* 123.
[7] Millar (1986) 295–318 at 277–78; Lactant. *De mort. pers.* 26.2.

regiments of imperial guard troops. Under Diocletian, the infantry guards were the praetorians, while the older cavalry regiment of the *equites singulares* was supplemented by a group of elite cavalry regiments known as the *scholae palatinae*. Constantine disbanded Maxentius' praetorians after the Battle of the Milvian Bridge in A.D. 312, and Licinius' (and probably his own) after Chrysopolis in 324. After this, the *scholae palatinae* remained as the imperial guard.[8] Although these regiments fought often and well, most of the combat power of the empire was provided by the imperial field armies. There were two of these from 285 (one led by Diocletian and one by Maximian), increased to four in 293 with the creation of the Tetrarchy. This system allowed the empire to deal simultaneously with problems on multiple fronts. Although the movements of some of these field armies can be traced, less can be said about many aspects of their activity.

Numbers are a difficult topic. Lactantius wrote that Diocletian quadrupled the number of Roman troops by creating a new army for each of the Tetrarchs.[9] It is unlikely that the number of troops actually quadrupled, but neither literary nor archaeological evidence allows anything to be said about how the total number of men in the army changed during the period under consideration here. This question is different from that of changing sizes of regiments. Legions in the mid-4th c. (probably 1,200 strong) were smaller than those of the early 3rd c. (10 cohorts, about 5,000 men), but the date and manner of this change is complicated (and it is probably better to think of different regiments developing their own organisations rather than a single centrally-mandated change).[10] Under the Tetrarchy, tile stamps from Galerius' palace at Gamzigrad in the early 4th c. mention 5 different cohorts from Legio V Macedonica, and when Diocletian raised a new series of 6 legions, three named Iovia for himself and three named Herculia for Maximian, these also had 10 cohorts; an inscription from Sitifis in Mauretania mentions cohorts VII and X of *Legio II Herculia*. Many frontier legions still had multiple cohorts at the end of the 4th c., though by the mid-4th c., field army legions were certainly smaller than 5,000 men.[11] How much smaller is currently debated. Duncan-Jones and Tomlin have suggested small regiments, based on Egyptian papyri from the end of the 3rd c. These arguments have been criticised by Coello and

---

8 *ILS* 2791; Lactant. *De mort. pers.* 19.6; Elton (2007) 270–309 at 279–80.
9 Lactant. *De mort. pers.* 7.2.
10 Elton (1996b) 89–90.
11 Veg. *Mil.* 1.17; *ILS* 4195; Christodoulou (2002) 275–81.

Zuckerman.[12] The discussion depends on two types of material, papyri which can be interpreted as referring either to complete units or to parts of units, and the archaeological evidence for small fortifications. Such arguments need to reflect the fact that at all periods there were many more bases than units and that out-posting parts of units to several locations was common.[13]

Drawing conclusions about unit structures from the design of fortifications is difficult since more is known about the defences than about the interior arrangements of these fortifications. Nor can the often smaller area of Late Roman forts be used to suggest smaller units since (unlike the usual pattern in the early Empire) the interior buildings for accommodation, administration and storage were often built directly against the fort wall, reducing the perimeter to be defended and thus the fort's area.[14] More excavation will help, but the great variety of types of Late Roman units, as well as the frequent modifications required by changing garrisons, resulted in many variations in accommodation. And, even though individual regiments or fortifications may have been smaller, this does not help assess whether there were fewer men under arms in a particular region.

One factor often connected with both the size of regiments and recruiting patterns is a difficulty in recruiting. Many of the soldiers in Late Roman armies were born outside the Roman Empire, a process often described as 'barbarisation'. This should not be linked to a hypothesised empire-wide manpower shortage. As I have argued elsewhere, the extent of non-Roman recruiting has often been exaggerated by modern writers and in the 4th c., the majority of Roman regular regiments were composed mostly of men born in the empire. There were some occasions when there were regiments recruited mostly of men of non-Roman origin, for example, some of the new *auxilia palatina* recruited from the Rhine by Constantius I and Constantine I, at around the end of the 3rd c., or the *foederati* regiments of the late 4th and early 5th c., but such units would in most cases have rapidly lost this special character.[15]

---

[12] Duncan-Jones (1990) 105–17, 214–21; Tomlin (2008) 143–66; Coello (1996) 37–42; Zuckerman (1988) 279–87.

[13] Out-posting has recently been rejected by Mackensen (1999) 221.

[14] Johnson (1983); Lander (1984) 259–61; Bidwell (1991) 9–15; compare with Richardson (2002) 93–107.

[15] Elton (1996b) 128–54.

Most of the evidence for recruitment is literary, and demonstrating the recruitment of soldiers of extra-imperial origin through archaeological evidence (whether they were men in their own units or parts of regular regiments) is difficult. Although we do not know how much equipment was issued by the state (though the existence of state arms factories (*fabricae*) suggests that most was state-provided), it seems unlikely that new recruits retained much native equipment.[16] However, even if intrusive material is recovered from military sites, this is not proof of non-Roman origin for all the troops based there. Roman soldiers were great travellers, and any 'intrusive' or 'non-Roman' find is as likely to be a military souvenir as it is evidence of soldiers of extra-imperial origin. Aurelius Gaius' tombstone from Phrygia in modern Turkey records a career at the end of the 3rd c. Although his epitaph is damaged, it mentions his service in Asia, Caria, Lydia, Lycaonia, Cilicia, Phoenicia, Syria, Arabia, Palestine, Egypt, Alexandria, India (perhaps Yemen or Axum), Mesopotamia, Cappadocia, Galatia, Bithynia, Thrace, Moesia, the Carpians' territory, Sarmatia four times, Viminacium, the Goths' territory twice, Germany, Dardania, Dalmatia, Pannonia, Gaul, Spain, Mauretania, and 10 other areas now lost from the stone.[17] Gaius could have collected souvenirs from almost anywhere in or outside the empire in the course of his travels.

Although Gaius may have been especially well-travelled, in the mid-4th c. the movements of the Celtae and Petulantes, two regiments of elite field army troops, can be followed. After campaigns against the Franks and Alamanni in Gaul in the late 350s, they marched east with Julian to Persia in 363, and then returned to the West in 364 with Valentinian I, where they campaigned in Gaul and Raetia.[18] Repairs and replacement of equipment meant that the appearance of those men who left Gaul in 361 was probably quite different from the men who returned in 364. And then there is the intriguing case of the macaque buried in military style from Les Colomines in the Pyrenees, perhaps to be viewed as a mascot?[19]

Even associating deposits of military equipment (with or without intrusive elements) with Roman military activity is difficult, since not all weaponry was military. Halsall's useful 1992 article on the Reihengräberzivilisation makes the point that weapon graves were common in the north-western provinces of the empire in the 3rd and 4th c. Moreover, the

---

[16] Coulston (2007); Woods (1993).
[17] *AE* 1981.777=*SEG* 31.1116; Drew-Bear (1981).
[18] Elton (1996b) 208.
[19] Guàrdia (2005) 65–106; and see Olesti *et al.* (in this collection).

presence of women and children in Roman camps was common, and categories such as military and civilian may not have been exclusive.[20] Even when material belongs to the Roman army, it may not reflect campaigning activity, since much material was abandoned or sold, buried or ritually deposited. Sometimes it does reflect campaigning, but the situation at Dura-Europos in Syria where soldiers were caught in a collapsed mine cannot be duplicated in the western Empire. Thus, the Deurne helmet from the Netherlands has an inscription identifying it as belonging to a member of the cavalry regiment *VI Stablesiani*, but it has recently been argued that this is a ritualised deposit, perhaps for a retirement, and so has little to do with campaigning.[21]

Regardless of the size, ethnic composition and equipment of these Roman regiments, they were combined to form field armies whose activities can sometimes be illustrated by archaeological evidence. Thus, a tombstone from Cologne records the death of a *protector* Viatorinus at the hands of a Frank in barbarian territory near Divitia, a fort on the right bank of the Rhine opposite Cologne. Providing a context for Viatorinus' death is impossible, and there is no way to suggest a date more precise than some point in the 3rd to 5th c.[22] Identifying a particular campaign is a problem for which literary sources are better suited, for instance, Ammianus Marcellinus described the 357 campaign against the Alamanni involving 13,000 men from the Gallic army under Julian, and 25,000 from the western praesental army under Barbatio, details that could never be gleaned from archaeology.[23]

Battlefield performance is a part of the story of imperial campaigning, but the archaeology of battlefields is of little use for a number of reasons.[24] If a battlefield can be identified, then military equipment can certainly be recovered from it. There are no Late Roman western examples, though the Kalkriese stands as a good western example for the early Empire.[25] But, given the poor knowledge of any Late Roman battle in terms of which events happened where and the difficulties in distinguishing between

---

[20] Halsall (1992); Harke (1990); Gardner (1999); Willems (1989).

[21] James (2004); van Driel-Murray (2004).

[22] *ILS* 2784.

[23] Amm. Marc. 16.11.2, 12.2.

[24] Freeman and Pollard (2001).

[25] Schlüter (1999) 125–59; Harnecker (2004).

Roman and non-Roman equipment,[26] rigorous scepticism is in order.[27] There are good modern examples of battlefield archaeology, the classic example being the Battle of Little Big Horn in 1876. However, it is worth noting with respect to this action the small size of the forces engaged (fewer than 1,000 men on either side), the fact that the battlefield was relatively undisturbed afterwards (designated as a National Cemetery in 1879), and that there are numerous first-hand accounts (including an official after-action enquiry in 1879). These conditions cannot be approached for a Late Roman battlefield and should give pause for reflection on how useful work on these battlefields could be. The evidence for sieges can be better, with Dura-Europos being the best Late Roman example, but though there were long sieges in the West, for example, Julian's actions at Aquileia in 361,[28] no western site has yet produced anything comparable.[29]

MILITARY BASES

Such large forces as the armies deployed by Julian and Barbatio in A.D. 357 were normally based at the 'Tetrarchic capitals', palace-cum-bases located either close to the frontier or on major communication routes. Thus, in Gaul, Trier was well-placed for action on the Rhine, in Italy, Milan or Aquileia were close to both the Rhine and Danube, and in the Balkans, Sirmium had good communications with both the Upper and Middle Danube. In Italy, Ravenna was used regularly as an imperial capital after 402, though less is known about where the army was based, perhaps at Ticinum (Pavia), which was certainly in use as an imperial capital in 408 during preparations for a campaign in Gaul. Elsewhere, there were less-developed facilities at temporary complexes at sites like Corduba (perhaps used by Maximian during his Spanish campaign) and London, where a complex whose construction is dated by dendrochronology to 294 was probably used by Carausius, Allectus, and then Constantius I. No such facilities are known in Africa, though there were presumably some government buildings in Carthage.[30]

---

[26] See Coulston (in this collection).
[27] See Lillington-Martin and Colvin (in this collection).
[28] See Whitby (in this collection).
[29] James (2004).
[30] Haley (1994); Williams (1993) 29–32.

These large bases were necessary to support the emperor and the *comitatus*, i.e. the emperor's household, the imperial administration, and the army. The household included all of the emperor's personal attendants, secretaries, cooks, grooms, barbers, etc., each with his own equipment and slaves. The imperial administration included senior officials like the praetorian prefect, *magister officiorum, comes sacrarum largitionum*, etc., allowing the emperor to issue laws, mint coins, hold trials and listen to appeals. There would also be large amounts of paperwork since a law of 319 issued in Sirmium demanded that summaries of all activities (*breves omnium negotiorum*) carried out by provincial governors should be sent to the offices of the praetorian prefect.[31] There was also the traffic of ambassadors from cities and of foreigners and messengers who kept on coming and going, including the regiments of imperial guards, and the imperial 'staff officers', the *protectores Augusti*.

And then there were the field armies whose troops became known as the *comitatenses* from the reign of Constantine onwards. On many occasions the whole apparatus was static, and much of it could be left behind when the emperor was campaigning a few days from one of these bases. Maximian spent most winters in Trier between 286 and 293, and campaigned in the summer against the Franks in the Rhineland, so many of his staff may have moved little at this point. But the *comitatus* needed to be ready to move at all times, and Maximian travelled extensively from 296, which necessitated mules, horses and wagons, as well as men to look after them. These logistical columns could be very long, and the Roman army marching under Julian in Mesopotamia in 363 is recorded as stretching over 4 miles of road.[32]

The local praetorian prefect had the role of supporting the *comitatus*. He thus had to find space to accommodate people and animals, to feed them, to provide equipment and replacement men and animals, and to store all this material until it was needed. The troops, whose numbers were always fluctuating, but which were probably always 10–20,000, and sometimes up to 50,000 men, would have been housed in a mixture of dedicated barracks, civilian quarters (a law of Valentinian I mentions soldiers having billeted themselves in synagogues in Trier), and hectares of tents.[33] Permanent bases probably also had a large parade ground (eastern

---

[31] *Cod. Theod.* 1.16.3 (319).
[32] Amm. Marc. 25.5.6.
[33] *Cod. Theod.* 7.8.2 (368/370/373).

examples are known at Constantinople and Antioch). Animals may have had stables or dedicated areas for grazing (though leaving animals outside in winter was not preferred).[34]

The continued provision of supplies for the *comitatus* was not a process which could have been improvised. The Panopolis Papyri show some of the measures required to support Diocletian's *comitatus* in Egypt in A.D. 299–300, e.g., a letter was received by Philo, *procurator* of the Upper Thebaid, recording the despatch to him of four bakers (all named with their villages) under a military escort, all needed for baking for the *comitatus*.[35] Detailed western examples are sparse, but when Constantius II was preparing to march against Julian in 361, he set up stockpiles of 3,000,000 *medimnoi* of wheat (*puroà*) in Brigantia in Switzerland, and 3,000,000 more in the Cottian Alps. Each of these stockpiles was the equivalent of *ca.* 120,000 metric tons in weight, and 340,000 m^3 in volume. A force of 50,000 men and 10,000 horses and mules could have been fed for three years from the quantities of wheat mentioned. In the field army bases, grain was stored in granaries to protect it from natural conditions (weather, wind, moisture), animals (rodents, birds, and insects), and micro-organisms, but for campaign depots, it was more likely that the grain was simply dumped in open stockpiles in the field. Assuming that there is no exaggeration in these figures, such stockpiles give an idea of the wastage that might be expected, and, therefore, the measures that had to be taken to ensure that operations were not constrained by lack of supplies.[36] Other ration items that were constantly supplied included meat, wine, and hard fodder (oats or barley) for the animals. To reduce transport costs, most of the supplies would have been brought from as close as possible to the army.

Roman armies also needed large amounts of equipment. Although there were state arms factories (*fabricae*), it is unclear whether the state provided all or only some items of equipment to troops, or how uniform issues of equipment were.[37] According to the *Notitia Dignitatum*, each province on the Rhine and Danube had a *fabrica scutaria* for the production of shields, while the three frontier dioceses of Gallia, Italia and Illyricum had two general factories which produced body armour and other equipment. There were also more specialised factories that produced swords (Lucca, Reims, Amiens), bows (Pavia), arrows (Concordia, Metz),

---

[34] Vegetius, *Mulomedicina* Book 2, prologue.
[35] *P.Beatty Panop.* 1.188–191.
[36] Julian. *Ep. ad Ath.* 286B.
[37] *Not. Dign. occ.* 9. 16–39; James (1988).

cataphract equipment (Autun), and artillery (Autun, Trier). Although production was highly centralised, the structure in the *Notitia* of all arrows in the western Empire being produced at two sites, and all bows at one, is highly unlikely, and most factories probably produced all types of equipment in small quantities.

In addition to the state production, units produced some of their own equipment; arrows, javelins and spears were relatively simple to make or repair. Sometimes local production was more sophisticated, and swords are known to have been produced in the Vindobona *canabae* in the 4th c.[38] The production of hobnails for boots might also have required large-scale smithing facilities. Smithing facilities might also have been required if Late Roman cavalry in western Europe normally used horseshoes. Although horseshoes were known in the Roman Empire, they seem not to have been standard military equipment. However, smiths are mentioned by Vegetius, and the regimental armourers listed by Mauricius could also have acted as smiths.[39]

An efficient system of replacement animals for the army was also required. Various areas of Europe had a reputation for producing good horses, e.g. Spain and Cappadocia, but all regions would have contributed animals, especially mules. A sense of the tremendous demand for horses comes from the fact that the sons of cavalrymen would only be enrolled as cavalry troopers if they provided their own horses.[40] The figures for Constantius' planned campaign give some perspective to the demand of the *comes Africae* Romanus for 4,000 pack camels and supplies from the city of Leptis in Africa *ca.* A.D. 364. Since 4,000 camels would be able to carry the rations for 40,000 infantry for a month, Romanus' demand may have been too much for Leptis (described by Matthews as 'seems, and perhaps was, excessive'), but it was the right sort of size to carry the supplies for a force of 10,000 for a summer's campaigning.[41]

These large quantities of supplies meant that warehouses were necessary for receiving and storing materials before issuing them to the troops. Archaeological remains of warehouses are known from almost all the Tetrarchic capitals. Trier has a number of preserved warehouses close to the Moselle, as do Aquileia, Milan and Sirmium.[42] As well as the warehouses

---

[38] Wilkes (2005) 197.
[39] Veg. *Mil.* 2.11; *Strategikon* 12.8.7; Southern and Dixon (1992) 229–33.
[40] *Cod. Theod.* 7.22.2 (326).
[41] Amm. Marc. 28.6; Matthews (1989) 281, 384–87; Haldon (1999) 287–92.
[42] Ward-Perkins (1981) 445–46, 464; Mócsy (1974) 312; Christie (2001).

in the bases themselves, there were storage and handling facilities on often-used routes, e.g. at Brittenberg or Jublains in northern Gaul, used for the transport of grain and meat from Britain to northern Gaul. The ships also used for transporting supplies could also carry troops.[43]

Although armies were often located in these bases, especially in the winter, they frequently left them. Sometimes the marches were short, only a few weeks if crossing the Danube from Sirmium for a raid into barbarian territory. On other occasions, however, the whole *comitatus* was on the move for years. In summer A.D. 296. Maximian fought on the Rhine, then moved to Spain in the autumn. By 297, he was in Mauretania, in 298, at Carthage and maybe in Tripolitania, and had crossed the Mediterranean to Rome by 299.[44] Roman emperors were very conscious of the strains this travel placed on their staff, and Constantine I mentioned the *palatini* 'who follow our standards, who always assist our actions, who, bent on their clerical duties, are exposed to lengthy journeys and difficult marches, are no strangers to the dust and toil of the camp'.[45]

Inscriptions can sometimes be cross-referenced with other information to add details of these travels. Thus a number of inscriptions can be related to the army of Maximian on its travels of 296–99. The time in Mauretania is probably documented by a stone from Sitifis, where two cohorts of Legio II Herculia erected a stone to mark their fulfilment of a vow to Mithras. The campaign is probably also recorded by a tombstone erected for Aurelius Dizo in Aquileia by his comrades in Legio XI Claudia; Dizo had served for 5 years before dying in Mauretania. The next stage in the campaign, in Tunisia, is probably attested by a tombstone from Theveste of Valerius Vitalis, a soldier of the regiment of the Martenses from the Gallic army.[46] Maximian then moved on to Italy, and this may be recorded by a tombstone from Rome erected by a certain Marcella, which records the life of her husband Martinus who 'served 5 years in *Legio I Minervia*, 4 years in *Legio XI*, 5 years in the *lanciaria*, 5 years in the pr(otectors)', though this could have come from one of the many other Tetrarchic armies that fought in Italy.[47] None of these stones is dated, but

---

[43] Napoli (2003); Pearson (2005) 83; Amm. Marc. 18.2.3; Julian. *Ep. ad Ath.* 279D–280A.

[44] Le Bohec (2004).

[45] *Cod. Theod.* 6.36.1 (326).

[46] *ILS* 4195; *CIL* V 893; *CIL* VIII 16551.

[47] *ILS* 2782; Mennella (2004) 359–69 tries to connect a number of un-dated funerary inscriptions in North Italy to Constantine's A.D. 312 campaign.

no other Tetrarchic field army campaigned in North Africa, and the names Aurelius and Valerius are particularly characteristic of the late 3rd c.[48] There are no known traces of marching camps along the route, though their construction was standard practice. However, Early Imperial Roman marching camps are only preserved in exceptional circumstances, so their apparent absence in the Late Empire should not be considered significant. Moreover, it may be that camps with ditches were dug only when close to the enemy, and in many cases these marching camps may have been little more than fenced areas.[49]

Although tracing the movements of armies and the infrastructure to support these is possible, it is far more difficult to find archaeological evidence for military activity, and what there is needs to be rigorously assessed. Destruction layers have sometimes been interpreted as evidence for military activity, e.g. in relation to the 367 barbarian conspiracy in Britain, or the 406 crossing of the Rhine, though such interpretations are usually rejected.[50] But, even if a destruction layer can be dated with confidence, without literary evidence, there are still great problems in understanding the context. A single destruction layer can as easily be the successful culmination of a barbarian raid as it can be the catalyst for a Roman counter-attack that could either wreak havoc in a barbarian society, as with the raids of Maximian in the late 3rd c., leading to the capture of the Frankish king Gennobaudes, or result in a disaster, as when Quintinus was ambushed in Francia in 388.[51] Coin hoards and deposits of treasure, like destruction contexts, are now cited less often as evidence for insecurity caused by warfare, but the tendency continues. Recent examples include ascribing the deposit of the Water Newton treasure to the 367 'barbarian conspiracy' or, when describing a coin hoard from Kellmünz with a latest date of 308, suggesting that 'the reason for its deposition is to be sought in the conflicts between Constantine I and Maxentius.'[52] In some cases, however, like the late 3rd c. Neupotz treasure, the case is more certain; here, a large collection of precious objects, packed into carts

---

[48] Keenan (1973).
[49] Elton (1996b) 247–48.
[50] Millet (1990) 215.
[51] *Pan. Lat.* 2.10.2; Gregory of Tours *Hist.* 2.9.
[52] Frend (1992) 121–31 and compare with Reece (1994); Mackensen (1999) 223.

and then lost in the river gravels of the Rhine, was presumably the booty from raids by Germans.[53]

Beyond these sorts of issues, studying the archaeological evidence alone, i.e. without considering the literary evidence or current military objectives and practices, is likely to give a misleading picture of what might have been going on in the western Empire during the 4th c. Thus, the best evidence for Roman campaigning in this period remains the surviving parts of the work (covering 354–78) of Ammianus Marcellinus, written by a soldier who had served in Gaul. But, apart from Ammianus' history, there is no other literature by soldiers, and, with the exception of some fragmentary historians, little detailed history. Book 7 of the *Codex Theodosianus* is devoted to military affairs, but this only covers legal matters, not campaign records. The *Notitia Dignitatum* includes lists of military officials and their staffs in around 400, though with some later updating. For military officials, the subordinate officers and sometimes their headquarters are listed, allowing the construction of an army list and some regional deployments, but allows little to be said about how the army was used.[54]

There are also many inscriptions which record the burial of soldiers, including a significant collection from a cemetery at Concordia, near Aquileia in northern Italy, and numerous individual stones from North Africa and the Rhineland. Many of the tombstones from Concordia have something to do with the presence of the western field army, but are unlikely to have much to do with Theodosius' campaign against Eugenius.[55] Focusing on western provinces also obscures the fact that the army in the West did not limit its activities to these areas, but was part of the Roman imperial army, as shown by the travels of Aurelius Gaius in the late 3rd c., and by the Celtae and the Petulantes under Julian. These logistical complications were also exacerbated by large operations on multiple fronts, e.g. in 357, Julian and Barbatio were fighting the Alamanni on the Rhine and, simultaneously, Constantius II was fighting the Sarmatians on the Danube. Modern scholars with a focus only on the West thus miss much of the best evidence for how the Roman army operated, with, for example, much of our information about the logistical efforts required to support the *comitatus* coming from Egyptian papyri.

---

[53] Künzl (1923).
[54] Seeck (1876); Brennan (1995); Kulikowski (2000b).
[55] Hoffmann (1963) 22–57; Tomlin (1972).

FORTIFICATIONS AND FRONTIER FACILITIES

Just as the location of the emperor and the army on the frontiers had an archaeological impact in the form of military bases, so the policy of aggressive strikes across the border of the empire can be documented archaeologically in various ways. These strikes often required crossing the Rhine or Danube, so bridges were built and then forts were built to protect the bridgeheads. In A.D. 294, Diocletian organised the construction of forts across the Danube at Aquincum (Budapest) and Bononia (Vidin). The fort opposite Aquincum probably contributed to Diocletian's victories against the Sarmatians, which were then commemorated with a series of coins with the legend *Victoria Sarmatica*.[56] There is a tendency in the primary sources (often followed by modern authors) to emphasise the role of individual emperors in the construction of fortifications. In particular, the gradual re-establishment of central imperial power under the Tetrarchy is often said to have brought in a new programme of fortification and deployment (especially in the East).[57] The existence of such a programme is usually documented by citing a passage of Zosimus:

> Constantine did something else which gave the barbarians unhindered access to the territory under the Romans. By the forethought of Diocletian, the frontiers of the Roman Empire everywhere were covered, as I have already said [in a lost section], with cities, fortresses, and towers. Since the whole army had its home in these, it was impossible for the barbarians to cross the frontier because they were confronted everywhere by forces capable of resisting their advances. (Zos. 2.34.1–2).

However, it is probably better to see construction of new fortifications and repair and upgrading of existing defences as ongoing tasks carried out by all administrations. A Latin inscription from Serdica in A.D. 152 records the construction of 4 *praesidia*, 12 *burgi* and 109 *phruri* to defend the province of Thrace, producing the results envisaged by a law of Valentinian I in 364, which instructed the *Dux Daciae Ripensis* to construct towers (*turres*) annually along the frontier.[58]

The ongoing nature of fieldwork and the length of the European frontiers mean that assessing trends is particularly dependent on regional

---

[56] Brennan (1980); Hydatius, *sa* 294; Mattingly-Sydenham, *RIC* 6.45.
[57] Lewin (2002) Vol. 1, 91–101; Reddé (1995).
[58] *AE* 2000.1291; *Cod. Theod.* 15. 1. 13 (364); Lenski (2002) Appendix A.

overviews.[59] In Africa, there was also ongoing fortification work and Carthage received a new city wall in the early 5th c.[60] City walls elsewhere were also upgraded or constructed, a process that may have involved civilian contractors and corvée labour.[61] For frontier defence, the maintenance of existing structures was probably more important than building new fortifications (though not as well documented). Re-building of fortifications was also common, and every time that a garrison was changed, buildings would receive new tenants and structural changes might be necessary. Besides the usual issues of building maintenance (probably carried out by the garrison), common problems for fortifications included the silting of ditches, subsidence of walls and towers, and rotting of gate timbers. Thus, Probus (praetorian prefect) was forced to clean up the defences of Sirmium in a hurry in 374, responding to an attack of Quadi and Sarmatians. According to Ammianus:

> He cleaned out the ditches which were choked with rubble and, thriving on his eagerness for building, he set right the greatest part of the walls, which had been neglected and ruined completely by the length of peace, as far as the battlements of the high towers.[62] (Amm. Marc. 29.6.11).

Two emperors in Britain, Carausius and then Allectus, were finally put down by Constantius I in A.D. 296, following the failure of an earlier expedition by Maximian against Carausius in 288/89. These wars are documented by a series of Carausian *antoniniani* naming legions and praetorian cohorts, as well as by issues of medallions, like the gold Arras medallion celebrating Constantius I's entry into London.[63] These wars were prolonged by the construction of a series of fortifications on the southern shore of Britain, known as the Saxon Shore forts, mostly built during the second half of the 3rd c. Recent dendrochronological work has firmly dated the construction of the fort at Pevensey to 293/94.[64] Such forts could be built quickly, and recent arguments have been made that Pevensey could have been built in a year by 570 men, a conclusion in line with an inscription from Gran in Pannonia boasting of building a fort

---

[59] Compare with James (2005) 499–502; Wilson (2006) 198–212; Haalebos and Willems (1999) 259–62; Visy (2003); Wilkes (1998) 635–43.

[60] Mattingly and Hitchner (1995); Le Bohec (2007) 431–41.

[61] E.g., Schwarz (2003) 644–47; Christie and Rushworth (1988).

[62] Elton (1996b) 167, 171.

[63] Mattingly-Sydenham, *RIC* 5.2.12, 55–86; Mattingly-Sydenham, *RIC* 6.34.

[64] Cotterill (1993); Pearson (1999); Pearson (2005).

from the ground up in 48 days.[65] Constantius I fought a second campaign in Britain against the Picts in 306, when York was presumably made into a temporary base for an imperial field army. In 309–10, Constantine built a bridge over the Rhine at Cologne, connecting the Roman bank with a new fort on the opposite bank at Divitia.[66]

A very different type of warfare was shown on the Arch of Constantine, which commemorated Constantine's victory over Maxentius, in this case over a civil war enemy.[67] It was common to remove troops from the borders to fight civil wars, an action which often provoked attacks by barbarians. Evidence for civil wars is often ephemeral, though one example is provided by an inscription from Ulmetum in Romania commemorating Valerius Victorinus, who fell at Chalcedon in A.D. 324.[68] Civil wars, despite their political importance, were only a temporary distraction from the ongoing process of providing frontier security, and coins of Crispus commemorating victories over the Alamanni and Sarmatians show continued campaigning across the Rhine and Danube, as does the construction of a stone bridge across the Danube at Oescus (Gigen) by Constantine in 328, and the Lower Danube fortified landing place at Constantiana Daphne (Tutrakan).[69] Other archaeological evidence for these sorts of campaigns is provided by the recently-published silver dish from Kaiseraugst which commemorates Constans' victory of 342 over some Franks.[70]

The continuing construction of fortifications thickened up the frontier defences, as in 357, when Julian built a fort at Tres Tabernae near Strasbourg, blocking a pass through the Vosges.[71] Julian's fortifications are known only from literature, but archaeology provides plentiful evidence for the building of walls and forts in the late 4th c. to block other passes such as those running through the Julian Alps.[72] In Britain, Hadrian's Wall continued to be garrisoned throughout the 4th c.[73] Ammianus Marcellinus' account of Theodosius the Elder in Africa shows how much evidence literature can contain about campaigning, though much valuable

---

[65] *ILS* 775; Pearson (1999).

[66] *Pan. Lat.* 6 (7).13.1–5.

[67] Pensabene and Panella (1999); Kleiner (2001) 661–63.

[68] *AE* 1976.631; Speidel (1995) 83–87; Woods (1997) 85–93.

[69] Mattingly-Sydenham, *RIC* 7.429; *Chron. Pasch. sa* 328; Lander (1984) 248–49.

[70] *AE* 1999.1123; Kaufmann-Heinimann (1999) 333–41; compare with Mattingly-Sydenham, *RIC* 8.124–29.

[71] Amm. Marc. 16.11.11.

[72] Christie (1991).

[73] Collins (2004); Casey (1993) 259–68; compare with Collins (2008) 256–61.

contextualisation is provided by archaeological evidence.[74] Construction
of forts along the Rhine and Danube continued into the early 5th c.

So far, these comments have focused on evidence that can be closely
dated, but there are many areas where the changes can only be dated
approximately. The problems of dating ephemeral events are brought
home by the campaigns of Theodosius against Magnus Maximus and
Eugenius in Italy in 388 and 394, for which there is literary but no archaeological evidence. From the end of the 4th c., the ephemeral nature of
the events is compounded by the difficulties in dating the archaeological
evidence that does survive. Changes in patterns of coin circulation and
diminished long-distance trade are reflected within the material record
by increasing residuality within 5th c. contexts. This combination of processes means that many military events such as the deposition of Gildo
in Africa in 397, or the actions of the Goths in Italy between 401 and 411
(including the sack of Rome by Alaric in 410), are for the most part either
archaeologically invisible or un-datable. In the case of the Rhine frontier,
even if there is archaeological evidence for early 5th c. warfare, it is uncertain whether it should be attributed to the 406 Rhine crossing, or to the
civil wars between Honorius and his rivals in Gaul, Constantine III and
Jovinus. The continued presence of Roman troops in Spain, perhaps in
416 or 418, is shown by the so-called *Letter of Honorius*, but what they
were actually doing is completely unknowable. Nonetheless, there would
have been logistical structures in place to support these movements of
troops.[75]

Both the changes in the nature of the Roman frontier in the 5th c.
and dating the abandonment of sites are difficult processes to be certain
about. These challenges are combined in the case of Britain from which
Constantine III moved many regiments to the continent.[76] This may have
involved the evacuation of border fortifications, and at some point in the
early 5th c., the fortifications on Hadrian's Wall were abandoned. However, whether this abandonment can be related to Constantine's actions
is unclear, despite the detailed excavations at Vindolanda and elsewhere.[77]
The small amount of dated evidence means that new finds can often
have great importance, but also means that interpretation of difficult

---

[74] Matthews (1985) 157–86; Elton (1996a) 131–35; Mattingly and Hayes (1992) 408–18.
[75] Kulikowski (1998) 247–52.
[76] Jones (1996).
[77] Hodgson (1991); Davies (1991) 52–57.

archaeology, especially that of timber-framed buildings becomes critical to the history of a region, as at Wroxeter.[78]

NAVAL RESOURCES

The western Empire also had large naval forces. Although the Roman army did not conceive of land and maritime forces as separate, it is convenient to do so analytically. The two major areas of deployment were the North Sea and the Mediterranean, each with different physical conditions, which meant that sailing vessels were more important in the North Sea, and oared vessels more important in the Mediterranean and for river flotillas in northern Europe. In both cases, fleets were composed of ships for fighting and for the supply and transport of troops. The North Sea fleet (known as the *classis Britannica* until the 3rd c.) was based around the English Channel and Rhine delta. The size of this fleet is unknown, but its duties included patrolling against raiders from the Rhineland and across the North Sea and, in particular, escorting supply convoys. These convoys could be large, with Julian ordering 600 ships to be built in A.D. 359 to support campaigns in the Rhineland against the Franks.[79] Other convoys transported troops, like the regiments sent from Gaul to Britain in 360 in response to raids on the northern frontier, or the movement of Constantine III's army from Britain to Gaul in 407. In addition to the seagoing forces, there were also flotillas of smaller ships on the Rhine and Danube.[80] In the Mediterranean, Ravenna was the most important western base, though other fleets were based at Misenum, Aquileia and Arles. These would have been used to move armies to Africa, like those of Theodosius in 373, Mascezel in 397, and Bonifatius and Aspar in 431.

Extensive facilities were required to build, house, and maintain these fleets and flotillas. A small shipyard on the Rhine at Mainz, where parts of five small vessels were found, may have been a repair facility for the Rhine flotilla.[81] The complexity of naval warfare only became visible during civil wars, which forced both sides to construct fleets rapidly. These included the wars against Carausius and Allectus in Britain, as well as the wars

---

[78] Fulford (2002) 639–45; compare with Johns and Bland (1994) 165–73.
[79] Zos. 3.5; Julian. *Ep. ad Ath.* 279D–280A.
[80] Elton (1996b) 100; compare with Bounegru and Zahariade (1996).
[81] Hockmann (1993) 125–35; compare with recent discoveries of Late Roman ships in Istanbul, Pekin (2007).

between Constantine I and Licinius, between Constantius II and Magnentius, and between Theodosius and first Magnus Maximus and then Eugenius. Improvising fleets was difficult, since there was a complex set of required raw materials: seasoned wood (especially long timbers), rope, and materials for caulking and sealing, etc. Moreover, crews could only be trained once the fleet was built. Despite these difficulties, large fleets could be produced in a hurry in an emergency, although many of their ships, especially the transports, were probably requisitioned rather than built from scratch. In 324, Constantine's fleet apparently numbered over 200 warships and over 2,000 transports, while Licinius had 350 warships.[82] Constantius II built a fleet in Egypt to support his campaign in Italy against Magnentius in 351–52, and then sent it against Carthage and, in turn, to Spain. Fleets could also be improvised out of merchantmen, as by Heraclianus in 413 when he used the African grain fleet to transport an army from Africa to Italy.[83]

THE ENEMIES OF ROME

The Roman army did not exist in isolation, but had developed in parallel with its enemies, responding to changes in barbarian practices, and, in turn, inspiring them. This continued interaction and exposure to Roman military techniques meant that the Roman Empire faced greater challenges from its 4th c. enemies than did it did in the 1st c. At the same time, the Roman army had also developed and was more effective in the 4th c. than in the 1st c. In particular, later burials outside the empire show an increasing volume of armour, and a greater tendency to use swords in addition to spears. However, these weapon burials show only the range of equipment available in particular regions, not what was typical, and so cannot be used, for example, to show whether the majority of barbarians wore armour. Nor can funerary archaeology address questions like the number of cavalry in a force, so any comments about the relative importance of Frankish cavalry must be misplaced.

Literary evidence is not necessarily better, and to reconstruct Alamannic military practice on the basis of a Roman statement that 'the Alamanni fight wonderfully on horseback' is clearly as inadequate as

---

[82] Zos. 2.22.1–2.
[83] Julian. *Or.* 1.40C; Marcell. com. *sa* 413.

reconstructing Alamannic armies based on funerary practices.[84] And, as with Roman troops, trying to identify any such groups within the Roman Empire depends on several assumptions. In the case of some early 5th c. sites in Britain, intrusive groups can clearly be identified on the basis of new styles of buildings, funerary practices and dress styles, but this intrusive nature does not define the role of these men. Thus, earlier theories interpreting many 4th c. settlements as those of *foederati* are now usually interpreted in the same way as the Reihengräberzivilisation weapon graves in Gaul.[85] Moreover, the rapid disappearance of any differences between locals and the Taifali settled in northern Italy in the 370s, the Goths settled in southern Gaul from 418, or the various Alan, Vandal, or Suevic settlements in Spain, suggests that whatever it was that set apart Romans from barbarians, it was not an approach to material culture.[86]

The increasing sophistication of individual equipment and the continued development of skills by barbarians were not matched by a developing state infrastructure. The archaeology of the various barbarian groups surrounding the empire can be characterised by the lack of central places and urban centres. The absence of a visibly centralised society and minimal writing both suggest a very limited ability to organise supplies, an argument that cannot be countered by pointing to occasional instances of literacy within a society, or the presence of imported experts. These features also suggest that any confederation of Franks or Alamanni could only have been temporary at best. And, though this is an argument from silence, the behaviour patterns of barbarian forces, i.e. their exhaustion of supplies, withdrawing because of supply shortages, dispersing widely and concentrating only to fight, suggest systems very different from those which existed for the Roman army. So, when Julian's men clamoured to fight at Strasbourg in 357, though outnumbered, it was because they were in a rare situation when they could see the enemy in front of them.[87] Thus, unlike the individual weapon sets, the material evidence for the nature of states and their ability to support armies in the *barbaricum* is very different from that of the Roman Empire, and suggests a different capacity for warfare.[88]

---

[84] Aur. Vict. *Caes.* 21.2.
[85] Welch (1993) 269–78; e.g. Eagles (2004) 236; compare Keay (2003) 200.
[86] James (1980) 223–42.
[87] Amm. Marc. 16.12.13; Elton (1996b) 80–81.
[88] Thompson (1965) 109–49, especially 109–11.

Outside the *Barbaricum*

Although most barbarian forces had weak supply systems, there were cases when there was an increased effectiveness. This development cannot be traced archaeologically, while literary knowledge of numbers is weak. Probably the best example of this increasing capacity is the Gothic forces led by Alaric in the 390s and 400s, though other groups that were in the field for a long time would have had similar abilities. In the case of the Goths, they may also have learnt something from being supplied by Roman armies during the campaigns against Maximus and Eugenius. This greater level of sophistication would probably have been limited to paying attention to collecting supplies and assembling large trains of wagons and pack animals.[89] And, although it is an argument from silence, it is difficult to conceive of these systems as being as complex as those practised by the Romans. Thus, the complex inter-relationship of logistics and operations does not always seem to have been well-managed, and the frequent recurrence of demands for grain for Gothic forces suggests that feeding a people, an army, and their accompanying animals, was always a major problem. Nonetheless, Alaric and Athaulf's Goths could keep armies in the field for long periods, even if rates of attrition would probably have been high. Some clear examples of this growing capacity are provided by the sieges of Athens in 396 and Rome in 408–410 by Alaric, and of Bazas in 414 by Athaulf.[90] Radical development, however, would not be possible until these barbarian groups ceased their peripatetic existence.

Conclusion

This paper has attempted to examine the archaeological evidence for military campaigning. Campaigning is like politics, an ephemeral and rapidly changing process of human interactions. Even when these interactions are well-understood, archaeological evidence is not especially well-suited to enhancing our knowledge of the pattern of events within a particular year, or to understanding any changes in the functioning either of the Roman army or the Roman Empire. But, in terms of enhancing our knowledge of the resources and processes, the archaeological evidence is more

---

[89] Heather (1991) 194.
[90] Zos. 5.5–6; Heather (1991) 213–18; Paul. Euch. 343–405.

useful. This evidence must, however, be understood within the context of the objectives of the Roman State, and there needs also to be an acknowledgment of the enormous differences between Rome and her enemies in the 4th c. West; focusing on frontier culture might suggest that there was little difference between the two, but focusing on warehouses, stables, or arms factories makes clear the differences between the Roman Empire and its enemies in the 4th c. In the 5th c., although there were changes in the threats posed by the enemies of Rome, and in the ability of the empire to support its forces, the archaeological evidence is not well-suited to discussing these.

BIBLIOGRAPHY

Primary Sources

Amm. Marc. = Rolfe J. C. (1963) ed. and trans. *Res Gestae* (London 1963).
AE = *L'Année Épigraphique* (Académie des inscriptions et des belles-lettres) (Paris 1888–).
Aur. Vict. *Caes.* = Gross-Albenhausen K. and Fuhrmann M. (2009) trans. and ed. Victor, Sextus Aurelius, *Die römischen Kaiser: lateinisch-deutsch* = Liber de Caesaribus (Düsseldorf 2009); Bird H. W. (1994) trans. *Liber de Caesaribus of Sextus Aurelius Victor* (Translated Texts for Historians 17) (Liverpool 1994).
Chron. Pasch. = Dindorf L. A. (1832) ed. *Chronicon Paschale* (Bonn 1832); Whitby M. and M. (1989) trans., intr. and notes. *Chronicon Paschale 284–628 AD* (Liverpool 1989).
CIL = Reimerum G. (1862) ed. *Corpus Inscriptionum Latinarum* (Berlin 1862).
Cod. Theod. = Mommsen Th., Meyer P. *et al.* (1905) edd. *Theodosiani libri xvi cum constitutionibus Sirmondianis* (Berlin 1905); Pharr C. (1952) trans. *The Theodosian Code and Novels and the Sirmondian Constitutions* (Princeton 1952).
Hydatius = Burgess R. W. (1993) *The Chronicle of Hydatius and the Consularia Constantinopolitana* (Oxford 1993).
Gregory of Tours *Hist.* = Krusch B. and Levison W. (1951) edd. *Decem libri historiarum* (MGH, SRM, I.1, 2nd ed.) (Hannover 1951); Thorpe L. (1974) trans. *History of the Franks* (Harmondsworth 1974).
Jer. *Ep.* = Hilberg I. and Kamptner M. (1996) edd. Jerome, *Epistulae* (Corpus scriptorium ecclesiasticorum Latinorum 54–56) (Vienna 1996); Wright F. A. (1933) *Selected Letters of St. Jerome* (London 1933).
Julian. *Ep. ad Ath.* and *Or.* = Wright W. C. F. (1913–23) ed. and trans. *The Works of the Emperor Julian* (London and Cambridge, Mass. 1913–23).
Lactant. *De mort. pers.* = Creed J. L. (1984) ed. and trans. Lactantius, *De mortibus persecutorum* (Oxford 1984).
Marcell. com. = Croke B. (1995) ed. and trans. *The Chronicle of Marcellinus: a Translation and Commentary with a Reproduction of Mommsen's Edition of the Text* (Sydney 1995).
Mattingly-Sydenham *RIC* 5 = Webb P. H., Mattingly H. and Sydenham E. A. (1968) *The Roman Imperial Coinage. Volume 5, Part 2: Probus to Diocletian* (London 1968).
Mattingly-Sydenham, *RIC* 6 = Sutherland C. H. V. and Carson R. A. G. (1967) *The Roman Imperial Coinage. Volume 6: From Diocletian's Reform (A.D. 294) to the Death of Maximinus* (London 1967).
Mattingly-Sydenham, *RIC* 7 = Bruun P. and Sutherland C. H. V. and Carson R. A. G. (1966) *The Roman Imperial Coinage. Volume 7: Constantine and Licinius, A.D. 313–337* (London 1966).

Mattingly-Sydenham, *RIC* 8 = Kent J. (1981) *The Roman Imperial Coinage. Volume 8: The Family of Constantine I, A.D. 337–364* (London 1981).

*Not. Dign. or.*and *occ.* = Seeck I. (1962) ed. *Notitia Dignitatum: accedunt notitia urbis Constantinopolitananae et Laterculi provinciarum* (Frankfurt 1962).

P. Beatty Panop. = Skeat T. C. (1964) *Papyri from Panoplis in the Chester Beatty Library* (Dublin 1964).

Pan. Lat. = Mynors R. A. B. (1964) ed. *XII Panegyrici Latini* (Oxford 1964); Nixon C. E. V. and Rodgers B. S. (1994) trans. *In Praise of Later Roman Emperors: the Panegyrici Latini* (Berkeley 1994).

Paul. Euch. = Evelyn-White H. G. (1924) ed. and trans. *Ausonius:* vol. 2: *The* Eucharisticus, *Paulinus Pellaius* (Cambridge, Mass. and London 1924).

SEG = *Supplementum Epigraphicum Graecum* (Leiden and Boston 1976-).

Strategikon = Dennis G. T. (1984) ed. *Maurice's Strategikon. Handbook of Byzantine Military Strategy* (Philadelphia 1984) and Dennis G. T. ed. and Gamillscheg E. trans. (1981) *Das Strategikon des Maurikios* (CFHB 17) (Vienna 1981).

Syn. Ep. = Garzya A. (1979) ed. *Synesii Cyrenensis epistolae* (Rome 1979); Fitzgerald A. (1926) trans. *The Letters of Synesius of Cyrene* (London 1926).

Veg. Mil. = Reeve M. D. (2004) ed. *Epitoma rei militaris* (Oxford 2006); Milner N. P. (1996) trans. *Epitome of Military Science* (Liverpool, 2nd ed. 1996).

Veg. Mulomedicina = Lommatzsch E. (1903) ed. *Prolegomena in Vegeti Digestorum artis mulomedicinale libros* (Leipzig 1903).

Zos. = Paschoud F. (1971–89) ed. and trans. *Zosime* (Paris 1971–89); Ridley R. T. (1982) trans. Zosimus, *New History* (Canberra 1982).

Secondary Works

Bidwell P. T. (1991) "Later Roman barracks in Britain", in *Roman Frontier Studies 1989: Proceedings of the XVth International Congress of Roman Frontier Studies*, edd. V. A. Maxfield and M. J. Dobson (Exeter 1991) 9–15.

Bounegru O. and Zahariade M. (1996) *Les forces navales du Bas Danube et de la Mer Noire aux Ier–VIe siècles* (Oxford 1996).

Brennan P. (1980) "Combined legionary detachments as artillery units in Late Roman Danubian bridgehead dispositions", *Chiron* 10 (1980) 553-67.

—— (1995) "The *Notitia Dignitatum*", in *Les littératures techniques dans l'antiquité romaine: statut, public et destination, tradition: sept exposés survis de discussions*, ed. P. Gros and C. Nicolet (Entretiens sur l'Antiquité classique 42) (Geneva 1995) 147–78.

Casey P. J. (1993) "The end of fort garrisons on Hadrian's Wall: a hypothetical model", in *L'armée Romaine et les barbares du IIIe au VII siècle*, edd. F. Vallet and M. Kazanski (Paris 1993) 259–68.

Christie N. (1991) "The Alps as a frontier", *JRA* 4 (1991) 410–30.

—— (2001) "War and order: urban remodelling and defensive strategy in Late Roman Italy", in *Recent Research in Late-Antique Urbanism*, ed. L. Lavan (JRA Supplementary Series 42) (Portsmouth, RI 2001) 106–22.

Christie N. and Rushworth A. (1988) "Urban fortification and defensive strategy in fifth and sixth century Italy: the case of Terracina", *JRA* 1 (1988) 73–88.

Christodoulou D. N. (2002) "Galerius, Gamzigrad and the fifth Macedonian legion", *JRA* 15 (2002) 275–81.

Coello T. (1996) *Unit Sizes in the Late Roman Army* (BAR International Series 645) (Oxford 1996).

Collins R. (2004) "Before 'the end': Hadrian's Wall in the fourth century and after", in *Debating Late Antiquity in Britain AD 300–700*, edd. R. Collins and J. Gerrard (BAR International Series 365) (Oxford 2004) 123–32.

—— (2008) "The latest Roman coin from Hadrian's Wall: a small fifth-century purse group", *Britannia* 39 (2008) 256–61.

Cotterill J. (1993) "Saxon raiding and the role of the Late Roman coastal forts of Britain", *Britannia* 24 (1993) 227–39.

Coulston J. C. N. (2007) "Art, culture and service: the depiction of soldiers on funerary monuments of the third century AD", in *Impact of the Roman Army (200 BC–AD 476): Economic, Social, Political, Religious and Cultural Aspects*, edd. L. de Blois, E. Lo Cascio *et al.* (Impact of Empire (Roman Empire, 27 B.C.–A.D. 476) 6) (Leiden 2007) 529–61.

Davies J. L. (1991) "Roman military deployment in Wales and the Marches from Pius to Theodosius I", in *Roman Frontier Studies 1989: Proceedings of the XVth International Congress of Roman Frontier Studies*, edd. V. A. Maxfield and M. J. Dobson (Exeter 1991) 52–57.

Drew-Bear T. (1981) "Les voyages d'Aurélius Gaius, soldat de Dioclétien", in *La Géographie Administrative et Politique d'Alexandre à Mahomet: actes du Colloque de Strasbourg, 14–16 juin 1979* (Travaux du Centre de recherche sur le Proche-Orient et la Grèce antiques 6) (Leiden 1981) 93–141.

Drinkwater J. F. (2007) *The Alamanni and Rome, AD 213–496* (Oxford 2007).

Duncan-Jones R. P. (1990) "Pay and numbers in Diocletian's army", in R. P. Duncan-Jones, *Structure and Scale in the Roman Economy* (Cambridge 1990) 105–17, 214–21.

Eagles B. (2004) "Britons and Saxons on the eastern boundary of the *Civitas Durotrigum*", *Britannia* 35 (2004) 234–40.

Elton H. (1992) "Defence in fifth-century Gaul", in *Fifth-Century Gaul: a Crisis of Identity?*, edd. J. F. Drinkwater and H. Elton (Cambridge 1992) 167–76.

—— (1996a) "Defining Romans, barbarians and the Roman frontier" in *Shifting Frontiers in Late Antiquity: Papers from the First Interdisciplinary Conferences on Late Antiquity, the University of Kansas, March, 1995*, edd. R. W. Mathisen and H. S. Sivan (Aldershot 1996) 126–35.

—— (1996b) *Warfare in Roman Europe, AD 350–425* (Oxford 1996).

—— (2007) "Roman military forces from the third to the seventh centuries", in *The Cambridge History of Greek and Roman Warfare*, edd. P. Sabin, H. Van Wees, and M. Whitby (Cambridge 2007) 270–309.

Freeman P. and Pollard A. (2001) edd. *Fields of Conflict: Progress and Prospect in Battlefield Archaeology* (BAR International Series 958) (Oxford 2001).

Frend W. H. C. (1992) "Pagans, christians, and "the Barbarian Conspiracy" of A.D. 367 in Roman Britain", *Britannia* 23 (1992) 121–31.

Fulford M. (2002) "Wroxeter: legionary fortress, baths, and the 'great rebuilding' of c.A.D. 450–550", *JRA* 15 (2002) 639–45.

Gardner A. (1999) "Military identities in Late Roman Britain", *OJA* 18 (1999) 403–18.

Guàrdia J. *et al.* (2005) "Enterrament d'època tardoromana correspondent a un macaco amb aixovar al jaciment de Les Colomines (Llívia)", *Ceretània: Quaderns d'Estudis Cerdans* 4 (2005) 65–106.

Haalebos J. K. and Willems W. J. H. (1999) "Recent research on the *limes* in the Netherlands", *JRA* 12 (1999) 247–62.

Haldon J. F. (1999) *Warfare, State and Society in the Byzantine World, 565–1204* (London 1999) 287–92.

Haley E. W. (1994) "A palace of Maximianus Herculius at Corduba?", *ZPE* 101 (1994) 208–14.

Halsall G. (1992) "The origins of the Reihengräberzivilisation: forty years on", in *Fifth-Century Gaul: a crisis of identity?*, edd. J. F. Drinkwater and H. Elton (Cambridge 1992) 196–207.

Harke H. (1990) "Warrior graves? The background of the Anglo-Saxon weapon burial rite", *PastPres* 126 (1990) 22–43.

Harnecker J. (2004) *Arminius, Varus and the Battlefield at the Kalkriese* (Bramsche 2004).

Heather P. J. (1991) *Goths and Romans* (Oxford 1991).

Hockmann O. (1993) "Late Roman Rhine vessels from Mainz, Germany", *IJNA* 22.2 (1993) 125–35.

Hodgson N. (1991) "The *Notitia Dignitatum* and the later Roman garrisons on Britain", in *Roman Frontier Studies 1989: Proceedings of the XVth International Congress of Roman Frontier Studies*, edd. V. A. Maxfield and M. J. Dobson (Exeter 1991) 84–92.

Hoffmann D. (1963) "Die spätrömischen Soldatengrabschriften von Concordia", *MusHelv* 20 (1963) 22–57.

James E. (1980) "Septimania and its frontier: an archaeological approach", in *Visigothic Spain: New Approaches*, ed. E. James (Oxford 1980) 223–42.

James S. (1988) "The *Fabricae*", in *Military Equipment and the Identity of Roman Soldiers: Proceedings of the Fourth Roman Military Equipment Conference*, ed. J. C. N. Coulston (BAR International Series 394) (Oxford 1988) 257–331.

—— (2004) *Excavations at Dura-Europos the Final Report. Volume VII: The Arms and Armour, and Other Military Equipment* (London 2004).

—— (2005) "Review article: Limesfreunde in Philadelphia: a snapshot of the state of Roman frontier studies", *Britannia* 36 (2005) 499–502.

Johns C. and Bland R. (1994) "The Hoxne Late Roman Treasure", *Britannia* 25 (1994) 165–73.

Johnson S. (1983) *Late Roman Fortifications* (London 1983).

Jones M. E. (1996) *The End of Roman Britain* (Ithaca 1996).

Kaufmann-Heinimann A. (1999) "Eighteen new pieces from the late Roman treasure of Kaiseraugst: first notice", *JRA* 12 (1999) 333–41.

Keay S. (2003) "Survey article: recent archaeological work in Roman Iberia (1990–2002)", *JRS* 93 (2003) 146–211.

Keenan J. G. (1973) "The names Flavius and Aurelius as status designations in Later Roman Egypt", *ZPE* 11 (1973) 33–63.

Kleiner F. S. (2001) "Who really built the Arch of Constantine?", *JRA* 14 (2001) 661–63.

Kulikowski M. (1998) "The *Epistula Honorii*, again", *ZPE* 122 (1998) 247–52.

—— (2000a) "Barbarians in Gaul, usurpers in Britain", *Britannia* 31 (2000) 325–45.

—— (2000b) "The *Notitia Dignitatum* as a historical source", *Historia* 49 (2000) 358–77.

Künzl E. (1923) ed. *Die Alamannenebeute aus dem Rhein bei Neupotz* (Mainz 1923).

Lander J. (1984) *Roman Stone Fortifications from the First Century AD to the Fourth* (BAR International Series 206) (Oxford 1984).

Le Bohec Y. (2004) "L'armée romaine d'Afrique de Dioclétien à Valentinien I", in *L'armée romaine de Dioclétien à Valentinien Ier*, edd. Y. Le Bohec and C. Wolff (Lyon 2004) 251–65.

—— (2007) "L'armée romaine d'Afrique de 375 à 439: mythes et réalités", in *The Late Roman Army in the Near East from Diocletian to the Arab Conquest: Proceedings of a Colloquium held at Potenza, Acerenza and Matera, Italy*, edd. A. Lewin and P. Pellegrini (BAR International Series 1717) (Oxford 2007) 431–41.

Lee A. D. (2007) *War in Late Antiquity: a Social History* (Oxford 2007).

Lenski N. (2002) *Failure of Empire: Valens and the Roman State in the Fourth Century* (Berkeley and London 2002).

Lewin A. (2002) "Diocletian: politics and *limites* in the Near East", in *Limes XVIII: Proceedings of the XVIIIth International Congress of Roman Frontier Studies held in Amman Jordan (September 2000)*, edd. P. Freeman, J. Bennett, Z. T. Fiema and B. Hoffmann (BAR International Series 1084) (Oxford 2002) 91–101.

Mackensen M. (1999) "Late Roman fortifications and building programmes in the province of Raetia: the evidence of recent excavations and some new reflections", in *Roman Germany: Studies in Cultural Interaction*, edd. J. D. Creighton, R. J. A. Wilson and D. Krausse (JRA Supplementary Series 32) (Portsmouth, RI 1999) 199–244.

Matthews J. F. (1985) "Mauretania in Ammianus and the *Notitia*", J. F. Matthews, *Political Life and Culture in Late Roman Society* (London 1985) 157–86.

—— (1989) *The Roman Empire of Ammianus* (London 1989).

Mattingly D. J. and Hayes J. W. (1992) "Nador and fortified farms in North Africa," *JRA* 5 (1992) 408–18.

Mattingly D. J. and Hitchner R. B. (1995) "Roman Africa: an archaeological review", *JRS* 85 (1995) 165–213.

Mennella G. (2004) "La campagna di Constantino nell'Italia nord-occidentale: la documentazione epigrafica", in *L'armée romaine de Dioclétien à Valentinien Ier*, edd. Y. Le Bohec and C. Wolff (Lyon 2004) 359–69.

Millar F. (1986) "Italy and the Roman Empire: Augustus to Constantine", *Phoenix* 40 (1986) 295–318.

Millet M. (1990) *The Romanization of Britain* (Cambridge 1990).

Mócsy A. (1974) *Pannonia and Upper Moesia* (London 1974).

Napoli J. (2003) "Le complexe fortifié de Jublains et la défense du littoral de la Gaule du Nord", *Revue du Nord* 85 (351) (2003) 613–29.

Pearson A. F. (1999) "Building Anderita: Late Roman coastal defences and the construction of the Saxon shore fort at Pevensey", *OJA* 18 (1999) 95–117.

—— (2005) "Barbarian piracy and the Saxon shore: a reappraisal", *OJA* 24 (2005) 73–88.

Pekin A. K. (2007) ed. *Gün Işığında* (Istanbul 2007).

Pensabene P. and Panella C. (1999) *Arco di Costantino tra archeologia e archeometria* (Rome 1999).

Reddé M. (1995) "Dioclétien et les fortifications militaires de l'antiquité tardive", *Antiquité Tardive* 3 (1995) 91–124.

Reece R. (1994) "353, 367, or 357? Splitting the difference or taking a new approach", *Britannia* 25 (1994) 236–38.

Richardson A. (2002) "Camps and forts of units and formations of the Roman army", *OJA* 21 (2002) 93–107.

Schlüter W. (1999) "The battle of the Teutoburg Forest: archaeological research at Kalkriese near Osnabrück", in *Roman Germany: Studies in Cultural Interaction*, edd. J. D. Creighton, R. J. A. Wilson and D. Krausse (JRA Supplementary Series 32) (Portsmouth, RI 1999) 125–59.

Schwarz P. A. (2003) "The walls of Augsburg, provincial capital of Raetia", *JRA* 16 (2003) 644–47.

Seeck O. (1876) ed. *Notitia Dignitatum* (Frankfurt 1876).

Southern P. and Dixon K. R. (1992) *The Roman Cavalry* (London 1992).

Speidel M. P. (1995) "A horse guardsman in the war between Licinius and Constantine", *Chiron* 25 (1995) 83–87.

Thompson E. A. (1965) *The Early Germans* (Oxford 1965).

Tomlin R. S. O. (1972) "*Seniores-Iuniores* in the Late Roman field army", *AJP* 93 (1972) 253–78.

—— (2008) "A.H.M. Jones and the army of the fourth century", in *A.H.M. Jones and the Late Roman Empire*, ed. D. Gwynn (Brill's Series on the Early Middle Ages) (Leiden 2008) 143–66.

van Driel-Murray C. (2004) "A Late Roman assemblage from Deurne (Netherlands)", *BJb* 200 (2004) 293–308.

Visy Z. (2003) *The Ripa Pannonica in Hungary* (Budapest 2003).

Ward-Perkins J. B. (1981) *Roman Imperial Architecture* (Harmondsworth 1981).

Welch M. G. (1993) "The archaeological evidence for federated settlement in Britain in the fifth century", in *L'armée Romaine et les barbares du IIIe au VII siècle*, edd. F. Vallet and M. Kazanski (Paris 1993) 269–79.

Wilkes J. J. (1998) "Recent work along the middle and lower Danube", *JRA* 11 (1998) 635–43.

—— (2005) "The Roman Danube: an archaeological survey", *JRS* 95 (2005) 124–225.

Willems W. J. H. (1989) "An officer or a gentleman? A Late-Roman weapon-grave from a villa at Voerendaal (NL)", in *Roman Military Equipment: the Sources of Evidence: Proceedings of the Fifth Roman Military Equipment Conference*, ed. C. van Driel-Murray (BAR International Series 476) (Oxford 1989) 143–56.

Williams T. (1993) *The Archaeology of Roman London*, vol. 3 (London 1993).

Wilson R. J. A. (2006) "What's new in Roman Baden-Wurttemberg?", *JRS* 96 (2006) 198–212.

Woods D. (1993) "The ownership and disposal of military equipment in the Late Roman Empire", *JRMES* 4 (1993) 59–69.

—— (1997) "Valerius Victorinus again", *Chiron* 27 (1997) 85–93.

Zuckerman C. (1988) "Legio V Macedonica in Egypt", *Tyche* 3 (1988) 279–87.

THE ARCHAEOLOGY OF WAR AND THE 5TH C. 'INVASIONS'

Michael Kulikowski

Abstract

This paper examines the extent to which warfare is particularly characteristic of the 5th c. and whether the typical scholarly focus on barbarian invasion in this period is justified by the evidence. It then examines the ways in which archaeological and literary evidence do and do not shed light on one another in the context of 5th c. warfare, taking a series of specific examples, including the re-occupation of high places in northern Spain, the ethnic interpretation of artefacts in Mesetan cemeteries, and the evidence of violence from Late Roman *Emerita Augusta*.

The 5th c. A.D. and its tangled politics involved a great deal of warfare, although we may well doubt whether warfare was dramatically more common than in previous centuries of Roman history. It is impossible to find a Roman century, the golden age of the 2nd c. A.D. not excepted, in which the Roman State was more often at peace than at war: thanks to political imperatives of varying sorts—aristocratic rivalry on the one hand, imperial ideology and legitimacy on the other—both Republican and Imperial history are dyed a bloody red, no doubt part of Roman history's eternal appeal to the popular audience. Despite this, warfare undoubtedly tends to loom larger in accounts of the 5th c. than it does in earlier periods, even for professional historians. The most charitable explanation might put this scholarly emphasis down to sparseness in the extant evidence, in which warfare consumes a disproportionately large amount of space. Alternatively, and more plausibly, it may simply be that modern narratives of invasion and imperial collapse—many provinces did, after all, cease to be governed by a Roman emperor in the 5th c.—have conditioned us to overlook much of the empirical evidence in front of us, a problem exacerbated by the recent tendency to make ethnicity and ethnogenesis the focus of research on the late ancient barbarians, to the exclusion of almost everything else.

Another question altogether is raised when archaeological evidence is brought into the equation. After all, 5th c. warfare would seem to raise no unique methodological considerations for either historian or archaeologist,

A. Sarantis, N. Christie (edd.) *War and Warfare in Late Antiquity: Current Perspectives*
(Late Antique Archaeology 8.1–8.2 – 2010–11) (Leiden 2013), pp. 683–701

war being war in the ancient world, and its technology and effects largely invariant.[1] Nevertheless, the over-arching historiography of the 5th c. has indeed had a substantial—and, one can safely suggest, deleterious—effect on our understanding of both warfare and social changes more generally. What follows will consider three questions in turn. The first is historiographical, whether we ought really to mark the 5th c. out as a period especially characterised by invasions and by warfare consequent upon them. The second is methodological, and of wide application, whether we should try to link together the literary and archaeological evidence for 5th c. warfare, and if so, how closely. The third is illustrative, an exemplary case in which archaeological and literary evidence do indubitably cast light on, without necessarily serving to confirm, refute, or supplement, one another.

The larger interpretative question must be primary, because it conditions everything we do with the history of the period. Despite general assumptions, there is a real doubt over how much invasion really does set the 5th c. off from other periods of Roman history, and how much invasion and its consequences characterise the military history of the period. The 3rd c. witnessed demonstrably more invasions, over a greater area of the empire, than did the 5th c.; more imperial campaigns are attested along the Rhine and Danube in the 4th c. than in the 5th. c. Actual invasions of the western provinces from outside the empire are confined, during the 5th c., to two rather short periods, first between A.D. 405 and 409, with Radagaisus and the Rhine crossing, then between 451 and 453, when Attila turned from east to west. Yet, in the grand narratives, this century is, indelibly and perhaps inevitably, that of the great invasions, the culmination of *les vagues germaniques* or the *Völkerwanderung*. As historians' shorthand, that may be harmless enough, but only if it does not prejudge our analyses of specific historical data—as it most certainly has done.

Because at the start of the 5th c. there was a western Roman emperor and at its end there was not, narratives of foreign conquest remain persistent, and the world has recently been treated to a confident re-affirmation of the old, old narrative of violent, fundamentally alien barbarians destroying an Empire chronically incapable of realising that it should have fought back harder.[2] It is, therefore, worth our insisting upon a couple of points. Most of the warfare of the 5th c. took place between armies resident on imperial soil. The fact that some of those armies were commanded by

---

[1] That, at least, is one of the chief inferences to be drawn from Sabin *et al.* (2007).

[2] Heather (2005).

barbarian kings or generals of foreign origin (recent or distant) does not make them invading armies. When a Suevic king made a concerted effort to hold Lusitania in the 440s, he and his followers were as much children of the Spanish provinces as were the Lusitanian civilians they terrorized, or the Bagaudae with whom they occasionally made common cause.[3]

When Aëtius and Theoderic I went to war for several years in the later 430s, both were a part of western provincial society. Perhaps more significantly, from everything we can tell, Theoderic's 'barbarian' and 'Gothic' side fielded more men who had been born and raised inside the frontiers of the empire than did the imperial and 'Roman' side of Aëtius—recruited in large part beyond the frontiers. That is to say, many of the barbarians in the 5th c. West, whom we are conditioned to think of as invaders, were in fact first-, second- and third-generation inhabitants of the imperial provinces. However comforting it may be to cling to the old images of encroaching barbarian waves, the wars of the 5th c. West were not for the most part invasions, but rather civil wars within Roman provinces. They were fought between competing factions; some included or deployed foreigners; some included men of various foreign origins alongside men of various provincial origins. None can be broken down into simple dichotomies of barbarian and Roman, conqueror and collaborator, foreign victor and native vanquished.

The traditional invasion paradigm also obscures another important and demonstrable fact: that even among the actual invaders of the 5th c. West, close neighbours of the empire predominated, neighbours who had lived for generations within the imperial shadow, effectively within an imperial commonwealth.[4] However doggedly some writers insist upon centuries-long migrations from Vistula to Costa del Sol, they do so in willful ignorance of the fact that every barbarian army that actually crossed the 5th c. *limes*, and every barbarian *gens* that set up shop on the soil of the western provinces, came not from some primeval Germanic forest, but from within a 100 km of the *limes*.[5] They traded actively with the empire, they participated in its monetary economy, and those among them who were rich ate off the same place-settings as did well-off people inside the imperial

---

[3] Kulikowski (2004) 176–214.

[4] This does not, one may note and *pace* Ward-Perkins (2005), necessitate any particularly rosy view of neighbourly relations, nor any preference for gentle (European Union-style) transformation narratives over harsh, catastrophist models: one can embrace one's catastrophe without appeal to invaders.

[5] It is the great merit of Drinkwater (2007) to have recognised this patent fact within both 4th and 5th c. contexts.

frontier. One need not like one's neighbours, but one generally understands their habits very well indeed. I belabour this point because the standard narrative encourages, perhaps imposes, a sense that the western Empire fell because something irreducibly alien was injected into its constitution.[6] Scholarly concentration on ways of 'telling the difference' and the forms and processes of ethnogenesis subtly reinforces that sense of barbarian otherness, implying that ethnicity and difference are the key analytical category for understanding barbarians, while on the other side, Roman homogeneity or universalism is normative.[7] Yet, though it makes for a less exciting story, what we really ought to be insisting on is the basic familiarity of Roman and barbarian in the 5th c. This point is particularly worth making in the present context, if only for a relatively obvious reason: the straitjacket of barbarian invasion and alterity has severely constrained what archaeologists look for in the 5th c. evidence. That, in consequence, has had a deleterious impact upon the sorts of questions we can ask about changes in the material culture of our period.

With that, let us turn to the question of how we can use material evidence for the history of the 5th c. West. We may leave aside the problematical use of literary evidence to date stratigraphy—particularly destruction layers—and of material evidence to fill gaps in the literary narrative, although both practices still eviscerate investigations of such western provinces as Spain and Italy. For the purposes of argument, one should instead posit an ideal situation in which archaeologists excavate their sites without preconceptions, or preconceived chronologies, drawn from the literary evidence; in which they publish their excavations transparently enough for any reader to check the basis of their conclusions; and in which historians use archaeological evidence not merely to confirm or refute conclusions made on the basis of the literary sources, but rather read the archaeological evidence on its own terms before asking

---

[6] Compare Bradley (1889); Demougeot (1969–79); Heather (2005). Note that, prose register apart, their narratives do not differ in any significant analytical sense. Contrast Halsall (2007), usefully free of mass 'migrations' and undifferentiated 'barbarians' despite its title.

[7] See, e.g., Pohl (1998) and the whole of the European Science Foundation's *Transformation of the Roman World* project. While this approach and these assumptions can be excused, or at least make a certain sense, for scholars who have been trained as medievalists, it seems that when it comes to the 5th c., even those trained as Roman historians seem unable to apply the nuance which is now the norm in studies of Roman identity in earlier periods—e.g. Woolf (1998); Goldhill (2001); Dench (2005).

what it does, or does not, say about the literary narrative.[8] Even where such ideal circumstances obtain, there are still constraints on the way the two sorts of evidence shed light on one another in the 5th c., particularly in terms of how we expect them to overlap and intersect. How clearly and specifically, for instance, should we expect the evidence of invasion to appear in the material evidence?

Let us take the major invasion of A.D. 405–409 as our example. Until not too long ago, it was normal to deploy every possible scrap of material evidence to corroborate and extend the scope of invasions known in the first instance from the literary sources. All Gaul smoked as if from a single funeral pyre, as Orientius famously tells us, so historians and archaeologists were equally keen to find its charred remains.[9] From the literary side, Carolingian saints' lives of dubious quality could attest barbarian raids unknown from the late antique evidence itself. Toponymy, as attested in medieval cartularies, could find Alans, Vandals and Sueves in surprising places.[10] On the archaeological side, both coin hoards and burnt foundations confirmed Jerome, Zosimus or Orientius, and showed us ever more spots through which the invaders must have passed. This technique, as exemplified by Christian Courtois' monumental and still incomparable *Les Vandales et l'Afrique*, inevitably maximised the extent of, and damage done by, the invasion.[11] Of course, nobody really takes that sort of approach anymore, at least not on such a breathtaking scale, even if many writers continue to be tempted to link coin hoards to specific moments of invasion or destruction. All the same, the assumption still stands that we somehow ought to be able to trace the invading foreigners in the material record: since we know that Vandals, Alans and Sueves invaded Gaul and landed in Spain by 409, we should be able to find their tracks.

Except we can almost never do so. The problem is the interaction between the time-frames inherent in archaeological as opposed to historical evidence; historians, particularly those who continue to use old-fashioned narrative history as a way of communicating analysis, would very much like the material evidence to tell us things that it is incapable of telling us. We want specific confirmation that such and such an army devastated such and such a city in the year 439, or that Gothic settlement

---

[8] This is the approach attempted in Kulikowski (2004), evidently with mixed success: see the criticisms of Fear (2007).

[9] Orientius, *Commonitorium* 2.184.

[10] The approach is still with us: Perevalov (2000).

[11] Courtois (1955) 38–54.

really did stretch all the way from Toulouse to Bordeaux: entire conference proceedings still devote themselves to constructing distribution maps of ethnic groups in the landscape.[12] Sadly, though, archaeology almost never gives us that sort of information. Any historian who has read more than a few complete site reports will have learned to treat with caution any assertion of a direct connection between a particular aspect of a site and events attested in the documentary record. The material evidence gives us an interpretative context for the narrative, not a confirmation of it, and the narrative itself still has to come from the literary sources. What is more open to significant dispute is how far we want to go in drawing connections between the two categories of evidence. This consideration may be a particularly acute concern in the context of warfare, as a specific example from the Spanish north-west will help to illustrate.

In the *conventus* of *Lucus Augusti* and *Bracara Augusta*, two of the three *conventus* that comprised the late antique province of Gallaecia, we can observe in the archaeological record signs of an increased nucleation of population at highland sites, some of them obviously hill-forts, others perhaps unfortified highland villages.[13] The chronology of these sites is hard to pinpoint, in part because the imported finewares which are our primary dating criteria are largely absent. However, from the numismatic evidence, and seemingly from the ceramic coarseware evidence as well, these upland sites begin to be occupied in the middle of the 5th c., sometimes on top of a disused pre-Roman settlement, sometimes on land which, so far as we can tell, had not been occupied before the Roman conquest of the peninsula.[14] At roughly the same time, lowland agricultural sites and what were probably municipal centres seem to have been abandoned in some numbers. Neither of the latter statements is entirely unproblematical: on the one hand, determining what constituted a municipal centre in north-west Spain is controversial, while much of our evidence for rural

---

[12] See, e.g., for two recent examples, Tejral *et al.* (1997); and López Quiroga *et al.* (2006), but note that nearly all the publications of the Association Française d'Archéologie Merovingienne are devoted to just such exercises.

[13] Albertini (1923) is still basic on the administrative shape of the peninsula, but add now Alföldy (2000). For *Gallaecia* in Late Antiquity, see especially Torres (1977); *Suevos-Schwaben* (1998); *Galicia* (1993).

[14] For recent advances on the archaeology of Late and post-Roman Gallaecia, see Bello Diéguez and Bas López (2000); Pérez Losada (2002).

abandonment comes from older villa excavations which automatically dated the end of villa sites to the year 409, or just around it.[15]

It was, of course, in A.D. 409 that the Alans, Vandals and Sueves who had crossed the Rhine in 405/406 fought their way from the north of Gaul, across the Pyrenees and into Hispania.[16] In the sharing out of provinces that followed, the Sueves took part of Gallaecia, which they never relinquished until they were subsumed into the Visigothic *regnum* in the 580s. We have, in the chronicle of Hydatius, a detailed record of semi-annual, low-level warfare in Gallaecia, which at times flared up into major fighting in the years between 420 and 470. Given this, it might seem plausible to regard the possible abandonment of lowland sites, and the definitely attested occupation of highland sites, as evidence of the numerous wars recorded in the literary evidence. We might, in other words, conclude that the constant warfare attested by Hydatius' gloomy narrative is confirmed by the material evidence of the Gallaecian hill-forts.

But there is a problem, one which goes beyond the obvious difficulty of dating the material evidence precisely. In the *conventus* of Asturica Augusta, which neighboured those of *Lucus* and *Bracara*, and further to the east in the mountainous regions of Cantabria and Vasconia, a virtually identical process of re-occupation of upland sites had begun somewhat earlier, in the 4th c., when datable imported wares make the chronology rather more secure than it is at 5th c. sites. In the Asturican *conventus* and further east, it is generally agreed, changes to occupational patterns are linked to a reversion to kinship structures characteristic of the pre-Roman period.[17] These structures had been abandoned and/or submerged for a century or so, in the first flush of incorporation into the empire, but gradually re-asserted themselves because they had been abandoned only at the insistence of a small leading elite. By the beginning of the 4th c., that elite no longer needed to assert its prominence through ostentatious display of

---

[15] Gorges (1979), which remains the main corpus of Roman villas in Hispania, is in severe need of updating; Chavarría Arnau (2007) marks a substantial advance, though is perhaps still too incautious in accepting the terminal dates for villas asserted in older site reports.

[16] The date of the barbarians' entry in Spain is firmly attested in Hydatius 34. For an argument in favour of 31 December 405, rather than the transmitted 406, for the Rhine crossing, see Kulikowski (2000), but note that the arguments of Birley (2005) 455–60 are a cogent challenge.

[17] Fernández Ochoa and Morillo Cerdán (1999); Novo Guisan (1992).

Roman habits.[18] In light of that, it may be no coincidence that the author
of the Verona List of 314 counted the Cantabri among the *gentes barbarae*
effectively outside the empire.[19] For our purposes, however, another point
is more germane: if one cannot ascribe the habitational transformation of
4th c. Cantabria to warfare, insecurity, or external threat (because none is
anywhere documented), then it may be unwise to ascribe identical habitational change in 5th c. Gallaecia to the arrival of Suevic invaders.

That question is, to some extent, imponderable: different causes can
lead to identical effects. Yet it raises a further interpretative complication which is equally troubling. The Gallaecian highland sites are inevitably ascribed to a Romano-Gallaecian population retreating in fear of the
invaders to hill-tops from which they could resist the Sueves; that is to say,
the sites are never interpreted in terms of Suevic invaders fortifying hill-
tops from which they could keep the locals in line. The literary evidence
accounts for some of this interpretative approach: one line in Hydatius
tells us that the Gallaecians retreated into their *castella* in the face of the
invaders.[20] On the other hand, the word *castellum* does appear to have
been used as a synonym of *civitas* in the Gallaecian context, so we cannot
be certain that Hydatius is actually referring to a hill-fort of this sort.[21] His
chronicle, moreover, shows both Sueves and Gallaecians living in cities,
and sometimes together in the same city, in exactly the decades to which
our highland sites probably date. Both these points suggest that there is
no historical reason to deny at least some of these hill-forts to the Sueves.
Regardless, rather than this literary evidence, most investigators appeal
to an archaeological reasoning: upland sites are generally regarded as a
Hispano-Roman response to Suevic warfare because artefacts of types that
are thought to be Suevic have not been found in hill-forts.

That putative objection raises another point that has to be considered
in any discussion of archaeology and warfare in the 5th c.: the ways in
which discussions of barbarians and barbarian ethnicity have impeded
discussion of changes in 5th c. material culture. This is not the place for a
critique of the cult of ethnogenesis, which has enraptured early medievalists for the past two decades; what began as a concept of modest novelty
and utility has now metastasised so far from anything warranted by the

---

[18] The single best account of the impetus for, and epiphenomena of, romanisation
remains Woolf (1998).
[19] *Lat. Ver.* 14.9. See Barnes (1996) for the date.
[20] Hydatius 41. With López Quiroga and Lovelle (1999).
[21] Rodríguez Colmenero (1999) 13.

ancient evidence that it ought soon to collapse under its own convoluted weight![22] Far more problematical than any particular approach to barbarian ethnicity is its privileged position as a central (or *the* central) concept for understanding the 5th c. As noted above, the analytical model that dominates current study of the barbarians means that concern for ethnic difference is assumed *a priori* to define barbarian history, so that the productive and nuanced approaches to cultural difference which have proved so fruitful for the study of the High Roman Empire are reduced to a brute polarity of barbarian ethnic heterogeneity and Roman universal homogeneity. This is as much a feature of archaeological as of historical investigation of the 5th c. West, and the result is that ethnicity overwhelms other useful approaches to the material evidence—social status, for instance, or gender, both of which tend to be subordinated to ethnicity when they are discussed at all. The vast preponderance of effort continues to be expended on uncovering the presence of barbarians in the material evidence, an exercise that admits of varying degrees of subtlety: in German-language publications, the school of thought that ascribes ethnicity to artefacts is alive and well, so that one brooch is Vandal, another is Gepidic, and a single piece of jewellery is enough to attest the presence of the Gepid element in a mixed Vandal-Gepidic force.[23] In France, meanwhile, the measuring of skulls is once again in vogue, an approach that German archaeologists sensibly avoid for reasons of more recent history. At its most sophisticated, this sorting of barbarian ethnic groupings can make appeal to computer models that map funerary assemblages across whole regions, so that the relative frequency of axe- versus spear-heads in graves can tell Frank from Alaman in the Rhineland.[24]

There is, to be sure, a considerable theoretical and practical literature demonstrating the flaws of even this most recent, and most nuanced, take on ethnic ascription.[25] For our purposes, however, it is more important to underscore the way in which the whole conceptual approach circumscribes how we analyse the 5th c., in a number of damaging ways. The focus on ethnicity in the 5th c. evidence—on finding barbarians, and telling one set apart from the others—assumes two things: first, that nothing

---

[22] See cogent critiques in Bowlus (1995); Gillett (2002); Goffart (2006).

[23] The many works of Volker Bierbrauer e.g. (1992) and (1994) are the main representatives of this approach.

[24] Siegmund (2000).

[25] See in particular Brather (2004) for the theoretical, and von Rummel (2007) for a concrete example.

is more important to the 5th c. than the introduction of newcomers into the Roman provinces; and second that those newcomers were essentially alien. That, in turn, confirms the natural prejudice of ancient historians to view this century in terms of the destruction of a Roman culture by alien outsiders, and as a Very Bad Thing. It also confirms the natural prejudices of early medievalists, who discern the outline of medieval and modern Europe in the triumph of Germanic *Gentilismus* over Roman universalism, and who think it a Very Good Thing.[26] In both cases, however, it is implicitly assumed that the basic cultural interaction must have been antagonistic, at least to begin with, and that the new social phenomena of the 5th c. West must be read as the result of ethnic change in a given region.

The first problem, the catastrophist reading, can be dealt with quite rapidly: the material culture of the western elites collapsed in the course of the 5th c., and no quantity of mitigating data can alter the scale of material decline—one need only contrast a 4th c. senatorial life, with its townhouses and indoor plumbing, to the down-at-heel, semi-fortified *castella* of the 5th c.[27] But to admit that the 5th c. witnessed the catastrophic decline of bijou lifestyles does not necessarily admit its frequent, assumed, corollary—that the catastrophe was caused by the imposition of new populations. Alternatives to the ethnic interpretation of 5th c. change have been suggested, and specific examples will demonstrate how valuable those alternatives are.[28] The famous *Reihengräberfelder* of the Rhineland had since 1950 been identified as the graves of incoming Frankish settlers into the Roman provinces of the Lower Rhine, an idea that went unchallenged for many decades. More recently, and with increasing confidence and supporting data over the years, Guy Halsall has demonstrated that these row cemeteries are not indices of migration or barbarian settlement. His work, and that of Frans Theuws, has, though along rather different lines, conclusively proved that whoever was buried in the *Reihengräber*, it was not a new Frankish elite who dominated the old Gallo-Roman population and introduced new burial customs.[29]

---

[26] This tension permeates the literature generated by the European Science Foundation's Transformation of the Roman World project: although both ancient historians and medievalists are represented, the overall tone privileges the transformative, continuity discourse of medievalists over the catastrophist approach favoured by the ancient historians who took part.

[27] That is to say, the central assertion of, e.g., Ward-Perkins (2005), is undeniable.

[28] Wickham (2005), with its continuous focus on the local and regional over the global, accepts invasion and population change without privileging them as explanations.

[29] Halsall (1992), (1995) and (2008); Theuws (2000).

The central insight is not that the brooch types and funerary deposition styles are by no means necessarily 'Germanic', or primarily comparable to those found deep in the *barbaricum*; on the contrary, even if one grants that some brooches found in the Gallic *Reihengräber* are indeed 'Germanic', deposition in the *Reihengräber* differs considerably more from depositions in the interior of the *barbaricum* than it does from local traditions of deposition in Late Roman Gaul. We know that immigration into this region occurred. We know that emigration from this region occurred. Some of the bodies in the *Reihengräber* may have been Franks, some may have been Romans, but all of them were participating in the creation of a new rite, of local origin, which presumably had something to do with the symbolic assertion of authority in a region that had lost its firm grounding in the political structure of the empire. The *Reihengräber* did not, that is to say, represent the imposition of a new, foreign rite in the midst of an indigenous population.

It has now been suggested that a similar reading makes good sense of the 5th and 6th c. evidence of the Spanish Meseta.[30] These giant cemeteries, most of them badly excavated in the 1920s and 1930s, have always been taken as decisive material evidence for the settlement of Goths beginning in the last years of the 5th c. and accelerating rapidly after the battle of Vouillé in 507. The most recent, and very thorough, typology of the artefacts found in these cemeteries goes so far as to periodise them according to a chronology drawn rigidly from the few known historical dates of the period, a couple of lines in the *consularia* of Zaragoza and the chronicle of John of Biclar.[31] Yet the interpretation of these cemeteries in terms of Gothic migration and settlement is fundamentally flawed. In fact, if archaeologists and historians were not so intent upon finding traces of alien barbarians inside the Roman provinces, one would not imagine a site like El Carpio de Tajo to be anything other than an indigenous development, with profound similarities to the older 4th c. burial styles of the Duero valley and the southern Meseta. As in northern Gaul, invasion and population replacement make less sense of the new form of funerary display than does evolution within a local culture in response to political change. The Meseta cemeteries are first found at a time when imperial authority had ceased to make even token efforts at claiming Spain as part of the empire; geographically, they lie not far beyond the region in which

---

[30] Kulikowski (2007a).
[31] Ripoll (1993–94) and (1998).

we have good evidence for Suevic hegemony; and they lie on the very edge
of the zone into which Gothic kings at Toulouse, and later at Narbonne
and Barcelona, were able to project their authority by means of periodic
incursions.[32] They are, in other words, located in a place where both age-
old and more recent structures of authority at best half-functioned, and
where new means of asserting local authority in public, representative
ways, might well be created.

The Meseta cemeteries are physically designed like the old Duero
necropolises; like the Duero necropolises, and unlike any putatively barbarian graves in the western provinces, they often contain a small knife,
probably a hunting knife; but unlike the Duero necropolises, such jewellery as they contain is modelled on the military styles favoured in the Late
Roman army, and on the increasingly international 'Danubian' fashions of
the Hunnic period—as prominent symbols of Roman military authority
as the belt buckles of the *Reihengräber*.[33] Thus both the *Reihengräber* and
the Meseta cemeteries are examples of new social phenomena which are
visible archaeologically, and which help give insight into the way political
relationships changed under the pressure of frequent warfare in the later
5th and the 6th c. They are, in other words, a response to endemic warfare and the collapse of a stable government that went with it. As importantly, they are representative examples of the interpretative *culs-de-sac*
one travels down if one presumes that ethnic change is the primary causal
factor in the period.

This paper has thus far focused on examples in which the relationship of archaeological and literary evidence in the history of the 5th c.
is connected to warfare and invasion in rather indirect ways. We may
conclude with a single, concrete example where that relationship is clear
and informative.[34] The south-western Spanish city of Mérida, Roman
Emerita Augusta, was founded in 25 B.C. and became the capital of the
Roman province of Lusitania, remaining a city of great importance until
the destruction of its walls by the Córdoban Emir Muhammad I in 868.
Mérida's ancient and medieval remains are very well preserved, mainly
because it remained something of a provincial backwater until the later

---

[32] For the political history, Kulikowski (2004) 256–86.

[33] For the Duero necropolises, see especially Fuentes Domínguez (1989).

[34] I have treated this material several times before: Kulikowski (2004) 111–12, 210–14,
(2006) and (2007b). The latter two articles reflect the state of research prior to 2003 despite
their date of publication. What follows should be regarded as superseding my earlier
treatments.

1990s, and although the city has grown very fast in the recent, decade-long Spanish property boom, the city's historic core has been excavated with exemplary care since the late 1980s. Although the main public spaces of the Roman city are very well-documented, and individual excavations have taken place within almost every *insula* of the ancient city, the two neighbourhoods that reveal the most about the late ancient city are the extensively excavated and well-published zones of the Morería, and the area around and beneath the Church of Saint Eulalia. The Morería excavations preserve several blocks of the Roman city, two in their entirety;[35] Santa Eulalia preserves a suburban villa property of the High Empire, over which a large necropolis developed, several mausolea and numerous burials pre-dating the erection of the earliest basilica in the 5th or 6th c.[36]

Both sites display evidence of a very substantial destruction phase in the 5th c. At the Church of Santa Eulalia, lavish mausolea were razed to ground level, sealing chambers that lay underground. Simpler grave markers were systematically demolished and the entire area flattened. In the 5th c. Morería, many of the *domus* that had been expensively furnished and re-modelled in the 4th c. property boom that accompanied the city's rise in status, were badly damaged; two bodies lay crushed beneath the roof tiles of one house. In another, a body had been carefully buried. In light of Roman taboos about intramural burial—and the absence of comparable intramural burials in Mérida before the 7th c.—the Morería grave could suggest a period of siege, in which people within the walls could not reach the cemeteries outside them. At both sites, all the documented destruction took place at the same time: the extremely careful publication of the stratigraphy at each site, and its good state of preservation in the Morería, if not Santa Eulalia, allows readers to check the respective excavators' confidence in that assertion. Whether the 5th c. destruction at the Morería was precisely contemporary with that at Santa Eulalia cannot be determined on the basis of the evidence uncovered. But despite that fact, the excavator of Santa Eulalia has often stated that the destruction at both Santa Eulalia and the Morería can be correlated to a known and

---

[35] There is no comprehensive report on the Morería; instead all the relevant excavation reports appear in volumes 1–5 of the annual *Mérida: Excavaciones Arqueológicas*. Especially important are Alba Calzado (1997) and (1998); Sánchez Sánchez (2000); there are useful overviews in Ripoll and Gurt (2000); and Mateos Cruz and Alba Calzado (2000).

[36] Here, see the highly detailed site report of Mateos Cruz (1999).

well-dated historical event, namely the attack on the city of Mérida by the Suevic king Hermigarius in 429, attested by Hydatius.[37]

While possible, this connection is unlikely. In the Morería, close dating of the destruction phase is impossible, because trenches with reliable stratigraphy did not contain diagnostic artefacts. At Santa Eulalia, where the stratigraphy is less good, datable material was present in greater quantity, comprising, as so often, mainly ceramics, some of which might date to the 420s, but the preponderance of which dates from later in the century. That is to say, the archaeological evidence does not on its own suggest a date in the 420s, but rather somewhat later—the 429 date has been pulled from Hydatius without any warrant in the material evidence itself. What is more, even if the material evidence did show an earlier date than it seems to, there would still be no good reason to suppose that it documents the Suevic siege attested in the chronicle of Hydatius. For most of the 5th c., Mérida was the hinge on which the political vicissitudes of the peninsula swung, standing as it did at the heart of Spain's most disputed region: as the diocesan capital, *Emerita Augusta* was the prize for which various competing powers constantly fought. Our literary evidence—and thus our access to a historical narrative—consists of a single chronicle of rather greater literary complexity than is immediately obvious: for a variety of reasons, Hydatius demonstrably leaves out information we can be certain he knew.[38] In light of that fact in particular, there is no reason at all that the destruction attested in the archaeological record should bear a necessary connection to any of the handful of historical episodes preserved in Hydatius. It is just as likely to document some other episode of violence which no extant source documents—and which might never have been documented in any literary source at all. That is to say, even here, in circumstances close to ideal by late ancient standards, there is no logical reason to correlate the literary and material evidence in any direct way: attempts at such correlation are instead driven by the deeply held desire for alternative sources of evidence to confirm what is known from traditional textual sources.

Fortunately for scholars, the Morería and Santa Eulalia excavations were published with such care that readers of the site reports can draw conclusions that differ from those of the reports' authors. As any reader

---

[37] Hydatius 80.
[38] Recent work on Hydatius has made a very substantial difference to the way we read his chronicle: Burgess (1993); Arce (1995); Kulikowski (2004) 153–56, with further references. On chronicles more generally, see Burgess and Kulikowski (2013).

of excavation reports will know, that is a rare luxury, though one that has been more common in Mérida than is the norm elsewhere; it is, therefore, particularly troubling to find a substantial number of recent publications on excavations within the walls of Roman Mérida confidently ascribing material remains to the destructive efforts of Hermigarius, even where the remains are too indistinct, or the area excavated too small to allow for dating more precise than 'late 4th or 5th c.'.[39] Doing this imports unwarranted assumptions into the material evidence and casts doubt upon every other aspect of a site report, particularly since so few recently-excavated intramural sites show signs of violent destruction; changing patterns of intramural land use, rather than violence, seem to better explain developments at these sites.[40] That said, the historian of warfare can still draw very useful conclusions from the archaeological evidence at both the Morería and Santa Eulalia, if not from less extensively documented sites inside the city walls, namely how, in the unstable conditions of the 5th c., a great Spanish city could suffer badly in moments of severe and sudden violence. On the other hand, that same evidence does allow us to understand what the periods of siege recorded abundantly in the narrative record were really like, and what they meant for the inhabitants of afflicted cities. In Hydatius or John of Biclar, the siege and capture of a city rarely merit more than a single line, and, where we get a longer description, it tends to be confected from literary sources like the Latin Josephus.[41] Yet behind the bald declarative statements of the chroniclers lies the physical destruction of an old urban landscape, as is made plain by the thorough publication of sites like the Morería and Santa Eulalia, and the literary sources make more sense as a result of that.

The foregoing observations have been somewhat diffuse, so it may, by way of conclusion, be worthwhile to reiterate the most important caveat about interpreting 5th c. changes, historical, social and material: not everything in the 5th c. is about the barbarians. Modern scholars may feel little sympathy with the direction in which Roman society was changing during the 5th c., but we have a better chance of understanding it if we do more than look for signs of barbarian invaders. That warfare was

---

[39] E.g. Sánchez Sánchez (2002a) and (2002b); Palma García (2004). Silva Cordero and Sánchez Sánchez (2006), however, rightly shows that the 5th c. collapse of the roof of a rich extramural house, not very far from the funerary zone of Santa Eulalia, cannot be proved to have suffered violent destruction as opposed to natural collapse.

[40] E.g. Sánchez Sánchez (2004); Ayerbe Vélez (2005); Pizzo (2005); Palma García (2005).

[41] See here the important insight of Arce (1995).

endemic to the 5th c. West is indisputable, and that most of this warfare looks more like local civil war than grand barbarian invasions does not in itself minimise the fact of warfare: in a place like Mérida, the facts of war are vividly illustrated in the (excavated) material record. On a larger scale, the endemic insecurity which war produced can help explain major social changes—new forms of burial display, new settlement patterns in the countryside, etc. But it is deeply reductionist to see these and other social changes as simple products of conquest and the response to it. The western provinces of the empire changed in the 5th c., and that change made them look less and less classical, but neither archaeological nor historical analysis is advanced by assuming that barbarians can explain every aspect of that change.

BIBLIOGRAPHY

Primary Sources

Hydatius = Burgess R. W. (1993) *The Chronicle of Hydatius and the Consularia Constantino-politana* (Oxford 1993).
Lat. Ver. = *Laterculus Veronensis*/Verona List, in Barnes T. D. (1982) *The New Empire of Diocletian and Constantine* (Cambridge, Mass. 1982) 201–208; Lowe E. A. (1934–71) ed. *Codices Latini antiquiores: a Palaeographical Guide to Latin Manuscripts prior to the Ninth Century* (Oxford 1934–71) 4.477.
Orientius, *Commonitorium* = Petschenig M. *et al.* (1889) edd. *Poetae Christiani Minores, Pars I* (Corpus Scriptorum Ecclesiasticorum Latinorum 16) (Vienna 1889).

Secondary Works

Alba Calzado M. (1997) "Ocupación diacrónica del área arqueológica de Morería (Mérida)", *Mérida: Excavaciones Arqueológicas 1* (1997) 285–315.
—— (1998) "Consideraciones arqueológicas en torno al siglo V en Mérida: repercusiones en las viviendas y en la muralla", *Mérida: Excavaciones Arqueológicas 2* (1998) 361–85.
Albertini E. (1923) *Les divisions administratives de l'Espagne romaine* (Paris 1923).
Alföldy G. (2000) *Provincia Hispania Superior* (Heidelberg 2000).
Arce J. (1995) "El catastrofismo de Hydacio y los camellos de la Gallaecia", in *Los últimos romanos en Lusitania*, edd. A. Velázquez, E. Cerrillo Martín de Cáceres and P. Mateos Cruz (Cuadernos Emeritenses 10) (Mérida 1995) 219–29.
Ayerbe Vélez R. (2005) "La llamada 'Basílica de Laborde': identificación, ubicación y cronología. Intervención arqueológica realizada en el solar no. 8 de la calle Calvario (Mérida)", *Mérida: Excavaciones Arqueológicas 8* (2005) 89–120.
Barnes T. D. (1996) "Emperors, panegyrics, prefects, provinces and palaces (284–317)", *JRA* 9 (1996) 532–52.
Bello Diéguez J. M. and Bas López B. (2000) edd. *A arqeoloxía galega hoxe: de 1988 a 1998: A Coruña, Outubro–Novembro de 1998: Actas* (A Coruña 2000).
Bierbrauer V. (1992) "Die Goten vom 1.–7. Jahrhundert n. Chr.: Siedelgebiete und Wanderbewegungen aufgrund archäologischer Quellen", *Peregrinatio Gothica* 2 (1992) 9–43.
—— (1994) "Archäologie und Geschichte der Goten vom 1.–7. Jahrhundert", *Frühmittelalterliche Studien* 28 (1994) 51–171.

Birley A. R. (2005) *The Roman Government of Britain* (Oxford 2005).

Bowlus C. R. (1995) "Ethnogenesis models and the age of migrations", *Austrian History Year-book* 26 (1995) 147–64.

Bradley H. (1889) *The Goths from the Earliest Times to the End of the Gothic Dominion in Spain* (London 1889).

Brather S. (2004) *Ethnische Interpretationen in der frühgeschichtlichen Archäologie: Geschichte, Grundlagen und Alternativen* (Berlin 2004).

Burgess R. W. (1993) *The Chronicle of Hydatius and the Consularia Constantinopolitana* (Oxford 1993).

Burgess R. W. and Kulikowski M. (2013) *Mosaics of Time: the Latin Chronicle Tradition from the First Century BC to the Sixth Century AD, Volume I: A Historical Introduction to the Chronicle Genre from its Origins to the High Middle Ages* (Turnhout 2013).

Chavarría Arnau A. (2007) *El final de las villae en Hispania (siglos IV–VIII)* (Turnhout 2007).

Courtois C. (1955) *Les Vandales et l'Afrique* (Paris 1955).

Demougeot E. (1969–1979) *La formation de l'Europe et les invasions barbares*. 2 vols (Paris 1969–1979).

Dench E. (2005) *Romulus' Asylum: Roman Identities from the Age of Alexander to the Age of Hadrian* (Oxford 2005).

Drinkwater J. (2007) *The Alamanni and Rome, 213–496* (Oxford 2007).

Fear A. T. (2007) "Review of *Late Roman Spain and its Cities*, by Michael Kulikowsi", *CR* 57 (2007) 198–200.

Fernández Ochoa C. and Morillo Cerdán A. (1999) *La tierra de los astures: Nuevas perspectivas sobre la implantación romana en la antigua Asturias* (Gijón 1999).

Fuentes Domínguez Á. (1989) *La necrópolis tardorromana de Albalate de las Nogueras (Cuenca) y el problema de las denominadas "necrópolis del Duero"* (Cuenca 1989).

Galicia (1993) *Galicia: da romanidade á xermanización. Problemas históricos e culturais. Actas do encontro científico en homenaxe a Fermín Bouza Brey (1901–1973)* (Santiago de Compostela 1993).

Gillett A. (2002) ed. *On Barbarian Identity: Critical Approaches to Ethnicity in the Early Middle Ages* (Studies in the Early Middle Ages 4) (Turnhout 2002).

Goffart W. (2006) *Barbarian Tides: the Migration Age and the Later Roman Empire* (Philadelphia 2006).

Goldhill S. (2001) ed. *Being Greek under Rome* (Cambridge 2001).

Gorges J.-G. (1979) *Les villes hispano-romaines* (Paris 1979).

Halsall G. (1992) "The origins of the *Reihengräberzivilisation*: forty years on", in *Fifth-Century Gaul: A Crisis of Identity?*, edd. J. F. Drinkwater and H. Elton (Cambridge 1992) 196–207.

—— (1995) *Settlement and Social Organization: the Merovingian Region of Metz* (Cambridge 1995).

—— (2007) *Barbarian Migrations and the Roman West, 376–568* (Cambridge 2007).

—— (2008) *Cemeteries and Society in Merovingian Gaul: Selected Studies in History and Archaeology, 1992–2007* (Leiden 2008).

Heather P. (2005) *The Fall of the Roman Empire: a New History of Rome and the Barbarians* (London 2005).

Kulikowski M. (2000) "Barbarians in Gaul, usurpers in Britain", *Britannia* 31 (2000) 325–45.

—— (2004) *Late Roman Spain and Its Cities* (Baltimore and London 2004).

—— (2006) "The Late Roman city in Spain", in *Die spätantike Stadt—Niedergang oder Wandel?*, edd. J.-U. Krause and C. Witschel (*Historia* Einzelschriften 190) (Stuttgart 2006) 129–49.

—— (2007a) "Wie Spanien gotisch wurde. Der Historiker und der archäologische Befund", in *Zwischen Spätantike und Mittelalter*, ed. S. Brather (Berlin 2007) 27–43.

—— (2007b) "Drawing a line under antiquity: archaeological and historical categories of evidence in the transition from the ancient world to the Middle Ages", in *Paradigms and Methods in Early Medieval Studies*, edd. C. M. Chazelle and F. Lifshitz (New York 2007) 171–84.

López Quiroga J. and Lovelle M. R. (1999) "Castros y 'castella tutiora' de época sueva en Galicia y norte de Portugal. Ensayo de inventario y primeras propuestas interpretativas", *HispAnt* 23 (1999) 355–74.

López Quiroga J., Martínez Tejera A. M., and Mórin de Pablos J. (2006) edd. *Gallia e Hispania en el contexto de la presencia 'germánica' (ss. V–VII): Balance y perspectivas. Actas de la Mesa Redonda hispano-francesa celebrada en la Universidad Autónoma de Madrid (UAM) y Museo Arqueológico Regional de la Comunidad de Madrid (MAR), 19/20 Diciembre 2005* (BAR International Series 1534) (Oxford 2006).

Mateos Cruz P. (1999) *La basílica de Santa Eulalia de Mérida. Arqueología y urbanismo*. (Anejos de *Archivo Español de Arqueología* 19) (Madrid 1999).

Mateos Cruz P. and Alba Calzado M. (2000) "De *Emerita Augusta* a Marida", in *Visigodos y Omeyas: Un debate entre la Antigüedad Tardía y la alta Edad Media*, edd. L. Caballero Zoreda and P. Mateos Cruz (Madrid 2000) 143–68.

Nodar Becerra R. (2005) "Aproximación a la arquitectura doméstica en el cerro del Calvario desde época romana hasta la actualidad. Intervención arqueológica realizada en el solar no. 48 de la C/ Adriano (Mérida)", *Mérida: Excavaciones Arqueológicas* 8 (2005) 45–65.

Novo Guisan J. M. (1992) *Los pueblos vasco-cantábricos en la Antigüedad Tardía, siglos III–IX* (Alcalá de Henares 1992).

Palma García F. (2004) "Secuencia ocupacional de un espacio extramuros de la *Colonia Augusta Emerita*. Intervención arqueológica realizada en el solar no. 44 de la calle Augusto", *Mérida: Excavaciones Arqueológicas* 7 (2004) 139–54.

—— (2005) "De la *domus* altoimperial al moderno hospital de San Juan de Dios. Intervención arqueológica realizada por la construcción del nuevo hemiciclo de la Asamblea de Extremadura en Mérida", *Mérida: Excavaciones Arqueológicas* 8 (2005) 159–208.

Perevalov S. M. (2000) "Bazas 414: la rupture de l'alliance alano-gothique", *Dialogues d'Histoire Ancienne* 26 (2000) 175–93.

Pérez Losada F. (2002) *Entre a cidade e a aldea. Estudio arqueohistórico dos "aglomerados secundarios" romanos en Galicia.* (*Brigantium* 13) (A Coruña 2002).

Pizzo A. (2005) "Intervención arqueológica realizada en el solar de la Calle San Juan, 7 (Mérida)", *Mérida: Excavaciones Arqueológicas* 8 (2005) 121–29.

Pohl W. (1998) ed. *Strategies of Distinction: the Construction of Ethnic Communities, 300–800* (Transformation of the Roman World 2) (Leiden 1998).

Ripoll G. (1993–1994) "La necrópolis visigoda de El Carpio de Tajo. Una nueva lectura a partir de la topochronología y los adornos personales", *Butlletí de la Reial Acadèmia Catalana de Belles Arts de Sant Jordi* 7–8 (1993–1994) 187–250.

—— (1998) *Toréutica de la Bética (siglos VI y VII d.C.)* (Barcelona 1998).

Ripoll G. and Gurt J. M. (2000) edd. *Sedes regiae (ann. 400–800)* (Barcelona 2000).

Rodríguez Colmenero A. (1999) *Aquae Flaviae II: O tecido urbanístico da cidade romana* (Chaves 1999).

Sabin P., van Wees H. and Whitby M. (2007) edd. *The Cambridge History of Greek and Roman Warfare.* 2 vols (Cambridge 2007).

Sánchez Sánchez G. (2000) "Intervención arqueológica en el solar de la c/ Almendralejo, no. 2, c.v.a la c. Morería. Nuevas aportaciones al conocimiento de la red viaria en *Augusta Emerita*", *Mérida: Excavaciones Arqueológicas* 4 (2000) 115–36.

—— (2002a) "Arquitectura doméstica en las proximidades de la plaza de toros. Intervención arqueológica realizada en un solar de la calle Legión X, no. 25", *Mérida: Excavaciones Arqueológicas* 6 (2002) 111–21.

—— (2002b) "Nuevos datos sobre el entorno del Arco de Trajano. Intervención arqueológica en un solar de la c/ Félix Valverde Lillo no. 9", *Mérida: Excavaciones Arqueológicas* 6 (2002) 193–202.

—— (2004) "Nuevas aportaciones a la red viaria de *Augusta Emerita*. Intervención arqueológica realizada en el solar no. 39–41 de la calle Legión X", *Mérida: Excavaciones Arqueológicas* 7 (2004) 127–38.

Siegmund F. (2000) *Alemannen und Franken* (Berlin 2000).

Silva Cordero A. and Sánchez Sánchez G. (2006) "La evolución urbanística de un espacio extramuros al norte de *Augusta Emerita*. Intervención arqueológica realizada en el solar no. 43 de la C/ Muza (Mérida)", *Mérida: Excavaciones Arqueológicas* 9 (2006) 61–84.

Suevos-Schwaben (1998) *Suevos-Schwaben: das Königreich der Sueben auf der iberischen Halbinsel (415–585) Interdisziplinäres Kolloquium. Braga, 1996* (Tübingen 1998).

Tejral J., Friesinger H. and Kazanski M. (1997) edd. *Neue Beiträge zur Erforschung der Spätantike im mittleren Donauraum* (Brno 1997).

Theuws F. (2000) "A kind of mirror for men: sword depositions in late antique northern Gaul", in *Rituals of Power: from Late Antiquity to the Early Middle Ages*, edd. F. Theuws and J. L. Nelson (Transformation of the Roman World 8) (Leiden 2000) 401–76.

Torres C. (1977) *Galicia Sueva* (A Coruña 1977).

von Rummel P. (2007) *Habitus barbarus: Kleidung und Repräsentation spätantiker Eliten im 4. und 5. Jahrhundert* (Berlin 2007).

Ward-Perkins B. (2005) *The Fall of Rome and the End of Civilization* (Oxford 2005).

Wickham C. (2005) *Framing the Middle Ages: Europe and the Mediterranean 400–800* (Oxford 2005).

Woolf G. (1998) *Becoming Roman: the Origins of Provincial Civilization in Gaul* (Cambridge 1998).

CONTROLLING THE PYRENEES: A MACAQUE'S BURIAL FROM LATE ANTIQUE *IULIA LIBICA* (LLÍVIA, LA CERDANYA, SPAIN)

Oriol Olesti,[1] *Jordi Guàrdia, Marta Maragall, Oriol Mercadal, Jordi Galbany*[2] *and Jordi Nadal*

Abstract

The remains of a primate's burial (a *Macaca sylvanus*, or a Barbary Macaque) were discovered in 2001 on the site of Les Colomines (Llívia), comprising the skeleton of the animal and some objects arranged as an offering. These offerings included decorated metallic pieces and some bronze military belts typical of the Late Roman period. The grave can be connected with the late antique phase of occupation of *Iulia Libica* in the 5th–6th c. A.D., and with several military episodes that occurred in the Pyrenees during this period. The macaque may have belonged to an officer. Some of the osteological and biometric studies on the macaque are presented at the end of the paper.

INTRODUCTION

Llívia was a Roman city located in the middle of the eastern Pyrenees, at an altitude of 1,220 m above sea level, and in a natural pass between southern Gaul and the Ebro Valley. This pass followed the course of the Segre River. Llívia now lies on the border between France and Spain. Ptolemy mentions the city as *Iulia Libica*, the sole *polis* of the *Cerretani*, and Pliny the Elder describes the *Cerretani* as *Iuliani* and *Augustani* who possessed Latin rights.[3] There is a limited corpus of Roman inscriptions in the region, and a recently discovered civic inscription naming a member

---

[1] Olesti-Vila's research was funded by "Programa Nacional para la movilidad de profe- sores de Universidad e investigadores españoles y extranjeros" (2006), "Programa mobili- tat del Professorat, Universitat Autònoma de Barcelona", Project HUM2007-64250/HIST, "Vencedores y vencidos: imperialismo, control social y paisajes antiguos". GDR AREA, Generalitat de Catalunya.

[2] Jordi Galbany's research was funded by the Spanish DGICYT BMC2000-0538 and CGL2004-0775/BTE projects.

[3] Ptol. *Geog.* 2.6.68; Plin. *HN* 3.3.22.

---

of the *gens Manlia*, which may be connected to an important presence of this *gens* in the Province of Narbonensis.[4]

Between 1997 and 2001, several excavations were carried out in Roman Llívia by J. Guàrdia (Arqueociència SC SL),[5] in the sector called 'Les Colomines'. Previously, Roman remains were only known through casual findings or minor interventions. The recent Les Colomines excavations, however, identified both an important public area of the urban centre (zone 'A') and a private quarter (zone 'B'), both dating from the Augustan period to the 5th–6th c. A.D. It was during these excavations that the burial of a Barbary Macaque was found and connected with the structures dating to Late Antiquity.

THE ARCHAEOLOGICAL CONTEXT: THE MACAQUE'S BURIAL

The burial of the macaque was found in the portico area of the 'A' zone of the Roman city of Llívia, close to an early imperial public building which was re-used in Late Antiquity (fig. 1).

The burial lay outside room 4, immediately (1 m) east of wall 26, and in the former covered zone of the portico. This Barbary Macaque (*Macaca sylvanus*) appeared in stratigraphic unit (US) 74, lying just under floor layer US 8 (fig. 2); the burial was cut into US 10 (a late antique ground surface) and US 23 (a collapsed layer of the early imperial building).

The grave measured 1 × 0.25 m, was oriented east-west, and had a preserved height of 15 cm (fig. 3). The upper part of the grave and the contemporary level of occupation, or floor, were lost. The skeleton of the cercopithecus was *in situ*, almost complete, and measured 78 cm high; the skull was in a lateral position, the hands clasped over the pelvis, and the legs laterally bent.

As shown by the osteological and biometric studies (see Appendix below), this macaque was a male sub-adult, probably in the last stages of its growth, and had not suffered any episodes of alimentary stress. The anthropic and deliberate origin of the grave is shown by the digging of the burial cutting, the disposition of the macaque's body, and especially by the deposition of several objects to accompany the Barbary Macaque.

---

[4] *IRC III*; Rodà and Olesti (in press).
[5] S. Aliaga, J. Campillo, M. Grau, M. Maragall, A. Rojas.

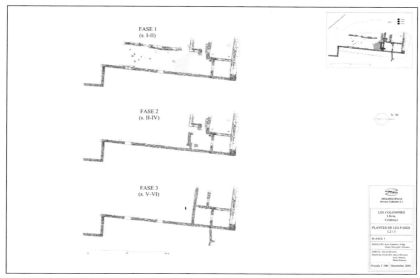

Fig. 1   'Les Colomines', archaeological phases of sector A.

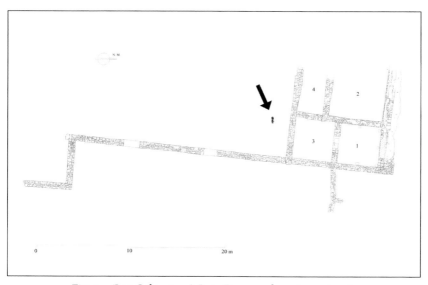

Fig. 2   'Les Colomines', Late Roman phase in sector A.
Location of the macaque burial.

Fig. 3   The macaque burial.

Objects Present in the Grave

The most important group of artefacts connected with this burial comprised metallic objects, some of them located under the bones (fig. 4): there were 7 bronze objects (a belt buckle, a screw or nail, the ring of a chain, and 4 decorative plates) and one iron belt pin.

Also found in the ditch were a rim of late antique pottery (made on a slow potter's wheel),[6] and the fragment of an ovicaprid jaw that might be considered a food offering. We will describe some of these objects in this section.

The bronze belt buckle (fig. 5; register number LL LC 01-73/2) is kidney-shaped and measures 3.7 × 1.7 cm; it features a decoration of incised parallel lines. This type of belt has been identified in a necropolis in Dijon, and in a burial in Bavaria linked to an early Merovingian presence. Recent studies consider these belts to be Merovingian, dating from the second

---

[6] This kind of pottery seems to be connected with African Red Slip ware D in other stratigraphic units of the site. It was no longer present by the time that medieval pottery begun to appear in Llivia.

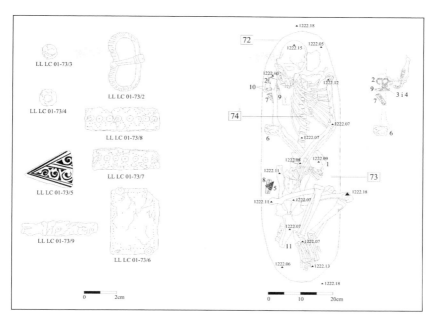

Fig. 4   The macaque burial and the location of the deposited objects.

half of the 5th c. The belt buckle appeared under the right arm of the macaque, close to its skull.[7]

The bronze counter-plate (fig. 6; LL LC 01-73/5) belonged to a military belt commonly used in the Late Roman army. It has a triangular shape, 3 cm long and 1 mm thick, and is decorated with volutes only on the upper side. It was cut out, and probably re-used. We consider it as an example of the Böhme type A, identified on the Rhine and in northern France, and dating from the end of the 4th c. A.D. to the first half of the 5th c. There are some parallels in northern Gallia, at the Pouligny necropolis, in Germania, in an Alamannic soldier's grave in Frankfurt Prannheim, and in Hispania, at Totanés, Paredes de Nava.[8] This counter-plate appeared next to the right side of the macaque's pelvis, over element 73/8.

---

[7] Vallet (1993); Martin (1993). A directly comparable belt buckle has also been unearthed in l'Aiguacuit (Terrassa, Barcelona), see Coll and Roig (2003). This object should provide the closest dating for the macaque's burial, as it is the latest find. Legoux *et al.* (2004) n° 105, 30, 52 date this belt buckle to A.D. 440/50.

[8] Böhme (1978); Pilet *et al.* (1993) on Pouligny; Die Alamannen (1997) on Frankfurt Prannheim; Aurreocoechea *et al.* (2001) on Totanés, Paredes de Nava.

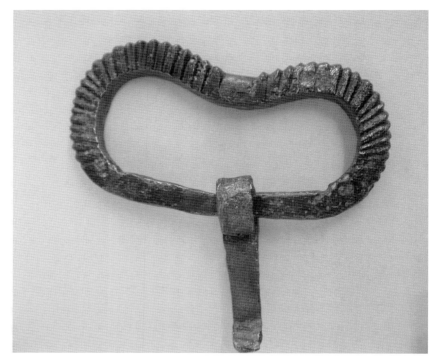

Fig. 5   Bronze belt-buckle (LL LC 01-73/2).

There were also three thin bronze plates (LL LC 01-73/6, 73/7, 73/8) of rect-angular shape (4.7 × 3 cm, 4.1 × 1.8 cm, 4.6 × 1.8 cm), two of which appeared over and under the right arm of the macaque, and the other under the pelvis. All belonged to the applied decoration of a belt, and exhibit an incised decoration of circles and dotted lines known from belt pieces from the Frénouville necropolis in Gaul, and which were typical of the buckles from Hispania known as 'Bienvenida', 'Cabrina' and 'Villasequilla'.[9]

Finally, an iron military belt piece (LL LC 01-73/9; 4.5 × 0.7 cm wide and 4 mm thick) was found. It has a piece of linen cloth stuck to it, and potentially derived from a soldier's attire (see below). This piece appeared under the macaque's right arm, between locations 73/2, 73/3, 73/4 and 73/7.

---

[9] Pilet *et al.* (1993); Aurrecoechea *et al.* (2001); compare with Sommer (1984) Tafel 82 on Merovingian buckles.

Fig. 6   Bronze counter-plate (LL LC 01-73/5).

The Chronology of the Macaque Burial

The arrangement of these objects suggests that the buckle (and the screw and the ring chain which were placed next to it) was used as part of a leash. The decorative plates could derive from a belt. They had probably originally belonged to different belts, and were perhaps re-used in this context. For instance, the chronology of the bronze counter-plate (end of 4th c./first half of 5th c. A.D.) is earlier than that of the belt buckle, which means that it could have initially been Roman army equipment. The belt buckle appears to date from a later period and perhaps belongs to the Merovingian tradition. This re-use of both Roman and Merovingian equipment can also be seen in several *foederati* graves, whose decorative objects likewise came from different traditions.[10]

Whatever the case, the military context of all of these pieces seems clear. They belong to a set of important Late Roman military clothing. Dur-

---

[10] The presence of similar metallic objects in human burial ritual is evident in necropolises of this period in Catalonia: Coll and Roig (2003); Ripoll (1986).

ing the Late Roman Empire, infantry armour gradually disappeared (*lorica segmentata* and *lorica scutata*), to be replaced by a tunic held by a belt. This military *tunica* was frequently made of linen—matching the piece of linen cloth found with the macaque. Despite the likely Germanic origin of this army dress piece, the *tunica* was commonly used by the Roman army from the mid-4th c., especially as a result of the pre-eminence of Germanic officers. This new military clothing accessory would naturally have also been worn by Hispano-Roman troops and Visigothic *foederati*.[11] The metallic objects found with the macaque could date from the 5th c. A.D.—most probably the second half—in keeping with the late antique pottery present in the grave. Radiocarbon dating of the IX left rib by the Beta Analytic Laboratory corroborates this dating, giving a calibrated date of AD 430 to 600 (Cal BP 1520 to 1350).[12] Therefore, a late 5th to mid-6th c. chronology for the burial seems most likely.

THE ARCHAEOLOGICAL CONTEXT: THE ROMAN CITY OF LLÍVIA

To understand the wider archaeological context of this burial, it is necessary to outline data regarding the character and sequence of activity at the Roman city of Llívia itself.

Llívia during the High Empire

Llívia was established as a native settlement during the Iron Age, when the current site and also a site on top of the Puig del Castell hill (where a castle was erected in the Middle Ages) were simultaneously occupied. This indigenous settlement, which included some huts and silos, was transformed during the Augustan period with the foundation of the Roman city.

The first early imperial structures to be identified were domestic buildings, situated in different zones of the current village of Llívia. Scattered materials were also found at the top of the Castle Hill, which was in all likelihood a defensive watch-post. The early imperial city also had a domestic and industrial area situated in sector B of 'Les Colomines', to the north

---

[11] Rovira (1997). We thank Prof. Roger Tomlin (Wolfson College, Oxford) for sharing his thoughts on Roman clothing with us.

[12] Beta Analytic Inc sample 317223. Bone collagen extraction with alkali. Measured Radiocarbon Age, 1420 +/- 30 BP. Conventional Radiocarbon Age (2 Sigma Calibration), 1530 +/- 30 BP.

of the city, where a *hypocaustum* was found. The relative wealth of the citizens is shown by the presence of oysters, glass, marble, *tessellae*, and pottery and amphorae imported from across the Mediterranean basin. But the most interesting structures were found in zone 'A', where the remains of an important building indicated the use of this space as a public area.[13] This building, which has only been partially excavated, measured 40 m long by 25 m wide, and included a peristyle, a portico area and two rooms (fig. 1). One of the rooms included 4 bases in the middle of its walls, probably indicating the former presence of pilasters. These structures could be linked to a public sector of the city, and some of the materials identified—such as a significant number of pieces of architectural marble (some fragments of *opus sectile*, decorative mouldings and *arae*), and a bust of a naked man in Carrara marble—allow us to place the forum of the city not far from this area. The marble recovered in this building came from several quarries in the Mediterranean region, chiefly in Greece, Italy and Africa.

The chronology of this building, and also of sector 'B', runs from the start of the 1st c. A.D. to the mid-2nd c. There was some usage of the area thereafter, but without new constructions or repairs. The city centre was abandoned from the mid-3rd c. There are a few scarce finds from Llívia after this point, but no secure layers of the second half of the 3rd and 4th c. There may have been a continued occupation in other sectors, but not in 'Les Colomines'.

Late Antiquity

The city centre was occupied again from the 5th c. A.D. (Archaeological Phase 3, 5th–6th c.), the period to which the macaque burial belongs. Scattered materials from this period have also been found on the Castle Hill. No occupation is evident in the domestic and industrial sector (zone 'B') during this period, but the public area was re-used, and some changes were made to the public building in zone 'A'. These included the modification of its former rooms 1 and 2 to create two new adjoining rooms (3 and 4), all interconnected by doors; the newly-constructed room 3 extended into the former portico.[14]

---

[13] Guardia *et al.* (2000).
[14] For the chronological sequence of this development, see Guàrdia and Maragall (2004); Guàrdia *et al.* (2005).

Rooms 1 and 3 contained occupation layers with domestic materials and a paved surface (stratigraphic units US 34, 60, 47, plus the sandy level of the courtyard US 10). These contexts yielded many materials from the collapse of the early imperial building. A hoard of 204 bronze coins was found in room 3, under the pavement (US 47), and within the fill of the foundation layer of the pavement (US 62). These coins are imitations of the official coins of the second half of the 4th c. A.D., and, despite their poor preservation, it is possible to identify some legends.[15] The chronology of the coins could be placed in the late 5th c., but coin 116, a possible *nummus* of Justinian, could push the chronology later. This hoard could be connected to two 5th c. hoards found in Barcino and Tarraco, both of which have been linked to a military presence. The pottery in US 62 and 10 also supports a 5th–6th c. chronology, in particular, the examples of African Red Slip ware D (Hayes 58, 78).

There is no archaeological evidence in 'Les Colomines' dating to later than the 6th c. A.D. Our limited Visigothic literary sources describe Llívia as a *castrum* or *oppidum*, and no longer as a *civitas/urbs*. This suggests that in the 7th c., Llívia was probably simply a fortress on Castle Hill, a secondary centre linked to the Pyrenean defensive system.[16]

A MACAQUE IN THE PYRENEES?

Nowadays the *Macaca Sylvanus* can be found in Morocco, Algeria, and in Europe, on the Rock of Gibraltar. It is highly likely that its habitat was much more extensive in Antiquity, and included Tunis and part of Libya (although ancient writers do not mention its presence in Gibraltar).[17] How then can we explain the presence of a macaque in Llívia, in a central Pyrenean valley? To do so, we must consider the wider role of primates in the Roman world.

---

[15] Marot (forthcoming). Group 1 type *GLORIA EXERCITUS* (4–14: 10 coins). Group 2 type *VIRTVS AVGVSTI* (15–25: 10 coins). Group 3 type *SPES REIPVBLICAE I* (26–62: 35 coins). Group 4 type *SPES REIPVBLICAE II* (63–87: 24 coins). Group 5 type *FEL TEMP REPARATIO* (88–115: 27 coins). Group 6 (116: 1 coin). One *Nummus* depicts what may be a Justinianic monogram.

[16] Julianus Toletanus, *MGH, 5, Scriptorum rerum merovingiarum. Historia Wambae Regis auctore Iuliano episcopo*, 10–11; and the so-called *Corduba Anonymous*. Later roles of the site are discussed in Mercadal and Olesti (2005).

[17] McDermott (1938) 56.

Primates in the Roman World

It was not uncommon for members of Roman high society to own primates, especially macaques. Literary sources mention this habit, for example, Plautus, who refers to the presence of small *simia* as pets in some wealthy *domus*.[18] These *simia* were generally small and came from North Africa: from Egypt, Ethiopia and Libya. Some Roman writers, notably Pliny,[19] classified primates according to the length of their tail, and used *simius* as a general term to describe them, and *pithecium* as a scientific one. The *cercopithecium* was the most frequently owned primate, especially the macaque and the *cynocephalus* (possibly the baboon), whereas the *satyrus* was less common. The ownership and display of primates, usually as pets and clowns, became more frequent during the High Empire. The *cercopithecum* was supposedly the cleverest and easiest to train of the primates. Cicero, Martial and Juvenal certainly refer to elites owning such animals, which also occasionally appear in Roman art.[20] According to Pliny, the *cercopithecum* could be bred within the *domus*. Sometimes they were dressed as men, or specifically as soldiers, to amuse visitors. *Simia* were also used by street artists as actors, as dancers, to drive little carts, or to perform roles in mythological plays. Further, *simia* could be put on show in the *ludi*, as happened under Pompey in 55 B.C., when some *cephi* resembling human beings were exhibited there.[21]

Simia were sometimes (but infrequently) eaten, and sometimes used to create rare medical products.[22] More interestingly, *simia* could be used as sacred animals: Juvenal mentions the use of *cercopitheci* as sacred animals in Egypt (note that the burial of sacred baboons was traditional here), and Tertullian duly highlights their association with the Osiris cult.[23] Primates continue to be attested in Late Roman society, being mentioned frequently in metaphorical contexts, for instance, by Ammianus Marcellinus, Avianus, the Latin Anthology and Isidore of Seville.[24]

From an archaeological point of view, the regular artistic depiction of these apes wearing a collar links them to the Llívia macaque. Otherwise,

---

[18] In general, McDermott (1938); Toynbee (1990) 59.
[19] Plin. *HN* 8.80.
[20] Cic. *Att.* 6.1.25; Mart., *Ep.* 7.87.4; Juv. 5.153.5. See McDermott (1938); Amat (2002) 109. Artistic imagery: Toynbee (1990) 59.
[21] See Juv. 5.153; Ael. *NA* 6.10, 5.26; Plin. *HN* 8.28.
[22] Phaedrus 3.4; Gal. 2.222 (Kühn (1821–33) ed. vol. 1, 222).
[23] Juv. 15, 1; Tert. *Apol.* 6. Discussed by Goudsmit and Brandon-Jones (1999).
[24] Amm Marc. 17.11.1; Avianus, *Fab.*14: *AL R* 330; Isid. *Etym.* 12.2.30. See, in general, Amat (2002) 109.

there are few examples of primates in the archaeological evidence. The
best known of these is the macaque found in the Moselle region, northern
France, in a military (legionary) necropolis. Unfortunately, details have
not been published.[25] It has been interpreted as evidence for the presence
of African soldiery, the assumption being that the macaque accompanied
its owner to northern France as a pet. Another key example, comprising
the skull of a Barbary macaque, was found at Emain Macha (Navan Fort,
County Armagh), Ireland, a site which was initially considered to be a
'fort', but was more likely to have been a ritual or ceremonial site dating
to the 1st c. B.C. This animal was interpreted as an exotic gift.[26]

   Finds of macaques in Egypt differ from these European examples. In
Egypt, macaques, baboons and other *simia* were buried in necropolises
like the one north of Saqqara, where an old tradition of burying mum-
mified sacred animals existed. At Saqqara, whose necropolis was in use
from the 4th c. B.C. to the Roman conquest, the majority of the *simia*,
notably baboons, came from Sudan, although a group of *Macaca sylvanus*
will have originated in the mountainous zones of north-west Africa. The
arrival of macaques in Egypt from the 2nd c. B.C. has been viewed as a
consequence of increased Punic trade in the area, as the Phoenicians were
traditionally traders of macaques throughout the Mediterranean basin.[27]

   In fact, the movement of exotic animals from North Africa to Europe
was not uncommon during the Roman period, as recent studies show.[28]
For instance, remains of peacocks (*Pavo cristatus*) were found in several
French sites (e.g. at Besançon in the 1st c. A.D.), Austria (from the 1st to
the 3rd c. A.D.) and the Netherlands (Velsen, 1st c. A.D.); remains of camels have been found in late antique sites in Belgium, and at Marseille and
Bordeaux (where a possible military context has been suggested, despite
the likely usage of the camels in the *ludi*). Another exotic animal imported
in Roman times was the caribou, identified in the Netherlands (at Valken-
burg), Switzerland (*Augusta Raurica*), England (Portchester) and France
(Rouen, Chartres). Finally, we might note the written reference to camels
in late antique *Hispania*: Hydatius' account of the Visigothic army's use of
camels to sack *Braccara* in 456.[29]

---

[25] Poplin (1986); Lepetz and Yvinec (2002) 39.
[26] Aston and Taylor (1999).
[27] Goudsmit and Brandon-Jones (2000).
[28] Lepetz and Yvinenc (2002).
[29] Hydatius 456, though Arce (1995) 224 considers these camels as one of Hydatius'
inventions, despite evidence elsewhere of the existence of camels in other late antique
military contexts.

A Hypothesis: a Military Presence in Llívia

Considering the likely military origin of the metal objects present in the macaque grave, the relative absence of urban life in *Iulia Libica* at that time, and the parallel find of a macaque in a military necropolis in the Moselle region, we believe that this macaque was a military pet, perhaps associated with an officer, which possibly played a symbolic role as a mascot, totem or *signum* within the unit as a whole.[30] Certainly, there are some known examples of exotic animals living or dying in a military context. For instance, a Breton bronze medallion from the 3rd c., depicting several exotic animals in front of military troops, has been interpreted as a representation of a *ludus* being performed in a military context.[31] There were no primates among these exotic animals, but there were peacocks or caribous, imported animals which, as noted above, are attested by some of the exotic zooarchaeological remains recorded in Rome's European provinces.[32] Furthermore, the performance of *ludi* inside *castra* is documented in ancient sources.[33]

The macaque might then be connected to a temporary and undocumented Late Roman military presence in Llívia, charged with defensive duties in the Pyrenean passes.[34] However, there is no clear military function evident from the archaeological evidence from Phase 3 of 'Les Colomines', the site of this intriguing burial. One explanation may be that this area of partial ruins acted as a secondary settlement to a fortress or *castrum* sited on 'Castle Hill'; the presence of a bronze hoard, which can be related to other archaeological finds from military sites and contexts in Catalonia, reinforces the idea that it had a military function. Effectively, this sub-settlement could be considered a *burgus* or *cannabae*, providing accommodation space for civilians linked to the army,[35] but not a fortress in itself.

Finally, it might be speculated that some of the troops present in Llívia were African on the basis of the North African origin of the macaque. The stationing of troops from the African province of Tingitana in Hispania,

---

[30] We do not think that the macaque is linked to a civilian context since, after the 3rd c., as the archaeology so far shows, the site's status and conditions were not conducive to attract an urban elite who might possess such animals (as pets or animals for the *ludi*).

[31] Tomlin (2000).

[32] Lepetz and Yvinec (2002).

[33] E.g. Suet. *Galb.* 6.

[34] See below.

[35] Compare Marin (1956) 436.

attested in the Early Roman Empire, has previously been suggested in connection with the conflicts in Hispania between Asterius and Mauro-cellus and the Vandals in A.D. 419–21.[36] The occupation of North Africa by the Vandals in 429 entailed the end of this relationship, but some former Mauretanian troops potentially remained in Hispania, especially in Tarraconensis, a province loyal to the emperor. Indeed, there were frequent contacts between Hispania and Africa during the first half of the 5th c. A.D., as shown by the distribution of North African coins in Hispania, and also by the use of camels in Theodoric II's army in 456, as mentioned earlier.[37]

THE HISTORICAL CONTEXT OF THE BARBARY MACAQUE

As highlighted above, by the 5th c. A.D., Llívia was no longer a real *urbs*; no late antique literary sources name the city, and the Visigothic texts simply refer to it as *Castrum Lybiae*. The archaeological data confirm this image: the industrial areas were abandoned, and the early imperial public buildings were re-used as domestic space from the 5th c. Nonetheless, some archaeological materials of this period have been recovered on the 'Puig del Castell' or 'Castle Hill'. Whilst we cannot identify the structures from which these materials derive—as the construction of the medieval castle destroyed the ancient layers—the sector where the Late Roman pottery was found occupies the north-eastern corner of the hill (the same place where the main tower of the medieval castle was built), which over-looks the Roman road from Gaul and the course of the Segre River; thus, the most strategic sector of the hill and ideal for a garrison.

In fact, Visigothic sources confirm the site's strategic role.[38] For example, in A.D. 672, during *dux* Flavius Paulus' uprising, King Wamba had to cross the Pyrenees, and we are told that one third of the king's army advanced from Tarraco through the *Strata Ceretana*, and occupied the *Castrum Lybiae*. This *castrum* was defended by Araugisclus and a bishop, Jacintus. From Llívia, the army reached the *castrum Sardonia*, probably also in the Cerdanya region. The larger portion of Wamba's army crossed the Pyrenees through the Ausonia and by the coast. This episode shows the

---

[36] Hydatius 74.26; Villaverde (2001) 284–85.
[37] Marot (2001) 138.
[38] See n. 11.

existence of several fortresses in the Pyrenees, including the *Clausurae*—a full defensive line across the mountain range. Some years later, in 731, the *Corduba Anonymous* mentions Llívia as *Cerritanensem oppidum*.

Is Llívia's defensive role also evident in the Late Roman period? Are there any precedents for a military presence in the Pyrenees before the 7th c. A.D.? Certainly, there are several historical episodes during which the Pyrenees were fortified. In A.D. 350, Emperor Constantius II sent troops to the Pyrenees to capture the *comes* Magnentius; 10 years later Constantius II reinforced the borders of Hispania following the uprising of his Caesar, Julian, in Gaul.[39] During the usurpation of Constantine III, in 408–409, the Spanish relatives of Emperor Honorius, Didimus and Verinianus, recruited a private army to counter the usurper's army, commanded by Constans and Gerontius, who were based in Caesaraugusta.[40] Part of this conflict took place in the Pyrenees, especially in the *Pyrenaei claustra*, where the *Honoriaci*, recently recruited barbarian troops (*in foedo recepti*), defeated the 'private' army. These *Honoriaci* were subsequently stationed in the Pyrenean *montis claustrorumque*, keeping watch and replacing the former troops, the *rusticani* (*eius cura permissa est remota rusticanorum fideli et utili custodia*).[41] Later, however, these *Honoriaci* allowed other barbarian troops to enter Hispania (Alans, Vandals and Suevi) by not defending the *claustra* (*prodita Pyrenaei custodia claustrique patefactis*).[42]

These episodes demonstrate the existence by the second half of the 4th c. of a defensive system in the Pyrenees, articulated around fortresses, or *claustra*, which could hinder and/or observe any crossings of the mountain range. The crossing into Hispania by Alans, Vandals and Suevi is usually placed in the western Pyrenees, but the role of the eastern range also seems important. Noticeably, after their defeat in A.D. 409, Didimus and Verinianus were executed at Arles, and some time later, when Gerontius appointed Maximus as Augustus of the Hispanian diocese, he settled in Tarraco. This possible garrisoning of the Pyrenees could help explain some archaeological remains, for instance, those at Roc d'Enclar

---

[39] A.D. 350: Julian. *Or*. 1.33. These episodes have been connected to the building of the *Clausurae*, a double fortress which controlled the crossing of the coastal Pyrenees.

[40] Zos. 6.4; Oros. 7.40.

[41] Oros. 7.40.8.

[42] Isid. *Hist. Vand.* 71 mentions the same episode, but in his version, the private army of Didimus and Verinianus and their *claustra* took three years to stop the usurper's army in the Pyrenees (*privato praesidio Pyrenaei claustra tuebantur*).

in Andorra.[43] Gerontius allowed the *Honoriaci* to remain and protect the Pyrenean passes. These troops, recruited by Stilicho, were made up of Gauls, Franks and other Germanic soldiers, and were perhaps distributed at and along several key sites and sectors.[44]

One year later, in A.D. 410, Gerontius himself rose up in arms against Constantine III, and designated Maximus as emperor. Maximus settled in Tarraco and Barcino. Discoveries of coins of Maximus in Tarraco, Barcino (the usurper's mint), Girona and the Rousillon[45] testify to the presence of his army in the north-east of the peninsula, close to the Gallic border and Arles, Constantine III's capital.

The military presence in the Pyrenees during the first half of the 5th c. could also be linked to campaigns against the Bagaudae in the Ebro valley, for instance in Ilerda. The probable aim of such activity was to control the main roads.[46] The instability caused by the actions of the Bagaudae on both sides of the Pyrenees could explain the stationing of garrisons at key points. In fact, we know that the Kingdom of Toulouse, with Theodoric II and his brother Federic, also fought against the Bagaudae in Tarraconensis *ex auctoritate romana* in A.D. 454, with the permission of Valentinian III.[47] Two years later, Theodoric II's army, allied with Avitus, used camels in its campaign against the Suevi in Braccara.[48] Another interesting episode was the expedition of Majorian to Spain in 460: the emperor, after negotiating with Theodoric II, arrived at Caesaraugusta from Gaul, and his crossing of the Pyrenees presumably required him to take control of the *claustra* system there.[49]

Despite Visigothic activity, the province of Tarraconensis remained under Roman control. Finally, King Euric's Visigoths attacked the Ebro valley in A.D. 473–75 (the cities of Caesaraugusta, Pompaelo and Tarraco)

---

[43] This site, placed on a hill controlling the Valira River (Andorra), has been considered a *castellum*—Bosch (1997) 101. The architectural remains are scarce, but some metallic objects, like a bronze buckle typical of barbarian troops serving the Late Roman army (4th c. AD), are significant—Rovira (1997) 147. Coins of both Honorius and Magnus Maximus are known here; similarly, in the Cerdanya region, a coin of Honorius, another of Constantine III, and a possible coin of Magnus Maximus (AE3, Les Colomines, Llívia), have been found.

[44] Halsall (2007) 210–13; Arce (2005) 49. There are *Honoriaci* troops placed in Pompaelo in the *Epistula* of Honorius (Códice de Roda), and also some scholars identify these forces as the *auxiliarii Honoriani* mentioned in the *Notitia Dignitatum*—Arce (2005) 49.

[45] Arce (2005) 58.

[46] Hydatius 142.

[47] Hydatius 454.

[48] See n. 39.

[49] Hydatius 192, 195; *Chronica Caesaraugustana, s.a.* 460; Halsall (2007) 263–65.

and again in 494, in an attempt at annexing Tarraconensis. The province was only finally taken in 506–507, after the battles at Dertosa and Vouillé, and the whole Pyrenean region came under Visigothic control. In this context, the Kingdom of Toledo will certainly have developed a coherent defensive system in the mountain ranges.[50]

As well as such military conflicts, other factors can be used to strengthen the notion of Llívia's military role within a system of Pyrenean fortifications. Recent research shows that a network of fortified cities in Hispania (especially in the north of the Meseta and the Cantabrian area) played an important role in the *annona militaris* system from the end of the 3rd c. A.D. As key centres for the collection of taxes and for the control of the main roads, these fortified cities were strategically situated within the structure of the *annona militaris*. The presence of *limitanei* in these areas during the 3rd and 4th c. may be connected with this system. This network also included the north-east of Tarraconensis, and it is not at all unreasonable to suggest that Llívia, strategically located between two provinces, could have played an important part in this *annona militaris* system.[51] The presence of Bagaudae in the Ebro Valley and the Pyrenees area during the 5th c. would have reinforced the need to control these important economic territories.

To summarise, between the 4th and early 6th c. A.D., several military episodes would have necessitated the installation and maintenance of troops and fortresses in this region, which effectively acted as a frontier between the 'wealthy' and 'loyal' Hispaniae and unstable regions, like Gaul and its Bagaudae, the Visigothic kingdom, and later the Franks. Unfortunately, the *Notitia Dignitatum* offers no clear evidence for this defensive system in Hispania, except perhaps via references to the presence of *comitatenses* troops in some regions: the *Undecimani, Gallicani* and the *auxilia palatina Salii iuniores Gallicani* in Hispania, and the *Lanciarii Gallicani Honoriani* and *Salli Gallicani* in Gallia.[52]

From the 4th c. AD., literary sources mention a rebellious imperial army, which, due to a lack of regular supplies, was forced to billet in the

---

[50] Arce (2005); Halsall (2007).

[51] Ochora-Morillo (2002) 584–85 and (2005); Olesti (2009).

[52] *Not.Dign. occ.* 7.234, 210, 239. Gallicani (documented in the 11th c. A.D. as Chalichano; and as Galliça in A.D. 1064) and Undecimani (Undecesse, a 9th c. attestation) are medieval place names in the Cerdanya, and both sites controlled the Roman road—see Mercadal and Olesti (2005). Late antique coins were collected in Challichano. In fact, the troops quartered in the province of Tarraconensis were based in Veleia, and their unit was the *Cohors prima Gallica—N.D.* 42, 32.

local cities and obtain its supplies from local communities; the disruption to supplies potentially stemmed from the activities of the Bagaudae. Old, partly-ruined Llívia may have been adopted as a base by part of this army. In the 5th c., the imperial government faced a number of problems maintaining the army, the 'barbarisation' of which increased with the recruitment of *foederati* troops; internal political instability and frequent usurpations accelerated this process, as shown, for instance, by the example of the Honoriani in Pompaelo. In fact, where loyalty to the empire is concerned, Tarraconensis appears to have been a relatively stable province. In contrast, the Visigoths had many problems controlling this territory, facing the assaults of Euric, the resistance of Burdullenus (in A.D. 496) and Petrus (in 506), and the eventual deposition of the *praefectus Hispaniarum* in Gerunda. These conflicts show that it was a province which remained linked to the empire until its very end. There is even an inscription honouring the Emperor Artemius in Tarraco (467–72, *RIT*), which may in part reflect state investment in preserving a defensive system in the Pyrenees, giving stability to this region and relative independence from the turbulent northern provinces.[53] The complex military activity in this region during the first half of 6th c. A.D., including some Byzantine activity from A.D. 551, could also explain the military presence in some key points, like Llívia.

If we place the archaeological material (including the buried macaque, and especially the recent C14 results) from *Iulia Libica* within this historical context, particularly the Romano-Visigothic operations of the second half of the 5th c., or the conflicts of first half of 6th c., it can be interpreted as evidence for the presence of imperial military units in Tarraconensis. We might hypothesise that these troops were recruited in different parts of the empire, were dressed and armed like typical Late Roman soldiers, and were stationed at *Iulia Libica* to man the defensive system in the north of Hispania and the Pyrenees, and to help in guarding the flow of the *annona militaris*. It is not necessary—nor is it easy—to link these troops and the macaque to any specific military activity or any specific military tradition (as the use of camels in the Visigothic army shows); rather, any troops at Llívia reflect wider processes of militarisation in the Roman Empire and in Spain in the 5th-6th c. The macaque was somehow caught up in all of this, perhaps giving the troops some light relief as they went about their duties in this last phase of Roman control in Hispania.

---

[53] Mayer (1993–94).

APPENDIX: BIOLOGICAL STUDIES OF THE LLÍVIA MACAQUE

Osteological and Biometrical Conclusions

Visual analysis of the dentition shows permanent and totally erupted incisors, canines, premolars and first and second molars, with unfinished growth in some roots. Meanwhile, third molars are half erupted or included in the corresponding crypts. This fact would indicate that the macaque was a sub-adult age, although probably in the last stages of its growth. Regarding the postcranial skeleton bones, most show one or more totally-free centres of ossification, the epiphyses have not joined, and the rest seem to be recently halfway or totally closed (an epiphyseal line is present). The biometrics show the following results: in the upper extremity, the arm (humerus) is robust and eurybrachic (typical of catarrhini primates), while in the forearm, the ulna or cubitus is very flat or hyperplatholenic, and the radium is not very robust but quite long. In the lower extremity, the femur shows a null pilaster and is stenomeric (i.e. has transverse flattening), while the tibia is platycnemic (with transverse flattening). The intermembral index (humerus + radium / femur + tibia) shows, logically, an upper extremity proportionally longer than the lower one.

Palaeopathological Conclusions

We detected some morphological anomalies on the tenth right rib, the left patella, a carpal bone, several phalanxes, one metacarpal, and several metatarsals, predominantly on the left side. Even though the literature describes multiple malformations of these bones for many species of primates, and regards them as a frequent phenomenon, we believe that in our case, the great majority of these anomalies or pathologies result from biomechanical causes and are of an external type (perhaps even anthropic or intentional causes), more than they are deviations of the anatomic normality. However, this question is still being investigated.

Other Relevant Issues

Attention can be drawn to the green dyes on some of the bones on the right side, which are due to the conversion of copper into carbonate, and to the oxidation of the iron in the objects found with the bones. Undoubtedly, the burial allows us to directly relate bones and objects, as well as verify if there were any displacements after their deposit and the partial or total

Table 1. Bones that present anomalies and/or pathologies

Bone	side	anomaly/pathology
Carpal bone (triquetral?)	unknown	Morphological difference between both sides
Fifth metacarpal (V)	left	Thickening of the diaphysis and proximal epiphysis changes
Proximal phalanx from the MTC V	left	Thickening of the diaphysis
Patella	left	Changes on the articular surface (knee joint); potential osteophytes
First metatarsal (I)	left	Considerable deformity of the head and extra bone formation
Metatarsal III	left	Changes and flattening of the diaphysis distal end and on the metaphyseal area
Metatarsal IV	left	Changes of the diaphysis distal end
Phalanx I of the MTT III	right	Changes on the head (or distal epiphysis)
Phalanx I of the MTT V	right	Flattening of the diaphysis

covering of the grave. Thus, while some objects were still in contact with the bones (like the humerus and the right scapula), others were located a long way from them—from the right clavicle and both ribs. Finally, other objects would have to have been *in situ* and further away from the body (the rectangular and triangular bronze platelets), since there is no evidence of them left on the nearest bones, such as the right coxal. Another point worth highlighting is the predominant location (perhaps intentional rather than accidental) of most of the objects found with the body on its right side. This was noticed during the excavation of the grave, as well as from the colour of the dyes of the bones.

Age, Sex and Species Attribution

The individual is attributable to the 'Superfamily' *Cercopithecoidea*. More specifically, it is a *Cercopithecidae* family and *Macaca sylvanus* species. Its morphological characteristics show that it was masculine and of a sub-adult age. The attribution of its sex is possible because the *Macaca sylvanus* is a dimorphic species in its dental size, especially where the canine teeth, but also the molars and premolars, are concerned. The occlusal wear is reduced or absent in all teeth, even though a light exposure of dentine can be observed in the incisors, in the maxilla as well as in the jaw. This leads us to infer that the macaque died at the age of 5 and a half years.[54]

This species has very terrestrial habits and is clearly dimorphic. Males weigh between 7–10 kg, while females only weigh 4–7 kg. Its current area of distribution is restricted to small regions of the Atlas Mountains in Morocco, and to Algeria and Gibraltar, although, until relatively recently, it occupied all of the southern coastal regions of the Mediterranean basin, from Morocco to Libya. In Plio-Pleistocene times this species inhabited south-western zones of Europe.[55] The species prefers to inhabit cedar forests, up to an altitude of 2,000 m, as well as bushy areas within coastal zones, or cliffs with dense vegetation and oak groves. Their feeding ecology is omnivorous, and is based on leaves, fruits, roots, nuts, several insects and small vertebrates. However, it shows a certain regional and seasonal variability: in the cedar forests, it is mainly based on leaves of cedar and herbs during winter and spring, while this diet changes during the summer and autumn to one centred on nuts, caterpillars and bulbs. Seasonal dietary differences are also noted in the oak groves, where nuts are the main food from June to November, while in winter, herbs, lichens and tree barks are eaten. In spring, the macaques incorporate into their diet several invertebrates, such as caterpillars, along with roots, bulbs and fungi. Seasonal and geographical differences in diet are very common in several species of extant primates, as many ecological studies of feeding patterns show.[56]

Bucco Dental Microwear Pattern

The buccal dental microwear pattern of the macaque has been analysed following the standard methodology on which several previous studies have been based.[57] SU74 *Macaca* presents a relatively high number of dental microstriations in comparison with the dental microwear patterns

---

[54] See Swindler (1976); and Harvati (2000) on sexing and ageing.
[55] For data here, see Kingdom (2001); James (1960).
[56] Doran and McNeilage (1998); Rogers *et al.* (2004); Alberts *et al.* (2005).
[57] Pérez-Pérez *et al.* (1999); Galbany and Pérez-Pérez (2004); Galbany *et al.* (2003), (2004a) and (2005a).

of other primate species. Its total number of microstriations (NT) is similar to that of the other wild *Macaca* specimens, gorilla (*Gorilla gorilla*) and guenons (*Cercopithecus sp.*),[58] but is higher than that of baboons (*Papio anubis*) or colobus (*Colobus sp.*). In contrast, SU74 presents a high length of microstriations (XT), with values comparable to chimpanzees (*Pan Troglodytes*) or gorillas (*Gorilla gorilla*) (fig. 7).

The fact that the SU74 macaque was not a wild animal makes it possible to extrapolate the typology of its likely feeding ecology by comparing its dental microwear with other wild primates. This will show how abrasive its diet was. We can confirm that this macaque had quite an abrasive diet, since the statistics place its analysed dental microwear variables close to that of guenons (*Cercopithecus sp.*), which are mainly fruit-eaters and hard-object eaters, and that of gorillas (*Gorilla gorilla*), who base their diet on varied leaves, stems, barks and some fruits. At the same time, its diet was very different from that displayed by the buccal dental microwear of the *Colobus sp.*, which fed mainly on leaves (fig. 8).

Conclusions of the Dental Study

The specimen SU74, found in a Roman-era grave in the Cerdanya, has been identified as a sub-adult male of the *cercopithecidae Macaca sylvanus* family by using odontometric criteria and the dental eruption pattern. This species inhabits North African areas. The macaque's teeth do not show a great deal of occlusal wear, even though there is slight dentine exposure in the incisors.

Macroscopically, no dental hypoplasias were observed, although with the Scanning Electron Microscope a very small one in the first lower right premolar is evident. The correct development of the teeth shows us that this animal suffered no episodes of alimentary stress during its growth. At microscopic level, a great number of growth lines or perykimata, even the enamel prisms, attributable to chemical alterations, can be observed in the premolars and molars. They seem to be due to post-depositional or taphomomic causes, typical of acid or basic grounds. Some teeth display punctual regions where the enamel has come off them. This characteristic may also be due to post-mortem processes. Despite the large surfaces with exposed growth lines, the first molars present areas where the enamel has been preserved and alimentary microstriations can be observed.

---

[58] Data obtained at the teeth cast collection at the Universitat de Barcelona.

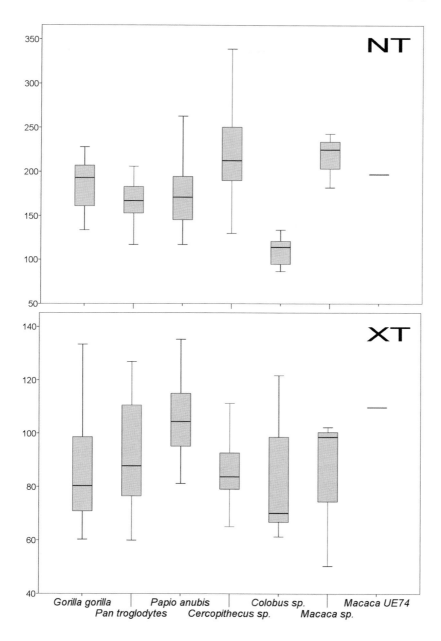

Fig. 7   Box-Plot of total number of microstriations (NT) and the mean length of
microstriations (XT) of all species analysed.

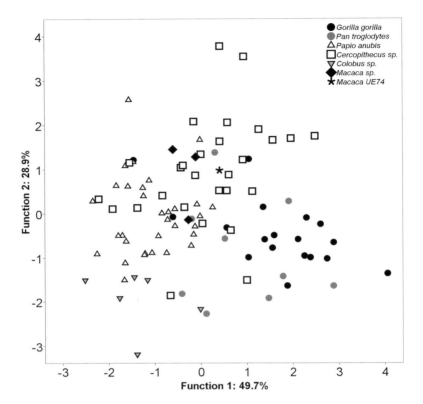

Fig. 8   Plot of the two first functions obtained from the Discriminant Function analysis of the 15 variables for extant primate species and the SU74 macaque. The first function explains 49.7% of total variability, and the second 28.9%.

They differ greatly from the microstriation marks found in the distal sides of the teeth, and originated exclusively from taphonomic causes, when these are present. The absence of great dental hypoplasias suggests that SU74 macaque did not suffer any alimentary stress in its life. Buccal dental microwear in the areas where the enamel has been preserved is similar to that of the extant gorillas, guenons and other macaques. Despite the difficulty in interpreting the data, the SU74 macaque probably had a diet not based exclusively on leaves, but also one of an abrasive and hetero-geneous nature, with the inclusion of hard objects, such as stems or bark, and also fruits.

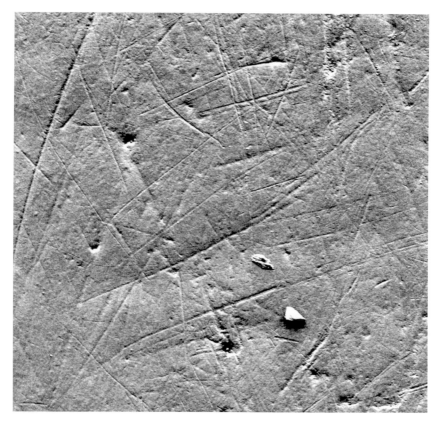

Fig. 9   Area of well-preserved enamel on the left upper first molar. 100x.

Acknowledgements

We would like to extend thanks to Esther Aliaga Rodrigo and Neil Christie for their help in checking the English version of this paper; to Joan Pinar and M. Carme Rovira for their help in identifying the metal objects; to the institutions that granted permission to study the extant primate speci-mens; to Alejandro Pérez-Pérez (Universitat de Barcelona) for his help and support; and to Núria Garriga (Universitat de Barcelona) for help with the statistical software. All SEM images were obtained at the *Serveis Cien-tíficotècnics* of the Universitat de Barcelona.

Bibliography

Primary Sources

Ael. *NA* = Scholfield A. F. (1958–59) ed. and trans. Aelian, *On the Characteristics of Animals* (London and Cambridge, Mass. 1958–59).
Amm. Marc. = Rolfe J. C. (1963) ed. and trans. *Res Gestae* (London 1963).
Avianus, *Fab.* = Gaide F. (1980) ed. and trans. Avianus, *Fables* (Paris 1980).
Chronica Caesaraugustana = Mommsen Th. (1894) ed. *MGS. Auctor antiquiss. XI. Chron. Min. II. Chronicorum Caesaraugustanorum reliquiae a. CCCCL–DLXVIII* (Berlin 1894).
Cic. *Att.* = Shackleton Bailey D. R. (1999) ed. and trans. Cicero, Marcus Tullius, *Letters to Atticus* (Cambridge, Mass. and London 1999).
Gal. = Kühn K. G. and Cnobloch C. (1821–33) edd. *Claudii Galeni Opera omnia* (Leipzig 1821–33).
Hydatius = Burgess R. W. (1993) *The Chronicle of Hydatius and the Consularia Constantinopolitana* (Oxford 1993).
IRC = Fabre G., Mayer M. and Rodà I (1984–) edd. *Inscriptions romaines de Catalogne, volume* 3: *Gérone* (Paris 1984–).
Isid. *Etym.* and *Hist. Vand.* = Isidore of Seville, *Etymologie sive Origines* and *Historia Vandalorum*, in Donini G. and Ford G. B. (1970) edd. and trans. *Isidore of Seville's History of the Goths, Vandals and Suevi* (2nd ed., Leiden 1970).
Julian. *Or.* = Wright W. C. F. (1913–23) ed. and trans. *The Works of the Emperor Julian* (London and Cambridge, Mass. 1913–23).
Julianus Toletanus = Migne J. P. (1851) ed. Iulianus Toletanus, *Historia rebellionis Pauli adversus Wambam Gothorum regem*, in *Patrologia Latina* 96 (Paris 1851) 759–98.
Juv. = Allcroft A. H. (1984) trans. Juvenal, *Satires i–viii* (London 1894).
Mart. *Ep.* = Shackleton Bailey D. R. (1993) ed. and trans. Martial, *Epigrams* (Cambridge, Mass. and London 1993).
Oros. = Raymond I. W. (1936) ed. and trans. Orosius, Paulus, *Seven Books of History against the Pagans: the Apology of Paulus Orosius* (New York 1936).
Phaedrus = Walpole, A. S. (1884) ed. with notes. Phaedrus, *Select Fables* (London 1884).
Plin. *HN* = Rackham H. and Jones. W. H. S. (1938–63) edd. and trans. Pliny the Elder, *Natural History* (Cambridge, Mass. and London).
Ptol. *Geog.* = Ptolemy, *Geographia*, in Stückelberger A., Grasshoff G. and Mittenhuber F. (2006) edd. and trans. *Klaudios Ptolemaios Handbuch der Geographie: Griechisch-Deutsch* (Basel 2006).
Suet. *Galb.* = Suetonius, *Galba*, in Murison C. L. (1992) ed. and trans. Suetonius, *Galba, Otho, Vitellius* (London 1992).
Tert. *Apol.* = Becker C. (1952) ed. and trans. Tertullian, *Apologeticum = Verteidigung des Christentums: lateinisch und deutsch* (Munich 1952).
Zos. = Ridley R. T. (1982) ed. and trans. Zosimus, *New History* (Canberra 1982).

Secondary Works

Alberts S. C., Hollister-Smith J., Mututua R. S., Sayialel S. N., Muruthi P. M., Warutere J. K. and Altmann J. (2005) "Seasonality and long term change in a savannah environment", in *Seasonality in Primates: Studies of Living and Extinct Human and Non-human Primates*, edd. D. K. Brockman and C. P. van Schaik (Cambridge Studies in Biological and Evolutionary Anthropology 44) (Cambridge 2005) 157–96.
Amat J. (2002) *Les Animaux familiers dans la Rome Antique* (Paris 2002).
Andritsakis D. P. and Vlamis K. F. (1986) "A new generation of the elastomeric impression materials", *Odontostomatologike Proodos* 40(3) (1986) 133–42.
Arce J. (1995) "El catastrofismo de Hidacio y los camellos", in *Los últimos romanos en Lusitania*, ed. A. Velázquez *et al.* (Mérida 1995) 219–29.
—— (2005) *Bárbaros y romanos en Hispania. 400–507 A.D.* (Barcelona 2005).

Aston M. and Taylor J. (1999) *Atlas de Arqueología* (Madrid 1999).

Aurrecoechea J. (2001) *Los cinturones romanos en la Hispania del Bajo Imperio* (Rome 2001).

Böhme H. W. (1978) "Tombes germaniques des IVᵉ et Vᵉ siècles en Gaule du Nord: chronologie, distributions, interprétation", in *Problèmes de chronologie relative et absolut concernant les cimetières mérovingiens d'entre Loire et Rhin*, edd. M. Fleury, and P. Périn (Actes du IIᵉ colloque archéologique de la IVᵉ Section de l'Ecole Pratique des Hautes Etudes) (Paris 1978) 32–35.

Campillo D. (2001) *Introducción a la paleopatología* (Bellaterra 2001).

Coll J. M. and Roig J. (2003) "Les sivelles de cinturó d'època visigoda (s. VI–VIII) à les comarques de Barcelona", in *II Congrés d'Arqueologia Medieval i Moderna à Catalunya*, vol. 2 (Sant Cugat del Vallès 2003) 831–36.

Die Alamannen (1997) = *Die Alamannen* (Exhibition catalogue, Archäologischen Landesmuseum Baden-Württemberg) (Stuttgart 1997).

Doran D. and McNeilage A. (1998) "Gorilla ecology and behavior", *Evolutionary Anthropology* 6 (1998) 120–31.

Duday H. and Masset C. (1987) *Anthropologie physique et archéologie: Méthodes d'étude des sépultures* (Paris 1987).

Galbany J., Pérez-Pérez A., Moyà-Solà S. and Farrés M. (2003) "Análisis del patrón de microestriación dentaria en primates Hominoidea actuales: un modelo alimentario para los primates fósiles del Mioceno *Dryopithecus laietanus y Oreopithecus bambolii*", in *Antropología y Biodiversidad*, edd. P. Aluja, A. Malgosa and R. M. Nogués (Barcelona 2003) 148–55.

Galbany J. and Pérez-Pérez A. (2004) "Buccal enamel microwear variability in Cercopithecoidea primates as a reflection of dietary habits in forested and open savannah environments", *Anthropologie* 42(1) (2004) 13–19.

Galbany J., Martínez L. M., Hiraldo O., Espurz V., Estebaranz F., Sousa M., Martínez López-Amor H., Medina A. M., Farrés M., Bonnin A., Bernis C., Turbón D. and Pérez-Pérez A. (2004) *Teeth: Catálogo de los moldes de dientes de homínidos de la Universitat de Barcelona* (Barcelona 2004).

Galbany J., Martínez L. M. and Pérez-Pérez A. (2004) "Tooth replication techniques, SEM imaging and microwear analysis in primates: methodological obstacles", *Anthropologie* 42(1) (2004) 5–12.

Galbany J., Moyà-Solà S. and Pérez-Pérez A. (2005) "Dental microwear variability on buccal tooth enamel surfaces of extant Catarrhini and the Miocene fossil *Dryopithecus laietanus* (Hominoidea)", *Folia Primatologica* 76(6) (2005) 325–41.

Galbany J., Martínez L. M., López-Amor H. M., Espurz V., Hiraldo O., Romero A., De Juan J. and Pérez-Pérez A. (2005) "Error rates in buccal-dental microwear quantification using Scanning Electron Microscopy", *Scanning* 27 (2005) 23–29.

Goudsmit J. and Brandon-Jones D. (1999) "Mummies of olive baboons and barbary macaques in the Baboon Catacomb of the sacred animal necropolis at north Saqqara", *JEA* 85 (1999) 45–53.

—— (2000) "Evidence from the Baboon Catacomb in north Saqqara for a West Mediterranean monkey trade route to Ptolemaic Alexandria", *JEA* 86 (2000) 111–19.

Guàrdia J., Grau M. and Campillo J. (2000) "*Iulia Lybica* (Llívia, Cerdanya). Darreres intervencions i estat de la qüestió", *Tribuna d'Arqueologia 1997–1998* (Servei d'Arqueologia de la Generalitat de Catalunya) (Barcelona 2000) 97–124.

Guàrdia J., Maragall M., Mercadal O., Olesti O., Galbany J. and Nadal J. (2005) "Enterrament d'època tardoromana corresponent a un macaco amb aixovar al jaciment de les Colomines", *Ceretània* 4 (2005) 65–106.

Halsall G. (2007) *Barbarian Migrations and the Roman West, 376–568* (Cambridge 2007).

Harvati K. (2000) "Dental eruption sequence among colobine primates", *American Journal of Physical Anthropology* 112 (2000) 69–85.

James W. W. (1960) *The Jaws and Teeth of Primates: Photographs and Commentaries* (London 1960).

Kingdom J. (2001) *The Kingdom Field Guide to African Mammals* (Princeton 2001).

Legoux R., Périn P. and Vallet F. (2004) *Chronologie normalisée du mobilier funéraire mérovingien entre Manche et Lorraine* (Bulletin de liaison de l'Association Française d'Archéologie Mérovingienne, n° hors serie) (Saint-Germain-en-Laye 2004).

Lepetz S. and Yvinec J. H. (2002) "Presence d'espèces animales d'origine méditerranéenne en France du Nord aux périodes romaine et médiévale: actions anthropiques et mouvements naturels", in *Mouvements ou déplacements de populations animales en Méditerranée au cours de l'Holocène*, ed. A. Gardeisen (BAR International Series 1017) (Oxford 2002) 39–55.

Marin M. (1956) *Instituciones militares romanas* (Madrid 1956).

Martin M. (1993) "Observations sur l'armement de l'époque mérovingienne précoce", *L'armée romaine et les barbares du IIIᵉ au VIIᵉ siècle*, edd. F. Vallet and M. Kazanski (Paris 1993) 395–410.

Mayer M. (1993–94) "Castrum quod vocatur clausuras", *Rivista di Studi Liguri* 59–60 (1993–94) 207–12.

McDermott W. C. (1938) *The Ape in Antiquity* (Baltimore 1938).

Mercadal O. and Olesti O. (2005) "La Cerdanya: transformacions d'un poble i d'un paisatge pirinenc en època antiga", in *II Congrés Internacional d'Història dels Pirineus*, edd. M. Cura, N. Soler and J. Maroto (Girona 2005) 181–274.

Marot T. (in press) "Aproximació a la circulació monetària a la Cerdanya (segle III dC-Antiguitat tardana)", in *Llívia i la Cerdanya a l'Antiguitat*, edd. O. Olesti, J. Guàrdia and O. Mercadal (Tarragona, in press).

Martínez L. M., López-Amor H. M. and Pérez-Pérez A. (2001) "Microestriación dentaria y alteraciones del esmalte dentario en homínidos Plio-Pleistocénicos de Laetoli y Olduvai", *Revista de Antropología Biológica* 22 (2001) 61–72.

McMinn R. M. H. and Hutchings R. T. (1996) *Atlas de anatomía humana* (Espaxs 1996).

Olesti O. (2009) "Transformaciones en el paisaje del Alto al Bajo Imperio: Rufinus Octavianus y el Noreste Hispano a principios del s. IV d.C.", in *Transforming Territories*, edd. T. Ñanco and B. Antela (Barcelona 2009) 213–24.

Pérez-Pérez A., Bermúdez de Castro J. M. and Arsuaga J. L. (1999) "Nonoclusal dental microwear analysis of 300.000-year-old Homo heidelbergensis teeth from Sima de los Huesos (Sierra de Atapuerca, Spain)", *American Journal of Physical Anthropology* 108(4) (1999) 433–57.

Pérez-Pérez A., Espurz V., Bermúdez de Castro J. M., De Lumley M. A. and Turbón D. (2003) "Nonoclusal dental microwear variability in a sample of Middle and Late Pleistocene human populations from Europe and the Near East", *Journal of Human Evolution* 44 (2003) 497–513.

Pilet C., Buchet L. and Pilet-Lemière J. (1993) "L'apport de l'archéologie funéraire à l'étude de la présence militaire sur le *limes* saxon, le long des côtes de l'actuelle Basse-Normandie", in *L'Armée romaine et les barbares du IIIᵉ au VIIᵉ siècle*, edd. F. Vallet and M. Kazanski (Paris 1993) 157–73.

Poplin F. (1986) "Introduction aux animaux et aux vegetaux du sejour des morts", *Anthropologie Physique et Archeologie* (Paris 1986) 281–87.

Ripoll G. (1986) "Bronces romanos, visigodos y medievales en el M.A.N.", *Boletín del Museo Arqueológico Nacional de Madrid* 4 (1986) 55–81.

Roda I. and Olesti O. (forthcoming) "Restes epigràfiques: la primera inscripció romana de Llívia", in *Llívia i la Cerdanya a l'Antiguitat*, edd. O. Olesti, J. Guàrdia and O. Mercadal (Tarragona, forthcoming).

Rogers M. E., Abernethy K., Bermejo M., Cipolletta C., Doran D., McFarland K., Nishihara T., Remis M. and Tutin C. E. G. (2004) "Western Gorilla diet: a synthesis from six sites", *American Journal of Physical Anthropology* 64 (2004) 173–92.

Rovira M. C. (1997) "Els accessoris dels vestits", in *Roc d'Enclar. Transformacions d'un espai dominant*, ed. X. Llovera (Monografies del Patrimoni Cultural d'Andorra 4) (Andorra 1997) 143–49.

Schultz A. (1979) *La vida de los primates: Historia Natural Destino*, vol. 18 (Barcelona 1979).

Sommer M. (1984) *Die Gürtel und Gürtelbeschläge des 4. und 5. Jahrhunderts im römischen Reich* (Bonner Hefte 22) (Bonn 1984).

Swindler D. R. (1976) *Dentition of Living Primates* (London and New York 1976).

Teaford M. F. and Oyen O. J. (1989) "*In vivo* and *In vitro* turnover in dental microwear", *American Journal of Physical Anthropology* 80 (1989) 447–60.

Tomlin R. S. O. (2000) "The legions in the Late Empire", in *Roman Fortresses and their Legions*, ed. R. J. Brewer (Cardiff 2000) 159–81.

Toynbee J. M. C. (1990) *Animals in Roman Life and Art* (London 1990; 1st ed. 1968).

Ubelaker D. H. (1978) *Human Skeletal Remains: Excavation, Analysis, Interpretation* (Washington 1978).

Vallet F. (1993) "Une implantation militaire aux portes de Dijon au Ve siècle", in *L'armée romaine et les barbares du IIIe au VIIe siècle*, edd. F. Vallet and M. Kazanski (Paris 1993) 249–58.

Villaverde N. (2001) *Tingitana en la Antigüedad Tardía (siglos III–VII)* (Madrid 2001).

LIST OF FIGURES

THE BALKANS

THE ARCHAEOLOGY OF WAR: HOMELAND SECURITY IN THE SOUTH-WEST BALKANS (3RD–6TH C. A.D.)

John Wilkes

Abstract

Between the 3rd and 6th c. A.D., external threat and internal stress gave rise to a proliferation of fortifications in the south-west Balkans either side of the Adriatic-Aegean watershed, a region for centuries under the unified administration of Roman Macedonia. Recent studies have identified two phases in this process. The earlier was a centrally-directed programme of new military bases, urban and other fortifications based on the network of Roman roads. The second followed the division between East and West, when the region became an uncontrolled border zone, and many sought safety in fortified upland settlements within a network of tracks and paths that replaced the earlier roads.

Introduction

Many regional studies of settlement in the Roman world confirm a consistent pattern. Initial conquest or occupation brought an evacuation of fortified hill settlements in favour of open sites in the plain, many of which became urban centres within a network of engineered roads; later external threat and internal stress brought a reversal of this trend, as the old upland settlements offered a measure of security within refurbished defences. Recent studies of many such locations in the south-west Balkans have suggested a similar pattern of change in two phases, one more centrally directed in the late 3rd and early 4th c. A.D., and a second, less co-ordinated, in the late 5th and 6th c.[1] Yet this particular region lay at the centre of the unified Roman Empire until the separation of east and west at the end of the 4th c., when it became a borderland astride the line of fracture between the two halves. That state of affairs evidently prevailed until the disintegration of the latter and the consolidation of the East brought the entire region under a measure of imperial control

---

[1] Baçe (1976); Popović (1984) 198 n.47; Mikulčić (2002).

A. Sarantis, N. Christie (edd.) *War and Warfare in Late Antiquity: Current Perspectives*
(Late Antique Archaeology 8.1–8.2 – 2010–11) (Leiden 2013), pp. 735–757

from late in the 5th c. The earlier phase amounted to a comprehensive refurbishment of the imperial infrastructure, including roads, in response to the political and military fragmentation of the 3rd c. following large-scale invasion from both north and east. The later phase appears to have been the result of the devolution of control to local centres, as the major highways between East and West ceased to function, to be replaced by a network of paths and tracks.

PROVINCIAL ORGANISATION BEFORE THE LATE 3RD C.

From the initial Roman conquest and occupation of Macedonia in the 2nd c. B.C., the lands on either side of the Adriatic-Aegean watershed in the south-west Balkans were placed under unified control. The provinces of Macedonia and Illyricum, created a century later, embraced territories on either side of the physical barrier formed by the mountains of the modern countries Bosnia-Hercegovina, Montenegro, Albania and Greece. The province of Dalmatia (Illyricum south of the River Sava) extended down the Adriatic to the River Drin in northern Albania, and eastwards as far as the Drina and Ibar rivers to a boundary with the central Balkan province, Moesia (later Moesia Superior). Further south, the province of Macedonia was extended from its historic heartland around the northern Aegean westwards, across the watershed to the Adriatic, to include the historic regions of Illyris and Epirus. The only change to this arrangement came in the 2nd c. A.D., when historic Epirus west of the Pindus range, the coastlands between the River Aous (Vijosë) in the north and the Gulf of Corinth in the south, was detached from the imperial province of Achaia and placed under an imperial official (*procurator*).[2]

THE IMPERIAL ROAD NETWORK

The effective administration of the Roman Empire between the 1st and 4th c. depended on safe and reliable communications, and the movement of supplies on a network of engineered highways, reaching to every province. As a result, the state imposed heavy burdens on provincial communities

---

[2] On the boundaries of Roman Macedonia, see Papazoglu (1988) 73–89 (late Republic and early Empire), 90–98 (late Empire).

to ensure the maintenance of the road system that was to prove vital in times of military emergency. The major routes of the empire are depicted on the Peutinger Map, and in the Itineraries that describe journeys along the roads with lists of stopping-places (*mansiones*) and relay-stations (*mutationes*), with intervening distances in Roman miles (*milia passuum*). Traffic in the south-west Balkans used four major roads recorded in these sources: (a) the Adriatic coast road from Narona in the Narenta (Neretva) valley to Nicopolis on the Gulf of Arta, a Greek city created by Augustus to mark his victory at Actium in 31 B.C.; (b) the main N-S route of the western Balkans, linking Thessalonica to the Danube via Scupi (Skopje) and Naissus (Niš). These two roads were linked by two recorded routes across the watershed; (c) between Lissus (Lezhë) on the Adriatic, and Ulpiana (Lipljan) in Kosovo via the Drin and White Drin valleys; (d) the western section of the historic *Via Egnatia* between Dyrrachium (Durrës) and Thessalonica, via the Genusus (Shkumbin) valley, the lakeland basins of Ohrid and Prespa, and Heraclea Lyncestis (Monastir/Bitola) in the Pelagonia basin. The territorial limits of this study are more or less defined by these roads, except in the south-east, where the limit is the important route, also recorded on the Peutinger Map, across the southern Balkans, linking Heraclea on the Egnatia, and Stobi on the Naissus-Thessalonica route, that continued north-east to Pautalia (Kjustendil), Serdica (Sofia) and Oescus (Gigen) on the Lower Danube.[3]

(a) The Adriatic coast road was created after the final Augustan conquest of Illyricum in A.D. 9 to link a chain of newly-established military bases, including two legionary *castra* and several auxiliary *castella*. South of the Narenta, the line of the road is marked by a large number of milestones, most without inscription, crossing the barren coastal hinterland of Hercegovina and Montenegro, to reach Scodra and Lissus via the Zeta valley. The branch to Epidaurum (Cavtat) on the Adriatic has yielded a milestone of A.D. 47, while several inscribed stones of the 3rd and early 4th c. are known from the line of the main highway. In the Macedonian (Albanian) section, the coastal road crossed, in one case by a bridge, several large rivers that seasonally flooded the coastal plain (Mat, Erzen, Shkumbin, Seman and Vijosë). A road-station, Pistum, between Lissus and Dyrrachium, is yet to be

---

[3] Talbert (2000) Maps 21 and 49 (by J. J. Wilkes), for Roman roads and stations in the southern Balkans.

located on the ground. The section between Dyrrachium, Apollonia and Aulon (Kepi Treportit), also a terminus of the *Via Egnatia*, has yielded milestones of the 3rd and early 4th c. Further south, in the Province of Epirus (later Epirus Vetus), there was an inland route to Nicopolis via the Drinos valley and the Ioannina basin, and a coastal road via Buthrotum (Butrint).[4]

(b) The Balkan N-S route is well documented between Thessalonica and Scupi, and followed the Vardar throughout. The key road junction was Stobi (Gradsko), ancient capital of Paeonia, at the confluence of the Erigon (Crna Reka) and the Axius (Vardar), where the major road between the south-west and north-east Balkans crossed the Axius. Between Stobi and Scupi, the importance of the road is indicated by milestones of the 2nd, 3rd and 4th c. North of Scupi, two routes led to Naissus: the more direct line by Vranje and the valley of the Southern Morava (recorded only on the Peutinger Map) had to confront several natural obstacles, and the road-stations on this section are yet to be located; the preferred route was the longer western line along the River Lepenica, through the Kačanik gorge, through eastern Kosovo, and down the Toplica valley (where the 4 road-stations are also yet to be located), to join the Morava a few miles south of Naissus. Milestones, including one recording 65 miles from Ulpianum, and another offering an almost unique record of the short-lived Emperor Aemilianus (A.D. 253), indicate regular repair.[5]

(c) Though recorded only on the Peutinger Map, and with no surviving milestones or historical record of its origin, the road between Lissus and Naissus was part of the shortest link between the Adriatic and the Lower Danube, via the River Timacus (Timok). It may have been once a road of great strategic value in the era of Roman conquest, and argument has been advanced for an Augustan date. The line of the Roman road likely matches that of the modern road via Pukë (possibly Ad Picaria?), crossing the Drin at Vau Spas (possibly Creveni?), and from Kukës, following the White Drin to Prizren (possibly Gabuleum?) and Suva Reka (possibly Theranda?) to a junction with the Scupi-Naissus road south of Ulpiana.[6]

---

[4] Hammond (1974) 189–92, for the coast road between Lissus and Apollonia.

[5] Hammond (1972) 78–84, for details of these routes.

[6] The military significance of this route, the most direct between the southern Adriatic and the Lower Danube, was many years ago stressed by Syme (1999) 130 (written in 1932–34).

(d) Apollonia's role as one of the western terminals of the *Via Egnatia* had evidently been assumed by Aulona in Late Antiquity, but both were always of lesser importance than Dyrrachium, still Albania's principal seaport. The two branches met in the Genusus valley west of Scampa (Elbasan), but the intervening stations on both cannot be located for certain, partly because of corruption of the literary sources, and partly because of changes in the courses of rivers in the coastal plain. Above Scampa, the river passes through the Candavian Mountains, where the road ascended to a mountain shelf above the left bank to by-pass its narrow gorges. The road crosses to the right bank of the river, and leaves the valley to climb steeply to the Përrenjas plateau before crossing a mountain range into the Ohrid basin. After Lychnidus (Ohrid), the road crosses two further ranges to reach the Resen basin north of Lake Prespa, and then Heraclea Lyncestis at the western edge of the Pelagonia basin. Settlements on the road between Heraclea and Stobi are recorded on the Peutinger Map with intervening distances (*Heraclea—[XIIII Styberra]—xi—Ceramis—xxiiii—Euristo—xii—Stobis*), and continued across the Axius to Pautalia in north-west Thrace. The omission of Styberra, which lay at the crossing of the Erigon, here and in other late sources, may be a consequence of its abandonment following the invasions of the 3rd c. After the settlement at Ceramiae (near Prilep), the road crosses the Pletvar Pass into the Raec valley, and after the Drenovo gorge, passes the settlement of Au(da)ristus (Drenovo) to reach the Axius (Vardar) at Stobi.[7]

The region defined by these Roman roads contains several mountain ranges and few major settlements. While remote from the military crises in the Danube lands that led to the separation of East and West at the end of the 4th c., it lay astride the resulting fissure between the two halves of the empire. As a result, it became a classic example of an uncontrolled borderland, remote from the centres of power. Yet it was a region of great strategic importance, and remained so during the Byzantine era, and in modern times, when Albania, Kosovo and the former Yugoslav Macedonia have been the scenes of conflict between major powers with interests in the area.

---

[7] Hammond (1972) 19–78, with revisions for Albania in Hammond (1974) 185–89.

Cities and Other Major Settlements in the South-West Balkans

There is abundant evidence that overland links with the peoples of the interior were an important element in the economy of the early Greek settlements of Epidamnus (later Dyrrachium) and Apollonia, and this was also the case with Roman settlements on or near to the Adriatic coast, established at Salona, Narona, Epidaurum (the predecessor of Ragusa/ Dubrovnik), Scodra, Lissus and Dyrrachium. In the Late Hellenistic period (2nd–1st c. B.C.), the silver coinages of Apollonia and Dyrrachium circulated widely in the Balkans.

East of the watershed, two major cities were both situated on the River Axius: Stobi had been the chief settlement in the region of Paeonia; Scupi, in the ancient region of Dardania, lay in the Upper Vardar basin. The former, a Hellenistic foundation, was later reconstituted with a Roman constitution (*municipium*), though remained predominantly Greek-speaking; the latter, a Roman veteran colony founded in the late 1st c. A.D., retained its Latin character. Other urban settlements that developed in the Hellenistic era include Heraclea Lyncestis (Bitola/Monastir), Au(da) ristus and Lychnidus, all described later as *poleis*, and probably originally the chief settlements of rural communities (*koina*), as were also Neapolis, Dostoneis, Styberra, the principal settlements of Derriopus, and Geneatae, the chief settlement in a mining area. In the early Empire, Alkomena is recorded as a village (*kome/vicus*), and the same status is recorded for Kolobaisa (where there was a shrine of Apollo and Artemis). There is little sign, however, that urban settlements developed in the border regions between Macedonia, Dardania, Praevalitana and Epirus Nova.[8]

The Impact of the 3rd c. Invasions

It was the Marcomannic wars under Marcus Aurelius (A.D. 167–80), and in particular the raid by the Costobocci in 170 that penetrated as far south as Greece, which generated an increased concern for internal security across the southern Balkans. In areas where the authority of the state had probably never been entirely effective, attention was given to the physical

---

[8] On these locations, see Papazoglu (1988) 313–23 (Stobi), 259–68 (Heraclea), 327 (Audaristus), 312–13 (Neapolis), 289–90 (Dostoneis), 298–302 (Styberra), 302–303 (Alkomena), 291 (Kolobaisa); *IG* 2.2.175 (Lychnidus); *IMS* 6 (1982) 20–40 (Scupi).

protection of the cities and to the security of the major roads. The full impact of increasing pressures from peoples bordering the Danube came in the middle decades of the 3rd c.: in 258, Sarmatians penetrated Moesia Superior and advanced south, probably via Naissus and Ulpianum, as far as Scupi, where they were halted by the Roman general Regalianus at the south exit from the Kačanik gorge—a victory commemorated by a monument to the Emperor Gallienus set up at the site;[9] a decade later, the Heruli passed through the area on their homeward march from the Aegean; and in 269, a force of Goths and other peoples reached Macedonia but were halted at Thessalonica, and then dispersed to settle in Thrace. In general, the area appears to have been unaffected by the subsequent imperial counter-offensives against invaders from beyond the Danube.

Under the Tetrarchy, the Prefecture of Illyricum was in the domain of Galerius, but after his death, it became the scene of intermittent conflict between the rival emperors, Constantine and Licinius. In 316, Licinius was forced to cede all the Balkans except for Thrace, but the conflict only ended in 324 after a decisive victory by Constantine. The impact of more than a decade of hostility that left the Balkans a borderland between the two may have caused the construction of forts and road posts along the border between Thrace and Macedonia, while a fort in Epirus Vetus, at Paleokastër on the inland route along the Drinos valley, appears to be dated by inscription to 311/13. External dangers were still present, and in 322/23, Constantine is credited with driving away Goths from Thessalonica, who are likely to have retreated north through Macedonia.

LATE ROMAN PROVINCIAL ORGANISATION

The impact of provincial changes made in the later 3rd c. under Diocletian and the Tetrarchy—the subdivision of existing provinces and the grouping of the new provinces into dioceses—was to reinstate the mountains of the region as a demarcation between East and West. The Scodra basin and the western part of Kosovo were detached from Dalmatia to form the province Praevalitana (or Praevalis); further south, the region of Illyris, west of the watershed, and comprising the coast between the rivers Drin and Aous, was detached from Macedonia as the province of New Epirus (Epirus Nova), the ancient region to the south henceforward being designated

---

[9] Mikulčić (2002) 157 Abb. 48 (based on Evans (1885) 115 fig. 55).

Old Epirus (Epirus Vetus). The boundary between Praevalitana and New Epirus probably followed the existing line between Dalmatia and Macedonia, that is south of Lissus between the rivers Drin and Mat. Inland, the watershed between the valley of the Black Drin between Ohrid and Kukës, and the White Drin in Kosovo, formed the inland limit of Praevalitana and New Epirus, beyond which were Dardania and Macedonia. Eastern Kosovo and the Skopje basin were detached from Upper Moesia (Moesia Superior) to form a separate province with the historic name Dardania. Further north, the New Dacia, carved out of the Moesian provinces and Thracia, created by Aurelian (270–75) following the evacuation of Dacia north of the Danube, was divided into Dacia Ripensis along the river Danube and Inland Dacia (Dacia Mediterranea), the latter comprising the regions around Naissus, Pautalia and Serdica (Sofia). Macedonia east of the watershed was unaffected by these changes. Later, there is record of a division between Upper Macedonia (Macedonia Salutaris) west of the River Haliacmon, and the historic heartland around the mouth of the River Axius; this arrangement evidently did not last, and in the following century, a new division left that region in Macedonia Secunda, though its limits evidently differed from the earlier arrangement.[10]

The Beginning of Militarisation

During the early Empire, Macedonia was reckoned to be among the 'unarmed provinces', with its military personal being seconded from provinces with legionary and auxiliary garrisons for the service of the governor, including the manning of police posts along the major roads. During the Dacian wars of Trajan, it appears that an auxiliary unit (*cohors I Hispanorum*) was for a time stationed at Stobi, although the papyrus register that furnishes this information indicates that a large proportion of its manpower was variously engaged throughout the Danube lands. That deployment may have been a temporary arrangement at a time when large numbers of troops were drawn from the rest of the empire for major campaigns on the Upper and Lower Danube. Yet it indicates the lasting strategic importance in the Balkan road network of the ancient Paeonian capital, which was to re-appear in Late Antiquity. In the 4th c. register, the *Notitia Dignitatum*, an army unit (*lanciarii Stobenses*) was

---

[10] On the boundaries of the later provinces, see Popović (1984) 182–85.

stationed there, and remained until the capture of the city by the Goths of Theodoric in 479 caused its transfer to Thrace. The same source lists two garrisons in Dardania, at Scupi (*Pseudocomitatenses Scupenses*) and at Merion (*Pseudocomitatenses Merenses*), perhaps to be located at Nikuštak north east of Skopje, although no record of either unit is known from the area.[11]

The huge programme of re-fortifying the defences of the northern frontiers carried through under Diocletian and Constantine was extended to include new forts at strategic locations in the interior. The south-west Balkans was an obvious region for such deployment, given that it lay astride major routes between north and south and between east and west. In Epirus Nova, the massive new *castrum* (348 × 308 m) at Scampa commanded the entry to the mountain section of the *Via Egnatia*. A smaller fort of similar design at Vig, on the road between Lissus and Kosovo, has been linked with the road-station *Ad Picaria*, recorded on the Peutinger Map; another at Paleokastër, on the road south along the Drinos valley in Epirus Vetus, is dated by an inscription to the reign of Constantine (311–13). Both of these smaller forts (*ca.* 100 m²) probably held infantry units. It remains uncertain whether the massive hill-top fortifications at Petrela, south of Tirana, belong to this network of forts, but similar constructions are known further north in Praevalitana, at Riječani and Nikšić in Montenegro, and at Bashtovë in Albania.[12]

East of the watershed, three forts are proposed as belonging to this phase of construction, two in Macedonia and one in Dardania. The regular fort at Dolenci (125 × 122 m) has circular towers at the corners and U-shaped interval towers, and may well be the earliest of the series known in Macedonia. The place is named in the Itineraries as Castra Nicea, and controls the Šemnica valley west of Herclea Lyncestis through which the *Via Egnatia* approaches the Diavat Pass. The earlier phase of the fort at Debreste, an irregular quadrilateral (175 × 157 m), appears also to date from the early 4th c. Its situation commands the western approach to the Barbara Pass, in the Velika valley, by which a road branched from the Scupi-Lychnidus road at Kičevo, leading to Ceramiae in the north of the Pelagonia Basin. The fort was subsequently much altered and strengthened in the 6th c. In Dardania, the fort at Bader occupied a terrace above the River Pčinja, and controlled the Axius valley road where it approached

---

[11] On this deployment, see Mikulčić (2002) 63–65.
[12] Popović (1984) 195–206; Baçe (1981) with *AE* 1984, 814–15 (Paleokastër).

the provincial boundary with Macedonia. It is almost certainly the road-station Praesidium on the Peutinger Map, since its location fits precisely with the recorded distance of 21 miles west of Scupi. As originally constructed, it was a large fortification (280/200 × 150/40 m), enclosing 3.6 ha, but it was later divided into two separate perimeters; the modern name Bader suggests an identification with the Bederiana of Procopius.[13]

RECONSTRUCTION AND PROTECTION OF URBAN CENTRES IN THE LATE 3RD AND EARLY 4TH C.

The impact of the 3rd c. invasions appears to have been greater for the small settlements in the longer term than was the case for the larger urban centres. Some, such as Au(da)ristus and Geneatae, survived within much reduced perimeters, but the larger cities, Heraclea, Stobi and Scupi, were reconstructed, and continued to fulfil an important role until the late 4th c. When they emerge again in the Early Byzantine period, the urban fabric is much reduced and their role significantly altered.[14]

West of the watershed there is less evidence for notable changes in the later larger urban centres, where the most destructive event of the period was the great earthquake of the mid-4th c. In the case of Dyrrachium, the port's importance may have caused the central authorities to construct a barrier wall at Porto Romano, guarding the northern approach to the city. At Scodra, recent investigations suggest that a reduced perimeter of defences enclosing the acropolis and the lower city is dated to the 4th c.; coin circulation here appears to have ceased at the end of the 4th c., but to have resumed by the early 6th, and then continued until the end of the century. A widespread evacuation of exposed settlements appears to have been the cause for the re-occupation of more protected sites of Hellenistic date (Pogradec, Antipatrea [Berat], Basse-Selcë [Pelion?], and others), although with much reduced defensive perimeters. Other less protected settlements close to the plain (Zgërdesh [Albanopolis?] and Gajtan near Scodra) were abandoned in favour of more secure situations (Krujë and Sarda). This shift of occupation appears to date to the late 4th and early

---

[13] Mikulčić (2002) 271 no. 179 (Dolenci), 348–50 nos. 274–74 (Debrešte), 145–46 no. 17 (Bader)—Procop. *Aed.* 4.1.

[14] Papazoglu (1988) 290–91 (Geneatae); for other locations see n. 8 above.

5th c., but at several sites, excavators have identified an interval between this phase and a 6th c. re-occupation.[15]

Most scholars now agree that, in the past, archaeologists have been too ready to link evidence for the demolition of buildings in both town and country directly with the presence of invaders from outside the empire, or even local dissidents. Some of this can be attributed to the over-dramatised accounts of the invasions in literary sources. Yet, even if destruction and demolition of buildings were not caused directly by the invaders in person, their arrival in regions where for centuries none had known anything but the Roman Peace, must have impacted on the local economy: the minting of local city coinages in the Balkans now ended, and the production of portrait sculpture ceased under Gallienus. The presence of the invaders also undermined any sense of security, and began the flight to fortified settlements, and the impoverishment and urgent re-fortification of the larger urban centres. The pattern is the same everywhere: at Resava, a dozen miles south-west of Stobi, a large villa was constructed above a large destruction deposit of the mid-3rd c.; within Stobi itself, the construction of several buildings early in the 4th c. overlay the debris of earlier buildings. The earlier defences were replaced with a reduced perimeter, with further reconstruction later in the same century. The impact on the city of Theodosius' defeat by the Goths in 379/80 in the vicinity is not known, but the emperor is recorded 8 years later residing in the city, while a monument was erected there to commemorate his victory over 'Saxones'.

The picture in the cities of Pelagonia is similar. At Styberra, the deposit of earlier statues of the gymnasium lying in a deep destruction deposit may indicate that the city was abandoned altogether. At Mojno, a dozen miles further south, fragments of a large marble statue of Gallienus probably came from the site of Pelagonia. In Heraclea Lyncestis, the defences were reconstructed and a basilica was constructed above the remains of the forum, both perhaps affected by destruction in the 3rd c. A different picture has emerged at Scupi in Dardania, where occupation continued, apparently without significant interruption, from the 2nd into the 4th c., around and below the Constantinian basilica.[16]

---

[15] Hoxha (2003) for Scodra; Baçe (1976) for other sites.
[16] Mikulčić (2002) 15–18 (historical survey) and 78–87 (evidence for impact of invasions).

Local Road Networks

Between the major Roman roads that linked the centres of population with stopping-places and relay-stations, which supported travellers on horseback or in carriages, and the transit of goods in heavy wagons, ran a network of tracks and paths by which pack-animals could follow remote valleys, and, when the seasons allowed, cross high mountains. With few bridges and no trace of engineering works, there is little direct evidence to indicate the use of such routes. On the other hand, there is a significant body of evidence for the use of such tracks in the Byzantine and Ottoman eras, when new market centres grew up for the reception and departure of caravans of pack-animals; one function of this traffic was to transport minerals out of mining settlements in some of the remotest and inaccessible locations.

The lines of movement in the pre-Roman era within the territory of Epirus Nova, that is Albania north of the Vijosë, are indicated by fortified settlements, some of which were followed by the Late Roman highways. These include the Drin valley between the coast and Kosovo, its northern tributary the Valbones, and the valley of the Black Drin south to its source in Lake Ohrid. Other routes existed along the Mat and Erzen rivers. The River Shkumbin was, before Rome, used more to reach the Korçë basin than to reach the Ohrid and Resen basins across the mountains. In both pre-Roman and Medieval periods, the principal route between the Adriatic and Macedonia via the Korçë basin followed the River Seman and its tributaries, the Osum and Devoll. How much local security was improved by Roman rule in these areas is open to debate, but there is a consistent picture that some high settlements in inconvenient locations were evacuated, perhaps in favour of open valley situations. The attraction of the Roman roads may, for some at least, have drawn many to settlements in their vicinity, at the expense of the more dispersed pattern of the pre-Roman era.[17] East of the watershed, various routes across the mountain ranges were linked to a major N-S passage in the west, between Skopje and Ohrid, not recorded in the Roman itineraries, and in the east, the well-documented route down the Vardar valley between Scupi and Stobi. Most of the routes that branched from these two lines led to the Pelagonia basin in the south.

The ancient road between Scupi and Lychnidus is followed by the modern highway for most of its distance of 200 km. West of the former there

----

[17] Avramea (1996).

was apparently a passage through the narrows of the northern loop of the Vardar, but the main road followed a direct route to Tetovo. From there, a track crossed the great massif of the Scardus Mons (Šar planina) by the Vesala Pass to Prizren in Kosovo, on the Drin route to the Adriatic. After Tetovo, the road continued south through the Polog basin to Gostivar, then crossed into the Velika valley and the Kičevo basin by the Korta Pass. From there, it crossed another range by the Preseka Pass to reach Ohrid by the Sateska valley. Kičevo lay on an important E-W herders' route that began at Dibër/Debar, at the confluence of the Radika with the Black Drin, that crossed the high Jama Pass to Kičevo, from where it continued east along the Velika valley to Brod, and then to the Barbara Pass into the Pelagonia basin to meet the main Heraclea-Stobi road at Ceramiae. Another path ran south from Skopje along the Velika to Brod, where it met the Kičevo-Ceramiae route. On this road again, a few miles east of Kičevo, a route branched south and crossed via the Turla Pass into the upper valley of the Erigon, and then proceeded down the valley through an important mining area, passing the settlements of Bryanium and Alko-menae, to enter Pelagonia from the west, where it met the Heraclea-Stobi highway at the crossing of the Erigon, close to the site of the (now abandoned) Hellenistic foundation, Styberra.

North of the Heraclea-Stobi road, a route led south-west from Bylazora (Titov Veles), an historic fortress in the Axius valley, to Ceramiae, that may have been the preferred approach to Pelagonia from the north. The road initially followed the Topolka, and crossed into the Babuna valley near the Hellenistic foundation and later fortification of Neapolis, from where it crossed the Prisat Pass. Both this route and a longer detour west-wards through the Derven Gorge passed through populated areas, where epitaphs of Hellenistic and Roman date have been recorded. An even more circuitous route followed the Topolka, to reach the Velika basin by the Korab Pass, and then join the Kičevo to Ceramiae route.[18]

Late 4th c. Invasions and the Separation of East and West

In A.D. 394, the Emperor Theodosius I led an army overland through Thracia and Illyricum to Italy, where, on 6th September, he defeated Eugenius at the 'Icy River' (*Fluvius Frigidus*) east of Aquileia. That event was the last assertion of a unified imperial control over East and West

---

[18] For these routes, see Mikulčić (2002) 41–47 with references to catalogue of sites.

that had endured for more than four centuries. In Milan, during games to celebrate the presence of the emperor in the western capital, Theodosius fell ill and died on 17th January 395. The empire was divided between his sons, Arcadius in the East and Honorius in the West, and although a formal constitutional unity continued, the interests of the two regimes soon diverged, and they came close to open conflict through those controlling affairs in the two capitals. In the original division, the Prefecture of Illyricum had been controlled from the West, but by the death of Honorius in 423, when most of the territories of the West had already passed out of direct imperial control, the balance of power in the Balkans had shifted decisively to the East.

While Dalmatia and the Pannonian provinces remained notionally with the West, the line of imperial fracture followed the Dinaric watershed of Bosnia and Hercegovina, leaving the dioceses of the Dacias and Macedonia with the East. When, shortly after the death of Honorius, an expedition was sent from the East to remove a usurper and install Valentinian III at Ravenna, the main body travelled via the Adriatic, but a cavalry force under Aspar came overland via Sirmium through Pannonia to northern Italy. A decade later, in 435, the Pannonian provinces Savia and Valeria were ceded to the Huns, and the area around Sirmium between the lower Sava and Drava, once the strategic centre of Roman control over the Danube lands, now marked the western limit of the East in Illyricum. When, after the collapse of the Hunnic Empire, Marcian granted most of Pannonia to the Goths (454/55), he was disposing of territories no longer under imperial control. The formal transfer of Illyricum to the East was part of the marriage agreement between Valentinian III and Eudoxia in 437.[19]

In regard to the south-west Balkans, some of the Goths moved in the direction of Macedonia following the Roman disaster at Adrianople in 378, but were forced to withdraw from Thessalonica because of plague. In winter 379/80, their victory over Theodosius at Stobi left Macedonia and Thessaly open to them. Some years later, after the Goths under Alaric had been driven away from Constantinople into Macedonia, an attempt by the western General Stilicho to confront them was frustrated by the rivalry between the two courts, and they were permitted to cross the mountains into Epirus Vetus and Nova, where Alaric was granted the status of Roman general in Illyricum by Arcadius. The region may then in fact have enjoyed

---

[19] For these events and the problem of the administration of Illyricum, see Wozniak (1981).

a few decades of peace that was ended by the destructive impact of the Huns, who, in 447, passed through the region and penetrated as far as Thermopylae. Their presence in the region is generally agreed to mark the end of whatever survived of major cities linked by still passable roads, and a transition to a form of settlement based on fortified towns and fortresses significantly different from the former system.[20]

In 479, Goths under Theodoric the Amal entered Macedonia from the north-east by the Serdica-Stobi route. They captured the latter town and drove out the garrison, then moved on to seize Heraclea Lyncestis before moving westwards along the *Via Egnatia* via Lychnidus to Dyrrachium, where they sought to retrieve losses suffered in an ambush by imperial forces while descending from the mountain section of the road east of Scampa. Five years later, they left the Balkans, marching overland to Italy by the northern route. The next invaders to enter the region were the Bulgars who, like the Huns, reached Thermopylae, but also looted Scupi, forcing its population to take refuge in the surrounding area. Most commentators are agreed that Procopius' account of annual devastations of the Balkans by Huns, Slavs and Antae, is overdrawn, but in 540, the Hunnic Kutrigurs penetrated to the Chalkidiki peninsula and beyond, in the course of which, according to Procopius, they destroyed many fortified places. A Slav raid that reached Dyrrachium in 548 probably followed the road from Naissus to Scodra via Kosovo. Two years later, the Slavs who moved south-west from the Serdica region to winter in Dalmatia probably followed the same route. In 558/59, the Kutrigurs, along with Bulgars and Slavs, entered Macedonia and Thessaly either by the Serdica-Stobi route, or perhaps by the Thracian section of the *Via Egnatia*. In 580/81, Slavs reached Greece, where they are said to have remained for 4 years. In 586, Slavs and Avars moved south through the area to reach Thessalonica on 22nd September. The evidence of coin hoards implies that these events marked the end of several major centres, including Stobi and Heraclea Lyncestis. There appears now to have been no significant circulation of imperial coins, and by 615, the Slav occupation of Macedonia seems complete.[21]

---

[20] For these events, see the discussion of Heather (1991) 147–56.

[21] For Illyricum in the late 5th and 6th c., see Croke (2001) 48–77. A detailed account of Theodoric's advance along the *Via Egnatia* is furnished by the historian Malchus fragment 20; Blockley (1983) 434–51 furnishes a text and translation. On the topography, see Hammond (1972) 34–35.

The Fortifications of Urban Settlement in the Late 5th and 6th c.

In the north, the Balkan highway between Constantinople and the Sirmium/ Singidunum (Belgrade) region survived as an imperial military axis down to the late 6th c. Further south, the *Via Egnatia* between Constantinople and Thessalonica remained just about accessible to imperial forces, but further west had lost its dominant role to a network of tracks passable only with pack-animals. A register of cities by province, compiled by Hierocles early in the reign of Justinian, for the use of officials, is the principal source for surviving urban centres around the mid-6th c. From this we see how in Praevalis (Praevalitana), Scodra is the provincial capital, along with Lissus, but Dorakion metropolis (i.e. Dyrrachium) appears where Doclea might have been expected. In Epirus Nova, Dyrrachium is listed first, followed by Scampis, Apollonia, Byllis, Amantia, Poucheropolis, Aulona and Lychnidus, the last being designated metropolis. Two further places, Alistron and Scepton, cannot be located, although the Mat valley has been suggested for both.

The duplication of Dyrrachium, the absence of Doclea, and the title metropolis for Lychnidus, have been attributed to later changes following the creation of the Byzantine theme of Dyrrachium in the 9th c. In the list of Constantine Porphyrogenitus, the cities of the no longer existing province Praevalis, that is Lissus, Ulcinium (Ulcinj) and Antibaris (Bar), appear as forts (castella) of Dyrrachium. The last in the list marked the southern limit of Dalmatia and was included in the *terra Dyrracenorum*. By that time, ancient Lychnidus, now Achris (Ohrid), the centre of a large ecclesiastical territory under the Bulgars, had become the centre of a small military theme created in the 11th c. Ancient Doclea had ceased to function during the Slav invasions, but its name survived (Duklja) for that region.

In Procopius' list of towns and fortresses for Epirus Nova, the Epirotes extend now as far north as Epidamnus ('now named Dyrrachium'), where begins Prekalis (Praevalis). The absence of places in the latter might be due to the Gothic occupation. In Epirus Nova, 32 newly-constructed fortresses and 26 repaired fortresses are named, of which only three appear in the list of Hierocles—Dyrrachium, the un-located Alistros and Amantia, to which (in the 'Secret History') he adds Lychnidus. Some names can be located with reasonable certainty: Pakoue (Pukë), Deuphrakos (Dibër/ Debar), Peteon (ancient Pelion = / Basse-Selcë), Klementiana (in the Kelmend region north of Lake Scodra). Other possible locations include Stephaniakon (Shtefni in the Mat valley) and Scemnites (Scampa— Elbasan). Scydreonopolis is almost certainly Scodra, the metropolis of

Praevalis, to which Klementiana and Antipagrai, listed after Scodra, and almost certainly to be identified with Antibaris, also belong.[22]

Archaeological evidence from this area is consistent in indicating a re-occupation in the late 5th and 6th c. A.D., after an interval of desertion in the defensible settlements already occupied in the late 4th and early 5th c. Overall, this evidence appears to complement the documentation of urban settlement provided by Hierocles. The embellishment with new public buildings, including a hippodrome and monumental defences, by the Emperor Anastasius of his native city Dyrrachium may be exceptional, but a measure of revival may well account for the later survival of several coastal settlements, including Lissus, Scodra, Ulcinium and Antibaris. On the southern border of Epirus Nova, inscriptions record that the reduced perimeter of defences provided for Byllis, in its secure hill-top situation, was constructed under the supervision of Justinian's General Victorinus.[23]

Under Justinian, both Praevalitana and Epirus Nova retained an eccle-siastical link with Rome through the *vicarius* at Thessalonica, but after A.D. 535, the former province was placed under the authority of Justiniana Prima, and the metropolitans of both provinces were based respectively at Scodra and Dyrrachium, with suffragans at Lissus and Doclea in the former, and at Lychnidus, Scampa, Apollonia, Amantia, Byllis and Aulona in the latter. There is material evidence that several churches flourished down to the time of the Slav migrations, illustrating the wealth of the organised Church when compared with a secular impoverishment.[24]

After Zeno, the seats of bishops had the status of cities, including those of suffragans such Nicea, Čučer in the Kačanik Gorge and Antania (near Zovik on the Crna Reka). In most cases, they had begun life as forts that after the end of the 4th c. are generally described as *oppida*, urban centres whose buildings retained their military character down into the Early Byz-antine period—a pattern also evident in some of the provinces north of the area. Generally, a distinction between military fort and civil town can no longer be drawn, either from the physical remains or from the lists of fortifications provided by Procopius. The principal fortified centres in the 6th c. were Heraclea Lyncestis and Nicea in Macedonia I, Stobi, Pelagonia (?) and Ceramiae in Macedonia II, Scupi, Merion and Ulpianum and Čučer (8 km from Scupi) in Dardania. Arguments have even been advanced for

---

[22] Popović (1984) 182–85 (for Praevalitana and Epirus Nova in Hierocles and Procopius).
[23] Gutteridge (2003) for Dyrrachium; *AE* 1989, 645–47 (Byllis inscriptions).
[24] Popović (1984) 206–207.

locating Justiniana Prima at Scupi, a reconstruction of the city following the disastrous earthquake in 518, rather than at Caričin Grad in southern Serbia, an identification that is now widely accepted. These include Procopius' statement that the city lay in Dardania, when the latter location does not, while the 6th c. monumental facade of the Kale fortress at Skopje is also significant.[25]

THE FORTIFICATION OF RURAL SETTLEMENT

Though much improved in recent years, the record of Late Roman and Early Byzantine rural settlement west of the watershed, in Praevalitana and Epirus Nova, is still less complete than that from the territories east of the mountains. Yet it is clear that from the late 4th c. onwards, there was a widespread re-use of ancient fortified locations, and the construction of new defended settlements that served as refuges for local communities in time of emergency. In Epirus Nova, the great *castrum* at Scampa became the centre of a network of fortified sites designed to maintain local security, based on a series of forts to control movement along the Genusus valley, in similar fashion to that known in greater detail for the section further east, between Lychnidus (Ohrid) and Heraclea Lyncestis (Bitola). Most of the sites linked with Scampa appear to have been occupied from the late 4th c., and the same appears to be the case with another group controlling the section between the Shkumbin valley and the Ohrid basin via the Përrenjas Plateau. Another series of fortified sites is dated to the 6th c.; some are new constructions, but many are refurbished earlier locations.[26]

Further north, in Praevalitana, the Drin valley route between the Adriatic and Kosovo was also controlled by fortified sites, also found in the tributary Valbones valley. More recent research has recorded many more sites in western Kosovo, not only along the line of the main road, but along local routes that linked the ancient predecessors of the modern centres Djakovica and Peć, and in the White Drin and Klina basins. Further south, in northern Epirus Nova, fortifications have been recorded in the inland valleys of the upper Mat (14 sites) and along the Black Drin between Kukës and Dibër (9 sites). A cross-country route north-east from

---

[25] Mikulčić (2002) 51–58. Notwithstanding the arguments of Mikulčić 57–58, the balance of the evidence appears to favour Caričin Grad, but the question remains unresolved.

[26] Baçe (1976).

Dyrrachium to Peshkopi in the Drin valley is indicated by a line of 10 sites. South of the *Via Egnatia*, the more ancient passage between the coast and Macedonia, via the Osum and Devoll valleys and the area of Lake Prespa, re-emerged as a major transit in Late Antiquity, commencing either from Scampa (7 sites) or Berat (6 sites).[27]

Further east, the passage of the *Via Egnatia* between Heraclea Lyncestis and Lychnidus had already been under surveillance from forts constructed in the late 3rd or early 4th c., and from late in the 4th c., was flanked by many new enclosures. Some of these may have served originally as refuges for the local population, but later grew into large permanent settlements with churches. South of Heraclea, there were three controlling forts, and a further four on the section west leading to Resen north of Lake Prespa, including the military fort at Nicea (Dolenci), later becoming a major urban centre with a bishop. Between Resen and Lychnidus, the earlier route by the Bukova Pass was apparently replaced by a more direct passage for pack-animals across the Istok (Petrina) range by the Bigla pass (1663 m); this was controlled by three fortifications. West of Lychnidus, the line of the ancient route around the lake shore remained in use, but was now secured by three new fortifications.[28]

Several fortified units controlled the main route between Scupi (Skopje) and Lychnidus: north of Tetovo, the fort and fortified settlement at Lešok was an administrative and economic centre for the northern part of the Polog basin from the 4th c. onwards; between Tetovo and Gostivar, the fort and tower at Gradec, constructed on a spur overlooking the passage of the road across the plain, was first constructed in the 3rd c. and remained occupied until the late 6th. Another fort constructed at the same time at Kičevo became the nucleus of a large civil settlement that survived into the 6th c. Around a dozen miles east of Kičevo, a new oval fort was constructed in the 6th c. at Miokazi in the Velika valley, on the remains of a Hellenistic settlement, and lay close to the point where the road to Derriopus and Heraclea crossed the boundary from Epirus Nova into Macedonia. The final section of the road to Lychnidus, down the Sateska valley to Struga on Lake Ohrid, was protected by a large triangular fortification at Trebenište (4th–5th c.), and also controlled the branch route east to join the *Egnatia*. Further south, another fort at Velmei controlled the place

---

[27] Perzhita and Hoxha (2003) for the sites in Kosovo. On the importance of the Devoll route before construction of the *Via Egnatia*, see Hammond (1972) 97–100 with Map 10.

[28] Mikulčić (2002) 36–37 (*Via Egnatia*) and 476 Abb. 394 (Istok/Bigla Pass).

where a route branched to the east to reach the Erigon valley in Macedonia by the Ilinska pass.[29]

Many of the fortifications constructed after the late 4th c. may, like
the earlier regular military forts, have been part of centrally-directed measures to combat a general state of insecurity, and in particular the hazardous state of road travel, but their design and construction were a product
of local organisation: while few have regular perimeters, their situations
were clearly chosen with care, with a view to controlling road traffic in
the vicinity. None has so far yielded any epigraphic evidence. In the area
under consideration, several locations appear to have developed as major
urban centres by the 6th c., some with Episcopal churches. For some, origins may have been as 4th c. military forts: Čučer, which has an acropolis
and a fortified lower town, commanded the main Scupi-Ulpiana road at
its southern exit from the Kačanik gorge; likewise the fort at Taor, which
controlled the Pčinja crossing of the Scupi-Thessalonica highway, became
a major urban centre in the 6th c., and is identified with Tauresium, birthplace of Justinian I; and further downstream, another fort and settlement
at Viničani, which controlled the section of the highway north of Stobi.[30]

If the surveillance of major junctions and river crossings served the
need of the central authority, there is also evidence that some of these
many fortified locations were part of locally-devised defence networks
created to protect exposed and densely-populated areas. An obvious area
was the Pelagonia basin, throughout history a means of passage between
north and south. At least 8 fortifications were placed to guard routes into
the area from the north and the north-east. This may have been a local
initiative designed to ward off the destructive passage of invaders heading
south from the direction of Bylazora (Titov Veles) and Stobi—something
that occurred more than once in the Late Roman period.[31]

A similar form of local control involving the crossings of provincial
boundaries is more likely to have been centrally-inspired rather than the
result of local initiative. Such traffic was from the time of the early Empire
subject to control by the customs agency (*portorium publicum*), managed
by imperial bureaux. There was a station on the Scupi to Ulpiana road
in the Kačanik Gorge where the road crossed from Dardania into Prae-

---

[29] Mikulčić (2002) 41–43 (*Scupi-Lychnidus* route), with area maps indicating sites,
451 Abb. 366 (Gostivar), 458 Abb. 374 (Tetovo), 472 Abb. 390 (Kičevo), 486 Abb. 406
(Struga), 437–38 (Velmei).

[30] Mikulčić (2002) 153–58 no. 26 with Abb. 44–49 (Čučer), 187 no. 56 (Taor), 441–42
no. 381 (Viničani).

[31] Mikulčić (2002) 66.

valitana. One factor in the increasing control over road traffic between different provinces may have been the importance of the mining activity in areas of the south-west Balkans. The boundary crossing from Dardania into Macedonia on the Axius highway was controlled by a station named Praesidium (see above). The actual crossing lay in the Sopot Gorge, where a pair of forts either side of the river have been identified with the station *Ad Cephalon*, where a barrier wall 600 m long closed off a by-pass route from the north—a construction that may date to the 4th c. The most elaborate crossing control was that from Dardania into Praevalitana, on the route between Scupi and Tetovo in the Polog basin; here, one major fort and several smaller posts were linked with a barrier wall several miles long.[32]

A recent study of 180 fortified upland sites dating from between the 3rd and the 6th c. in the area east of the watershed (FYR Macedonia) provides the following statistical summary regarding date and function,[33] where that evidence is available:

Table 1. Regions and Categories

Region	Nos of sites	Type:	Frontier	Road	Mines
Skopje basin	(25)		12	5	8
North west (Polog basin)	(23)		15	5	3
West (Dibër, Kičevo and Brod)	(28)		5	3	3
South west (Ohrid, Struga and Resen)	(38)		6	5	3
South (Pelagonia basin, Bitola, Demir Hisar, Kruševo and Prilep)	(41)		13	9	10
South east (Vardar valley, Titovo Veles and Kavardarci)	(25)		4	5	3

Table 2. Dating

3rd–4th centuries	8
4th century	5
3rd–5th centuries	5
3rd–6th centuries	19
4th–6th centuries	23
5th–6th centuries	31
6th century	38

---

[32] Mikulčić (2002) 67–68.
[33] Compiled from the lists of sites in Mikulčić (2002).

Conclusion

The impact of war, or rather the fear of war, in the south-west Balkans between the 3rd and 6th c. was both profound and lasting. By the end of the period, we see a fortified landscape, where towns, road-stations, border stations and mining administration all existed within the protection of walls. Many of these fortified locations were linked to observation towers on surrounding hills. Against this evidence, the total of more than 400 fortified locations listed by Procopius for the area in the 6th c. seems entirely credible, a response to the fragmentation of imperial authority from the late 4th c. How these were created and controlled remains uncertain. The general uniformity of the military fortifications created in the late 3rd and 4th c.—in terms of regular perimeters, massive external towers and narrow entrances—provided a model for later constructions, but most of the later fortifications were less regular in shape (e.g. triangular, oval), and sometimes entirely irregular to fit the terrain. Despite the huge investment in construction, it seems that most of these strongholds ceased to function in the face of the Slav migrations in the late 6th and early 7th c., although the extent and nature of Slav settlement west of the watershed, that is in Albania, have been fiercely contested in recent decades.

Bibliography

Primary Sources

AE = *L'Année Épigraphique* (Académie des inscriptions et des belles-lettres) (Paris 1888-).
IG = Edson C. F., Papazoglou F., Milin M. and Ricl M. (1972–) edd. *Inscriptiones Graecae Epiri, Macedoniae, Thraciae, Scythiae* (Inscriptiones Graecae 10) (Berlin 1972–).
IMS = Papazoglou F., Mirković M., Dragojević B. (1976–) edd. *Inscriptions de la Mésie supérieure* (Belgrade 1976–).
Procop. *Aed.* = Dewing H. B. (1940) ed. and trans. Procopius, *The Buildings* (Cambridge, Mass. and London 1940).

Secondary Works

Avramea A. (1996) "Trace et function de la Via Egnatia. Du IIᵉ siècle avant J.-c. au VI siècle après J.-c.", in *The Via Egnatia under Ottoman Rule (1380–1699): Halcyon Days in Crete II: a Symposium held in Rethymnon 9–11 January 1994*, ed. E. A. Zachariadou (Rethymnon 1996) 3–7.
Bace A. (1976) "Fortification de la Basse Antiquité en Albanie", *Monumentet* 11 (1976) 45–74.
—— (1981) "La forteresse de Paleokastra", *Iliria* 11.2 (1981) 193.
Blockley R. C. (1983) ed. *The Fragmentary Classicising Historians of the Later Roman Empire: Eunapius, Olympiodorus and Malchus. Volume II: Text, Translation and Historiographical Notes* (ARCA Classical and Medieval Texts, Papers and Monographs 10) (Liverpool 1983).

Croke B. (2001) *Count Marcellinus and his Chronicle* (Oxford 2001).

Evans A. J. (1885) "Antiquarian researches in Illyricum III and IV", *Archaeologia* 49 (1885) 1–167.

Gutteridge A. (2003) "Cultural geographies and 'The ambition of Latin Europe': the city of Durres and its fortifications c. 400–c. 1501", *Archeologia Medievale* 30 (2003) 19–65.

Hammond N. (1972) *A History of Macedonia. Vol. 1: Historical Geography and Prehistory* (Oxford 1972).

—— (1974) "The western part of the Via Egnatia", *JRS* 64 (1974) 185–94.

Heather P. (1991) *Goths and Romans 332–489* (Oxford 1991).

Hoxha G. (2003) *Scodra and Praevalis in the Late Antiquity* (Shkodër 2003).

Koch G. (1989) *Albanien: Kunst und Kultur im Land der Skipetaren* (Cologne 1989).

Mikulčić I. (2002) (ed. M. Konrad) *Spätantike und frühbyzantinische Befestigungen in Nordmakedonien. Städt- Vici- Refugien- Kastelle* (Münchner Beiträge zur Vor- und Frühgeschichte Bd. 54) (Munich 2002).

Oikonomides N. (1996) "The medieval Via Egnatia", in *The Via Egnatia under Ottoman Rule (1380–1699): Halcyon Days in Crete II: a Symposium held in Rethymnon 9–11 January 1994*, ed. E. A. Zachariadou (Rethymnon 1996) 8–16.

Perzhita L. and Hoxha G. (2003) *Late Antiquity Castles in Western Dardania (4th–6th cent.)* (Tirana 2003).

Papazoglu F. (1988) *Les villes de Macédoine à l'époque romaine* (Bulletin de Correspondance Hellénique Supplement 16) (Athens and Paris 1988).

Popović V. (1984) "Byzantins, Slaves et Autochtones dans les provinces de Praevalitane et Nouvelle Epire", *Villes et peuplement dans l'Illyricum protobyzantin* (Collection de l'École française de Rome 77) (Rome 1984) 181–243.

Syme R. (1999) (ed. A. Birley) *The Provincial at Rome; and Rome and the Balkans 80 BC–AD 14* (Exeter 1999).

Talbert R. J. A. (2000) ed. *Barrington Atlas of the Greek and Roman World* (Princeton 2000).

Wilkes J. J. (2006) "The significance of road-stations for the archaeology of Albania in the Roman era", in *New Directions in Albanian Archaeology: Studies Presented to Muzafer Korkuti Tiranë*, edd. L. Bejko and R. Hodges (Tirana 2006) 169–76.

Wozniak F. E. (1981) "East Rome, Ravenna and Western Illyricum", *Historia* 30 (1981) 351–82.

Zachariadou E. (1996) ed. *The Via Egnatia under Ottoman Rule (1380–1699): Halcyon Days in Crete II: a Symposium held in Rethymnon 9–11 January 1994* (Rethymnon 1996).

MILITARY ENCOUNTERS AND DIPLOMATIC AFFAIRS
IN THE NORTH BALKANS
DURING THE REIGNS OF ANASTASIUS AND JUSTINIAN

Alexander Sarantis

Abstract

Balkan history in the late 5th to 6th c. A.D. period is viewed by scholars as, at best, a respite from a series of devastating barbarian raids and, at worst, as another stepping-stone on the path to the inevitable loss of imperial control over the region. This paper redresses these perceptions by portraying the reigns of Anastasius and Justinian as a period in which the Romans/Byzantines were taking the initiative and 'winning' in their military and diplomatic dealings with the barbarians. These emperors devoted considerable political energy and economic and military resources to restoring imperial military authority in the northern Balkans.

Introduction

The history of military encounters and diplomatic affairs in the northern Balkans between the late 5th and late 6th c. A.D. has not been treated in great detail by secondary works. Modern histories of the late antique Balkans have focused predominantly on the 4th to 5th c. and 6th to 7th c. periods, during which the area was invaded and colonised by Visigoths, Ostrogoths and the Huns of Attila; and the Avars and Slavs, respectively.[1] The works that cover the Anastasian and Justinianic periods of Balkan history have done so in the context of broader histories on the late antique or 6th c. Balkans, or in studies of the barbarian groups that are attested in the Balkans in this period.[2] Meanwhile, histories of the Anastasian and

---

[1] On the Goths and the Romans, Heather (1991) and (1996); Wolfram (1988). On the Balkans in the context of the fall of the Roman Empire, Heather (2005). On the Huns, see Thompson (1948) and (1996); Gordon (1966); Kelly (2008). On the Avars, see Pohl (1988). On Slavs and Avars, see Whitby (1988). Curta (2001a) considers the ethnogenesis of the Slavs in the 6th c. A.D.

[2] The articles in Poulter (2007a) examine the history and archaeology of the Balkans in Late Antiquity. However, although these cover the Justinianic period, none take into account large-scale Anastasian and Justinianic military campaigns in the region. On the

A. Sarantis, N. Christie (edd.) *War and Warfare in Late Antiquity: Current Perspectives*
(Late Antique Archaeology 8.1–8.2 – 2010–11) (Leiden 2013), pp. 759–808.

Justinianic periods have generally concentrated on the Persian Wars, and, for Justinian, the reconquest of the West Roman provinces.[3]

There has been an associated tendency to view the Balkan region in this period as a backwater, a low priority to the imperial authorities, which, still reeling from the invasions and settlement by Goths and Huns during the 4th to 5th c. A.D., would be doomed as soon as a barbarian group as powerful as Attila's Huns emerged once again north of the Danube.[4] Even though historians have credited Justinian for his fortification programme and diplomatic policies in the Balkans, they have not recognised his strategic prioritisation of the region and deployment of field armies there.[5] The nature of the textual sources is partly to blame. What little material has survived on Balkan affairs in the Anastasian and Justinianic periods comprises isolated references in chronicles or narrative histories.[6] For example, Procopius' passages on the Balkans are brief and fragmentary in comparison with those on the Persian, Vandalic and Gothic wars, to which he devoted entire books. Further, this major historian portrays imperial policies in the Balkans in a negative light, using hyperbolic phrases to exaggerate the impact and frequency of barbarian raids, and to play down imperial successes on the battlefield.[7]

Archaeologists have contributed to this gloomy portrayal of the 5th to 6th c. A.D. Balkans. Because most of the material evidence cannot be accurately dated to a particular reign, they have understandably tended

---

Lombards, Christie (1995); Pohl and Erhart (2005); Pohl (1996) and (1997); Christou (1991). For the Gepids, see Bóna (1976); Croke (1982a); Diculescu (1923); Pohl (1980). On the Heruls, Brandt (2005); Ellegård (1987); Schwarcz (2005). On the Slavs, Curta (2001a) and (2005).

[3] Cameron (2005); Evans (1996); Maas (2005) on Justinian. See Haarer (2006) on Anastasius. These works do not include chapters specifically devoted to the Balkans.

[4] Jones (1964) 299; Liebeschuetz (2007) 101; Stein (1949–59) volume 2, 310 refers to the Balkans as "une entrave génante".

[5] Wozniak (1978) 147 and 157 recognises Justinian's diplomatic skill in dealing with the Pannonian barbarians, but sees this as an example of "conciliatory opportunism", driven by military vulnerability in the Balkans. Similarly, although Whitby (2007) 140–41 acknowledges the recovery in imperial fortunes and interest in the Balkans from the reign of Anastasius, he stresses that the region was a low strategic priority and denuded of mobile field troops. Curta (2005) 181–86 highlights the effectiveness of the Justinianic fortification of the Lower Danube frontier, but sees it as a sign that, after a brief period following the 'Endless Peace' with Persia, Roman troops were drawn from the region and re-deployed in other areas of the empire. Liebeschuetz (2007) 112–13 highlights barbarian raids, but does not refer to imperial military responses, which he relates to the lack of field forces in the Balkans.

[6] Procop. *Pers.* and *Goth.*; Malalas; Marcell. com.; Agath.; Menander.

[7] Especially in Procop. *Anec.* For instance, when discussing barbarian raids on the Balkans at 2.11, he states: 'from year's end to year's end they all took it in turn to plunder and pillage everything within their reach'. For a detailed analysis of Procopius' treatment of the Balkans, see Sarantis (forthcoming).

to focus on the bigger picture—the transformation of the Balkans across Late Antiquity from the Roman to the Dark Age periods.[8] Consequently, they present the region as experiencing a downward spiral, punctuated by a succession of destructive invasions, prior to the eventual, inevitable collapse of imperial control at the hands of the Avars and the Slavs in the late 6th to 7th c.[9] The material evidence for an end to the villa economy, the disappearance of un-walled cities in open plains, and the proliferation of fortifications in isolated locations are used to highlight military insecurity, dislocation and decline. Indeed, in light of the widespread barbarian invasions and settlement of the Balkan provinces in the late 4th to 5th c., life was, unsurprisingly, in many ways not as rosy as it had been in the Roman era. Within this narrative, the late 5th to 6th c. period is seen at best as a brief and limited respite.[10]

However, this paper will present a more optimistic picture of the northern Balkans during the reigns of Anastasius and Justinian. It will do this by suggesting that, in comparison with the preceding period of Gothic and Hunnic migrations and invasions, this was a period in which the Romans gained the upper hand in their military confrontations with barbarian groups.

In its first half, the paper will piece together the literary evidence to examine the considerable military resources and diplomatic energy that Anastasius and Justinian devoted to countering internal and external barbarian threats to the Balkans, and to spreading Roman influence both north and south of the Danube. There is no doubt that the literary evidence has important limitations.[11] For the late 5th to mid-6th c. it is especially fragmentary, and, as already noted, skewed by subjective views and rhetoric in the case of Procopius. We cannot assume any comprehensive coverage of Balkan military affairs in this period. Indeed, we must accept that, as with all reconstructions of late antique history, there were almost certainly barbarian raids and Roman campaigns about which we will never learn. However, on a more positive note, what literary evidence we have derives from numerous sources which were written by politically well-connected contemporary authors, and the coverage provided is not at all

---

[8] Poulter (2007a).

[9] Poulter (2007b) 40 recognises a degree of imperial control was re-established in the 6th c., but 46–48 sees this as limited and ultimately doomed. Crow (2007) interprets the strength of the Anastasian Long Wall as evidence for the weakness of the north Balkan defences.

[10] Liebeschuetz (2007) 106–14; Poulter (2007b) 14–15.

[11] Poulter (2007b) 12–15.

patchy.[12] Although Procopius' Balkan passages digress from his Gothic, Vandalic and Persian Wars narratives, this does not mean that we only learn about Balkan affairs whenever they impacted on other military arenas. Instead, Procopius' Balkan excursuses sit uncomfortably within these works, and are loosely connected to the main subject matter, implying that Procopius considered the Balkan arena important in its own right, but, writing mainly in the early 550s, felt that it was too late to devote a separate book to it, and so inserted this material wherever he could.[13]

If we add Procopius' material to the chronicle entries written by Malalas and Marcellinus Comes, and the relevant passages of Agathias', Menander's and Jordanes' histories, most of which were not written in the context of other campaigns, our coverage of Justinianic Balkan affairs is actually fairly good, with only a few hiatuses.[14] We may surmise that these sources furnish us with the highlights of Roman-barbarian military affairs in this period, and would not have neglected to cover equally significant invasions and battles. Although such literary material is not as good as archaeological evidence for discussing socio-economic conditions on the ground, it is the best evidence that we have for the dating and nature of military and political events.[15]

The second part of the paper will consider epigraphic and archaeological evidence for Balkan fortification work, and legislative evidence for administrative reforms, and assess how these drives may have related to Anastasius' and Justinian's military and diplomatic strategies. Like the literary evidence, the archaeological record is far from comprehensive, and a precise match between the two bodies of evidence will not be attempted here.[16] Instead, the paper will examine the ways in which the

---

[12] See Appendix below for a timeline of events.

[13] See Sarantis (forthcoming) for a fuller discussion of Procopius' treatment of the Balkans.

[14] See Appendix at the end of this paper. On Malalas, Croke (1990); Jeffreys (1990). On Marcellinus Comes, Croke (2001) chapters 1 and 2. On Agathias, Cameron (1970) 1–2. On Procopius, Cameron (1985); Greatrex (2003); Howard-Johnston (2000); Kaldellis (2001).

[15] Poulter (2007b) 12 and 15 doubts whether literary evidence can be used to construct a continuous framework of periods and sub-periods in which the relative gravity of the various barbarian raids can be assessed. While he is right in suggesting that this will never be an exact science, this does not mean that ancient historians should not attempt to reconstruct historical phases from the available literary evidence. Thompson (1996); Heather (1991) and (1996); Whitby (1988); and Pohl (1988) are among the works which have been invaluable to our understanding of the different periods in late antique Balkan history.

[16] Poulter (2007b) 2–4 on the problematic use of archaeological material by historians.

archaeological evidence can provide a general socio-economic and physical context for the documented political and military events; in doing so, it will cover both areas in which the archaeological and literary sources support each other and areas in which they contradict one another. For instance, archaeology can cast light on exaggerations in the literary evidence and help assess wider changes that may have been caused by particularly disruptive political or military developments; meanwhile, the documented events might help explain specific characteristics of the settlement pattern and delineate possible sub-periods within the archaeological evidence.

It must be stated at the outset that the paper will inevitably be skewed toward the reign of Justinian—inescapable given that the majority of the events related by the literary sources occurred then. This may relate to the accidental survival of more texts from the reign of Justinian, or simply to the fact that his reign really was more eventful.[17]

4TH TO 5TH C. BACKGROUND

The Balkans suffered along with the West Roman provinces during the era of migrations and invasions by Gothic and Hun groups between the late 4th and late 5th c. A.D. By the accession of Anastasius in A.D. 491, northwestern Illyricum had been lost to barbarian groups, such as the Gepids and the Suevi, many parts of the frontier provinces in Thrace and Illyricum had been settled by the Gothic and Hunnic remnants of Attila's Empire, and the Danube only nominally represented the frontier between the Roman Empire and *barbaricum*.[18] Pannonia had been lost as early as the late 4th to early 5th c., while the loss of control over the Danube region between Singidunum and Novae to Attila in the 5th c. further restricted imperial control over the northern frontier region.[19] Subsequently, central control over the military administration of the north Balkans had been placed in question by a series of rebellions by Germanic generals and soldiers

---

[17] See Crow (2007) 402 for the former argument.

[18] On the post-Attila settlement of Pannonia, see Pohl (1980) 264–68; Jord. *Get.* 50.264–56.288; Wolfram (1988) 258–68; Heather (1991) 240–72. More generally on Pannonia in this period, see Eadie (1982); Christie (1992). On the Goths in the Balkans, see Malchus 15, 18 and 20.

[19] On the Huns' settlement in Pannonia: Marcell. com. 422. On Roman accession to Attila's demand that Lower Moesia and Dacia Ripensis Upper Moesia be evacuated, Thompson (1996) 108–10.

serving as federate troops in the Roman armies.[20] These were particularly
serious during the three decades after Attila's death in 453. The dislocation of central control over many regions of the Balkans meant that their
surviving populations were compelled to fight for their own interests—a
situation well illustrated by the decision of the citizens of Thessalonica
to rebel against the Prefect of Illyricum when threatened by the Goths
in 479.[21]

The archaeological record closely mirrors this situation, showing a rupture in socio-economic life and earlier settlement patterns. A number of
excavated north Balkan sites, such as Sucidava, have brought to light evidence for destruction in the mid-5th c.[22] This evidence correlates what is
known from the literary sources regarding the destruction of numerous
cities, including provincial capitals and secondary cities, by Attila's armies
during his attacks of A.D. 441, 443 and 447.[23] The principal result of the
barbarian invasions and migrations of the late 4th to mid-5th c. seems to
have been the end of any lingering vestiges of 'classical' Roman provincial
life in the frontier regions,[24] to be replaced by a 'militarised' landscape
that will be discussed in the second half of this paper.

DIPLOMACY AND MILITARY CONFRONTATIONS IN THE NORTHERN BALKANS FROM A.D. 491 TO 565

Diplomatic Policies[25]

After the disintegration of Attila's Empire in A.D. 453, and the departure
of the Ostrogoths in 488, the Balkans no longer faced a unified barbarian threat. Instead, during the reigns of Anastasius and Justinian, its geo-
political situation was fragmented: Germanic Goths, Gepids, Lombards
and Heruls competed at various points for control of Pannonia to the

---

[20] Heather (1991) 253–69 on the two Gothic leaders named Theoderic.
[21] On A.D. 479: Malchus 20, lines 59–62. On the dislocation between central and local
interests: Heather (2007) 170–78.
[22] On Nicopolis ad Istrum: Poulter (1995), (1998), (2007a) and (2007d). See n.10 of Guest
(2007) for references to numismatic evidence for the destruction of Balkan cities in the
mid 5th c. A.D.
[23] Marcell. com. 441, 444 and 447; Priscus 8.
[24] Poulter (2007b) 27–48 on the transition to Late Antiquity in the northern Balkans.
[25] For fuller analysis of the literary evidence for Justinian's Balkan policy, see Sarantis
(forthcoming).

north-west; Slavic Antae and Sklaveni vied for control of modern Walla-chia, north of the Lower Danube; and nomadic Bulgars, Bosporus, Utigur and Kutrigur Huns, and finally Avars, did the same in the Black Sea region to the north-east.

Anastasius and Justinian sought to maintain this balance of power and prevent the emergence of another superpower, pursuing this goal through Machiavellian divide and rule diplomacy, forming alliances with groups before playing them off against each other, and consistently building net-works of allies against any groups threatening to become too powerful. As well as forging alliances north of the frontier, they absorbed tribes into the military establishment of the Balkan provinces. Their methods included grandiose receptions in Constantinople, at which barbarian leaders were sometimes baptised; the payment of tribute; the promise of military sup-port in inter-barbarian wars; and, less frequently, marriage alliances. These policies ensured that there was no great threat to the Balkan provinces, created a series of buffer zones north of the Danube comprising allied states willing to defend the empire from powers further north, and pro-vided the empire with access to an invaluable manpower resource.

1. *Pannonia and the Germanic Kingdoms*

The Germanic groups that occupied Pannonia were sedentary kingdoms which competed with one another for imperial tributary payments and military and diplomatic support. This meant that imperial policy in the area consisted in the main of diplomatic initiatives and occasional mili-tary campaigns. Anastasius and Justinian tended to form alliances against the groups in control of the former Illyrian capital of Sirmium:[26] the Ostrogothic Kingdom of Italy from A.D. 491 to 535; and the Gepid King-dom of Pannonia and Dacia from 536 to 552. This policy owed much to the strategic importance of the city, which commanded routes into Illyri-cum from the Middle Danube area. Whichever group controlled Sirmium could, therefore, regulate the movement of Slavic and Hunnic raiders into the Balkans. These groups were at times willing to cross the Carpathians in order to enter the Balkans through Gepid territory, thereby avoiding the heavily defended lower reaches of the Danube frontier.[27]

---

[26] For cities, rivers and mountains mentioned in this paper see fig. 2.

[27] Procop. *Goth.* 8.18.17 on the reasoning behind the Gepids' decision to ferry Kutrigur Huns into the Balkans: 'but since the Romans were guarding carefully the crossing of the Ister River both in Illyricum and in Thrace, they themselves ferried these Huns across the Ister at the point where their own territory touched the river.'

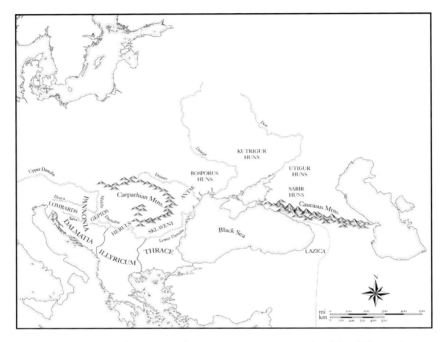

Fig. 1   Approximate locations of non-Roman groups north of the Balkans during
the reign of Justinian (map produced by Carlos García).

During the 500s, the major concern for Anastasius was to prevent any further expansion of Theoderic's Gothic Kingdom beyond Pannonia and to
contain this threat to eastern Illyricum. In 505, Anastasius dispatched the
Illyrian field army, commanded by Sabinianus the Younger and comprising
10,000 Bulgars, to attack the Gothic ally, the Gepid warlord Mundo, in the
Middle Danube/Sava area. Although Mundo was victorious and the Goths
took control of Pannonia Sirmiensis, Anastasius subsequently ensured
that the Goths did not proceed further than the Sava region. He seems to
have encouraged the Lombards' annihilation of the Goths' Herul allies in
the Upper Danube area in 508, and in 512, secured an alliance with one
group of these Heruls. In 510, he negotiated the return to imperial control
of Pannonia Bassianae, the south-eastern quarter of Pannonia Sirmiensis.

Justinian gave the Herul federates land to settle and defend about Singidunum, and received and baptised the Herul King, Grepes, in Constantinople in 527.[28] The emperor also instituted an alliance with the Gepid

---

[28] Malalas 18.14.

Kingdom of Dacia, and recruited the former Gothic general and Gepid warlord, Mundo, as *Magister Militum per Illyricum*, in 529.[29] A Roman-sponsored Gepid-Herul attack on the Goths at Sirmium was repelled in about 530.[30] This pressure on the Goths culminated in the Roman invasion of Dalmatia in 535. Although Procopius focuses on Belisarius' invasion of Sicily and southern Italy, the biggest and bloodiest confrontation between the Roman and Gothic field armies actually took place in Dalmatia between 535 and 536.[31]

Gepids and Lombards took advantage of the Goths' defeat in 536 by settling Pannonia.[32] Justinian forged alliances with both groups between 536 and 552, but consistently favoured the Lombards when Gepid-Lombard disputes threatened to boil over in the late 540s and early 550s.[33] The danger that the Gepids were on the verge of achieving total domination of Pannonia lay at the root of this approach, since during the 540s, they had strengthened their military resources by recruiting rebel Heruls fleeing the Roman Empire, and the Lombard warlord Ildiges;[34] they had also begun to exploit their naval domination of the Middle Danube by ferrying into Illyricum Sklaveni and Kutrigur Hun raiding groups.[35] Justinian responded by instigating two large military campaigns: in 549, a Roman-Herul army numbering over 25,000 crushed the Gepids' Herul allies west of the Iron Gates; and in 552, a Roman-Lombard force invaded Gepid territory and inflicted a decisive defeat.[36] We hear of no major threat emanating from the Pannonian area for the remainder of Justinian's reign.

2. *Wallachia and the Slavic Tribes*

The Slavic tribes are first documented in the early 520s, when Procopius records an invasion of Thrace by a group called the 'Antae'.[37] Although

---

[29] Malalas 18.46.

[30] Cassiod. *Var.* 11.1; Procop. *Goth.* 5.3.12–21. On the dating of the attack: Christou (1991) 65; Diculescu (1923) 121; Wolfram (1988) 323; Schmidt (1954) 534.

[31] Procop. *Goth.* 5.5.2, 5.7.1–10, 5.7.23–36. On the Roman campaigns in Dalmatia, see Sarantis (2009) 25–27.

[32] On the chronology of these developments, see Sarantis (2009) 25–27; Diculescu (1923) 134; Stein (1949–59) volume 2, 528; Christie (1995) 35; Schmidt (1954) 580; Wozniak (1978) 148; Werner (1962) 140; Pohl (1997) 89.

[33] Croke (2005); Pohl (1997); Wozniak (1978); and Sarantis (2009) 27–38 on the Gepid-Lombard dispute of the late A.D. 540s.

[34] Procop. *Goth.* 6.14.37, 7.34.42–43 and 7.35.12–22.

[35] Procop. *Goth.* 8.18.15–17 and 8.25.10.

[36] Procop. *Goth.* 7.34.40–47 and 8.25.14.

[37] Procop. *Goth.* 7.40.4–7. Many scholars claim that the 'Getic' attack of A.D. 517 attested by Marcell. com. 517 represents the first attack by a Slavic group: Croke (2001) 70; Vasiliev

the Slavs' origins are unclear, most likely they had been expanding into modern Wallachia from the steppe and forested regions of Russia since the 5th c.[38] The two major groupings of Slavs were the Sklaveni, who inhabited the regions just north of the Lower Danube, and the Antae, who lived to the north-east of the Sklaveni, in the vicinity of the Black Sea.[39] The Sklaveni were politically amorphous, consisting of numerous small tribes with no overall leader.[40] These groups united periodically to launch invasions of the Balkans, which they did more than any other group in the Justinianic era, especially in the late 540s and early 550s, when they raided the Balkans in 545, 548, 550, 550–51 and 551.[41] The exaction of booty and prisoners was apparently the main aim of these expeditions.

As a result, military force rather than diplomatic negotiation tended to be Justinian's general approach to dealing with the Sklaveni. The Thracian field army led by Germanus annihilated the Antic raiders of northern Thrace in the early 520s.[42] A series of Roman incursions into Slav territory then took place between 531 and 534 under another general of Thrace, Chilbudius.[43] The Sklaveni raids of the late 540s and early 550s were all repelled from the Balkans. The most notable imperial victory was achieved in the Astice region of Thrace by a large Roman army commanded by the eunuch, Scholasticus, in 551.[44] This success was all the more important given how deep into Thrace the Sklaveni raiders had managed to penetrate on this occasion.

The Antae seem to have had a better defined political organisation and territorial base:[45] after the Sklaveni-Antae war of the late 530s, Justinian signed an agreement with the Antae in 545, acknowledging their settlement of Tyras on the Black Sea coast, in return for their promise to form

---

(1950) 302–12; Liebeschuetz (2007) 111. However, the first source to use the term Getae to refer to the Slavs is the 7th c. Theoph. Sim. 3.4.7. Contemporary sources use the term 'Getic' to refer to Germanic groups—as, for example, Procop. *Goth.* 3.2.3–6; Marcell. com. 505; and Jordanes, whose history of the Goths is, of course, called the *Getica*.

[38] Barford (2001); Dolukhanov (1996); Shchukin (1986–1990). Curta (2001a) for the revisionist view that the ethnogenesis of the Slavs instead occurred *in situ* among groups already living north of the Danube in the 6th c.

[39] Procop. *Goth.* 7.14.30; Jord. *Get.* 5.33–38.

[40] *Strategikon* 11.4 refers to the Slavs' lack of government.

[41] Procop. *Goth.* 7.13.21–26, 7.29.1–3, 7.38, 7.40.1–8, 7.40.30–45, and 8.25.1–6.

[42] Procop. *Goth.* 7.40.4–7.

[43] Procop. *Goth.* 7.14.1–6.

[44] Procop. *Goth.* 7.32.41–45.

[45] Curta (2001a) 36–44.

a buffer against Hunnic invasions from the north.[46] This imperial favou-
ritism towards the Antae may explain the Sklavenis' subsequent dealings
with the Gepids and invasions of the Balkans.

Following the defeat of the Gepids in A.D. 552, we hear nothing more
of Slavic raids until 559, when Kutrigur-Slav forces invaded the Balkans.[47]
This established the dangerous precedent of Hunnic and Slavic tribes
combining to invade the Balkans, a characteristic of many of the late 6th
to early 7th c. Avaro-Slav attacks.

3. *The Black Sea and the Hunnic Tribes*

The steppe regions north of the Black Sea were occupied by a changing
kaleidoscope of nomadic Hunnic tribal confederations. The disintegration
and reformation of these groups would explain why we encounter the
largest number of ethnonyms in the literary sources from the area in this
period. Because the leaders of such groups needed to satisfy their followers by giving them booty, raiding was an important characteristic of Hunnic relations with the Roman Empire.[48] Hunnic raiding parties tended to
be larger than the Slavic groups and better organised, as suggested by the
fact that the literary sources identify their leaders.

Anastasius and Justinian employed the whole range of diplomatic and
military responses to the Hunnic world. Bulgar tribes raided Illyricum on
three occasions in the 490s.[49] Anastasius reacted by settling a large group
of Bulgars as federate troops in the Lower Danube area; these participated
in Sabinianus' campaign against Mundo in A.D. 505. This absorption of
the Bulgars was apparently successful insofar as we hear nothing more
of the Bulgars as aggressors until 530.[50] In the 520s, Justinian courted the
Bosphorus Huns through missionary activity and the reception of their
King, Grod, in Constantinople in 528.[51] Subsequently, a rebellion against
Grod provoked Justinian to dispatch an expedition by land and sea to
restore imperial control over the Huns of the Crimean region. In the same
year, two Hun armies crossed the Lower Danube and defeated the frontier

---

[46] Procop. *Goth.* 7.14.31–33. Curta (2001a) 80; and Madgearu (1992) on the possible locations of Tyras.

[47] Curta (2005) 183 sees this as a sign that Justinian's fortification system was in place
by this point. Liebeschuetz (2007) 114 also recognises the respite post-552.

[48] Procop. *Pers.* 1.3.3–5 on the Hunnic peoples; Thompson (1996); Maenchen-Helfen
(1973).

[49] Marcell. com. 493, 499 and 502; Croke (1980) 188–90.

[50] On Bulgar federates, see Marcell. com. 502; Malalas 16.16, line 402.

[51] Malalas 18.14 and 21 on the Grod affair and the Hun attack of A.D. 528.

forces of Lower Moesia and Scythia Minor.[52] They were then crushed by the field armies of Thrace and Illyricum on the Thracian plain south of the Haemus Mountains. A Bulgar invasion was defeated at Iatrus in 534 by the praesental army led by the Armenian, Tzittas.[53] Major Hunnic incursions took place in 539, 551 and 559.[54] The last two of these attacks were carried out by Huns of the Kutrigur confederation, which seems to have coalesced by the late 540s, at the same time as a rival Utigur group, in the vicinity of the Sea of Azov. On each occasion, Justinian persuaded the Kutrigurs to leave the Balkans by inciting the Utigurs to lay waste to Kutrigur territory west of the River Tanais (the modern River Don).

The Avars posed the final, and, possibly, greatest threat to the Balkan provinces during the Justinianic era. During the late 550s, they swept across the Caucasus and steppe regions, subjugating tribes such as the Kutrigurs, Utigurs and Antae;[55] in 562, they arrived on the north banks of the Lower Danube, demanding settlement in Scythia Minor. Through a mixture of delaying tactics, and the build-up of military forces in the Lower Danube area, Justinian first rejected this proposal and then ensured that Avar attempts to cross the river were repelled by imperial defences.

Imperial Military Campaigns North and South of the Danube Frontier

Anastasius' and Justinian's Balkan diplomacy has often been portrayed as an attempt to compensate for a lack of military resources in the Balkans.[56] However, Machiavellian diplomatic policies and a Balkan-wide fortification plan, to be discussed in the following section, were not enough to ensure security, and both were pursued in conjunction with military force. As seen, numerous major military campaigns were conducted in Pannonia during the 500s, 530s, 540s and 550s. These included the invasion of Gothic Dalmatia in A.D. 535 by the Illyrian field army led by Mundo, and two large campaigns versus the Gepid-Herul alliance in 549 and the Gepids in 552. The latter two campaigns highlight Justinian's use of the 'stick' in equal measure to the 'carrot' in his Gepid-Lombard diplomacy. The Gepid and Lombard envoys who arrived in Constantinople in A.D. 548 were not

---

[52] For the Balkan provinces in this period, see fig. 3.
[53] Marcell. com. 534.
[54] On A.D. 539 and 551: Procop. *Goth.* 2.4.4–12. On 559: Malalas 18.129; Agath. 5.11.25.
[55] On the Avars in the late 550s and early 560s, see Menander 5.1–5.4; Theophanes AM6050; Stein (1949–59) volume 2, 544.
[56] See n.5.

merely seeking diplomatic support from Justinian in order to end their dispute, but were requesting military assistance.[57] Justinian chose to side with the Lombards, and saw to it that substantial field armies were deployed in their favour. Further, Justinian twice used military force north of the Lower Danube to reinforce his diplomatic policies: first against the Bosphorus Huns in A.D. 528; and second, when he instructed Chilbudius to campaign against the Sklaveni tribes between 531 and 534.

In spite of such clever use of diplomatic and military policies, barbarian raids on the Balkans could not be blocked entirely. The abiding impression one gets from a surface reading of Procopius' *Anecdota* is that the Balkans were regularly left to be devastated by these invasions without military reply.[58] Piecing together the literary evidence for this period, however, it becomes apparent that the majority of these attacks were, in fact, confronted by Roman military forces:[59] Anastasius deployed large armies against the Bulgars, Vitalian's rebellious federate troops and the Heruls;[60] in the 520s, the Antae attack was defeated, and Hun, Bulgar and Getic raiders repelled;[61] Bulgar raiders were again crushed in 534; and Justinian dispatched armies to defeat most of the Slavic and Hunnic attacks of the 540s and 550s.

The regular deployment of large armies commanded by first-rate generals is a striking element of this Roman policy in the Balkans that has not been recognised. For example, in A.D. 548, the Illyrian field army numbering 15,000 men was deployed against the Sklaveni.[62] The following year, the same army was sent alongside 11,500 cavalry troops against

---

[57] Procop. *Goth.* 7.34.4: 'they sent envoys to the Emperor Justinian begging him to send them an army'.

[58] Procop. *Anec.* 18.15. Secondary works tend to follow Procopius and emphasise the frequency and severity of barbarian attacks in this period, and play down imperial military responses: Liebeschuetz (2007) 111–13; Popović (1975); Lemerle (1954). Poulter (2007b) 14 refers to the numerous barbarian raids down to the end of Justinian's reign and argues that we are reliant on *Buildings* Book 4 for Justinian's counter-measures. He does not mention Procopius' accounts of Roman military campaigns in the *Wars*.

[59] Naturally, there may have been unopposed barbarian assaults which did not make it into the surviving texts; by the same token, though, there may have been additional, unreported Roman military successes.

[60] On the Bulgar and Gothic campaigns: Marcell. com., 493, 499 and 505. On the Herul campaign: Procop. *Goth.* 6.14.29–30. For the chronology and causes of Vitalian's rebellion between 514 and 516, see Martindale (1992) 1170–76; Croke (1995) 116–20.

[61] On the Antae campaign: Procop. *Goth.* 7.40.4–7. On the defeat of the Huns in 529: Malalas 19.46. On the defeats of both Getae and Bulgars: Marcell. com. 530.

[62] Procop. *Goth.* 7.29.1–3.

the Gepids.[63] The size of these forces is placed in context by the fact that Belisarius was only able to recruit a force of 4,500 for his second Italian campaign of the 540s, while Dagistheus arrived in Lazica in 548 with an army of 8,000.[64]

A flexible use of *comitatenses, limitanei* and *foederati* forces was an important feature of Roman campaigns.[65] Although there were occasions on which the Thracian field army confronted barbarians in Thrace, and the Illyrian field army fought barbarians in Illyricum, both armies were deployed in the other areas if necessary. For instance, Mundo led the Illyrian field army into the Lower Danube region in A.D. 530 in order to repel Bulgar raiders.[66] Similarly, in 528, the Illyrian field army was diverted to Thrace to help the Thracian field army defeat the Huns. Earlier, the frontier forces of the *duces* of Lower Moesia and Scythia Minor had been called upon to confront the same Hun invaders.[67] In addition, high-ranking generals who happened to be present in Constantinople were recruited to lead armed forces on specific campaigns: Narses in A.D. 545, Buzes in 549, Scholasticus in 551, and Belisarius in 559 are obvious examples. In 534, the *Magister Militum Praesentalis*, Tzittas, led the praeseantal field army based in the Balkans against Bulgar raiders at Iatrus. Naval forces were also important to the defence of the frontier, presumably employed in the naval expedition against the Bosphorus Huns in 528 and in the Wallachian campaigns of the early 530s.[68]

Most importantly, barbarians, whether semi-independent federate units, or commanders of field armies, were deployed in the majority of the military encounters. Following the repeated rebellions of the post-Attila period, the barbarian peoples left behind by the 4th–5th c. A.D. Visigothic, Hunnic and Ostrogothic invasions had been absorbed by the Balkan military establishment by the reign of Justinian.[69] The sources are full of references to barbarian allied, federate and military leaders loyally serving the imperial cause in the Balkans. Malalas mentions Goths, Huns and

---

[63] Procop. *Goth.* 7.34.40–43.

[64] Procop. *Goth.* 7.10.3 and *Pers.* 2.29.10.

[65] Whitby (2007) 145–46 makes the point that by the 6th c., the Balkan military was less rigidly organised into field and frontier units and more flexible in its deployment.

[66] Marcell. com. 530.

[67] Malalas 18.21.

[68] Bounegru and Zahariade (1996) on the Danube navy in Late Antiquity.

[69] On the integration of barbarian manpower in the late antique Balkan military infrastructure: Whitby (2007) 148–54; Sarantis (2010); Gillett (2002); Pohl and Reimitz (1998); Pohl and Wood (2000). See Heather (2007) 186; and Whittow (2007) 385–87 for a positive view regarding the survival of Roman elites in the northern Balkans.

Bulgars among the federate forces in Scythia Minor in the 510s. Mundo was perhaps the most effective of the barbarian generals:[70] this Gepid chieftain and former ally of the Goths fought a series of victorious campaigns in Illyricum, served in the East against the Persians, and, along with Belisarius and Constantiolus, rescued Justinian from the Nika riot in 532.[71]

The most serious internal barbarian threat to imperial military authority in the Balkans during this period was posed by Vitalian's revolt from A.D. 514 to 517. It is notable, however, that only two such episodes occurred subsequently, and both were relatively small-scale and short-lived. First, the Lombard leader of the *scholae*, Ildiges, fled the Balkans to the Gepid Kingdom of Thorisin in A.D. 551.[72] Second, 3,000 Herul federate troops rebelled in the mid-540s and went over to the Gepids. However, 1,500 Heruls led by Philemuth remained loyal to the empire and accompanied Roman cavalry divisions in annihilating their rebellious countrymen in 549.[73] The Heruls are, in fact, more consistently portrayed by the literary sources as loyal and important players in the various Justinianic wars: Herul *Magistri Militum* such as Philemuth, Suartas and Beros served imperial forces all over the empire.[74]

Although the Balkans formed a principal source of manpower for the Justinianic wars in Africa, Italy and the East, this did not mean that it was a low strategic priority, or that its defences were left un-manned. Justinian could still spare troops for the Balkans when other campaigns were in full swing. For instance, although the General Narses departed for Italy in spring A.D. 552 with an army of 30,000 men, recruited principally from the Balkans, Justinian retained a sufficiently large military force at his disposal to both put down a religious uprising at Ulpiana and aid the Lombards in the invasion and defeat of the Gepids in Pannonia, in summer 552.[75] In 550, the General Germanus was ordered to postpone his recruitment drive at Serdica for a new offensive against Gothic Italy in order to deal with a Sklaveni incursion which was threatening Thessalonica.[76] Justinian was

---

[70] Croke (1982a).

[71] Procop. *Pers.* 1.24.40–42.

[72] Procop. *Goth.* 7.35.12–22.

[73] Procop. *Goth.* 7.34.42–43 on the numbers of the Gepid and Roman Herul contingents in 549.

[74] See Sarantis (2010) on the importance of Herul manpower (and Balkan manpower in general) in the Justinianic wars.

[75] Procop. *Goth.* 8.25.11–13.

[76] Procop. *Goth.* 7.40.1–3.

clearly unwilling to order a new invasion of Italy without first resolving problems in the Balkans.

It should be pointed out that a minority of invasions were, at least initially, unopposed. For example, the Getic invasion of Illyricum in A.D. 517 swept through Thessaly, Epirus and Macedonia without encountering imperial forces.[77] During the reign of Justinian, the most obvious examples are the Hunnic invasions of 539 and 559. The Balkan defences were unprepared for these attacks because they took place following periods in which the region had enjoyed a respite from barbarian raids, not because the Balkans were unimportant strategically. Thus, although Justinian's response to the attack of 559 would suggest that it had taken him by surprise, the response was not in reality slow: first, hastily assembled troops, many of them irregular, under the command of the by now retired Belisarius, managed to repulse the Kutrigur Huns from Constantinople, while garrisons of the Chersonese and Thermopylae cross walls defeated and turned back from Asia Minor and Greece other divisions of the invaders; second, in the aftermath of the invasion, Justinian bolstered the naval forces of the Lower Danube by sending additional vessels, re-built the Long Wall defences which had fallen into disrepair, and re-deployed units of *scholae* palatine guards to the garrisons of southern Thracian cities.[78] He also re-assigned the General Justin from Lazica to the Lower Danube frontier, probably appointing him 'Quaestor of the Army'.[79] By the time the Avars threatened in A.D. 562, the Roman defences of the Lower Danube were able to repel them, Justin playing an important role in organising the defensive operation.[80]

Although Procopius includes verbose statements that the whole of the Balkan Peninsula was littered with corpses and ravaged annually from coast to coast, a look at the precise facts included in his work and in other literary sources suggests that the devastations may be exaggerated. In contrast with the 'migratory' invasions of Visigoths, Huns and Ostrogoths of the late 4th to 5th c., the invasions of the first half of the 6th c. were short-lived forays into the Balkan provinces by groups who tended to return north as soon as they had exacted sufficient booty to justify their

---

[77] Marcell. com. 517.
[78] Malalas 18.132.
[79] Martindale (1992) 241–42.
[80] Evagr. 5.1 refers to Justin's successful defence of the Lower Danube from the Avars in 562.

expeditions.[81] They were largely perpetrated by Hunnic and Slavic groups from regions north of the Lower Danube, who tended to cross the Carpathians in order to enter Illyricum via Gepid territory, thereby avoiding Roman defences of the Lower Danube.[82] The few occasions on which the literary sources give figures regarding the sizes of these raiding parties suggest that they were frequently small, numbering 2,000 to 3,000.[83] In contrast with the Huns and the Goths of the 5th c., who captured and destroyed prominent provincial cities on a regular basis, the intruders of the Justinianic period were not adept at storming walls: only Topirus in Rhodope, Anastasiopolis in Thrace, Cassandria in Macedonia, and Odessos in Lower Moesia, are mentioned as having fallen to barbarian forces during Justinian's reign.[84] Given Procopius' sensationalist portrayal of the attacks, he would surely have included more information regarding the fall of other major cities had this happened. He does mention that 32 *frouria* fell to the Hun raiders of 539, although this is only a small proportion of the hundreds of fortified settlements which existed in Macedonia at that time.[85]

Rather than spending time laying siege to fortified centres, barbarian raiders regularly stuck to inhospitable mountain terrain away from open

[81] Procop. *Aed.* 4.7.13 mentions that Sklaveni groups were wont to lay ambushes in the vicinity of the new fort of Adina in the Lower Danube region, implying that some groups did not return northward, but remained in the Balkans. However, this is the only reference to this phenomenon, most other texts suggesting that Sklaveni raiders returned northward. Indeed, Procop. *Goth.* 7.40.33 views the fact that the Slav raiders of 550–51 wintered in the Balkans as exceptional: 'they actually spent the winter as if in their own land'.

[82] Curta (2005) 183; and Liebeschuetz (2007) 111 put the respite from barbarian attacks after A.D. 552 down to the success of Justinian's fortification programme. However, much of this will have been in place by the time of the Slav and Hun raids of A.D. 545–52: see the section on the Balkan fortification system below. Conversely, Poulter (2007b) 14; and Crow (2007) 400 are sceptical regarding the effectiveness of the Lower Danube defences. Yet Procopius explicitly states that the Kutrigur Huns avoided this heavily-defended frontier, and sought to use the Gepid ferry service instead (see n.27). Although Procopius only mentions this on two occasions, it can surely be no coincidence that Slav and Hun invasions proliferated during the period of Roman-Gepid hostility in the late 540s and early 550s, and petered out subsequent to the Lombard-Roman defeat of the Gepids in 552. Further, the majority of these raids appear to have initially affected Illyricum, which would make sense had they crossed Gepid territory

[83] For instance, Procop. *Goth.* 7.38.3.

[84] Topirus fell to the Sklaveni in A.D. 551: Procop. *Goth.* 7.38.9–18, Cassandria fell to the Huns in A.D. 539: Procop. *Pers.* 2.4.5, and Anastasiopolis and Odessos fell to the Huns in 563: Malalas 18.132.

[85] See Wilkes (in this collection). Procop. *Pers.* 2.4.5.

plains, presumably so as to avoid Roman forces.[86] In particular, this strategy was employed by the Sklaveni, who, according to the military treatise,
Maurice's *Strategikon*, were well-known for their reliance on a 'guerrilla'
style of warfare.[87] Indeed, Roman forces in A.D. 548 in Epirus and in 551
in northern Illyricum spent their time chasing and attempting to harass
Sklaveni raiding parties without managing to engage them. Furthermore,
the Sklaveni achieved significant victories over Roman forces by exploiting an element of surprise, in their ambush of Chilbudius' raiding party
north of the Danube in 534, and in their victory near Adrianople in 551.[88]
On the latter occasion, the Sklaveni exploited their dominance of higher
ground to inflict a defeat on Roman forces left exposed on the plain
below. But when the Romans could pin down and engage the Sklaveni on
their own terms, as in 551 in Astice, they achieved resounding victories.
The same can be said of the majority of the Romans' military encounters
with barbarians in the Balkans, against the Huns in 528, Bulgars in 534,
Heruls in 549 and Gepids in 552. Unfortunately, we lack sufficient literary
evidence to discuss the tactical, technological and topographical factors
that contributed to these Roman successes.

Summary

Thus, by Justinian's death in A.D. 565, the Gepid and Avar threats had
been assuaged, and, with the exception of the Kutrigur-Slav raid of 559,
there had been no major invasion of the Balkans since 551. Most invasions
had been met with military force and repelled, while there had been no
serious military unrest in the Balkans since Vitalian's rebellion of the 510s.
The River Danube remained the northern frontier of the Roman Empire,
while Justinian was still in a position to influence the barbarian groups
beyond it through a combination of diplomacy and military force. The
next section will set these diplomatic and military achievements within
the context of the fortification work and internal reforms which took
place in the Balkans during the early 6th c.

---

[86] Procop. *Goth.* 7.38.7 on the Sklaveni: 'they neither had any experience in attacking
city walls, nor had they dared to come down to the open plain'. Procop. *Goth.* 7.40.5–7: 'the
Sklaveni, upon learning from their captives that Germanus was in Serdica .... immediately
turned aside from their march on Thessalonica and no longer dared to descend to the
plain'. This shows that they did come down from the mountains when Roman forces were
absent, but would not dare to do so otherwise.

[87] *Strategikon* 9.4 warns Roman troops to guard against Slav ambushes.

[88] Procop. *Goth.* 7.14.4–5 and 7.40.38–40.

The Role of the Balkan Fortification System
in Military Campaigns

Procopius' Buildings *Book 4 and Material Evidence for Fortification Work
in the Late 5th to 6th c.*

The material remains of urban and rural settlements and Book 4 of Procopius' *Buildings* suggest that a large-scale, Balkans-wide fortification plan was carried out during the late 5th to mid-6th c. This provided the physical backdrop to the north Balkan military campaigns and diplomatic initiatives just discussed. The lists and narrative passages of *Buildings* Book 4 describe building works that can be divided into three main categories: major provincial cities, principal routes, frontiers, both internal and external, and interior cross walls; secondary provincial cities and forts away from major strategic routes or zones; and finally, fortified rural farmsteads and isolated watchtowers. The rigid organisation of this material by geographical and administrative area and the density of place names included leads most commentators to suggest that Procopius was exploiting maps and lists of building works drawn up by provincial or municipal authorities.[89]

As a result, some archaeologists have taken a positivistic approach to Book 4, seeking to match it precisely to the archaeological evidence and geography of the Danube region;[90] often, they use Procopius' work as the basis of their analysis of the material evidence, and date the majority of 6th c. A.D. works to Justinian's reign. Conversely, other archaeologists choose to highlight the inaccuracies of Procopius' text—the occasions on which Procopius mentions a fortification not evident in the material record, or vice versa, or makes a mistake regarding the location of a settlement.[91] In particular, these scholars take issue with the text's rhetorical exaggeration of Justinianic building work. They point out that many Balkan settlements first acquired monumental fortifications and/or moved to more defensible sites prior to Justinian, either during the 5th c. and/or in the reign of

---

[89] Cameron (1985) 84–85; Howard-Johnston (2000); Whitby (1988) 72–80 and (2000) 718–19. Others, such as Elsner (2007), see the lists as a literary ploy.

[90] Torbatov (2000a) and (2000b); Vašić (1999).

[91] For instance, Poulter (2007b) 9–10. Crow (2007) states the case against the optimistic approaches to Procopius of certain archaeologists, although he takes a balanced view in his contribution to this volume. Gregory (2000) 105 sums up criticisms of Procopius on the Balkans. Bowden (2003) 85–86 and 173–80 criticises archaeologists who have defined Epirote architecture in terms of its Justinianic date and inclusion in Procopius' *Buildings*.

Anastasius.[92] They also highlight that much of the work Procopius attributes to Justinian was more likely to have been carried out by local populations.[93]

However, given the limited nature, inconsistencies, inaccuracies, and subjectivity of both Book 4 and the archaeological reports, it is surely unrealistic to expect any greater correlation between the two bodies of evidence;[94] there is no way that the hundreds of place names Procopius mentions in his text could be matched precisely to the probably isolated locations of many of these sites.[95] Procopius was relatively ignorant of Balkan affairs, having not spent much time there, with the exception of a return trip from Italy in A.D. 540, during which he may have learnt details of building work at sites such as Diocletianopolis in Thessaly.[96] This would explain why he misinterprets his documentary sources in certain cases. Such inexperience can in fact be used in defence of Book 4. Had Procopius been more in tune with and interested in Balkan developments, the inaccuracies of his work would be more damning. Nonetheless, the documentary basis of the text means that it represents an invaluable source for a Justinianic building plan, however much this has been exaggerated by the rhetoric of the author. Rather than attempting to prove its accuracy or inaccuracy, we must place in context the limitations of Book 4, and appreciate its significance as a contemporary literary record of 6th c. building work, which, in its general geographical scope and descriptions of settlement patterns, actually fits in very well with the archaeological record to date.

In fact, the work Procopius actually credits Justinian with is predominantly reconstruction rather than new construction work, which concurs with the archaeological evidence from many places, which points to new

---

[92] Especially Crow (2007).

[93] Bowden (2006).

[94] Poulter (2007b) 43–46 highlights the amount of work yet to be done on late antique Balkan archaeology and the problematic and erratic nature of much of the work that has been carried out to date. Whitby (1988) 72–80 and (2000) 718–19; and Dunn (2004) 575–77 make the best cases for the validity of *Buildings* Book 4 as evidence for a Justinianic fortification programme, and Dunn points to the futility in attempting to match precisely the archaeological record to Procopius' lists, but does not see this as a reason to doubt the book's reliability.

[95] Poulter (1999) 207 on the discovery of 268 sites in an area of 2,000 km², which highlights the number that could yet be found in such areas; Mikulčić (2002) and Milinković (2011) show the existence of hundreds of hill-top sites in the FYROM and Serbia alone.

[96] Karagiorgou (2001a) 143–50 makes this point.

fortification work in the 4th or 5th c. and multiple subsequent repairs.[97] Procopius' references to the contraction of sites, their relocation to more defensible higher ground, fortifications erected around towers, and the proliferation of smaller fortified sites in rural areas surrounding provincial cities, all also correlate what is known from the 6th c. archaeological evidence, even if not all of this work was directly co-ordinated by central authorities. There is good epigraphic evidence to suggest that some of this work was carried out during the Anastasian era.[98] This consists of inscriptions from Istros, Tomis and Dinogetia in Scythia Minor, the small fortress of Vavovo Kale near modern Gradec, in Lower Moesia, which protected a key mountain pass in the eastern Haemus range, and the city of Ratiaria in Dacia Ripensis. Most importantly, Anastasius at the very least initiated a significant reconstruction of the 65 km Long Wall of Thrace.[99]

There is also good epigraphic evidence for Justinian's contributions hereabouts. Justinianic building inscriptions come from cities as far apart as Byllis in Epirus Nova, Corinth in Achaia, Callatis and Mesembria on the Black Sea coast, and a site near modern Prijepolje in Upper Moesia.[100] Those of Byllis and Corinth, which advertise the involvement of a military architect named Victorinus, are of particular interest: inscription 2 from Byllis refers not only to the Justinianic fortification of the city walls, but to Victorinus' completion of similar work throughout Moesia, Scythia, Thrace and Illyricum.

Furthermore, it has been convincingly argued that the site of Caričin Grad should be associated with Justiniana Prima, the new Illyrian capital founded in the early 530s.[101] Excavation has revealed that this was a fortified city of approximately 10 ha, situated on an elongated plateau between Mount Radan and the plain of Leskova, modern Serbia. It was apparently

---

[97] Iatrus, discussed by von Bülow (2007), is a typical example. Crow (2001) on the initial 4th and 5th c. fortification of major centres. Dinchev (2007) gives an excellent overview of the chronology and nature of late antique northern Balkan fortified settlements.

[98] For a discussion of this evidence, see Crow (2007) 400–402.

[99] Croke (1982b); Crow and Ricci (1997); Crow (2007) support an Anastasian dating of the Long Walls. Whitby (1985) prefers a construction in the 5th c. Procop. *Goth.* 4.9.6–7 attributes their construction to Anastasius.

[100] Feissel (1988) on the Byllis inscriptions. Kent (1966) 168–69; and Gregory (1979) 254–55 on the Corinth inscriptions. Beševliev (1964) 103 on Mesembria. Barnea (1977) 79 on Callatis. Feissel (2000) 91 on Prijepolje. Crow (2007) 405 argues that the Mesembrian inscription may in fact have been imported from Constantinople at a later date. This argument is plausible but not possible to confirm. Less persuasive is Crow's attempt to discredit this evidence on the basis of its absence from *Buildings* Book 4.

[101] Ivanišević (2010); Bavant and Ivanišević (2008), (2007) and (2003); Bavant (2007); Bavant *et al.* (1990); Duval and Popović (1984).

studded with administrative complexes and churches, baths, colonnaded streets and an aqueduct, and had three sets of fortifications (enclosing the acropolis and upper and lower cities). This correlates broadly what is written by Procopius at the outset of Book 4 of the *Buildings*, even if the relevant passage naturally exaggerates the splendour of what was in fact a typically small, fortified late antique urban centre.[102]

Bearing in mind the roughly equal amount of material evidence for Anastasian and Justinianic fortification work, and the general 6th c. dating of many fortifications, it is not implausible that Anastasius started and Justinian finished off a 'tri-partite' policy, combining an official reinforcement of frontier forts, strategic cross-walls and major routes, with a defence-in-depth drive aimed at interior cities, and finally a rural shelter programme.

The majority of the Anastasian frontier fortification or refortification works were presumably carried out prior to A.D. 514 and Vitalian's rebellion. Work on the Long Wall has plausibly been dated to the early 500s, pre-A.D. 507;[103] this also seems a good chronological context for the Anastasian work in Scythia Minor and Dacia Ripensis. Justinianic building work probably took place predominantly during the late 520s and 530s, in the context of the early Justinianic administrative reforms, to be discussed below, and in light of the corpus of Justinianic building inscriptions looked at by Denis Feissel, which date principally to the early part of the reign.[104] It is less likely that such work was carried out on as large a scale after 542, given the outbreak of the plague, a proliferation of barbarian raids, and the financial difficulties caused by military reversals in Italy, Africa and the East. Finally, most commentators argue that Procopius had completed the *Buildings* by 554.[105]

The Configuration of Balkan Fortifications

Putting chronological precision and *Buildings* Book 4 aside, the majority of 5th to 6th c. A.D. archaeological sites did not fall out of use until the late 6th to 7th c., when coin series die out and destruction layers are noted

---

[102] While Poulter (2007b) argues that Procopius' account is "fictitious and bears no semblance to the reality", Whittow (2007) 377; and Ćurčić (2010) 209 observe that Procopius' account does include the main archaeologically identified features.

[103] Croke (1982b) 71–74.

[104] Feissel (2000) 85.

[105] For instance, Howard-Johnston (2000) 21; Greatrex (2003) 50–51.

at numerous sites.[106] This means that they provide us with a physical context within which we can envisage the Anastasian and Justinianic military operations outlined above.

The network of fortifications outlined in Procopius' Book 4 is borne out by the material record, revealing that there was little difference between urban and rural and military and civilian settlements in this period.[107] Urban, semi-urban and fortified rural settlements all acquired large fortifications, such as U- and horseshoe-shaped towers and curtain walls. Tiny watchtowers and fortresses proliferated, not only along major routes and in the vicinity of important provincial cities and military bases, but along isolated valleys and defiles, and on rocky outcrops.[108] Fortresses the length of the Danube, from Singidnum to the Black Sea, in places on both sides of the river, represented the initial barrier to barbarian raiders. In Upper Moesia, the city of Viminacium was apparently replaced by one, or possibly two, smaller forts on hill-tops in the vicinity of the original site;[109] these more defensible locations will have also served as look-out points. Ceramic and numismatic evidence from the fortresses of the Iron Gates region of the Danube in the province of Dacia Ripensis, has led archaeologists to point to their construction or reconstruction in the Justinianic era.[110] The excavation of portuary installations at sites such as Hajdučka Vodenica sheds light on the importance of the Danube navy to military operations, control of the Iron Gates gorges being presumably vital to the co-ordination of Illyrian and Thracian campaigns, and to preventing the most powerful opponents of the empire, usually based in Pannonia, from by-passing interior defences and launching naval attacks on Thrace.

In Lower Moesia, studies at Novae and Iatrus reveal how both witnessed continued occupation and building phases in the 6th c.: Novae acquired a number of basilicas and retained a relatively large intramural area, while Iatrus served as a military base and supply depot.[111] Fortifications

---

[106] See, for example, Madgearu (2001).

[107] Surveys of northern Balkan urbanism: Poulter (1983), (1995), (1996), (1999), (2007a) and (2007d); Dinchev (1997), (2000), (2007) and (2008); Ćurčić (2010) and (2001b); Băjenarov (2010); Ivanov (1999); Torbatov (2002); Wilkes (2005); Conrad and Stancev (2002); von Bülow and Milceva (1999); and relevant sections of Hoddinott (1974); Velkov (1977); and Biernakca-Lubanska (1982). See the section on the Balkans of the 'Fortifications in the East: A Bibliographic Essay' (in this collection) for a fuller discussion of the literature.

[108] See Băjenarov (2010) for a catalogue of sites in the dioceses of Dacia and Thrace.

[109] Milošević (2002) 154.

[110] Petrović and Dušanić (1996); Vasić (1994); Wilkes (2005) 189–92; Kondić (1984). See Băjenarov (2010) 93–124 for a gazetteer of sites.

[111] Biernacki (2005); and Dyczek (2008) on Novae. von Bülow (1995) and (2007) on Iatrus.

Fig. 2   Cities, rivers and mountains in the Balkans during the reign of Justinian
mentioned in this paper (map produced by Carlos García).

at Durostorum and Abritus were maintained and renovated in the 6th c.[112] In Scythia Minor, Tropaium Trainani, Dinogetia and Sucidava are examples of fortified cities and military bases of various sizes along the frontier.[113] Lower Moesia and Scythia Minor also possessed large cities on the Black Sea coast, such as Odessus, Istria and Tomis.[114] Evidence for naval installations, warehouses and commercial districts at these ports testifies to their important commercial function and reception of ships carrying military supplies destined for the frontier forces.[115]

Meanwhile, fortified settlements existed in regions behind the Danube frontier. In Illyricum, the strategically vital province of Dacia Mediterranea was replete with fortifications along its major routes, within both valleys and upland basins, to defend approaches to the Thracian and Macedonian plains. For example, the valley of the River Timok, which runs from Naissus across the Haemus range to the Lower Danube plain, was dotted with fortifications, watchtowers and barracks;[116] further south, cities such as Justiniana Prima, Serdica and Pautalia were surrounded by a number of small forts;[117] Serdica acquired monumental walls and various churches in the 6th c., while Pautalia was relocated to a more defensible location on a hill-top overlooking the former city.[118] Isolated areas of northern Illyricum acquired the sorts of rural refuges mentioned in Procopius.[119]

Major routes across the Lower Danube plain to the south of the river also featured constellations of fortified settlements.[120] For instance, reports on fortifications in the vicinity of the Marcianopolis-Dorostorum road in Lower Moesia have been used to correlate Procopius' reference to fortresses such as Palmatae along the same route.[121] A variety of fortified settlements and bases existed in the south of the Lower Danube plain: the much smaller successor to the city of Nicopolis ad Istrum, an annexe of barely 5 ha, was used primarily as an administrative and military base, while the fortress of Dichin seems to have been populated by

---

[112] Radoslavova (2011) on Abritus, and Angelova and Buchvarov (2007) on Durostorum.
[113] Zahariade (2006) on Scythia Minor, especially 61–126. See also Torbatov (2002); and Doncheva-Petkova and Torbatov (2001).
[114] Preshlenov (2002) on Odessus. Opait (2004) 104–11 on Tomis.
[115] Bounegru and Zahariade (1996) 75–76 and 78–80.
[116] Petrović (1994–95).
[117] Bavant (2007) 340–42; Băjenaru (2010) 143–50.
[118] Hoddinott (1974) 269–85 and 285–86; Băjanarov (2010) 42.
[119] Mikulčić (2011).
[120] See Băjenarov (2010) 25–32 on Balkan roads.
[121] Torbatov (2000a).

soldier-farmers and used as a grain depot;[122] further south, a number of settlements existed on defensible hill-tops in the foothills of the Haemus Mountains, notably the fortress at Veliko Tărnovo, which has been associated with Zikideva.[123] Watchtowers and fortresses guarded the major passes of the Haemus Mountains, such as the Pass of Djulino in the east,[124] the Succi Pass,[125] and the Kotel Pass.[126] Finally, major cities south of the Haemus Mountains in the north Thracian plain were also heavily defended. The remarkable remains of *ca.* 2,000 m of fortifications at Diocletianopolis, still over 10 m high in some places, replete with interior galleries and monumental gates, bear impressive witness to the fortified landscape of the 6th c. Balkans.[127]

The Defensive and Offensive Roles of the Fortification System

Such a monumental, widespread fortification system would explain why so few cities fell to barbarian raiders according to the literary sources. Datable finds from destruction or burning layers do attest the demise of some cities, including Iatrus in Lower Moesia at some point in the 520s (perhaps attacked by Antae or Huns). This required complete rebuilding subsequently, possibly as part of Justinian's fortification drive.[128] Similarly, a destruction layer at Dinogetia, in Scythia Minor, has been dated to the late 550s and convincingly associated with the Kutrigur Hun attack of 559.[129] The minor fort at Ovidiu in Scythia Minor also has a destruction layer containing a coin of 539/40.[130] The wolf-gnawed limbs of a dismembered skeleton have been discovered in a destruction layer at Dichin (a site also later rebuilt) that is dated to the end of the 5th c.[131]

---

[122] Poulter (1995), (1998) and (2007c) 51–82 on Nicopolis, and (2007c) 82–96 on Dichin.

[123] Dinchev (1997).

[124] Preshlenov (2001).

[125] Dinchev (2007) 524–25; Băjenaru (2010) 144–45.

[126] Dinchev (2007) 519.

[127] Madzharov (1989). According to Hoddinott (1975) 198 and 300, the walls at modern Hissarya suffered from damage, possibly at the hands of the Visigoths, during the third quarter of the 4th c. According to Hierocles 6.35.3–5 they were still in use in the mid-6th c., and Theoph. Sim. 2.17.1 recounts that they later held firm during the Avar attack of 587. Velkov (1977) 129–30: stylistic factors have suggested a 5th to 6th c. dating of basilicas within the walls, confirming a functioning city in this period.

[128] von Bülow (2007) 472.

[129] Barnea (1966) 537–59; Mitrea (1974) 49–72.

[130] Băjenarov (2010) 133–35; Torbatov (2002) 182–87.

[131] Poulter (2007c) 86.

However, these are isolated examples, and Procopius' claims that Huns and Slavs regularly caused major damage to the Balkans, from the Ionian coast to Constantinople, are not truly borne out by the archaeological evidence. There is no sign of any great rupture in the society and economy of the Balkan Peninsula comparable with that of the 4th to 5th c., when major cities such as Naissus and Nicopolis ad Istrum were destroyed by the Huns, or the late 6th to 7th c., when Avaro-Slav invasions and migrations spelt the beginning of the end of imperial control in the Balkans, and burnt cities and the end of coin series characterise the material record.[132] In addition, Popović and Lemerle's use of coin hoards to trace the barbarian raids of the Justinianic era has been placed in serious doubt by the works of Metcalf and Curta.[133]

Rural areas and the smaller fortified settlements within them may have suffered more. For instance, according to Procopius, 32 *frouria* fell during the A.D. 539 Hunnic raid.[134] This figure can be placed in context by the large geographical scope of this attack and the hundreds of fortified settlements and fortlets that existed in each Balkan region.[135] The fortification of not only major urban centres, but rural backwaters, farmsteads, and, in some cases, churches, combined with the ineptitude of the barbarian invaders at storming walls, would explain why these raiders travelled such long distances, and places in doubt how badly they damaged rural areas.

Although the fortification system was put in place to defend local populations and resources, it also served an aggressive purpose. The existence of a network of fortified bases gave the Roman army an excellent platform from which to conduct campaigns within the Balkans. Those armies responsible for pursuing often elusive barbarian raiders over long distances and inhospitable terrain must have used the various fortified granaries and barracks for rest and supply. At the same time, the numerous watchtowers will have played an important role in surveillance and reconnaissance activities.

---

[132] For the destruction of settlements in the mid-5th c., see Guest (2007) 300 n.10. See Dinchev (2007) 516 on the mid-6th c. high-point for Balkan fortified settlements and their later 6th c. demise, and Madgearu (2001) on the decline of cities in Scythia Minor from the late 6th c.

[133] Popović (1975); Lemerle (1954); Curta (1996); Metcalf (1991).

[134] Procop. *Pers.* 2.4.5. The word *frourion* suggests the existence of a military garrison at the sites in question, although we cannot expect Procopius to accurately delineate the varying roles of different types of settlement, given his confusion on other matters.

[135] Over 200 in Serbia alone: Milinković (2011) 285.

During peacetime, the Thracian and Illyrian field armies will have been dispersed over the fortifications of the Balkans, frequently away from the frontier.[136] The failure of the Roman army to oppose certain barbarian attacks may be down to the failure of local commanders to muster these troops, rather than their absence from the area.[137] Two of the principal bases of the generals of Thrace and Illyricum are believed to be Odessus and Naissus, respectively.[138] Evidence for an organised military within fortresses is less transparent in 6th c. than in 4th c. phases of fortresses. However, this may simply owe something to the blurring of civilian and military life by this period. It is also likely that, in many cases, soldiers lived in regions surrounding a fortress or minor fort, unsurprising given the small size of many of these installations. Further, evidence does exist for buildings used as barracks at settlements throughout the region, from fortresses in the Timok valley, to the Markova Mehana site in the vicinity of the Trajan Gates, to Nicopolis ad Istrum, and cities such as Tropaium Traiani in Scythia Minor. Inscriptions attesting field units have been discovered at Ulmetum and Tomis in Scythia Minor.[139] Weaponry has been found at a number of sites, including Caričin Grad/Justiniana Prima, testifying to infantry and cavalry units.[140] This correlates the literary evidence, which shows that many of the major engagements between Roman armies and barbarian raiders took place in the interior, as well as frontier, areas of Thrace and Illyricum—as against the Sklaveni in Europa in 551 and Epirus Nova in 548.

Meanwhile, federate, frontier and naval forces at bases close to the frontier were responsible for dealing with immediate threats and policing duties. In A.D. 528, the initial Hun invasion was met by the frontier forces of the Lower Danube, before field armies confronted it on the Thracian plain. Helmets, shields, swords and arrow-heads discovered at Scythian frontier forts, such as Sucidava, Capidava and Dinogetia, and dated to the 6th c., presumably attest *limitanei* or *foederati*.[141] There is stylistic evidence to support the suggestion in literary sources that many of the

---

[136] Dunn (2004) on the militarisation of interior regions. *Cod. Theod.* 7 on the blurring of military and civilian life in the Late Roman period.

[137] As suggested by Whitby (2007) 143.

[138] Whitby (2007) 144.

[139] Barnea (1977) Inscription 108 refers to the *lanciarium iuniorum* as having erected part of the fortification at Ulmetum. Barnea (1977) Inscription 23 refers to the *sagittarii iuniores* at Tomis.

[140] Ivanišević (2010) 770–71.

[141] Zahariade (2006) 182.

frontier forces were of barbarian descent; this includes weaponry and jewellery from tombs at Singidunum, helmets and buckles from Scythia Minor and the northern Balkans in general, and the increasingly prominent use of a type of grey, burnished pottery, which resembles types discovered north of the Danube.[142]

This brings us to the intimidating nature of the frontier fortifications vis-à-vis barbarian groups inhabiting regions beyond the Balkan provinces. Roman fortresses in Scythia, Moesia and Dacia Mediterannea served as the bases from which Roman troops were gathered and mobilised to fight in the various campaigns north of the Danube discussed earlier. For instance, the General Germanus used the Dacian city of Serdica as his base while recruiting an army to invade Pannonia and then Ostrogothic Italy in 550. Chilbudius' invasions of Wallachia must have been launched from Lower Danube ports. Fortified granaries and supply depots, such as Dichin and Iatrus, and Danubian portuary installations, testify to the operation of provisioning and supporting the Roman army on such campaigns. This frontier system must have appeared ominous to barbarian groups living on the opposite banks of the Danube.[143]

Administrative Reforms and Local Initiative

Central Imperial Initiatives: the Administrative Re-integration of the North Balkans

Justinian's attempt to re-assert imperial administrative and political control over the north Balkans also provides a context for the military campaigns discussed above. In A.D. 536, logistical support for the frontier forces was bolstered with an administrative innovation, the *Quaestura Exercitus*.[144] The 'Quaestor of the Army', Bonus, was to administer a *de facto* military prefecture, concentrated on the frontier provinces of Lower

---

[142] Ivanišević and Kazanski (2002) 101–57 on the late antique tombs at Singidunum; Vagalinski (2002) on barbarian pottery and (1998) on a late antique helmet from Voivoda; Vagalinski *et al.* (2000) on eagle-headed buckles.

[143] Curta (2005) 175–83 on the intimidating nature of the Justinianic frontier fortifications vis-à-vis the barbarian world to the north. It could be argued, however, that this was not just because of their defensive effectiveness, but because of their potential to operate as a platform for offensive campaigns.

[144] *Nov. Iust.* 41, in Schöll and Kroll (1892–95) 262–63. Secondary literature on the *Quaestura Exercitus*: Karagiorgou (2001b); Curta (2002); Torbatov (1997); Swan (2007).

Moesia and Scythia Minor, but also incorporating the eastern Mediterranean provinces of the Aegean islands, Caria and Cyprus. *Novellae* 41 of 536 and 50, instituted the following year, make clear that the Quaestor was to supervise and make more efficient the delivery of the military *annona* from the interior provinces to forces based in the region.

Recovery of transport containers, such as the LR2 pots, in 6th c. contexts along the Danube, is indicative of this military supply system.[145] The Odessan funerary inscription devoted to an Asian ship-owner named Oxiholios, and the inscription from Tomis referring to 'Sepponos the wine merchant', cast light on the shipping putting in at Moesian and Scythian ports.[146] From these coastal centres, the *annona* must have reached Danubian fortresses and cities on vessels sailing up the Danube, or wagons moving along the latitudinal military roads traversing the frontier region.

The primary aim of the *Quaestura Exercitus* was to ensure the effective military performance of the Lower Danube frontier forces.[147] The regular and efficient provisioning of these troops was especially desirable bearing in mind the military encounters that had already taken place in the region by A.D. 536, including the Hun and Bulgar invasions of 528, 530 and 534, and the expeditions launched from the area into Wallachia by Chilbudius between 531 and 534. Indeed, the defeat and death of Chilbudius must have provoked some fear of Sklaveni reprisals, and may explain Justinian's intention to maximise the effectiveness of the frontier defences.[148]

From a strategic perspective, the combination of the civil, and, possibly, military, commands of Lower Moesia and Scythia Minor, ensured a unified response to barbarian attempts to cross the Danube. This will have been preferable to a divided military command in the area, which enabled the Huns to defeat the ducal forces of both provinces in separate encounters in A.D. 528. The reform was also designed to strengthen the Danube navy

---

[145] Karagiorgou (2001b) 148–49; Opait (2004) 104–109.

[146] Barnea (1977) Inscription 6 from Tomis; Beševliev (1964) Inscription 96 from Odessus.

[147] Torbatov (1997) 79 emphasises the judicial, but not military power of the Quaestor. Curta (2002) 11 sees the post as designed "to secure both militarily and financially the efficient defence of the Danube frontier". Swan (2007) 253 and 262–65 stresses that the reform was designed to improve an extant supply system.

[148] Curta (2005) sees Chilbudius' defeat as inaugurating a more defensive approach to the security of the Lower Danube. Certainly, the setback will have encouraged the imperial government to improve the logistical support of frontier troops, whether on defensive or offensive missions.

Fig. 3   Balkan provinces during the reign of Justinian (map produced by Carlos García).

by putting the ship-building facilities and naval manpower of the islands and Caria at its disposal.[149]

---

[149] Stein (1949–59) volume 2, 474–75. Giorgos Deligiannakis' paper given to the After Rome Seminar at Trinity College, Oxford on 3rd June 2004 entitled "Grey zones of Late

The construction of a new ecclesiastical and administrative capital in northern Illyricum by 535 points to similar efforts in the western Balkans. The new capital, Justiniana Prima, was installed in the vicinity of the emperor's birthplace, in the province of Dacia Mediterranea, not far from its border with Dardania. *Novella* 11, promulgated in 535, proudly announces that this foundation was not only to serve as the new seat of the Archbishop of Illyricum, Catelliano, but had already been established as the new capital of the Illyrian prefecture.[150] Although subsequent *Novellae* from the mid-540s signify the return of the Illyrian prefect to Thessalonica, there is no evidence to suggest that he had not been previously based at Justiniana Prima.[151]

Leaving aside the issue of the praetorian prefect, it is nonetheless indisputable that a strong ecclesiastical presence was now established in northern Illyricum. This is significant considering the power wielded by ecclesiastical leaders in urban and provincial politics in Late Antiquity.[152] Indeed, the gist of *Novella* 11 is the re-assertion of imperial administrative and cultural authority over an area that had been largely lost to barbarian immigrants by the late 5th c.;[153] it contrasts the southward movement of the Illyrian capital from Sirmium to Thessalonica in the mid-440s as a result of the Hunnic attacks. The new centre of Illyrian power was Dacia Mediterranea and its triangle of key cities: Serdica, the provincial capital and gateway to the Iron Gates pass; Naissus, the base of the general of Illyricum; and Justiniana Prima, the new political and ecclesiastical capital. This zone was crucial because, through it, ran the major routes from Pannonia to Thrace and the fertile interior Illyrian plains of Macedonia and Thessaly. Like Lower Moesia and Scythia Minor, Dacia Mediterranea was the platform from which the interior Balkans could be defended, and diplomatic and military influence projected into barbarian-held lands further north. The energetic military activity of the general of Illyricum, Mundo, increasingly close cultural and political ties with the Herul federates, and Justinian's designs on Gothic-held southern Pannonia further west provide the diplomatic and military contexts within which *Novella* 11 can be understood.

Antiquity: the Aegean islands" demonstrated the numerous late antique harbours, portuary installations, and ship-building capabilities on Rhodes and the Dodecanese islands.

[150] *Nov. Iust.* 11, in Schöll and Kroll (1892–95) 94.

[151] Bavant and Ivanišević (2003) 45.

[152] For instance, Jones (1964) 874–79 and 933–37; Liebeschuetz (2001) 137–55.

[153] *Nov. Iust.* 11, in Schöll and Kroll (1892–95) 94, lines 13–21.

Local Initiatives: Archaeological and Legislative Evidence for Balkan Urban and Rural Populations

Thus far, imperial military campaigns, fortification drives and administrative reforms have been discussed with little thought for the role played by local societies. However, rather than viewing fortification work as either imperial or local, it makes more sense to see its initiation, organisation and implementation as resulting from an intersection of local, regional and central authorities, varying depending on the circumstances. While there was undoubtedly a projection of central authority over the Balkans in this period, the amenability of local populations was still vital to the success of imperial policies. The literary evidence for the 5th and 7th c. barbarian invasions and imperial military campaigns in the Balkans includes numerous examples of urban and rural populations distant from Constantinople throwing their lot in with the barbarians and/or refusing to co-operate with Roman military commanders.[154] That we hear little of such obstructive behaviour toward Roman military campaigns during the reigns of Anastasius and Justinian indicates, presumably, that local populations were by this point willing to support them.[155]

But who were these local populations? The notion that the Balkan settlement pattern merely consisted of isolated administrative or military outposts, with little connection to the surrounding countryside, and provisioned entirely from without, often permeates the secondary literature.[156] This is the easiest conclusion to draw given the lack of archaeological evidence for large urban or rural populations, and the literary evidence for centralised reforms and external logistical support. However, there is archaeological and epigraphic evidence to suggest that this view has been exaggerated.

---

[154] See Heather (2007) 173–86 on the damage to Roman culture in the frontier regions, and the dislocation between their provincial populations and a central government unable to protect them.

[155] The only documented uprising occurred at Ulpiana in Dardania in A.D. 551, and, according to Procop. *Goth.* 8.25.13, was motivated by an unspecified religious cause— perhaps Justinian's poor treatment of Pope Vigilius and his promulgation of the Edict of the Faith the previous year.

[156] Curta (in this collection) sees a sea of military settlements largely supplied from without, playing down any large-scale agricultural activity. Whitby (2007) 140 points to insecurity as far south as Rhaedestus, and paints a picture of inhabitants cowering behind walls. Liebeschuetz (2007) 113 states that, beyond fortified settlements, the countryside lay open to barbarian devastation.

First, rather than seeing the widespread fortification of the Balkans as simply a sign of insecurity, it can also be viewed as an indication that there were populations and wealth worth protecting in this period, and the central, provincial and local initiative and resources to do so. Sizeable urban populations still existed in a number of cities judging by their remains. For instance, although some cities, such as Nicopolis ad Istrum, came to represent extremely small, fortified areas, dominated by administrative, military and ecclesiastical buildings, with very little sign of residential settlement, others, like Novae and Zikideva, retained relatively large intramural areas and acquired public buildings and basilicas.[157] The Black Sea cities of Odessus, Tomis and Istria retained large intramural areas, street grids, and buildings typically associated with classical cities, such as townhouses and bathing complexes.[158] Archaeological evidence for extramural residential and artisanal areas and forts exists at sites such as Zikideva and Caričin Grad.[159]

Military and ecclesiastical building work carried out during the reigns of Anastasius and Justinian was not necessarily all the result of a 'top-down' process, organised and funded by Constantinople, as Procopius' work and some of the epigraphic evidence suggests. In reality, the part played by local groups in initiating, organising and appointing architects to carry out building projects was also important. A 5th–6th c. A.D. building inscription from Ulmetum shows that one section of its wall had been contributed by the local butchers' guild;[160] another, from Mesembria, advertises the role of a local division of soldiers.[161] Even inscriptions which appear to show off an imperial work may be deceptive. Thus Inscription 2 from Byllis proclaims:

> Victorinus, with his commanding nature, with the foresight of God and the Virgin Mother of God, correctly serving the aim and methods of Justinian the most-powerful lord, having erected the fortresses of the Moesians and Scythians and of Illyricum together with the whole of Thrace, piously builds the wall (*teixos*) at Byllis. (Feissel (1988) 137–38).

---

[157] Conrad and Stancev (2002) 674 on 23 ha Novae. Dinchev (1997) 54 on 21.4 ha Zikideva.

[158] Zahariade (2006) 73–79 on the spectacular growth of Tomis from 60 to 70 ha in the Justinianic period; Preshlenov (2002) 18 on 35 ha Odessos.

[159] Dinchev (1997) 64–65 on Zikideva's satellite settlements with residential and economic purposes; Bavant (2007) 340–42 on the proliferation of fortresses in valleys surrounding Justiniana Prima, and 371 on the evidence for an extramural settlement.

[160] Popescu (1976) Inscription 8.

[161] Barnea (1977) Inscription 108.

Given that Byllis was a secondary provincial city, we cannot be certain that Victorinus was centrally appointed to carry out this work. Indeed, the reference to Justinian, as to God, could well have been merely a symbolic gesture.[162] According to the inscription, Victorinus had worked on fortresses throughout Moesia and Scythia, Thrace and Illyricum. Whether or not directly employed by the central authorities, it may be presumed that specialised, itinerant architects such as this man did very well out of the building boom. Even if the fortification work at Byllis was organised and funded locally, the inscription makes clear that inhabitants of secondary provincial cities distant from Constantinople were doffing their caps to the central authorities. The notion of a Balkan-wide Justinianic fortification drive may have been exaggerated by imperial propaganda, but the fact that local communities felt the need to buy into it further contributes to the impression that it was in their interests to promulgate the imperial cause.

Rather than islands of Roman administration, shut off from lawless and dangerous rural areas, cities such as Byllis and Justiniana Prima can be viewed as cultural, military and political foci, from which surrounding rural populations could be governed by local, regional or provincial elites.[163] The lack of evidence for non-fortified rural settlements should not lead us to conclude that no-one inhabited the areas between such centres. Given that residential buildings in many excavated fortresses were made of light materials, such as wood, rural populations now largely dwelt in buildings that are much less visible archaeologically.[164] Indeed, archaeologists make

---

[162] Poulter (2007b) 11; Bowden (2006) 280–83.

[163] Although Dunn (2004) 578–80 argues that the Justinianic fortification or militarisation of the Macedonian countryside resulted in depressed economic activity from the 540s, mainly indicated by the fall in the amount of bronze coinage recovered from this period. He alleges that it did this by causing a structural imbalance between local, regional and imperial interests through the arrival of too many soldiers and officials in the region who needed to be fed, and the deleterious effect of this development on settlements without salaried garrisons. This interesting argument is contradicted, however, by the limited evidence for any significant Balkan-wide economic decline before the late 6th c.; the decline in bronze coinage could relate to other factors such as the plague.

[164] Poulter (1999) 207 points out the large number of sites that have already been identified in northern Bulgaria, despite the early stage of research into rural areas, and (2007) 46–48, on how much work remains to be carried out on rural areas. Dinchev (2007) 510 on the poor quality of building materials used in smaller, 'local', rural settlements. Vašić (1994) 66 on how the apparent lack of residential structures from the remains of forts may be explained by the perishable materials with which they were built.

clear how much work is yet needed in order to build up a more accurate impression of rural settlement patterns in this period.[165]

Furthermore, networks of tiny forts in isolated non-strategic rural areas would not have been necessary unless used as periodic local shelters for people and agricultural equipment and produce. Evidence from sites such as Iatrus, Dichin and Gradishte on the Lower Danube plain has led archaeologists to suggest that they were used at least in part as supply centres, or fortified granaries, in which agricultural produce generated from the surrounding land was stored.[166] The hypothesis that Germanic soldier-farmers inhabited such centres is attractive, and Procopius' passage on the changing status of federate troops would tie in neatly with this proposition.[167] The historian claims that, by the Justinianic period, federate troops were essentially little different from traditional *limitanei*. This contrasted to their 4th c. predecessors, who had been autonomous allies of the empire.[168] If the *limitanei* were indeed being scaled down, perhaps it owed something to the availability of barbarian *foederati* in the frontier zones.

Had there been no peasant or soldier cultivators and/or middle landowning groups, there would have been no need for the promulgation of *Novellae* 33–35 in the mid-530s.[169] These warned larger landowners, who were *milites* in some cases, off making usurious loans of money and equipment to poorer peasants. The *Novellae* were promulgated in Thrace, the Lower Danube frontier region and Illyricum. These decrees might be interpreted as evidence for rural poverty and dislocation, bearing in mind their descriptions of bankrupt and landless peasants fleeing the area; however, more likely, such legislation bears witness to an agricultural system in which a large enough surplus existed for landowners, possibly local military commanders, administrators or bishops, to profit from.

The proliferation of ecclesiastical centres throughout the northern Balkans in this period, from major ecclesiastical monuments and centres, such

---

[165] Poulter (2007b) 41–46.

[166] von Bülow (2007) on Iatrus; Poulter (1999) on Gradishte; Poulter (2007b) 82–94; Swan (2007); and Grinter (2007) on Dichin. Their reconstructed picture shows that the Lower Danube frontier zone was not solely reliant upon supply from without, but that communities, especially in more inhospitable areas, also generated agricultural surpluses from farming the surrounding land.

[167] Poulter (2007b) 94; Procop. *Vand.* 3.11.1–4.

[168] On the changing status of the *foederati* in Late Antiquity: Elton (1996) 91–96; Chrysos (1989) 13–24 and (1997) 185–206; Heather (1998); Pohl (1997) 78–87. On the blurring of distinction between barbarian and Roman in the Late Roman army, see Greatrex (2000).

[169] *Nov. Iust.* 33–35, in Schöll and Kroll (1892–95) 239–41.

as the Episcopal complex in Novae, to rural churches placed in isolated locations, such as those in the Timok valley, serves as further evidence that this was not an unpopulated wasteland.[170] The unfortified five-aisled basilica at Draganovets, in one of the eastern passes of the Haemus range, is a good example: it was situated in an open space, in close proximity to numerous fortifications that occupied higher, more defensible positions. The religious element in the integration of barbarian populations is highlighted by the number of ecclesiastical monuments that have been associated with a baptismal purpose.[171]

CONCLUSIONS

To sum up, during the reigns of Anastasius and Justinian, considerable energy was expended in re-asserting Roman administrative and military authority over the north Balkans, and projecting diplomatic influence into the barbarian regions beyond them. This took the form of internal reforms and building work, time-honoured diplomatic measures, and the deployment of large field armies. Piecing together the literary sources for military encounters in this period, large armies were regularly deployed within and beyond the Balkan provinces, and were largely successful in their operations; Justinian in particular ensured that they destroyed or harried the majority of barbarian attacks. Even when field armies were not deployed, the network of fortifications, reinforced under both emperors, stood firm, and barbarian raiders were forced to cover large distances in search of plunder before returning home. Little archaeological evidence exists for widespread destruction, and the literary sources testify that very few major urban settlements fell. Further, in contrast with the 4th to 5th c. barbarian invaders, who spent years, sometimes decades, south of the Danube, with wives, children and wagons in tow, attacks in the Justinianic period were short-lived, targeted strikes by small raiding parties, often designed to renegotiate settlements with the imperial authorities. In fact, imperial armies carried out similar raids in the Black Sea area in the 520s and on Sklaveni territories in Wallachia in the 530s.

---

[170] Biernacki (2005) on Novae; Vašić (1994) 49–50 for churches in the Timok valley.

[171] A point made by Curta (2001c) 50, who highlights the important role played by church building and religion in the cultural integration of the barbarian population of the Balkans.

Although there is no literary or archaeological evidence for the technological, tactical or strategic details which determined the course and nature of military confrontations, it seems likely that the emperors' diplomatic, administrative and fortification policies provided the basis for Roman military successes. After all, military campaigns do not exist in a vacuum: success depends on the relationships of armies with local populations, whether in foreign or domestic territory, the contentedness of troops with socio-economic or cultural factors, adequate logistical provisioning, a network of defensive and/or offensive bases and structures to fall back on, or launch campaigns from, and strategic and numerical advantages when engaging in battle.

Without successful diplomatic preparations, troops were more likely to be fighting in unfavourable circumstances. The ability of Anastasius and especially Justinian to manipulate inter-barbarian rivalries meant that the majority of military encounters were fought on Roman terms: against individual barbarian groups; on a number of occasions with the support of military allies; and with the Romans holding the initiative. These campaigns were never carried out against entire federations, and rarely resulted in tactical surprises, as had been the case on numerous occasions in the 4th and 5th c. A.D., most notoriously at the Battle of Adrianople in 378. Furthermore, by engineering and maintaining a favourable balance of power in the barbarian world north of the Danube, Justinian could draw upon the vast manpower resources of groups occupying an area between the Alps and the Caucasus; these not only bolstered the military resources of the Balkans, but were drawn upon to fight in the wars in Italy, Africa and the East.

A network of fortifications, communications and supply centres provided the infrastructure for internal military operations and the platform for campaigns north of the Danube. At the same time, the more effective control and manipulation of populations now settled in the north Balkan provinces is evident from the fact that there were no major rebellions subsequent to that of Vitalian in the 510s. Administrative innovations, such as the *Quaestura Exercitus* and the establishment of a new Illyrian capital at Justiniana Prima, along with imperial propaganda concerning the fortification plan, all point to concerted efforts to tighten control. Their success is suggested by the limited evidence for local opposition to Roman military campaigns, and the loyalty of barbarian soldier-residents, such as Bulgars, Heruls, Huns and Goths, who played key roles not only in defending the Balkans, but in fighting wars beyond the Danube.

Despite this optimistic outlook on diplomatic and military successes and a political re-integration of the Balkan population, it should be reiterated that there had been no restoration of 'classical' Roman civic and provincial life in the northern Balkans. Archaeological studies have shown that the 6th c. northern Balkan landscape had changed significantly from that of the 4th c. Roman villas and cities built on 'classical' lines no longer dominated the region, and militarised settlements were largely inhabited by first- and second-generation barbarian groups, although we should not rule out the survival and adaptation of some Roman elites. Only a small number of cities, including those on the Black Sea coast, retained 'classical' elements, such as large circuit walls, town houses, street grids, and baths.

However, this paper has sought to refrain from comparing the era of Anastasius and Justinian to the period before the great barbarian migrations, a few hundred years earlier, and has instead considered it in light of the periods immediately preceding and subsequent to it. Archaeological evidence from the reigns of Anastasius and Justinian suggests no major rupture in the Balkan settlement pattern comparable with those of the 5th or late 6th to 7th c. Therefore, while playing down Procopius' more exaggerated descriptions of grandiose imperial building works in the Balkans, the work of archaeologists to date at the same time places in context his claims regarding the gravity of barbarian invasions in the Balkans and the impotence of the Romans.

The importance of imperial agency in exploiting the imbalance between the empire and the barbarian world is highlighted by the rapid reversal in Roman fortunes following the accession of Justin II. His refusal to apply Justinian's expedient diplomatic policies and his confrontational approach to the Avars at the very least did nothing to prevent them from uniting Pannonia, and, at the very worst, contributed to this unfavourable development. From Pannonia, the Avars were able to circumvent the northern Balkan defensive system and become the most significant threat since Attila's Hunnic confederation. They not only wrought havoc on the Balkans through their invasions, but, in the late 6th and 7th c., made possible the gradual migration of Slavic tribes into interior Illyricum. Hopefully, however, this paper has shown that, ignoring this benefit of hindsight, this loss of imperial control over the Balkans was not inevitable in A.D. 565.

Appendix: Timeline of Balkan Military Affairs 491–565

493 *Magister Militum per Illyricum* Julian killed in skirmish with Bulgars.

499 Bulgars defeat Thracian field army of 15,000 men and 520 wagons, commanded by Aristus beside the River Tzurta.

502 Bulgar invasion of Illyricum is unopposed.

504 Gothic General Pitzas captures Sirmium from the Gepids.

505 Mundo the Gepid warlord defeats Illyrian field army and 10,000 Bulgar federate troops commanded by Sabinianus the Younger.

508 Lombards defeat and annihilate the Heruls in the Upper Danube region.

508–10 Anastasius forges an alliance with the Lombards.

510 Anastasius negotiates the return of Pannonian Bassianae to the empire with Ostrogothic King, Theoderic.

512 Anastasius settles the Heruls in north-western Illyricum.

514–17 Rebellion of the *Comes Foederatum*, Vitalian.

517 Invasion by Getae (probably the Gepids given Marcellinus' use of the term throughout his chronicle to refer to this group) sweeps through interior Illyricum unopposed.

early 520s Invasion by Antae of northern Thrace is defeated by Germanus, *Magister Militum per Thraciam*.

527 Justinian reinforces agreement with the Herul federates through the baptism of King Grepes in Constantinople and donation of lands about Singidunum.

528 Justinian baptises the Bosphorus Hun King Grod in Constantinople. After Grod is murdered by rebels upon his return to Bosphorus, a Roman expedition is launched against the Huns by land and sea.

528 Invasion of Thrace by two Hunnic armies is defeated on the Thracian plain by the Illyrian and Thracian field armies led by Askum the Hun and Godilas.

529 Appointment of Mundo the Gepid as *Magister Militum per Illyricum*. Mundo defeats mixed barbarian invading force including Huns upon his arrival in Illyricum.

530 Mundo defeats Getae (probably the Gepids) in Illyricum and then Bulgars in Thrace, killing 500 of the latter.

late 520s Roman-sponsored Gepid attack on the Goths at Sirmium. Gothic counter-attack ends with the sack of Gratiana.

531–34 *Magister Militum per Thraciam*, Chilbudius, defends the Lower Danube from barbarian attack, and carries out a series of raids on Sklaveni territories north of the frontier. He is killed in 534, when his expeditionary force is ambushed by the Sklaveni.

534–35 Bulgar attack is intercepted at Iatrus and repulsed by the *Magister Militum Praesentalis*, Tzittas.

535–36 Mundo leads Roman invasion of Dalmatia. Although Mundo and his son, Mauricius, are killed in the initial fighting, Roman control is established with Constantianus' capture of Salona in 536.

536 The Gepids seize control of Sirmium following the departure of the Goths.

536–39 At some point in these years, a Roman-Lombard agreement is reached, according to which Justinian ratifies the Lombards' annexation of territories in Pannonia Savia and Noricum Mediterranea.

539 Hun invasion of Illyricum and Thrace leads to the fall of Cassandria in Macedonia and 32 forts.

534–45 Sklaveni-Antae war won by the Sklaveni. Followed by Antae raid on Thrace.

544 Hun attack on Illyricum.

545 *foedus* signed with the Antae.

545 Sklaveni raid on Illyricum defeated and repelled by Herul force recently recruited by Narses.

545–48 At some point in these years, the political division and rebellion of the Herul federates takes place. This is followed by the defection of an anti-Roman group of Heruls to the Gepids.

548 Sklaveni raiders pursued in Epirus by 15,000 strong Illyrian force.

548–49 The first Gepid-Lombard dispute results in the arrival of envoys from both sides in Constantinople requesting imperial military support. Justinian chooses to side with the Lombards. A large Roman army of 10,000 cavalry and 1,500 Herul allies, alongside the Illyrian field army, defeats a 3,000-strong force of the Gepids' Herul allies. The Gepids agree to a truce with the Lombards.

550 Sklaveni raid the Balkans, splitting into two forces, of 1,800 and 1,200. One of these sacks the city of Topirus in Rhodope before returning north. The other captures and kills Asbadus, the leader of a cavalry division based at Tzurullum in Thrace.

550 Sklaveni incursion into Illyricum disrupts Germanus' recruitment campaign at Serdica. The Sklaveni travel from Dacia Mediterranea to Dalmatia.

550 The second Gepid-Lombard dispute results in a stand-off between the two armies before another agreement is reached, this time for two years.

551 The Sklaveni that had moved into Dalmatia the previous year unite with another group and invade the Balkans. They put to flight a Roman army led by John the Glutton, Nazares, Scholasticus, Aratius and Justin, at Adrianople, before being crushed by the same force in the Astice region.

550–51 The Gepids ferry into Illyricum an army of 12,000 Kutrigur Huns led by Chinialon. Justinian arranges for the invasion of the Kutrigur homeland by his allies, the Utigur Huns led by Sandil. The Kutrigurs agree to leave the Balkans, although 2,000 led by Sinnion remain as federate troops.

551 Sklaveni force invades Illyricum before being engaged by the armies of the Generals Justin and Justinian, the sons of Germanus.

551 The Gepids ferry these Sklaveni out of the Balkans, charging two pieces of gold per head. Justinian responds by seeking and reaching a truce with the Gepids, which is signed by Gepid notables in Constantinople.

551 The Lombard warlord Ildiges leaves his post as head of the *scholae* palatine guards and flees the Balkans with co-conspirator, Goar the Goth. They take 300 Lombard troops from Apri in Europa, and steal horses from the imperial horse pastures in Thrace. En route to the Gepids' territory in Pannonia, they defeat a Kutrigur Hun division, presumably the 2,000 settled in Thace, and ambush a Roman army in Illyricum.

552 Roman army of 30,000 led by Narses embarks on the invasion of Gothic Italy. It comprises Herul, Gepid and Lombard contingents.

552 When the Gepids ferry another group of Sklaveni into the Balkans, Justinian uses the end of the two-year Gepid-Lombard truce as an excuse to support a Lombard invasion of Gepid territory; Roman force led by Amalafridas fights alongside the Lombards. The Gepids suffer a crushing defeat and treat with the Romans and the Lombards. The truce involves an exchange of the Lombard and Gepid exiles, Ildiges and Ustrigothus. Another Roman force led by Justin, Justinian and Suartas is waylaid by a religious uprising at Ulpiana which it quells and does not make it to Pannonia.

557 Avar envoys arrive in Constantinople. Agreement reached according to which the Avars defeat Roman enemies in the Caucasus region, including Sabir Huns, Zali and Unigurs.

559 Kutrigur Hun-Slav invasion of the Balkans led by Zabergan. Three forces are repulsed by the garrisons of the Chersonese and Thermopylae cross walls, and by a scratch force led by Belisarius in the Long Wall region. Justinian once again arranges an Utigur invasion of the Kutrigurs' homeland to persuade them to depart. Justinian sends additional double-prowed ships to the Danube, and supervises reconstruction of Long Wall defences from Selymbria.

557–62 Avars twice attack the Antae.

562 Avars arrive north of Lower Danube demanding to be given land to settle in Scythia Minor. Justinian uses delaying tactics to keep Avar envoys in the capital, while Justin reinforces Lower Danube defences. The Avars fail to breach the frontier after the outbreak of hostilities and move westward.

562 Seven divisions of *scholarii* are transferred to Heraclea in Europa.

562 Hunnic attacks result in the sack of Odessus and Anatsasiopolis. Marcellus, the brother of the future emperor, Justin II, is sent to recapture Odessus and repel the Huns.

ACKNOWLEDGEMENTS

I would like to thank the two anonymous referees for their feedback on this paper. I would also like to thank Carlos García for his work on the maps. Any remaining errors are my own.

BIBLIOGRAPHY

Primary Sources

Agath. = Frendo J. D. (1975) trans. Agathias, *The Histories* (Berlin 1975); Keydell R. (1967) ed. *Agathiae Myrinaei Historiarum libri quinque* (Berlin 1967).

Cassiod. *Var.* = Mommsen T. (1894) ed. *Cassiodori Senatoris Variae* (Berlin 1894); Barnish S. J. B. (1992) ed. and trans. *The Variae of Magnus Aurelius Cassiodorus Senator, the Right Honourable and Illustrious Ex-Quaestor of the Palace, Ex-Ordinary Consul, Ex-Master of the Offices, Praetorian Prefect and Patrician: Being Documents of the Kingdom of the Ostrogoths in Italy Chosen to Illustrate the Life of the Author and the History of his Family* (Translated Texts for Historians 12) (Liverpool 1992).

Cod. Theod. = Mommsen Th., Meyer P. *et al.* (1905) edd. *Theodosiani libri xvi cum constitu-tionibus Sirmondianis* (Berlin 1905); Pharr C. (1952) trans. *The Theodosian Code and Novels and the Sirmondian Constitutions* (Princeton 1952).

Evagr. = Whitby M. (2000) trans. and ed. *The Ecclesiastical History of Evagrius Scholasticus* (Liverpool 2000); Bidez J. and Parmentier L. (1898) ed. *The Ecclesiastical History of Evagrius with the Scholia, ed. with intr., critical notes and indices by J. Bidez and L. Parmentier* (London 1898).

Hierocles = Honigmann E. (1939) ed. *Le synekdémos d'Hiéroklès et L'opuscule géographique de Georges de Chypre: texte, introduction, commentaire et cartes* (Brussels 1939).

Jord. *Get.* = Mierow C. C. (1915) trans. *The Gothic History of Jordanes* (Princeton 1915).

Malalas = Thurn I. (2000) ed. *Ionnis Malalae Chronographia* (Berlin 2000); Jeffreys E., Jeffreys M. and Scott R. (1986) trans. *The Chronicle of John Malalas* (Byzantina Australiensia 4) (Melbourne and Sydney 1986).

Malchus = Blockley R. C. (1983) ed., trans. and notes. *The Fragmentary Classicising Historians of the Later Roman Empire: Eunapius, Olympiodorus, Priscus and Malchus Vol.2* (Liverpool and Cairns 1983).

Marcell. com. = Croke B. (1995) ed. and trans. *The Chronicle of Marcellinus: a Translation and Commentary with a Reproduction of Mommsen's Edition of the Text* (Sydney 1995).

Menander = Blockley R. C. (1985) ed. and trans. *The History of Menander the Guardsman* (ARCA, classical and medieval texts, papers and monographs 17) (Liverpool 1985).

Nov. Iust. = Schöll R. and Kroll W. (1892–95) edd. *Corpus Juris Civilis* III: *Novellae* (Berlin 1892–95, repr. 1945–1963).

Priscus = Blockley R. C. (1983) ed., trans. and notes. *The Fragmentary Classicising Historians of the Later Roman Empire: Eunapius, Olympiodorus, Priscus and Malchus Vol.2* (Liverpool and Cairns 1983).

Procop. *Goth.*, Procop. *Vand.*, Procop. *Pers.* = Dewing H. B. (1914–54) ed. and trans. Procopius, *History of the Wars 1–5* (Cambridge, Mass. and London 1914–54).

Procop. *Aed.* = Dewing H. B. (1914–54) ed. and trans. Procopius, *Buildings 7* (Cambridge, Mass. and London 1914–54).

Procop. *Anec.* = Dewing H. B. (1914–54) ed. and trans. Procopius, *The Secret History 6* (Cambridge, Mass. and London 1914–54).

Strategikon = Dennis G. T. (1984) ed. *Maurice's Strategikon: Handbook of Byzantine Military Strategy* (Philadelphia 1984); Dennis G. T. ed. and Gamillscheg E. trans. (1981) *Das Strategikon des Maurikios* (CFHB 17) (Vienna 1981).

Theophanes = Mango C. A. and Scott C. (1997) edd. *The Chronicle of Theophanes Confessor: Byzantine and Near Eastern History, A.D. 284–813* (Oxford 1997); de Boor C. (1883, 1885) ed. *Theophanis Chronographia* 2 vols. (Leipzig 1883, 1885).

Theoph. Sim. = de Boor C. (1887) *Theophylacti Simocattae Historia* (Leipzig 1887; rev. and amended ed. P. Wirth, Stuttgart 1972); Whitby M. and Whitby M. (1986) trans. *The History of Theophylact Simocatta: an English Translation with Introduction and Notes* (Oxford 1986).

Secondary Works

Angelova S. and Buchvarov B. (2007) "Durostorum in Late Antiquity (fourth to seventh centuries)," in *Post-Roman Towns, Trade and Settlement in Europe and Byzantium, Vol. 2: Byzantium, Pliska and the Balkans*, ed. J. Henning (Berlin 2007) 61–87.

Băjenaru C. (2010) *Minor Fortifications in the Balkan-Danubian Area from Diocletian to Justinian* (Cluj-Napoca 2010).

Barford P. M. (2001) *The Early Slavs* (London 2001).

Barnea I. (1966) "L'incendie de la cité de Dinogetia au VIᵉ siècle", *Dacia* 66 (1966) 237–59.

—— (1977) *Les monuments paleochrétiennes de Roumanie* (Vatican City 1977).

Bavant B., Kondic. V. and Spieser J.-M. (1990) *Caričin Grad II: le quartier sud-ouest de la ville haute* (Belgrade 1990).

Bavant B. and Ivaniševič V. (2003) *Iustiniana Prima-Cariĉin Grad* (Belgrade 2003).

—— (2007) "Iustiniana Prima (Cariĉin Grad). Eine spätantike Stadt vom Reissbrett", in *Roms Erbe auf dem Balkan. Spätantike Kaiservillen und Stadtanlagen in Serbien*, edd. U. Brandl and M. Vašić (Mainz 2007) 108–29.

—— (2008) "Cariĉin Grad (Serbie), les campagnes de fouille de 2007 et 2008", *MÉFRM* 120.2 (2008) 443–51.

Beševliev V. (1964) *Spätgriechische und spätlateinische Inschriften aus Bulgarien* (Berlin 1964).

Biernacka-Lubanska M. (1982) *The Roman and Early Byzantine Fortifications of Lower Moesia and Northern Thrace* (Wrocław 1982).

Biernacki A. (2005) "A city of Christians: Novae in the 5th and 6th c. AD", *Archaeologia Bulgarica* IX (2005) 53–74.

Bóna I. (1976) *The Dawn of the Dark Ages: the Gepids and the Lombards in the Carpathian Basin* (Budapest 1976).

Bounegru O. and Zahariade M. (1996) *Les forces navales du bas Danube et de la Mer Noire aux Ier–VIe siècles* (Oxford 1996).

Bowden W. A. (2003) *Epirus Vetus: the Archaeology of a Late Antique Province* (London 2003).

—— (2006) "Procopius' *Buildings* and the late antique fortifications of Albania", *New Directions in Albanian Archaeology: a Festschrift for Muzafer Korkuti Tiranë*, edd. L. Bejko and R. Hodges (Tirana 2006) 223–32.

Brandt T. (2005) "The Heruli", accessed at http://www.gedevasen.dk/heruleng.html (2005).

Cameron A. (1970) *Agathias* (Oxford 1970).

—— (1985) *Procopius and the Sixth Century* (London 1985).

Christie N. (1992) "The survival of Roman settlement along the Middle Danube: Pannonia from the 4th to the 10th century A.D.", *OJA* 11 (1992) 317–39.

—— (1995) *The Lombards: the Ancient Langobards* (Oxford 1995).

Christou K. (1991) *Byzanz und die Langobarden: von der Ansiedlung in Pannonien bis zur endgültigen Anerkennung (500–680)* (Athens 1991).

Chrysos E. (1989) "Legal concepts and patterns for the barbarians' settlement on Roman soil", in *Das Reich und die Barbaren*, edd. E. Chrysos and A. Schwarcz (Vienna 1989) 13–24.

—— (1997) "Conclusion: *de foederatis iterum*", in *Kingdoms of the Empire: the Integration of Barbarians in Late Antiquity*, ed. W. Pohl (Transformation of the Roman World 1) (Leiden 1997) 185–206.

Conrad S. and Stancev D. (2002) "Archaeological survey on the Roman frontier on the Lower Danube between Novae and Sexaginta Prista", in *Limes XVIII: Proceedings of the XVIIIth International Congress of Roman Frontier Studies, held in Amman, Jordan (September 2000)*, edd. B. Freeman, B. Bennek, Z. T. Fiema and B. Hoffmann (BAR International Series 1084) (Oxford 2002) 673–84.

Croke B. (1980) "Justinian's Bulgar victory celebration", *Byzantinoslavica* 41 (1980) 188–95.

—— (1982a) "Mundo the Gepid: from freebooter to Roman General", *Chiron* 12 (1982) 125–35.

—— (1982b) "The date of the Anastasian Long Wall in Thrace", *GRBS* 23 (1982) 59–78.

—— (1990) "Malalas, the man and his work", in *Studies in John Malalas*, edd. E. J. M. Jeffreys, B. Croke and R. Scott (Byzantina Australiensia 6) (Sydney 1990) 1–25.

—— (1995) ed. and trans. *The Chronicle of Marcellinus: a Translation and Commentary with a Reproduction of Mommsen's Edition of the Text* (Sydney 1995).

—— (2001) *Count Marcellinus and his Chronicle* (Oxford 2001).

—— (2005) "Jordanes and the Immediate Past", *Historia* 54.4 (2005) 473–94.

Crow J. (2001) "Fortifications and urbanism in Late Antiquity: Thessaloniki and other eastern cities", in *Recent Research on Late Antique Urbanism*, ed. L. Lavan (JRA Supplementary Series 42) (Portsmouth, RI 2001) 91–107.

—— (2007) "Amida and Tropeum Traiani, a comparison of two late-antique frontier cities", in *The Transition to Late Antiquity: on the Danube and Beyond*, ed. A. G. Poulter (Proceedings of the British Academy 141) (Oxford 2007) 435–55.

Crow J. and Ricci A. (1997) "Investigating the hinterland of Constantinople: interim report on the Anastasian Long Wall", *JRA* 10 (1997) 235–62.

Ćurčić S. (2010) *Architecture in the Balkans from Diocletian to Süleyman the Magnificent* (New Haven 2010).

Curta F. (1996) "Invasion or inflation? Sixth- to seventh-century Byzantine coin hoards in eastern and southeastern Europe", *AIIN* 43 (1996) 65–224.

—— (2001a) *The Making of the Slavs: History and Archaeology of the Lower Danube Region, c. 500–700* (Cambridge 2001).

—— (2001b) "Peasants as 'makeshift soldiers for the occasion': sixth-century settlement patterns in the Balkans", in *Urban Centers and Rural Contexts in Late Antiquity*, edd. T. S. Burns and J. W. Eadie (East Lansing 2001) 199–217.

—— (2001c) "*Limes* and cross: the religious dimension of the sixth-century Danube frontier of the Early Byzantine empire", *Starinar* 51 (2001) 45–70.

—— (2002) "*Quaestura exercitus Iustiniani*: the evidence of seals", *Acta Byzantina Fennica* 1 (2002) 9–26.

—— (2005) "Frontier ethnogenesis in Late Antiquity: the Danube, the Tervingi, and the Slavs", in *Borders, Barriers, and Ethnogenesis: Frontiers in Late Antiquity and the Middle Ages*, ed. F. Curta (Studies in the Early Middle Ages 12) (Turnhout 2005) 173–204.

Diculescu C. (1923) *Die Gepiden: Forschungen zur Geschichte Daziens im frühen Mittelalter und zur Vorgeschichte des rumänischen Volkes* (Leipzig 1923).

Dinchev V. (1997) "Household substructure of the Early Byzantine fortified settlements on the present Bulgarian territory", *Archaeologia Bulgarica* 1 (1997) 47–63.

—— (2000) "The definitions of urban area in the late antique dioceses of Thrace and Dacia: the overestimated centres", *Archaeologia Bulgarica* 4.2 (2000) 65–84.

—— (2007) "The fortresses of Thrace and Dacia in the Early Byzantine period", in *The Transition to Late Antiquity: on the Danube and Beyond*, ed. A. G. Poulter (Proceedings of the British Academy 141) (Oxford 2007) 479–546.

—— (2008) *Arheologicheskoto proouchvane na Haemus Thores* (Razkopki i prouchvaniya 37) (Bulgarian=*Archaeological Study of the Haemus*) (Sofia 2008).

Dolukhanov P. (1996) *The Early Slavs* (London 1996).

Doncheva-Petkova L. and Torbatov S. (2001) "Zur Chronologie der Architektur der spätrömischen und frühbyzantinischen befestigten Siedlung bei Odărci (Provinz Skythien)", in *Karasura: Untersuchungen zur Geschichte und Kultur des alten Thrakien. Volume 1: 15 Jahre Ausgrabungen in Karasura: Internationales Symposium Čirpan/Bulgarien, 1996*, edd. M. Wendel , J.-K. Bertram and M. Minkova (Weissbach 2001) 237–45.

Dunn A. (1994) "The transition from polis to kastron in the Balkans", *Byzantine and Modern Greek Studies* 18 (1994) 60–80.

—— (2004) "Continuity and change in the Macedonian countryside, from Gallienus to Justinian", in *Recent Research on the Late Antique Countryside*, edd. W. Bowden, L. Lavan and C. Machado (Late Antique Archaeology 2) (Leiden and Boston 2004) 535–86.

Duval N. and Popović V. (1984) edd. *Caričin Grad I* (Belgrade and Rome 1984).

Dyczek P. (2008) ed. *Novae: Legionary Fortress and Late Antique Town* (Warsaw 2008).

Eadie J. W. (1982) "City and countryside in Late Roman Pannonia: the *Regio Sirmiensis*", in *City, Town and Countryside in the Early Byzantine Era*, ed. R. L. Hohlfelder (New York 1982) 25–43.

Ellegård A. (1987) "Who were the Eruli?", *Scandia* 53 (1987) 5–34.

Elsner J. (2007) "Ekphrasis as panegyric: the rhetoric of buildings in the *De Aedificiis* of Procopius", in *Art and Text in Byzantine Culture*, ed. E. James (Cambridge 2006) 33–57.

Elton H. (1996) *Warfare in Roman Europe, AD 350–425* (Oxford 1996).

Evans H. J. A. S. (1996) *The Age of Justinian* (London 1996).

Feissel D. (1988) "L'architecte Viktorinos et les fortifications de Justinien dans les provinces balkaniques", *BAntFr* (1988) 136–46.

—— (2000) "Procope et les autres sources: les édifices de Justinien au temoignage de Procope et de l'Épigraphie", *Antiquité Tardive* 8 (2000) 81–104.

Gillett A. (2002) ed. *On Barbarian Identity: Critical Approaches to Ethnicity in the Early Middle Ages* (Studies in the Early Middle Ages 4) (Turnhout 2002).

Gordon C. D. (1966) *The Age of Attila: Fifth Century Byzantium and the Barbarians* (New York 1966).

Greatrex G. (2000) "Roman identity in the sixth century", in *Ethnicity and Culture in Late Antiquity*, edd. S. Mitchell, G. Greatrex and K. Adshead (London 2000) 267–92.

—— (2003) "Recent work on Procopius and the composition of *Wars* Book VIII", *Byzantine and Modern Greek Studies* 27 (2003) 45–67.

Gregory T. E. (1979) "The Late Roman wall", *Hesperia* 48 (1979) 264–80.

—— (2000) "Procopius on Greece", *Antiquité Tardive* 8 (2000) 105–14.

Grinter P. (2007) "Seeds of destruction: conflagration in the grain stores of Dichin", in *The Transition to Late Antiquity: on the Danube and Beyond*, ed. A. G. Poulter (Proceedings of the British Academy 141) (Oxford 2007) 281–86.

Guest P. (2007) "Coin circulation in the Balkans in Late Antiquity", in *The Transition to Late Antiquity: on the Danube and Beyond*, ed. A. G. Poulter (Proceedings of the British Academy 141) (Oxford 2007) 295–308.

Haarer F. (2006) *Anastasius I: Politics and Empire in the Late Roman World* (Cambridge 2006).

Heather P. J. (1991) *Goths and Romans, 332–489* (Oxford 1991).

—— (1996) *The Goths* (Oxford 1996).

—— (1998) "Disappearing and reappearing tribes", in *Strategies of Distinction: The Construction of Ethnic Communities, 300–800*, edd. W. Pohl and H. Reimitz (Transformation of the Roman World 2) (Leiden 1998) 95–112.

—— (2005) *The Fall of the Roman Empire* (London 2005).

—— (2007) "Goths in the Roman Balkans, c. 350–500", in *The Transition to Late Antiquity: on the Danube and Beyond*, ed. A. G. Poulter (Proceedings of the British Academy 141) (Oxford 2007) 163–90.

Hoddinott R. F. (1975) *Bulgaria in Antiquity* (London 1975).

Howard-Johnston J. D. (2000) "The education and expertise of Procopius", *Antiquité Tardive* 8 (2000) 19–30.

Ivanišević V. (2010) "Caričin Grad—the fortifications and the intramural housing in the lower town", in *Byzanz—das Römerreich im Mittelalter, 2.2*, edd. F. Daim and J. Drauschke (Mainz 2010) 747–78.

Ivanišević V. and Kazanski M. (2002) "La necropole de l'époque des grandes migrations à Singidunum", in *Singidunum 3*, ed. M. Popović (Belgrade 2002) 101–57.

Ivanov R. T. (1980) *Abritus: a Roman Castle and Early Byzantine Town in Moesia Inferior* (Sofia 1980).

—— (1999) *Dolnodunavskata otbranitelna sistema mezhdu Dortikum i Durostorum ot Avgust do Mavrikii* (Bulgarian=*The Defence System along the Lower Danube between Dorticum and Durostorum from Augustus to Maurice*) (Sofia 1999).

Jeffreys E. J. M. (1990) "Malalas' Sources", in *Studies in John Malalas*, edd. E. J. M. Jeffreys, B. Croke and R. Scott (Byzantina Australiensia 6) (Sydney 1990) 167–216.

Jones A. H. M. (1964) *The Later Roman Empire, 284–602: a Social, Economic and Administrative Survey* (Oxford 1964).

Kaldellis A. (2004) *Procopius of Ceasarea: Tyranny, History and Philosophy at the End of Antiquity* (Philadelphia 2004).

Karagiorgou O. (2001a) *Urbanism and Economy in Late Antique Thessaly (3rd–7th century AD): the Archaeological Evidence* (D.Phil diss., Univ. of Oxford 2001).

—— (2001b) "LR2: a container for the military annona on the Danubian border?", in *Economy and Exchange in the East Mediterranean during Late Antiquity: Proceedings of a Conference at Somerville College, Oxford, 29th May, 1999*, edd. S. Kingsley and M. Decker (Oxford 2001) 188–205.

Kelly C. (2008) *Attila the Hun: Barbarian Terror and the Fall of the Roman Empire* (London 2008).

Kent J. H. (1966) *Corinth, vol VIII: The Inscriptions, 1926–1950* (Princeton 1966).

Kondić V. (1984) "Les formes des fortifications protobyzantines dans la région des Portes de Fer", in *Villes et peuplement dans l'Illyricum protobyzantin: Actes du colloque organisé par l'École française de Rome, Rome, 12–14 mai 1982* (Rome 1984) 131–61.

Lemerle P. (1954) "Invasions et migrations dans les Balkans depuis la fin de l'époque romaine jusqu'au VIIIᵉ siècle", *RHist* 211 (1954) 295–300.

Liebeschuetz J. H. W. G. (2001) *Decline and Fall of the Roman City* (Oxford 2001).

—— (2007) "The Lower Danube region under pressure: from Valens to Heraclius", in *The Transition to Late Antiquity: on the Danube and Beyond*, ed. A. G. Poulter (Proceedings of the British Academy 141) (Oxford 2007) 101–34.

Maas M. (2005) ed. *The Cambridge Companion to the Age of Justinian* (Cambridge 2005).

Madgearu A. (1992) "The placement of the fortress Turris", *BalkSt* 33 (1992) 203–208.

—— (2001) "The end of town-life in Scythia Minor", *OJA* 20.2 (2001) 207–17.

Madzharov M. (1989) "Diocletianopolis, ville paléochrétienne de Thrace", in *Actes du XI-e Congrès International d'Archéologie Chrétienne. Lyon, Vienne, Grenoble, Genève et Aoste (21–28 septembre 1986) vol. 3* (Rome 1989) 2521–37.

Maenchen-Helfen O. J. (1973) *The World of the Huns: Studies in their History and Culture* (Berkeley 1973).

Metcalf D. M. (1991) "Avar and Slav invasions into the Balkan peninsula (*c.* 575–625): the nature of the numismatic evidence", *JRA* 4 (1991) 140–48.

Martindale J. R. (1992) *The Prosopography of the Later Roman Empire* 3 (Cambridge 1992).

Mikulčić I. (2002) (ed. M. Konrad) *Spätantike und frübyzantinische Befestigugungen in Nordmakedonien. Städt- Vici- Refugien- Kastelle* (Munich 2002).

Milinković M. (2008) "Die spätantik-frühbyzantinischen befestigten Höhenanlagen in Serbien", in *Höhensiedlungen zwischen Antike und Mittelalter von den Ardennen bis zur Adria*, edd. H. Steuer and V. Bierbrauer (Berlin and New York 2008) 533–57.

—— (2011) "Höhensiedlungen des 6. und 7. Jahrhunderts in Serbien", in *Keszthely-Fenékpuszta im Kontext spätantiker Kontinuitätsforschung zwischen Noricum und Moesia*, ed. O. Heinrich-Tamáska (Budapest, Leipzig, Keszthely and Rahden 2011) 285–302.

Milošević G. (2002) "New data on the topography of Viminacium", in *The Roman and Late Roman City: the International Conference, Veliko Turnovo, 26–30 July 2000*, edd. L. Ruseva-Slokoska, R. T. Ivanov, V. Dinchev (Sofia 2002) 151–58.

Mitrea B. "Les monnaies et l'ecroulement de Dinogetia à la fin du VIᵉ siècle", *Pontica* 7 (1974) 49–72.

Opait A. (2004) *Local and Imported Ceramics in the Roman Province of Scythia (4th–6th centuries AD): Aspects of Economic Life in the Province of Scythia* (BAR International Series 1274) (Oxford 2004).

Petković S. (2011) "Late Roman Romuliana and mediaeval Gamzigrad from the end of 4th to 11th centuries A. D.", in *Keszthely-Fenékpuszta im Kontext spätantiker Kontinuitätsforschung zwischen Noricum und Moesia*, ed. O. Heinrich-Tamáska (Budapest, Leipzig, Keszthely and Rahden 2011) 267–84.

Petrović P. (1994–95) "Les fortresses de la basse antiquité dans la region du Haut Timok", *Starinar* 45–46 (1994–95) 55–66.

Petrović P. and Dušanić S. (1996) edd. *Roman Limes on the Middle and Lower Danube* (Belgrade 1996).

Pohl W. (1980) "Die Gepiden und die gentes an der Mittleren Donau nach dem Zerfall der Attillareiches", in *Die Völker an der mittleren und unteren Donau im fünften und sechsten Jahrhundert*, edd. H. Wolfram and F. Daim (Vienna 1980) 239–305.

—— (1988) *Die Awaren: ein Steppenvolk im Mitteleuropa, 567–822 n. Chr.* (Munich 1988).

—— (1996) "Die Langobarden in Pannonien und Justinians Gotenkrieg", in *Ethnische und kulturelle Verhältnisse an der Mittleren Donau im 6.–11. Jahrhundert*, edd. D. Bialeková and J. Zabojnik (Bratislava 1996) 27–35.

—— (1997) "The empire and the Lombards: treaties and negotiations in the sixth century", in *Kingdoms of the Empire: the Integration of Barbarians in Late Antiquity*, ed. W. Pohl (Transformation of the Roman World 1) (Leiden 1997) 75–134.

Pohl W. and Erhart P. (2005) edd. *Die Langobarden: Herrschaft und Identität* (Vienna 2005).

Pohl W. and Reimitz H. (1998) edd. *Strategies of Distinction: the Construction of Ethnic Communities, 300–800* (Transformation of the Roman World 2) (Leiden 1998).

Pohl W., Wood I. and Reimitz H. (2001) edd. *The Transformation of Frontiers from Late Antiquity to the Carolingians* (Transformation of the Roman World 10) (Leiden and Boston 2001).

Popescu E. (1976) *Inscriptiile Grecesti si Latine din secolele IV–XIII descoperite in Romania* (Bucharest 1976).

Popović M. (1991) *The Fortress of Belgrade* (Belgrade 1991) (trans. from original publication of 1982).

Popović V. (1975) "Les témoins archéologiques des invasions avaro-slaves dans l'Illyricum Byzantin", *MÉFRA* 87 (1975) 445–504.

Poulter A. G. (1983) ed. *Ancient Bulgaria: Papers Presented to the International Symposium on the Ancient History and Archaeology of Bulgaria, University of Nottingham, 1981* (Nottingham 1983).

—— (1995) ed. *Nicopolis ad Istrum: a Roman, Late Roman and Early Byzantine City* (London 1995).

—— (1996) "The use and abuse of urbanism in the Danubian provinces during the Later Roman Empire", in *The City in Late Antiquity*, ed. J. Rich (London 1996) 99–135.

—— (1998) ed. *Nicopolis ad Istrum: the Pottery and Glass* (London 1998).

—— (1999) "Gradishte near Dichin: a new late Roman fortress on the Lower Danube", in *Der Limes an der unteren Donau von Diokletian bis Heraklios*, edd. G. von Bülow and A. Milceva (Sofia 1999) 211–31.

—— (2007a) ed. *The Transition to Late Antiquity: on the Danube and Beyond* (Proceedings of the British Academy 141) (London 2007).

—— (2007b) "The transition to Late Antiquity", in *The Transition to Late Antiquity: on the Danube and Beyond*, ed. A. G. Poulter (Proceedings of the British Academy 141) (Oxford 2007) 1–50.

—— (2007c) "The transition to Late Antiquity on the Lower Danube: the city, a fort and the countryside", in *The Transition to Late Antiquity: on the Danube and Beyond*, ed. A. G. Poulter (Proceedings of the British Academy 141) (Oxford 2007) 51–97.

—— (2007d) ed. *Nicopolis ad Istrum: a Late Roman and Early Byzantine City: the Finds and the Biological Remains* (London 2007).

Preshlenov H. (2001) "A late antique pattern of fortification in the eastern Stara Planina Mountain (the Pass of Djulino)", *Archaeologia Bulgarica* 5 (2001) 33–43.

—— (2002) "Urban spaces in Odessus (6th c. BC–7th c AD)", *Archaeologia Bulgarica* 6 (2002) 13–43.

Radoslavova G. (2011) "Abritus—eine spätrömische-byzantinische Stadt in Moesia Secunda", in *Keszthely-Fenékpuszta im Kontext spätantiker Kontinuitätsforschung zwischen Noricum und Moesia*, ed. O. Heinrich-Tamáska (Budapest, Leipzig, Keszthely and Rahden 2011) 249–56.

Sarantis A. (2009) "War and diplomacy in Pannonia and the north-west Balkans during the reign of Justinian: the Gepid threat and imperial responses", *DOP* 63 (2009) 15–40.

—— (2010) "The Justinianic Herules: from allied barbarians to Roman provincials", in *Neglected Barbarians (40th International Congress on Medieval Studies, Kalamazoo, 2005)*, ed. F. Curta (Turnhout 2011) 361–402.

—— (forthcoming) *The Balkans during the Reign of Justinian* (Cambridge, forthcoming).

Schmidt L. (1954) *Die Ostgermanen* (Munich 1954).

Schwarcz A. (2005) "Die Heruler an der Donau", in *Sprache als System und Prozess. Festschrift für Günter Lipold zum 60. Geburtstag*, ed. C. M. Pabst (Vienna 2005) 504–12.

Shchukin M. B. (1986–90) "The Balto-Slav forest direction in the archaeological study of the ethnogenesis of the Slavs", *Wiadowosci Archeologiczne* 51/1 (1986–1990) 3–30.

Stein E. (1949–59) *L'Histoire du Bas-Empire*, 2 vols. (Paris 1949–59).

Swan V. (2007) "Dichin (Bulgaria): interpreting the ceramic evidence in its wider context", in

The Transition to Late Antiquity: on the Danube and Beyond, ed. A. G. Poulter (Proceedings of the British Academy 141) (Oxford 2007) 251–80.

Thompson E .A. (1996) *The Huns* (Oxford 1996).

Torbatov S. (1997) "Quaestura exercitus: Moesia Secunda and Scythia under Justinian", *Archaeologia Bulgarica* 1 (1997) 78–87.

—— (2000a) "The Roman road Durostorum—Marcianopolis", *Archaeologia Bulgarica* 4 (2000) 59–72.

—— (2000b) "Procop. De Aedif. IV, 7,12–14 and the historical geography of Moesia Secunda", *Archaeologia Bulgarica* 4 (2000).

—— (2002) *Ukrepitelnata sistema na provinciia Skitiia (kraia na III–VII v.)* (Bulgarian=*The Defence System of the Late Roman Province of Scythia (Late 3rd to 7th Century)*) (Veliko Tărnovo 2002).

Vagalinski L. (1998) "Ein neuer spätantiker Segmentenhelm aus Voivoda, Schumen Gebiet (nordost Bulgarien)", *Archaeologia Bulgarica* 2.1 (1998) 96–106.

—— (2002) *Burnished Pottery from the First Century to the Beginning of the Seventh Century A.D. from the Region South of the Lower Danube* (Sofia 2002).

Vagalinski L., Atanassov G. and Dimitrov D. (2000) "Eagle-Head buckles from Bulgaria (6th–7th c AD)", *Archaeologia Bulgarica* 4 (2000) 78–91.

Vašić M. (1994) "Le limes protobyzantin dans la province de Mésie Premiere", *Starinar* 45–46 (1994–1995) 41–53.

—— (1999) "Transdrobeta (Pontes) in Late Antiquity", in *Der Limes an der unteren Donau von Diokletian bis Heraklios: Vorträge der Internationalen Konferenz Svištov, Bulgarien (1.–5. September 1998)*, edd. G. von Bülow and A. Milceva (Sofia 1999) 27–35.

Vasiliev A. A. (1950) *Justin the First: an Introduction to the Epoch of Justinian* (Cambridge 1950).

Velkov V. (1977) *Cities in Thrace and Dacia in Late Antiquity* (Amsterdam 1977).

von Bülow G. (2007) "The fort of Iatrus in Moesia Secunda: observations on the Late Roman defensive system on the Lower Danube (fourth–sixth centuries AD)", in *The Transition to Late Antiquity: on the Danube and Beyond*, ed. A. G. Poulter (Proceedings of the British Academy 141) (Oxford 2007) 459–78.

von Bülow G. and Milceva A. (1999) edd. *Der Limes an der unteren Donau von Diokletian bis Heraklios: Vorträge der Internationalen Konferenz Svištov, Bulgarien (1.–5. September 1998)* (Sofia 1999).

Werner J. (1962) *Die Langobarden in Pannonien: Beiträge zur Kenntnis der Langobardischen Bodenfunde vor 568* (Munich 1962).

Whitby M. (1985) "The Long Walls of Constantinople", *Byzantion* 55 (1985) 560–83.

Whitby M. (1988) *The Emperor Maurice and his Historian: Theophylact Simocatta on Persian and Balkan Warfare* (Oxford 1988).

—— (2000) "The Balkans and Greece 420–602", in *The Cambridge Ancient History. Volume 14: Late Antiquity, Empire and Successors AD 425–600*, edd. A. Cameron, B. Ward-Perkins and M. Whitby (Cambridge 2000) 701–30.

—— (2007) "The role of the Roman army in the defence of the Balkans", in *The Transition to Late Antiquity: on the Danube and Beyond*, ed. A. G. Poulter (Proceedings of the British Academy 141) (Oxford 2007) 135–61.

Wilkes J. J. (2005) "The Roman Danube: an archaeological survey', *JRS* 155 (2005) 124–225.

Wolfram H. (1988) *History of the Goths* (Berkeley 1988).

Wozniak F. (1978) "Byzantine diplomacy and the Lombard-Gepidic wars", *BalkSt* 20 (1979) 139–58.

Zahariade M. (2006) *Scythia Minor: a History of a Later Roman Province (284–681)* (Amsterdam 2006).

LIST OF FIGURES

HORSEMEN IN FORTS OR PEASANTS IN VILLAGES? REMARKS ON THE ARCHAEOLOGY OF WARFARE IN THE 6TH TO 7TH C. BALKANS

Florin Curta

Abstract

Conspicuously absent from 6th to early 7th c. fortified sites in the Balkans are stirrups and other elements of equipment signalling the presence of cavalry troops. Hoards of iron implements containing stirrups have been wrongly dated to Late Antiquity; they are in fact of a much later date (9th–11th c. A.D.). Those hoards which can be dated to the 6th c. with some degree of certainty lack agricultural tools associated with large-scale cultivation of fields. As most such hoards found in Early Byzantine hill-forts typically include tools for the garden-type cultivation of small plots of land, they show that no agricultural occupations could be practised inside or outside 6th c. forts, which could satisfy the needs of the existing population. Those were, therefore, forts, not fortified villages.

'Now, every year a force of cavalry (στρατιῶται ἔφιπποι) from the other cities of Dalmatia used to collect at, and be dispatched from Salona, to the number of a thousand, and they would keep guard on the river Danube, on account of the Avars'. After defeating the Dalmatian cavalry force on their own territory, the Avars:

> held the survivors captive and dressed themselves up in their clothes, just as the others had worn them, and then mounting the horses and taking in their hands the standards and the rest of the insignia which the others had brought with them, they all started off in military array and made for Salona. And since they had learnt by enquiry also the time at which the garrison was wont to return from the Danube (which was the Great and Holy Saturday), they themselves arrived on that same day. When they got near, the bulk of the army was placed in concealment, but up to a thousand of them, those who, to play the trick, had acquired the horses and uniforms of the Dalmatians, rode out in front. Those in the city [of Salona], recognising their insignia and dress, and also the day, for upon this day it was customary for them to return, opened the gates and received them with delight. But they, as soon as they were inside, seized the gates and signalising their exploit to the army, gave it the cue to run in and enter with them. And so they put to the sword all in the city, and thereafter made themselves masters of all the country of Dalmatia and settled down in it. (Const. Porph. *DAI* 30.18–58, trans. in Moravcsik and Jenkins (1967) 141 and 143).

A. Sarantis, N. Christie (edd.) *War and Warfare in Late Antiquity: Current Perspectives*
(Late Antique Archaeology 8.1–8.2 – 2010–11) (Leiden 2013), pp. 809–850

Thus did Emperor Constantine Porphyrogenitus explain in the mid-10th
c. the fall of Salona, an event of the early 7th c. There are many reasons
for not taking this story literally: the tale has long been recognised as a re-
hashing of that in chapter 29 of the *De administrando imperio* (itself based
on information obtained probably from local sources in Split), with Avars
replacing Slavs.[1] Moreover, ever since J. B. Bury, scholars have regarded
the story in chapter 30 as a later addition, perhaps even following the
death of Emperor Constantine Porphyrogenitus.[2] The numismatic evidence shows that the destruction of Salona could not have possibly taken
place as described by Constantine Porphyrogenitus, since in the early 630s
Salona had still not been deserted.[3] At no point during its long history did
the Roman province of Dalmatia expand as far to the north or north-east
as the Danube. Despite claims to the contrary, no evidence exists so far of
an Avar settlement in Dalmatia.[4] One might suppose, therefore, that the
episode of the Avar conquest of Salona in the *De administrando imperio* is
a strategy its author adopted to explain both the reduction of the Roman
population of Dalmatia to the 'townships on the coast' and the subsequent conquest of the interior by Croats.[5]

But not everything in this episode is made up. An independent cavalry
corps recruited from among inhabitants of Dalmatia was known since the
3rd c., and there are good grounds to believe that some remnants of that
survived into the early 7th c. Some are ready to take Constantine Porphyrogenitus' testimony at face value and argue that the 'force of cavalry'
recruited in the early 600s from the cities of Dalmatia and dispatched to
Salona was an urban militia.[6] Others maintain that that force was indeed
the reinforcements, which in the early 580s were expected to relieve
Sirmium from the Avar siege.[7] Either way, the point about Emperor

---

[1] Novaković (1972) 5–52; Jakšić (1984) 322. Const. Porph. *DAI* 29.33 calls the Slavs Avars
(Σλάβοι οι καὶ Ἄβαροι καλούμενοι). For a re-assessment of the testimony of Constantine
Porphyrogenitus as a source for the history of late antique and early medieval Dalmatia,
see Rajković (1997); and Goldstein (2005).

[2] Bury (1906) 52.

[3] Marović (1984) and (2006).

[4] Advocates of an Avar presence in Dalmatia were both historians (Klaić (1990) 13–14)
and archaeologists (Kovačević (1966)). For far more skeptical treatments of sources, see
Pohl (1988) 282 and (1995); Rapanić (2001).

[5] Const. Porph. *DAI* 30.58–60. For the story of the Croat conquest of Dalmatia, see Fine
(2000); and Margetić (2001) 41–113, 121–48, and 155–70.

[6] Ferluga (1978) 73.

[7] Pillon (2005) 55–56 citing Menander the Guardsman. There is, however, no mention
of cavalry units from Dalmatia in any of the surviving fragments from Menander's work—
see Blockley (1985).

Constantine's story of how the Avars conquered Salona was that the military equipment of the Dalmatian horsemen was radically different from that of the Avars: it was only by disguising themselves as Dalmatian horsemen that barbarians could enter the city. The unexpected loss of Dalmatia to the barbarians was brought about by Avar travestiers.

However, the impression one gets from examining sources chronologically closer to the events narrated in the *De administrando imperio* is that the military travesty actually worked in the opposite direction. When the author of a late 6th or early 7th c. military treatise known as the *Strategikon* made recommendations as to the organisation and equipment of Roman cavalry troops, he left no doubt as to the source of inspiration for his advice:

> The horses, especially those of the officers and the other special troops, in particular those in the front ranks of the battle line, should have protective pieces of iron armor about their heads and breast plates of iron or felt, or else breast and neck coverings such as the Avars use (κατὰ τὸ σχῆμα τῶν Ἀβάρων). The saddles should have large and thick cloths; the bridle should be of good quality; attached to the saddles should be two iron stirrups, a lasso with thong, hobble, a saddle bag large enough to hold three or four days' rations for the soldier when needed. There should be four tassels on the back strap, one on top of the head, and one under the chin. The men's clothing, especially their tunics, whether made of linen, goat's hair, or rough wool, should be broad and full, cut according to the Avar pattern (κατὰ τὸ σχῆμα τῶν Ἀβάρων), so they can be fastened to cover the knees while riding and give a neat appearance.[8] (*Strategikon* 1.2.35–49, trans. Dennis (1984) 13).

Even though stirrups are not specifically attributed to the Avars, they are mentioned here in a passage marked twice and with the same words by reference to Avar practices. This is in fact a chapter of the *Strategikon* in which its author insists that Roman cavalrymen employ a number of devices, all said to be of Avar origin: cavalry lances, 'with leather thongs in the middle of the shaft and with pennons'; round neck pieces 'with linen fringes outside and wool inside'; horse armor; long and broad tunics; and tents, 'which combine practicality with good appearance'.[9] In this context, the mention of pairs of stirrups to be attached to saddles must also be interpreted as a hint to Avar practices. After all, cavalry lances, horse armour, and tents are also attributed to the Avars in the chapter

---

[8] Stirrups are also mentioned, without any reference to the Avars, in *Strategikon* 2.9.22–28.

[9] *Strategikon* 1.2.10–22. See also Szádeczky-Kardoss (1986) 208–209.

dedicated to 'Scythians, that is Avars, Turks, and others whose way of life resembles that of the Hunnish people', from which stirrups are nonetheless absent.[10]

Primarily on the basis of the *Strategikon*, scholars have by now accepted the idea that "contacts with nomadic groups who inhabited or passed through steppe regions north of the Danube and Black Sea made it possible for central Asian or even more easterly military equipment and practices to be transferred to the Balkans"; such is the case of the stirrup, which was adopted by Roman cavalrymen in the late 6th c. from the Avars, "who ultimately brought it from the eastern steppes and China".[11] Others, however, refuse to give the Avars any credit for the introduction of the stirrup to Europe, and instead maintain that the earliest Avar stirrups were either imports from, or imitations of specimens originating in the empire.[12] The 'stirrup controversy' has generated a considerable amount of literature, which had very little, if any impact, on studies dedicated to the Late Roman or Early Byzantine army.[13] There is to date no special study dedicated to the archaeology of the Avar influence on Roman military equipment and tactics.[14]

Nor has any attempt been made to assess the testimony of the *Strategikon* in the light of the archaeological evidence pertaining to the Early Byzantine period.[15] Were Roman troops in the 6th c. Balkans equipped and armed as recommended by the author of the *Strategikon*? Were Avar attacks on the Balkan provinces of the empire repelled by means of cavalry troops, or was defence based more on the network of hill-forts that had been built during the long reign of Emperor Justinian? Were such fortified settlements a military response to a particular form of warfare, which was prevalent in the 6th c., or did they serve as refuge for the rural population in their environs? Can weapons and agricultural implement

---

[10] *Strategikon* 11.2.1–3. See Bachrach (1984) 25.

[11] Haldon (2002) 66. The case for an Avar influence on Roman or Early Byzantine military equipment was made by Szádeczky-Kardoss (1981). For Avar innovations in military equipment, see Hofer (1996); and Nagy (2005).

[12] White (1962) 22; Freeden (1991) 624. For a critique of such views, see Schulze-Dörrlamm (2006).

[13] For an excellent survey of the 'stirrup controversy', see DeVries (1998) 95–103. Neither Kolias (1988) nor Haldon (2002) seem at all interested in the works of Lynn White and Bernard Bachrach.

[14] By contrast, Early Byzantine influence on Avar culture has recently been the object of several studies, most prominently Garam (2001).

[15] For the archaeology of Early Byzantium, see Rautman (1990); Sodini (1993); Zanini (1994).

finds, especially those from hoard assemblages excavated on Early Byzantine hill-fort sites, help determine whether their primary function was
military or civilian?

In this essay I argue that answers to those questions, although implicit
in the abundant literature on the archaeology of the 6th and early-7th c.
Balkans, constitute a compelling basis for rejecting the current interpretation of the military infrastructure of the region during the last century
of Roman rule. My discussion of the partial conclusions drawn from the
analysis of Avar-age stirrups and hoards of iron implements and weapons
found on Early Byzantine hilltop sites is intended as a reminder that one
cannot simply use the archaeological evidence as an illustration of what
is already known from written sources.

STIRRUPS

No stirrups have so far been found that could be dated, with any degree
of certainty, before the Avar conquest, in the late 560s, of the Carpathian
Basin.[16] The earliest stirrups that could safely be attributed to the Avar age
are apple-shaped, cast specimens with elongated suspension loops and
flat treads slightly curved inwards, such as that found in a sacrificial pit
in Baja (fig. 1/1).

Equally early are the stirrups with circular bow and eyelet-like suspension loop. Apple-shaped stirrups with elongated suspension loops
do not appear after *ca.* A.D. 630, but those with circular bow and eyelet-
like suspension loops remained in use throughout the 7th c., and can
be even found in assemblages dated to the early 8th c.[17] Two stirrups
with elongated suspension loops have been found in association with
Byzantine gold coins struck for Justin II (at Szentendre) and Maurice

---

[16] Ambroz (1973) 91; Bálint (1993) 210. The year 568 is traditionally viewed as the beginning of the Avar age, primarily because that is when, according to the written sources, the
Avars defeated the Gepids and forced the Lombards to migrate to Italy. However, there is
so far no solid argument against dating the earliest Avar-age assemblages to before 568, see
Stadler (2005) 128. 'Early Avar' is a technical term referring to the first stage of the chronological model of Avar archaeology, which was established by Ilona Kovrig (1963) on the
basis of her analysis of the Alattyán cemetery and recently refined by Peter Stadler on the
basis of calibrated radiocarbon and dendrochronological dates, see Stadler (2008) 47–59.

[17] Garam (1992) 160. For stirrups with elongated attachment loops as the earliest Avar-
age stirrups, see Nagy (1901) 314; Kovrig (1955) 163; Garam (1990) 253; Daim (2003) 468.
Aibabin (1974) called this the 'Pereshchepyne type' of stirrup. According to Iotov (2004)
140, 142, such stirrups belong to his class IA.

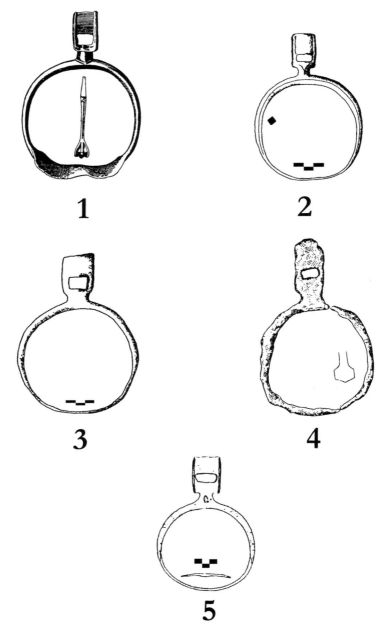

Fig. 1   Early Avar, apple-shaped cast stirrups with elongated suspension loop: 1—Baja, sacrificial pit; 2—unknown location in northeastern
Bulgaria; 3—Pernik, Early Byzantine hill-fort; 4—Nevolino, grave 122;
5—Strezhevo, hoard of iron implements. (After Hampel (1905); Iotov
(2004); Goldina and Vodolago (1990); and Janakievski (1980).)

(at Nyíregyháza-Kertgazdaság).[18] Neither one of these could be dated to the 6th c., but such a date could nonetheless be advanced for other, similar specimens found both within and outside the area of the Carpathian Basin, which was controlled *ca.* 600 by the Avars.[19] Several apple-shaped stirrups with elongated attachment loops found in Hungary (Mikebuda, Bicske, and Szeged-Öthalom) were richly decorated with a damascened ornament, which is most typical for artefacts found in assemblages firmly dated to *ca.* 630.[20]

Elsewhere in eastern Europe, the evidence for pre-7th c. stirrups is equally ambiguous (fig. 2).

Three stirrups with circular bow and eyelet-like suspension loop have been found in two separate burial chambers of the Klin Iar cemetery near Kislovodsk in the northern Caucasus region. Because the two burial chambers also produced *solidi* struck for emperors Maurice and Heraclius, respectively, the stirrups are regarded as among the earliest, if not *the* earliest specimens of their kind in the entire Caucasus region.[21] Another stirrup of an unknown type was associated with a drachma struck in 545 for the Sassanian King Khusro I in a burial assemblage of a large cemetery excavated in the 1980s in Verkhniaia Saia, at the foot of the Ural Mountains.[22] An apple-shaped specimen with elongated attachment loop

---

[18] Hampel (1905) 343–45; Csallány (1958) 49–50 and 66–68. The coin found together with the Szentendre stirrup was a *tremissis* struck for Justin II in Constantinople between 565 and 578, while that found together with the Nyíregyháza stirrup was a light (23 carat-) *solidus* struck for Emperor Maurice in Constantinople between 584 and 602. See Somogyi (1997) 67 and 87.

[19] Curta (2008a) 306–307.

[20] Heinrich-Tamáska (2005) 29 and 24 figs. 3–4.

[21] Härke and Belinskii (2000) 201–202. Two stirrups have been found beside a male skeleton in burial chamber 341, together with pressed silver belt mounts. Two *solidi* struck for Maurice (582–602), one freshly minted, the other worn, were found with the neighboring skeleton. Stirrups and *solidi* are therefore not necessarily contemporary. A fragmentary stirrup (most likely another specimen with eyelet-like suspension loop) came from burial chamber 363, together with two skeletons, a male and a female. A pendant made of a *solidus* struck for Heraclius of 634–41 was found next to the skull of the female skeleton. Again, the association of stirrup and coin is not warranted. I am grateful to Heinrich Härke for the details of his unpublished excavations in Klin Iar, including the complete illustration of the grave goods found in burial chambers 341, 360, and 363.

[22] Grave 19: Goldina and Vodolago (1990) 29–30. Another stirrup was found in grave 45 of that same cemetery together with a Soghdian imitation of a Sassanian drachma of Varakhran V (421–39), see Goldina and Vodolago (1990) 31. Such imitations are known as 'Bukharkhudat' coins because they were struck in Bukhara, but they are notoriously difficult to date; no agreement exists on their exact chronology and historical circumstances surrounding their production. The coin from grave 45 could have just as well been minted in the 6th as in the 7th c.

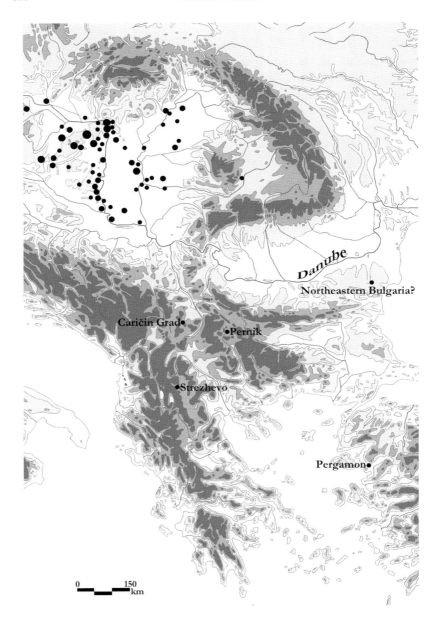

Fig. 2   Distribution of late 6th to 7th c. stirrups in south-eastern Europe. The cluster in the Carpathian Basin is of Early Avar, apple-shaped cast stirrups with elongated suspension loop and flat tread slightly bent inwards. Smallest circle, thereafter up to 2, 3, and 7 specimens, respectively.
(Data after Stadler (2005), with additions.)

is known from a burial assemblage from Burakovo in Tatarstan, found with a double-edged sword and belt mounts with open-work decoration known as 'Martynovka mounts', dated to the second half of the 6th or to the early 7th c.[23] Several stirrups with circular bow and eyelet-like suspension loop from the Ural region and the steppe lands north of the Black Sea were also found in association with such typically 6th c. artefacts as belt mounts with open work decoration, foil mounts with pressed ornament, or shoe buckles with rectangular plates.[24] Grave 122 in Nevolino produced an apple-shaped stirrup with elongated suspension loop (fig. 1/4); unfortunately, there were no coins and no chronologically sensitive artefacts among the grave goods from that burial assemblage.[25] A comparable stirrup was in the fill of a robbed inhumation grave from the Birsk cemetery in Bashkortostan; the grave produced a Khwarazmian coin struck between 750 and 760—which must be regarded as a stern warning against hastily assuming early dates for all stirrups with elongated attachment loops.[26]

Nonetheless, where available, the archaeological evidence points unmistakably to a 7th c. date. Such is the case of the stirrup of an unknown type, found together with a solidus struck between 661 and 663 for Emperor Constans II, in a barrow of the Romanovskaia cemetery on the Lower Don River.[27] Likewise for the apple-shaped stirrup from the rich burial assemblage from Malo Pereshchepyne in Left-Bank Ukraine, which was attributed to Kubrat, the Bulgar ruler allied with Emperor Heraclius

---

[23] Izmailov (1990) 64 and 70 fig. 2. For Martynovka mounts, see Somogyi (1987); Bálint (1992); Gavritukhin and Oblomskii (1996) 25–28. Such mounts were produced by means of two-piece moulds, such as that found in a workshop in Caričin Grad: Bavant (1990) 221–23.

[24] Belt mounts with open work decoration: Goldina and Vodolago (1990) 30 (grave 28 in Verkhniaia Saia) and 51 (grave 95 in Nevolino). Foil mounts with pressed ornament: Semenov (1988) 97–99 and 100 fig. 2.3, 4 (grave 17 in Novohryhorivka). Shoe buckles with rectangular plate: Goldina and Vodolago (1990) 124 pl. 27.43 and 146 pl. 49.11 (grave 140 in Brody); Rashev (2000) 24 (Portove, barrow 12, grave 5). For 6th and 7th c. assemblages in the steppe lands north of the Black Sea, see also Curta (2008b).

[25] Grave 122: Goldina and Vodolago (1990) 53 and 146 pl. 49.10. The grave also produced a bridle bit, an iron buckle and a handmade bowl. On the other hand, grave 122 was situated in the middle of the cemetery, a position strongly suggesting a date earlier than that of graves found on the fringes, which could be dated to the late 7th, 8th, or even 9th c.

[26] Grave 382: Mazhitov (1990) 261, 264–65, and 263 fig. 2/16. The Khwarazmian coin was perforated, an even stronger indication of a late date. Among other grave goods from that burial assemblage, there was also a so-called pseudo-buckle. The chronology of such belt mounts cannot be pushed beyond A.D. 700, see Garam (2000) and Gavritukhin (2001). The association between stirrup and pseudo-buckle is also attested in grave 202 in Nevolino, for which see Goldina and Vodolago (1990) 59 and 146 pl. 49.12.

[27] Semenov (1988) 109.

against the Avars. The last coins from that assemblage were 18 light
(20 carat) *solidi* struck for Constans II between 642 and 646.[28] Most other
stirrups from the steppes north of the Black Sea should date to the later
7th c., if not after 700.[29]

Given the insistence with which the author of the *Strategikon* recommended imitating Avar practices, as well as the abundance of stirrups
found in the region adjacent to the northern frontier of the empire, the
number of specimens from the Balkans that could be dated to the late 6th
or early 7th c. is surprisingly small (fig. 3).

Leaving aside misidentified artefacts and mounting devices occasionally found on Early Byzantine sites, there are so far just two early stirrups known from the Balkans.[30] One is an isolated find from Pernik, more
likely from the Early Byzantine than from the early medieval occupation
phase on that site (fig. 1/3);[31] the other, unprovenanced, is said to be from
north-eastern Bulgaria (fig. 1/2).[32] No stirrup with circular bow and eyelet-
like suspension like that from Pergamon has so far been found on any 6th
or early 7th c. site in the Balkans.[33] Why are there not more stirrup finds
from Early Byzantine hill-forts in the Balkans? The presence of cavalry
troops in the region is clearly documented for the period during which
some of the earliest apple-shaped stirrups with elongated attachment

---

[28] Aibabin (1974) 32 and 33 fig. 3; Werner (1984) pl. 7.15. The Malo Pereshchepyne stirrup was made of silver, not bronze. For the coins, see Sokolova (1995). All light *solidi* struck
for Constans II were perforated, and 9 of them had precious stones set on the obverse. For
Kubrat and Malo Pereshchepyne, see Werner (1985); Werner (1992b); L'vova (2000). For a
chronological *mise-au-point* of the problem, see Gavritukhin (2006).

[29] Novopokrovka: Kukharenko (1952) 36–37 and 39; Hlodosy: Smilenko (1965); Zach-
epilovki: Smilenko (1968); Iasinovo: Aibabin (1985) 191–96 and 192 fig. 1.2; Voznesenka:
Grinchenko (1950) pls. 1.1–4 and 6.9 and Ambroz (1982). The stirrup found in grave 204
of the large cemetery excavated in Shokshino (north-western Mordovia) may also be of
7th c., although no other grave goods are known from that assemblage. See Cirkin (1972)
163 and 162 fig. 2.21. Seventh century stirrups are also known from cemeteries excavated
in the present-day Kaliningrad *oblast'* of Russia, not far from the Baltic Sea shore, see
Kleemann (1956) 115 and pl. 31a.

[30] Misidentified artefacts: Herrmann (1992) 175. I owe a debt of gratitude to Kristina
Rauh for clarifying the identification of the iron artefact from Rupkite as definitely *not* a
stirrup. See Werner (1984b) for mounting devices, whose function was probably not unlike
that of the stirrups Early Byzantine corpsmen attached to the front and back of their saddles in order to transport the wounded on horseback (*Strategikon* 2.9.22–28). None of the
other stirrups mentioned in Bugarski (2007) 258 can be dated to the 6th or 7th c.

[31] Changova (1992) 181 and fig. 168.1; Iotov (2004) pl. 71.754.

[32] Iotov (2004) pl. 71.753.

[33] Gaitzsch (2005) 121 and pl. 56.V29.

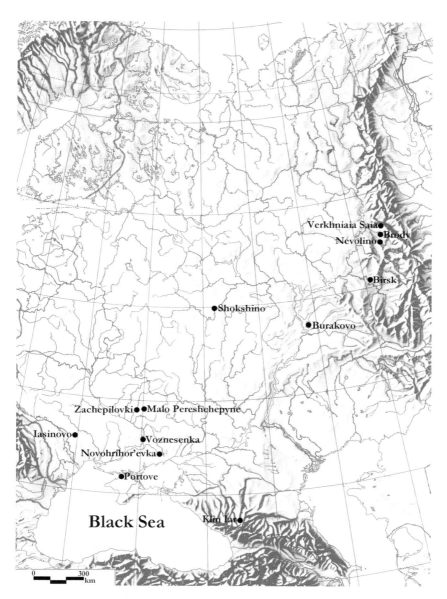

Fig. 3   Distribution of 6th and 7th c. stirrups in Eastern Europe.

loops were deposited in Early Avar burials.[34] Moreover, the presence of at least some horses on Early Byzantine sites is betrayed by occasional finds of bridle bits, such as those from Caričin Grad and Pazarište (Ras).[35] But were there any troops stationed in the forts scattered across the Balkans, which employed the equipment of Avar inspiration recommended by the author of the *Strategikon*?

Besides 'Avar', three-edged arrow heads and battle axes, there is some evidence of armour and composite bows.[36] Missing, however, are lance-heads such as those found together with Early Avar stirrups. It has recently been noted that in Hungary, Early Avar stirrups appear more often with lance-heads than with any other kind of weapon.[37] Lance-heads appear

---

[34] Cavalry troops accompanying Tatimer to Constantinople in 593: Theoph. Sim. 6.7.13. During the attack on the 600 Sclavenes returning from a raid in the region of Zaldapa, Aquis, and Scopi (594), the barbarians were throwing javelins at the horses of the Roman cavalrymen: Theoph. Sim. 7.1.7. Those were clearly cavalrymen, but were they members of the local garrisons or troops from the field armies moved into the region? In the case of the 593 episode, the answer is very simple: Tatimer had been sent by Priscus (the general in command of the field army operating north of the Danube) to Emperor Maurice in Constantinope with the prisoners captured after the attack on Ardagastus' territory. Tatimer was ambushed by Sclavenes and escaped only when infantry troops stationed in the area intervened, an indication that there were no cavalry troops available. Similarly, the episode of 594 involved the advanced guard of the field army under Peter (Emperor Maurice's brother). The Romans who dismounted and approached the wagon circle were soldiers in the field army, not members of local garrisons. There is no indication that the Armenian troops mentioned by Sebeos (*History* 15, in Thomson (1999) 31) were about to move permanently to the Balkans. There is no mention of cavalrymen in Sebeos, but assuming that troops included cavalry units, then it is significant that horsemen needed to be brought from outside. Therefore, the idea that the cavalry troops occasionally mentioned in relation to military events in the Balkans "are likely to have been drawn from those units stationed in the Balkans" has absolutely no support in the existing evidence.

[35] Bavant (1990) 242 fig. 171 and pl. 43.288–90; Popović (1999) 73 and 112 fig. 59.7.

[36] Three-edged arrow heads: Stoichev (2005); Dimitrov *et al.* (1965) 56 fig. 25; Herrmann (1992) 175; Uenze (1992) pl. 31.24–25; Janković (1981) 179 fig. 72a; Gabričević (1986) 89 fig. 22.3, 6; Mano-Zisi (1958) 326 fig. 36; and Bavant (1990) pl. 40. 237–42; Jeremić and Milinković (1995) 223 figs. 28g; Milinković (1995) 235 fig. 10 d; Sretenović (1984) 233 fig. 216.1; Popović (1999) 112 fig. 59.4; Mikulčić (2002) 126 fig. 15.1–3, 156 fig. 47.12–13, and 290 fig. 185.7; Milinković (2006) 249 fig. 4. Battle axes: Uenze (1992) pl. 21.2,3; Bavant (1990) pl. 38.216–18; Jeremić (1995) 206, fig. 23b; Sretenović (1984) 233, fig. 216.6. For lamellar armour, see Bugarski (2005). Bone or antler reinforcement plates for composite bows are known both from frontier forts and from sites in the interior; however, not all of them are securely dated to the late 6th or early 7th c., see Petković (1995) 102 and pl. 38.3; Čermanović-Kuzmanović (2004) 241; Ivanišević and Špehar (2005) 147–48 and 148 fig. 9/1; Uenze (1992) pl. 43.4; Milinković (2006) 249 fig. 4. For the reconstruction of the composite bow on the basis of the archaeological record of early Avar-age burial assemblages, see Fábián and Ricz (1991); Ricz and Fábián (1993). For the archaeological evidence of Avar lamellar armour, see Csallány (1958–1959), (1969–71) and (1982).

[37] Curta (2008a) 310–11. Almost half of all burial assemblages with lances excavated in Hungary and the neighbouring regions are of the Early Avar age, see Szentpéteri (1993) 216.

singly in Early Avar graves, but there are also instances of two or three per burial assemblage, often of different types. The strong correlation between stirrups and lance-heads suggests that stirrups were employed primarily by lancers. Stirrups, on the other hand, were particularly important when the amount of body armour increased and, when wielding multiple weapons, especially when switching from bow to lance in action, they made the rider more top-heavy and susceptible to lose his balance.[38] In other words, stirrups were the hallmark of a class of 'professional' mounted warriors, who could afford armour for themselves and for their war horses, a multitude of high-quality weapons, and a special training for a highly versatile form of warfare. Early Avar lances had narrow, short, and solid blades of high-quality steel, designed to pierce armour.[39] These may well have been the κοντάρια, to which the author of the *Strategikon* refers in relation to the Avars, and which modern commentators translate as either 'throwing spears' or 'stabbing lances'.[40] Some argue that, much like apple-shaped stirrups with elongated attachment loops, such lance-heads were of Byzantine manufacture.[41] If so, their absence from the archaeological record of the 6th to early 7th c. Roman provinces in the Balkans is remarkable. None of the lance- or spearheads found on Early Byzantine hill-fort sites in the region bears any resemblance to the weapons accompanying Avar warriors to their graves.[42]

Equally different from Avar weapons are the swords from Sadovec, Caričin Grad, and Balajnac.[43] Excavations of several Early Byzantine sites produced shield bosses or handles, which are otherwise absent from Early Avar burial assemblages with stirrups.[44] Judging from the existing evidence, the garrisons of 6th to 7th c. Balkan hill-top sites were more likely to have fought as infantry than as cavalry troops. Those were soldiers equipped with spears, swords, battle axes, and shields; some may

---

[38] Curta (2008a) 312. For switching from bow to lance, see *Strategikon* 1.12–16; for switching from lances to bows, a particularly Avar speciality, see *Strategikon* 11.2.24–27.

[39] Csiky (2007) 310–11 and 309 fig. 2 (type I/1).

[40] *Strategikon* 1.2.17 (κοντάρια καβαλλαρικά) and 11.2.24 and 26. See also Nagy (2005) 137.

[41] Freeden (1991) 624.

[42] For lance- and spear-heads on Early Byzantine hill-fort sites, see Gabričević (1986) 89 fig. 22.5, 7 (Rtkovo); Deroko and Radojčić (1950) 138 fig. 41; and Bavant (1990) pl. 40.246, 247 (Caričin Grad); Jeremić and Milinković (1995) 223 fig. 28 c-f and 224 fig. 30 c-e (Bregovina); Marušić (1962) pl. 4.1, 2 (Nezakcij); Lazaridis (1965) 327–34 (Nea Anchialos); Romiopoulou (1973–74) 697 (Kitros); Agallopoulou (1975) 239 (Ladochori).

[43] Uenze (1992) pl. 43.3, 5–8; Deroko and Radojčić (1949) 137 fig. 39; Jeremić (1995) 193–94. For Avar swords, see Simon (1991).

[44] Milošević (1987) fig. 24; Jeremić and Milinković (1995) 224 fig. 30; Bavant (1990) pl. 41.255; Mikulčić (2002) 468 fig. 385.1; Majewski *et al.* (1974) 179 and 181 fig. 5a.

have used composite bows, but, again, they were not mounted archers. While horses may have indeed existed in some forts, there is no sign of the permanent presence of horsemen with equipment of Avar inspiration. If any Roman cavalrymen battled the mounted Avar warriors in the Balkans, they must have been highly mobile troops coming from outside the region. They most certainly were not from units stationed on a longer term in any of the forts excavated so far in the Balkans.

HOARDS

In spite of the incontrovertible testimony of the *Strategikon*, there is very little evidence for the use of stirrups in the late 6th or early 7th c. Balkans. Nonetheless, some scholars have recently claimed that not only were stirrups used during the Early Byzantine period, but they were also produced in the Balkans.[45] Their main support for this is the presence of an apple-shaped specimen with elongated suspension loop among the 15 stirrups found in the Strezhevo hoard (figs. 1/5; 4).[46]

Given that apple-shaped stirrups with elongated suspension loops are typical for Early Avar assemblages in Hungary and the surrounding regions, the conclusion was drawn that the hoard itself must be dated to the same period. A 6th c. date was also advanced for some of the artefacts with which the stirrups were associated in the hoard assemblage, especially two L-shaped keys and a processional cross. Analogies for the keys were found among artefacts from a number of Early Byzantine sites in Serbia (Caričin Grad, Jelica, Gornij Streoc, Bregovina, and Gamzigrad), even though none of them was found in an archaeological context securely dated to the 6th or early 7th c. In fact, L-shaped keys with twisted handles very similar to one of the two Strezhevo keys come from Early Medieval hoard assemblages in Bulgaria and Moravia,[47] some found

---

[45] Bugarski (2007) 262.

[46] Janakievski (1980). The hoard was found during salvage excavations carried out in 1979 next to the basilica with mosaic pavement within the Early Byzantine fort at Kale.

[47] Chelopech (Bulgaria): Mutafchiev (1914) 266 fig. 243.6. Dălgopol (Bulgaria): Zlatarski (1960) 103–109 and fig. 8. Žabokreky (Slovakia): Bartošková (1986) 61–62 and 63 fig. 20.24. Staré Zámky (Moravia, Czech Republic): Staňa (1961) 112 fig. 29.7. Gajary (Slovakia): Bartošková (1986) 15 fig. 5.32. Mikulčice (Moravia, Czech Republic): Bartošková (1986) 29 fig. 10A.48. Moravský Jan (Slovakia): Müller (1996) 370 fig. 5.323. In Bulgaria, L-shaped keys are also known from late 9th to 10th c. burial (Oborochishte) and settlement assemblages (house 32 in Garvan), see Văzharova (1976) 333 and 335 fig. 211.3; Văzharova (1986) 109 and 107 fig. 99.2.

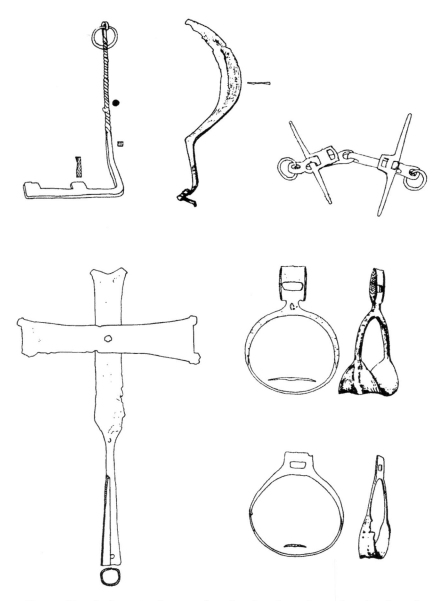

Fig. 4   Hoard of iron implements found in Strezhevo (Macedonia), selected artefacts: L-shaped key, sickle, bridle bit, processional cross, and stirrups. (After Janakievski (1980).)

together with precisely-dated artefacts, such as Late Avar strap-ends and belt mounts (which cannot be earlier than *ca.* 750), or Byzantine coins struck for Emperor John Tzimiskes (969–76).[48] Conversely, keys known from assemblages securely dated to the 6th c. are of a completely different kind and bear no resemblance to those from the Strezhevo hoard.[49] Similarly, the best analogy for the iron processional cross from Strezhevo is the 10th or early 11th c. specimen at Sredishte (Bulgaria), and not the crosses from Caričin Grad, Sadovec, or Gamzigrad, all of which were suspension, and not processional crosses.[50] A late, most likely 10th c. date for the Strezhevo stirrup is also strongly supported by the chronology of the 14 stirrups of Iotov's class 5A, none datable before *ca.* 900.[51]

Tenth and 11th c. stirrups are known from two other hoard assemblages found on Early Byzantine hill-fort sites in the Balkans. One of them was found behind the eastern gate of the Early Byzantine fort in Troianov most near Kladovo, on the right bank of the Danube, in Serbia, together with a bronze censer. The latter bears no resemblance to any of the 6th c. censers known from the Balkans, and despite claims to the contrary, cannot be dated before the 10th c.[52] The Troianov most hoard must therefore be associated with the later, medieval (10th to 12th c.) occupation of the site.[53] Similarly, the hoard found within the Early Byzantine fort in Dolishte, not far from Varna, in Bulgaria, is of a much later date, containing, among other implements, a stirrup with elliptic bow of Iotov's class 8A, which can only be dated after *ca.* 900, if not 1000.[54]

---

[48] Coins of John Tzimiskes: Chelopech (Mutafchiev (1914) 264). Late Avar strap ends and belt mounts: Moravský Jan (Bartošková (1986) 35 fig. 12. 3, 5–6, and 8–10; Müller (1996) 370 fig. 5.327). The strap ends and belt mounts from Moravský Jan are specimens of Zábojník's classes 90, 113, 229, and 251, respectively. Such belt fittings are most typical for the Late Avar III phase (*ca.* 750-*ca.* 780). See Zábojník (1991) 241; Stadler (2008) 59.

[49] See, for example, keys from a small hoard of casts found in Drobeta Turnu-Severin: Bejan (1976). This hoard must dated to the (late) 6th c., as affirmed by the presence within this of cast fibulae with bent stem—see Curta (2001) 245.

[50] Bugarski (2007) 260. For the processional cross from Sredishte, see Iotov (2004) 83 and 81, fig. 39.546. For iron processional crosses in Bulgaria, all dated after *ca.* 900, see Totev (2002) and (2005).

[51] Iotov (2004) 147 and 151–52 and (2007).

[52] For the hoard, see Garašanin and Vašić (1987) 94, 101 fig. 12, and 102 fig. 13–14. For the dating of the stirrup, see Iotov (2004) 152. Bugarski (2007) 258 wrongly insists on a 7th c. date. For finds of 6th c. censers in the Balkans, see Rendić-Miočević (1952) 202 fig. 1; Čorović-Ljubinković (1954) and (1956); Atanasov (2004) pl. 6.

[53] For the medieval occupation in Troianov most, see Marjanović-Vujović (1987); and Milenković (1997).

[54] Kouzov (2000). For the chronology of stirrups with elliptic bow, see Iotov (2004) 158.

These are stern reminders that not all assemblages found on sites otherwise known to have been occupied during the 6th and 7th c. should automatically be attributed to the Early Byzantine phase of occupation. More than 20 hoards have so far been found on Early Byzantine fortified sites in the Balkans (see Table 1; fig. 5).

Some of them have been used as an illustration not only of a late antique occupation of those sites, but also of their 'ruralisation', given the presence of agricultural tools among items found with such assemblages.[55] In at least two cases, the hoards themselves have been dated to the 6th or

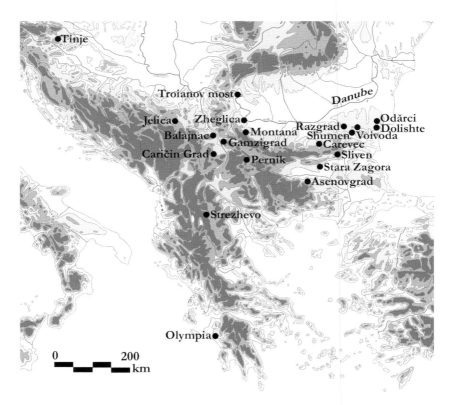

Fig. 5   Distribution of hoards of iron implements and weapons found on Early Byzantine hill-fort sites in the Balkans.

---

[55] Most typical for this approach is Popović (1990) and (1994–95). For the ruralisation of Balkan urban centers in the Balkans between the 5th and the 7th c., see Popović (1982).

7th c. because of being found on Early Byzantine sites.[56] Single or hoard finds of agricultural implements have then been used to determine the function of such sites: in spite of their fortification, they were supposedly not military, but civilian settlements.[57] That besides agricultural tools, some hoards have also produced weapons, does not seem to have been an impediment for such an interpretation, nor was the existence of a medieval occupation phase at many of these hoard sites.[58]

A very different interpretation, however, may be advanced on the basis of a seriation of hoards of iron implements (including those with stirrups) by correspondence analysis. With this technique, which has been introduced to archaeology only during the last 20 years or so, the relationships between hoards, those between artefact categories, and those between artefact categories and hoards, may be analysed together and represented in the same scattergram or series of scattergrams produced by the plotting of pairs of orthogonal axes. In addition to 21 hoards found on Early Byzantine sites, the analysis has also taken into consideration 11 other hoards of a certainly medieval date.[59] The scattergram displaying the relationships between hoards shows a cluster in the first, and another in the third and fourth quadrants (fig. 6).

Judging from the scattergram displaying the relationships between artefact categories (fig. 7), a few outliers (Preslav 2, Stambolovo, and Montana 2) include such typically medieval tools as bill-knives of Henning's class G5, sickles of Henning's class H4, scythes of Henning's class I5, and so-called 'ogribki'.[60]

---

[56] Antonova (1973) 139; Milinković (2001) 102.

[57] Henning (1986) 107; Werner (1992) 415. The most recent advocate of this idea is Kirilov (2007).

[58] For Troianov most, see above, n. 53. For Pernik, Shumen, Odărci, Montana, Razgrad, and Gamzigrad, see Changova (1992); Antonova (1975) and (1985); Doncheva-Petkova (1986); Kurnatowska and Mamzer (2007); Stanilov and Aleksandrov (1983); Georgieva (1961); Bikić (1997). A medieval, possibly 10th or 11th c. occupation of the site at Jelica is betrayed by potsherds of Combed Ware found within the basilica A. See Milinković (2001) 71–74, 80, and 102.

[59] For the 21 hoards found on Early Byzantine sites, see Table 1. For the other, later hoards, see Bobcheva (1972); Mutafchiev (1914); Zlatarski (1960); Dzhingov (1966) 52–53; Vitlianov (1978); Pleterski (1987); Stanchev (1985); Baracki (1960). The definition of tool types follows Henning (1987) 43, that of axes the classification of Bartošková (1986) 6 fig. 1, and that of lance-heads and stirrups the classification of Iotov (2004) 79–83 and 140–58. For correspondence analysis, see Shennan (1990) 283–86; Bølviken et al. (1982). For an exemplary application to the analysis of burial assemblages, see Nielsen (1988).

[60] Short scythes with shortened 'half handles' (Henning's class I 5) were found in relatively large numbers on 9th c. sites in Bulgaria and north of the Lower Danube, see Curta (1997) 220–21. Sickles of Henning's class H4 are considerably later than others, perhaps first

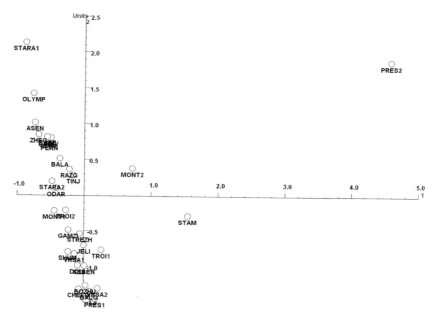

Fig. 6   Correspondence analysis plot of 32 hoards of iron implements and weapons:
ASEN—Asenovgrad; BALA—Balajnac; BOZHU—Bozhurovo; CARE—Carevec;
CARG—Caričin Grad; CHELO—Chelopech; DALG—Dălgopol; DOLI—Dolishte;
GAMZI—Gamzigrad; JELI—Jelica; MONT1—Montana 1; MONT2—Montana 2;
ODAR—Odărci; OLYMP—Olympia; PERN—Pernik; PRES1—Preslav 1; PRES2—
Preslav 2; RAZG—Razgrad; SEBEN—Sebenje; SHUM—Shumen; SLIV—Sliven;
STAM—Stambolovo; STARA1—Stara Zagora 1; STARA2—Stara Zagora 2; STR-
EZH—Strezhevo; TINJ—Tinje; TROI1—Troianov most 1; TROI2—Troianov most
    2; VOIV—Voivoda; VRSA1—Vršac 1; VRSA2—Vršac 2; ZHEG—Zheglica.

One hoard in the first quadrant (Stara Zagora 1) stands out as the only
assemblage combining such items as a copper-alloy kettle, two bronze
candlesticks, and several bronze vessels, including four 2nd to 3rd c.
authepsae.[61] That the Stara Zagora 1 hoard must be of a later date emerges
from the examination of the candlesticks and of 6 bells, all of liturgical
use. One bell has an inscription mentioning a certain presbyter named
Sergios, another bears the monogram of Emperor Justin II—the latest

---

appearing in the 10th c. Similarly, bill-knives of Henning's class G5 were in use in the 900s:
one was found among the grave goods of a 10th c. burial in Oborochishte—Henning (1987)
90, 96. 'Ogribki' are commonly interpreted as tools for scraping the kneading trough, but
there is no solid argument for that interpretation.
    [61] Cholakov and Ilieva (2005) 54–56 and 57 pl. 1.1–4.

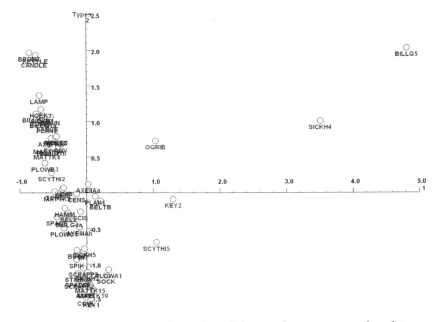

Fig. 7   Correspondence analysis plot of the artefact categories found in 32 hoards of iron implements and weapons: ANV—anvil; AXEFAN—battle axe, fan-shaped; AXEIIAa—battle axe, Bartošková's class IIAa; AXEIIIAb—battle axe, Bartošková's class IIIAb; AXEIIIB—battle axe, Bartošková's class IIIB; BELL—cattle bell; BELTB—belt buckle; BILLG1a—bill-knife, Henning's class G1a; BILLG1b—bill-knife, Henning's class G1b; BILLG2b—bill-knife, Henning's class G2b; BILLG4a—bill-knife, Henning's class G4a; BILLG5—bill-knife, Henning's class G5; BIT—bridle bit; BRONZE—bronze vessels; BUCK—bucket handles; CANDLE—candlestick; CENS—censer; CHAIN—plow chain; CHIS—chisel; COMB—currycomb; COUL—coulter, Henning's class E 1; HAMM—hammer; HOEK3—drag hoe, Henning's class K3; KETTLE—kettle; KEY1—key, L-shaped; KEY2—key, anchor-shaped; LAMP—lamp; LANCE—lance head, Iotov's class 1B; MATTK4—mattock, Henning's class K4; MATTK5—mattock, Henning's class K8; MATTK8—mattock, Henning's class K 8; MATTK10—mattock, Henning's class K10; MATTK15—mattock, Henning's class K15; OGRIB—tool ("ogribka"); PICKL1—pickaxe, Henning's class L1; PICKL2—pickaxe, Henning's class L 2; PLAN1—plane, curved; PLAN2—plane, straight; PLOWA1—ploughshare, Henning's class A1; PLOWB3—ploughshare, Henning's class B3; PLOWC1—ploughshare, Henning's class C1; SCIS—scissors; SCRAPP2—scraping tool, Henning's class P2; SCRAPP3—scraping tool, Henning's class P3; SCYTHI2—scythe, Henning's class I2; SCYTHI5—scythe, Henning's class I5; SOCK—socketed share; SPADE—spade, Henning's class F1; SPIK—spike; STIRR8A—stirrup, Iotov's class 8A; TONGS—tongs; WHETS—whetstone; WIMB—wimble.

chronological indication within the entire assemblage.[62] A 6th c. date may also be advanced for the Olympia hoard, which, besides iron tools and bronze vessels, included 22,252 copper coins, mostly *minimi*, but also coins struck for Justinian and Justin II.[63]

Can the same date be therefore assigned to other hoards from the cluster in the first quadrant? The Zheglica hoard includes a measuring cup with Greek inscription, which is believed to be of a 6th or early 7th c. date, although no convincing analogies are so far known.[64] The Caričin Grad hoard was found within a smithy built within the portico of a street excavated in the south-western section of the Upper City; the smithy has been dated to the last phase of occupation at Caričin Grad, *ca.* AD 600.[65] Similarly, the Odărci hoard is said to have been buried during the last phase of occupation on the site, which is coin-dated to the 610s.[66] To be sure, many of the items included in hoards from the cluster in the first quadrant are known only from 5th or 6th c. assemblages. For example, ploughshares of Henning's class B3 are attested on 6th c. monastic sites and hill-forts.[67] One such ploughshare, as well as a scythe of Henning's class I2, was recovered on the site of the *villa rustica* in Obelia near Sofia (Bulgaria), which was abandoned shortly before 450.[68] A sickle of Henning's class H1 was found in a house of the Early Byzantine fort in Pazarište (Ras) together with a half-*follis* struck for Justin II in Thessalonica in 569/70.[69] All known mattocks of Henning's class K4 have been found in assemblages or on sites dated to Late Antiquity; mattocks of classes K4 and K8, as well as bill-knives of Henning's class G1a, were among the items discovered in a large (still unpublished) hoard from Voivoda, which also produced a copper-alloy kettle, bronze lamps, and a clasp-helmet of the Baldenheim class.[70]

The seriation by correspondence analysis has isolated in the first quadrant a group of hoards which appear to be of an early, most likely

---

[62] Cholakov and Ilieva (2005) 58. A good analogy for the Stara Zagora candlesticks are two silver candlesticks from Sadovec with control stamps from the reign of Justinian— Iurukova (1992) 287.

[63] Völling (1995) 425–41. All coins have since been lost.

[64] Gerasimov (1946) 204.

[65] Popović (1990) 295.

[66] Cholakova (2005) 149.

[67] Henning (1987) 59–60. The distribution of B3 ploughshares is restricted to the territory of the 5th and 6th c. Roman provinces in the northern Balkans. For finds from monastic sites, see Dzhambov (1956) 188 fig. 29. For hill-fort finds, see Velkov (1935) fig. 5.

[68] Stancheva (1970) 535–38.

[69] Popović (1999) 95–96 and 115 fig. 61.13.

[70] Henning (1987) 154. For the helmet, see Vagalinski (1998).

6th c. date. They typically include several agricultural tools of distinct types, such as pick-axes, mattocks, drag hoes, bill-knives, sickles, and scythes, in combination with lance-heads of Iotov's class 1B and battle-axes, either fan-shaped or of Bartošková's class IIAa. A ploughshare of Henning's class B3 may also appear occasionally in such an assemblage. However, the overwhelming presence of gardening tools, such as mattocks of Henning's classes K4, K 5, and K8, and pick-axes strongly suggests that the agriculture practised in the 6th c. Balkans was restricted to areas sufficiently small to be cultivated with little or no use of draught animals. This has often been explained in terms of the specific landscape surrounding the 6th c. fortified sites in the Balkans. Hence, the small number of agricultural tools found in Caričin Grad, in sharp contrast to the comparatively larger number of blacksmithing or carpentry tools, was related to the hilly and densely-forested hinterland of the city, with no signs of agricultural cultivation even during the centuries pre-dating its foundation.[71] Others have pointed out the causal link between the disappearance during the 5th c. of *villae rusticae*, and the drastic changes in the rural economy of the 6th c. Balkan provinces. Farming implements, such as mattocks and pick-axes, often of larger size than those of earlier periods, could be indications of this new economic profile, characterised by a drastic reduction of areas under cultivation, and by the emphasis placed on human labour, with little or no use of draught animals.[72]

A very different picture emerges from the examination of hoards from the third and fourth quadrants of the correspondence analysis plot. They produced a number of agricultural tool categories almost equal to that from late antique hoards, but of quite different quality. Mattocks of Henning's classes K4, K5, and K8 have been replaced by 'light' specimens of his classes K10 and K15, most typical for work in the early medieval vineyards.[73] Similarly, ploughshares of Henning's class A1 and C1 appear in great numbers (as many as 9 specimens in the Dălgopol hoard), often in combination with coulters of Henning's class E1—indicative of the cultivation of larger fields by means of ploughs with mouldboards, such as depicted in graffiti on the walls of the royal palace in Pliska, dated

---

[71] Popović (1990) 293 and (1994–1995) 69. There is a significantly smaller number of ploughshares from Early Byzantine than from Roman sites in the northern Balkans.

[72] Henning (1987) 79.

[73] Henning (1987) 83; Curta (1997) 220.

to the 9th c.[74] Ploughshares, especially where found in a great number of specimens, often appear together with socketed ard-shares of Central Asian origin, an association most typical for early medieval hoards found in north-eastern Bulgaria and south-eastern Romania.[75]

Spades and tanged shares in the form of spade irons (Henning's class F2) have also been regarded as indicators of a type of agriculture associated with the early medieval nomads.[76] To the same direction points the presence of scraping tools of Henning's class P2, the earliest European specimens of which are known from 8th to 9th c. assemblages of the Saltovo-Mayaki culture of southern Ukraine and Russia, which is commonly associated with the Khazar Qaganate.[77] It is therefore no surprise that hoards from the third and fourth quadrants combine agricultural tools with bridle bits and stirrups, as well as weapons typically associated with mounted shock combat, such as the spear-shaped battle axe from Shumen or axes of Bartošková's class III.[78] This is true not only for hoards, for which a medieval date may be advanced on the basis of the associated stirrups (fig. 8), but also for others, such as Shumen, Jelica, Montana 1, or Gamzigrad, which were until now believed to be of late antique date (Table 1).

Moreover, a late, possibly 9th c., date may be tentatively advanced for at least some of the hoards from the first quadrant, on the basis of the presence in such assemblages of such typically medieval items as axes of Bartošková's class III, 'ogribki', ploughshares of Henning's class A1 or 'light' mattocks (classes K9–11) (fig. 9).

If so, then such hoards have nothing to do with the Early Byzantine forts in which they were found, and must instead be attributed to the Early Medieval occupation of those sites, and are part of a phenomenon linked to the political, administrative and military changes taking place in 9th c. Bulgaria.

---

[74] Henning (1987) 49–69. With few exceptions, ploughshares of Henning's class A1 are not known from 6th c. assemblages in the Balkans.

[75] Curta (1997) 219.

[76] Vagarelski (1929); Henning (1987) 73. The earliest evidence of ards equipped with tanged shares comes from China under the Han dynasty—see Pleterski (1987) 275.

[77] Kovács (1981) 94. Along with various battle axes, scraping tools of Henning's class P2 may have served as markers of social status for burials of Khazar warriors of the so-called *afsad* class—see Afanas'ev (1993) 141–42.

[78] For spear-shaped axes, see Henning (1989) 91. On the use of such weapons, as well as of battle axes of Bartošková's classes II and III, in mounted combat, see Curta (1997) 225.

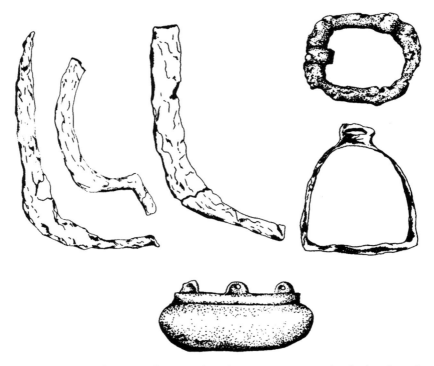

Fig. 8   Hoard of iron implements found in Troianov most (Serbia), selected
artefacts: sickle, scythes, belt buckle, stirrup, and censer.
(After Garašanin and Vašić (1987).)

FORTS

There are several conclusions to be drawn from the above discussion.
First, it appears that very little, if any, evidence exists for the presence of
large numbers of horsemen garrisoned in Balkan forts. According to Procopius, a commander of the cavalry cohorts stationed 'from ancient times'
at Tzurullum (present-day Çorlu, in Turkey) was defeated, captured, and
savagely executed by marauding Sclavenes in A.D. 549.[79] But Tzurullum
was a major city in the hinterland of Constantinople, and the presence of

---

[79] Procop. *Goth.* 7.38.5. The Sclavenes of A.D. 549 were probably horsemen, for Procopius calls them an 'army' (στράτευμα), a word he commonly uses for cavalry troops
(e.g., Procop. *Pers.* 1.12.6, 1.21.15, 2.4.4, Procop. *Vand.* 3.18.13). See Ivanov *et al.* (1991) 234.

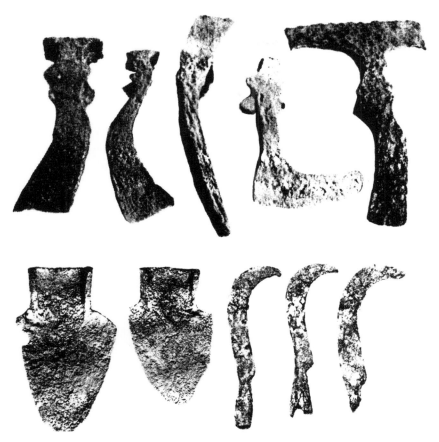

Fig. 9   Hoard of iron implements found in Razgrad (Bulgaria), selected artefacts:
     battle axes, ploughshares, and billknives. (After Ivanov and Stoianov (1985).)

cavalry troops there may be explained in connection with the defence of
the Anastasian Long Wall. There is nothing in the archaeological evidence
so far known from Çorlu that could be used either to confirm or to reject
Procopius' information.[80] But the much richer archaeological record of
6th c. forts in the northern Balkans is unambiguous: there were very
few, if any, cavalry units in Early Byzantine garrisons. No horsemen are
mentioned in the garrison of Asemus, which so much impressed Peter, the

---

[80] The only Early Byzantine remains from Çorlu known so far are the city walls, for
which see Pralong (1988) 185–86. For the archaeology of the Anastasian Long Wall: Crow
(2007) and (in this collection).

general at the head of the army sent by Emperor Maurice in A.D. 594 against the Sclavenes north of the Danube.[81] The evidence of weapons found on 6th c. fortified sites in the northern Balkans and discussed in the first part of this paper also suggests that the garrisons stationed there were made up of foot-soldiers, not horsemen.

But were those full-time soldiers, or were they peasants like those at Thermopylae, whom Procopius describes as suddenly becoming 'make-shift soldiers for the occasion', abandoning their agricultural occupations until Justinian replaced the inexperienced garrison with regular troops?[82] Some scholars have interpreted the archaeological evidence of 6th c. forti-fied settlements as indicating not military, but civilian sites.[83] According to Archibald Dunn, fortified hilltop sites in northern Greece offered shel-ter to the urban and rural populations fleeing the lowlands under the con-tinuous threat of barbarian raids.[84] Andrew Poulter denies the existence of any identity or even similarity between the hill-top sites in northern Balkans, which he regards as temporary refuges, and those "regularly built fortifications on the frontier, which more obviously performed a military role".[85] Chavdar Kirilov points to the archaeological evidence of agricul-tural occupations as an argument in favour of the idea that hilltop sites were fortified villages, not military forts.[86] Because of farming implements from hoards, Pernik, Shumen, and Odărci are therefore re-interpreted as defended villages, although, in all three cases, there is plenty of evidence of an early medieval occupation phase.[87]

---

[81] Theoph. Sim. 7.3.1–10.

[82] Procop. *Aed.* 4.10. For the archaeological evidence of a Justinianic garrison guarding the pass at Thermopylae, see Rosser (2001).

[83] Kirilov (2007) 333 with a critique of Ovcharov (1982). See also Milinković (2007) 166–79.

[84] Dunn (1997) 144; Dunn (2004) 551–52.

[85] Poulter (2004) 247, repeated verbatim in Poulter (2007) 380. While criticising others for being "too quick to assume that they [the fortified sites] all served a military func-tion", Poulter then hastily attributes the last phase of occupation on fortified sites in the northern Balkans to "newcomers arriving about 500 AD", either Slavs or other "nomadic migrants"—Poulter (2004) 248 and (2007) 381. As the archaeological evidence of the last phase of occupation has nothing in common with that of sites north of the Lower Danube attributed to the 6th c. Slavs, his remarks must be treated with extreme caution, especially his idea that the "Slav pottery does not exist or is exceedingly rare because the nomadic Slavs did not use it"—Poulter (2004) 250 and (2007) 382.

[86] Kirilov (2007) 333–35, on the basis of the results of Dimităr Nikolov's excavations at Mezideva, near Krăn, for which see Nikolov (1990). However, it is not clear from either whether the abundance of agricultural tools on the site must be dated to the 5th or to the 6th c. Judging by the numismatic evidence, Mezideva was flourishing *ca.* A.D. 400.

[87] Kirilov (2007) 337–38.

We have seen that the Shumen hoard has in fact been misdated, together with other assemblages such as Jelica and Gamzigrad. As for hoards securely dated to Late Antiquity, it is important to note that farming implements, especially those used in tillage (as opposed to those used for harvesting) represent only a small percentage of the entire assemblage: the Olympia hoard, dated with coins struck for Justinian and Justin II, includes 12 harvesting implements (5 bill knives and 7 sickles), but only 6 tilling tools (two mattocks and 4 pick-axes). None of those tilling tools may be associated with any form of large-scale cultivation, and some of them were instead a natural accompaniment to forest clearing activities. The Sliven hoard (with three mattocks, one pickaxe, and 7 drag-hoes) is the only assemblage in which tilling tools predominate. For Pernik, although its hoard produced a ploughshare, two drag-hoes, three mattocks, and a pick-axe, the largest number of items comprise tools for harvesting (4 bill-knives, one scythe and 8 sickles). The same is true for the Odărci and Stara Zagora 2 hoards, in which tools for harvesting, especially sickles and scythes, appear in much greater numbers than those for tilling. Despite the presence of mattocks and pick-axes, the Carevec, Tinje, and Voivoda hoards have produced more carpentry tools (especially chisels, wimbles, saws, burins, planes, and other carving tools) than either farming implements (for both tilling and harvesting) or weapons. The only hoard in which weapons predominate is Razgrad, which is probably not of late antique date.

Observation of the scattergram showing the relationships between artefact categories reveals the combination of tools and weapons underlying the structure of the late antique hoards. The cluster of hoards in the first quadrant is based on a combination of tilling (mattocks of Henning's classes K4 and K8, pick-axes of classes L1 and L2, drag-hoes of class K3, and ploughshares of class B3), harvesting (bill-knives of Henning's classes G1 and G2b, sickles of class H1, and scythes of class I2), and primarily carpentry tools (straight planes, wimbles and chisels). If fan-shaped axes were also used in carpentry, then the number of craftsman tool types is as large as that of tilling tool types. The 'grammar' of late antique hoards seems to be based on the conceptual association of vineyard or field harvesting with tilling. Judging from the tools themselves, the latter was an activity linked to work in the garden or on small fields, and cannot therefore serve for the identification of the function of any site as 'agricultural' and not 'military'.

The mattocks and pick-axes, as well as the sickles and bill-knives found in abundance in late antique hoards, fit very well within the picture of small-scale cultivation of crops either within or just outside the city or fort

walls. Large 'open spaces' existed, for example, on the northern side of the
Early Byzantine fort built in the south-eastern corner of the ancient city of
Nicopolis ad Istrum (Nikiup); there is no sign of large-scale grain cultivation, and the open spaces may have been used for garden cultivation of
millet and legumes.[88] Analysis of palaeobotanical assemblages from Iatrus
(Krivina) has revealed that the diet of the soldiers in the fort's garrison
consisted of oats and peas, both of which may have been cultivated on
site.[89] This is further substantiated by the evidence of written sources:
in 583, when attacking Singidunum by surprise, the Avars 'encountered
the majority of the city's inhabitants encamped in the fields, since the
harvest constrained them to do this; for it was summer season and they
were gathering in their subsistence'.[90]

However, there is also evidence to suggest that the small-scale cultivation on plots inside or outside city walls was not sufficient for the
subsistence of the relatively large number of people living inside 6th c.
hill-top sites. The distribution of 6th c. amphorae (particularly LR1, LR2,
and *spatheia*) on such sites in the Balkans has been interpreted as evidence of a state-run distribution of food supplies to the garrisons stationed in forts.[91] Palaeobotanical assemblages from the late 6th and early
7th c. military site at Svetinja comprised mixes of wheat, rye, barley, and
millet—an indication of supplies of corn coming from outside the military settlement, probably from neighbouring Viminacium, to which they
may have been shipped via the *annona*-like distributions signaled by finds
of Late Roman amphorae.[92] The author of the *Strategikon* recommends
that when campaigning north of the Danube River, in Sclavene territory,
Roman troops do not destroy provisions found in the surrounding countryside, but instead ship them on pack animals and boats 'to our own
country'.[93] That Roman soldiers needed to rely on food supplies captured
from the enemy suggests that there was no large-scale production of food
in or around the fortified sites in the Balkans. Similarly, the analysis of

---

[88] Poulter (1995) 166 and 181.

[89] Hajnalová (1982) 232. According to Beech (2007) 244 and 247, the analysis of 6th c.
samples from Nicopolis ad Istrum suggests "continued supply" of cereals, but it remains
unclear whether those were locally cultivated or brought to the site from afar.

[90] Theoph. Sim. 1.4.1–2 (trans. Whitby and Whitby (1986) 24–25). For a similar episode
in Thessalonica during the early years of Heraclius' reign, see the *Miracles of St. Demetrius*
2.2.199.

[91] Curta (2001b) 209–10. For LR1 amphorae as an indicator of *annona*-type distributions
to the army stationed in the northern Balkans, see Karagiorgou (2001).

[92] Borojević (1987) 67 and 70.

[93] *Strategikon* 11.4.8.

faunal remains from Iatrus shows that the soldiers in the garrison relied heavily on hunting for meat procurement.[94]

Even if some inhabitants of fortified sites in the 6th c. Balkan provinces of the empire turned to small-scale, garden cultivation of crops in order to supplement (insufficient or irregular?) *annona* distributions, no evidence exists that such activities were anything more than temporary or economically marginal. Hill-top sites in the Balkans may not have all been military, but none of them appears to have functioned as a fortified village. Behind or just outside the walls of the 6th c. forts, no agricultural occupations could be practised in such a way as to satisfy the needs of the existing population. The 'ruralisation' of the late antique Balkans must instead be understood as the militarisation of the countryside.

CONCLUSION

This discussion brings into focus a number of themes which have relevance to an understanding of the wider social issues underpinning the 6th c. changes in the settlement pattern of the empire's Balkan provinces. As part of the military strategy implemented by Emperor Justinian, a great number of fortified sites perched on hill-tops appeared almost everywhere in the Balkans. It is difficult to prioritise the various factors, since they must be considered interdependent. However, the lack of sufficient troops in the Balkans, the disappearance of the old administrative structure, especially of *civitates* and *provinciae*, and the need to provide an efficient response to devastating raids by barbarian horsemen—'Huns', Cutrigurs, or Avars—all contributed to the implementation of a vast program of fortification, the size of which the Balkans had never witnessed before. The picture to emerge from the evidence reviewed is one of "landscapes of *kastra*",[95] a conclusion supported by the relative paucity of weapons or military equipment of Avar inspiration in relation to the existence of large numbers of cavalry units permanently stationed in the Balkan provinces.

On the other hand, reflecting upon the specific range of farming implements discovered in hoard assemblages from Early Byzantine fortified

---

[94] Bartosiewicz and Choyke (1991) 191. The situation at Iatrus sharply contrasts that at Butrint (Albania) and Tinje (Slovenia), two sites on which early and mid-6th c. animal bone assemblages are dominated by pig, with no traces of game. See Powell (2004) 306 Table 17.1; Ciglenečki (2000) 167–71.

[95] Dunn (2004) 578.

sites, a more general tendency towards garden cultivation of small fields that could be tilled by hand, without the use of draught animals, seems to suggest that among 6th c. fortified sites, some, at least, had a civilian, and not military function. That distinction, however, is currently too ill-defined to be operational: the identification of certain fortified sites as 'military' is based on "the strengths of their fortifications, their relationships to lines of communication, and the edge of the plain, and on the presence of particular internal features"; conversely, civilian sites "do not in practical terms control the Plain, or its points of egress and entry, or its roads".[96]

In reality, no criteria currently exist to enable a clear-cut distinction between 'military' and 'civilian' fortified sites on the basis of the archaeological evidence alone. To the extent that all 6th c. sites in the Balkans had defensive walls, it is perhaps safer to assume that they were *all* 'military', despite the wide variation in the number and quality of troops stationed in every one of them. Moreover, the sheer number of forts precludes the possibility that some of them were fortified villages meant to supply the others with food. There is simply no evidence of a settlement hierarchy in the 6th c. Balkans, which could possibly mirror the distinction currently, but artificially, drawn between various hilltop sites. The agrarian technology revealed by the analysis of hoards is one of limited resources, which could in no way be linked to a self-sufficient rural economy. Since the size of the fields is dependant on the implements being used to till them, one might ask how it was possible to feed the population—military or otherwise—living within the ramparts of the numerous 6th c. Balkan forts.

The emerging picture is one of contrasting lines of development. On one hand, the great number of forts must have created an enormous demand for food supplies, even if we allow for the possibility that not all forts were permanently occupied. On the other hand, there is now clear evidence of a generalised collapse of the rural economy.[97] Whether or not the garrisons of 6th c. forts were made up of 'makeshift soldiers for the occasion', by A.D. 500 there were certainly fewer peasants in the Balkans than in 400, and virtually no peasants at all by 600. If hoards of iron implements and weapons are to be regarded as evidence of civilian sites with agricultural

---

[96] Dunn (2004) 551–52.
[97] Curta (2001b). The much rosier picture in Dunn (2005) can hardly apply to the 6th c. Much closer to reality seems to be Dunn (2004) 579: "A countryside largely divided between supposedly self-sufficient, but actually impoverished, *kastra*, albeit of diverse origins, was a stagnant and probably disaffected one".

functions, it is perhaps no accident that such hoards were found inside forts without 'open spaces', in which very little room was left for the possible garden cultivation of small fields. Unless we assume that the agricultural tools found in hoards were employed for working on fields outside the fort walls, there is no way to solve the contradiction between the concept of many, overcrowded forts providing shelter for the rural population from the lowlands, and the absence of any material culture indicators of a vibrant rural economy capable of feeding the inhabitants of forts.

So, were forts built as refuges or were they part of a much broader strategy of immediate response to barbarian raids from across the Danube frontier of the empire? The idea that Justinian's programme of fortification in the Balkans was based on a defence-in-depth strategy has been vehemently rejected by some or hesitantly accepted by others.[98] Instead of debating whether the concept of 'defence in depth' had any application in the 6th c., it may be wiser to give the last word to the author of the *Strategikon*, that savvy Roman army officer with a good knowledge of the situation on the frontier of the empire:

> If an enemy force, superior in strength or even equal to ours, invades our country, especially at the beginning of the invasion, we must be sure not to engage it in pitched battle. We should instead carefully lay ambushes by day or by night, block the route it is taking, seize strong points beforehand, destroy supplies along its line of march... All necessary supplies must be collected in very strong fortresses... Forts which are not in a strong natural setting should be made more secure. Part of the army, depending on the progress of the fighting, should be assigned to their defence. Preparations should be made to transfer the inhabitants of weaker places to more strongly fortified ones. (*Strategikon* 10.2).

Acknowledgements

I wish to acknowledge the contribution of the two anonymous readers to the final version of this chapter. Although I disagree with both of them on almost every aspect of interpretation, their comments and recommendations helped sharpen the focus of this research and have forced me to re-think some of the implications of my conclusions.

---

[98] Poulter (2007) 380: "There exists no evidence whatsoever that imperial Roman or Early Byzantine policy adhered to the principle of defence in depth". Meanwhile, Crow (2007) refers to the Anastasian Long Wall as the 'final frontier'.

Table 1. Re-dating of the hoards found on Early Byzantine sites

Hoard	Previous dating	New dating
Balajnac	Late antique (6th c.)	Late antique (6th c.)
Carevec	Late antique (6th c.)	Late antique (6th c.)
Caričin Grad	Late antique (6th c.–7th c.)	Late antique (6th–7th c.)
Odărci	Late antique (7th c.)	Late antique (5th–6th c.)
Olympia	Late antique (6th–7th c.)	Late antique (6th–7th c.)
Pernik	Late antique (5th–6th c.)	Late antique (5th–6th c.)
Sliven	Late antique (5th–6th c.)	Late antique (5th–6th c.)
Zheglica	Late antique (6th c.)	Late antique (6th c.)
Stara Zagora 1	Late antique (6th c.)	Late antique (6th c.)
Gamzigrad	Late antique (5th–6th c.)	Early medieval (9th–10th c.)
Jelica	Late antique (6th–7th c.)	Early medieval (9th–10th c.)
Montana 1	Late antique (5th–6th c.)	Early medieval (9th–10th c.)
Razgrad	Late antique (5th–6th c.)	Early medieval (9th–10th c.)
Shumen	Late antique (5th–6th c.)	Early medieval (9th–10th c.)
Stara Zagora 2	Late antique (5th–6th c.)	Early medieval (9th–10th c.)
Strezhevo	Late antique (7th c.)	Early medieval (10th–11th c.)
Tinje	Late antique (5th–6th c.)	Early medieval (8th–9th c.)
Voivoda	Late antique (5th–6th c.)	Early medieval (9th–10th c.)
Dolishte	Early medieval (9th–10th c.)	Early medieval (9th–10th c.)
Montana 2	Early medieval (9th–10th c.)	Early medieval (9t–10th c.)
Troianov most 1	Early medieval (10th–11th c.)	Early medieval (10th–11th c.)
Troianov most 2	Early medieval (9th–10th c.)	Early medieval (9th–10th c.)
Asenovgrad	Early medieval (8th–9th c.)	Late antique (5th–6th c.)

BIBLIOGRAPHY

Primary Sources

Const. Porph. *DAI* = Moravcsik G. and Jenkins R. J. H. (1967) edd. Constantine Porphyrogenitus, *De administrando imperio* (Washington 1967).

Menander = Blockley R. C. (1985) ed. and trans. *The History of Menander the Guardsman*
(Liverpool 1985).

Miracles of St. Demetrius = Lemerle P. (1979–81) *Les plus anciens recueils des miracles de
Saint Démétrius et la pénétration des Slaves dans les Balkans* (Paris 1979–81).

Procop. *Goth.*, Procop. *Vand.*, Procop. *Pers.* = Dewing H. B. (1914–54) ed. and trans. Procopius, *History of the Wars 1–5* (Cambridge, Mass. and London 1914–54).

Procop. *Aed.* = Dewing H. B. (1914–54) ed. and trans. Procopius, *Buildings 7* (Cambridge,
Mass. and London 1914–54).

Sebeos = Thomson R. V., Howard-Johnston J. D. and Greenwood T. (1999) trans., comm.
and notes. *The Armenian History Attributed to Sebeos* (Translated Texts for Historians
31) (Liverpool 1999).

Strategikon = Dennis G. T. (1984) trans. *Maurice's Strategikon: Handbook of Byzantine Military Strategy* (Philadelphia 1984).

Theoph. Sim. = Whitby M. and M. (1986) trans. *The History of Theophylact Simocatta: an English Translation with Introduction and Notes* (Oxford 1986).

Secondary Works

Afanas'ev G. E. (1993) "Sistema social'no-markiruiushchikh predmetov v muzhskikh pogrebal'nikh kompleksakh Donskikh alan", *Rossiiskaia Arkheologiia* 4 (1993) 131–44.

Agallopoulou P. (1975) "Ladochori Igoumenitsas", *ArchDelt* 30.2 (1975) 239.

Aibabin A. I. (1974) "Stremena Pereshchepinskogo tipa", *Soobshcheniia Gosudarstvennogo Ermitazha* 39 (1974) 32–34.

—— (1985) "Pogrebanie khazarskogo voina", *Sovetskaia Arkheologiia* 3 (1985) 191–205.

Aleksandrov G. (1977) "Rezultati ot razkopkite na 'Kaleto' v Mikhailovgrad", *Izvestiia na Muzeite v Severozapadna Bălgariia* 1 (1977) 267–92.

—— (1987) "Rezultati ot razkopkite na krepostta Montana (1971–1982)", in *Montana*, ed. V. Velkov (Sofia 1987) 54–85.

Aleksiev I. (1976) "Nakhodka na orădiia na truda i văorăzhenie ot Carevec", *Muzei i pametnici na kulturata* 16.2 (1976) 33–36.

Ambroz A. K. (1973) "Stremena i sedla rannego srednevekov'ia kak khronologicheskii pokazatel' (IV–VIII v.)", *Sovetskaia Arkheologiia* 4 (1973) 81–98.

—— (1982) "O Voznesenskom komplekse VIII v. na Dnepre—vopros interpretacii", in *Drevnosti epokhi velikogo pereseleniia narodov V–VIII vekov. Sovetsko-vengerskii sbornik*, edd. A. K. Ambroz and I. Erdélyi (Moscow 1982) 204–22.

Antonova V. (1973) "Arkheologicheksi prouchvaniia na Shumenskata krepost", *Izvestiia na Narodniia muzei Shumen* 6 (1973) 127–58.

—— (1975) "Grad Shumen do XI vek (V svetlinata na arkheologicheskite prouchvaniia)", *Vekove* 4.6 (1975) 22–30.

—— (1985) "Shumenskata krepost prez rannoto srednovekovie (VII–X v.) (obsht obzor)", *Godishnik na muzeite ot Severna Bălgariia* 11 (1985) 55–63.

Atanasov G. (2004) "De nouveau sur la localisation de la forteresse bas-byzantine St. Cyril en Scythie Mineure", in *Prinos lui Petre Diaconu la 80 de ani* (Brăila 2004) 405–11.

Bachrach B. S. (1984) "A picture of Avar-Frankish warfare from a Carolingian Psalter of the early ninth century in light of the Strategikon", *Archivum Eurasiae Medii Aevi* 4 (1984) 5–27.

Bálint Cs. (1992) "Kontakte zwischen Iran, Byzanz und der Steppe. Das Grab von Üç Tepe (Sowj. Azerbajdžan) und der beschlagverzierte Gürtel im 6. und 7. Jahrhundert", in *Awarenforschungen*, ed. F. Daim (Vienna 1992) 309–496.

—— (1993) "Probleme der archäologischen Forschung zur awarischen Landnahmen", in *Ausgewählte Probleme europäischer Landnahmen des Früh- und Hochmittelalters*, edd. M. Müller-Wille and R. Schneider (Sigmaringen 1993) 195–273.

Barački S. (1960) "Grupni nalazi starosrpskog gvozdenog alata iz Vršaca", *Rad Vojvodanskih Muzeja* 9 (1960) 186–95.

Bartosiewicz L. and Choyke A. M. (1991) "Animal remains from the 1970–1972 excavations of Iatrus (Krivina), Bulgaria", *ActaArchHung* 43 (1991) 181–209.

Bartošková A. (1986) *Slovanské depoty železných předmětů v Československu* (Prague 1986).

Bavant B. (1990) "Les petits objets", in *Caričin Grad II. Le quartier sud-ouest de la ville haute*, edd. B. Bavant, V. Kondić and J.-M. Spieser (Belgrade and Rome 1990) 191–257.

Beech M. (2007) "The environmental archaeology research programme at Nicopolis: methodology and results", in *The Transition to Late Antiquity: on the Danube and Beyond*, ed. A. G. Poulter (Proceedings of the British Academy 141) (Oxford 2007) 219–48.

Bejan A. (1976) "Un atelier metalurgic de la Drobeta-Turnu Severin", *Acta Musei Napocensis* 13 (1976) 257–68.

Bikić V. (1997) "Srednjovekovna trapezna keramika sa Gamzigrada", in *Arheologija istočne Srbije. Zbornik radova*, ed. D. Srejović (Belgrade 1997) 319–24.

Blockley R. C. (1985) ed. and trans. *The History of Menander the Guardsman* (Liverpool 1985).

Bobcheva L. (1972) "Orădiia na truda ot srednovekovieto v muzeia v Tolbukhin", *Muzei i pametnici na kulturata* 12. 2 (1972) 9–12.

Bølviken E., Ricka Helskog E., Helskog K., Holm-Olsen I. M., Solheim L. and Bertelsen R. (1982) "Correspondence analysis: an alternative to principal components", *WorldArch* 14 (1982) 41–60.

Borojević K. (1987) "Analiza ugljenisanog semenja sa lokaliteta Svetinja", *Starinar* 38 (1987) 65–71.

Bugarski I. (2005) "A contribution to the study of lamellar armours", *Starinar* 55 (2005) 161–79.

——— (2007) "Ostava iz Strezheva: uzengije u ranovizantijskom kontekstu", in *Niš and Byzantium. Vth Symposium, Niš, 3.–5. June 2006. The Collection of Scientific Works 5*, ed. M. Rakocija (Niš 2007) 251–67.

Bury J. B. (1906) "The treatise *De Administrando Imperio*", *ByzZeit* 15 (1906) 517–77.

Čermanović-Kuzmanović A. (2004) *Tekija* (Belgrade 2004).

Changova I. (1992) *Krepostta Pernik VIII–XIV v.* (Pernik 3) (Sofia 1992).

Cholakov I. M. and Ilieva P. (2005) "Ein Hortfund von Metallgegenständen der frühbyzan-tinischen Epoche aus Stara Zagora (Südostbulgarien)", *Archaeologia Bulgarica* 9.3 (2005) 53–85.

Cholakova A. (2005) "Rannovizantiiksi kompleks ot zhelezni sechiva i predmeti ot Odărci (aspekti v izsledvaneto na koletivnite nakhodki)", *Arkheologiia* 46 (2005) 147–58.

Ciglenečki S. (2000) *Tinje nad Loko pri Žusmu. Poznoantična in zgodnjesrednjeveška naselbina* (Ljubljana 2000).

Cirkin A. V. (1972) "Shokshinskii mogil'nik", *Sovetskaia Arkheologiia* 1 (1972) 155–70.

Conchev D. (1950) "Prinos kăm bălgarskata materialna kultura", *Izvestiia na Arkheolog-icheskiia Institut* 17 (1950) 298–305.

Čorović-Ljubinković M. (1954) "L'encensoir des environs de Kuršumlja", *ArchIug* 1 (1954) 83–89.

——— (1956) "Ranokhrishtjanska kadionica iz Pepeljevca", in *Konzervatorski i ispitivachki radovi*, ed. M. Panić-Surep (Belgrade 1956) 139–40.

Crow J. (2007) "The Anastasian Wall and the Lower Danube frontier before Justinian", in *The Lower Danube in Antiquity (VI c. B.C.–VI c. AD): International Archaeological Conference, Bulgaria-Tutrakan, 6.–7.10.2005*, ed. L. Vagalinski (Sofia 2007) 397–410.

Csallány D. (1958) "Szabolcs-Szatmár megye avar leletei", *Jósa András Múzeum Evkönyve* 1 (1958) 31–87.

——— (1958–59) "A hajdúdorogi avar mellpáncél", *A Debreceni Déri Múzeum Évkönyve* 35 (1958–59) 17–23.

——— (1969–71) "Avar páncélok a Kárpát-medenceben", *Jósa András Múzeum Evkönyve* 12–14 (1969–71) 7–44.

——— (1982) "Avar kori páncélok a Kárpát-medenceben", *Jósa András Múzeum Evkönyve* 15–17 (1982) 5–12.

Csiky G. (2007) "A kora avar lándzsák tipológiája", *Archaeologiai Értesitő* 132.1 (2007) 305–23.

Curta F. (1997) "Blacksmiths, warriors and tournaments of value: dating and interpreting early medieval hoards of iron implements in Eastern Europe", *Ephemeris Napocensis* 7 (1997) 211–68.

——— (2001a) *The Making of the Slavs: History and Archaeology of the Lower Danube Region, c. 500–700* (Cambridge Studies in Medieval Life and Thought 52) (Cambridge and New York 2001).

——— (2001b) "Peasants as 'makeshift soldiers for the occasion': sixth-century settlement patterns in the Balkans", in *Urban Centers and Rural Contexts in Late Antiquity*, edd. T. S. Burns and J. W. Eadie (East Lansing 2001) 199–217.

—— (2008a) "The earliest Avar-age stirrups, or the 'stirrup controversy' revisited", in *The Other Europe in the Middle Ages: Avars, Bulgars, Khazars, and Cumans*, ed. F. Curta (East Central and Eastern Europe in the Middle Ages 450–1450 2) (Leiden and Boston 2008) 297–326.

—— (2008b) "The northwestern region of the Black Sea during the sixth and early seventh centuries", *Ancient West & East* 7 (2008) 149–85.

Daim F. (2003) "Avars and Avar archaeology", in Regna *and* Gentes: *the Relationships between Late Antique and Early Medieval Peoples and Kingdoms in the Transformation of the Roman World*, edd. H.-W. Goetz, J. Jarnut and W. Pohl (Transformation of the Roman World 13) (Leiden and Boston 2003) 463–570.

Damianov S. (1976) "Prouchvaniia na sgrada no. 8 ot kăsnoantichniia grad pri s. Voivoda, Shumensko", *Godishnik na muzeite ot Severna Bălgariia* 2 (1976) 17–27.

Dennis G. T. (1984) trans. *Maurice's Strategikon: Handbook of Byzantine Military Strategy* (Philadelphia 1984).

Deroko A. and Radojčić S. (1950) "Otkopavanje Carichina grada 1947 godine", *Starinar* 1 (1950) 119–42.

DeVries K. (1998) *Medieval Military Technology* (Peterborough 1998).

Dimitrov D. P., Chichikova M., Sultov B. and Dimitrova A. (1965) "Arkheologicheskie raskopki v vostochnom sektore Nove v 1963 godu", *Izvestiia na Arkheologicheskiia Institut* 28 (1965) 43–62.

Doncheva-Petkova L. (1986) "Selishte ot vremeto na Părvoto bălgarsko carstvo pri s. Odărci, Tolbukhinski okrăg", in *Zbornik posveten na Boshko Babich. Mélange Boško Babić 1924–1984* (Prilep 1986) 165–68.

Dunn A. W. (1997) "Stages in the transition from the late antique to the Middle Byzantine urban centre in southern Macedonia and southern Thrace", in *Aphieroma ston N. G. L. Hammond*, (Etaireia Makedonikon Spoudon) (Thessalonica 1997) 137–50.

—— (2004) "Continuity and change in the Macedonian countryside from Gallienus to Justinian", in *Recent Research on the Late Antique Countryside*, edd. W. Bowden, L. Lavan and C. Machado (Late Antique Archaeology 2) (Leiden and Boston 2004) 535–86.

—— (2005) "The problem of the Early Byzantine village in eastern and northern Macedonia", in *Les villages dans l'empire byzantin, IVe-XVe siècles*, edd. J. Lefort, C. Morrisson and J.-P. Sodini (Paris 2005) 267–78.

Dzhambov Kh. (1956) "Rannokhristiianska cărkva pri s. Isperikhovo, Peshterska okoliia", *Godishnik na Narodniia Arkheologicheski Muzei Plovdiv* 2 (1956) 175–92.

Dzhingov G. (1966) "Prinos kăm materialnata kultura na Preslav i negovata okolnost", *Arkheologiia* 8, no. 2 (1966) 42–58.

Fábián G. J. and Ricz P. (1991) "Ujabb adatok az avarok úgynevezett reflex íjáról (Ijtanulmány a bácskai avar kori leletek alapján)", *A Herman Otto Múzeum Évkönyve* 30–31.2 (1991) 127–40.

Ferluga J. (1978) *L'amministrazione bizantina in Dalmazia* (2nd ed., Venice 1978).

Fine J. V. A. (2000) "Croats and Slavs: theories about the historical circumstances of the Croats' appearance in the Balkans", *Byzantinische Forschungen* 26 (2000) 205–18.

Freeden U. v. (1991) "Awarische Funde in Süddeutschland?", *JRGZM* 38 (1991) 593–627.

Gabričević M. (1986) "Rtkovo—Glamija I—une forteresse de la Basse époque. Fouilles de 1980–1982", *Đerdapske sveske* 3 (1986) 71–91.

Gaitzsch W. (2005) *Eisenfunde aus Pergamon. Geräte, Werkzeuge und Waffen* (Berlin and New York 2005).

Garam É. (1990) "Bemerkungen zum ältesten Fundmaterial der Awarenzeit", in *Typen der Ethnogenese unter besonderer Berücksichtigung der Bayern*, edd. H. Friesinger and F. Daim (Vienna 1990) 253–72.

—— (1992) "Die münzdatierten Gräber der Awarenzeit", in *Awarenforschungen*, ed. F. Daim (Vienna 1992) 135–250.

—— (2000) "Über die Beziehung der byzantinischen Goldschnallen und der awarenzeitlichen Pseudoschnallen", in *Kontakte zwischen Iran, Byzanz und der Steppe im 6.-7. Jahrhundert*, ed. Cs. Bálint (Varia Archaeologica Hungarica 10) (Budapest 2000) 215–28.

—— (2001) *Funde byzantinischer Herkunft in der Awarenzeit vom Ende des 6. bis zum Ende des 7. Jahrhunderts* (Budapest 2001).

Garašanin M. and Vašić M. (1987) "*Castrum* Pontes. Izveshtaj o iskopavanjima u 1981. i 1982. godina", *Đerdapske sveske* 4 (1987) 71–116.

Gavritukhin I. O. (2001) "Evoluciia vostochnoevropeiskikh psevdopriazhek", in *Kul'tury Evraziiskikh stepei vtoroi poloviny I tysiacheletiia n.e. (iz istorii kostiuma)*, edd. D. A. Stashenkov, A. F. Kochkina and L. V. Kuznetsova (Samara 2001) 31–86.

—— (2006) "La date du 'trésor' de Pereščepina et la chronologie des antiquités de l'époque de formation du Khaganat khazar", in *La Crimée entre Byzance et le Khaganat Khazar*, ed. C. Zuckerman (Monographies du Centre de recherche d'histoire et civilisation de Byzance 25) (Paris 2006) 13–30.

Gavritukhin I. O. and Oblomskii A. M. (1996) *Gaponovskii klad i ego kul'turno-istoricheskii kontekst* (Moscow 1996).

Georgieva S. (1961) "Srednovekovnoto selishte nad razvalinite na antichniia grad Abritus", *Izvestiia na Arkheologicheskiia Institut* 24 (1961) 9–36.

Gerasimov T. (1946) "Nakhodki v razvalinite na rannovizantiiskogo gradishche pri s. Zheglica", *Izvestiia na Arkheologicheskiia Institut* 15 (1946) 203–205.

Goldina R. D. and Vodolago N. V. (1990) *Mogil'niki Nevolinskoi kul'tury v Priural'e* (Irkutsk 1990).

Goldstein I. (2005) "Discontinuity/continuity in Croatian history from the sixth to the ninth century", in *L'Adriatico della tarda Antichità all'età carolingia. Atti del convegno di studio Brescia 11–13 ottobre 2001*, edd. G. Brogiolo and P. Delogu (Rome 2005) 195–211.

Grinchenko V. A. (1950) "Pam'iatka VIII st. kolo s. Voznesenky na Zaporizhzhi", *Arkheolohiia* 2 (1950) 37–63.

Hajnalová E. (1982) "Archäobotanische Funde aus Krivina", in *Iatrus-Krivina: Spätantike Befestigung und frühmittelalterliche Siedlung an der unteren Donau* (Berlin 1982) 207–35.

Haldon J. F. (2002) "Some aspects of Early Byzantine arms and armour", in *A Companion to Medieval Arms and Armour*, ed. D. Nicolle (Woodbridge and Rochester 2002) 65–80.

Hampel J. (1905) *Alterthümer des frühen Mittelalters in Ungarn* (Braunschweig 1905).

Härke H. and Belinskii A. (2000) "Nouvelles fouilles de 1994–1996 dans la nécropole de Klin Yar", in *Les sites archéologiques en Crimée et au Caucase durant l'Antiquité tardive et le Haut Moyen Age*, edd. M. Kazanski and V. Soupault (Leiden and Boston 2000) 193–210.

Heinrich-Tamáska O. (2005) *Studien zu den awarenzeitlichen Tauschierarbeiten* (Innsbruck 2005).

Henning J. (1986) "Bulgarien zwischen Antike und Mittelalter im Spiegel der Wirtschaftsarchäologie", *Das Altertum* 32.2 (1986) 100–12.

—— (1987) *Südosteuropa zwischen Antike und Mittelalter: Archäologische Beiträge zur Landwirtschaft des I. Jahrtausends u. Z.* (Berlin 1987).

—— (1989) "Vostochnoe po proiskhozhdeniiu oruzhie i snariazhenie vsadnikov v kladakh sel'skokhoziaistvennykh zheleznykh izdelii v iugo-vostochnoi Evrope (VIII–X vv.)", *Problemi na prabălgarskata istoriia i kultura* 1 (1989) 87–104.

—— (2007) ed. *Post-Roman Towns, Trade, and Settlement in Europe and Byzantium*, 2 vols. (Berlin and New York 2007).

Herrmann J. (1992) "Karasura 1981–1991. Zu den bisherigen Ergebnissen von Ausgrabungen und Forschungsarbeiten in Südthrakien zwischen Stara Zagora und Plovdiv", *ZfA* 26 (1992) 153–80.

Hofer N. (1996) "Bewaffnung und Kriegstechnologie der Awaren", in *Reitervölker aus dem Osten. Hunnen und Awaren. Burgenländische Landesausstellung 1996. Schloß Halbturn, 26. April-31. Oktober 1996*, edd. F. Daim, K. Kaus and P. Tomka (Eisenstadt 1996) 351–54.

Iotov V. (2004) *Văorăzhenieto i snariazhenieto ot bălgarskoto srednovekovie (VII–XI v.)* (Varna 2004).

—— (2007) "Otnosno datirovkata na sbornata nakhodka ot Strezhevo, Bitolsko", *Problemi na prabălgarskata istoriia i kultura* 4.2 (2007) 171–80.

Iurukova I. (1992) "Trouvailles monétaires de Sadovetz", in *Die spätantike Befestigungen von Sadovec. Ergebnisse der deutsch-bulgarisch-österreichischen Ausgrabungen 1934–1937*, ed. S. Uenze (Munich 1992) 279–333.

Ivanišević V. and Špehar P. (2005) "Early Byzantine finds from Čečan and Gornji Streoc (Kosovo)", *Starinar* 55 (2005) 133–59.

Ivanov S. A., Gindin L. A. and Cymburskii V. L. (1991) "Prokopii Kesariiskii", in *Svod drevneishikh pis'mennykh izvestii o slavianakh*, edd. L. A. Gindin, S. A. Ivanov and G. G. Litavrin (Moscow 1991) 170–249.

Ivanov T. and Stoianov S. (1985) *Abritus: its History and Archaeology* (Razgrad 1985).

Izmailov I. L. (1990) "Poiavlenie i rannaia istoriia stremian v Srednem Povolzh'e", in *Voennoe delo drevnego i srednevekogo naseleniia Severnoi i Central'noi Azii. Sbornik nauchnykh trudov*, edd. Iu. S. Khudiakov and Iu. A. Plotnikov (Novosibirsk 1990) 61–70.

Janakievski T. (1980) "Kale, s. Strezhevo-Bitolsko (izveshtaj od zashtito arkheoloshko istrazhuvanie)", *Macedoniae Acta Archaeologica* 6 (1980) 97–110.

Janković Đ. *Podunavski deo oblasti Akvisa u VI i pochetkom VII veka* (Belgrade 1981).

Jakšić N. (1984) "Constantine Porphyrogenetus as the source for destruction of Salona", *Vjesnik za arheologiju i historiju Dalmatinsku* 77 (1984) 315–26.

Jeremić M. (1995) "Balajnac, agglomération protobyzantine fortifiée", *Antiquité Tardive* 3 (1995) 193–207.

Jeremić M. and Milinković M. (1995) "Die byzantinische Festung von Bregovina (Südserbien)", *Antiquité Tardive* 3 (1995) 209–25.

Karagiorgou O. (2001) "LR2: a container for the military annona on the Danubian border?", in *Economy and Exchange in the East Mediterranean during Late Antiquity: Proceedings of a Conference at Somerville College, Oxford—29th May, 1999*, edd. S. Kingsley and M. Decker (Oxford 2001) 129–66.

Kirilov Ch. (2007) "Der rissig gewordene Limes. Höhensiedlungen im östlichen Balkan als Zeugnis für die Schwache des oströmischen Reiches in der Spätantike", in *The Lower Danube in Antiquity (VI c. B.C.–VI c. AD): International Archaeological Conference, Bulgaria-Tutrakan, 6.–7.10.2005*, ed. L. Vagalinski (Sofia 2007) 329–52.

Klaić N. (1990) *Povijest Hrvata u srednjem vijeku* (Zagreb 1990).

Kleemann O. (1956) "Samländische Funde und die Frage der ältesten Steigbügel in Europa", in *Documenta archaeologica Wolfgang La Baume dedicata 8.II.1955* (Bonn 1956) 109–22.

Kolias T. (1988) *Byzantinische Waffen* (Vienna 1988).

Kouzov Kh. (2000) "A find of medieval iron objects from the fortress near the village of Dolishte, Varna district (Bulgarian Black Sea coast)", *Archaeologia Bulgarica* 4.2 (2000) 85–91.

Kovačević J. (1966) "Avari na Jadranu", in *Referati sa simpozijuma praistorijske i srednjevjekovne sekcije Arheološkog Društva Jugoslavije*, ed. N. Tašić (Belgrade 1966) 53–81.

Kovács L. (1981) "Der landnahmezeitliche Grabfunde von Hajdúböszörmeny-Erdős tanya", *ActaArchHung* 33 (1981) 81–103.

Kovrig I. (1955) "Contribution au problème de l'occupation de l'Hongrie par les Avares", *ActaArchHung* 6 (1955) 163–92.

—— (1963) *Das awarenzeitliche Gräberfeld von Alattyán* (Budapest 1963).

Kukharenko Iu. V. (1952) "Novopokrovskii mogil'nik i poseleniia", *Arkheolohiia* 6 (1952) 33–50.

Kurnatowska Z. and Mamzer H. (2007) "Ergebnisse und Erfahrungen aus den polnischen Untersuchungen", in *Post-Roman Towns, Trade, and Settlement in Europe and Byzantium*, 2 vols., ed. J. Henning (Berlin and New York 2007) 527–42.

Lalović A. (1985) "Gamzigrad/Romuliana", *Arheološki pregled* (1985) 164–65.

Lazaridis P. (1965) "Nea Anchialos", *ArchDelt* 20, no. 2 (1965) 326–34.

Liubenova V. (1981) "Selishteto ot rimskata i rannovizantiiskata epokha", in *Pernik I. Poselishten zhivot na khălma Krakra ot V khil. pr. n. e. do VI v. na n. e.*, ed. T. Ivanov (Sofia 1981) 107–203.

L'vova Z. A. (2000) "Pogrebeniia v Maloi Pereshchepine i Voznesenke i Kubrat, kagan Velikoi Bulgarii", *Stratum* 5 (2000) 145–60.

Majewski K., Press L., Kolkuna S., Sokhatski Z., Tabash Z., Shubevt V. and Kolendo J. (1974) "Arkheologicheski izledvaniia v zapadniia sektor na Nove", *Izvestiia na Arkheologicheskiia Institut* 34 (1974) 176–203.

Mano-Zisi Đ. (1958) "Iskopavanja na Carichinom Gradu 1955 i 1956 godine", *Starinar* 7–8 (1958) 311–28.

Margetić L. (2001) *Dolazak Hrvata* (Split 2001).

Marjanović-Vujović G. (1987) "Pontes-Traianov most. Sredniovekovna ostava B", *Đerdapske sveske* 4 (1987) 136–42.

Marović I. (1984) "Reflexions about the year of the destruction of Salona", *Vjesnik za arheologiju i historiju Dalmatinsku* 77 (1984) 293–314.

—— (2006) "O godini razorenja Salone", *Vjesnik za arheologiju i historiju Dalmatinsku* 99 (2006) 253–72.

Marušić B. (1962) "Neki nalazi iz vremena seobe naroda u Istri", *Jadranski zbornik* 5 (1962) 159–75.

Mazhitov N. A. (1990) "Kompleksy s monetami VIII v. iz Birskogo mogil'nika", *Sovetskaia Arkheologiia* 1 (1990) 261–66.

Mikulčić I. (2002) (ed. M. Konrad) *Spätantike und frühbyzantinische Befestigungen in Nordmakedonien: Städte-Vici-Refugien- Kastelle* (Munich 2002).

Milenković M. (1997) "Kostol-Pontes u XI–XII veku", in *Slavianskii srednevekovyi gorod*, ed. V. V. Sedov (Moscow 1997) 243–51.

Milinković M. (1995) "Die Gradina auf dem Jelica-Gebirge und die frühbyzantinischen Befestigungen in der Umgebung von Čačak, Westserbien", *Antiquité Tardive* 3 (1995) 227–50.

—— (2001) "Die byzantinische Höhenanlage auf der Jelica in Serbien—ein Beispiel aus dem nördlichen Illyricum des 6. Jh.", *Starinar* 51 (2001) 71–133.

—— (2006) "Osvrt na nalaze vremena seobe naroda sa juga Srbije i iz susednikh oblasti", in *Niš and Byzantium. IV Symposium, Niš, 3–5 June 2005: the Collection of Scientific Works 4*, ed. M. Rakocija (Niš 2006) 245–63.

—— (2007) "Stadt oder 'Stadt': frühbyzantinische Siedlungsstrukturen im nördlichen Illyricum", in *Post-Roman Towns: Trade and Settlement in Europe and Byzantium*, 2 vols., ed. J. Henning (Berlin and New York 2007) 159–91.

Milošević G. (1987) "Ranovizantijska arhitektura na Svetinji u Kostolcu", *Starinar* 38 (1987) 39–57.

Müller R. (1996) "Die Awaren und die Landwirtschaft", in *Reitervölker aus dem Osten. Hunnen und Awaren. Burgenländische Landesausstellung 1996: Schloß Halbturn, 26. April-31. Oktober 1996*, edd. F. Daim, K. Kaus and P. Tomka (Eisenstadt 1996) 365–71.

Mutafchiev P. (1914) "Sondazhi pri s. Chelopech", *Izvestiia na Varnenskoto arkheologichesko druzhestvo* 4 (1914) 264–66.

Nagy G. (1901) "Sírleletek a régibb középkorból III. Némedi (Tolna m.)", *Archaeologiai Értesítő* 21 (1901) 314–18.

Nagy K. (2005) "Notes on the arms of the Avar heavy cavalry", *ActaOrHung* 58 (2005) 135–48.

Nielsen K. H. (1988) "Correspondence analysis applied to hoards and graves of the Germanic Iron Age", in *Multivariate Archaeology: Numerical Approaches to Scandinavian Archaeology*, ed. T. Madsen (Aarhus 1988) 37–54.

Nikolov D. (1990) "Mezideva: a Thracian settlement in Late Antiquity", *Terra antiqua balcanica* 5 (1990) 166–72.

Nikolov D. and Kalchev K. (1986) "Razkopki na obekt 'Mladezhki dom' v Stara Zagora prez 1982 g.", *Izvestiia na muzeite ot Iugoiztochna Bălgariia* 9 (1986) 39–66.

Novaković R. (1972) "Neka zapazhanja o 29. i 30. glavi De administrando imperio", *Istorijski časopis* 19 (1972) 5–54.

Ovcharov D. (1982) *Vizantiiski i bălgarski kreposti V–X vek* (Sofia 1982).

Petković S. (1995) *Rimski predmeti od kosti i roga sa teritorije Gornje Mezije* (Posebna izdanja 28) (Belgrade 1995).

Pillon M. (2005) "Armée et défense de l'Illyricum byzantin de Justinien à Héraclius (527–641). De la réorganisation justinienne l'émergence des 'armées de cité'", *Erytheia* 26 (2005) 7–85.

Pleterski A. (1987) "Sebenjski zaklad", *ArhVest* 38 (1987) 237–330.

Pohl W. (1988) *Die Awaren: Ein Steppenvolk im Mitteleuropa 567–822 n. Chr.* (Munich 1988).

——— (1995) "Osnove Hrvatske etnogeneze: Avari i Slaveni", in *Etnogeneza Hrvata*, ed. N. Budak (Zagreb 1995) 211–23.

Popović I. (1990) "Les activités professionnelles Caričin Grad vers la fin du VIᵉ et le début du VIIᵉ siècle d'après les outils de fer", in *Caričin Grad II: Le quartier sud-ouest de la ville haute*, edd. B. Bavant, V. Kondić and J.-M. Spieser (Belgrade and Rome 1990) 269–306.

——— (1994–1995) "Les particularités de l'outillage protobyzantin dans les Balkans du Nord", *Starinar* 45–46 (1994–95) 67–75.

Popović M. (1999) *Tvrđava Ras* (Belgrade 1999).

Popović V. (1982) "Desintegration und Ruralisation der Stadt im Ost-Illyricum vom 5. bis 7. Jahrhundert n. Chr.", in *Palast und Hütte: Beiträge zum Bauen und Wohnen im Altertum von Archäologen, Vor- und Frühgeschichtlern*, edd. D. Papenfuss and V. M. Strocka (Mainz 1982) 545–66.

Poulter A. G. (1995) *Nicopolis ad Istrum: a Roman, Late Roman, and Early Byzantine City* (London 1995).

——— (2004) "Cataclysm on the Lower Danube: the destruction of a complex Roman landscape", in *Landscapes of Change: Rural Evolutions in Late Antiquity and the Early Middle Ages*, ed. N. Christie (Aldershot and Burlington 2004) 223–53.

——— (2007) "The Bulgarian-British research programme in the countryside and on the site of an Early Byzantine fortress: the implications for the Lower Danube in the 5th to 6th centuries AD", in *The Lower Danube in Antiquity (VI c. B.C.–VI c. AD): International Archaeological Conference, Bulgaria-Tutrakan, 6.–7.10.2005*, ed. L. Vagalinski (Sofia 2007) 361–84.

Powell A. (2004) "The faunal remains", in *Byzantine Butrint: Excavations and Surveys, 1994–99*, edd. R. Hodges, W. Bowden and K. Lako (Oxford 2004) 305–20.

Pralong A. (1988) "Remarques sur les fortifications byzantines de Thrace orientale", in *Géographie historique du monde méditrannéen*, ed. H. Ahrweiller (Paris 1988) 179–200.

Rajković S. (1997) "Vizantijska Dalmacija u spisu *De administrando imperio*—nove dileme", *Zbornik radova Vizantološkog Instituta* 36 (1997) 221–32.

Rapanić Ž. (2001) "Dai coloni greci ai missionari franchi", in *Bizantini, Croati, Carolingi: Alba e tramonto di regni e imperi*, edd. C. Bertelli, G. P. Brogiolo, M. Jurković, I. Matejčić, A. Milošević and C. Stella (Milan 2001) 31–59.

Rashev R. (2000) *Prabălgarite prez V–VII vek* (Sofia 2000).

Rautman M. (1990) "Archaeology and Byzantine studies", *Byzantinische Forschungen* 15 (1990) 137–65.

Rendić-Miočević D. (1952) "Nekoliko zanimljivih nalaza iz starokršćanskog Solina", *Vjesnik za arheologiju i historiju Dalmatinsku* 54 (1952) 199–204.

Ricz P. and Fábián G. J. (1993) "Interdisciplinarni pristup rekonstrukciji avarskog luka. Kratak prikaz stanja problematike", *Rad Vojvodanskih Muzeja* 35 (1993) 79–85.

Romiopoulou E. (1973–74) "Agios Demetrios Kitrou", *ArchDelt* 29.2 (1973–74) 697.

Rosser J. (2001) "Evidence for a Justinianic garrison behind Thermopylae at the Dhema Pass", in *Mosaic. Festschrift for A. H. S. Megaw*, edd. J. Herrin, M. Mullett and C. Otten-Froux (London 2001) 33–41.

Schulze-Dörrlamm M. (2006) "Awarische Einflüsse auf Bewaffnung und Kampftechnik des ostfränkischen Heeres in der Zeit um 600?", in *Arms and Armour as Indicators of Cultural Transfer: the Steppes and the Ancient World from Hellenistic Times to the Early*

Middle Ages, edd. M. Mode and J. Tubach (Nomaden und Sesshafte 4) (Wiesbaden 2006) 485–507.

Semenov A. I. (1988) "K vyiavleniiu central'noaziatskikh elementov v kul'ture rannesrednevekovykh kochevnikov Vostochnoi Evrope", *Arkheologicheskii sbornik Gosudarstvennogo Ermitazha* 29 (1988) 97–111.

Shennan S. (1990) *Quantifying Archaeology* (Edinburgh 1990).

Shtereva I. and Radeva M. (2001) "Kolektivna nakhodka ot rannovizantiiski orădiia na truda ot Sliven", *Arkheologiia* 42.1–2 (2001) 79–84.

Simon L. (1991) "Korai avar kardok", *Studia Comitatensia* 22 (1991) 263–346.

Smilenko A. T. (1965) *Hlodos'ki skarbi* (Kiev 1965).

—— (1968) "Nakhodka 1928 g. u g. Novye Senzhary (Po materialam obsledovaniia A. K. Takhtaia)", in *Slaviane i Rus'. Sbornik statei. K shestdesiatiletiiu akad. B. A. Rybakova*, edd. E. I. Krupnov, V. I. Buganov, S. A. Pletneva, I. P. Rusanova and G. F. Solov'eva (Moscow 1968) 158–66.

Sodini J.-P. (1993) "La contribution de l'archéologie à la connaissance du monde byzantin (IVᵉ–VIIᵉ siècles)", *DOP* 47 (1993) 139–84.

Sokolova I. V. (1995) "Monety pereshchepinskogo klada. Katalog", *Vizantiiskii Vremennik* 56 (1995) 305–19.

Somogyi P. (1987) "Typologie, Chronologie und Herkunft der Maskenbeschläge: zu den archäologischen Hinterlassenschaften osteuropäischer Reiterhirten aus der pontischen Steppe im 6. Jahrhundert", *ArchAustr* 71 (1987) 121–54.

—— (1997) *Byzantinische Fundmünzen der Awarenzeit* (Innsbruck 1997).

Sretenović M. (1984) "Mokranjske stene. Visheslojno naselje. Izveshtaj o arkheoloshkim istrazhivanjima u 1980. godini", *Đerdapske sveske* 2 (1984) 221–30.

Stadler P. (2005) *Quantitative Studien zur Archäologie der Awaren I* (Vienna 2005).

—— (2008) "Avar chronology revisited, and the question of ethnicity in the Avar qaganate", in *The Other Europe in the Middle Ages: Avars, Bulgars, Khazars, and Cumans*, ed. F. Curta (East Central and Eastern Europe in the Middle Ages 450–1450 2) (Leiden and Boston 2008) 47–82.

Staňa Č. (1961) "Depot želez a žernovů na slovanském hradišti Staré Zámky u Líšně", *Sborník československé společností archeologické pri ČSAV* 1 (1961) 110–20.

Stanchev D. (1985) "Nakhodka na zhelezni predmeti ot s. Stambolovo, Rusenski okrăg", *Godishnik na muzeite ot Severna Bălgariia* 11 (1985) 31–34.

Stancheva M. (1970) "Epanouissement et disparition de deux *villae rusticae* près de Serdica", in *Actes du Premier Congrès international des études balkaniques et sud-est-européennes, Sofia, 26 août-1septembre 1966*, edd. V. Georgiev, N. Todorov and V. Tăpkova-Zaimova, vol. 2 (Sofia 1970) 535–38.

Stanilov S. and Aleksandrov G. (1983) "Srednovekovno ezichesko svetilishte v razvalinite na Montana", *Arkheologiia* 25.1–2 (1983) 40–52.

Stoichev S. (2005) "Triperite vărkhove na streli ot Shumenskiia region", in *Prof. d.i.n. Stancho Vaklinov i srednovekovnata bălgarska kultura*, edd. K. Popkonstantinov, B. Borisov and R. Kostova (Veliko Tărnovo 2005) 171–77.

Szádeczky-Kardoss S. (1981) "Der awarisch-türkische Einfluss auf die byzantinische Kriegskunst um 600 (Anmerkungen zum *Strategikon* des Maurikios)", *Studia turco-hungarica* 5 (1981) 63–71.

—— (1986) *Avarica: Über die Awarengeschichte und ihre Quellen* (Szeged 1986).

Szentpéteri J. (1993) "Archäologische Studien zur Schicht der Waffenträger des Awarentums im Karpatenbecken I", *ActaArchHung* 45 (1993) 165–246.

Totev K. (2002) "Tri vizantiiski procesiini krăsta ot Preslav", *Arkheologiia* 43.3 (2002) 57–65.

—— (2005) "Vizantiiski procesien krăst ot părvite razkopki v Pliska", in *Prof. d.i.n. Stancho Vaklinov i srednovekovna bălgarska kultura*, edd. K. Popkonstantinov, B. Borisov and R. Kostova (Veliko Tărnovo 2005) 216–19.

Uenze S. (1992) *Die spätantiken Befestigungen von Sadovec. Ergebnisse der deutsch-bulgarisch-österreichischen Ausgrabungen 1934–1937* (Munich 1992).

Vagalinski L. (1998) "Ein neuer spätantiker Segmenthelm aus Voivoda, Schumen Gebiet (Nordostenbulgarien)", *Archaeologia Bulgarica* 2.1 (1998) 96–106.

Vagarelski Kh. (1929) "Iz veshtestvennata kultura na bălgarite (rala)", *Izvestiia na Narodniia Etnografskiia Muzei* 8–9 (1929) 98–110.

Văzharova Zh. (1976) *Slaviani i prabălgari po danni na nekropolite ot VI–XI v. na teritoriiata na Bălgariia* (Sofia 1976).

—— (1986) *Srednovekovnoto selishte s. Garvăn, Silistrenski okrăg (VI–XI v.)* (Sofia 1986).

Velkov V. (1935) "Eine Gotenfestung bei Sadowetz (Nordbulgarien)", *Germania* 19 (1935) 149–58.

Vitlianov S. (1978) "Kolektivna nakhodka—zhelezni orădiia na truda ot Preslav", *Vekove* 7.4 (1978) 76–78.

Völling Th. (1995) "Ein frühbyzantinischer Hortfund aus Olympia", *AM* 110 (1995) 425–59.

Werner J. (1984) *Der Grabfund von Malaja Pereščepina und Kuvrat, Kagan der Bulgaren* (Munich 1984).

—— (1984b) "Ein byzantinischer 'Steigbügel' aus Caričin Grad", in *Caričin Grad I: Les basiliques B et J de Caričin Grad, quatre objets remarquables de Caričin Grad, le trésor de Hajdučka Vodenica*, edd. N. Duval and V. Popović (Belgrade and Rome 1984) 147–55.

—— (1985) "Kagan Kuvrat, fondatore della Magna Bulgaria. La sua tomba a Malaja Pereščepina presso Poltava", *Archeologia Medievale* 12 (1985) 709–12.

—— (1992) "Golemanovo Kale und Sadovsko Kale: Kritische Zusammenfassung der Grabungsergebnisse", in *Die spätantiken Befestigungen von Sadovec (Bulgarien): Ergebnisse der deutsch-bulgarisch-österreichischen Ausgrabungen 1934–1937*, ed. S. Uenze (Munich 1992) 391–417.

—— (1992b) "Neues zu Kuvrat und Malaja Pereščepina", *Germania* 10.2 (1992) 430–36.

Whitby M. and M. (1986) trans. *The History of Theophylact Simocatta: an English Translation with Introduction and Notes* (Oxford 1986).

White L. (1962) *Medieval Technology and Social Change* (Oxford 1962).

Zábojník J. (1991) "Seriation von Gürtelbeschlaggarnituren aus dem Gebiet der Slowakei und Österreichs", in *K problematike osídlenia stredodunajskej oblasti vo včasnom stredoveku*, ed. Z. Čilinská (Nitra 1991) 219–321.

Zanini E. (1994) *Introduzione all'archeologia bizantina* (Rome 1994).

Zlatarski D. (1960) "Kolektivna nakhodka ot slavianski sechiva ot s. Dălgopol", *Izvestiia na Varnenskoto arkheologichesko druzhestvo* 11 (1960) 103–109.

LIST OF FIGURES

Fig. 6 Correspondence analysis plot of 32 hoards of iron implements and weapons: ASEN—Asenovgrad; BALA—Balajnac; BOZHU—Bozhurovo; CARE—Carevec; CARG—Caričin Grad; CHELO—Chelopech; DALG—Dălgopol; DOLI—Dolishte; GAMZI—Gamzigrad; JELI—Jelica; MONT1—Montana 1; MONT2—Montana 2; ODAR—Odărci; OLYMP—Olympia; PERN—Pernik; PRES1—Preslav 1; PRES2—Preslav 2; RAZG—Razgrad; SEBEN—Sebenje; SHUM—Shumen; SLIV—Sliven; STAM—Stambolovo; STARA1—Stara Zagora 1; STARA2—Stara Zagora 2; STREZH—Strezhevo; TINJ—Tinje; TROI1—Troianov most 1; TROI2—Troianov most 2; VOIV—Voivoda; VRSA1—Vršac 1; VRSA2—Vršac 2; ZHEG—Zheglica.

Fig. 7 Correspondence analysis plot of the artefact categories found in 32 hoards of iron implements and weapons: ANV—anvil; AXEFAN—battle axe, fan-shaped; AXEIIAa—battle axe, Bartoškova's class IIAa; AXEIIIAb—battle axe, Bartoškova's class IIIAb; AXEIIIB—battle axe, Bartoškova's class IIIB; BELL—cattle bell; BELTB—belt buckle; BILLG1a—bill-knife, Henning's class G1a; BILLG1b—bill-knife, Henning's class G1b; BILLG2b—bill-knife, Henning's class G2b; BILLG4a—bill-knife, Henning's class G4a; BILLG5—bill-knife, Henning's class G5; BIT—bridle bit; BRONZE—bronze vessels; BUCK—bucket handles; CANDLE—candlestick; CENS—censer; CHAIN—plow chain; CHIS—chisel; COMB—currycomb; COUL—coulter, Henning's class E 1; HAMM—hammer; HOEK3—drag hoe, Henning's class K3; KETTLE—kettle; KEY1—key, L-shaped; KEY2—key, anchor-shaped; LAMP—lamp; LANCE—lance head, Iotov's class 1B; MATTK4—mattock, Henning's class K4; MATTK5—mattock, Henning's class K8; MATTK8—mattock, Henning's class K 8; MATTK10—mattock, Henning's class K10; MATTK15—mattock, Henning's class K15; OGRIB—tool ("ogribka"); PICKL1—pickaxe, Henning's class L1; PICKL2—pickaxe, Henning's class L 2; PLAN1—plane, curved; PLAN2—plane, straight; PLOWA1—ploughshare, Henning's class A1; PLOWB3—ploughshare, Henning's class B3; PLOWC1—ploughshare, Henning's class C1; SCIS—scissors; SCRAPP2—scraping tool, Henning's class P2; SCRAPP3—scraping tool, Henning's class P3; SCYTHI2—scythe, Henning's class I2; SCYTHI5—scythe, Henning's class I5; SOCK—socketed share; SPADE—spade, Henning's class F1; SPIK—spike; STIRR8A—stirrup, Iotov's class 8A; TONGS—tongs; WHETS—whetstone; WIMB—wimble.

Fig. 8 Hoard of iron implements found in Troianov most (Serbia), selected artefacts: sickle, scythes, belt buckle, stirrup, and censer. (After Garašanin and Vašić (1987).)

Fig. 9 Hoard of iron implements found in Razgrad (Bulgaria), selected artefacts: battle axes, ploughshares, and billknives. (After Ivanov and Stoianov (1985).)

THE EAST

MILITARY INFRASTRUCTURE IN THE ROMAN PROVINCES NORTH AND SOUTH OF THE ARMENIAN TAURUS IN LATE ANTIQUITY

James Howard-Johnston

Abstract

Rome's eastern defences were re-modelled and extended from the 3rd c. to cope with the enhanced power of Persia under the Sassanian dynasty. There were four main phases of development—under the Tetrarchate, in the 4th, early 6th and later 6th c. A.D. The defensive system was well adapted to the terrain, with several distinct components: fortified cities, fortresses, forts, fortified highland redoubts, defended passes, support and lateral roads. A marked shift of attention north of the Armenian Taurus and an increasing reliance on Bedouin clients in the south characterised the final phase.

INTRODUCTION

Material evidence casts light on but a few aspects of warfare. The thoughts of the main protagonists, their hopes and fears, the objectives they define, the plans they formulate, the orders issued by them, and their myriad *ad hoc* responses to changing circumstances in the course of campaigns and individual engagements—none of these can be caught from durable traces left on the ground. This is equally true of corporeal activity on the part of troops under their command, their marching, counter-marching, battle formations, battle manoeuvres and individual actions in combat. For the whole process of combat and planning beforehand, we have to turn to written, narrative sources; they alone can reveal something of the prime moving forces in war, namely the aspirations and decisions of the small groups in command of large forces of fighting men, and the movements and actions instigated by them.

It is only parts of the infrastructure of war which have left traces in the material record, together with a minuscule proportion of the debris of conflict. For the remote past, painstaking survey may trace lines of communication and supply through more or less well preserved sections of paved roads, artificial cuttings and remains of bridges. If very lucky, we might also learn something of logistics systems by finding vestiges of

A. Sarantis, N. Christie (edd.) *War and Warfare in Late Antiquity: Current Perspectives*
(Late Antique Archaeology 8.1–8.2 – 2010–11) (Leiden 2013), pp. 853–891

specialised warehouses built to hold military supplies, in ports and at key points on support roads. The most plentiful evidence, however, is that provided at numerous sites, large and small, both civilian and purely military, by fortifications. Built to withstand sustained physical attack by all the siege machines devised by man, some have survived the assault of time over many centuries; it has only been quarrying of ruins for building stone in the relatively recent past, in districts witnessing rapid population growth, and destructions caused by rapid urban expansion, which have erased these crucial historical monuments. So it is possible to outline the main features of defensive systems, which might also provide bases for offensive action. For the Roman Empire, both in its heyday and in its beleaguered later life, much of the outer zone of defence, its northern and eastern *limites*, can be reconstructed—walled cities, smaller fortified towns, major and minor military bases connected by networks of roads. *Limes* studies have, for some time, constituted a distinct sub-discipline of Ancient History.

There is rather less of the debris of conflict for the historian to sift through. The more scientific the approach to war, the less detritus is likely to be found on the battlefield. For properly educated commanders—and that includes Late Roman generals, inspired to emulate the finest fighting forces known to them, those of the Huns and their Turkic successors—strove to pare down the phase of head-to-head engagement to a short bout of bloody combat, squeezed between a preliminary phase of tactical manoeuvring designed to maximise the chances of victory and a final phase of pursuit and destruction of the disordered remnants of the defeated foe. In any case, we cannot expect to find much debris on battlefields, a millennium and a half or so later, if we allow both for systematic collection of weapons and equipment by victors, and for corrosion and decay of the arrows and other missiles which might once have littered the ground. Nor are there Roman analogues to the horse burials of nomads or the rich graves of Germanic warriors, to yield up evidence about arms and armour away from the battlefield. Close study of pictorial evidence, military handbooks, narrative sources, and scattered archaeological finds is required to piece together a picture of the Roman cavalryman and infantryman in Late Antiquity.[1]

---

[1] See the contribution by Coulston (in this collection) on extant Late Roman weaponry.

The only engagements of which we can hope to find physical traces might be related to extended sieges of cities and fortresses. Siege-works may be observed if the stronghold targeted was in a powerful natural position and its capture was regarded as militarily vital: siege-mounds rising to a great height, requiring movement of massive amounts of earth and stone, may still be seen outside Masada in Palestine and Cremna in Pisidia.[2] Whilst mobile armoured shelters, stone-throwing artillery, crossbows, rams, fire-weapons and siege-towers have left no trace beyond a few of the stone projectiles and metal arrow-heads which were discharged, their presence in aggregate may be inferred from damage detected in destroyed and subsequently repaired sections of circuit wall. Tell-tale evidence of the successful conclusion of a siege, of a city's sack and looting, is to be found in widespread fire-damage to public monuments and residential dwellings.

The most useful material evidence about armed conflict between organised states in the distant past lies in natural features of the landscape: the military historian must travel and cover the ground in the principal arenas of war to acquire some proper appreciation of the constraints under which generals operated in the past. For campaigns and conflicts, staff officers will have had to take note of the articulation of the terrain, of the alignment, elevation and relief of mountain ranges, of tracks cut by rivers through mountains and plains, of the distribution of large arable plains and thus food. Narrow, easily defensible pathways through mountain ranges acquired extraordinary strategic value for the side which could command them; by securing such gaps, a mountain range might form a formidable obstacle to an enemy. River valleys and open uplands, by contrast, offered inviting routes of attack, from whatever base area was chosen for the assembly of an expeditionary force to the targeted enemy territory. Campaigns can only be understood if they are placed in geographical context—terrain and man's constructions together forming something akin to a pinball machine, within which much ingenuity, at the strategic and tactical level, was required to secure safe passage and to maximise the chance of success in battle.

---

[2] Richmond (1962); Mitchell (1989).

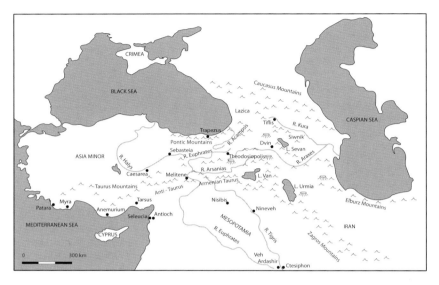

Fig. 1   Roman-Persian war zone.

Relief, Routes and the Strategic Balance
in Mesopotamia and Armenia

The two established great powers of western Eurasia in Late Antiquity were the East Roman and Sassanian Persian Empires. Both encompassed a wide range of peoples and geographically variegated territory, each was conscious of past greatness (recent for the Romans, distant for the Persians) and with aspirations to future universal rule, but each was wary of the other. By the late 4th c., after two long series of wars, the first initiated by the Persians (A.D. 230–98), the second by the Romans (A.D. 337–87), they had finally taken each other's measure and had acknowledged the high cost of attempting to gain a clear advantage. The accommodation reached in *ca.* 387 was undoubtedly prompted in part by awareness of the potential danger posed to both by the appearance of a dangerous nomadic people in the north, the Huns from east Eurasia, who themselves had pretensions to rule on the grand scale. The danger did not abate after the waning of Hun power: threats from without, from Germanic peoples emancipated from Hun overlordship and from other nomadic arrivals from the East, strengthened Roman and Persian commitment to the agreed settlement and a long phase of stability set in; punctuated by two short crises, it lasted throughout the 5th c.[3]

By the beginning of this long peaceful interlude, the Romans had developed an elaborate system of defence-in-depth in what was the principal theatre of war, northern Mesopotamia, while relying on a few key strongholds, supplemented by occasional military intervention and client-management in western Transcaucasia north of the Armenian Taurus. Whereas the looser-organised Parthian Empire had mainly targeted Roman Armenia, the offensive thrust of the Sassanians was directed north from lower Mesopotamia, for it was to the rich alluvium between the Tigris and the Euphrates that they shifted the centre of gravity of the Persian Empire. There the twin cities of Ctesiphon and Veh Ardashir which straddled the Tigris grew in size and wealth, feeding off the trade channelled up the Persian Gulf from the Indian Ocean and the increased agricultural production of their hinterlands, boosted by grand irrigation schemes. It was consequently the Roman provinces fronting this wealthy Sassanian heartland which bore the brunt of attacks in a first expansionist phase, and to which investment in military infrastructure was mainly directed.[4]

The Sassanian threat forced the Romans to concentrate their defensive installations in northern Mesopotamia and the Anti-Taurus region behind the Euphrates, but their distribution on the ground was primarily determined by nature: thus route junctions, river crossings, passes, and natural strongholds were the prime sites, wherever they were to be found within striking distance of the political frontier. The fortified zone ran north from the Arabian Desert to the Caucasus and the Black Sea. The nearer reaches of the desert could be kept under loose control through Arab clients—a single ruling dynasty in the case of the Persians, a series of Bedouin chiefs watched over by frontier commanders on the Roman side.[5] The interior of Arabia beyond was a tribal world of flux, upon which external influences could play, that of each great northern power (attenuated as it was disseminated through intermediaries), and that of the Kingdom of Himyar in South Arabia which could be cast more widely through direct military action and was

---

[3] Dodgeon and Lieu (1991); Greatrex and Lieu (2002); Howard-Johnston (1995).
[4] Gray (1973); Howard-Johnston (1995) 198–205.
[5] Fisher (2011).

more pervasive because it was more familiar.[6] Rome's great danger lay in the far north, where the Black Sea offered an inviting direct route to Constantinople, if ever the Persians were to establish a secure base on the coast of Lazica or Abasgia, while a relatively easy coastal route exposed Trebizond (classical Trapezus) to attack by land from Lazica.[7] The Caucasus and its multitudinous highland peoples formed a virtually impenetrable barrier (save for the central Dariel Pass and the Caspian Gates at the eastern end) which sheltered both Persian and Roman sectors of Transcaucasia from the northern nomadic world.

Between the desert and these northern limits lay the zones of conflict, where the territories of the two empires, whether directly or indirectly, controlled, abutted, and where their interests, territorial and commercial, clashed most clearly. The frontier between them was artificial, cutting across relatively homogeneous terrain: in the south the Fertile Crescent which arches over the desert from lower Mesopotamia to Syria and Palestine in the west, and, to the north, the elevated uplands of Armenia, studded with volcanoes and fertile alluvial basins, which form a huge natural causeway linking the Iranian and Anatolian plateaux. Both zones were also ethnically and culturally homogeneous. The higher powers might strive to pull them apart, but the natural trend was for intensive cross-border interplay, political as well as commercial, between their subjects and clients.[8]

A series of contiguous mountain ranges separates the Fertile Crescent from the higher lands of Iran, Armenia and Anatolia. The Zagros range, beginning with wide, beneficent valleys which constituted Persia proper, the kernel of the Sassanian Empire as long before of its Achaemenid predecessor, runs north-north-west until it merges with a formidable gathering of mountains, in what is now the heartland of Kurdistan, straddling the modern Iranian, Iraqi and Turkish frontiers. From this tangle of virtually impenetrable highlands, a line of mountains runs west as a virtually continuous barrier, separating south-west Armenia from northern Mesopotamia (the Armenian Taurus). It pens in Lake Van and pushes on to the weak point where the Euphrates breaks through to the south, between the districts of Hanzit (classical Anzitene) and Malatya (classical Melitene). Beyond, this single range splays out into the Anti-Taurus, comprising some seven distinct ridges, which encircle a fertile basin around modern

---

[6] Hoyland (2001).
[7] Procop. *Pers.* 2.28.23; Agath. 2.18.7.
[8] Whitby (1988) 197–202.

Elbistan (not far from classical Arabissus). The Anti-Taurus then contracts to form a single, massive range, the Taurus proper, which separates Cilicia from Cappadocia and then runs on west towards the Aegean, with a great northern curve around the bay of Antalya (classical Attaleia).

Numerous routes threaded their way up and over this long chain of mountains, but few were feasible for organised fighting forces. Two lay within Persian territory, one involving a long detour to the east to cross the Zagros south of Lake Urmia, the other connecting the Tigris valley to south-west Armenia via Bitlis and the west end of Lake Van. The Romans controlled a pass which crosses the Armenian Taurus diagonally from the Upper Tigris basin past Ergani and on to the district around the powerful medieval castle of Harput (in Hanzit), and two to the west of the Euphrates, one running north from Tarsus to Tyana through the Cilician Gates, the other picking its way across Rough Cilicia, the fissured and somewhat flattened section of the Taurus immediately west of the Cilician plain, north-west to Iconium in the southern angle of the Anatolian plateau.[9]

Given their strategic function as pathways between two distinct theatres of war, much of Rome's (and probably likewise Persia's) investment in defensive infrastructure was directed at securing the passes in their territory. For assured command of a direct route south-north brought with it a very significant gain, that of inner lines, and the closer that route to the frontier, the greater its potential strategic value both in attack and defence. The final concentration of a strike force could then be delayed to the very eve of the attack, when the opposing troops were still divided between two fronts, north and south of the intervening mountains, while, if it was a case of countering invasion, a force could be discharged into the advancing enemy's rear.

The general alignment of the mountains which bounded Armenia on the north was likewise east-west and consisted of a number of distinct components: the mountainous region of Siwnik' (modern Nagorno Karabakh) around Lake Sevan, which separates the Araxes valley from that of the Kura to the north, can be circumvented to east and west; then come the highlands of Tao, a contested region between Armenia and Georgia,

---

[9] The geographical remarks which follow are based, to a large extent, on direct observation during travels in Turkey and Iran, supplemented by armchair research. The most convenient surveys of terrain are in two volumes issued by the Naval Intelligence Division in its Geographical Handbook Series during the Second World War and subsequently made available to the public: NID, *Turkey*, I (April 1942) 19–194, and NID, *Persia* (September 1945) 34–86.

into which deep canyons have been cut by the Çoruh River (classical Boas/Acampsis) and its tributaries; it is virtually impassable for any but small irregular bodies of fighting men. It extends west on either bank of the Çoruh and develops into the Pontic range which forms the northern margin of the Anatolian plateau. A single route of great strategic importance runs south from Trebizond over the Zigana Pass towards the Upper Euphrates valley.

A third set of mountains, again aligned roughly east-west, transects both Azerbaijan (classical Atropatene, together with Caucasian Albania to the north) in the east and Armenia in the south-west. First come mountains separating the basin of Lake Urmia from the Araxes valley to the north, then the huge shoulders from which the cone of Mount Ararat rises to 5,122 m, and, adjoining it, a range which marches along the northern side of the elongated plain of Bagrewand, and, to the south of Erzurum (classical Theodosiopolis), the Bingöl Dağ, a huge, spreading, coneless volcano, which feeds the upper waters of the Araxes. Two distinct ranges run west from the Bingöl Dağ, the first a grim line of close-packed peaks (known now as the Mountains of Satan), the second the high, Taurus-like Munzur Dağ which abuts the Euphrates.

The eastern approaches to Anatolia are thus divided into two relatively broad avenues: the northern follows the Araxes valley, crossing a series of alluvial plains and passing north of Mount Ararat, as far as the plain of Basean; beyond rises a low, easily traversable ridge, the watershed between the Araxes and the Euphrates, which marked the frontier between the two empires, and, immediately to the west, the plain of Erzurum. The Upper Euphrates valley then offers an inviting route as far as the Tercan plain (classical Derzene), where the river is pushed south for a while. The Roman road continued west to Satala, which commands the junction between the east-west route and that running north over the Pontic Mountains to Trebizond. The southern avenue runs west from the basin of Lake Urmia, passing south of Mount Ararat and skirting the northern edge of the mountains of Kurdistan and the volcanoes which pen in Lake Van to the north. It then enters a broad swathe of open, undulating country, drained by the Murat Su (classical Arsanias), and continues to the Euphrates, crossing between Hanzit and Malatya.

The political frontier ran diagonally across Armenia, from the middle of the Armenian Taurus to the Bingöl Dağ, then continuing along the watershed east of Theodosiopolis and over impenetrable mountains to the Black Sea coast to the east of Rize (classical Rhizaeum). The Romans were at a considerable strategic disadvantage, since there was only one route, skirting the western side of the Bingöl Dağ, along which troops could be dispatched from one potential avenue of invasion to the other. The Persians, by contrast, had a choice of south-north routes, all debouching (or starting) in the Araxes valley: (1) close to the frontier, immediately to the east of the Bingöl Dağ; (2) running north across a narrow point in the intervening range, from the north-west end of Bagrewand; (3) across the western shoulder of Ararat, from the south-east end of Bagrewand; and (4) crossing the northern rim of the Urmia basin.

The strategic advantage thus lay with the Persians on their western frontier throughout the century or more of peace which followed the settlement of *ca.* A.D. 387. This compensated them for their comparative weakness at the grand strategic level, caught as they were between a mighty sedentary empire in the West and the natural centres of nomad power in central Asia. The Bitlis Pass which they controlled was closer to the frontier than the Romans' Ergani Pass. In western Armenia, they had several reserve routes behind that skirting the Bingöl Dağ, while the Romans could only fall back on routes on the far, western bank of the Euphrates where it turns south for good, cutting its way through a series of canyons. It is true that, in the north, the Romans had an important route over the Pontic mountains, connecting Trebizond to Satala, which had no Persian analogue. But its primary function was logistic, as a conduit for supplies shipped into Trebizond for troops manning the Euphrates defences to the south. It was too far from the frontier to be of operational use.

Development of Road-System and Frontier Defences, 1st to 4th c.

In interludes of peace, the Romans made massive investments in military infrastructure along the whole length of their eastern frontier. This was necessary since it was a largely open frontier and man had to make good the deficiencies of nature, especially in the south, on the eastern frontage of the fertile strip which separates the desert from the East Mediterranean, where manufacturing and commerce were most advanced. Asia Minor likewise lay all too exposed to attack from the east across Armenia (not to mention the nightmare possibility of naval expeditions across the Black Sea).

Inscriptions provide vital chronological information about individual building projects, but, overall, few have survived. Data are even scantier regarding road-construction projects, since milestones were only put up exceptionally, perhaps because of the importance of a scheme or the status of the governor responsible, or the proximity of a great urban centre.[10] This epigraphic evidence can be supplemented with archaeological finds (stray and excavated), as also from literary sources. Once lives of saints come on stream in Late Antiquity, historians have no shortage of narrative material to exploit. To this should be added a few unusual texts (notably, the problematic *Peutinger Table, The Buildings* of Procopius, and George of Cyprus' survey of the Roman world) which supply much remarkably detailed information.[11] Nonetheless, most of the extant stretches of visible roadway and most extant fortifications are unlabelled, do not figure in narrative sources, and have not seen systematic excavation; scholars often therefore have to resort to conjecture about their dating, relying on circumstantial evidence or comparative analysis of masonry and defensive designs.

A massive scholarly infrastructure underlies this short paper—but not mine, for I have only travelled in the Mesopotamian and Armenian sectors of the Roman frontier zone, while my observations (hasty and limited) lack the precision and authority of a professional archaeologist; instead I rely on the work of others, who may, like Tim Mitford, Shelagh Gregory, Thilo Ulbert, David Kennedy and Anthony Comfort, draw primarily on the evidence of their own eyes (*autopsy*, in its correct, classical usage),[12] or whose main service has been to survey and analyse the results of third-party autoptic research, as Benjamin Isaac, Clive Foss and Greg Fisher have done.[13] In addition, there are those, like Michael Whitby, whose primary focus has been textual, but who have also striven to identify places named in written sources (primarily Procopius and Theophylact Simocatta in his case), by scouring the archaeological literature and by investigation on the ground.[14]

In what follows, I simply offer a synthesis, conjectural in places, outlining the main features of the Roman defensive system as it had developed by the late 4th c., followed by somewhat fuller analysis of the large investment programme initiated by Anastasius (491–518) and carried on by Justin I (518–27) and his successors in the 6th c. Such an analysis is made possible by the volume of specific information provided by Procopius and George of Cyprus. My aim is to discern the overall shape of the defensive

---

[10] Compare French (1980); Isaac (1990) 108–11; Mitchell (1993) 1, 124–27.
[11] *Tabula Peutingerana*, segment 10; Procop. *Aed.* 2–3; Georgius Cyprius, nos. 949–57.
[12] Mitford (1980); Gregory (1997); Ulbert (2000); Kennedy (2004); Comfort (2008).
[13] Isaac (1990); Foss (1997); Fisher (2011).
[14] Whitby (1984), (1986a), (1986b) and (1987); Whitby and Whitby (1986).

system, the underlying principles which shaped it, and the degree of variation between different sectors of the frontier. As already indicated, it is
the two central zones in northern Mesopotamia and western Armenia on
which attention is concentrated, but comments will also be made on the
desert frontage of Syria and Palestine to the south and the Black Sea littoral in the north.

Of course, the Sassanian defensive system should be subjected to similar scrutiny. That, however, is a yet more difficult task. Not only is there
minimal epigraphic evidence and virtually no usable literary material
except that provided by Roman sources, but there has been much less
field work on the Persian side of the late 4th c. frontier. The most useful survey, one carried out in a small segment of northern Iraq, between
the Tigris and Jebel Sinjar, on the eve of the filling of the Saddam dam
reservoir, gives a tantalising glimpse of a defensive network of small rectangular forts watching over routes, and four larger fortified settlements
acting as nodal points.[15] As for the wider context in north Mesopotamia,
Procopius' account of 6th c. operations suggests that the primary role in

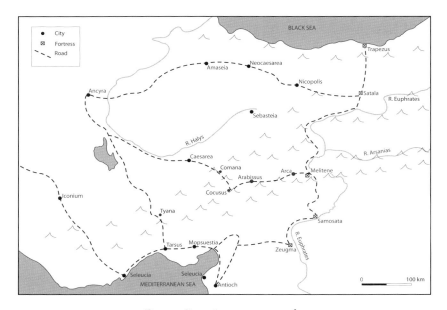

Fig. 2   Frontier support roads.

---

[15] Wilkinson and Tucker (1995) 70–71, 188–89 (figs. 46–47).

defence was played by the regional capital, Nisibis, which, in time of war, housed large forces capable of operating independently in the field. Dvin, Nisibis' analogue to the north of the Armenian Taurus, may have had an equally central role in regional defence, with the added advantage that the narrow passage at the west end of its plain could be blocked; if so, the Sassanians may have been more inclined than the Romans to concentrate their fire power in a few well-defended cities.[16]

The basic lineaments of a defensive system in the East can be traced by the time of Hadrian's formal progress through different provinces of the Middle East in A.D. 129–31, which probably included a tour of inspection of the Euphrates frontier just before he sailed back to Athens in autumn 131.[17] The imperial government's evident confidence in the security of the region points unequivocally to the completion of the elaborate programmes of road-construction and fortification, initiated under the Flavians in the 70s. The two programmes were, of course, closely connected: the better the communications, the more forces could be concentrated at nodal points in the defensive system when things were quiet, and deployed at speed when there were problems to be dealt with. In the south, an old caravan route from the head of the Red Sea to Bostra was upgraded and paved, after the annexation of the Nabataean kingdom of Arabia in A.D. 106. Completion of different sections of the *Via Nova Traiana* is marked by milestones dated 111 and 114. From Bostra a spur to the south-west (dated 120) connected it to a transverse strategic route constructed earlier, around 69, which ran inland from Caesarea to Gerasa. In the mid-2nd c., another spur would be built across the rugged volcanic plateau of the Leja (classical Trachonitis) to link Bostra to Damascus.

Four legions, stationed at Aila, Bostra, Jerusalem and Raphanaea, were responsible for policing the whole length of this southern half of the frontier and the refractory districts in the interior.[18] Above Raphanaea, the Euphrates provided a clear demarcation and useful first line of defence, backed in the plains of northern Syria by the existing fortifications of long established cities, and in the highlands beyond by a defensive zone in which forts and fortresses, about a day's march apart, were linked by a paved road (datable probably to the 70s and 80s A.D.), which lacks milestones (such might, of course, have helped orient an enemy). Legionary

---

[16] Procop. *Pers.* 2.18.7–13 (Nisibis), 25.1–9 (Dvin).
[17] Birley (2000) 142–45.
[18] Isaac (1990) 110, 119–22, 134–36; Millar (1993) 92–94, 138–39; Kennedy (2004) 39–40.

fortresses guarded potential crossing points on the Euphrates on both flanks of the Anti-Taurus, at Zeugma and Samosata in Commagene (annexed in 72), and Melitene in eastern Cappadocia. The same function of control was performed further north by a further legionary base, Satala, commanding an important cross-roads south of the Pontic mountains, and by Trebizond.[19]

Supplies, equipment and additional troops could be conveyed most conveniently by sea to large artificial harbours at Seleucia (linked by canal to Antioch) in the south and Trebizond (built under Hadrian) in the north. One of the prime functions of the large granaries built at Patara and Myra in Lycia in Hadrian's reign was surely to provision the army on the frontier.[20] But, given the perils of navigation from late autumn to early spring, it was vital to possess secure land-based lines of supply, hence the upgrading in the later 1st c. of a support road running east from Ancyra along the northern edge of the Anatolian plateau to Satala (sections of which are documented by milestones as well as extant surface remains), and, possibly, a diagonal road crossing the plateau to Iconium and picking its way through difficult country to a second Seleucia, at the western extremity of the plain of Cilicia.[21]

At the end of the 2nd c., a second phase of development began with a drive to improve the road network in south-east Asia Minor, probably linked to Septimius Severus' push across the Euphrates, and his annexation of a large bridgehead in northern Mesopotamia between 195 and 199. Before long, however, the impetus changed when intelligence came of a new dynasty in the Persian heartland in the southern Zagros, and of the dynamic growth of its power as it spread over the whole Parthian Empire, in the 210s and 220s; there was no reason to suppose that it would be confined within existing political frontiers.[22] A high-standard road was built from Caesarea to Melitene, as an additional, southern, support road for forts on the Euphrates: its route ran east to the Anti-Taurus and then followed a sinuous course, south over the two northernmost ridges, past Comana and Cocusus, then east across the interior basin past Arabissus, and finally over the eastern mountain rim past Arca into the plain of

---

[19]   Mitford (1980) 1180–92. Mitford will be publishing a full study of the Euphrates frontier in the near future, which incorporates the results of extensive fieldwork. He has traced the course of the Roman road over the Pontic Mountains well to the east of the Zigana Pass.

[20]   Rickman (1971) 137–40; Millar (1993) 86–88, 103–104.

[21]   Mitford (1980) 1185; French (1980) 711; Mitchell (1993) 1, 122, 130 (map 8).

[22]   Millar (1993) 120–26, 147–50.

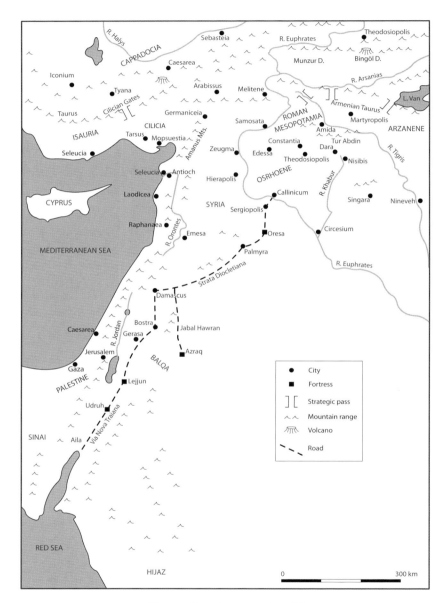

Fig. 3   Frontier zones (south)

Melitene. Initiated in 198–99, it saw intermittent work between 218 and 253, presumably to bring it up to proper military standard, in terms of width, paved surface, etc.[23]

The choice of this particular route is instructive, since it was by no means direct, and entailed extensive engineering work where it cut across the grain of the landscape. Security clearly dictated this: pushed as it was through mountains firmly controlled by the Romans, it could be denied without difficulty to an enemy; Roman forces could then be mobilised, without fear of attack, in the sheltered plain of Arabissus. It was this creation of a secure but aggressively positioned assembly area for a reserve force, close to the Euphrates frontier zone, which probably justified the expenditure. Such a reserve force provided additional exterior protection for Caesarea, the principal city of south-east Asia Minor, which, in time of war, could double as a powerful forward base. A contemporary road-scheme (datable between 217 and 238) involved (1) the upgrading of what had hitherto been no more than a caravan route between Tyana and Tarsus, which winds its way across the Taurus, at one point squeezing through a narrow passage between high cliffs (the Cilician Gates), and (2) repair and improvement work on bridges in Cilicia. This too may have been another component of a grand scheme to improve communications in an era of increasing apprehension about Persian attack.[24] Finally, a large fort, Şerefiye Kale (400 × 300 m), which commands the route (apparently not developed by the Romans) running up the Tohma valley on to the plateau at the Uzun Yayla, may date to this same critical period when Rome's defences were being strengthened in the south-east.[25]

The Euphrates defences proved their worth after the defeat and death of Gordian deep in Persian Mesopotamia in 244, which was not followed up by a Persian counter-invasion of Roman territory. They were tested properly and held, when Persian raiding forces, exploiting the defeat of Philip the Arab at Barbalissus, raided at will over northern Syria in 252 or 253, but made no inroads into Cilicia or the Anatolian plateau, save for an isolated foray which reached Satala (possibly a year or two later). It was only after a third catastrophic defeat in 260 near Carrhae (modern Harran) in Osrhoene, at which the Emperor Valerian and his staff were captured, that the Euphrates defences were overwhelmed. If the order in which the

---

[23] Mitford (1980) 1184, n. 30, 1206–1208.
[24] French (1981) 18–22, 32–33, 88–93.
[25] Sinclair (1987–90) II, 456–59.

places devastated are listed in the *shahanshah* Shapur's triumphal inscription on the Cube of Zoroaster at Naqsh-i Rustam corresponds to the order in which they were attacked, Shapur's counterattack was directed first at Cilicia, from where one force raided west as far as Anemurium along the south coast, another used the old Rough Cilicia road to attack Laranda and Iconium, and a third (likely the main force) pushed north, probably through the Cilician Gates, to take out the Anti-Taurus sector of the Euphrates defences from the rear.[26]

There was no opportunity for anything but improvisation over the following two decades, as the empire fought for survival against a variety of Germanic invaders in the West, against Goths who attacked the Balkans and Asia Minor by land and sea, and Persians in the East, not to mention usurpers at home. The nadir of Roman fortunes was marked by the emergence of a single, half-Romanised, mercantile city, Palmyra, as an independent power in the Middle East between 260 and 272.[27] Herculean efforts were required first to stabilise the situation, then to re-assert Roman authority via a general programme of militarisation. A new stage in the state's mobilisation for war was inaugurated in 284, when imperial power was shared out among four partner rulers (the Tetrarchy headed by Diocletian), with a concomitant division of power and territories, and a concerted drive to improve government efficiency by wholesale reform of the tax system and the bureaucracy. As for defensive installations, only repairs and improvements could be carried out as and when necessary in the localities, principally on city fortifications, while the empire remained at war with the Persians.

This war was brought to an end on terms favourable to the Romans in 287. A successful expedition led by Carus in 283 into Lower Mesopotamia, in the course of which both halves of the Persian capital were captured, turned the tide. Roman superiority was emphasised again in a final brief flaring of war in 297–98, which culminated in a victory won by Galerius, Diocletian's junior partner in the East, over the *shahanshah* Narseh, and the capture of many prisoners, including the latter's womenfolk. Substantial territorial concessions were then secured: the frontier now embraced the whole Armenian Taurus as far as Corduene to the south of Lake Van, and the intervening stretch of land between the mountains and the left

---

[26] *ŠKZ*, cc.6–30, I, 25–43, II, 41–98; Dodgeon and Lieu (1991) 34–65; Millar (1993) 152–55, 159–67.

[27] Dodgeon and Lieu (1991) 68–110; Millar (1993) 167–73.

bank of the Tigris.[28] Refurbishing of the southern half of the Roman Empire's eastern defences, put in hand in 287, could now be developed into an elaborate system of forward defence, without fear of Persian intervention. As elsewhere, the guiding principle was that of asserting Roman authority on the margins: forts, large and small, lined the frontier road from the Euphrates in the north to the head of the Gulf of Sinai in the south. The bulk of the empire's military manpower was deployed as far forward as possible, in smaller and larger garrisons, which could move swiftly to each other's support or, if action on a larger scale were required (say to cut off an invader's retreat or to project Roman authority), might coalesce into larger field forces.

Palmyra's independence as a client-state was ended, the city being incorporated into a new, outer defensive shield for the rich Middle Eastern provinces. The *Via Nova Traiana* continued to act as the spine of the defensive system in the far south, endowed with new forts. North of Damascus, which was linked to Bostra by a 2nd c. road cutting across the Leja, a new road, watched over by forts, ran to Palmyra and thence north to the Euphrates and a new forward base at Circesium. It was joined near Dumayr by an outer road coming from the oasis of Azraq far to the south (already secured in the Severan period with a support road from the Hawran and at least two forts), which skirted the eastern edge of the Jebel Hawran where it protrudes into the desert from the Leja. This great natural redoubt was incorporated into the new defensive system, known as the *Strata Diocletiana*. Larger garrisons, with *ca.* 1,000 men, were placed at intervals to police the frontier, based at Aela, Udruh, Lejjun, Bostra, Danaba, Palmyra, Oresa, Sura and Circesium.[29]

Diocletian himself visited Antioch and Emesa in A.D. 290, probably to supervise the start of the grand project, as well as to obtain formal submission from neighbouring Arab tribes. He was credited with putting 'the bonds of captivity' on the Saracens and winning laurels from the conquered nations bordering Syria, in a panegyric delivered to his colleague Maximian at Trier in 291.[30] The senior emperor's personal interest (he returned in 300–302) and the massive expenditure involved prove the very high priority given to improvement of imperial security along the whole desert frontage. The rise of Palmyra to regional hegemony had evidently

---

[28] Dodgeon and Lieu (1991) 112–34; Millar (1993) 174–80.

[29] Killick (1986); Isaac (1990) 162–218: Millar (1993) 137–38, 179–89; Gregory (1997) II, 171–73, 181–83, 189–224; Kennedy (2004); Parker (2006).

[30] *Pan. Lat.* 11.5.4 and 7.1. Compare Nixon and Rodgers (1994) 76–103.

delivered a massive shock to the Roman body politic. Large forces had been mobilised, which far exceeded the city's own military capability. There can be little doubt that the main body of fighting men who went on to conquer much of the Roman Middle East were Arabs. The Roman guise of the city and of its leaders' imperial claims should not mislead us as to the real source of its military strength, the great reservoir of nomad Bedouin in northern Arabia. Diocletian and his fellow-rulers could have no illusions about the danger which the Arabs would pose to the exposed provinces of Syria, Palestine, Arabia and Egypt, if they again came to be united around a single political centre.[31]

No significant developments are recorded under the Tetrarchy further north. Work on the Euphrates *limes* and its frontage beyond the river (the provinces of Osrhoene and Mesopotamia) probably comprised chiefly repairs to existing fortifications. Rather more surprising is the dearth of evidence about fortification projects in the five annexed satrapies on the far bank of the Tigris. The remains of only one readily identifiable Roman fort have been found, at Gayda Kale. This was large with an irregular plan, measuring 240 × 190 m, and capable of holding a garrison of 1,000 men for conducting operations in the mountains; it was virtually impregnable, with massive walls of ashlar masonry (some 5 m thick), strengthened with round towers at 20 m intervals. These features and its location point to a construction date between A.D. 298 and 363. It commands a small plain on a difficult route across the Armenian Taurus south of Lake Van, which bypasses the main Bitlis Pass. While it was clearly intended to block the route at a pinch point, its prime function was probably to act as a powerful forward base, securing the Bitlis Pass for exclusive Roman use.[32]

Given its scale, the Diocletianic programme may have taken decades to complete. It was followed up with some work in northern Mesopotamia, up to the right bank of the Tigris, notable being the fortification of Amida, which was given massive defences of the most up-to-date kind and was thus transformed into a bastion of Roman power commanding the Upper Tigris basin. Two key points on the perimeter of the Tur Abdin hills to the south were also fortified, Cepha and Rhabdium, both completed probably after the death of Constantine in 337, since they are credited to Constantius II; they should be associated with plans for a renewal of hostilities against the Sassanians (in 337). The renaming of Tella, which

---

[31] Compare Millar (1993) 173, 327–36.
[32] Mitford (1986).

commanded the main route west from the Tur Abdin, after Constantius (as Constantia), indicates that its defences too were strengthened at this time so as to make it a secure reserve base.[33]

The war initiated by Constantine dragged on for half a century. The balance of power in 363 shifted with the failure of Julian's grand army, thwarted in the irrigated alluvium of Mesopotamia, then trapped on the left bank of the Tigris, far from Roman territory, and demoralised after Julian's death. His successor, Jovian, had to offer major concessions to extricate the army, namely much of the territory on the left bank of the Upper Tigris ceded by the Persians in 298, and a swathe of territory to the east of Amida and the Tur Abdin, including Nisibis; north of the Armenian Taurus, he agreed to the cession of Armenia.[34] Since there was a better prospect of reversing some of these losses through diplomacy and client-management, and it would be easier to find a diplomatic cloak for aggression, the epicentre of the fighting over the following decades moved north to Transcaucasia. At the same time, attempts were made to improve the Roman position in the far north by constructing forts guarding the approaches to Pityus and Sebastopolis on the Black Sea coast under Valens. The last two projects to be completed before a durable peace was agreed in *ca.* 387 were both named after the reigning emperor, Theodosius I: a Syrian Theodosiopolis (previously Resaena) commanded the desert front-age south-east of Constantia, while an Armenian Theodosiopolis watched over the Euphrates-Araxes watershed.[35]

To judge by the terms of later, better-documented treaties, the two sides agreed to refrain from future military construction projects.[36] It is unlikely that repair and maintenance work was precluded, however, since dilapidation could not be assumed to proceed in tandem on both sides of the frontier; minor improvements may also have been allowed, since some might be structurally necessary. But no major project, whether to strengthen existing fortifications, or to create a new installation, was permitted. This froze the defensive systems of the two sides in the state they had reached in *ca.* 387. Neither is likely to have been much concerned about their southern defences. Insofar as was humanly possible, Diocletian and his successors had secured Rome's long desert frontage. Sassanian Mesopotamia, with its much shorter frontage, was protected by an outer

---

[33] Matthews (1989) 54–55.
[34] Matthews (1989) 130–87; Blockley (1992) 24–30.
[35] Zuckerman (1991) 533–40; Garsoïan (2004).
[36] Procop. *Pers.* 1.2.15, *Aed.* 2.1.5; Menander 6.1 (lines 354–58).

screen of forts and an inner line of defence along the Euphrates.[37] On both sides of the new frontier in north Mesopotamia, networks of defensive installations had been developed, with Amida and Nisibis as focal points. This meant rough parity in the military infrastructure of the two sides south of the Armenian Taurus. The same was probably true to the north, but the allocation to the Persian sphere of four-fifths of Transcaucasia, including the regional capitals of Armenia and Iberia, gave them a distinct strategic advantage. With only one advance base at Theodosiopolis and some positions on the east coast of the Black Sea, the Romans would have to rely on forces in the field to keep enemies out of the Armenian approaches to Asia Minor, if ever relations were to deteriorate. The only alternative would be to cede their sector temporarily and to fall back on the old Flavian defences behind the Euphrates.

FORTIFICATION PROGRAMMES IN THE 6TH C. A.D.

However, the peace did hold for over a century, apart from two short, rapidly defused crises. In general, both sides proved remarkably restrained, refraining from exploiting crises affecting the other, until the temporary eclipse of the Sassanian Empire after the defeat and death of Peroz at the hands of the Hephthalites in A.D. 484. Even then, the Romans did no more than withhold the offset payments which they were probably obliged to make towards the cost of Caucasus defence, on the good grounds that they would simply be passed onto the Hephthalites in the form of Persian tribute.[38] In due course, this provided the *shahanshah* Kavad I (488–96; 499–531) with a pretext for breaking the peace, there being then, as now, no better way for a leader to boost his position at home than by garnering prestige from a successful foreign adventure.

The Romans were taken completely by surprise when Kavad attacked in force in late August 502. Whatever intelligence was received of Persian preparations was evidently disregarded in an age of peaceful symbiosis. Kavad, taking personal charge of operations, sliced through the Roman frontier. Theodosiopolis fell after a short siege. He then cut south, apparently unopposed, through south-west Armenia where local administration was delegated to local satraps, crossed over the Armenian Taurus,

---

[37] Finster and Schmidt (1976).
[38] Greatrex (1998) 14–18, 47–52.

again apparently unopposed, and appeared before Martyropolis where the satrap put up no resistance and submitted. He then closed in on his main objective, the city of Amida, the lynch-pin of Roman defence in northern Mesopotamia. The city resisted sturdily for over three months, countering the machines deployed by the Persians and the great mound which they built. Eventually it fell after a commando raid captured a tower on the night of 10th–11th January 503.[39]

Kavad thus managed, in less than 6 months, to rip away the whole forward zone of defence built up by the Romans over some two centuries. The western fifth of Armenia, allocated to the Romans in *ca.* 387, was completely exposed once Theodosipolis was captured. The loss of Amida did not have such dire strategic consequences, since Roman forces could fall back on the Tur Abdin as well as to two rear bases, Constantia and Theodosiopolis. But the whole of northern Mesopotamia was more open to attack than before, as already shown during the siege of Amida when an Arab force ranged west and raided the territories of Carrhae and Edessa.[40] The security of northern Syria and Asia Minor once again depended on the Euphrates and the Flavian defensive system which backed it north and south of the Armenian Taurus.

Kavad's opponent, Anastasius, a quintessentially civilian emperor, had no choice but to wage war on the grandest possible scale to recover the lost ground. By 504, after transferring troops from the Balkans, he deployed something close to 100,000 Roman troops in the Mesopotamian theatre. This gave the Roman supreme commander, Celer, a decisive advantage, which he exploited to the full. The Persian position was weakened when Huns attacked in the north. Co-ordinated operations by Celer's subordinate generals secured control of the Tigris basin and isolated Amida, which was put under an effective blockade; starvation eventually forced the Persians to yield. They agreed to evacuate Amida, in return for a facesaving payment, and to open peace negotiations.[41]

While negotiations dragged on through 505 and 506, the Romans set about strengthening their defences. Emergency repairs were carried out on fortifications which had failed to hold out during the fighting—Edessa, Batnae, Birta and Dura.[42] Two major projects were also begun: Theodosiopolis, given its strategic importance as the sole Roman fortress in Roman

---

[39] Greatrex (1998) 76–94.
[40] Greatrex (1998) 87.
[41] Greatrex (1998) 108–15.
[42] Josh. Styl. cc. 87, 89, 91.

Armenia, was endowed with a larger circuit wall, construction of which probably took several years.[43] In northern Mesopotamia, a start was made on construction of a new hard-point military base at Dara, a mere 5 km or so from the frontier and menacingly close to Nisibis. This was a highly provocative project. Hence the presence nearby of two field armies, one based at Amida, the other at Edessa, in the early stages of construction, and then, for several critical months during the 506 campaigning season, of Celer with a powerful army at the site itself.[44] The Persians objected vociferously but were unable to disrupt what was a very effective building campaign. They had no choice but to stomach Dara, where work finished in 507/508, and, yet worse from their point of view, to accept a Roman proposal for a 7-year truce from 506 and its subsequent extensions.[45]

They thus, in effect, allowed the Romans to embark on a massive fortification programme along the whole northern half of their mutual frontier, from the Black Sea to the great bend of the Euphrates in northern Syria. Military protection was still required as a deterrent against any Persian breach of the truce, but there was no need to concentrate Roman forces for successive building campaigns, each limited to one or two sites. Naturally, Kavad attempted to disrupt the work, but without provoking war. Surrogates were brought into play: Sabir Huns from north of the Caucasus in 515 entered Roman territory and caused extensive damage in Cappadocia; Persia's Arab clients raided in 519 or 520; and a north Caucasus Hunnic ruler was inveigled into attacking the Romans (only the last was thwarted by swift Roman counter-action).[46] But the Romans were not deterred, and the rolling programme—a slow-moving offensive in stone—continued for some 20 years, until, by winter 527–28, their strategic position immeasurably strengthened, they were ready to take action to avenge the wrong done to them in 502.

This early 6th c. fortification programme is better documented than any of its predecessors.[47] In addition to extant remains, remarkably well preserved in some cases, inscriptions, and historical reports about individual projects or local defence schemes, there is that extraordinary text, *The Buildings* of Procopius, an encomium of Justinian, which is narrowly

---

[43] Procop. *Aed.* 3.5.4–5.

[44] Josh. Styl. cc. 90, 92, 97, 100; Zach Myt. 7.6.

[45] Compare Greatrex (1998) 116–22, arguing that fortification work was prohibited during the truce.

[46] Malalas 16.17 (Sabir Huns), 17.10 (Hunnic ruler); *Chron.724* 111, a. 830; and Michael the Syrian 9.16, trans. Chabot, II, 178 (Arabs). Compare Greatrex (1998) 130–34.

[47] Compare Whitby (1986a); Howard-Johnston (1989).

focussed on his building activity, including road improvements and bridge-work. Procopius, who served on the eastern frontier with Belisarius and had the connections to gain access to official records, devotes more than a third of his survey to military projects in the Mesopotamian and Arme-nian frontier zones. Naturally he stresses the Emperor Justinian's input, exaggerating the scale of repair and restoration work where he limits himself to brief, general descriptions, but he also includes an impressive amount of detailed information about a number of sites.

It is hard to believe that Procopius invented specific improvements (e.g. the heightening of circuit-walls or construction of a fore-wall where none had existed), which he enumerates whether in full descriptions or in pithy summaries, or that he slips projects from the category of reconstruction

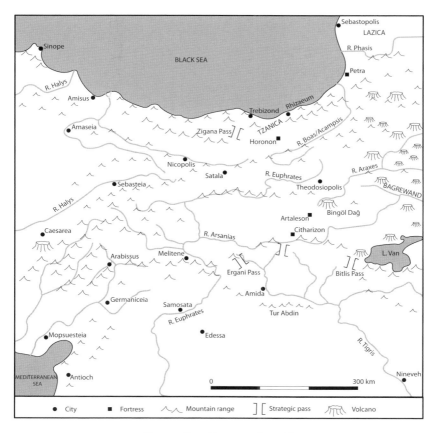

Fig. 4   Frontier zone (north).

to that of new construction. It looks as if the historian prevailed over the encomiast whenever his interest was aroused in the details of projects. Indeed, so extensive and detailed is his coverage in places, that it is tempting to suppose that he had a professional interest in the subject.[48] His information makes it possible to identify several distinct elements in the programme and to discern something of the strategic objectives pursued. It should be noted, though, that his coverage is not complete. He restricts himself to projects which could be credited to Justinian, that is projects completed after Justin I's accession in A.D. 518, when Justinian first took an active part in government. He carefully excludes projects started and completed under Anastasius, confining his coverage to those late Anastasian starts which were not finished when he died, and subsequent starts under Justin. He makes this clear in the case of the refortification of Melitene, a vital improvement on the weakest sector of the frontier, which he credits primarily to Anastasius, but notes was completed by Justinian (i.e. under Justin).[49]

For the opening 5 or 6 years of the programme, *ca.* 509–513/14, we have to turn instead to reports in the principal contemporary and near-contemporary sources, pseudo Joshua the Stylite, Malalas and pseudo Zachariah of Mitylene. It is a pity too that there is a gap in the rich Armenian historical tradition from the later 480s to the 570s, depriving us of information about the Persian response on the ground, and about Armenian attitudes to what may well have become an arms race between the two great powers.

The outer defences of the East Roman Empire were weakest in Armenia. An earlier arms race had been halted in or about 387, after the full militarisation of northern Mesopotamia, but before the construction of anything akin to a defensive system north of the Armenian Taurus and east of the Euphrates. Theodosiopolis, at the head of the Upper Euphrates valley, was more a symbolic marker than an effective bulwark of Roman power, since it could easily be by-passed. As for the southern half of the Roman sector of Armenia, there was no Roman military or governmental presence, since local satraps were left in place.[50] Thus the empire was extraordinarily vulnerable on the eastern approaches to Asia Minor by land. The Persians' defences were probably no stronger, but they had the great advantage of

---

[48] Howard-Johnston (2000).
[49] Procop. *Aed.* 1.3.3, 3.4.15–20.
[50] Procop. *Aed.* 3.1.17–27.

controlling a far larger proportion of Transcaucasia, which thus formed a buffer-zone, the circuit walls of its principal cities providing serviceable fortifications for any troops deployed for forward defence.

It comes as no surprise, then, that a large number of new forts and fortresses were built from scratch to improve security in Roman Armenia. In the far north, the Tzan, who lived in the fissured country of the Upper Boas/Acampsis, were subjected to the last recorded campaign of intensive pacification and development undertaken by a Roman government. Communications were improved by new road schemes, which involved forest clearance and engineering work in difficult country. A church was founded to act as a focal point for the evangelising of the population. It was probably built on a grand scale, for maximum effect, and may (though this is a highly speculative conjecture) even have provided the inspiration for the magnificent romanesque churches built elsewhere in Tzanica, Lazica and in Iberia over the following centuries. Four new forts were built and two existing ones were refurbished, to form a grid of control over Tzanica, fronted by a major new fortress at Horonon, a strategic route-junction where the borders of Tzanica, Persarmenia and Roman territory converged. By these well-tried methods, which had proved their worth in northern Spain, Wales, Pisidia, etc. in the heyday of the empire, a refractory highland region was transformed in a few decades into a well-defended forward Roman redoubt.[51] Given its position, pacified Tzanica both enhanced Roman standing and influence at the east end of the Black Sea, and could act as a platform for raiding Lazica or the Araxes plain around Dvin, capital of Persarmenia.

Depth and solidity were imparted to the defences by other measures in the hinterland of Tzanica: there were six backing forts, one moved to a more defensible site, three built from scratch, two renovated.[52] Further away, Satala's defences were rebuilt and strengthened with the addition of a fore-wall, and major restoration work was undertaken at three important cities on or near the northern support road—Colonia, Sebasteia and Nicopolis. Finally, the government produced funding for a general upgrading of local rural defences in the hinterland of Colonia.[53]

Reliance was placed above all on diplomacy to maintain security at the eastern end of the Black Sea. It was only through the exercise of

---

[51] Procop. *Aed.* 3.6.9–26.
[52] Procop. *Aed.* 3.4.10–11, 5.13–15.
[53] Procop. *Aed.* 3.4.2–9, 11.

influence over Laz rulers that Romans could be sure of preventing the establishment of a Sassanian base on the Black Sea. This policy was crowned with success in 522, when the king of the Laz came over to the Roman side (a move marked publicly by his baptism on a ceremonial visit to Constantinople).[54] The Romans responded with an aid programme, designed both to improve his security *vis à vis* the Persians (a new fort was built at Losorium and the passes leading into Lazica were blocked with defensive walls) and to enhance his domestic standing (Petra on the coast was fortified and built up into a fine-looking city).[55] The nearest Roman fortress was Rhizaeum, which commanded the coastal strip to the east of Trebizond, and which gained formidable, ingeniously designed defences.[56] Flanking Tzanica to the south, Theodosiopolis also benefited from improvements to its Anastasian defences, the walls upgraded to the standard of those at Dara—heightened, with two tiers of embrasures and strong towers—and protected by a new fore-wall and ditch.[57]

Further south, the valley of the Arsanias and the rolling uplands on the right bank remained under the control of local satraps, albeit now selected and appointed by the Romans. There was thus no question of developing a system of layered defence. Anastasius' government had to limit its efforts to construction of two fortresses right on the frontier, Artaleson (commanding the open country of Chorzane south of the Bingöl Dağ) and Citharizon (commanding the Arsanias valley and the northern approaches to the central pass over the Armenian Taurus), and to the re-fortification of Melitene, strategically placed to bar entry to the routes leading up to the Anatolian plateau. All of these were major projects, the first two on virgin sites, the third, Melitene, comprising a complete over-haul of the defences, involving construction of new walls enclosing the large built-up area around the old legionary fortress.[58] Behind, a scheme for improving regional security, by fortifying previously unfortified large villages, was funded by central government in the wake of the depredations of the Sabir Huns in Cappadocia.[59]

Work in northern Mesopotamia was not on the same scale, since a formidable network of defences already existed. Once dilapidated walls had

---

[54] Malalas 17.9.
[55] Procop. *Aed.* 3.7.5–7, *Pers.* 2.17.3.
[56] Procop. *Aed.* 3.7.3–4.
[57] Procop. *Aed.* 3.5.6–11.
[58] Procop. *Aed.* 3.3.7–14, 4.15–20.
[59] Malalas 16.17.

been made good and the balance of power had been changed dramatically by the construction of Dara right on the frontier. The chief task was to deter the Arab clients of the Persians from wide-ranging and damaging forays, like those made during Kavad's war. At least 12 forts were built north of Circesium (itself renovated and provided with a fore-wall), along the line of the Khabur River, up to Magdalathon and Great and Lesser Thannurius, in what looks like a throw-back to a much earlier, more confident frontier policy. They were placed on sites which were weakly defended by mud walls, if at all. They were clearly intended to police the frontier, especially a frequented crossing-point near Great Thannurius, and, indeed, to make the frontier a reality by advertising Rome's military presence. The effect sought, evidently at considerable expense, was primarily psychological, namely one of daunting the neighbouring Bedouin and declaring the hinterland of the Khabur an arena of combat against intruders.[60]

Defences were also repaired and improved on the Euphrates upstream from Circesium, and in the interior, on the left bank. A powerful backing fortress, with an enlarged and re-modelled circuit wall, was built on the ruins of Zenobia. Together with a restored fort on the opposite bank, it assured Roman control of a narrow strategic passage in the river-valley. Away from the river, work was carried out at the two cities, which commanded the natural avenue of invasion leading along the *badiya* south of the Tur Abdin—Theodosiopolis and Constantia (the latter a major project, including the construction of additional interval towers).[61] Security in the Upper Tigris basin was improved by updating the defences of forts in the vicinity of Amida (itself repaired after its recovery), while construction of new forts, together with renovation of those dating from the 4th c. (a total of 14 are named), solidified the Roman grip on the Tur Abdin massif between Amida and Dara. Like Tzanica, far to the north, the Tur Adbdin also had considerable offensive potential, since it protruded deep into Persian territory. It was a secure forward base, from which to launch expeditions north into the Upper Tigris basin and Arzanene on the far side of the river, or south, to raid the *badiya* (the environs of Nisibis were indefensible) and its small Sassanian analogue, the Jebel Sinjar.[62]

The defences of cities and forts behind the great bend of the Euphrates, in the north Syrian province of Euphratesia, were also restored and

---

[60] Procop. *Aed.* 2.6.1–8, 13–16.
[61] Procop. *Aed.* 2.5.1–8, 6.12, 8.8–25.
[62] Procop. *Aed.* 2.3.27–28, 4.1–21. Compare with Whitby (1986a) 727–28.

upgraded, notably at Hierapolis, the chief city and command centre of the region, which was given a new, reduced circuit of walls.[63] Procopius' systematic coverage does not reach further south, and so we are left in the dark about work carried out in the rest of Syria and further south, in the provinces of Palestine and Arabia, save for occasional information culled from texts, literary and epigraphic. It looks as if the great majority of Diocletianic forts and fortresses were no longer manned, reliance being placed instead on the prosperous towns, like Umm al-Rasas, Umm el-Jimal and Khirbet es-Samra, which had grown up in the *badiya* since the 4th c.[64] Local, rural-based defence forces, consisting of *limitanei* settled on small-holdings, seem to have been run down. Their role was probably taken over by urban militias, reinforced at times of danger by detachments sent from major bases like Palmyra, Damascus, Bostra, Udruh, Aila.

The defensive strategy was different from Diocletian's, its principal components being (1) concentration of force and (2) rapid deployment along high-standard roads to critical points in time of war. More reliance was placed on the Beduin tribes fronting the settled lands, after many generations of careful client-management. A 6th c. innovation was the elevation of the leading family of the Ghassan, the Jafnids, to royal status in A.D. 529, and delegation to them of authority over all the tribes fronting the Roman provinces, in the hope of replicating the military effectiveness of the Lakhm, the Persians' Arab clients.[65] Two cities, Sergiopolis in the north (a beneficiary of the fortification programme) and Bostra in the Hawran, were developed into regional cult-centres and show-pieces of Late Roman architecture, to act both as focal points for the Christian Arab tribes, and as secure bases from which to monitor their behaviour.[66]

There were thus several distinct components to the fortification programme initiated by Anastasius and brought to completion by Justinian: (1) artificially strengthened natural redoubts (Tzanica and the Tur Abdin); (2) powerful new or re-modelled fortresses at key points on the frontier north and south of the Armenian Taurus (Horonon, Theodosiopolis, Artaleson, Citharizon, Dara, Circesium); (3) networks of defended sites stretching deep into the interior, except in the region of the satrapies in south-western Armenia, where the task of backing up the forward bases

---

[63] Procop. *Aed.* 2.9.10–20.

[64] Piccirillo and Alliata (1994); Foss (1997) 245–54; de Vries (1998); Humbert and Desreumaux (1998).

[65] Procop. *Pers.* 1.17.40–48; Whittow (1999).

[66] Procop. *Aed.* 2.9.3–9; Fowden (1999) 60–100; Foss (1997) 237–54.

fell on a single base, Melitene; and (4) projects designed to project Roman influence more effectively over the Bedouin (the Khabur screen of forts and the prestige buildings of Sergiopolis and Bostra).

A fifth component, equally important, was the creation of direct, secure north-south routes of communication within the two arenas of war (between Theodosiopolis and Citharizon in the north and across the Tur Abdin in the south), and, even more important, between the two arenas, across the Armenian Taurus. At this strategic level, there had been a rough balance during the long period of peaceful co-existence from the late 4th c., each great power controlling a convenient route set back from their mutual frontier (the Romans the Ergani Pass, which ran south-east from Anzitene towards Amida, the Persians the Bitlis Pass, which linked the west end of Lake Van to Arzanene on southern flank of the mountains). The Romans had a useful forward position facing Arzanene at Martyropolis, where the *shahanshah* Yazdgerd I, in a remarkably conciliatory act, had allowed the bones of Christians martyred in Persia in the past to be deposited.[67] Martyropolis, which had surrendered without a fight in 502, had its defences strengthened to transform it into a secure base controlling the southern approach to the central Pheison Pass over the Armenian Taurus. Given that Citharizon commanded the northern outlet of the pass, the Romans only needed to build forts at its southern entrance (Pheison) and the two narrowest passages (at Illyrisus and Saphchae), to secure it for their own exclusive use. Procopius rightly gave this group of Justinianic projects pride of place in his survey of military construction north of Mesopotamia.[68] It meant that they had not only enhanced their regional defences along the whole length of the frontier, but had gained the vital advantage of inner lines where it mattered most, between the two main theatres of war.

The whole ambitious scheme of defence improvement was nearing completion in 527, when Justinian was crowned emperor in succession to his uncle Justin. At the same time, the armed forces were being put on a war footing. The phase of uneasy co-existence from 505, which had been punctuated by diplomatic fencing and occasional strikes by surrogates, was coming to an end. Units under the command of dukes were stationed in the main new or refurbished frontier fortresses in Armenia and Mesopotamia, as well as at the outpost in the north-western desert,

---

[67] Fowden (1999) 48–56.
[68] Procop. *Aed.* 3.2.10–3.6.

Palmyra.[69] The war opened in 528 with a three-pronged Roman advance into Lazica, aimed ultimately at Iberia, which went disastrously wrong, and with a defeat in northern Mesopotamia. The fortification programme had perforce to come to an end.[70] Improvements could be made, in time of war, to the command structure: a new field command was created in the north, covering the Armenian theatre with its headquarters at Theodosiopolis; greater cohesion was imparted to the Romans' Arab clients in the south by the elevation of the ruling Ghassan clan of the Jafnids to royal status.[71] Troop deployments could also be varied. But only emergency repair work to physical defences could be carried out in wartime (as, for example, at Callinicum in 542),[72] unless a field army commander felt confident enough to abandon operations and stand guard over a building site.[73]

In the event, the pause in the fortification programme was to last for over two decades, until the late 540s. The 'Peace Without End' which brought the war to a close in 532 assuredly included a clause prohibiting fortification work in frontier areas.[74] Then, after Kavad's son Khusro I launched a surprise attack in 540, gaining large ransoms from the cities he passed and even capturing Antioch, first the fighting, then the fiscal crisis, induced by the coming of plague to the Mediterranean in 541–42, precluded any resumption of the fortification programme.[75] Probably only from the late 540s, when the fiscal crisis was beginning to ease and the conflict was confined to Lazica, was an attempt made to remedy the principal defect in the Roman defensive system as it had been left in the late 520s, namely the absence of forts and fortresses to back up Artaleson and Citharizon in south-west Armenia. Direct rule had been imposed and the satrapies

---

[69] Procop. *Aed.* notes, without dating, the establishment of new ducal commands at Circesium (2.6.9), Martyropolis (3.2.1), Citharizon (3.2.1, 3.7–8), Artaleson (3.3.13–14), and Horonon (3.6.16–17). Two, the Martyropolis and Palmyra commands, both at highly sensitive places, are dated by Malalas, 18.2 and 5 to 527.

[70] Malalas 18.4 and 26.

[71] Malalas 18.10; Procop. *Aed.* 3.1.16 and 5.12, *Pers.* 1.17.45–48.

[72] Procop. *Pers.* 2.21.30–32.

[73] Two earlier building campaigns, at Thannuris and Melebasa, in 527, ended in failure (Zach. Myt. 9.2.5).

[74] Procop. *Pers.* 1.22.3–6 and 16–17 simply picks out major new clauses dealing with the length of the peace, the large payment to be made by the Romans, the partial demilitarisation of Dara, and an exchange of captured forts. Many other clauses, probably lifted from earlier treaties, were needed to regulate relations, commercial and diplomatic, between the two sides and their clients, and to deal with potential sources of conflict, such as cross-border disputes and fortification projects in frontier areas.

[75] Procop. *Pers.* 2.5–13, 22–23; Ps.Dionysius 74–98. Compare Sarris (2002).

Fig. 5   Roman forts in south-west Armenia.

abolished in 536 (without infringing the 532 treaty which said nothing about domestic constitutional or administrative arrangements)[76] and the void between Melitene and the frontier could now be filled, good use being made of natural strong-points first fortified in prehistoric times.

George of Cyprus, writing in the 590s, lists the forts and fortified towns which comprised the new regional defensive system: four linked Artaleson with the inner defensive line on the Euphrates—Baïuluus (modern Bağın), Merticertum (modern Mazgırt), Chozanum (modern Hozat) and Chosomachum (modern Çemişkezek), each commanding a river crossing in the open, rolling country to the north of the Arsanias; three others stood in the river valley—Palius (modern Palu), Arsamosata (Haraba, now beneath the Keban dam reservoir) and Dadimum (modern Tadım).[77] Their construction, in a final, delayed phase of the Anastasian fortification programme, can be placed before the 562 peace treaty, since, once again, fortification work was prohibited in frontier zones, and, after the renewal of warfare in 572 (initiated this time by the Romans), it would

[76] *Nov. Iust.* 31.1.3. The satraps must have lost their military authority earlier, before the outbreak of war in 528, to the dukes of Martyropolis and Citharizon. Compare Procop. *Aed.* 3.1.28–29, who conflates this with their later abolition.

[77] Georgius Cyprius 48–49 (nos. 948–57). Compare Howard-Johnston (1983) 246–51, 255–57 and (1989) 221–22.

have required the commitment of a whole field army to a building campaign. This only happened at times when the fighting died down: first during the Mesopotamian truce of 575–78 when, to compensate for the loss of Dara in 573, the defences of Monocarton were probably beefed up to guard the eastern approach to the reserve base at Constantia (the renaming of Monocarton in honour of Tiberius, Caesar and *de facto* ruler from December 574, can be taken to mark the completion of the work); and second in two relatively quiet years (586 and 587), when warfare had become attritional, and refortification could be put in hand at several sites (to tighten Roman control over the southern access to the Bitlis and Illyrisus passes and over the central Tur Abdin).[78]

Conclusions

Half a millennium of investment in military infrastructure, culminating, between 506 and 562, in a comprehensive programme of refurbishing, improving and extending the eastern frontier defences, virtually guaranteed the security of the heartlands of the Roman Empire in the eastern Mediterranean. Western Armenia had been transformed into a fortified outer shield for Asia Minor; northern Mesopotamia performed a similar function for Syria, the Euphrates in both cases forming the inner line of defence. Threats from the East, whether emanating from the Mesopotamian alluvium, the economic centre of gravity of the Parthian-Persian world, or the highlands of Iran, its military and cultural centre, were effectively countered along the whole length of the frontier from the Black Sea to the great sweep of the Euphrates as it turned south and east.

Two guiding principles were evident from first to last: (1) regular forces were deployed close to the frontier, either dispersed in a large number of fortified places or concentrated in a smaller number of larger bases; and (2) the frontier was regarded as a sharp divide between the civilised world where law and order reigned, and a heterogeneous outer world, which the Romans sought to overawe by advertising their power in the tangible form of forts, fortresses, great cities and the fine public buildings, especially churches, adorning them. By exploiting every advantage offered by terrain in a broad swathe behind the frontier to create secure assembly areas, large, well-protected refuge zones, and routes for strategic movement

---

[78] Whitby (1988) 268, n. 33, 282–86.

which could be denied to others, the Romans laid down defined arenas for manoeuvre against intruder forces. Each military installation built to command a nodal point in the network of natural and manmade communications, and each of the heavily fortified cities distributed across these combat zones, not only rooted Roman authority in what might have been contested territory, but also posed a potential threat to an invading force, since detachments large enough to operate independently in the field might lurk in any one of the defended bases.

Taken in aggregate, Roman frontier and backing bases north and south of the Armenian Taurus constituted a formidable bipartite defensive zone. The most that the Persians could hope for, in normal circumstances, was to take out a single stronghold in a campaigning season, when they were in a position to undertake siege operations (as happened at Dara in 573), or to sweep past the defended sites, if they were known to be undermanned, and push on into the interior, plundering and slowing only momentarily to gather ransom money from frightened cities (as in 540).[79] The only alternative was to prepare for a long war of attrition, as Khusro II did on receiving news of the execution of his benefactor, the Emperor Maurice, in November 602. He knew that the Romans would be unable to match his armies in the field, because the *magister militum per Orientem* had refused to recognise the regime of the usurper Phocas and had come out in open rebellion; but, even with this initial advantage, it took 8 years of hard fighting and a second, yet more serious Roman domestic crisis for his forces to reach and then breach the inner Euphrates line of defence.[80]

Whereas the trend in the north was for a deepening and strengthening of the defensive zones, south of the Euphrates bend the purely military installations on the frontier were thinned out. The remaining bases with larger concentrations of troops were supplemented by the towns which had grown up in the *badiya* in Late Antiquity, and by the Arab tribes fronting the *badiya* whose loyalties had been long cultivated. The Roman authorities did not drop their guard *vis à vis* the nomads of the desert. The Mediterranean coast, from Laodicea in the north to Gaza in the south, was, together with the Nile valley, the industrial and commercial heartland of the empire. Prosperity had spread inland, especially in the 6th c., with increasing interchange with the Arabs,[81] and there would be a huge

---

[79] Theoph. Sim. 3.10.4–11.2; Procop. *Pers.* 2.5–13.
[80] Thomson and Howard-Johnston (1999) xxii–xxiii, 197–203.
[81] Johns (1994) 4–8; Walmsley (2007) 34–45, neither of whom seeks the explanation in trade outside the borders of the empire.

price to pay if security could not be guaranteed. However, the fertile strip of land, studded with prosperous towns and cities, squeezed between the desert and the sea, which constituted the Roman Levant, was inherently more exposed than northern Syria, Cilicia and Asia Minor. There was no room for a buffer zone between frontier and interior. Hence a high priority continued to be attached to preclusive defence, as was made evident by the retention of the main military bases of the Diocletianic system, and the continuing presence of ducal military commands in frontier provinces. Hence, too, the grant of supra-tribal authority to the Ghassan, in an effort to improve the military performance of the client tribes.

In the event, the new system worked well. The desert frontage remained secure, save in A.D. 573, when Roman defences were in disarray after a catastrophic defeat in northern Mesopotamia. This second crisis was engineered by the Persians, who managed to neutralise the Ghassan and catch a Roman field army outside Nisibis unawares, by advancing up the Khabur and attacking them in the rear. Even so, pro-active diplomacy, a vital ingredient of preclusive defence, limited the damage which the temporary defection of the Ghassan caused. The tribes who traditionally looked to the Romans for benefits in cash and kind continued to be responsive. After the dissolution of the Ghassan system of tribal management in 582, no rival nexus of tribes rose in north-west Arabia to challenge Roman hegemony.[82]

When Roman control was eventually prised loose from the Levant, the force which prevailed was that of Persian field armies, with the aid of a new client-management system devised to protect the whole desert frontage of the Fertile Crescent, from the head of the Persian Gulf to the head of the Red Sea.[83] By that stage, however, both the north Mesopotamian and the west Armenian defensive zones had been conquered and the whole East Roman Empire was under pressure from without. So the Persian conquest of Syria, Cilicia, Palestine and Egypt, between 611 and 621, is not attributable to weakness in the southern sectors of the defensive system. It is to be explained rather by Roman political division and by the determination and commitment of the reigning *shahanshah*, Khusro II (590–628).[84]

Khusro, however, over-reached himself, and all his gains were lost in the last two years of that long war. The Roman authorities returned to

[82] Whitby (1988) 256–58, 264, 272–76, 280.
[83] Howard-Johnston (2006b) 20–22.
[84] Thomson and Howard-Johnston (1999) xxiii–xxiv, 203–13.

Syria and Palestine in 629–30, and Roman forces re-occupied their bases. The old client-management system was reinstated, headed once again by the Ghassan. But it was only a momentary restoration of the old order, for a new danger flared up within four years, in a quite unexpected quarter.[85] The Hijaz had long lain near the horizon of Roman diplomatic vision in the south, an intermediary zone between the two natural power-centres of the Arabian peninsula, in the Yemen and in the north-west. The new, tightly-bonded nexus of alliances, centred on Medina, which appeared in the decades when the great war in the north was reaching its climax, was poised to strike north, once its hegemony was assured within Arabia. With the impetus imparted by commitment to a new, enveloping and ener-gising faith, the armies sent north from the Hijaz were likely to prove invincible, whatever the circumstances.[86] Buoyed up though they were by their recent victory over Persia, Roman forces could not match them in the field, despite the stalwart support of their Ghassan allies. Worse still, there were too few forward bases on the southern section of the *Via Nova Traiana* for them to mount an effective defence, and no second line of fixed defence on which they could fall back.

So it was that within two years of the death of the Prophet, with Arabia unified (by force), Muslim armies were able to attack Palestine from the south in 634, and, after winning a decisive victory a few miles inland from Gaza, could dispatch raiding forays over the defenceless country to the north. Within a year, Palestine submitted to Muslim rule, and the battle for Syria began, a battle which was not to last much longer.[87] Remarkably, within a generation, the Romans would be stripped of their lands in the Middle East and forced to withdraw behind the natural and manmade defences of Asia Minor.

POSTSCRIPT

The above outline is a rough interpretation only, since much work remains to be done. Tim Mitford's forthcoming book on the Euphrates *limes* will add greatly to our knowledge of installations and roads north of the Arme-nian Taurus. If security were to improve significantly in the zone to the

---

[85] Howard-Johnston (1999).
[86] Donner (1981) 11–90.
[87] *Chron.724* 18–19; Sebeos 135–36. Compare Thomson and Howard-Johnston (1999) 240–43.

east of the Euphrates and it were possible to carry out similarly thorough survey work there, attention should be directed in the first instance at Tzanica, where neither the church nor the ducal base (Horonon) mentioned by Procopius have been identified on the ground, and, in the second, at the region around the Bingöl Dağ where a major Justinianic fortress, Artaleson, awaits discovery. As for excavation, the priorities should be Erzurum (both intra-urban rescue work and investigation of the extant remains of the city wall), Afşin (Arabissus) and other sites in the Armenian Taurus (Elbistan) basin. South of the Anti-Taurus, the main task is to improve knowledge of urban life and military infrastructure on the Sassanian side of the frontier, beginning with the important site of Nisibis on the modern Syrian-Turkish frontier. On the Roman side, the flourishing of archaeology and research in Jordan is steadily improving our knowledge and understanding of the development of the *badiya* and its hinterlands in Late Antiquity. It would be a great boon if the authorities in Syria and south-eastern Turkey were equally supportive of archaeological research.

BIBLIOGRAPHY

Primary Sources

Agath. = Keydell R. (1967) ed. Agathias Myrinaeus, *Historiarum libri quinque* (Berlin 1967).
Chron 724 = Chabot J.-B. (1955) trans. *Chronicon miscellaneum ad annum Domini 724 pertinens* (CSCO, Scriptores Syri 4, Chronica Minor II) (Louvain 1955) 63–119.
Georgius Cyprius = Gelzer H. (1890) ed. Georgius Cyprius, *Descriptio Orbis Romani* (Leipzig 1890).
Josh. Styl. = Trombley F. R. and Watt J. W. (2000) trans. *The Chronicle of Pseudo-Joshua the Stylite* (Translated Texts for Historians 32) (Liverpool 2000).
Malalas = Thurn J. (2000) ed. Ioannes Malalas, *Chronographia* (Berlin 2000); Jeffreys E., Jeffreys M and Scott R. (1986) trans. *The Chronicle of John Malalas* (Melbourne 1986).
Nov. Iust. = Schöll R. and Kroll W. (1892–95) edd. *Corpus Juris Civilis* III: *Novellae* (Berlin 1892–1895, repr. 1945–1963).
Menander = Blockley R. C. (1985) ed. and trans. *The History of Menander the Guardsman* (ARCA, classical and medieval texts, papers and monographs 17) (Liverpool 1985).
Michael the Syrian = Chabot J. B. (1899–1910) ed. and trans. *Chronique de Michel le Syrien* 4 vols. (Paris 1899–1910).
Pan. Lat. = Mynors R. A. B. (1964) ed. *XII Panegyrici Latini* (Oxford 1964).
Procop. *Aed.* = Dewing H. B. and Downey G. (1971) ed. and trans. Procopius, *De Aedificiis* (Cambridge, Mass. 1971).
Procop. *Goth*, Procop. *Pers.* and Procop. *Vand.* = Dewing H. B. (1962–71) ed. and trans. Procopius, *History of the Wars*, 5 vols. (Cambridge Mass. 1962–71).
Ps.Dionysius = Witakowski W. (1996) trans. Ps.Dionysius of Tel-Mahre, *Chronicle*, Part III (Translated Texts for Historians 22) (Liverpool 1996).
Sebeos = Thomson R. trans. in Thomson R. W. and Howard-Johnston J. (1999) edd. *The Armenian History Attributed to Sebeos* (Translated Texts for Historians 31) (Liverpool 1999).

ŠKZ = Huyse P. (1999) ed. and trans. *Die dreisprachige Inschrift Šabuhrs I. an der Ka'ba-i Zardušt (ŠKZ)*, (Corpus Inscriptionum Iranicarum, 3.1), 2 vols. (London 1999).
Tabula Peutingerana = Miller K. (1962) ed. *Die Peutingersche Tafel* (Stuttgart 1962).
Zach. Myt. *Chron.* = Hamilton F. J. and Brooks E. W. (1899) trans. *The Syriac Chronicle Known as that of Zachariah of Mitylene* (London 1899).

Secondary Works

Birley A. R. (2000) "Hadrian to the Antonines", in *Cambridge Ancient History, Volume II: The High Empire, A.D. 70–192*, edd. A. K. Bowman, P. Garnsey and D. Rathbone (Cambridge 2000) 132–94.
Blockley R. C. (1992) *East Roman Foreign Policy: Formation and Conduct from Diocletian to Anastasius* (Leeds 1992).
Comfort A. (2008) *Roads on the Frontier between Rome and Persia: Euphratesia, Osrhoene and Mesopotamia from AD 363 to 602* (Ph.D. diss., Univ. of Exeter 2008) http://eric.exeter.ac.uk/exeter/handle/10036/68213.
de Vries B. (1998) ed. *Umm el-Jimal, a Frontier Town and its Landscape in Northern Jordan, I: Fieldwork 1972–1981* (JRA Supplementary Series 26) (Portsmouth, RI 1998).
Dodgeon M. H. and Lieu S. N. C. (1991) *The Roman Eastern Frontier and the Persian Wars AD 226–363: a Documentary History* (London 1991).
Donner F. M. (1981) *The Early Islamic Conquests* (Princeton 1981).
Finster B. and Schmidt J. (1976) *Sasanidische und frühislamische Ruinen im Iraq* (Baghdader Mitteilungen 8) (Berlin 1976).
Fisher G. (2011) *Between Empires: Arabs, Romans and Sasanians in Late Antiquity* (Oxford 2011).
Foss C. (1997) "Syria in transition, A.D. 550–750: an archaeological approach", *DOP* 51 (1997) 189–269.
Fowden E. K. (1999) *The Barbarian Plain: St. Sergius between Rome and Iran* (Berkeley and Los Angeles 1999).
Freeman P. and Kennedy D. L. (1986) edd. *The Defence of the Roman and Byzantine East: Proceedings of a Colloquium held at the University of Sheffield in April 1986* (BAR International Series 297) (Oxford 1986).
French D. H. (1980) "The Roman road-system of Asia Minor", in *Aufstieg und Niedergang der römischen Welt*, II.7.2, ed. H. Temporini (Berlin 1980) 698–729.
—— (1981) *Roman Roads and Milestones of Asia Minor*, I: *the Pilgrim's Road* (Oxford 1981).
French D. H. and Lightfoot C. S. (1989) edd. *The Eastern Frontier of the Roman Empire: Proceedings of a Colloquium held at Ankara in September 1988* (BAR International Series 553) (Oxford 1989).
Garsoïan N. G. (2004) "La date de la fondation de Théodosioupolis-Karin", *RÉB* 62 (2004) 181–96.
Gray E. W. (1973) "The Roman eastern *limes* from Constantine to Justinian—perspectives and problems", *Proceedings of the African Classical Associations* 12 (1973) 24–40.
Greatrex G. and Lieu S. N. C. (2002) *The Roman Eastern Frontier and the Persian Wars, Part II AD 363–630: a Narrative Sourcebook* (London 2002).
Gregory S. (1997) *Roman Military Architecture on the Eastern Frontier*, 3 vols. (Amsterdam 1997).
Howard-Johnston J. D. (1983) "Byzantine Anzitene", in *Armies and Frontiers in Roman and Byzantine Asia Minor: Proceedings of a Colloquium held at University College Swansea, in April 1981*, ed. S. Mitchell (BAR International Series 156) (Oxford 1983) 239–88, repr. in Howard-Johnston (2006a) chapter III.
—— (1989) "Procopius, Roman defences north of the Taurus and the new fortress of Citharizon", in *The Eastern Frontier of the Roman Empire: Proceedings of a Colloquium held at Ankara in September 1988*, edd. D. H. French and C. S. Lightfoot (BAR International Series 553) (Oxford 1989) 203–29, repr. in Howard-Johnston (2006a) chapter II.

—— (1995) "The two great powers in Late Antiquity: a comparison", in *The Byzantine and Early Islamic Near East*, III: *States, Resources and Armies*, ed. A. Cameron (Princeton 1995) 157–226, repr. in Howard-Johnston (2006a) chapter I.

—— (1999) "Heraclius' Persian campaigns and the revival of the East Roman Empire, 622–630", *War in History* 6 (1999) 1–44, repr. in Howard-Johnston (2006a) chapter VIII.

—— (2000) "The education and expertise of Procopius", *Antiquité Tardive* 8 (2000) 19–30.

—— (2006a) *East Rome, Sasanian Persia and the End of Antiquity: Historiographical and Historical Studies* (Aldershot 2006).

—— (2006b) "Al-Tabari on the last great war of antiquity", in Howard-Johnston, *East Rome, Sasanian Persia and the End of Antiquity: Historiographical and Historical Studies* (Aldershot 2006), ch. VI.

Hoyland R. G. (2001) *Arabia and the Arabs from the Bronze Age to the Coming of Islam* (London 2001).

Humbert J.-B. and Desreumaux A. (1998) edd. *Fouilles de Khirbet es-Samra en Jordanie*, I: *La voie romaine, le cimetière, les documents épigraphiques* (Turnhout 1998).

Isaac B. (1990) *The Limits of Empire: the Roman Army in the East* (Oxford 1990).

Johns J. (1994) "The *Longue Durée*: state and settlement strategies in southern Transjordan across the Islamic centuries", in *Village, Steppe and State: the Social Origins of Modern Jordan*, edd. E. L. Rogan and T. M. M. Tell (London 1994) 1–31.

Kennedy D. L. (2004) *The Roman Army in Jordan* (2nd ed., London 2004).

Killick A. C. (1986) "Udruh and the southern frontier", in *The Defence of the Roman and Byzantine East: Proceedings of a Colloquium held at the University of Sheffield in April 1986*, edd. P. Freeman and D. L. Kennedy (BAR International Series 297) (Oxford 1986) 431–46.

Matthews J. F. (1989) *The Roman Empire of Ammianus Marcellinus* (London 1989).

Millar F. (1993) *The Roman Near East 31BC-AD337* (Cambridge, Mass. 1993).

Mitchell S. (1989) "The siege of Cremna", in *The Eastern Frontier of the Roman Empire: Proceedings of a Colloquium held at Ankara in September 1988*, edd. D. H. French and C. S. Lightfoot (BAR International Series 553) (Oxford 1989) 311–28.

—— (1993) *Anatolia: Land, Men and Gods in Asia Minor*, 2 vols. (Oxford 1993).

Mitford T. B. (1980) "Cappadocia and Armenia Minor: historical setting of the *Limes*", in *Aufstieg und Niedergang der römischen Welt*, II.7.2, ed. H. Temporini (Berlin 1980) 1119–228.

—— (1986) "A Late Roman fortress south of Lake Van", in *The Defence of the Roman and Byzantine East: Proceedings of a Colloquium held at the University of Sheffield in April 1986*, edd. P. Freeman and D. L. Kennedy (BAR International Series 297) (Oxford 1986) 565–73.

—— (in prep.) *Rome and Armenia: The Euphrates Frontier* (Oxford).

Naval Intelligence Division (1945) Geographical Handbook Series: *Persia* (1945).

—— (1942–43) Geographical Handbook Series: *Turkey*, 2 vols. (1942–43).

Nixon C. E. V. and Rodgers B. S. (1994) *In Praise of Later Roman Emperors* (Berkeley and Los Angeles 1994).

Parker S. T. (2006) *The Roman Frontier in Central Jordan: Final Report on the Limes Arabicus Project, 1980–1989* (Washington D.C. 2006).

Piccirillo M. and Alliata E. (1994) edd. *Umm al-Rasas, Mayfa'ah, I: Gli scavi del complesso di Santo Stefano* (Jerusalem 1994).

Richmond I. A. (1962) "The Roman siege-works of Masada, Israel", *JRS* 52 (1962) 142–55.

Rickman G. (1971) *Roman Granaries and Store Buildings* (Cambridge 1971).

Sarris P. (2002) "The Justinianic Plague: origins and effects", *Continuity and Change* 17 (2002) 169–82.

Sinclair T. A. (1987–90) *Eastern Turkey: an Architectural and Archaeological Survey*, 4 vols. (London 1987–90).

Thomson R. W. and Howard-Johnston J. D. (1999) edd. *The Armenian History Attributed to Sebeos* (Translated Texts for Historians 31) (Liverpool 1999).

Ulbert T. (2000) "Procopius, *De Aedificiis*: Einige Überlegungen zu Buch II, Syrien", *Antiquité Tardive* 8 (2000) 137–47.

Walmsley A. (2007) *Early Islamic Syria: an Archaeological Assessment* (London 2007).

Whitby M. (1984) "Procopius' description of Martyropolis (*De Aedificiis* III.2.10–14)", *Byzantinoslavica* 45 (1984) 177–82.

—— (1986a) "Procopius and the development of Roman defences in Upper Mesopotamia", in Freeman *The Defence of the Roman and Byzantine East: Proceedings of a Colloquium held at the University of Sheffield in April 1986*, edd. P. Freeman and D. L. Kennedy (BAR International Series 297) (Oxford 1986) 717–35.

—— (1986b) "Procopius' description of Dara (*Buildings* II.1–3)", in *The Defence of the Roman and Byzantine East: Proceedings of a Colloquium held at the University of Sheffield in April 1986*, edd. P. Freeman and D. L. Kennedy (BAR International Series 297) (Oxford 1986) 737–83.

—— (1987) "Notes on some Justinianic constructions", *Byzantinisch-neugriechischen Jahrbücher* 23 (1987) 89–112.

—— (1988) *The Emperor Maurice and his Historian: Theophylact Simocatta on Persian and Balkan Warfare* (Oxford 1988).

Whitby M. and Whitby M. (1986) trans. *The History of Theophylact Simocatta* (Oxford 1986).

Whittow M. (1999) "Rome and the Jafnids: writing the history of a 6th c. tribal dynasty", in *The Roman and Byzantine Near East, II: Some Recent Archaeological Research*, ed. J. H. Humphrey (JRA Supplementary Series 31) (Portsmouth, RI 1999) 207–24.

Wilkinson T. J. and Tucker D. J. (1995) *Settlement Development in the North Jazira, Iraq: a Study of the Archaeological Landscape* (Warminster 1995).

Zuckerman C. (1991) "The early Byzantine strongholds in eastern Pontus", *TravMém* 11 (1991) 527–53.

LIST OF FIGURES

EL-LEJJŪN: LOGISTICS AND LOCALISATION
ON ROME'S EASTERN FRONTIER IN THE 6TH C. A.D.

Conor Whately

Abstract

This paper re-evaluates some of the conclusions reached by the contributors to the published final excavation report for the fortress of el-Lejjūn in Jordan, particularly regarding its occupation in the first half of the 6th c. A.D. I argue that there was still a significant military presence, likely composed of *limitanei*, during that period, and that much of their food was sourced locally. This is in keeping with what we know about the provisioning of Roman frontier fortresses in other parts of the empire, and trends in the trade networks of the 6th c. East in general. Furthermore, the essay highlights the value that detailed archaeological reports have for elucidating Late Roman military logistics.

INTRODUCTION

In his book, *Framing the Early Middle Ages*, Chris Wickham remarks, "surprisingly, not much work has been done on the supply aspect of Late Roman military logistics."[1] He also notes that he has trouble seeing how archaeology could help illuminate the situation, though significantly he is concerned with amphorae distribution.[2] Wickham may be right, insofar as Late Roman amphorae (LRA) cannot prove the existence of the supply of grain,[3] but there are many other ways that archaeology can help us

---

[1] Wickham (2005) 78. Mitthof's (2001) detailed study focuses primarily on the administrative end of military supply in Egypt, using papyri, and to a lesser extent, legal and literary texts. Decades earlier, Jones (1964) discussed logistics, and like Mitthof, made little use of the material evidence.

[2] Wickham (2005) 78.

[3] In a paper focused almost entirely on the material evidence, there is bound to be some confusion about nomenclature, particularly as regards the time periods under study. Generally, I disagree with arguments on the suitability of using the term 'Byzantine' for the post-324 East, such as those advocated by Tsafrir and Foerster (1997) 85, n. 1. As this paper focuses on the 6th c., I avoid many of these problems, and as such, I shall, by and large, stick with 'Late Roman' when referring to the state and army, rather than 'Late Byzantine', the name usually given by archaeologists working on 6th c. Palestine, save for when I

A. Sarantis, N. Christie (edd.) *War and Warfare in Late: Current Perspectives*
(Late Antique Archaeology 8.1–8.2 – 2010–11) (Leiden 2013), pp. 893–924.

to better understand military supply. John Haldon's edited volume, *General Issues in the Study of Medieval Logistics*, highlights just how valuable the material evidence is, particularly when integrated with other modern research techniques and tools, such as computer modelling.[4] Indeed, in a volume devoted to archaeology and war in Late Antiquity, there is perhaps no other military issue for which the material evidence plays such an important part as logistics.[5]

Thus, this paper will focus on one element of Late Roman military logistics, namely the provisioning of food for the frontier forces, especially the *limitanei*, in the East.[6] To do this, I concentrate on the recently published final excavation report for the *Limes Arabicus* and el-Lejjūn, perhaps the best excavated late antique military site on the eastern frontier.[7] Detailed though the evidence published in the report may be, problems exist with the conclusions that the team have drawn, which I shall highlight.[8] I then discuss the relevance of this evidence from the Arabian frontier and put my conclusions into a broader context, before asking whether it has some bearing on the degree of state involvement in frontier supply and organisation, while pointing out important distinctions between peace and wartime logistics.

---

critique conclusions drawn from Parker's (2006a) final report, in which the chronological periods used have some bearing on my conclusions.

[4] Haldon (2006a). Some papers in the volume explore select issues pertaining to logistics by using techniques developed for other disciplines, such as landscape archaeology and GIS. The collection demonstrates just how valuable modern research tools can be for analysing the issues of supply and demand, both as regards the Byzantine army, and society at large. Haldon's introductory chapter (2006b) provides an excellent overview of the main issues concerned with military logistics for any ancient or medieval state.

[5] Note Toplyn's (2006) 482 pertinent comments.

[6] At least two works have concentrated on the provisioning of Roman soldiers in the East during the Imperial period: Adams (1976); and Kissel (1995). My paper is inspired in part by Toplyn (2006), building on his dissertation (1994).

[7] Parker and Betlyon (2006).

[8] This paper addresses some of the same concerns raised by Magness (1999), who points out problems with the conclusions drawn about the chronology of the forts of En Boqeq, Upper Zohar, and those of the area east of Mount Hebron. That re-evaluation has important implications for this paper (see below).

THE BACKGROUND: *LIMITANEI* AND THE EASTERN FRONTIER[9]

The fort of el-Lejjūn is located in central Jordan, to the east of the Dead Sea, on the eastern edge of the Jordanian plateau (see fig. 1).[10] The Central Moab—the part of the Jordanian plateau where the fort is located—is characterised by hot and dry summers and cold and moist winters; rainfall was far from abundant, with the yearly average between 200 mm and 300 mm. The area is almost totally devoid of trees, and dominated by shrubs and bushes. Roman Arabia—later Arabia and Palestine—was the southern portion of the eastern frontier, which stretched from the Caucasus in the north to the Red Sea in the south. Imperial Rome's great eastern foe, Persia, first under the Arsacids, and in our period under the Sassanids, concentrated most of its attacks in the northern sector of that frontier. During the reign of Justinian, for example, the wars with Persia were in Mesopotamia and the Caucasus.

Nevertheless, in the late 3rd/early 4th c., a period of intense re-organisation on the eastern frontier, new fortifications were constructed, and old ones were re-built in both the north and south along the old road *via nova Traiana*, which became the *Strata Diocletiana*. It is during this period that el-Lejjūn was built (see fig. 2). Though one can plausibly argue that the fortifications—forts, fortlets, and towers—in the northern half of the frontier were erected in response to a perceived Persian threat, it is less so for the southern half. The Arabs were the only potential external threat, and opinion is divided over the danger they posed.[11]

Regardless of the strategic context of el-Lejjūn and its contemporaries along the *Strata Diocletiana*,[12] the fort would have had a number of functions pertaining to both internal and external security as well as trade. It is generally accepted that a unit of *limitanei*, the legio IV Martia, was based at the legionary fortress of el-Lejjūn. This attribution is based on

---

[9] The best overview of frontiers in Late Antiquity is by Mark Graham (2006), who focuses (ix), on "the place of imperial frontiers in [the] Late Roman worldview". On frontiers throughout the Imperial period, see Whittaker (1994).

[10] My discussion of the geography and topography is based on that of Toplyn (1994) 1–9. For a broader overview of the eastern desert frontier, see Kennedy and Riley (1990) 24–26.

[11] Some scholars, such as Parker, believe that the Arabs were a credible threat, while others, such as Isaac, dispute this.

[12] I sidestep here the vexed issue of defence-in-depth, first raised by Luttwak (1976). Suffice to say, such a description does fit the evidence, even if the Romans themselves never conceived of their purpose in such a way.

an entry in the *Notitia Dignitatum*, which lists the aforementioned legion with the site of Betthorus.[13] Given that we do not know the ancient name for el-Lejjūn, or the modern location of Betthorus, and the absence of any epigraphic or literary material that might support this, we are left with no alternative.[14]

Next I need to address concerns about the continued existence, or disbandment, of the *limitanei* at the site, and in the empire at large, during the reign of Justinian.[15] Although no one would deny a military presence at the site in the 4th and early 5th c., there is some debate concerning its occupancy in the second half of the 5th and first half of the 6th c.

On a wider setting, much of the debate about the change in fortunes of the *limitanei* stems from an over-quoted, yet poorly understood, passage from Procopius' *Secret History*, a vitriolic supplement to his more measured *Wars*, and in stark contrast to his panegyrical *Buildings*. Where the narrator of the *Secret History* is overly harsh towards Justinian, his counterpart in

---

[13] *Not. Dign. or.* 37.21.22.

[14] Toplyn (2006) 502; and Parker (2006c) 542–43, for example, accept that a limitanean unit resided in the fort. Parker (2006c) 543 at least recognises the absence of any confirmation of the unit's type. El-Lejjūn was constructed in the late 3rd or early 4th c., so coinciding with the military reorganisations of Diocletian and Constantine. Other than from the *Notitia Dignitatum*, the legio IV Martia is unknown. By the late 1st c., legions across the empire were becoming stationary, a process reaching its zenith a century later. Then, when troops were needed elsewhere, smaller units, vexillations, were drawn from the parent legion. There is reason to believe that these vexillations evolved into the mobile 4th c. *comitatenses*, while the legions left behind evolved into the *limitanei*, the stationary units. On the other hand, by the 6th c. the distinction between *limitanei* and *comitatenses* had become blurred so that the latter were also often now stationary (Whitby 1995) 70–71; Casey (1996) 216. Carrié (1995) 33 suggests that the primary distinction between the members of the armed forces under Justinian was between palatine and provincial troops. The gradual emergence of the *buccellarii* also causes problems of identification, for many of the alleged limitanean units from Egypt may have been units of *buccellarii*, which in turn casts doubt on similar assertions here (Haug (2007) 216; Sarris (2006) 162–75). On army changes in the 2nd and 3rd c., see Rankov (2007) 70–75. For Late Antiquity, see Elton (2007) 272–78. On Late Roman legions, see Tomlin (2000).

[15] The best guide to the primary evidence pertaining to the *limitanei*, at least for the 3rd through 5th c., is Isaac (1998) 366–78. The notion that the *limitanei* were little more than peasant militia goes back nearly a century: Grosse (1920) 63–70, 275–76. Stein (1949) 86 agreed: "but their military valour did not cease to diminish". Van Berchem (1952) 20–21; and Jones (1964) 649–54 were generally more positive in their assessments. MacMullen (1963) argued strongly in favour of their role as soldier-farmers. Despite the convincing assertions of the *limitanei*'s effectiveness by Isaac (1990) 208–13; Elton (1996) 200–208; and Nicasie (1998) 18–22, doubts still remain, as the works of Richardot (2005) 171–75; and Le Bohec (2006) 143–44; and, to a lesser degree, Southern and Dixon (1996) 35–37; and Greatrex (1998) 34–36 indicate.

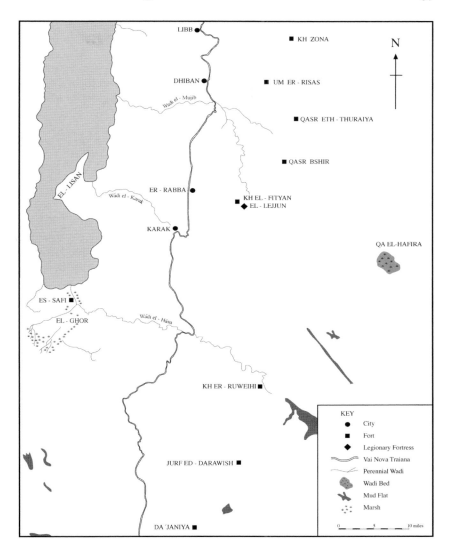

Fig. 1   Map of the Frontier in Central Jordan in Late Antiquity.

the *Buildings* is the opposite; possibly reality lies somewhere in the middle.
In a later part of the passage in question, Procopius claims that:

> a long time ago those who ruled Rome deployed a host of soldiers at all of
> the furthest points of the commonwealth to guard the frontiers of the Roman
> Empire, especially the eastern part, from Persian and Saracen incursions;
> they called these troops *limitanei*. The Emperor Justinian at first treated

these men harshly and as second-class troops, so that those responsible for paying their wages were four or five years in arrears, and whenever peace broke out between the Romans and Persians, the poor souls were forced, since they were meant to benefit from the blessings of peace, to give freely to the office of the public treasury that which was owed to them for some time; later they were deprived of this classification as legitimate soldiers. (Procop. *Anec.* 24.12–13).

A positivistic reading of this passage, taken in isolation, suggests a significant change in Justinian's frontier policy in the region at this time. However, mining a text for evidence, particularly an author as complex as Procopius, is hazardous.[16] A lawyer from Caesarea with the requisite education in rhetoric, Procopius was well-versed in the art of persuasion. As with his other texts, in the *Secret History*, Procopius has a point to prove; so when it is read in its broader context, and in light of the broader themes in the *Secret History*, the passage's veracity is undermined. About midway through the *Secret History*, Procopius turns his attention from his issues with Belisarius, Antonina, and Theodora, to Justinian's depredations of the empire, which, unsurprisingly, take up most of the text. Although Procopius has a number of gripes, there are three particular themes that are pertinent here, all of which probably impacted on Procopius himself: economic matters, foreign policy, and those groups wronged by Justinian.[17] In this passage, from his discussion of the sad plight of all 6th c. soldiers,[18] Procopius is afforded the chance to check off all three of these complaints, and this is how we should understand this piece of narrative. He has discussed the foreign policy blunders of Justinian, the plight of people such as the landowners, and the emperor's economic depredations. This passage enables Procopius to bring all of these issues together.

On the other hand, though not necessarily a conscious deceiver of his audience,[19] whomever that may have been, Procopius is considerably manipulative, carefully selecting and including details when and where

---

[16] Kaldellis (2004) is one of the most recent scholars to bring attention to this problem, particularly for complex historians like Procopius; see also Cameron (1985).

[17] The former issue, economic matters, has recently been the subject of a study by Sarris (2006) 5–6.

[18] Procop. *Anec.* focuses on soldiers from 24.1 to 24.29.

[19] However, Procopius (Procop. *Anec.* 23) erroneously claims that the Saracens continually ravaged the empire, when in fact there were two possible points when they posed any threat, notably around A.D. 503/504, and in 527, both when the empire was busy dealing with the Persians to the north. Significantly, we do not know the extent of the damage these Arab incursions caused. Tates (2004) 391–92 instead calls the period A.D. 330–540 the 'Byzantine Peace', while noting that in Arabia, more territory was occupied than before.

he saw fit. The payment of soldiers may have been in arrears, peace may not have given them their deserved respite, and the *limitanei* may not have been well-respected by all, but these episodes may not have been concurrent, despite the fact that this is suggested by the Procopian passage. As with the issue of the expansion of frontier construction as set out in the *Buildings*, much of what Procopius attributes to Justinian may have been the work of an earlier emperor, such as Anastasius.[20] As such, this quote should not be taken at face value, particularly when we consider the wider context.

There are a number of sources, both literary and papyrological, that suggest that the *limitanei* retained a prominent role throughout the 6th c.[21] They seem to be attested at Elephantine in southern Egypt, as both papyri and a few comments in Procopius' *Wars* make clear.[22] Justinian's *Novel* 103 notes the importance of the *limitanei* in Palestine in the first half of the century.[23] Generally, the novel maintains the distinction between civilian and soldiery in the province,[24] though as a result of the unrest involving the Samaritans,[25] the proconsul was able to co-opt frontier soldiers based in the province to quell any serious disturbances. Tackling civilian unrest is different from fighting an organised army; nevertheless, in some ways, the former can be more challenging than the latter, and so here we have evidence for the *limitanei*'s continued importance.

Staying with Roman Palestine, we also have evidence for the existence of units of *limitanei* from A.D. 505 to the end of the 6th c. from Nessana,[26] as well as in the mid 6th c. from the fortresses at Upper Zohar, and En Boqeq.[27]

---

[20] Anastasius (Haarer (2006) 214) is known to have instituted a number of reforms for the benefit of the army, which, prior to his accession, was in a poor state. Plus, Procopius is vague about when this is meant to have happened, and given the regularity of war in the 6th c., it is hard to imagine that the soldiery was paid consistently throughout. Again, the evidence points towards Procopius' careful manipulation of his material.

[21] Isaac (1998) 462: "To conclude, it must be said again that so far there is little evidence of any large-scale reduction of the provincial army in Palestine before the early 7th c."

[22] The papyri pertaining to Elephantine are collected and translated by Porten (1996). The pertinent passage in Procopius is found at Procop. *Pers.* 1.19.27–37, summarising the region's military and diplomatic history as he knew it.

[23] *Iust. Nov.* 103. The province in question was Palestina Secunda. On this interesting piece of legislation, see Mayerson (1988) 65–71.

[24] This process was initiated by Diocletian. Barnish *et al.* (2000) 199 sensibly note that this distinction was difficult to maintain in practice; compare Isaac (1998) 467–69.

[25] Mayerson (1988) 68.

[26] Kraemer (1958) 5 dates the archive to the period between A.D. 505 and 596, while Isaac (1990) 209 says that the Theodosian *numerus* was there from at least 548.

[27] Magness (1999).

Units of *limitanei* appear in Syria during this period, as a passage in John Malalas dated to 527 indicates.[28] Probably the most convincing evidence comes from a further piece of Justinianic legislation, and yet another passage from Procopius. After the re-conquest of Africa in 533, Justinian attempted to re-assert imperial control by reforming the new province's administration, and to maintain/establish peace, he deployed units of *limitanei*. The importance of this action is highlighted by Procopius' comments about the security problems in Africa at what had initially seemed to be the end of the Vandal War.[29] If the *limitanei* were no longer a viable military option, it is hard to understand why Justinian would have used them. There is also evidence that they continued to be paid regularly, at least in the Danube, though I know of no evidence to suggest that those in the Balkans would have fared better than those in Arabia.[30]

The continued presence of *limitanei* on the south-eastern frontier, however, remains contentious; although they continued to be used throughout the 6th c., on this frontier, allied soldiers, particularly Arab federates, played an increasingly prominent role. By the mid-6th c., scholars agree that the southern frontier in the East was firmly in the hands of the Ghassanid federates, who came to act, for all intents and purposes, as *limitanei*.[31] What we do not know, however, is when exactly they became involved, and the specific nature of their defensive role. Sartre notes that between the treaty of A.D. 502/503 and Arethas' promotion to phylarch in 528/29, we have very little evidence of Arab involvement.[32] The most vociferous supporter of the Arabs, Irfan Shahîd, suggests that the *limitanei* continued to be used, at least for a time, following Arethas' promotion.[33] Others have claimed that the frontier was abandoned or dismantled as early as the second half of the 5th c., or certainly by A.D. 500, and that the strategic alliances with the Kindites and then Ghassanids (or possibly concurrently from 502/503) were a response to this deficiency.[34] Unfortunately, support for this supposition is usually sought in Parker's monograph on Romans and Saracens, which does not include the results of the interim

---

[28] Malalas 18.2.
[29] *Iust. Cod.* 1.27.2.8; Procop. *Vand.* 4.8.21.
[30] Casey (1996) 218.
[31] Sartre (1982) 172; Casey (1996) 220–22; Shahîd (2002) 42; Fisher (2004) 56–57; Zuckerman (2004) 160; Lewin (2007b) 476–77.
[32] Sartre (1982) 163. Where Sartre dates Arethas' promotion to A.D. 528, Shahîd (2002) 24 dates it to 529.
[33] Shahîd (2002) 33.
[34] Casey (1996); Fisher (2004); Fiema (2007); Lewin (2007a), (2007b).

report from el-Lejjūn, let alone the results of the final report, which is the subject of this paper.[35] In other words, there is no consensus and much uncertainty, so highlighting the need to re-evaluate the evidence from the fortress.

THE *LIMES ARABICUS* PROJECT

1. *A Reconsideration of the Evidence: Military Occupation*

The excavations from central Jordan carried out by S. Thomas Parker's team from 1980–1989 uncovered a wide range of material; indeed, the quantity and quality of their investigations are notable. Since my primary focus is military food supply, the plant remains analysed by Patricia Crawford,[36] and the zooarchaeological evidence analysed by Michael Toplyn,[37] are particularly important. To determine the relevance of the evidence, we need to know whether the site was even occupied in the first half of the 6th c. and to what degree. This will clearly have a huge impact on whether it is possible to generalise from the material for the 6th c. Unfortunately, it is here that that the authors of the report stumble, for a significant number of the conclusions drawn are not supported by the evidence that they have uncovered,[38] as detailed below.

The consensus among the excavators is that the fortress was used much less intensively in the second quarter of the 6th c. leading up to the earthquake of A.D. 551, after which the unit that had been posted there left.[39] Does the evidence support the claims for less-intensive occupation? I begin my critique of their conclusions by looking at the church. The excavation of the church at el-Lejjūn is often cited as support for the decline in the fortress's fortunes.[40] The church, a basilica located in the north-west quadrant of the fortress, was first built during the reign

---

[35] Fiema (2007) 316 is one such example.

[36] Crawford (2006b).

[37] Toplyn (2006).

[38] Nevertheless, it is a testament to the high standard of the papers collected that such a re-evaluation of the evidence is possible.

[39] See, for example, Parker's (2006d) 562–71 discussion in his overview of the frontier east of the Dead Sea.

[40] Parker (2006c) 564: "the church at el-Lejjūn is also suggestive of local conditions in the early 6th c. The church is among the smallest known in Transjordan and is rather shoddy in construction." His comments match those made elsewhere, though as we shall see, the excavation of the church itself does not support these claims.

of Anastasius.[41] Schick identifies three main phases in the church's history. The first phase, he remarks, was difficult to dissociate from the pre-church phase;[42] the second was the 'most elaborate', and had a *terminus post quem* of 534 based on the discovery of a coin;[43] while the final stage was the crudest, and there was some evidence that the function of the building had changed.[44] Based on Schick's reconstruction of the church's history, it seems that the fortress was most prosperous early in the reign of Justinian, contrary to Parker's assertions.[45]

One of Parker's main concerns is the lack of decorative flair in the church, such as frescoes and mosaics, particularly in comparison to other sites in the region.[46] The problem with this assertion is that the other sites were, in all likelihood, civilian, while el-Lejjūn was military. Given the profound lack of comparable military sites in Jordan or elsewhere, we should reserve these sorts of comparisons for military sites alone, since there is no reason to suggest that civilian and military churches would necessarily be comparable. Sixth century soldiers, officers aside, were by no means wealthy, and since it is reasonable to suggest that a majority of them would have had to support a family, it is hard to deduce where the extra money to decorate the church would have come from. Besides, it is not yet clear that the army of the 6th c. was uniformly Christian; this cannot be securely stated for the state, or for society at large for that matter.[47] As such, we should not point to the church as evidence for a low standard of living in the fortress during the Justinianic period.

---

[41] Schick (1987) 371. The excavations of the church were published in the interim report for the *Limes Arabicus*.

[42] Schick (1987) 365.

[43] Schick (1987) 372.

[44] Schick (1987) 376–82.

[45] Parker (2006c) 564; compare Parker (2006a) 121.

[46] Another issue, of course, is that little of the church actually remains, and so any possible decorations might have been removed in antiquity.

[47] Most, if not all, of the soldiers based at this fortress would have been recruited locally, and given the Christian character of 6th c. Palestine, it is quite reasonable to assume that they would, therefore, have been Christian. The process of recruitment, as always in Roman history, was not uniform across the empire, as a number of the soldiers identified by Procopius in his descriptions of the various military campaigns during Justinian's reign hailed from isolated regions that likely had had little exposure to Christianity, such as Isauria. A shrine for the *aedes*, the military standard, was maintained until the mid-6th c., which casts some doubt on the full Christianisation of the soldiers. On the Christianisation of the Late Roman army, see MacMullen (1984) 41–44; Shean (2010) 177–215; and Lee (2007a) 176–93. On the Christianisation of the region, see Parker (2006c) 569–71.

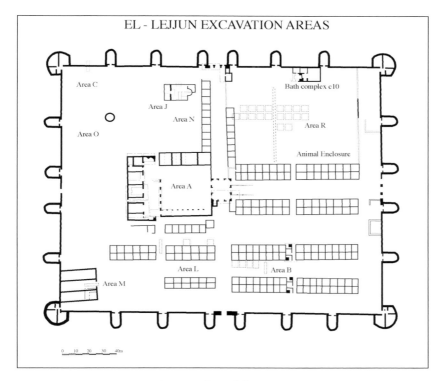

Fig. 2   Plan of el-Lejjūn.

Parker points to the pottery for further signs of reduced occupation in the 6th c.: "in quantitative terms and as expected from the initial surface survey, the vast bulk of the pottery from four of the five excavated forts dated to the Late Roman/Early Byzantine period. Within the legionary fortress, fully 76.5% of all datable sherds were Late Roman/Early Byzantine, that is, 4th/5th century."[48] This is, of course, in stark contrast to our period, for which, though the stratum contained a 'relatively large amount of Late Byzantine pottery', it amounted to only 22.7%.[49] The difference between the two percentages is indeed rather marked, at least until we look closer at the respective chronological periods that Parker is comparing. The dates for Parker's Late Roman/Early Byzantine period run from 284 to 502, which is where the 76.5% comes from, while the Late

---

[48] Parker (2006d) 363.
[49] Parker (2006d) 363.

Byzantine period runs from 502 to 551. The first period referred to is nearly four times longer than the second. If we break up the Late Roman/Early Byzantine period into four smaller chunks, and then divide the percentage by four, the percentage per chunk is around 19%, and suddenly the difference is much less profound. Without being able to date the sherds more precisely, my suggestion is purely speculative; nevertheless, it does underscore the problem with comparing the evidence from two widely different chronological periods.

The coinage is also often cited in support of the diminished 6th c. activity in the fortress, particularly from around 530 onwards.[50] Yet again, however, the conclusions drawn are not secure: at el-Lejjūn, 482 coins were found that date to the Early Byzantine period, A.D. 324–491; conversely, only 48 coins were found in the Late Byzantine layer, which Betlyon dates from A.D. 491–565.[51] At first glance we again find a rather pronounced difference; of those 482 Early Byzantine coins, 249 bronze coins were from a hoard found in the *principia*.[52] Of the remaining 233 coins, 95 cannot be dated with any certainty, though Betlyon dates some of them to points ranging from the mid 4th c. to the 5th.[53]

This leaves us with 138 datable coins for the period running from A.D. 324–491. As with the pottery, what initially seemed to be a rather profound difference is no longer so: hoard aside, we now have 138 coins for a period of 167 years, and 48 coins for a period of 74 years.[54] Although the difference is still seemingly significant, there are a number of reasons why many more coins were in circulation during the 4th c. than the 6th:[55]

---

[50] Parker (2006a) 121.

[51] As regards the coinage totals, I am only referring to those coins that were found within the fortress itself. It should be clear that there is some disagreement among the contributors about the dates used.

[52] Betlyon (2006) 432.

[53] Betlyon (2006) 430–31.

[54] Betlyon (2006) 443 does admit that "small but significant numbers of coins reappear at el-Lejjūn in the reign of Anastasius (491–518) and continue through the reigns of Justin I (518–27) and Justinian I". On Anastasius' reform of the coinage, see Haarer (2006) 202–206. The newly-introduced Anastasian coins, such as the *nummus*, and the *folles*, were quite large, and so much more difficult to lose, which might also have contributed to the relatively small number of Late Byzantine coins. I thank Stanley Ireland for advice on this matter.

[55] Betlyon (2006) gives conflicting suggestions about why this might be so. While on 420 discussing the Early Byzantine coins, he notes that most pre-date the earthquake of A.D. 363; he suggests that this might reflect the inflationary problems which plagued the state. Later, however, on 443, he argues that the small number of coins from the period from the late 4th to the 5th c. might be due to a reduction in the size of the garrison. He

Constantius' campaigns in the East, and the subsequent transfer of troops from the West, might explain the prominence of coins from western mints, and so the relative abundance of Early Byzantine coins.[56] Inflation had been a problem at the end of the 3rd c. and the beginning of the 4th before Constantine's reforms, and this might be what is reflected in the relatively high numbers of coins from the reigns of Diocletian during the Tetrarchy, and later Constantine.[57] There were also a number of succession problems during the reign of Constantine's sons, and the high of number of coins dating to their reigns might reflect their eagerness to promote their own case to the soldiers. Finally, the number of coins that date to the decades before the earthquake of 363 might reflect the increased importance of cash payments to the soldiers, who, though initially paid primarily in kind in the early years of the 4th c., were increasingly paid in cash[58] as the state came to realise the greater ease with which this could be affected.[59] All in all then, and as with the pottery, the coinage does not support the theory of a reduced standard of living, and the difference in totals is easily explained away.

Other evidence published in the final report raises doubts about the conclusions as well, although they do, by and large, point towards reduced occupation in the fortress itself.[60] I want next to look at the evidence of the small finds,[61] the *principia*,[62] and the barracks.[63] Regarding the small finds, we learn that the bulk comes from stratum III, a layer dating to the first half of the 6th c.[64] Most of that material was found

---

follows this in his conclusion when he posits that the number of coins may reflect a large population at the fortress pre-363. This change in theory is unconvincing.

[56] Compare Betlyon (2006) 443.

[57] Depeyrot (2006) 234–47 discusses inflation in the 3rd and early 4th c., as well as Constantine's attempts to stabilise the economy.

[58] What is more, whether paid in cash, in kind, or some combination, the soldiers continued to receive cash donatives throughout the period. See Lee (2007a) 57–60 for donatives in Late Antiquity.

[59] Lee (1998) 220–21; Depeyrot (2006) 240; Lee (2007a) 87.

[60] It is still not possible to equate the size of a fortress with the size of the unit residing inside, and I must re-emphasise this point as this seems to be the assertion of the team who worked at el-Lejjūn—Groot *et al.* (2006) 161. Granted, it is possible that fewer of the buildings may have been occupied, but that does not unequivocally mean a smaller unit. As imperial 'era' evidence, such as Hunt's *pridianum* (and granted that it describes wartime conditions), shows, troops were continuously engaged in duties far beyond their home base, and often for extended periods of time.

[61] McDaniel (2006) 293–327.

[62] Lain and Parker (2006) 123–59.

[63] Groot *et al.* (2006) 161–85.

[64] McDaniel (2006) 305–11, 318–20.

CONOR WHATELY

in either the barracks, or the *principia*, which might suggest that at least significant portions of these buildings were still in use throughout this period, though it could also point towards their use as dumping grounds.[65] Indeed, Lain and Parker note in regard to the *principia* that "this stratum produced the best-preserved evidence of occupation excavated between 1980 and 1985".[66]

Yet, there seems to be little doubt that a smaller percentage of the fortification was occupied during the 6th c., particularly in those two areas of greatest relevance to the presence of soldiery, the barracks and the *principia*; and some of the post-502 earthquake reconstructions were of a lower quality than those of the comparable post-363 earthquake.[67] Lain and Parker remark that the reconstructions of the *principia* were unpretentious.[68] Yet there was no reason for lavish repairs considering the site's isolation, and the concurrent military crisis to the north, which meant that most imperial expenditure on the military at this time would have been diverted there.[69] We are reminded of the comments about el-Lejjūn's church. I would suggest that this lack of pretension is indicative of changing cultural practices, rather than changing economic conditions.[70]

---

[65] It also seems that the small finds were not concentrated in any single barracks building, but were scattered fairly evenly throughout the fortress—McDaniel (2006) 305–11. That said, Groot *et al.* (2006) 170 tell us that barracks block L was largely unoccupied in the 6th c., and, significantly, no more than a handful of the small finds were found in block L in the Late Byzantine stratum. Several finds are jewellery, found not only in the *principia*, but the barracks as well.

[66] Lain and Parker (2006) 131.

[67] I have trouble equating the re-use of materials with economic turmoil. Presumably, when an ancient structure such as this fortress suffered significant damage as the result of a disaster like the 502 earthquake, a good sign of resilient and able inhabitants would be the almost immediate reconstruction of those important structures. It probably would have taken far too long to bring in new materials for repairs, and it would have been much easier and more practical to use what was immediately available, namely, the fallen debris. On the shoddy reconstructions of the *principia*, see Lain and Parker (2006) 131–32, 152–55. On the barracks, see Groot *et al.* (2006) 169–70, 180–82.

[68] Lain and Parker (2006) 132.

[69] Whereas in other parts of the empire, city walls, and other sorts of military architecture, were monumentalised in part to intimidate locals, it is not clear to whom something comparable here would have been directed, particularly considering the reduced, or even non-existent, civilian population outside of the fortress in the *vicus*, which was no longer occupied in the 6th c. For example, Elsner's (1998) 131 comments on some of the monumental architecture from 4th c. Trier: "The walls [of Constantius Chlorus' palace] boasted imposing gates, like the surviving Porta Nigra . . . which were designed at least as much to *impress* [sic] both insiders and outsiders as they were to be functional defences." Though the location and date are quite different from 6th c. Arabia, they are relevant.

[70] Compare Wickham (2005) 448, 620, as regards the hotly-debated economic situation in 6th c. Syria and Palestine. Kennedy (2007) 89, on the other hand, seems to imply that the construction of churches is not a sign of economic prosperity, in the context of

It is when we look at the results of the excavations of the barracks that we find evidence of reduced occupation. Barracks blocks K and L seem to have been scarcely occupied in the 6th c.[71] Parker suggests the same for block B, yet he bases this interpretation on a single room.[72] In fact, several of the rooms were re-used following the earthquake, as the earlier excavations indicated.[73] Thus, despite the seemingly reduced levels of occupation, the evidence of the small finds, the *principia*, and the barracks suggests that the living conditions were not of such a poor quality as originally supposed.

The remaining question concerns whether this continued occupation was military. Of the small finds recovered for the period from A.D. 502–551, 14.28% were deemed military.[74] This is down from the 22.53% recovered for the previous period (A.D. 363–502)—which, again, encompasses a much longer time-frame. In the latter period, there is a much higher percentage of domestic objects, particularly those, such as jewellery, usually associated with women, and those with the disposable income to afford them.[75] On the other hand, McDaniel, in the more recent discussion of the small finds, notes that, period percentages aside, nearly one-third (12 of 35) of all military objects found at the fortress date to the period from A.D. 502–551.[76] Furthermore, McDaniel says that the relatively small number of military items overall is what we would expect for a site occupied by soldiers, since the majority of the artefactual record left behind by soldiers is not necessarily 'military' in character; indeed, 235 items date to A.D. 502–551, 70 of which are domestic, generally concerned with food preparation, and from the barracks (unsurprising given that soldiers would have prepared their own food).

As regards the barracks block, Groot, in the interim report, noted that it was renovated in the period from 400–500, with the addition of storage

the Justinianic plague. As regards this plague, Little's (2007) recent collection of papers provides the best overview of the major issues, with acceptance generally of quite a severe impact on 6th c. society, not only Roman, but elsewhere; nevertheless, without knowing more about fertility rates, we should be cautious about asserting that there was an irreversible decline following its arrival.

[71] Groot *et al.* (2006) 170, 181.

[72] Parker (2006c) 563.

[73] Groot (1987a) 302–309; compare Groot *et al.* (2006) 162. For the *horreum*, see Crawford (2006a) 237, who notes that: "in terms of the relative quantity of ceramic remains and soil volume excavated, the Late Byzantine period was the best-represented period in Area M [the so-called *horreum*] in all three squares."

[74] Groot (1987b) 497–98.

[75] Groot (1987b) 498.

[76] McDaniel (2006) 295–96.

facilities and the re-surfacing of two thirds of the flooring.[77] After the 502 earthquake, significant portions of the barracks were rendered unusable, though repairs were carried out, where possible, and the useable portions continued to be inhabited.[78] Additional lodging was set up along the *via vicinaria* to compensate for the shortfall. The most significant evidence, however, for a continued military presence at the fortress in the half century both before and after 502 comes from the *principia*. Haeckel (in the interim report) and Lain and Parker (in the final report) all note restoration following the earthquake.[79] Perhaps the most significant part of that reconstruction for the soldiers concerned the *aedes*, the shrine for the standard, the floor of which was in the process of being re-surfaced. Despite this interruption, a new floor, though probably not the one originally conceived, was installed.[80] Taken together then, it is hard to interpret the occupation of the site as anything other than military from A.D. 450–550, and the continued attention given to the *aedes* is most significant in this regard, though we must bear in mind that civilians, particularly women, also seem to have been living in the fort at the time.

2. *Food Supply*

What of food at el-Lejjūn? There is evidence for a wide variety of different plants both cultivated and wild, including cereals, both wheat and barley; legumes, such as lentils, vetch, and/or peas; and fruit, for example, olives, dates, grapes, figs, and peaches.[81] Most of the remains found were common in the Near East; moreover, with the exception of dates and peaches, all of these plants were found in all periods. As regards the locally-cultivated cereals, wheat was more common than barley;[82] but Crawford does note the limited evidence for the implements used in the production of these.[83] For legumes, no clear evidence for local cultivation emerged,[84] whereas fruit, such as olives and grapes, was produced locally, though on a limited scale, and Crawford notes that "the absence of processing installations for olives or grapes may also indicate that production, if local, was not suf-

---

[77] Groot (1987a) 290.
[78] Groot (1987b) 303–307.
[79] Haeckel (1987) 244; Lain and Parker (2006) 156.
[80] Haeckel (1987) 244.
[81] Crawford (2006b) 454.
[82] Crawford (2006b) 454.
[83] Crawford (2006b) 459; compare McDaniel (2006) 298–327.
[84] Crawford (2006b) 460.

ficient for oil or wine production, but limited to quantities sufficient for table consumption as fruit."[85] Indeed, the presence of imported amphorae suggests that some wine and oil was imported, if on a limited scale, which might also have been the case for some of the other fruits. Still, the weight of evidence points towards a focus on local production and consumption, particularly for wheat, barley, and oil.[86]

The zooarchaeological remains similarly provide evidence for localisation in food supply, or at least preferences. All sorts of animal remains were uncovered at el-Lejjūn, of which 18% were identifiable.[87] Of those, the bones of domestic sheep and goats (caprines) are the most common by some margin, followed by chickens, and then cattle and pigs; remains of donkeys, dromedaries, hares, foxes, and possibly horses have also been found.[88] Sheep, goats, chickens, cattle, and pigs were the animals that would have been consumed by the soldiers.[89] The restricted evidence for wild animals suggests that these did not make up a big part of a soldier's diet.[90] This evidence supports the increasingly accepted view that meat made up a substantial portion of a Roman soldier's diet.[91] Interestingly, since no clear evidence of a significant difference exists between the consumption of meat in the barracks or the *principia*, it seems that both officers and foot soldiers had relatively equal access to the meat available.[92]

Of the animals found, sheep tend to outnumber goats during the archaeological Byzantine periods, and Toplyn plausibly suggests that they were primarily exploited for meat, and that their consumption was mostly local.[93] Cattle seem to have been used primarily 'for traction power' rather than meat production.[94] In the earlier imperial West the opposite may have been true,[95] though on the Upper Danube, pork apparently

---

[85] Crawford (2006b) 460.

[86] Crawford (2006b) 461.

[87] Toplyn (2006) 464. To my mind, Toplyn's paper on the zooarchaeological evidence is the most insightful, and provocative, of the collection.

[88] Toplyn (2006) 466–67. Donkeys, mules, dromedaries, and horses were used for transportation purposes rather than for meat, while foxes and hares were presumably hunted occasionally for sport (489–98).

[89] Toplyn (2006) 467. Noticeably, their remains are distributed almost identically throughout the fortress' history.

[90] Toplyn (2006) 468–69.

[91] Davies (1971) 126; King (1999a) 139; Roth (1999) 27–32; Toplyn (2006) 467.

[92] Toplyn (2006) 474.

[93] Toplyn (2006) 478. Wool and hair products, however, were also important—476.

[94] Toplyn (2006) 483.

[95] Roth (1999) 30. King (1999a) 139, for example, concluded that British sites have much higher numbers of cattle in comparison to caprine and pig bones. He (139–42) compares

was more popular.[96] At the Late Roman fortress of Dichin, there is an increase in the percentage of cattle and pig remains, with a concomitant drop in the percentage of caprine remains in the 6th in comparison to the 5th c.[97] Conversely, at el-Lejjūn, Toplyn posits that pork served as a supplement to the meat consumed from other animals, notably sheep and goats.[98] This is in keeping with what we know about other sites in the Near East. Cope, discussing food remains found in late antique Caesarea, sees sheep and goats as the mainstays of local meat production.[99] Decker observes that at Androna in Syria, which shares a number of geographical features with el-Lejjūn, sheep were the dominant livestock.[100] King too, in a broader study of meat in the Roman diet, notes that at most sites in the Fertile Crescent, whether urban, rural, or military, caprine remains are dominant.[101]

We do know that pork was consumed in other parts of the 6th c. Roman world by soldiers, as two recently published Justinianic-period papyri from Egypt attest.[102] While these documents do give us some indication of the mechanics of food supply for the army in Egypt, they do not tell us how common pork consumption was.[103] Of the animals found at the site that were exploited for consumption, poultry shows a most surprising presence.[104] Generally speaking, poultry is never discussed as a source of meat and protein for Roman soldiers, and yet at el-Lejjūn, chicken bones outnumbered pig bones. Toplyn contends that chickens do not compete with

---

these data with sites in Switzerland and Germany, and the results, for both auxiliary and legionary fortresses, were similar; he points to a rise in sheep and goat numbers in the Late Roman period. To my knowledge, most studies of Roman military diet using zooarchaeological material focus on the West, and the Imperial period—for example, the recent valuable collection edited by Stallibrass and Thomas (2008a).

[96] Pork was the meat of choice in Roman Italy, as the evidence of Apicius seems to suggest. Roth (1999) 29 remarks that pig remains are generally lower than cattle on military sites, and that there tend to be fewer references to pork in the literary sources; compare Toplyn (2006) 484–85.

[97] Johnstone (2007) 291.

[98] Toplyn (2006) 487.

[99] Cope (1999) 407.

[100] Decker (forthcoming).

[101] King (1999b) 185–87; compare Toplyn (2006) 506.

[102] Haug (2007).

[103] On the workings of the *annona militaris* in Egypt from the 4th to 6th c., see the important contribution of Mitthof (2001). This study, based on the papyri, only touches on military supply under Justinian (259–66).

[104] When Maurice (*Strategikon* 7.A.10) lists the sorts of food to be brought along and stored in saddlebags on campaign, he just says meat (*kreous*; *Strategikon* 7.A.10.4), without specifying the kind. Given that he is concerned with an army on the move, we can assume that he is referring to salted meat, and quite probably pork.

humans for food, and so are much more efficient converters of protein than pigs.[105] On the other hand, the small finds evidence points towards the presence of civilians amongst those living inside the fortress during this period, despite the fact that the *vicus* had long since been abandoned (A.D. 363 earthquake). Thus, it was quite possibly the civilians who were eating chicken. Nevertheless, in addition to its probable consumption by civilians, poultry, like pork, probably served as a supplementary meat source to the soldiers, though this could change when and if they were ever besieged.[106]

Toplyn's findings, as he notes, have two important implications: "(1) project sites [el-Lejjūn and its environs] were not regularly engaged in supplying each other with processed meat cuts or caprine meat on the hoof, and (2) livestock exploitation strategies practiced in the environs of project sites were conducive to states of self-sufficiency in meat production."[107] Indeed, he argues that the evidence points towards the unit's reliance "on agropastoralism rather than a marked dependence on imported or hunted food".[108] This suggestion, when considered in light of the faunal evidence, is an important one for military supply empire-wide, and merits further consideration.

FOOD SUPPLY ON THE FRONTIER AND LOCALISATION

Based on my re-evaluations, the fortress of el-Lejjūn was still occupied at a significant level in the first half of the 6th c. and featured both civilian and military inhabitants; as seen, Crawford and Toplyn persuasively

---

[105] Toplyn (2006) 489. Chicken remains from the contemporary Danubian site of Dichin make up a tiny portion of the total bone assemblage: Johnstone (2007) 289–90. Compare Veg. *Mil.* 4.7: 'However, not only pork but all other kinds of animal which cannot be protected by an enclosure ought to be cured, so that with meat serving as a supplement, the grain supplies will suffice. But the city's birds can be fed without imposing on the citizenry, and are needed for the sake of the infirm.' Neither King (1999a) nor Roth (1999) address poultry in their discussion of imperial food supply. The same is true for Engels (1978) 123–30, on the provisions of Alexander's Macedonian army; see Haldon (1997) 124–25, (1999) 139–43 and (2006b) on the medieval Byzantine army; and Van Creveld (1977) 5–26 for the armies of the Early Modern period.

[106] Veg. *Mil.* 4.7.

[107] Toplyn (2006) 479, with important qualifications about these findings, and their implications.

[108] Toplyn (2006) 504—a conclusion supported by the fact that there is considerable evidence for the production of secondary objects like milk, cheese, and wool. Compare Toplyn (1994) 124–25.

argue in favour of local provenance for the unit's food supplies.[109] These conclusions raise questions about the degree of direct state involvement in the provisioning of units on the frontier, particularly as regards cereals. From Diocletian through the 4th c., soldiers had generally been paid in kind through a complex system generally called the *annona militaris*, a response to the monetary instability that surfaced in the 'Third-Century Crisis'.[110] Supplies, collected as a type of tax, were sent to depots before being redistributed to the armed forces where needed;[111] much was done at a regional level, though demand often outstripped supply. Thus, the state was engaged in the long distance transport of goods to the army, a practice which was particularly important for units based in more remote locations.[112] In Egypt this tax in kind was collected and redistributed by the civilian local administration.[113]

By the 6th c., however, it has been suggested that the soldiers were paid entirely in cash, a process believed to have been completed by Anastasius, and most prevalent among the *limitanei*.[114] This simplified the provisioning of the army, and lessened the need for expensive long distance transport. On the other hand, the praetorian prefect is still thought to have played a major role in food provisioning for the army in the 6th c.[115] The evidence of el-Lejjūn, however, points towards localised supply for both meat and grain.[116] Toplyn doubts that soldiers had the knowledge of husbandry to breed the sorts of animals found at the site, and as such, they would have had to buy or requisition them from settled neighbouring areas to the west.[117] Haldon has noted that the economy in Late Antiquity was "intensely local and regionalised".[118] The frontier soldiers, often some of the biggest drivers of the local economy, tended to be well integrated into society, being largely recruited locally.[119]

---

[109] Compare Stallibrass and Thomas (2008b) 6–9, focusing on food supply in the northwest provinces, note that most animals and plants would be local (148).

[110] Zuckerman (2004) 172; Whitby (2007) 324. Compare *Cod. Theod.* 7.4.

[111] Lee (2007b) 404; Whitby (2007) 324.

[112] Jones (1964) 671; Haldon (2005) 34; Fear (2007) 447; Lee (2007b) 404.

[113] Fear (2007) 447; Palme (2007) 259. Compare Mitthof (2001).

[114] Jones (1964) 671; Haarer (2006) 186–99; Lee (2007b) 407.

[115] Haldon (2005) 44.

[116] By 'localised'—without necessarily getting into who specifically was involved—I mean that the food was supplied by the fort itself and/or the surrounding area.

[117] Toplyn (2006) 481–82.

[118] Haldon (2005) 35.

[119] As argued by Ravegnani (1988) 19; Whitby (1995) 69, 79–81; Fiema (2007) 316; Palme (2007) 260–61.

The best documentary evidence that we have for both these tendencies—local recruitment and integration in their region—on the southern frontier comes from the Nessana papyri. The local unit, the 'Company of the Most Loyal Theodosians',[120] seems to have procured its camels from the village of Nessana.[121] The soldiers here were recruited locally, and they seem to have been involved in a number of transactions with the community.[122] Although these papyri do not tell us whether the soldiers were growing their own crops or whether they were involved in animal husbandry, they certainly do own land. Indeed, upon retirement, *limitanei* seem to have been given land to farm, though whether they cultivated it themselves is another matter.[123] Although there are papyri in the collection that pertain to grain, including the disposition and requisition of wheat,[124] soldiers are not explicitly mentioned, and so we do not know how exactly they received their grain.

Fiema has looked at the military as depicted in the Petra papyri, and has ultimately concluded that the government was still responsible for the distribution of the *annona militaris*.[125] These papyri provide evidence for payment in kind of a number of foodstuffs, including meat, wheat, and wine.[126] This limited pool of evidence does, as with el-Lejjūn, point towards local supply.[127] This connection between local produce and tax collection also points towards localised food acquisition. Taken together, the papyri of Nessana and Petra, and the zooarchaeological and faunal evidence from el-Lejjūn, suggest that, at least for the southern portion of the East Roman frontier, the units of *limitanei* were localised as regards the supply of food and animals.

What about other parts of the empire? Some evidence exists for the methods of supply in Egypt, the Balkans, and Mesopotamia; each area

---

[120] Kraemer (1958) 5.

[121] *P. Nessana* 35.

[122] Isaac (1998) 458–62 says that the unit at Nessana was probably recruited locally, and that it was well integrated in local affairs; compare *P.Nessana* 14–30; Whitby (2000) 492–93.

[123] Lee (2007b) 409.

[124] *P. Nessana* 40, 61–67, 82–83; compare Mayerson (1962).

[125] Fiema (2002) 225–31 and (2007) 316.

[126] Fiema (2007).

[127] At el-Lejjūn, it would seem that it was their families, or possibly their servants, who were involved in the farming, whereas at Nessana, given the presence of the town, they may have sought their grain from the community—thus both were local means of acquisition, just of different types. When the site was abandoned, the inhabitants probably took most of their tools with them, hence the lack of farming implements found.

seems to have had its own principal mechanism. Egypt, of course, had the capacity to produce the goods required by its army.[128] Like their Jordanian and Palestinian counterparts, they were well-integrated into local society, a fact particularly evident in the papyri from Elephantine and Syene.[129] There, some of the local *limitanei*, and perhaps to some degree as well, the *buccellarii*,[130] relied on procuring their supplies from the Great Estates,[131] though originally they might have done this through the local *curiae*.[132] The various rations required were collected as part of the tax and then redistributed to the soldiers.[133] By the mid-6th c., however, we have what seems to be evidence for Egyptian soldiers purchasing rations, such as meat (pork) from butchers, for themselves and their dependents.[134] This reliance on civilian tax authorities probably changed, however, during the reign of Justinian, as the soldiers were given a more direct role in their acquisition of their food requirements.[135]

Moving north, the Balkans were some remove from the bread baskets of the empire, and the units based around the Danube more often than not had to rely on provisions shipped by the state. Indeed there is evidence that this was a widespread practice, particularly along the Lower Danube, as indicated in the abundance of LR1 and LR2 amphorae.[136] Also of note is the creation of the *Quaestura Exercitus* in A.D. 536,[137] a piece of Justinianic legislation designed, at least in part, to regularise the transportation of supplies for the *limitanei*.[138] As regards meat, although pig and caprines continued to be local in origin, at least at Dichin, cattle seems

---

[128] Lee (2007a) 86.

[129] Porten (1996); compare Palme (2007) 260–61.

[130] Alston (2002) 414 notes other types of soldiers listed in the papyri from the Apion archive, such as Scythians and Goths. Compare Josh. Styl. 86, 96 (Trombley and Watt (2000) xxxviii).

[131] Alston (2002) 411; Sarris (2006) 164–66. Sarris (2006) discusses in detail the mechanics of the Great Estates in Egypt, as well as their respective places in society.

[132] Lee (2007a) 86.

[133] Mitthof (2001) 168–257; Palme (2007) 259.

[134] Haug (2007). Mitthof (2001) 266 suggests that under Justinian soldiers were paid in gold rather than kind, a fact which seems to be supported by the papyri discussed by Haug.

[135] Mitthof (2001) 259–66.

[136] Karagiorgou (2001).

[137] *Iust. Nov.* 41. Compare *Iust. Nov.* 50; Stein (1949) 474–75; Jones (1964) 661; Sarantis (2006) 244–48; Lee (2007a) 109–11.

[138] This legislation originally also contained a schedule for the provisioning of soldiers. *Iust. Nov.* 41.11–13.

to have been imported—a significant point given that the percentage of cattle bone assemblages found here increases at the expense of caprines in the 6th c.[139]

The *Chronicle of Pseudo-Joshua the Stylite* provides a mass of information about the provisioning of troops in Mesopotamia,[140] showing soldiers provisioned in a manner similar to that stipulated by *Novella* 41 in the Balkans, in that a praetorian prefect is sent to Edessa to furnish the troops;[141] moreover, like Egypt, he in turn gets the supplies from the Edessenes. Pseudo-Joshua also notes the importance of local merchants.[142] The communities on the Tur Abdin plateau flourished in the 6th c. with a seeming explosion of new constructions after the creation of Dara, thanks to the substantial influx of state funds. An army of perhaps 10,000 men would have needed to be supplied with food, and these villages provided the most obvious source.[143] As I noted above, the geography of Androna in Syria is similar to that of el-Lejjūn, though farming, even dry farming, seems to have been more restricted. To compensate, *qanat* lines and water reservoirs were constructed.[144] In these three regions, Egypt, the Balkans, and Syria, we likely have three distinct, if complementary, procedures for food provisioning for the frontier forces. The latter two cases, however, raise another issue, notably the distinction between peace- and wartime logistics.

The divisions of the Roman army based in Egypt never experienced the sorts of instability, at least in regard to external foes, that the units in the Balkans and Mesopotamia did. Indeed, the same is essentially true of the units based in Palestine. The main theatre of operations during the eastern campaigns in the 6th c. was the northern frontier, running from northern Syria and the Euphrates, northwards into the Caucasus and the

---

[139] Johnstone (2007) 292.

[140] Interesting that Pseudo-Joshua, instead of closing several of his years in Thucydidean (and Procopian, at least as regards the *Gothic Wars*) fashion by noting the end of the campaign year, on at least one occasion, Pseudo-Joshua does so by recording the price of wheat (Josh. Styl. 27). Moreover, food prices serve as a barometer for how good or how bad things are, and they are occasionally described within a Christian morality-based framework (Josh. Styl. 44–45).

[141] Josh. Styl. 54. This *Chronicle* is by far the best literary text as regards 6th c. logistics.

[142] Josh. Styl. 66.

[143] Whitby (2000) 492; compare Liebeshuetz (1972) 80, who notes the army's economic impact on Syria, especially near Antioch, and Chalcis.

[144] Decker (forthcoming) 18–20; compare with Mango (2002) 314–5 and (2008) 5–8.

Black Sea. There is an obvious problem with concentrating on an Arabian fortress in a study on logistics in the 6th c.: the southern frontier
was some distance from the main theatres of action, in Mesopotamia and
the Caucasus.[145] Whether the evidence from el-Lejjūn could serve as a
model for the empire at large is, therefore, debatable. Alston, for example,
explicitly states that the system that he was describing for Egypt pertained
to peace-time.[146] The Balkans were heavily militarised in the 6th c., and
one could well read the creation of the Quaestor of the Army as a reflection of this insecurity.[147] On the other hand, Lee equates it with Thrace's
economic difficulties, and the subsequent logistical problems.[148] Pseudo-
Joshua is describing the Anastasian war with Persia, and so the procedures which he outlines, such as bringing in Appion (praetorian prefect)
to Edessa, might be specific to wartime situations. Yet do the wartime
contexts necessarily preclude an emphasis on localised mechanisms for
the supplying of frontier forces?

Greatrex has recently drawn attention to the administrative reforms
of Justinian on the frontiers, particularly the transfer of dukes from provinces to cities in the early 6th c.;[149] in addition, Kelly has discussed the
decentralisation of authority under Justinian.[150] Of course, the localisation of food supply evident among the *limitanei* in Jordan might be part
of a wider regional phenomenon, for Wickham[151] and Haldon[152] have
both suggested that the economy in Syria and Palestine was localised
and regionalised. At the same time, other frontiers used local solutions to
problems of supply. During the first three centuries of the imperial period,
a significant portion of the army's food needs were met locally.[153] In the
3rd c., there was a shift towards centralisation, though by the 6th c., par-

---

[145] Note Wheeler (2007) 236–37 regarding the importance of the northern frontier during the Principate.

[146] Alston (2002) 410.

[147] Stein (1949) 475; Sarantis (2006) 247. The establishment of the *Quaestura Exercitus* might simply be the formalisation of what was already regular practice in the 5th c.,
namely the "appointing of a special deputy praetorian prefect to oversee the logistical
arrangements for major campaigns"—Barnish *et al.* (2000) 196, n. 145; compare Jones
(1964) 627–28.

[148] Lee (2007a) 109. Compare Whitby (1988) 70; and Haarer (2006) 164–79 on the revolt
of Vitalian, which contributed significantly to the unrest in Thrace.

[149] Greatrex (2007).

[150] Kelly (2004) 64–104.

[151] Wickham (2005) 772.

[152] Haldon (2006b) 36.

[153] Cherry (2007); Stallibrass and Thomas (2008c).

ticularly during the reign of Justinian, this process seems to have reversed. The paying of soldiers in cash should be seen in this light.

This emphasis on local responses to military matters in the 6th c. was also suggested by Whitby, who approached the question largely from the literary material.[154] The conclusions that I have drawn from the material evidence from el-Lejjūn are in line with his views and in keeping with what we know about the economy in Palestine in general, and the military empire-wide. Justinian was keen to make units more efficient at responding to problems at the local level, particularly in regions where the threat was minimal, such as Jordan. This change may also reflect his predecessor Anastasius' realisation that the state could not respond to military problems quickly, a situation that had worsened since the failed invasion of Africa in 468; by granting more local autonomy, the units could, in theory, respond quicker to smaller problems than the state could ever hope to.[155]

CONCLUSIONS

This paper has highlighted the value of a long-term archaeological excavation for the study of food supply, pointing towards the detailed picture of military life it can provide. I have also indicated some of the problems with the conclusions that were drawn from el-Lejjūn, something that would not have been possible without such a detailed final report. Ideally we need more such excavations, particularly at sites such as Dara, which had a more central role in combat operations. At present, we must rely on Michael Whitby's description (already over 20 years old) of the site, particularly the granary.[156] Regrettably, a comparatively detailed multi-year study of northern Mesopotamia, one of the principal theatres of operations on Rome's eastern frontier in the 6th c., is difficult to conduct due to the security problems in the region. Though somewhat more politically stable, the same applies to the Caucasus. In the absence of surveys and excavations then, and until archaeologists are afforded the opportunity, we are forced to extrapolate data from other areas, such as Late Roman

---

[154] Whitby (1995) 111–13 and (2005) 378–79.

[155] This, of course, evokes the hotly debated issue of 'grand strategy', which is beyond the scope of this paper. A recent and provocative contribution to this debate is Kagan (2006), who uses contemporary discussions of strategy, and grand strategy, to formulate important new questions about Roman foreign policy and imperial decision-making.

[156] Whitby (1986) 748, 750. Mango identified the structure as a granary (1982) 103–104. Compare with Gregory (1996) 85–86.

Jordan, to build up a model for how the central portion of the frontier operated. Finally, we are also in need of studies that incorporate the wide variety of evidence at hand for military logistics in Late Antiquity, from the reports of contemporary histories, to the law codes and to the papyri.[157] As shown, however, the material evidence must not be overlooked, as it too can highlight important problems that have considerable bearing on phenomena empire-wide.

Acknowledgements

I want to thank Michael Whitby, the editors of this volume, those who attended my presentation of this material at a University of Warwick Department of Classics and Ancient History Research seminar, and the two anonymous reviewers for their valuable comments on earlier drafts of this paper. I am also grateful to Debbie Miles-Williams (University of Leicester) for redrawing the two figures.

Bibliography

Primary Sources

Cod. Iust. = Krüger P. (1892–95) ed. *Corpus Juris Civilis* III: *Codex Iustianianus* (Berlin 1892–95).

Cod. Theod. = Mommsen Th., Meyer P. *et al.* (1905) edd. *Theodosiani libri xvi cum constitutionibus Sirmondianis* (Berlin 1905); Pharr C. (1952) trans. *The Theodosian Code and Novels and the Sirmondian Constitutions* (Princeton 1952).

Iust. Nov. = Schöll R. and Kroll W. (1892–95) edd. *Corpus Juris Civilis* III: *Novellae* (Berlin 1892–95).

Josh. Styl. = Trombley F. R. and Watt J. W. (2000) trans. *The Chronicle of Pseudo-Joshua the Stylite* (Translated Texts for Historians 32) (Liverpool 2000).

Not. Dign. or. = Seeck I. (1962) ed. *Notitia Dignitatum: accedunt notitia urbis Constantinopolitananae et Laterculi provinciarum* (Frankfurt 1962).

P. Nessana = Kraemer Jr. C. J. (1958) ed. *Excavations at Nessana, conducted by H. D. Colt, Jr.*, volume 3: *Non-Literary Papyri* (Princeton, NJ 1958).

Procop. Anec. = Dewing H. B. (1914–54) ed. and trans. Procopius, *The Secret History 6* (Cambridge, Mass. and London 1914–54).

Procop. Pers., *Procop. Vand.* = Dewing H. B. (1914–54) ed. and trans. Procopius, *History of the Wars 1–2* (Cambridge, Mass. and London 1914–54).

Strategikon = Dennis G. T. (1984) ed. *Maurice's Strategikon: Handbook of Byzantine Military Strategy* (Philadelphia 1984); Dennis G. T. ed. and Gamillscheg E. trans. (1981) *Das Strategikon des Maurikios* (CFHB 17) (Vienna 1981).

---

[157] Compare with Adams (2001).

Veg. *Mil.* = Reeve M. D. (2004) ed. *Epitoma rei militaris* (Oxford 2006); Milner N. P. (1996) trans. *Epitome of Military Science* (2nd ed., Liverpool 1996).

Secondary Works

Adams J. P. (1976) *Logistics of the Roman Imperial Army: Major Campaigns on the Eastern Front in the First Three Centuries A.D.* (Ph.D. diss., Yale Univ. 1976).
Adams C. E. P. (2001) "Feeding the wolf: logistics and the Roman army", *JRA* 14 (2001) 456–72.
Alston R. (2002) "Managing the frontiers: supplying the frontier troops in the sixth and seventh centuries", in *The Roman Army and the Economy*, ed. P. Erdkamp (Amsterdam 2002) 398–419.
Barnish S., Lee A. D. and Whitby M. (2000) "Government and administration", in *The Cambridge Ancient History, volume 14: Late Antiquity: Empire and Successors A.D. 425–600*, edd. A. Cameron, B. Ward-Perkins and M. Whitby (Cambridge 2000) 164–206.
Betlyon J. W. (2006) "The coins", in *The Roman Frontier in Central Jordan: Final Report on the* Limes Arabicus *Project, 1980–1989*, edd. S. T. Parker and J. W. Betlyon (Dumbarton Oaks Studies 40) (Washington 2006) 413–44.
Cameron A. (1985) *Procopius and the Sixth Century* (London 1985).
Carrié J.-M. (1995) "L'état à la recherche de nouveaux modes de financement des armées (Rome et Byzance, IVe—VIIIe siècles)", in *The Byzantine and Early Islamic Near East III: States, Resources and Armies*, ed. A. Cameron (Princeton, NJ 1995) 27–60.
Casey P. J. (1996) "Justinian, the *limitanei*, and Arab-Byzantine relations in the 6th c.", *JRA* 9 (1996) 214–22.
Cherry D. (2007) "The frontier zone", in *The Cambridge Economic History of the Greco-Roman World*, edd. W. Scheidel, I. Morris and R. Saller (Cambridge 2007) 720–40.
Cope C. R. (1999) "Faunal remains and butchery practices from Byzantine and Islamic contexts", in *Caesarea Papers 2: Herod's Temple, the Provincial Governor's Praetorium and Granaries, the Later Harbor, a Gold Coin Hoard, and Other Studies*, edd. K. G. Holum, A. Raban and J. Patrich (JRA Supplementary Series 35) (Portsmouth, RI 1999) 405–17.
Crawford P. (2006a) "The *Horreum* at el-Lejjūn (Area M)", in *The Roman Frontier in Central Jordan: Final Report on the* Limes Arabicus *Project, 1980–1989*, edd. S. T. Parker and J. W. Betlyon (Dumbarton Oaks Studies 40) (Washington 2006) 239–40.
—— (2006b) "The plant remains", in *The Roman Frontier in Central Jordan: Final Report on the* Limes Arabicus *Project, 1980–1989*, edd. S. T. Parker and J. W. Betlyon (Dumbarton Oaks Studies 40) (Washington 2006) 453–61.
Davies R. W. (1971) "The Roman military diet", *Britannia* 2 (1971) 122–42.
Decker M. (forthcoming) "Agriculture at Androna", in *Oxford Excavations at Andarin (Androna)*, edd. M. Mango *et al.* (Oxford, forthcoming).
Depeyrot G. (2006) "Economy and society", in *The Cambridge Companion to the Age of Constantine*, ed. N. Lenski (Cambridge 2006) 226–52.
Elsner J. (1998) *Imperial Rome and Christian Triumph: the Art of the Roman Empire, A.D. 100–450* (Oxford 1998).
Elton H. (1996) *Warfare in Roman Europe, AD 350–425* (Oxford 1996).
—— (2007) "Military forces (the Later Roman empire)", in *The Cambridge History of Greek and Roman Warfare, volume 2: Rome from the Late Republic to the Late Empire*, edd. P. Sabin, H. Van Wees and M. Whitby (Cambridge 2007) 325–67.
Engels D. W. (1978) *Alexander the Great and the Logistics of the Macedonian Army* (Berkeley 1978).
Fear A. (2007) "War and society (the Later Roman empire)", in *the Cambridge History of Greek and Roman Warfare, volume 2: Rome from the Late Republic to the Late Empire*, edd. P. Sabin, H. Van Wees and M. Whitby (Cambridge 2007) 424–58.

Fiema Z. T. (2002) "Late-antique Petra and its hinterland: recent research and new interpretations", in *The Roman and Byzantine Near East* 3, ed. J. H. Humphrey (JRA Supplementary Series 49) (Portsmouth, RI 2002) 191–252.

—— (2007) "The Byzantine military in the Petra Papyri—a summary", in *The Late Roman
Army in the Near East from Diocletian to the Arab Conquest: Proceedings of a Colloquium
held at Potenza, Acerenza and Matera, Italy (May 2005)*, edd. A. S. Lewin and P. Pellegrini
(BAR International Series 1717) (Oxford 2007) 313–19.

Fisher G. (2004) "A new perspective on Rome's desert frontier", *BASOR* 336 (2004) 49–60.

Graham M. W. (2006) *News and Frontier Consciousness in the Late Roman Empire* (Ann
Arbor 2006).

Greatrex G. (1998) *Rome and Persia at War, 502–532* (Leeds 1998).

—— (2007) "Dukes of the eastern frontier," in *Wolf Liebeschuetz Reflected: Essays Presented
by Colleagues, Friends and Pupils*, edd. J. F. Drinkwater and B. Salway (Bulletin of the
Institute of Classical Studies 91) (London 2007) 87–98.

Gregory S. (1995–97) *Roman Military Architecture on the Eastern Frontier*, 3 vols. (Amsterdam 1995–97).

Groot J. C. (1987a) "The barracks of el-Lejjūn", in *The Roman Frontier in Central Jordan:
Interim Report on the* Limes Arabicus *Project, 1980–1985*, ed. S. T. Parker (BAR International Series 340) (Oxford 1987) 261–310.

—— (1987b) "The small finds", in *The Roman Frontier in Central Jordan: Interim Report on
the* Limes Arabicus *Project, 1980–1985*, ed. S. T. Parker (BAR International Series 340)
(Oxford 1987) 497–521.

Groot J. C., Jones J. E. and Parker S. T. (2006) "The barracks in el-Lejjūn (Area K, L, R,
and B.6)", in *The Roman Frontier in Central Jordan: Final Report on the* Limes Arabicus
Project, 1980–1989, edd. S. T. Parker and J. W. Betlyon (Dumbarton Oaks Studies 40)
(Washington 2006) 161–85.

Grosse R. (1920) *Römische Militärgeschichte von Gallienus bis zum Beginn der byzantinischen Themenverfassung* (Berlin 1920).

Haarer F. K. (2006) *Anastasius I: Politics and Empire in the Late Roman World* (Cambridge
2006).

Haeckel A. E. (1987) "The *Principia* of el-Lejjūn", in *The Roman Frontier in Central Jordan:
Interim Report on the* Limes Arabicus *Project, 1980–1985*, ed. S. T. Parker (BAR International Series 340) (Oxford 1987) 203–60.

Haldon J. F. (1997) "The organisation and support of an expeditionary force: manpower
and logistics in the Middle Byzantine period", in *Byzantium at War (9th–12th Century)*,
ed. K. Tsiknakis (Athens 1997) 111–51.

—— (1999) *Warfare, State and Society in the Byzantine World 565–1204* (London 1999).

—— (2005) "Economy and administration: how did the empire work?", in *The Cambridge
Companion to the Age of Justinian*, ed. M. Maas (Cambridge 2005) 28–59.

—— (2006a) ed. *General Issues in the Study of Medieval Logistics: Sources, Problems and
Methodologies* (Leiden 2006) 1–35.

—— (2006b) "Introduction", in *General Issues in the Study of Medieval Logistics: Sources,
Problems and Methodologies*, ed. J. F. Haldon (Leiden 2006) 1–35.

Haug B. (2007) "Military pork: two receipts for rations", *ZPE* 160 (2007) 215–19.

Isaac B. H. (1990) *The Limits of Empire: the Roman Army in the East* (Oxford 1990, 2nd ed.,
Oxford 1992).

—— (1998) "The meaning of *limes* and *limitanei* in ancient sources", in B. H. Isaac, *The
Near East under Roman Rule: Select Papers* (Mnemsyne, bibliotheca classica Batava,
Supplementum 177) (Leiden 1998) 345–87.

James S. (1988) "The *fabricae*: state arms factories of the later Roman empire", in *Military
Equipment and the Identity of Roman Soldiers: Proceedings of the Fourth Roman Military
Equipment Conference*, ed. J. C. N. Coulston (BAR International Series 394) (Oxford 1988)
257–331.

Johnson S. (1983) *Late Roman Fortifications* (Totowa, NJ 1983).

Johnstone C. (2007) "A short report on the preliminary results from the study of the mammal and bird bone assemblages from Dichin", in *The Transition to Late Antiquity: on the Danube and Beyond*, ed. A. G. Poulter (Proceedings of the British Academy 141) (Oxford 2007) 287–94.

Jones A. H. M. (1964) *The Later Roman Empire 284–602: a Social, Economic and Administrative Survey* (Oxford 1964).

Kagan K. (2006) "Redefining Roman grand strategy", *Journal of Military History* 70 (2006) 333–62.

Kaldellis A. (2004) *Procopius of Caesarea: Tyranny, History, and Philosophy at the End of Antiquity* (Philadelphia 2004).

Karagiorgou O. (2001) "LR2: a container for the military *annona* on the Danubian border", in *Economy and Exchange in the East Mediterranean during Late Antiquity*, edd. S. Kingsley and M. Decker (Oxford 2001) 129–66.

Kelly C. (2004) *Ruling the Later Roman Empire* (Cambridge, Mass. 2004).

Kennedy D. L. and Riley D. N. (1990) *Rome's Desert Frontier: from the Air* (Austin 1990).

Kennedy H. (2007) "Justinianic Plague in Syria and the archaeological evidence", in *Plague and the End of Antiquity: the Pandemicc of 541–750*, ed. L. K. Little (Cambridge 2007) 87–95.

King A. (1999a) "Animals and the Roman army: the evidence of animal bones", in *The Roman Army as a Community: Including Papers of a Conference held at Birkbeck College, University of London on 11–12 January 1997*, edd. A. K. Goldsworthy, I. P. Haynes and C. E. P. Adams (JRA Supplementary Series 34) (Ann Arbor 1999) 139–50.

—— (1999b) "Diet in the Roman world: a regional inter-site comparison of the mammal bones", *JRA* 12 (1999) 168–202.

Kissel T. (1995) *Untersuchungen zur Logistik des römischen Heeres in den Provinzen des griechischen Ostens (27 v. Chr.–235 n. Chr.)* (St. Katharinen 1995).

Kraemer C. J. (1958) *Excavations at Nessana, volume 3: the Non-Literary Papyri* (Princeton, NJ 1958).

Lain A. and Parker S. T. (2006) "The *Principia* of el-Lejjūn (Area A)", in *The Roman Frontier in Central Jordan: Final Report on the* Limes Arabicus *Project, 1980–1989*, edd. S. T. Parker and J. W. Betlyon (Dumbarton Oaks Studies 40) (Washington 2006) 123–159.

Le Bohec Y. (2006) *L'armée romaine sous le bas-empire* (Paris 2006).

Lee A. D. (1998) "The army", in *The Cambridge Ancient History, volume 13: the Late Empire A.D. 337–425*, edd. A. Cameron and P. Garnsey (Cambridge 1998) 211–37.

—— (2007a) *War in Late Antiquity: a Social History* (Oxford 2007).

—— (2007b) "Warfare and the state (the Later Roman empire)", in *The Cambridge History of Greek and Roman Warfare, volume 2: Rome from the Late Republic to the Late Empire*, edd. P. Sabin, H. Van Wees and M. Whitby (Cambridge 2007) 379–423.

Lewin A. S. (2007a) "'Amr Ibn 'Adī, Mavia, the Phylarchs and the Late Roman army: peace and war in the Near East", in *The Late Roman Army in the Near East from Diocletian to the Arab Conquest: Proceedings of a Colloquium held at Potenza, Acerenza and Matera, Italy (May 2005)*, edd. A. S. Lewin and P. Pellegrini (BAR International Series 1717) (Oxford 2007) 243–62.

—— (2007b) "The impact of the Late Roman army in Palaestine and Arabia", in *The Impact of the Roman Army (200 BC–AD 476)*, edd. L. De Blois and E. Lo Cascio (Leiden 2007) 463–80.

Liebeschuetz J. H. W. G. (1972) *Antioch: City and Imperial Administration in the Later Roman Empire* (Oxford 1972).

Little L. K. (2007) ed. *Plague and the End of Antiquity: the Pandemic of 541–750* (Cambridge 2007).

Luttwak E. N. (1976) *The Grand Strategy of the Roman Empire: from the First Century AD to the Third* (Baltimore 1976).

MacMullen R. (1963) *Soldier and Civilian in the Later Roman Empire* (Cambridge, Mass. 1963).

—— (1984) *Christianizing the Roman Empire* (New Haven 1984).

Magness J. (1999) "Redating the forts at Ein Boqeq, Upper Zohar, and other sites in SE Judea, and the implications for the nature of the *Limes Palaestinae*", in *The Roman and Byzantine Near East, volume 2*, ed. J. H. Humphrey (JRA Supplementary Series 31) (Portsmouth, RI 1999) 189–206.

Mango M. (1982) *The Churches and Monasteries of the Tur `Abdin* (London 1982).

—— (2002) "Excavations and survey at Androna, Syria: the Oxford Team 1999", *DOP* 56 (2002) 307–15.

—— (2008) "Baths, reservoirs and water use at Androna in Late Antiquity and the Early Islamic period", in *Residences, Castles, Settlements: Transformation Processes from Late Antiquity to Early Islam in Bilad al Sham: Proceedings of the International Conference held at Damascus, 5–9 November, 2006*, ed. K. Bartl (Orient-Archäologie 24) (Damascus 2008) 1–21.

Mayerson P. (1962) "Agricultural evidence in the Colt Papyri", in *Excavations at Nessana Vol. 1*, ed. I. H. D. Colt (London 1962) 224–69.

—— (1988) "Justinian's Novel 103 and the reorganization of Palestine", *BASOR* 269 (1988) 65–71.

McDaniel J. (2006) "The small finds", in *The Roman Frontier in Central Jordan: Final Report on the* Limes Arabicus *Project, 1980–1989*, edd. S. T. Parker and J. W. Betlyon (Dumbarton Oaks Studies 40) (Washington 2006) 293–327.

Mitthof F. (2001) Annona Militaris: *Die Heeresversorgung im spätaniken Ägypten* (Florence 2001).

Nicasie M. J. (1998) *Twilight of Empire: the Roman Army from the Reign of Diocletian until the Battle of Adrianople* (Amsterdam 1998).

Palme B. (2007) "The imperial presence: government and army", in *Egypt in the Byzantine World, 300–700*, ed. R. S. Bagnall (Cambridge 2007) 244–70.

Parker S. T. and Betlyon J. W. (2006) edd. *The Roman Frontier in Central Jordan: Final Report on the* Limes Arabicus *Project, 1980–1989* (Dumbarton Oaks Studies 40) (Washington 2006).

Parker S. T. (2006a) "The legionary fortress of el-Lejjūn", in *The Roman Frontier in Central Jordan: Final Report on the* Limes Arabicus *Project, 1980–1989*, edd. S. T. Parker and J. W. Betlyon (Dumbarton Oaks Studies 40) (Washington 2006) 111–22.

—— (2006b) "The pottery", in *The Roman Frontier in Central Jordan: Final Report on the* Limes Arabicus *Project, 1980–1989*, edd. S. T. Parker and J. W. Betlyon (Dumbarton Oaks Studies 40) (Washington 2006) 329–71.

—— (2006c) "History of the Roman frontier east of the Dead Sea", in *The Roman Frontier in Central Jordan: Final Report on the* Limes Arabicus *Project, 1980–1989*, edd. S. T. Parker and J. W. Betlyon (Dumbarton Oaks Studies 40) (Washington 2006) 517–74.

Porten B. (1996) *The Elephantine Papyri in English: Three Millennia of Cross-cultural Continuity and Change* (Leiden 1996).

Rankov B. (2007) "Military forces (the Late Republic and the Principate)", in *The Cambridge History of Greek and Roman Warfare, volume 2: Rome from the Late Republic to the Late Empire*, edd. P. Sabin, H. Van Wees and M. Whitby (Cambridge 2007) 30–75.

Ravegnani G. (1988) *Soldati di Bisanzio in età Giustinianea* (Rome 1988).

Richardot P. (2005) *La fin de l'armée romaine 284–476* (Paris 2005).

Roth J. P. (1999) *The Logistics of the Roman Army at War (264 B.C.–A.D. 235)* (Leiden 1999).

Sarantis A. (2006) *The Balkans during the Reign of Justinian: Barbarian Invasions and Imperial Responses* (D.Phil. diss. Univ. of Oxford 2006).

Sarris P. (2006) *Economy and Society in the Age of Justinian* (Cambridge 2006).

Sartre M. (1982) *Trois études sur l'Arabie romaine et byzantine* (Brussels 1982).

Shahîd I. (2002) *Byzantium and the Arabs in the Sixth Century, volume 2* (Washington, DC 2002).

Schick R. (1987) "The Church of el-Lejjūn", in *The Roman Frontier in Central Jordan: Interim Report on the* Limes Arabicus *Project, 1980–1985*, ed. S. T. Parker (BAR International Series 340) (Oxford 1987) 353–83.

Shean J. F. (2010) *Soldiering for God: Christianity and the Roman Army* (Leiden 2010).

Southern P. and Dixon K. R. (1996) *The Late Roman Army* (London 1996).

Stallibrass S. and Thomas R. (2008a) edd. *Feeding the Roman Army: the Archaeology of Production and Supply in NW Europe* (Oxford 2008).

—— (2008b) "For starters: producing and supplying food to the army in the Roman north-west provinces", in *Feeding the Roman Army: the Archaeology of Production and Supply in NW Europe*, edd. S. Stallibrass and R. Thomas (Oxford 2008) 1–17.

—— (2008c) "Food for thought: what's next?", in *Feeding the Roman Army: The Archaeology of Production and Supply in NW Europe*, edd. S. Stallibrass and R. Thomas (Oxford 2008) 146–69.

Stein E. (1949) *Histoire du Bas-Empire II* (Paris 1949).

Tates G. (2004) "La Syrie-Palestine", in *Le Monde Byzantin I*, ed. C. Morrisson (Paris 2004) 373–401.

Tomlin R. S. O. (2000) "The legions in the Late Empire", in *Roman Fortresses and their Legions*, ed. R. J. Brewer (London) 159–81.

Toplyn M. (1994) *Meat for Mars: Livestock, limitanei, and Pastoral Provisioning for the Roman Army on the Arabian Frontier (A.D. 284–551)* (Ph. D. diss., Harvard Univ. 1994).

—— (2006) "Livestock and *Limitanei*: the zooarchaeological evidence", in *The Roman Frontier in Central Jordan: Final Report on the* Limes Arabicus *Project, 1980–1989*, edd. S. T. Parker and J. W. Betlyon (Dumbarton Oaks Studies 40) (Washington 2006) 463–507.

Trombley F. R. and Watt J. W. (2000) trans. *The Chronicle of Pseudo-Joshua the Stylite: translated with notes and introduction* (Translated Texts for Historians 32) (Liverpool 2000).

Tsafrir Y. and Foerster G. (1997) "Urbanism in Scythopolis-Bet Shean in the fourth to seventh centuries", *DOP* 51 (1997) 85–146.

Van Berchem D. (1952) *L'armée de Dioclétien et la réforme constantinienne* (Paris 1952).

Van Creveld M. (1977) *Supplying War: Logistics from Wallenstein to Patton* (Cambridge 1977).

Wheeler E. L. (2007) "The Army and the *Limes* in the East", in *A Companion to the Roman Army*, ed. P. Erdkamp (Oxford 2007) 235–66.

Whitby M. (1986) "Procopius' description of Dara (*Buildings* II.1–3.)", in *The Defence of the Roman and Byzantine East: Proceedings of a Colloquium held at the University of Sheffield in April 1986*, edd. P. Freeman and D. Kennedy (BAR International Series 297) (Oxford 1986) 737–83.

—— (1988) *The Emperor Maurice and his Historian: Theophylact Simocatta on Persian and Balkan Warfare* (Oxford 1988).

—— (1995) "Recruitment in Roman armies from Justinian to Heraclius (*ca.* 565–615)," in *The Byzantine and Early Islamic Near East III: States, Resources and Armies*, ed. A. Cameron (Princeton, NJ 1995) 61–124.

—— (2000) "Army and society in the later Roman world", in *The Cambridge Ancient History, volume 14: Late Antiquity: Empire and Successors A.D. 425–600*, edd. A. Cameron, B. Ward-Perkins and M. Whitby (Cambridge 2000) 469–95.

—— (2005) "War and state in Late Antiquity: some economic and political connections", in *Krieg, Gesellschaft, Institutionen: Beiträge zu einer vergleichenden Kriegsgeschichte*, edd. B. Meissner, O. Schmitt, and M. Sommer (Berlin 2005) 355–85.

—— (2007) "War (the Later Roman Empire)", in *The Cambridge History of Greek and Roman Warfare, volume 2: Rome from the Late Republic to the Late Empire*, edd. P. Sabin, H. Van Wees, M. Whitby (Cambridge 2007) 310–341.

Whittaker C. R. (1994) *Frontiers of the Roman Empire: a Social and Economic Survey* (Baltimore 1994).

Wickham C. (2005) *Framing the Early Middle Ages: Europe and the Mediterranean 400–800* (Oxford 2005).

Zuckerman C. (2004) "L'armée", in *Le Monde Byzantin I*, ed. C. Morrisson (Paris 2004) 143–80.

List of Figures

CIVIL WAR

WARS WITHIN THE FRONTIERS:
ARCHAEOLOGIES OF REBELLION, REVOLT AND CIVIL WAR

Neil Christie

Abstract

Civil war is much documented by text, but far too little by archaeology. The later Roman world was one often afflicted by civil conflict and power struggles between rival emperors, generals and troops, and these all appear to have had serious impacts on communities, regions, economies and frontiers. In what ways though can archaeology offer a guide or additional insight into these many conflicts? Or are these wars intangible materially, despite their destructive human impact? This paper broadly considers the types of materials and evidence—from walls to coins—that might reveal something of the 3rd to 5th c. wars that damaged the Roman West in particular, and argues that much more weight needs to be placed on these internal traumas.

INTRODUCTION

His name, that is Antoninus, was erased by order of the Senate (that of Varius Heliogabalus remained), since he had held it under usurpation, wishing to appear to be the son of Antoninus...He alone of all *principes* was both dragged along and thrown into a sewer and hurled into the Tiber. This befell him as a result of the general hatred of all, which emperors must particularly guard against, seeing that those who do not earn the love of Senate, people and soldiers, do not earn a tomb. (SHA *Heliogab.* 17).

Although this emperor [Constantius II] in foreign wars met with loss and disaster, yet he was elated by his success in civil conflicts, and drenched with awful gore from the internal wounds of state. It was on this unworthy...ground that in Gaul and Pannonia he erected triumphal arches at great expense, commemorating the ruin of the provinces, and added records of his deeds, that men might read of him as long as those monuments would last. (Amm. Marc. 21.16.15).

Soldiers who have been so trained and exercised at their base, whether they are legionaries, auxilia or cavalry, when they come together for a campaign from their various units, inevitably prefer warfare to leisure in the rivalry for valour. No one thinks of mutiny, when he carries confidence in skill and strength. (Veg. *Mil.* 3.4).

A. Sarantis, N. Christie (edd.) *War and Warfare in Late Antiquity: Current Perspectives*
(Late Antique Archaeology 8.1–8.2 – 2010–11) (Leiden 2013), pp. 927–968

Whilst civil war was central to the creation of Empire and to the affir-
mation of strong imperial rule in the first centuries B.C. and A.D.—from
triumvirates to Actium and to the 'Year of the Four Emperors' in A.D. 69—
its traumas and human impacts are rarely registered in the archaeological
record. Arguably the evidence is almost all documentary and iconographic
(numismatic and sculptural) and certainly, without the narrative sources,
these major events, so core to so many historical analyses of Rome's
social, political, and military development, might be almost invisible and
even ignored. This may well overstate the case since, obviously, we can
identify provincial annexations, foundations of colonies, military changes,
and religious directives as consequences of new orders, but even here,
without the texts, these events and material impositions could be viewed
simply as responding to direct imperialism by a smooth-running state.
Similarly, the creation and evolution of the imperial cult, whilst intimately
tied to securing power and allegiance in contexts of upheaval (Octavian/
Augustus at the start of Empire to confirm a divinely sanctioned role;
Vespasian in A.D. 69/70 to reinforce and stabilise his hard-fought position), do not speak directly of the consequences of civil strife.[1] And, of
course, we have documented purges of rivals, kin, generals and supporters (religious, military or social) by new or intended emperors—these too
might be classed as 'civil conflict', but again leave no archaeological trace,
unless we count instances of *damnatio memoriae*, where names or images
of once accepted elites or imperial familial members are scratched, chiselled or blotted out.[2]

---

[1] On the imperial cult, see, in particular, Fishwick (1992) and (2002), who charts the
fluctuating role of the cult and the input of emperors in the first two centuries A.D.—but
with diminishing data subsequently; the epigraphy and actual sculpture from excavated
cult temples confirm specific peaks, often to be associated with imperial needs to affirm
(a generally new) authority. See discussion below on the later fates of imperial cult complexes. Much debate is available on Augustan imagery, but a valuable analysis comes in
Elsner (1995) 159–72 and 192–210. Too many books exist that cover the span of the Late
Republic and earlier Empire in terms of politics, war and succession, but, besides Tacitus'
and Suetonius' Histories, two colourful modern overviews are Leach (1978); and Greenhalgh (1975); and with Jones (1980), a compact and lucid review of Octavian to Augustus;
and Morgan (2007), an excellent new appraisal of A.D. 69.

[2] See introductory quote on Heliogabalus. Key is Varner (2004), with an emphasis on
defacings and re-workings of portrait sculpture. Regarding bloody removals of kin and
potential rivals, the Roman emperors were on a par with Germanic kings, as brought
out neatly in Merrills (2009), who explores the dynastic disputes and succession issues
amongst the Vandal royalty of North Africa, with Huneric in A.D. 480/81 being especially
brutal and thorough.

Civil war in its various guises—conflict and campaigns between emperor and usurper, between usurpers, between east and west emperors (of varied 'legitimacy'), between generalissimos and counts, between mutinous armies and the state, between breakaway provinces and governors, and caused by assassinations of generals, purges of bodyguards, the vicious exploitation of civilians by state forces, civil insurrections, and perhaps also banditry—is a feature, often a prevalent one, of the 3rd to 5th c. in both the West and East of Rome's Empire. Some, especially in the 4th c., gain as much documentary attention as those 350 years earlier, from chroniclers and poets alike. Arguably, these were less debilitating to the state than those of the 3rd c., which were, in their frequency and distribution, highly divisive, damaging and a sizeable drain on lives and resources. Patently, Rome did regroup, restore and endure, but the view stands of an Empire whose suicidal or blood-letting tendencies were never far from the surface, and were only partially kept in check by tougher imperialism, which in turn generated provincial discord with the core and a slow detachment from it.

Halsall and others point to the substantial manpower losses through civil wars won by Theodosius in the late 4th c., which must have destabilised the West and fractured the West Roman court's ability to sustain its internal controls; a much thinned frontier control thence created the openings through which non-Roman enemies started to push, whilst ineffective emperors chose entrenched positions.[3] Imbalances exist though in modern assessments of the impacts of these civil wars, with some seeing Rome's long-term endurance as signifying how these internal conflicts were only temporary—if very bloody—bursts of destabilisation;[4] yet internal damages and disunities may appear temporary, but can also be cumulative in their impacts. Whilst Drinkwater has observed how "barbarians did

---

[3] Selection by Theodosius of his weak son Honorius as his western counterpart further diluted the battered western Empire: see general summaries in Mitchell (2007) 84–93; and by Curran and Blockley in Cameron and Garnsey (1998). On Theodosian victories and western debilitation, see comments in Ferrill (1986) 75–77; Blockley (1998) 426–30; and, most usefully, Halsall (2005) 48–49. On emperors and war in this period, see also the valuable summary in Lee (2007) 21–37.

[4] E.g. Elton (1996) 152–55, who seems not to trust claims of manpower shortages in the period towards ca. A.D. 400, but does note the claimed 54,000 Roman troopers lost in Magnentius' general's defeat at Mursa in 351; perhaps over 30,000 fell in Eugenius' defeat at the *Fluvius Frigidus* in 394. Elton offers useful overviews on the nature of usurpers and civil wars and talks of the tactics documented, including sieges—193–98, 227–33—but he in no way highlights these as on a par with barbarian impacts. Also on the natures of civil war/conflict, see Lee (2007) 66–73.

not often take advantage of internal wars", he also identifies how many scholars have overplayed the intensity and scale of barbarian raids in the 3rd and 4th c. especially, and have ignored the fact that some 'campaigns' against these non-Roman groups were small-scale actions, partly pursued by emperors and generals to gain legitimate and praiseworthy victories (to balance out the damages and bad press caused by civil strife).[5]

There are problems in defining civil war in the latest phases of the empire, of course, since in the 5th c., warfare against non-Romans was as much inside as outside or on the fringes of the empire, and with many of these non-Romans, periodically at least, labelled and paid as federates or allies to fight for the imperial government—often against usurpers or insurrectionist groups viewed as working against the official state machinery. The Visigoths of south-west Gaul could even, in their shady federate status, dare to promote certain usurpers, though these usurpers might be viewed as more Roman to locals than the aggressive and never-seen emperor based in distant Italy, who might then send troops to bring even greater disruptions to their territory. Hydatius' chronicle, for the first half of the 5th c., is particularly busy in recounting the efforts and failures of the Goths as federates, alongside tracing Roman (Italian) campaigns against claimants such as Jovinus and Sebastian, to be matched by the moans of Prosper of Aquitaine, writing in the 430s and enumerating usurpers and intruders in the first third of the century.[6] How we define civil war is matched by how we define the power groups and their relationships with the central state—indeed, in the context of 5th c. coinages, King suggests that however we interpret the confusing issues of 'official' or 'unofficial' status (in our academic and historical eyes), "the answer lies in a more flexible approach to the definition of Roman and non-Roman in this period".[7]

---

[5] Drinkwater (1996).

[6] See Burgess (1992) on Hydatius; and Muhlberger (1992) on both Prosper and the 'Gallic Chronicler' of A.D. 452, whose emphasis, Muhlberger argues, is geared more to observing the dismemberment forced by external forces in the West. See also Kulikowski (in this collection). For 5th c. civil wars, see Ward-Perkins (2005) 43–49, highlighting how "As in other periods of history, failure against foreign enemies and civil war were very closely linked, indeed each fed off each other". Ward-Perkins singles out the long, but ineffective reign of Honorius as enabling the West's dismemberment. He makes little comment on 3rd and 4th c. civil conflicts. See Faulkner (2000) 168–74; and Snyder (1998) 95–99 on the main British usurpers/tyrants—Magnus Maximus and Constantine III.

[7] King (1992) 195, who observes how indeed "It is virtually impossible to assign the coins . . . to either locals or barbarians given the nature of the evidence" —however, whether

This paper, however, is not geared to seeking such definitions, or to contemplating further the depth of impact—short- and long-term—of civil wars on the late Empire and their contribution to the 'End'; rather, it aims to examine how far archaeology is able to trace civil war on its different levels, and whether its voice can contribute anything to an analysis of the textual evidence. The worry is that the traumas that must have been played out on battlefields, in camps, in sieges and towns, are largely lost to us despite the documented levels of upheaval and loss; as a result, it may be easy for historians and archaeologists alike to downplay the physical impact and even to doubt the damages inflicted on both military and civilian populations.[8] Below, I examine a variety of sources of evidence to start the debate on archaeological visibility: first, town and other defences, to consider state responses to insecurities; second, memorials—from epitaphs to official representations and commemorations; third, numismatic guides to wars, usurpers and victories; and finally, the topic of reprisals or retribution, where a new power defaces and seeks to blot out depictions of the defeated. Most of the data deployed here are not clear-cut, and may be read in different ways; but it is better to ask different questions of these than to stick to a simple reading and explanation.

WALLS

First we turn to the most tangible of manifestations of later Roman insecurities. The erection of powerful urban defensive circuits in the western Empire and in Gaul especially from the late 3rd c., and the shrinkage of urban spaces, in some instances of 'exposed' towns, are seen as fundamental components of a changing Roman world, and as reactions to growing external threats. New frontier works, the re-thinking and re-modelling of frontier control systems and of the Roman army in general, plus a revised emphasis on key (military) highways linking inner capitals to the frontier zones, add to the general image of change, and of efforts to preserve the whole Empire.[9]

we try to label these as local/barbarian/official/unofficial, the coins are unarguably efforts at a continuity of Roman forms and monetary display.

[8] In part, the problem is matched by the general invisibility of archaeological data for some of the major plagues documented in the Roman and Byzantine epoch—see comments in Christie (2006) 500–504 on the so-called Justinianic plague of the A.D. 530s.

[9] Poulter (2007a) provides one very full example where the emphasis is on Rome against the outsiders: the Danube provinces and frontiers see significant changes in the

But the emphasis is all too often on the threats beyond the empire's frontiers. Thus, in Stephen Johnson's invaluable volume *Late Roman Fortifications* (1983)—which surely merits a second edition to take on board so much new archaeology of defence—it is noticeable how civil conflict within the empire plays merely a bit part in his narrative of cause and effect, with the emphasis very much on the external, non-Roman threats.[10] Thus: "The Gothic raid of 267 came as a concerted culmination to a series of inroads made by the Goths from about 238 onwards. Spasmodic pressure on the Danubian frontier and on Thrace had been met by a succession of 3rd c. emperors, sometimes by cash subsidies (in effect payment to keep the peace) and sometimes by the withdrawal of this courtesy, and consequential further raids. Sustained resistance to the Gothic pressures was not assisted by the instability of the imperial office".[11] Johnson's maps pinpointing the distribution of 3rd c. coin hoards show the latter gathered around the imposed lines of arrows which the captions label as 'General direction of Barbarian invasions with dates'; hoards thus were panic responses to non-Romans according to Johnson, who effectively excludes the panics equally induced by Roman civil war and movements of Roman troops, and excludes the possibility that the hoards represent savings by Roman troops gathered in those spaces, or savings lost or given up as new coins with changed imagery—on the latest 'official' coins—took over in circulation.[12]

4th to 6th c. within the army, but especially in terms of fortifications and their design, content and supply. It is noticeable how minimal the comments are here on the impact of civil wars in this same period in the regions analysed—but this is as much due to the archaeological emphasis on the frontier line and on the related evidence. Poulter (2007b) 30, for example, notes the set of five Diocletianic inscriptions of A.D. 298/99 from Moesia II province, each recording *pro futurum in aeternum rei publicae praesidium constituerunt*: these defences refer to a securing of the line and the province, but arguably they also recall the need to secure the empire/State internally.

[10] Chapter 4 of Johnson (1983) has a very telling title: 'The pressures on Rome: barbarian invasions and tactics'. In this, significant internal disruptions such as the rise of the Gallic Empire on imperial soil are commented upon more in terms of opening up access to the empire for new barbarian raids, which Johnson perceives as the more damaging to the West, even though the civil wars probably extinguished far more soldiery. Too often Johnson speaks of 'invasions' or refers to war bands, implying a high numerical scale, although in many 3rd and even 4th c. instances, these were probably rapid and thus fairly small-scale raiding parties, exploiting voids created by distracted Roman forces. On the possible sizes of such raiding forces, see Elton (1996) 72–73, plus 48–54; and on the artificial (Roman and modern) inflation of their threat, see Drinkwater (1996), developed much more fully in (2007).

[11] Johnson (1983) 73. Witschel (2004) 256 points to the over-emphasis by modern commentators on barbarian impacts in 2nd and 3rd c. contexts.

[12] Johnson (1983) 71, 75, figs. 23 and 24.

Fig. 1   The canal defensive walls at Aquileia in north-east Italy. The multiple defences at this imperial city are assigned to various historical dates, many tied to civil war episodes. The image shows *spolia* as the main wall fabric, perhaps indicative in this instance of rushed works in advance of expected assault.
(Photo: Neil Christie)

There are urban sites and defences that have been associated closely with reactions to impending or actual civil war. The key example is Aquileia, a major port city, and imperial stopover at the head of the Adriatic in north-east Italy (fig. 1). Aquileia has seen extensive excavations since the early 20th c., including of its defensive curtains, some of whose phases and builds remain exposed. The various excavators have sought to identify defences—which overall span Republican to Byzantine times—to match some of the key moments in the city's history.[13] Thus we are informed of circuits tied to 169 B.C. and the Roman colony; A.D. 168—the Marcomannic assault; A.D. 238—civil war destruction/siege; 290/300—a revised imperial status; 361—civil war siege; 394—stopover point for Theodosius I; 452—Aquileia's destruction by the Huns; 490—siege by Theoderic; 556—a Byzantine restoration.

---

[13] Summarised with related bibliography in Christie (2006) 291–94. See Christie (2006) 322–24 for discussion of *spolia* in city walls, identifying varied uses and displays, whether practical, ornamental and/or symbolic (these valid for *spolia* usage in other contexts, such as in churches—Christie (2006) 130–33).

Should major documented events always equate with major structural responses? Arguably, there is too much effort to achieve this, when in reality some of the building works are of longer gestation. Thus, for the siege of Maximinus the Thracian in A.D. 238,[14] the use of artillery by both defenders and attackers (with women inside Aquileia cutting their locks to provide strings for bows and catapults) indicates a defended city, but was this via rapidly built new walls, or a modified old Republican circuit, itself perhaps hastily restored after the Marcomannic and Quadic incursions into north-eastern Italy in the 160s? The insertion of both imperial palace and circus in the city's western quarter, in the Tetrarchic and Constantinian period, is then linked to the addition of various projecting towers (pentagonal, octagonal, polygonal) on the wall circuit. Most evident is the *spolia*-laden canal/riverside circuit with towers (fig. 1), featuring re-used inscriptions and architectural material thought to come from buildings demolished (or already ruinous from other sieges!) to help build and defend the 4th c. townscape.

A further, later wall divided the old city in half, running through the ruinous forum-basilica and rejecting the old monumental and imperial zones, but enclosing the core religious buildings, including the *memoria* of S. Ilario, built *ca.* A.D. 400. *Spolia* incorporated in these defences relates to buildings demolished by the end of the 4th c., and with one partial inscription recording a likely emperor (*Theodo...*) and Hilarianus (praetorian prefect), in charge of restoration of works and walls; as the prefect is identified with Hesperius Hilarianus, son of the poet senator Ausonius, and in office in Gaul and Italy in the 380s, so the claim is that Theodosius the Great prompted defensive renewals or modifications at Aquileia, perhaps in the wake of the defeat at Adrianople, or after defeating Eugenius.

As stated, it is slightly incautious to attempt to tie walls in too closely to such documented events and names,[15] although an exposed and important city like Aquileia will undoubtedly have been forced to respond structurally—in terms of defence and repair of walls, buildings, population

---

[14] Herodian 8.3–4.

[15] See useful comments in Fernández-Ochoa and Morillo (2005) 300–301, 316–27 on dating, typological analyses, structural variances and related questions in connection to Late Roman circuits in Spain in particular. Rambaldi (2009) 122–28 offers an Empire-wide assessment of defensive building works in the 3rd c. anarchy period, although the related catalogue shows that dating of some circuits is often made by association with historical events, especially invasions, rather than through secure archaeological chronologies—though rarely will pots or coins prove a construction date.

displacement—to both Roman and non-Roman assails. It is also problematic to claim that strong (although clearly not always effective) defences could be raised at speed. If advance warning was good and an army at hand—as would be valid perhaps for a major city like Aquileia—then rapid response is feasible (such as refortifying or bolstering walls in a month or so), but with much necessarily brutal treatment of public and other structures to procure sufficient materials for both the core and the face of walls. Such may indeed be evident in the canal curtain, and this fits better a context of potential siege warfare, which would only be expected from an alternative or rebel Roman army.

Elsewhere in Italy, other defensive measures by key towns can fit equally into the context of internal instability, and in the case of Verona, the use of *spolia* in a curtain wall documented to A.D. 267, in the reign of Gallienus, contrasts with the ordered and more monumental Aurelianic walls of Rome, whose form and scale signify a longer programme of construction. 'Barbarian' incursions, notably by the Iuthungi/Alamanni, did hit Italy in the 260s, but just as important for Gallienus was the ongoing and fluctuating conflict with the so-called Gallic Empire, headed by Postumus.[16] We cannot exclude that both usurper and emperor began to secure strategic centres with walls as physical manifestations of the drawn-out power struggle (see also below on Britain): a rival Roman army would cause far more damage than swift Alamannic raiding parties, and establishing fortified urban strongholds where troops might be billeted and food supplies stored—or where civilians and administrators might find security while the military forces were elsewhere—makes major sense, even if the logistics of undertaking such measures would have been arduous at best in the timeframe.[17]

Rome's own defences certainly can be read in like fashion: a key political and civilian centre, secured in line with a new policy of fortification, prompted by upheavals of civil war and external barbarian raiding. This

---

[16] Rambaldi (2009) 127 and catalogue entries 168–88 for likely later 3rd c. walls in North Italy, preferring to emphasise these as responses to the "più massiccia invasione di Alamanni e Iutungi".

[17] In this context, a first appearance of a modified Roman army in terms of greater mobility—both in cavalry and particularly in field units—and in provision of bodyguards for emperors, is logical, as 'Gallic' and 'Roman' usurpers and emperors roved to meet rival threats and external raids; Gallienus is suggested by some as the author of this new military template, later formalised under Constantine or Diocletian: Southern and Dixon (1996) 11–14; Whitby (2004) 160–62; Tomlin (2000) stressing the small sizes of the new field units/legions. On later Roman military equipment, see also Bishop and Coulston (1993) and see Coulston in this collection.

Fig. 2   A 19th c. engraving of Burgh Castle wall and circuit tower, one of the
Saxon Shore fort installations active by the final quarter of the 3rd c. (From:
Knight (1845)).

marks the start of a formal process of defensive investment in cities in
the West, developed under the Tetrarchs and Constantine.[18] Potentially,
therefore, walls first appear as expressions of new security, or of efforts to
maintain control, with an emphasis both on key strategic urban seats, but
also on significant population foci—the threat being real or perceived.
With stability restored, this process of strengthening urban defences is
extended outward, in recognition of the value of such secure bases for
populations, food and troops.

Perhaps one of the more secure linkages between urban and military
defence and Roman civil war is evident in Roman Britain towards the end
of the 3rd c., in the wake of the collapse of the 'Gallic Empire' and Britain's continued separation from 'official' Roman rule. Here we can trace

---

[18] Urban and wider defensive processes in Late Roman Italy are examined in Christie
(2006) 294–348 with related references. For wider patterns, refer again to Johnson (1983);
for Spain, see the careful review by Fernández-Ochoa and Morillo (2005), who pinpoint a
first phase of urban defensive reconfiguration under the Tetrarchy (pp. 327–29) centred
on the north-west of the province.

extensions and reinforcements to the series of coastal bases and depots labelled the Saxon Shore forts, extending from the central south coast base of Portchester to at least Brancaster in Norfolk, or further north still, to Skegness and Brough-on-Humber (fig. 3).[19] Some of these belong to the early 3rd c. or earlier, and may have served as shipment points, depots, fleet bases for military campaigns, such as under Severus, and as simple supply bases for the forts and towns of the interior; forts at these sites and accompanying walls were thus intended to define military units and defend supplies.

But reversion to defences and new installations can be identified for the A.D. 270s onwards, at seats like Richborough (a new fort replacing a signal-tower), Dover and Portchester, and the temptation has been to link these works with the name of the rebellious general, Carausius, dominant in Britain and on the near continent from A.D. 286, until he was murdered and replaced by his minister Allectus in 293, who endured until 296.[20] Both were viewed as usurpers, and both were active in issuing coins, but both sought recognition for long spells—hence many of the issues of Carausius duly found in the earliest layers of the Shore forts depict him alongside the more easterly *imperatores* (and 'brothers'), Diocletian and Maximian. The recent excavations at Pevensey, meanwhile, have uncovered timber foundation piles to the south curtain wall, dendrochronologically attributable to A.D. 280–300, but with associated coins of Carausius and Allectus, tying the fortress to A.D. 293.

As noted, some forts were earlier in date, and some seem to show fair activity in the 270s, as at Portchester, Bradwell and Lympne (such as with coins of Tetricus), which might even be an indication of military provisioning and entrenchment during the period of the Gallic Empire—and not just reactions to possible largely undocumented seaborne raids along the Channel coasts by Saxons and others. The efforts at Pevensey in 293 should certainly indicate expectation of a seaborne attack, and the form of the defences here, as in the other 'new' forts, are observed as of a scale to counter siege, which was not a likely tactic of any small-scale raiding

---

[19] Pearson (2002) provides the most recent review of functions and chronologies to the Saxon Shore forts.

[20] Coarelli (1999) 32–33 notes the references in panegyrics to Constantius and to Maximianus first to victory and restoration of *Britannia*, and then to glorification of the naval victories in the East and West through displaying the prows of conquered vessels (i.e. of Carausius) on the Rostra in the Roman Forum.

force.[21] Magnus Maximus and other mid- and later 4th c. British usurpers may well have utilised the forts again in their stands to gain the purple, but more as launch-pads for campaigns on the continent, and for securing rearguard supplies; otherwise their role against external threats—Saxons, Franks and others—was heightened in the 4th c., as marked by the provision of new signal towers along the north-eastern and western coasts of the province.

Alongside the military coastal bases, we might question whether politics and civil war affected also urban contexts in Britain, most specifically at the governor's capital of London. Both new work and re-assessment of old excavation data from London, and specifically at and near Newgate, identify a re-modelling of the city walls in the second half of the 3rd c., reinforcing the earlier and substantial stone circuit of *ca.* A.D. 190–225; the re-modelling more generally included provision of the riverside wall as well as of bastions and re-cut ditches.[22] Whilst this review prefers not to see the first circuit as tied to the name of the governor Clodius Albinus (A.D. 193–97) in resistance to Septimius Severus, and argues for an extended building campaign, the later 3rd c. work remains linked to historical events from our few textual guides—"at a time when Saxon shore raids were becoming more frequent".[23]

Maloney earlier flagged the evidence from Shadwell, 1.2 km east of London, indicative of a signal station and tower of 8 m², which coin-finds identify as strongly active in the 280s and 290s, and with usage enduring perhaps until the mid-4th c.[24] Some coin issues at Shadwell go back to the 260s, and fit well with the revised dating of the riverside wall to A.D. 255–70; whilst this pre-dates the famous names of Carausius and Allectus, it does fit the wider context of the Gallic Empire and of upheavals and change active on the continent. Effectively, the generally imprecise

---

[21]   Pearson (2002) 56–64 and 125–38 reviews the dating evidence and context; see 136–37 on 'Defence against Rome'. Johnson (1983) 211 is more hesitant, saying that arguments to tie Carausius to fortification works "to secure his position after his usurpation . . . do not carry conviction", although, as in (1979) 111–14, he is happy to see Carausius exploiting and perhaps then upgrading pre-existing defensive bases after his usurpation.

[22]   Lyon (2007), en route reviewing previous publications on London and its walls by Norman and Reader in the early 20th c., plus, from the 1960s to early 1990s, Merrifield, Maloney and Perring in particular. For the 3rd and 4th c. works, see 46–52, with the main emphasis on the bastions which belong mainly to the mid 4th c., although some can be shown now to have been medieval additions.

[23]   Lyon (2007) 52.

[24]   Maloney (1983) 104–105, although some evidence points to this being a funerary, not military structure. For wider discussion of Romano-British town defences, see Hobley (1983).

evidence from London (as elsewhere) can currently be read in a variety of ways, either to fit an historical context or more than one, or to 'float' and provide a patchwork image without being part of a rigid chronological system. But, since defensive works for some towns can be fairly securely attested in northern Gaul from *ca.* 270, a contemporary programme of fortification or reinforcement across the Channel at key sites is equally logical; a riverside wall at London in the 260s would fit the wider network of provincial security measures being instigated, in response to both civil war and heightened external threats.[25]

A contrast with the Saxon Shore forts, which were not disbanded following their likely role as a protective naval and supply cordon for Carausius and Allectus, can be made with the *Claustra Alpium Iuliarum*, established in the 4th c. across the north-east line of the Alpine chain, as a control and guard to access into Italy from the Danubian territories. Discussed more fully elsewhere, this military command comprised a network of road forts and associated valley walls and watchtowers, plus new legionary units, designed to observe and channel movement along key and lesser pass routes. The principal centres included pre-existing towns with revamped defences set near, rearward, or in advance of the defensive core, notably Castra (Ajdovščina), plus new forts, such as Ad Pirum (Hrušica), overseeing specific route-ways.[26] Text and archaeology combine well to indicate that the *Claustra* functioned fully perhaps only between *ca.* A.D. 310 and 395, and were exploited or misappropriated mainly for conflict between rival emperors, the best documented being the clash between Eugenius

---

[25] City walls in northern Gaul: Mertens (1983); and the wider review of the Gallic and Germanic provinces by Johnson (1983) 82–117; and Knight (1999) 26–34, noting only Grenoble with a date secured by inscriptions to Diocletian and Maximian. For a summary of studies on defences in Aquitaine, see Christie (1997). Chronologies for the defences remain much debated, with work further south in Gaul, such as that at Le Mans and Tours, preferring wall construction dates in the first half of the 4th c., and sometimes even as late as the mid 4th c., as recently proposed for Tours, whose compact circuit included the amphitheatre: Galinié (2007) 247–55, 359–61. As noted, for north-west Spain, Fernández-Ochoa and Morillo (2005) 331–39 argue for a first significant phase of urban defences at key centres under the Tetrarchy, and in fact "situate the construction of the first wall-circuits in Spain within this historical context [securing troop and supply movement], connecting fortification programs in Gaul and Britain with the contemporary phenomenon in Spain" (339). The authors hold back, however, from connecting these acts to the Gallic Empire, to Carausian efforts, to state efforts against Carausius, or to works in the aftermath of such civil conflicts. Again, the archaeology does not enable any such historical precision; we await suitably explicit epigraphic guides.

[26] An overview is offered in Christie (1991), but with the archaeology detailed by Ulbert (1981) for Ad Pirum.

(plus General Arbogast) and Theodosius in the Julian Alps in September 394, which saw terminal destruction to a variety of installations (and manpower); but, other actions between Roman forces are documented for 352 (Magnentius versus Constantius II), and for 388 (Magnus Maximus versus Theodosius), with possible traces of these evident in Ad Pirum's archaeology.[27]

The *Claustra* may well, therefore, have been disbanded as a formal military defensive system as a result of these internecine struggles, even if the defended towns persisted as depots, civilian bases and occasional billeting points. However, it appears that the *Claustra* installations were not reactivated when Stilicho was endeavouring to deal with the Gothic forces of Alaric in the last decade of the 4th c. and first decade of the 5th, when reliance was more on combining troop numbers (including of course those troops removed from the Rhine and from Britain), tracking the enemy, and selecting occasional pitched battles—with, as is well known, variable results (for Stilicho, Alaric and Rome).[28]

MEMORIALS

A defaced memorial in the Rome Forum bears witness to Stilicho's fights and fates in external and internal conflict (fig. 4). The stone (and now long lost statue), set up under the city prefect in A.D. 405, records, in good quality script, the victorious harrying and defeat (albeit not wholesale) of Gothic forces on Italian soil in 402 and 403—the text celebrates and (rather anxiously perhaps?) emphasises the 'fidelity and valour of the most devoted troops'. But subsequent failures to trap and destroy Alaric and his Visigoths, claims of collusion with this enemy, and losses incurred through the invasion of Radagaisus in 405/406, saw the Emperor Honorius order the arrest and execution of his general (and son-in-law) in 408, plus a purge of Stilicho's German bodyguard and other non-Roman units (as well as some unfortunate secular Roman officials). Some of these

---

[27] Ulbert (1981) 42–49 on these destructive episodes. On manpower losses, see below.

[28] Papers in the excellent conference volume edited by Buora (2002) utilise *militaria*—military equipment items—to explore not just dress and identity, but questions such as the militarisation of the landscape, garrisons, and provision of defensive posts. Cavada and Župančič, for example, attempt to tie fittings with the Rhenish and British troops summoned by Stilicho to defend Italy; Bolla, meanwhile, suggests some finds from the Lake Garda zone may help document both external/barbarian raids and even civil conflicts. The volume is reviewed by Christie in *JRA* 17 (2004) 699–705.

soldiers (an estimate is of 20,000) escaped to join Alaric, who in 410 finally entered and sacked Rome; these ex-Roman soldiers and bodyguards may even have seen that their former commander-general's name and honours had been chiselled out of existence on that same dedicatory stone in the Forum.[29]

A memorial, arguably, both to civil war and its human losses and impacts, as well as to frontier traumas and enemy plundering, is encapsulated in the much debated Augsburg altar dedication of A.D. 260/61, commemorating a victory against Iuthungi and Semnones by the provincial governor Genialis.[30] This was no powerful legionary force in victory, however, as we are told that Genialis' forces were a mix of Raetian troops, one body from one or both of the German provinces, as well as local recruits, either conscripts or local volunteers (*populares*—perhaps citizens protecting their lands). The scattered composition and the recourse to *populares* to bolster the regular soldiery reflect how the conflict with external enemies came in the midst of internal strife, since, as Drinkwater has recently argued, Genialis had declared in favour of the new 'Gallic Emperor' Postumus, who was elevated to the throne in 260. Genialis may well have gathered together both Raetian and German provincial and frontier troops to deal first with the returning Iuthungi, and then to offer his arms and services to Postumus. The latter, however, failed to exploit this offer, only for Gallienus to take back a rebellious Raetia and to remove Genialis.

The inscription shows the erasure of the names of both Postumus and a related Honoratianus—*damnationes memoriae* of vanquished usurpers— and of the Raetian army. A further element to note is the delay of Gallienus in dealing with both Iuthungian and Raetian threats, due largely to the usurpations in the Balkans of two other claimants, Regalianus and Ingenuus. Delays cost Rome dear, therefore: Iuthungi able to raid deep even into north Italy (the inscription records 'several thousand' Italians who were released by Genialis' victory—though with many no doubt also killed in Italy or at the battle), Genialis denuding the German *limes*,

---

[29] Claridge (1998) 84 notes how sockets remain on the stone to show the placement of the lost statue of Stilicho; she adds that the pedestal was in fact a re-used "old equestrian statue base set on its end".

[30] Drinkwater (2007) 53–61 offers a detailed contextualisation of the stone; its discovery and inscription are discussed fully in Bakker (1993), whose chronology for these events is slightly earlier than Drinkwater's. See also Carroll (2001) 132–33.

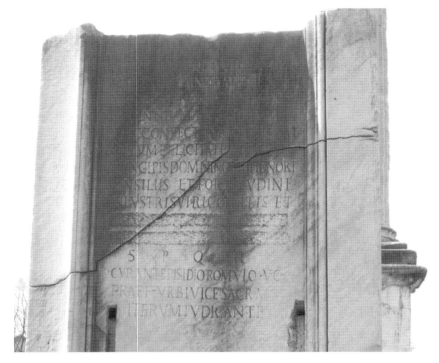

Fig. 3   Dedication in the Rome Forum set up by the city prefect, Pisidius Romulus in A.D. 405. Above the SPQR, the two lines which formerly heralded the name of the *magister militum* Stilicho have seen *damnatio memoriae* imposed following the Emperor Honorius' execution of his general in A.D. 408. (Photo: Pauline Carroll).

Postumus establishing himself as a lasting threat in the West, and then the full evacuation of Upper Germany.[31]

There are only occasional tombstones which provide a context for the loss of life, by soldiers in particular, in the 3rd and 4th c., and which testify to war, on and well within the empire's frontiers. Two epitaphs linked by location relate to the 4th c. fortified bridgehead at Deutz (Roman Divitia), opposite Cologne, in Germania II province on the northern Rhine: the first, probably of the mid 4th c., records the soldier and *protector* Viatorinus, perhaps officer to the mounted scouts stationed there, who was killed by

---

[31] Drinkwater (2007) 56–57 and 61–62 arguing down the numbers of captives to the high hundreds. On the Gallic Empire as a whole, see Drinkwater (1987), and with useful elements also in Knight (1999). Useful views on the evacuation of the former Upper Germany *limes* zone and the nature of the enemy are in Witschel (2004) 270–71.

a Frank on barbarian soil near his fort. The second is another *protector* (senior centurion), one Florius Baudio, *ex ordinario leg(ionis) II Ital(icae) Divit(ensis)*, who was killed in the campaigns of, and advances through Italy led by, Constantine in A.D. 312, en route to face Maxentius at Rome; his son, also in the unit—which may have been a select detachment from the *Divitia* fort—buried Baudio at Spoleto. Two other Divitian soldiers who died on the same campaign were buried in Otricoli and at Rome.[32]

Whilst the previous examples range from a generalissimo to governors and to soldiers, one of the most tangible and best studied (and most debated) memorials to late Roman civil war is the Arch of Constantine, sited between the Colosseum and the much older (but equally inspiring) Arch of Titus, with its own images of victory, spoils and triumph.[33] Constantine's arch commemorates in large measure victory against a fellow Roman, an established emperor at Rome, Maxentius, who contributed much to the Eternal City's urban and monumental fabric, yet who was suitably framed as a 'tyrant' (not former colleague) as Constantine marched on and conquered Rome.[34] The Arch is recorded as being set up in A.D. 315, in honour of Constantine by the Senate and people of Rome, on the occasion of his *decennalia* or tenth anniversary (thus, since his proclamation, and thus, at the outset of his civil war actions, rather than following his capture of Rome).

Whilst matching the arches and displays of earlier emperors such as Titus, Trajan and Severus, and duly repeating some of the imagery in terms of captured barbarians and winged victories and of *adventus* or triumphal entry and procession, the narrow horizontal friezes above the side arches portray episodes key to Rome's restoration from the tyrant— such as the advance from Milan, the assault and capture of Verona (fig. 4), and the battle at the Milvian Bridge. 'Borrowed' or re-located panels of Trajanic, Hadrianic and Marcus Aurelian date are viewed now as allying or equating the new western emperor with glorious *imperatores* of the

---

[32] See Carroll (2001) 136 with colour pl.22; and Tomlin (2006) 61, citing *ILS* 2777 for Baudio and *CIL* XI 4085 and *ILS* 2346 for the two other felled loyal Constantinian troopers. Carroll-Spillecke (1997) 148, however, identifies the pre-Constantinian origin to the *Divitenses*, implying an original fort base elsewhere.

[33] On the Arch of Constantine, a compact and current summary is by Liverani (2005), but with fuller discussion and bibliography by Elsner (2000), examining the imagery and meanings in detail; see also the brief but useful comments in Cameron (2005) 24.

[34] On Maxentian and Tetrarchic works in Rome and other capitals, see Rinaldi Tufi (2005); for Tetrarchic works in Rome, see Coarelli (1999). Maxentius as builder and restorer with grand designs is flagged by himself on coin issues as *conservator urbis suae*.

Fig. 4   The Arch of Constantine, Rome—view of the south face, left entrance
arch, depicting the siege by Constantine's troops of Verona (or Susa) in north
Italy; above are two of the roundels of Hadrianic date. (Photo: Neil Christie).

past, duly reinforced by instances of Constantine's head replacing those of
these 2nd c. emperors. As Elsner emphasises, the totality and syncretism
of the new and the (modified) old in form, fabric and detail make the
Arch (presumably its design had been approved and perhaps enhanced
by the emperor himself) a powerful and symbolic statement of renewal as
well as continuity: "The specific inauguration of Constantine's campaign
to overthrow Maxentius, and its setting in parallel with Trajan's Dacian
Wars, is valorized by the broader picture of Roman imperialism—the conquest and maintenance of the provinces—that is implicitly made possible
by such hard but responsible choices as that of Constantine to make civil
war against . . . 'tyranny' ".[35] This is, therefore, a monument to legitimacy.

---

[35] Elsner (2000) 173, 163–75 analyses this use of 'past and present'. The attic inscriptions
refer thereby to a 'just' use of army and weapons. However, it is important to recognise,
as Mayer (2006) has argued, that the Arch of Constantine and an anonymous panegyrist
do make reference to victory over northern barbarians too. Compare Drinkwater (1996)
26, highlighting how many a 3rd and 4th c. emperors had to have a convenient or more
appropriate barbarian victory to impress both state and provincials.

We might also note an important predecessor to Constantine's Arch (or the Senate's Arch to Constantine) in Rome's forum, which likewise exploited *spolia* in symbolic fashion to commemorate a restored empire. The *arcus Novus* was a Tetrarchic victory monument erected most probably in A.D. 303 as part of the *decennalia* and *vicennalia* celebrations of the emperors, and including as a presumed centre-piece, the triumph over the usurpers Carausius and Allectus in Britain. What seems evident is that this employed materials culled from the Arch of Claudius—itself of course commemorating a British triumph—of A.D. 51/52.[36]

In effect, Constantine's Arch was in line with a new practice of merging old and new, and showing how holding together the empire, through dealing with usurpers or enemies of a 'just' state, was as valid a victory as defeating the enemies over the frontiers. Hence the victory monuments proudly erected in the reign of Constantius II as recorded by Ammianus Marcellinus (see introductory quotes)—of which only the so-called 'Pagan Gate' (Heidentor) at *Carnuntum*-Petronell on the Danube frontier survives.[37] Mayer has provided an excellent overview of some of these Late Roman victory monuments recounting and also depicting conflict against fellow Romans—though often in union with victories gained against proper barbarians—and questions how their words and images were perceived.[38] Mayer highlights how legitimacy of rule was key to monuments of later civil conflict, most notably those erected in honour of Theodosius in Constantinople in the last two decades of the 4th c.; he quotes Pacatus, whose panegyric of A.D. 389 refers to justified imagery of defeated rivals, in this instance Magnus Maximus:

> It is important to the security of every age for what has been done to be seen so that if anyone has ever entertained any nefarious desires, he may review the monuments of our times and drink innocence with his eyes.[39] (Pacatus, *Pan. Lat.* 2 (12) 44.5–45.3 (trans. Nixon and Rodgers (1994) 512)).

---

[36] Coarelli (1999) 26–27, 31–32.

[37] Jobst (2002) identifies the varied chronologies proposed for the 'Pagan Gate', but confirms from the *spolia*—re-cycled brick, tile and stone, notably 22 altars from nearby sanctuaries, including one dedicated by the local *XIV legio* to *Iupiter Optimus Maximus*—and from finds excavated at and around the arch, a mid 4th c. date. The exploitation of the altars as building materials is postulated as an aggressive Christian policy against the old cult spaces at the fort and town.

[38] Mayer (2006).

[39] Mayer (2006) 150–51. Translation from Nixon and Rodgers (1994) 512 of *Pan. Lat.*2 (12) 44.5–45.3.

The spiral column of Arcadius celebrating the victory of the East over a rebellious Roman general in A.D. 400, the Goth Gainas, was arguably the most explicit visual statement of conflict between Roman forces, but again with the emphasis visually placed on legitimacy—hence, on the main column itself, Arcadius is depicted on the lost frieze as seated alongside the western Emperor Honorius, with soldiers ranged up either side, whilst battle rages above, and on the base the two are shown on three sides.[40]

Brief comment may also be made of the changing character of triumphs, recently analysed by Beard, who highlights how victory monuments in the first centuries A.D. were closely tied to imperial triumphs, comprising processions of victorious soldiery, with captured booty and prisoners, and the returning emperor—all neatly displayed in the art of the Arch of Titus. In the Late Empire, there was a transition to ceremonial arrivals (*adventus*), with related games and processions, not necessarily linked to actual victories. Far less scope existed for display of enemy booty, as often campaigns against non-Romans were on Roman soil and may have seen the re-capture of Roman goods and people (as with the Augsburg inscription noted above); exceptions were the triumphs held for Aurelian and Diocletian. Far more scope existed to display the heads of vanquished usurpers—as with that of Maxentius by Constantine. The *adventus* became more of a display of rulership and authority than of victories.[41]

MONEY

Money can act as a guide to later Roman civil conflict on a variety of levels: (i) first in terms of inflation, counterfeiting, weakened metal content and size as indications of internal politico-military and economic upheavals preventing production and circulation of and access to standard types; (ii) hoarding to signify either threat and panic and lost wealth, with the possible death/murder/flight of the owners reflected in the failure to recover the money, metal and other items, or hoards to signify avoidance—e.g.

---

[40] Mayer (2006) 152; Liebeschuetz (1991) 273–78; Lee (2007) 46.
[41] Beard (2007) 321–28. On the Arch of Titus, see 43–45. Amm. Marc. 16.10.1 viewed Constantius II's visit to Rome in A.D. 357 as "an attempt to hold a triumph over Roman blood"—but with the historian eager to find fault with this Christian stranger to the City. On imperial victories and media of display, see also Lee (2007) 37–50. On imperial or 'official' art and its forms on the arches and columns, see Reece (1999a) 19–31.

of tax-collectors, of looters (military or civilian), or of ties to failed usurpers and emperors, where the coin issues might implicate the owner;
(iii) imagery and legends on coins to guide us on names of potential usurpers, some unknown to extant written sources, and on the propaganda of
victory, appeals to gods, to unity, to harmony, etc.; (iv) savings and hoards
to indicate owners and their allegiance or conflict with the state or with
figures of power; and (v) coins as bribes/tribute to enemies and allies, and
as donatives to supporters and soldiers.

For the latter, the reinterpretation of the early 4th c. hoard of gold and
silver coin, jewellery and silverware found near Beaurains (Arras, near
Calais) in 1922 is significant. This material included the famous so-called
'Arras Medallion', depicting Constantius' triumphant entry and relief of a
supplicant Londinium in A.D. 296—this the formal numismatic resumé of
an imperial Roman re-capture of a breakaway province (the legend on the
reverse records the 'restorer of the eternal light').[42] This medallion is, with
others in the hoard, a special record and keepsake of the owner's military
life. From graffiti etched on the latest medallion, ownership appears to
have been both that of Vitalian, *protector*, and, probably, his father, Valerian, whose name appears on a ring with his wife's, and who may have
accumulated the older portion of the hoard. The coin issues and medallions appear to denote donatives, special payments made to troops and
staff at the start or end of campaigns, or at victories or imperial anniversa-
ries; key dates in the hoard are 297, 303 and 310. The need to tie army and
senior commanders to an emperor in the 3rd c. and beyond appears to be
borne out in the numismatic record, indicating donatives and especially
the medallions as more 'regular' displays and bestowals from the reign
of Gallienus.[43]

Heightened regular moneys and extras for the wider troop bodies across
the 3rd c. upheavals played a significant part in prompting the progressive
debasement to extremes of silver coin issues. This was partly caused by

---

[42] Abdy (2006) 55–56; Tomlin (2006) 59. The catalogue entries 11–59 in Hartley *et al.*
(2006) 122–31 cover the Arras hoard; items 18 and 19 (illustrated in colour on 57) comprise
additional medallions of Constantius depicting the emperor raising the personified *Britannia* from her knees, whilst being crowned by the winged Victory. The *PIETAS AUGG* "legend emphasises the pious duty of the emperors in helping a beleaguered province". Mayer
(2006) observes how both the medallion legend and a contemporary rhetor make no reference to civil war, but rather—at least in the poetical case—to victory over barbarians.

[43] Abdy (2006) 55, highlights the medallions as gifts to senior staff and argues how in
the Beaurains hoard, the owner's promotion up the senior ranks is seemingly matched by
a proportionate rise in the monies received.

(Source: http://classicaleconomies.com/mil_anarchy.shtml)

Fig. 5   AR *antoninianus* of Postumus (259–68). 19 × 23 mm, 3.13 g.
Mint: Mint city I (Treveri [Trier]), 1st *officina*. <u>Struck</u>: 1st emis-
sion, 1st phase, AD 260. Obv: IMP C M CASS LAT POSTIMVS P F
AVG Radiate, draped, and cuirassed bust right. Rev: SALVS PRO-
VINCIARVM River god Rhinus reclining left, resting right arm
on forepart of boat left in background, cradling reed in left arm,
which rests against urn to right. The river god and warship may
well symbolise the riverine and maritime strength of the 'Gallic
Empire'. Ref: Mattingly-Sydenham, *RIC* 5 87 corr. (obv. legend);
AGK 87a; Cunetio 2367

civil conflict creating fragmented state control over metal resources, sup-
pliers and mints.[44] As a result, we also observe episodes of 'coin copying',
whereby mints such as Trier and temporary military mints, as along the
Danube, issued cast bronzes and false silver coin, presumably to counter
short-term exigencies as official supplies ceased; striking are incidences of
copying in Britain and Gaul in the A.D. 260–80 period, and again in the
350s.[45] Noticeably, it is only after the demise of the 'Gallic Empire' and the
claimed restoration of empire that scope presented itself under Aurelian

---

[44] Duncan-Jones (2004) 43–47 highlights such output as tied particularly to the need
to provide largesse to the army, and with hoarding linked to Roman troop concentrations—45, n. 113. He argues thus that "the great third-century debasement was not merely
a result of heavier spending, but also indicates dwindling resources" with mining output—
or wider access to the metals—dramatically hit.
[45] King (1996) 239–41. Howgego (1996), meanwhile, determines how scrutiny of the
issues in mid 3rd c. hoards in these same areas testifies to a notable 'dislocation' between
East and West Roman Empires. For an in-depth study of the 3rd c. coin hoards of Gaul and
Germany, see Haupt (2001), recording over 1,700 hoards with end issues of between A.D.
180 and 280—but note the review by Peter Guest in *Britannia* 36 (2005) 514–15.

to seek to revive reasonable silver content, which might also then mean that 'Gallic' coins were discarded and hoards left unclaimed.[46]

Arguably, the internal Roman conflicts and crises of the 3rd c. are flagged by the coins, not just in terms of the often bewilderingly rapid change in emperors, names and faces—alongside the appearance of some usurper names, who never made it into general circulation through their rapid demise, and who, therefore, passed the bulk of the population by— but also on the imagery and legends of the issues of the later Empire.[47] Legends—such as on the Arras Medallion noted above—recalling (perhaps more in hope than in reality) 'restoration', 'renewal', 'peace', 'security' and 'piety' abound, framing images of supportive gods, trampled captives, walls and gates, or occasional warships (fig. 6). Words, ragged strikings of coins, and the struggling supply of these can only have added to the wider social tension which is sensed rather than seen in the archaeological record. As with the Arch of Constantine discussed above, the perception of the names, words and images, by elites and general public alike, cannot be traced, but the efforts of the emperors and moneyers to portray and name suggest an audience that did see and listen.

In the East, an emblematic example is provided by inscriptions and coin issues proclaiming new powers based at Palmyra. In Gallienus' reign, recognition of consular rank was awarded to one Odaenathus (Odeinath), a possible self-appointed governor, whose clan had perhaps only recently taken root in the city, but who provided Palmyra and distant Rome with victories—perhaps just localised affairs—against Persia, and in theory secured the eastern frontier; in local documents, Odaenathus also appears with the title of 'king of kings' in recognition of his achievements in safe-guarding Palmyra and her lands. This label of authority was passed on to his son Vaballathus when Odaenathus was assassinated along with

---

[46] By then signs existed of a fair level of demonetisation in many parts of the empire: thus Katsari (2005) charts changes and decay in silver and bronze issues (from hoards and excavated deposits) in 3rd c. Asia Minor. She highlights the reign of Gallienus as the most unstable coin-wise, matching the far-flung politico-military vicissitudes. See also Katsari (2003) and her wider analysis of gold and silver, observing the limited visibility of gold coin in hoarding in the 3rd and 4th c., perhaps indicating that gold was viewed more as bullion than coin; nonetheless, the presence of gold coin over the frontiers is seen as merchant-linked rather than as tribute, with the latter best served by gold bars.

[47] Reece (1999a) 35–38 offers useful comment on portraiture on 3rd and 4th c. coins: "The third century, which has... been called a desert of dated monuments, shows a quite remarkable free-for-all in coin portraits" with many a worried looking 3rd c. emperor— except for the very 'tranquil' Gallienus; Reece identifies how Gallic Empire coins show high-quality portraiture overall.

his elder son in A.D. 267—perhaps at the instigation of his wife Zenobia, who became effective regent over this junior son. Coins produced at
Antioch and Alexandria in 271–72 comprise doubled-headed issues, with
the new (western) Roman Emperor Aurelian on one side, and Vaballathus
on the other, and with legends denoting the latter as *rex*, *imperator* and
dux Romanorum. Potentially these issues reflect a call for shared power
at a time when Aurelian was still securing his own position in the West,
and reflect a route to sanction or authorise Vaballathus and Zenobia at
Palmyra. But, when Aurelian began forcibly to move eastwards against
these perceived usurpers, new coins start to proclaim Vaballathus alone
as Augustus, thus counter-attacking Aurelian "ideologically by claiming
imperial authority" —if not for long.[48]

Discerning civil war propaganda in coin issues is a research area to
be encouraged, to weigh up the value of legends and claims of *GLO-
RIA ROMANORUM*, *FEL TEMP REPARATIO*, *RESTITUTOR REIPUBLICAE*,

Fig. 6a and b   Billion *antonianus* of Vabalathus (268–72). 20 mm, Mint: Antiochia
272. Obv: IMP C AVRELIANVS AVG/H Radiate, draped, and cuirassed bearded
bust of Aurelianus right. Rev: VABALATHVS V C R IM D R Laureated, draped bust
of Vabalthus right. Ref: Mattingly-Sydenham, *RIC* 5 381 (Copyright image Andreas
Pangerl, www.romancoins.info).

---

[48] Long (1996). The creation of a fortress town (or at least a reinforcement and re-naming
of an older site) of Zenobia (Halabija) on the Euphrates was perhaps part of a Palmyrene
effort to secure control in Syria (as opposed to against Rome) in A.D. 270. Gerster and
Wartke (2003) 159–65 provide some fine aerial views of the well-preserved site which saw
Diocletianic renewal and then activity into the 6th c.

SPES ROMANORUM and *SALUS PROVINCIARUM* and *REIPUBLICAE* in their contemporary politico-military context in the 3rd to 5th c. Specific mint issues in divided rules, imagery before and after restorations, and coin qualities, are all routes of discussion. Two small examples might be Vetranio's 'illegal' coins, issued from Thessalonica and bearing the legends *VIRTUS EXERCITUM* and, more tellingly, *CONCORDIA MILITUM*; secondly, there is the series inscribed *DOMINO NOSTRO*, which is attributed to output from Carthage in the late 4th or early 5th c., probably during Gildo's or Count Boniface's revolts from the Italian government, when the issuer showed "evident reluctance . . . to inscribe a name or precise title on his coins".[49]

Finally in this section, we might observe how some coins may have taken on symbolic roles in episodes of civil upheaval. Thus, Morelli discusses how in the 3rd c., there is a perceptible increase in the use of coins, often gold issues, as pendants on necklaces, either in multiples (such as in an example reconstructed for the Beaurains hoard, and featuring 8 coins of 2nd to 3rd c. date), or singly, and occasionally used as settings in rings.[50] One pendant-coin is of Vittorinus, a usurper-successor to Postumus in the Gallic Empire in A.D. 268–70, found near Aja in the Low Countries; another is a rare Italian example (a majority of known finds coming from regions like Gaul, the Danubian provinces and Egypt) from Parma, featuring an *aureus* of Gallienus, whose deposition in a hoard may well have coincided with the assassination of Gallienus. In both instances, the use of gold, ornate border settings, and their display as pendants, can be viewed as signifying a desired visual impact, and a route to expressing a precise political leaning and loyalty—by both males and females (since the necklaces probably imply female owners).

Men (and Women)

The constancy and the brutality of the conflicts of the 3rd c. must have impacted on a wide variety of levels which drastically damaged populations

---

[49] Carson *et al.* (1978) 77, 58. Whitby (2004) 180 correctly observes how soldiers were the main audience for most of these coins.

[50] Morelli (2009), notably 89–93. Significantly, in many cases, the coins' settings in pendants appear to have been contemporary or near contemporary to their minting, suggestive of a particular or targeted output—might this equate with new-style donatives to loyal staff or soldiers?

in a number of areas, mentally, physically and socially: through trauma and death—family members lost, raped, dispossessed; through economic hardship—failures to gather in or have access to foodstuffs, with markets and supplies disrupted or commandeered, and lands not properly tended; and through reduced childbirth, as fear and food shortage impacted on the basics of living. As archaeology shows, frontier territories in many parts of the West show a reduced landscape, through a thinning out of farms and population.[51] Although frontiers and towns and forts did persist once reactivated or restored, as around Trier, supplies and manpower now often came from further afield—from deeper within the provinces, but also with an increasing reliance on non-Roman troops drawn from over the frontiers to counter the internal voids. It is easy to over-dramatise this, and at the same time it is easy to contrast this by identifying a fairly busy and effective army in the Tetrarchic and Constantinian periods, but we should not in any way minimise the manpower drain created by both civil and external conflict in the two generations before, as indeed in the conflicts of A.D. 310–20.

Whitby noticeably identifies how the evidence of later 4th c. laws may well reveal how very severe problems of recruitment are registered in the wake of the civil wars and suppressions of Magnus Maximus in A.D. 386 and Eugenius (in 394), with scared provincials damaged by the actions of the two sides, with uncertainties of who to support, flights and loss of life. We can note, for example, Eutropius' claim in his overview of the clash between Constantius II and Magnentius at Mursa in 351 that 'great resources were used up in that battle, sufficient for any foreign wars which could have won many triumphs and brought peace'.[52] Archaeologically, our problem lies in not being able to trace such losses, notably through burial evidence: as noted above, we have few tombstones that speak directly of the casualties in the many Roman civil wars, and there are even fewer known or excavated and published cemeteries in Italy, Gaul or elsewhere, that can be linked to communities affected by civil war—certainly, no mass

---

[51] Van Ossel and Ouzoulias (2000); and earlier work by Wightman (1981) for Trier, summarised in Duncan-Jones (2004) 32–33. Van Ossel and Ouzoulias show no single pattern prevailing, but with patches of loss. They do note, however, the numismatic and archaeological evidence for the Alf valley downstream of Trier, where fires and abandonment on some sites "can be linked to the events accompanying the usurpation of Magnentius and Decentius" (138). Wider comments and views on damage in the West in Witschel (2004).

[52] Eutr. 10.12; Whitby (2004) 164–70; Lee (2007) 74–79. Elton (1996) 152–55 prefers to see no sizeable shortage of manpower.

war graves are known, and instances of unburied or brutal killings near frontier sites are linked more to barbarian raids.[53]

Military historians generally agree that Roman manpower losses and military demands were prompts for increased use of non-Roman forces, notably Goths, in the Roman armies from the later 4th c., and, in the context of the early 5th c. West, events on the Rhine and the movements of the Goths in the Balkans and then Italy required that a reliance on non-Romans grew substantially—although this transition is still to be wholly recognised archaeologically along the frontiers and within provinces. As known, Italy's pull sees a weakening of military cover across Britain, Gaul and Raetia, all subsequently reflected in those provinces feeling forced to look to themselves and their own resources to ensure their survival, with new, more local centres of political gravity emerging within these provinces. New usurpers, local alliances with enemies, and the rise of what have been termed 'self-help' groups—seeking influential or wealthy leaders close at hand to guide and secure communities—are documented internal responses to the upheavals of the first decades of the 5th c.; all might count as 'civil war' or 'uprisings'.

New physical reactions might be expected—city walls repaired, villas fortified, refuges created, open weapon display: whilst the archaeology cannot be tight enough, arguably, to pinpoint these and their politico-military contexts, nonetheless, we might question the existing data more, so as to consider whether there was less of an external or 'barbarian' threat than there was an internal one. One example to note is the later Roman (considered 4th c. and pre-Visigothic) re-occupation or re-use of hilltop sites across sectors of the Duero plateau in the Burgos province of Spain, and proposed comparable refuges or upland seats in the area of the Roman town of Clunia; such movement of farming groups from plain (farm or villa) to hills represents local responses to insecurities, but we

---

[53] Urban cemeteries of later Roman date have been studied at Milan and Concordia (the latter the seat of an arms factory), but, perhaps unexpectedly, these lack indications of social episodes linked to war. Reece (1999b) reviews the publication of a cemetery of *ca.* 70 burials at Iutizzo Codroipo in Friuli, NE Italy, which the excavators, on the basis of belt fittings and coins, set to the mid 4th c. and, perhaps incautiously, they label the males as 'soldiers of Magnentius'; Reece accepts a change in rite in this older cemetery at this date, but queries whether these fittings imply newcomers and soldiers, or rather locals gaining a new employment and mode of display. More dramatic are the executed members of a Roman family on a farm at Harting in Bavaria—tortured, scalped and thrown into a well in *ca.* A.D. 260 and linked to Alamannic raids: Carroll (2001) 138.

need note how some hillforts were selected in regions like western Britain as new elite power centres.[54]

Such leaders and groups were also required in some regions to deal with other responses to state fracturing, such as elevated levels of rural banditry and urban dissensions. In terms of banditry, the law codes make clear that bouts of lawlessness, runaway slaves, army desertion, and the flight of some urban refugees, fuelled groups of bandits, the best documented being the Bagaudae or Bacaudae, though this label was perhaps applied with a broad brush to any rebellious rabble when the state sought a crackdown on lawlessness. Whilst better documented in 5th c. Gaul (Brittany notably) and northern Spain, reference to what appear to be larger, organised groups of Bagaudae as rural or peasant militia or bandits, begin already in the later 3rd c. (for example, the Emperor Maximianus suppressed a horde in A.D. 289). They are identified in various ways, but generally in the context of a breakdown in official control, with displaced or dispossessed groups of peasants and slaves, overburdened by tax or other demands, seeking their own form of order, organised around chiefs and would-be generals.

Their equation in state texts with 'barbarians' is not dissimilar to imperial triumphal images and panegyrics denouncing usurpers and fellow Romans who work against legitimate rule and order. Their origins in essence lie with the traumas of the 3rd c. crisis and civil wars, where state and non-state demands and exactions, and plundering by rivals and by barbarian raiders, forced groups into such 'self-help' units. How many and how unified such groups were is wholly unclear, and there is currently no archaeology to trace them, although conceivably some of the burials in parts of late 4th and early 5th c. Gaul with weaponry could be seen as belonging to estate militias and local leaders—who may or may not have been viewed centrally as Bagaudae, but who as landowners, may have been actively defending their properties as a matter of course in times of breakdown in normal order (civil war, Bagaudic raids, Gothic and Suevic attacks or threats from state officers, notably tax collectors and army recruitment gangs).[55]

---

[54] On northern Spain, see Cepas (2006) 205–206. For hill-fort re-use in the context of 5th c. Britain, see White (2007) 165–76; and Faulkner (2000) 178–79. For Italy, Christie (1991) and (2006) 473–77 discusses how far some upland sites were natural movements, refuges (temporary or permanent), or had military roles.

[55] Although landowners, by opposing state officials may have then been classed as Bagaudae; Drinkwater stresses a lack of continuity between the 3rd and 5th c. entities: Knight (1999) 54–56; Drinkwater (2007) 180–81 and (1992). On the burial evidence, see

Reprisals

Acts of aggression were not just by soldiery against soldiery, but also by soldiery against civilians, whether in the context of troops being billeted in towns or on estates, and forcibly requisitioning space and supplies, tools, animals and, of course, women, or where troops move in to clear out and often kill supporters (and their families) of failed usurpers or dethroned emperors. Authorised acts of ransacking and polluting properties as 'pay-back', or unauthorised acts by soldiers of theft, damage and rape against others, cannot be identified without text, graffiti or clear evidence of destruction and/or levelling of properties.[56] More often, a property might be confiscated (and its owners either killed or made slaves) and given to a new owner as a reward for their service to the empire. Some such events may have nothing to do with the military, but may be locals exploiting upheavals during, or in the aftermath, of civil conflict, and seeking to improve their own lot at the cost of others.

The earlier archaeological efforts to tie in destructions, fires, bodies and abandonment of Roman villas and farms in south-western England to Ammianus Marcellinus' tales of woe in the 'Barbarian Conspiracy' of A.D. 367—sites such as Keynsham with its main rooms fired and at least one body left in collapsed wall debris, and Nuthills, with claims of the villa having been "mercilessly raided" —in reality struggle to fit a tight chronology; yet their general association with the mid- to later-4th c. can as easily be tied into local and regional raids, civilian conflicts, slave and brigand attacks. Clearances and renewals at sites like Brislington may denote new owners, or the displaced former owners coming back once events had settled down.[57] In the case of Gadebridge Park (Herefordshire), demolition in the mid 350s has been linked to a rooting-out of supporters of the defeated Magnentius under Constantius II, whose agent Paul the 'Chain' took vicious exaction on the usurper's weakened homeland—'descending

---

Halsall (1992). Ward-Perkins (2005) 54 observes how the settlement of 'allied' Visigoths in A.D. 419 in south-west Gaul was partly designed to counter the revolt and movements of Bagaudae there. Faulkner (2000) 176–77 ponders peasant revolt parallels in early 5th c. Britain, but Snyder (1998) 227–28 sees no Bagaudae here.

[56] See the detailed comments by Lee (2007) in his ch. 5 'The Experience of War'. Elton (1996) 196–98 comments on the fate of usurpers and their supporters, arguing that "persecution of a rebelling or usurping faction was rarely carried out beyond its upper ranks, probably because it was counter-productive", though regiments might be disbanded and re-assigned—see n.57 below on troops in Tripolitania.

[57] Branigan (1976) 136–40.

like a sudden torrent upon the persons and estates of many people, [he] spread ruin and destruction in various forms'.[58]

The case of Palmyra can again be mentioned. Aurelian's vicious exactions against the city of Zenobia are suitably documented and, if only in part, traced archaeologically, and by the Tetrarchic period a new, reduced city, part military, had been imposed on the west flank. The old city spaces saw some continuity, however, although there is a likely significant change imposed here too: the palace and power centre of Odaenathus and Zenobia had been sited in the centre of the city, along the Great Colonnaded Street, and between the sanctuaries of Nabu, Balashamin and Bel, close to the agora; the street and tetrastyle were the focus for statues and dedications by the local princes and elite. Whilst little is known of the palace, it has been argued that, as an additional act of cancelling out Zenobian power politics, the site was replaced by the Baths of Diocletian, in service already by A.D. 284, and thus probably begun soon after Aurelian's actions.[59] Otherwise, in fact, the religious structures were little affected, the only exception being the sanctuary of the warrior goddess Allat, where statuary appears to have been bashed about and decapitated, with these materials re-used in a re-built precinct wall of *ca.* A.D. 300—such damage to statuary might well have been by eager Aurelianic troops, who may well have despoiled the sanctuary of portable wealth too.[60]

Civilians could suffer the consequences of their city councils favouring or siding with usurpers and rebels—even if, of course, such siding may have been the decision of just a few individuals, with the urban communities either ignorant of the rebellion, or the imperial struggles being

[58] Amm. Marc. 14.5—Paul continued his dirty (but presumably sanctioned) deeds against supporters of the tyrants Gallus (15.3) and Silvanus (15.6). Gadebridge: Neal (1974). The novel by Vansittart (1983) to my mind provides a very useful recreation of some of the mixed-up socio-political events of the second half of the 4th c. in Britain from the perspective of a would-be lead player, who in reality has little scope to make any mark in the military confusion.

[59] Yon (2001) 180. Stunning air photographs of the site, including the so-called Diocletianic Camp, are presented in Gerster and Wartke (2003) 117–30, nb. pl. 138, with the fortress-town of Halabija-Zenobia depicted on pp. 159–65. A lively history of Queen Zenobia comes in General Tlass (1986).

[60] Sauer (2003) 49–52 describes the Allat material, but hesitates in ascribing this closely to the emperor's reprisals; in contrast he more readily attributes the damage to the goddess' statuary in later 4th c. events to Christians: "The contrast between the at most half-hearted pagan iconoclasm even in a city responsible for repeated rebellion and what was to follow over a century later is striking. One cannot help thinking that Aurelian and his troops felt more fear or respect for the pantheon of the defeated city than hatred for their enemies"—52.

enacted elsewhere. Thus we are informed of the brutal retributions authorised by Maximinus via his legate Capellianus, following the unsuccessful
revolt of the Gordians (I and II) in North Africa, put down after just three
weeks in A.D. 238, and resulting in their execution in Carthage—only for
a third Gordian to gain more lawful (of a sort) accession to the throne,
also in 238. Archaeological traces of destruction of houses and damage to
public units, such as the amphitheatre at Thydrus (El Jem/El Djem), have
been attributed to the reprisals by Capellianus, whilst the massive refurbishment of the amphitheatre there is seen as an act of compensatory
munificence and renewal by Gordian III (perhaps also completing work
started by Gordian I/II). The association is tempting, although the dating
awaits corroboration.[61]

The image and value of the emperor were, I would argue, seriously
diluted across the 3rd c.: not only did citizenry in town and country
lose track—except by coin and legend—of the rise and fall of emperors,
pretenders, usurpers and generals (unless forcefully informed of a new
name in power by passing soldiery, tax collectors or deserters), but the
claim that these emperors were genuinely worthy of worship must have
sounded very hollow. A consequence might well have been the demise
of many an imperial cult shrine and centre in the West especially, and,
perhaps, attacks on shrines favoured by individual rulers or usurpers.
Charting the demise of imperial cult sites is not an easy task, as too few
have either been recognised or excavated to sufficient degree or quality
to identify sequences of decay; there is a temptation also to assume that
where destruction or loss occurs then it relates chiefly to a change in state
religion—i.e. the rise of Christianity—or to barbarian assault, rather than
considering an altered mentality of locals and Romans. Thus, the recent
archaeological analyses of the provincial cult centre at Tarragona in Spain,
and of the imperial cult temples at Narona in Dalmatia and Eretria in
Greece, have emphasised Christian iconoclasm as the lead player.[62] For
Narona, excavations in 1995–96 identified the well-preserved Augusteum,

---

[61] Bomgardner (1981), citing Herodian 7.9,10–11. Bomgardner argues that the amphitheatre was even then not completed after Gordian III's five-year reign, since the new
emperor, Phillip, duly shifted his imperial focus to founding a new city at his own birthplace. Gordian III, meanwhile, took out his own anger on the *legio III Augusta*, which
had helped put down the revolt of his father and grandfather: Mattingly (1995) 55 and
83, observing how in Tripolitania some traces exist of possible absorption of disbanded
legionaries into auxiliary or other detachments.

[62] Tarragona: Keay (1996). Narona: Marin (2001). Eretria: Schmid (2001). On the imperial cult in general in the West, see Fishwick (1992) and (2002).

whose interior had remained largely intact since destruction in the 4th c.: here were recovered, *in situ*, a series of at least 14 life-size and three lesser cult statues of good quality carving of the 1st and 2nd c., all toppled and all decapitated, with some of the heads wholly removed, and others discarded outside or cast down the forum steps.[63] The last statues belong to the 2nd c., but there is nothing to indicate any dedications of new works in the 3rd c. However, destruction of the statues and a deliberate in-filling of the building are set by the archaeologists only to the end of the 4th c. "suddenly and violently, probably following Theodosius' Edict".[64]

A comparable scenario is proferred for Eretria, in the sense of the presence in destruction deposits of the 4th c. of statuary belonging to seven figures, mainly cuirassed emperors of the first two centuries A.D., but with one base at least belonging to *ca.* A.D. 200, and a nearby statue base of Caracalla attested. It is argued that the coins from the destruction layer—which included debris from the statuary, which was smashed into small fragments and the heads destroyed—show the temple's demise after the 350s: "We seem therefore not to be dealing with a typical *damnatio memoriae* of one or more emperors; the destruction of heads and hands and the cutting of all the sculptures into minute pieces is more typical of Christian iconoclasm".[65]

Tarragona's case differs in part due to its role as provincial capital and seat of the provincial cult and council, and here, the scale of operations for the imperial cult was on a grand scale, with massive redevelopment coming under Vespasian, when the upper town there was conceived as the grandiose stage for the seat of both council and imperial cult—the latter with a precinct containing the temple to Rome and Augustus, the former occupying a lower terrace and featuring statues dedicated to and by the priesthood of the cult.[66] The city's high status ensured a constancy of elite benefactions, enabling construction of various public monuments,

[63] Marin (2001) 97–111 on identification of the statues, which include Augustus, Livia, Tiberius and Vespasian; three of the heads were recovered from the forum in 1874 and 1878. The lack of a statue of Nero could be seen as a *damnatio memoriae* (103). One might note, from Fishwick's study, how many imperial cult sites see a busy investment under Vespasian from A.D. 70, following the destabilising civil war of 69, in part to secure his own footing at the start of a new dynasty: he modified the whole cult to centre on Roma, on the deified dead and on the living emperor—the latter as a link between present and past; a fuller, more formalised priesthood was instituted too, and there is encouragement to municipal cult centres: Fishwick (2002) 223–26.

[64] Marin (2001) 91–92.
[65] Schmid (2001) 140–41.
[66] Keay (1996) nb. 28, 33, 36.

and competition for the honour of the priesthood. The picture is much changed by the mid 3rd c., by which time the priesthood statuary had come to an end, and urban activity as a whole was reduced (including the demise of the theatre); where new work occurs, such as restorations to the amphitheatre, or the setting up of honorary statues to the emperors in the 4th c. (some of their pedestals were actually re-cut from earlier ones), the effort comes from state officials or government grants, implying a removal of elite participation at Tarragona, and suggesting more widely a loss of confidence in state and cult. Although not an immediate reaction to civil war, the impact of warfare on society, economy and the status of the emperor are borne out in the data here and at Narona and Eretria. What we cannot glean at the latter sites, however, is how far imperial cult sites were ignored or even attacked by ordinary people in the wake of civil wars and usurpations; in moments of social upheaval, conflict can spill out on many levels, few of which can be traced archaeologically—notably the persecution of religious groups (see below).

Much is owed to Eberhard Sauer's provocative book (2003) which prompts us to look in a new way at Roman temple art and its survivals and fates, as he identifies strongly the contexts and modes of iconoclastic damage (defacing, smashing, decapitation, etc. of statues, murals, etc.). His over-riding intention is to highlight religious hatred and exactions against an enemy, and a recurrent theme is Christian acts against pagan cult images in the Late Roman period, which he examines to good effect, especially in the context of the destruction of Mithraic sites and cult works.[67] But, as seen, we ought not to ignore defacings and destructions much prior to these Christian acts of violence: *damnationes memoriae* are known, forming official deletions of names, faces, records of rulers and, occasionally, of lessers, but these effectively acted as a guide to individuals, whether governors, tribunes, bakers or slaves, in terms of how perceived evils and wrongdoers could be cancelled out.[68] Episodes of ransacking, raiding, looting by soldiers and thieves or by ordinary folk in the context

[67] Sauer (2003)—especially 79–88 on Mithraic cult images, and 131–56 on this and other oriental cults. Damage, mutilation or annihilation of faces and heads of statues and relief sculpture stand out—e.g. at the sanctuary at Sarsina with its cult statues of Isis, Cybele and Serapis brutally battered and scattered (139).

[68] See Rambaldi (2009) 139 with catalogue entries 1–2 for examples of 3rd c. anarchy period erasures of names of emperors from temple and other inscriptions, such as those of Philip the Arab and of Gallienus, at the temples of Jove and Serapis, respectively, at Abitina (Chouhoud el Bātin) in Africa Proconsularis.

of civil war must have been frequent—as statements of new authority, rejections of others, or simply as opportunities for gain.

Sauer overall sees the destroyers as either barbarian raiders/occupiers or Christians. In discussing episodes of statue-smashing in parts of the old Roman frontier province of Germany in town, sanctuary or villa contexts (e.g. Ladenburg, Dieburg and Bad Wimpfen), Sauer prefers to await the Alemannic take-over after A.D. 260 as the context, or to suggest earlier raids. He may well be correct, but in the case of the desecration (twice) of a Jupiter column at Ladenburg (a Roman town near modern Heidelberg), where, some time in the 3rd c., the Jupiter sculpture and other materials were thrown down a well, only then for the column to have been restored before a second dumping of a demolished and fire-damaged monument took place some time later, alternative views can be proferred.[69] Sauer's argument is that the giant Jupiter columns—about 13 existed in this one town—were highly visible symbols of Roman imperialism, which provoked reaction from invaders, and were a natural focus of aggression; yet surely we cannot exclude local reaction against Rome and the state in the context of 3rd c. civil war and the town's neglect by official arms, and local frustration meted out on the monuments to Roman security? Similarly, whilst the excavators of the imperial cult buildings at Narona and Eretria may well be perfectly correct in pinpointing desecration and destruction as sanctioned actions by Christians following imperial legislation, we do not know if these were acts by soldiers, monks, the local bishop, clergy and slaves, disgruntled citizens, or a mix of idealised churchmen and a suitably energetic group of locals, who enjoyed completing the looting that had gone before, and who might have hoped for possible booty from the exercise.

Christians play a different role of course in the 3rd c. upheavals and in the re-affirmation of the state under the Tetrarchs by being singled out for persecution in both military and civilian contexts. Aggressive persecutions in the mid-3rd c. under Decius and Valerian can be perceived as efforts to require loyalties to the struggling authorities in periods of insecurity, inside and without the empire, and can also be perceived as distrusts within communities as stresses took hold; renewed persecution under

---

[69] Sauer (2003) 55–57. Carroll (2001) 138, noting traces of destructions by raids, also points out how "The possibility that signs of violence in the third and fourth centuries could have been the result of Roman armies engaged in civil wars, however, is rarely considered" —e.g. feuding emperors inviting in German groups such as the Iuthungi and Alamanni, as seems to have occurred between Postumus and Gallienus.

Galerius (and Diocletian) at the start of the 4th c. was aimed at reinforcing the new image of emperors favoured by specific gods (notably Jove
and Hercules). Coin images, dedications and the re-naming of army units
and even a few towns (such as *Gorsium-Herculia* in Pannonia) stress this
Tetrarchic approach, although we have little to show a renewal of display
inside imperial cult centres, bar the chamber and its wall paintings in a
converted part of the Temple of Ammon at Luxor, Egypt, attached to the
Diocletianic fort; potentially more emphasis was made on display outside,
in public spaces and basilicas, through statuary, often of colossal dimensions (as, for example, Maxentius' Basilica Nova in Rome).[70]

Conclusion: Civil Conflict Present and Past

Modern parallels of civil war and their consequences, in African states
in particular, show frenzied gangs at work, despoiling and looting, setting cars on fire, hurling stones, controlling streets armed with makeshift
weapons, with minimal guidance, and with the 'authorities' overseeing
through hard-hand violence, and through hard-men bodyguards; how
often the individuals concerned are fighting for a specific cause, or are
simply caught up in the turmoil or even excitement, is never clear. Whilst
mention could be made of the civil war genocide impacts in Sudan, or
in Rwanda in 1994, when the Hutu government's murderous efforts to
exterminate the rival Tutsi population saw the massive loss of life and
the brutality of the Hutus, a recent event indicative of the upheaval and
confusion caused through civil violence, was the election in Kenya at the
end of 2007, marked by claims of the rigging of votes and counting, followed by riots and tribal conflict. If never spilling into the ethnic brutali-
ties of the Rwandan Hutu, by 19 January 2008, the death toll was set at
800 (including 30 burnt alive in a church on 1 January) and with a claimed
250,000 displaced refugees.[71] And the most recent upheavals (2011–12) in
Egypt and Syria especially have done plenty to flag to us the potential

---

[70] Janes (2002) 48–50 on the persecutions; Elsner (1995) 173–76 on the imagery at
Luxor. See Lee (2007) 193–98 on soldiers and persecutions as also on their role in destroying pagan shrines later. On evidence for Christian soldiery pre-Constantine, see Lee (2007)
176–82.

[71] *The Independent*, 29.1.2008 (issue no.6642), articles by Steve Bloomfield and Richard
Dowden, with the emotive headline: 'They killed our people, so now we will do likewise.
We are just revenging'. Acts of violence extended even against tourists, reporters and
hospitals.

impact of mob activity, ailing governmental responses, and resultant societal and urban breakdowns. The 'official' noises and words from the Syrian
President and his army were smokescreens to violence meted out against
opposition activists and civilians alike, and with the tension and damage
dragged out despite vague outside threats and denouncements.[72]

The looting by locals of shops, hospitals, state buildings and muse-
ums in the Iraq invasion by the US was not something sanctioned by the
incoming forces, but happened through the convenience and opportunities that confusion and upheaval and a loss of normal authority brought;
here, the toppling of the monumental statues of Saddam Hussein were
largely organised televised events, attracting onlookers and contributors,
with groups keen to side with the new powers.[73] The struggle for cohesion and order since, and the emergence of factions in particular, perhaps
parallel some of the events felt in civil conflict in later Roman times. Much
of the hurt and violence of the warfare is human and psychological; and
whilst bombs and tanks have meant that an archaeology of modern Iraq
would identify clearly the warfare, and whilst the civil strife is known and
reported, the latter may leave minimal trace—although the evidence of
executions and 'ethnic cleansing' under Saddam Hussein now made evident from uncovered mass burial pits, as likewise excavated to show the
conflicts in Bosnia and Spain, can yield a horrific graphic depiction of the
results of such wars.

A final point of comparison might be drawn with the events centred
around Chechnya and Russia, with the former resembling a breakaway
Roman province in the late Empire as centralised control deteriorates:
after the Soviet Union collapsed in 1991, Chechnya first ran as a republic
within the Russian Federation, and then drove for independence, a move
fiercely opposed by Russia: major military aggression by the latter across
1994–96, separatist reprisals, persistent diplomatic exchanges and breakdowns, economic hardships, and ongoing distrust, all ring loud as parallels
with the discussions above.[74]

---

[72] Besides numerous and ongoing newspaper, television and other press coverage,
see also outline summary of the Syrian uprisings at: http://en.wikipedia.org/wiki/Syrian
uprising(2011%E2%80%93present) noting a potential loss of life in the order of 30–50,000
[accessed 2.11.12].

[73] *The Independent*, 10.4.2008 (issue no.6704, Extra), *Picture Post: The Fall of Saddam—
and the 'Green Blob'*, article by Kim Sengupta, reports on the derided replacement sculpture called officially 'Survivor', but locally known as 'The Green Blob'.

[74] Rapid guide to 'Crisis in Chechnya' is presented in http://www.globalissues.org/
Geopolitics/Chechnya [accessed 23.5.08].

In our sketched 3rd to 5th c. Roman contexts, there are, as has already been seen, archaeological, iconographic and other indicators, which can point to conflict, propaganda, loss and response; destruction deposits and walls, however, remain too frequently tied to the non-Roman enemies, and we perhaps underplay how much in reality reflects the civil wars, which were as, if not at times, much more brutal and more debilitating than the barbarian assaults prior to the 5th c. What we should at least recognise is that military changes—defence (urban and military) as well as army composition and tactics—in the Late Empire, were responses to upheavals wrought by both internal and external threats; the architectural redefinition of towns especially links to an insecurity which prompted the uncertainties of internal Roman stability. Civil wars were powerful and debilitating realities under Rome: recognising the potential of observing the impact of civil war from other sources—coins, burials, cult desecration and so on—is important, although as yet far too few secure data exist to work with.

ACKNOWLEDGEMENTS

My thanks go especially to Andrew Merrills (Leicester) and Stanley Ireland (Warwick) for their helpful suggestions, corrections, etc. in modifying and tightening up this paper, and to the two anonymous referees for their additional guidance. And final thanks go to Andreas Pangerl for kindly supplying figs. 6a, b.

BIBLIOGRAPHY

Primary Sources

Amm. Marc. = Rolfe J. C. (1963) ed. and trans. *Res Gestae* (London 1963).
CIL = Reimerum G. (1862) ed. *Corpus Inscriptionum Latinarum* (Berlin 1862).
Eutr. = Santini S. (1979) ed. *Eutropii Breviarium ab urbe condita* (Leipzig 1979); Bird H. W. (1993) trans. *The Breviarium ab urbe condita of Eutropius, the Right Honourable Secretary of State for General Petitions: dedicated to Lord Valen, Gothicus Maximus and Perpetual Emperor* (Translated Texts for Historians 14) (Liverpool 1993).
Herodian = Stavenhagen K. (1967) ed. Herodian, *ab exessu divi Marci libri octo* (Stuttgart 1967).
ILS = Dessau H. (1856–1931) *Inscriptiones latinae selectae* (Berlin 1856–1931).
Mattingly-Sydenham *RIC* 5 = Webb P. H., Mattingly H. and Sydenham E. A. (1968) *The Roman Imperial Coinage, volume 5, part 2: Probus to Diocletian* (London 1968).
Pan. Lat. = Mynors R. A. B. (1964) ed. *XII Panegyrici Latini* (Oxford 1964); Nixon C. E. V. and Rodgers B. S. (1994) trans. *In Praise of Later Roman Emperors: the Panegyrici Latini* (Berkeley 1994).

964 NEIL CHRISTIE

SHA = Magie D. (1953) ed. and trans. *The Scriptores Historiae Augustae* (London 1953).
Veg. *Mil.* = Reeve M. D. (2004) ed. *Epitoma rei militaris* (Oxford 2006); Milner N. P. (1996) trans. *Epitome of Military Science* (Liverpool, 2nd ed. 1996).

Secondary Works

Abdy R. (2006) "In the pay of the emperor: coins from the Beaurains (Arras) treasure", in *Constantine the Great: York's Roman Emperor*, edd. E. Hartley, J. Hawkes, M. Henig and F. Mee (York 2006) 52–58.
Bakker L. (1993) "Raetien unter Postumus—das Siegesdenkmal einer Juthungenschlacht im Jahre 260 n. Chr. aus Augsburg", *Germania* 71 (1993) 369–86.
Beard M. (2007) *The Roman Triumph* (London and Cambridge, Mass. 2007).
Bishop M. C. and Coulston J. C. N. (1993) *Roman Military Equipment from the Punic Wars to the Fall of Rome* (London 1993).
Blockley R. C. (1998) "Warfare and diplomacy", in *The Cambridge Ancient History, Volume 13: the Late Empire, A.D. 337–425*, edd. A. Cameron and P. Garnsey (Cambridge and New York 1998) 411–36.
Bomgardner D. L. (1981) "The revolt of the Gordians and the amphitheatre at Thysdrus (El Djem)", in *The Roman West in the Third Century: Contributions from Archaeology and History*, edd. A. King and M. Henig (Oxford 1981) 211–14.
Bowes K. and Kulikowski M. (2005) edd. *Hispania in Late Antiquity: Current Perspectives* (The Medieval and Early Modern Iberian World 24) (Leiden and Boston 2005).
Branigan K. (1976) "Villa settlement in the West Country", in *The Roman West Country: Classical Culture and Celtic Society*, edd. K. Branigan and P. J. Fowler (Newton Abbot 1976) 120–41.
Buora M. (2002) ed. *Miles Romanus, Dal Po al Danubio nel Tardoantico: Atti del Convegno Internazionale, Pordenone-Concordia Sagittaria 17–19 Marzo 2000* (Pordenone 2002).
Burgess P. W. (1992) "From Gallia Romana to Gallia Gothica: the view from Spain", in *Fifth-Century Gaul: a Crisis of Identity?*, edd. J. F. Drinkwater and H. Elton (Cambridge 1992) 19–27.
Cameron A. (2006) "Constantius and Constantine: an exercise in publicity", in *Constantine the Great: York's Roman Emperor*, edd. E. Hartley, J. Hawkes, M. Henig and F. Mee (York 2006) 18–30.
Cameron A. and Garnsey P. (1998) edd. *The Cambridge Ancient History. Volume 13: the Late Empire, A.D. 337–425* (Cambridge and New York 1998).
Carroll M. (2001) *Romans, Celts and Germans: the German Provinces of Rome* (Stroud 2001).
Carroll-Spillecke M. (1997) "The late Roman frontier fort *Divitia* in Cologne-Deutz and its garrisons", in *Roman Frontier Studies 1995: Proceedings of the XVIth International Congress of Roman Frontier Studies*, edd. A. Groenman van Waateringe, B. L. van Beck, W. J. H. Willems and S. L. Wynia (Oxford 1997) 143–50.
Carson R. A. G., Hill P. V. and Kent J. P. C. (1978) *Late Roman Bronze Coinage A.D. 324–498, Parts I and II* (London 1978).
Cepas A. (2006) "The ending of the Roman city: the case of Clunia in the northern plateau of Spain", in *People and Space in the Middle Ages, 300–1300*, edd. W. Davies, G. Halsall and A. Reynolds (Turnhout 2006) 187–207.
Christie N. (1991) "The Alps as a frontier, AD 168–774", *JRA* 4 (1991) 410–30.
—— (1997) "Defences and defenders in Late Roman South-West Gaul", *JRA* 10 (1997) 489–94.
—— (2006) *From Constantine to Charlemagne: an Archaeology of Italy, AD 300–800* (Aldershot 2006).
Claridge A. (1998) *Rome: an Oxford Archaeological Guide* (Oxford and New York 1998).
Coarelli F. (1999) "L'edilizia pubblica a Roma in età tetrachica", in *The Transformations of Vrbs Roma in Late Antiquity*, ed. W. V. Harris (Portsmouth, RI 1999) 23–33.

Corney M. (1997) "The origins and development of the 'small town' of Cunetio, Mildenhall, Wiltshire", *Britannia* 28 (1997) 337–50.

Donati A. and Gentili G. (2005) edd. *Costantino il Grande: La civiltà antica al bivio tra Occidente e Oriente* (Milan 2005).

Drinkwater J. F. (1987) *The Gallic Empire: Separatism and Continuity in the North-Western Provinces of the Roman Empire, A.D. 260–274* (New York 1987).

—— (1992) "The Bacaudae of fifth-century Gaul", in *Fifth-Century Gaul: a Crisis of Identity?*, edd. J. F. Drinkwater and H. Elton (Cambridge 1992) 208–17.

—— (1996) "The 'Germanic threat on the Rhine frontier': a Romano-Gallic artefact?", in *Shifting Frontiers in Late Antiquity*, edd. R.W. Mathisen and H.S. Sivan (Aldershot 1996) 31–44.

—— (2007) *The Alamanni and Rome, 213–496 (Caracalla to Clovis)* (Oxford 2007).

Duncan-Jones R. (2004) "Economic change and the transition to Late Antiquity", in *Approaching Late Antiquity: the Transformation from Early to Late Empire*, edd. S. Swain and M. Edwards (Oxford 2004) 20–52.

Elsner J. (1995) *Art and the Roman Viewer: the Transformation of Art from the Pagan World to Christianity* (Cambridge and New York 1995).

—— (2000) "From the culture of *spolia* to the cult of relics: the Arch of Constantine and the genesis of late antique forms", *PBSR* 68 (2000) 149–78.

Elton H. (1992) "Defence in fifth-century Gaul", in *Fifth-Century Gaul: A Crisis of Identity?*, edd. J. Drinkwater and H. Elton (Cambridge 1992) 167–76.

—— (1996) *Warfare in Roman Europe AD 350–425* (Oxford 1996).

Faulkner N. (2000) *The Decline and Fall of Roman Britain* (Stroud 2000).

Fernández-Ochoa C. and Morillo Á. (2005) "Walls in the urban landscape of late Roman Spain: defense and imperial strategy", in *Hispania in Late Antiquity: Current Perspectives*, edd. K. Bowes and M. Kulikowski (Leiden and Boston 2005) 299–340.

Ferrill A. (1986) *The Fall of the Roman Empire: the Military Explanation* (London 1986).

Fishwick D. (1992) *The Roman Imperial Cult in the West* (London 1992).

—— (2002) *The Imperial Cult in the Latin West: Studies in the Ruler Cult of the Western Provinces of the Roman Empire, volume III: Provincial Cult, Part 1: Institution and Evolution* (Religions in the Graeco-Roman World 145) (Leiden, Boston and Köln 2002).

Galinié H. (2007) ed. *Tours antique et medieval: Lieux de vie, temps de la ville* (Tours 2007).

Gerster G. and Wartke R.-B. (2003) *Flugbilder aus Syrien: Von der Antike bis zum Moderne* (Mainz am Rhein 2003).

Greenhalgh P. A. L. (1975) *The Year of the Four Emperors* (London 1975).

Halsall G. (1992) "The origins of the Reihengräberzivilisation: forty years on", in *Fifth-Century Gaul: a Crisis of Identity?*, edd. J. Drinkwater and H. Elton (Cambridge 1992) 196–207.

Haupt P. (2001) *Römische Münzhorte des 3.Jhs. in Gallien und den germanischen Provinzen* (Provinzialrömische Studien 1) (Grunbach 2001).

Hobley B. (1983) "Roman urban defences: a review of research in Britain", in *Roman Urban Defences in the West*, edd. J. Maloney and B. Hobley (CBA Research Report 51) (London 1983) 78–84.

Howgego C. (1996) "The circulation of silver coins, models of the Roman economy, and crisis in the third century A.D.: some numismatic evidence", in *Coin Finds and Coin Use in the Roman World: the Thirteenth Oxford Symposium on Coinage and Monetary History, 25–27.3.1993*, edd. C. King and D. G. Wigy (Berlin 1996) 219–36.

Janes D. (2002) *Romans and Christians* (Stroud 2002).

Jobst W. (2002) "La Porta dei Pagani di *Carnuntum* e il *limes* danubiano pannonico nel IV secolo d.C.", in *Roma sul Danubio: Da Aquileia a Carnuntum lungo la via dell'ambra*, edd. M. Buora and W. Jobst (Rome 2002) 165–71.

Johnson S. (1979) *The Roman Forts of the Saxon Shore* (London 1979).

—— (1983) *Later Roman Fortifications* (London 1983).

Jones A. H. M. (1980) *Augustus* (London 1980).

Katsari C. (2003) "Bimetallism and the circulation of gold coins during the third and the fourth centuries AD", *Münstersche Beiträge zur antiken Handelsgeschichte* 22.1 (2003) 48–68.

—— (2005) "The monetization of Roman Asia Minor in the third century AD", in *Patterns in the Economy of Roman Asia Minor*, edd. S. Mitchell, C. Katsari and D. Braund (Swansea 2005) 261–88.

Keay S. (1996) "Tarraco in Late Antiquity", in *Towns in Transition: Urban Evolution in Late Antiquity and the Early Middle Ages*, edd. N. Christie and S. T. Loseby (Aldershot 1996) 18–44.

King A. and Henig M. (1981) edd. *The Roman West in the Third Century: Contributions from Archaeology and History* (BAR International Series 9) (Oxford 1981).

King C. E. (1981) "The circulation of coin in the western provinces, A.D. 260–295", in *The Roman West in the Third Century: Contributions from Archaeology and History*, edd. A. King and M. Henig (BAR International Series 9) (Oxford 1981) 89–106.

—— (1992) "Roman, local, and barbarian coinages in fifth-century Gaul", in *Fifth-Century Gaul: a Crisis of Identity?*, edd. J. F. Drinkwater and H. Elton (Cambridge 1992) 184–95.

—— (1996) "Roman copies", in *Coin Finds and Coin Use in the Roman World: the Thirteenth Oxford Symposium on Coinage and Monetary History, 25–27.3.1993*, edd. C. King and D. G. Wigy (Berlin 1996) 237–63.

Knight C. (1845) *Old England: a Pictorial Museum* (London 1845).

Knight J. (1999) *The End of Antiquity: Archaeology, Society and Religion AD 235–700* (Stroud 1999).

Kulikowski M. (2007) *Rome's Gothic Wars from the Third Century to Alaric* (Cambridge and New York 2007).

Leach J. (1978) *Pompey the Great* (London 1978).

Lee A. D. (2007) *War in Late Antiquity: a Social History* (Oxford 2007).

Liebeschuetz J. H. W. G. (1991) *Barbarians and Bishops: Army, Church and State in the Age of Arcadius and Chrysostom* (Oxford 1991).

Liverani P. (2005) "Il Arco di Costantino", in *Costantino in Grande: La civiltà antica al bivio tra Occidente e Oriente*, edd. A. Donati and G. Gentili (Milan 2005) 64–69.

Long J. (1996) "Two sides of a coin: Aurelian, Vaballathus, and eastern frontiers in the early 270s", in *Shifting Frontiers in Late Antiquity*, edd. R. W. Mathisen and H. S. Sivan (Aldershot 1996) 59–71.

—— (2007) *Within these Walls: Roman and Medieval Defences north of Newgate at the Merrill Lynch Financial Centre, City of London* (MOLAS Monograph 33) (London 2007).

Maloney J. (1983) "Recent work on London's defences", in *Roman Urban Defences in the West*, edd. J. Maloney and B. Hobley (CBA Research Report 51) (London 1983) 96–117.

Maloney J. and Hobley B. (1983) edd. *Roman Urban Defences in the West* (CBA Research Report No.51) (London 1983).

Marin E. (2001) "The temple of the imperial cult (Augusteum) at Narona and its statues: interim report", *JRA* 14 (2001) 81–112.

Mattingly D. J. (1995) *Tripolitania* (London 1995).

—— (2006) *An Imperial Possession: Britain in the Roman Empire* (London 2006).

Mayer E. (2006) "Civil war and public dissent: the state monuments of the decentralised Roman empire", in *Social and Political Life in Late Antiquity*, edd. W. Bowden, A. Gutteridge and C. Machado (Late Antique Archaeology 3.1) (Leiden 2006) 141–55.

Merrills A. (2010) "'The secret of my succession': dynasty and crisis in Vandal North Africa", *Early Medieval Europe* 18.2 (2010) 135–59.

Mertens J. (1983) "Urban wall-circuits in Gallia Belgica in the Roman period", in *Roman Urban Defences in the West*, edd. J. Maloney and B. Hobley (CBA Research Report No.51) (London 1983) 42–57.

Mitchell S. (2006) *A History of the Later Roman Empire, AD 284–641: the Transformation of the Ancient World* (Oxford 2007).

Morelli A. L. (2009) "Il gioiello monetale in età romana", in *Oreficeria antica e medieval: Tecniche, produzione, società*, edd. I. Baldini Lippolis and M. T. Guaitoli (Ornamenta 1) (Bologna 2009) 79–101.

Morgan G. (2007) *69 AD: the Year of Four Emperors* (Oxford 2007).

Muhlberger S. (1992) "Looking back from mid-century: the Gallic Chronicler of 452 and the crisis of Honorius' reign", in *Fifth-Century Gaul: a Crisis of Identity?*, edd. J. F. Drinkwater and H. Elton (Cambridge 1992) 28–37.

Neal D. S. (1974) *The Excavation of the Roman Villa in Gadebridge Park, Hemel Hempstead 1963–8* (London 1974).

Nixon A. and Rodgers B. (1994) *In Praise of Later Roman Emperors: the* Panegyrici Latini (Berkeley 1994).

Okamura L. (1996) "Roman withdrawals from three transfluvial frontiers", in *Shifting Frontiers in Late Antiquity*, edd. R. W. Mathisen and H. S. Sivan (Aldershot 1996) 11–19.

Pearson A. F. (2002) *The Roman Shore Forts: Coastal Defences of Southern Britain* (Stroud 2002).

Pollini J. (2006) "Review of Varner, *Mutilation and Transformation*: Damnatio Memoriae *and Roman Imperial Portraiture*", in *The Art Bulletin* 88.3 (Sept. 2006) 590–98.

Poulter A. G. (2007a) ed. *The Transition to Late Antiquity: on the Danube and Beyond* (Proceedings of the British Academy 141) (London 2007).

—— (2007b) "The transition to Late Antiquity", in *The Transition to Late Antiquity: on the Danube and Beyond*, ed. A. G. Poulter (Proceedings of the British Academy 141) (London 2007) 1–50.

Rambaldi S. (2009) *L'edilizia pubblica nell'impero romano all'epoca dell'anarchia militare (235–284 d.C.)* (Bologna 2009).

Reece R. (1999a) *The Later Roman Empire: an Archaeology AD 150–600* (Stroud 1999).

—— (1999b) "Two late Roman cemeteries in Italy", *JRA* 12 (1999) 793–97.

Rinaldi Tufi S. (2005) "La grande architettura fra Diocleziano e Costantino a Roma e nel mondo romano", in *Costantino in Grande: la civiltà antica al bivio tra Occidente e Oriente*, edd. A. Donati and G. Gentili (Milan 2005) 92–105.

Sauer E. (2003) *The Archaeology of Religious Hatred in the Roman and Early Medieval World* (Stroud 2003).

Schmid S. (2001) "Worshipping the emperor(s): a new temple of the imperial cult at Eretria and the ancient destruction of its statues", *JRA* 14 (2001) 113–42.

Snyder C. A. (1998) *An Age of Tyrants: Britain and the Britons, A.D. 400–600* (Stroud 1998).

Southern P. and Dixon K. R. (1996) *The Late Roman Army* (London 1996).

Swain S. and Edwards M. (2004) edd. *Approaching Late Antiquity: the Transformation from Early to Late Empire* (Oxford 2004).

Tlass M. (1986) *Zénobie: Reine de Palmyre* (Damas 1986).

Tomlin R. S. O. (2000) "The legions in the late Empire", in *Roman Fortresses and their Legions*, ed. R. Brewer (London 2000) 159–79.

—— (2006) "The owners of the Beaurains (Arras) treasure", in *Constantine the Great: York's Roman Emperor*, edd. E. Hartley, J. Hawkes, M. Henig and F. Mee (York 2006) 59–64.

Ulbert Th. (1981) *Ad Pirum (Hrušica), Spätrömische Passbefestigung in den Julischen Alpen: Der deutsche Beitrag zu den slowenisch-deutschen Grabungen 1971–1973* (Munich 1981).

Van Ossel P. and Ouzoulias P. (2000) "Rural settlement economy in Northern Gaul in the late Empire: an overview", *JRA* 13 (2000) 133–60.

Vansittart P. (1983) *Three Six Seven, Memoirs of a Very Important Man* (London 1983).

Varner E. R. (2004) *Mutilation and Transformation*: Damnatio Memoriae *and Roman Imperial Portraiture* (Leiden 2004).

Ward-Perkins B. (2005) *The Fall of Rome and the End of Civilization* (Oxford and New York 2005).

Whitby M. (2004) "Emperors and armies, AD 235–395", in *Approaching Late Antiquity: the Transformation from Early to Late Empire*, edd. S. Swain and M. Edwards (Oxford 2004) 156–86.

White R. (2007) *Britannia Prima: Britain's Last Roman Province* (Stroud 2007).

Wightman E. (1981) "The fate of Gallo-Roman villages in the third century", in *The Roman West in the Third Century: Contributions from Archaeology and History*, (BAR International Series 9), edd. A. King and M. Henig (Oxford 1981) 235–43.

Witschel C. (2004) "Re-evaluating the Roman West in the 3rd c. A.D.", *JRA* 17 (2004) 251–81.

Yon J.-B. (2001) "Euergetism and urbanism in Palmyra", in *Recent Research in Late-Antique Urbanism*, ed. L. Lavan (JRA Supplementary Series 42) (Portsmouth, RI 2001) 173–81.

LIST OF FIGURES

THE JUSTINIANIC RECONQUEST OF ITALY:
IMPERIAL CAMPAIGNS AND LOCAL RESPONSES

Maria Kouroumali

Abstract

This article examines a particular aspect of Justinian's campaigns against the Ostrogoths in Italy, one that is often overlooked, yet one that is essential to the understanding of these wars, namely the nature of the relations among the three sides caught up in the conflict: Romans, Goths and Italians. This study shows, through careful examination of the primary sources, notably the account of Procopius, that the relations of the inhabitants of Italy with the two warring sides were dependent on the Italians' needs and concerns to preserve their security, rather than on ideologically-driven alliances.

There are a number of issues which are of importance in understanding the events of any war. Here I will attempt to highlight an often overlooked aspect of the campaigns of the East Romans against the Ostrogoths in Italy in the A. D. 530s–550s: the impact of the war on the local population, the Italians. We should first note that the 'barbarians' who invaded not long after Rome's Fall—the Ostrogoths—were already to some degree Romanised before they entered the country. They maintained the pre-existing Roman social and political conditions in Italy, thereby ensuring the continuity of a still highly urbanised and functional society. The Ostrogoths also upheld the inherited Roman infrastructure and communications network, and, as will be seen, these remained active fully into the war decades while there was also considerable diplomatic activity between Ostrogoths and Romans. Scholarship has usually focused on these and other aspects, and yet the attitude of native inhabitants towards invading and resident armies during a war should be of equal importance, giving a fuller *human* face to the conflicts. After all, in this case, the situation is complicated by the fact that the Italians themselves were not the primary targets of Justinian's campaign, but rather their appointed overlords, the Ostrogoths. A considered study of the exact nature of the relationship between the native Italian population and the two opposing forces will potentially enable us to perceive some of the underlying tensions that influenced the often shifting allegiance of the Italian citizens during the long, drawn-out war.

A. Sarantis, N. Christie (edd.) *War and Warfare in Late Antiquity: Current Perspectives*
(Late Antique Archaeology 8.1–8.2 – 2010–11) (Leiden 2013), pp. 969–999

INTRODUCTION: ISSUES OF ETHNICITY, IDENTITY, PRIMARY SOURCES
AND THE ARCHAEOLOGICAL RECORD

Before we proceed to examine the relations between native Italians, Goths and Romans, some introductory comments must be made on several other topics. These are: the issue of ethnicity and self-identity and the related use of the terms 'Italian', 'Roman', 'Goth'; the primary written sources; the archaeological record of late antique Italy; and the limitations of both source types in helping to explore the subject of this article. These matters are not the central focus here, not because they are unimportant, but because they have received considerable scholarly attention elsewhere.

Ethnicity and Identity

Relatively recently a substantial, international collaborative project entitled *The Transformation of the Roman World* was sponsored by the European Science Foundation. The results of this research were published in a series of volumes, which not only include an entire volume devoted solely to questions of ethnicity and self-identity, but also contain many articles in other volumes dealing with several aspects of the problem.[1] As these publications were just starting, P. Amory wrote a thought-provoking study of self-identity with particular reference to the Goths in Italy. This work challenges a number of traditional theories on the subject, most of which accept that the various migrating tribes in Late Antiquity were members of distinct ethnic groups or, at least, contained a kernel of distinct, self-proclaimed ethnicity. Despite efforts to avoid doing so, Amory's theory sometimes falls into the trap of modernising the past. In summary, Amory argues that the various Germanic peoples, which migrated to and from the Balkans and onto Italy in particular, cannot be identified as belonging to a separate ethnic group with distinct identities. Rather he believes that references to individuals in the primary sources that distinguish them from 'Romans' and make them appear as members of a distinguishable ethnicity form part of an ethnographic language that was the product of

---

[1] Volumes: Pohl (1997a); Pohl and Reimitz (1998); Pohl (1999) 127–41; Pohl *et al.* (2001). Key articles: Hedeager (2000) 15–57; Chrysos (2003) 13–19; and Wormald (2003) 21–53.

the ideological constructs and prejudices of the authors of those texts, influenced by literary tradition and ignorance.[2]

Amory's theory of sophisticated ideological propaganda received strong criticism from a number of historians, most importantly, P. Heather and R. Markus.[3] I would add to this critique by pointing out that references to the specific places of origin of various people in the written sources reveals a simpler way of viewing things in the 6th c. It does not mean that matters were less complex, but that they must have had reasons to distinguish each individual's place of origin, thereby revealing the prejudices and concepts operating in their time. It should be kept in mind that most people in those times were distinguished either by the name of their father or their birthplace. When Procopius, for example, uses either one, he does so to inform his readers, either of the presence of barbarians in the army, or to distinguish native inhabitants (Italians) from those he considered to be Goths.

The debate on ethnicity, identity and self-identity, of course, is ongoing, but, for the purpose of this article, suffice to say that there were definable groups of Italians, Romans and Goths in Italy, who also viewed themselves as such, even though it is hard to arrive at definite conclusions regarding the exact components and modes of display of identity in each case. The most that can be said is that there certainly appears to have been a kin-based centre at the core of these groups with a considerable degree of cultural outflow and inflow on the edges. I have chosen to use the terms 'Italian', 'Roman' and 'Goth' to reflect the usage in Procopius' original Greek text rather than replacing 'Italian' with 'Roman' and 'Roman' with 'Byzantine', as this would be anachronistic.[4] Thus, throughout the paper, 'Italian' refers to the native inhabitants of Italy, 'Roman' to the citizens and army of the East Roman Empire, and 'Goth' to the Ostrogoths in Italy. When dealing with ancient sources, no terminology is perfect, but the adherence to the terminology of the primary sources in this case seems to me preferable.

---

[2] Amory (1997), esp. ch.5. On barbarian identity and the creation of a historical past, see Heather (1999) 234–58; and Wolfram (1994) 19–38.

[3] Heather (2003) 85–133; R. Markus (1998) 414–17.

[4] Christie (2006) 57–64 on labels and identities in post-Roman Italy.

Primary Sources

Equally, a few words need to be said on the primary written source material for the Gothic war. There are a number of texts which shed light on various aspects and events of the war. These are the *Variae* of the Italian senator Cassiodorus;[5] the *Getica* (*De origine actibusque Getarum*) and the *Romana* (*De Summa Temporum vel origine actibusque gentis Romanorum*) of Jordanes,[6] a Goth from Italy writing in Constantinople during the Gothic war, and the *Liber Pontificalis* (henceforth *Lib. Pont.*), the title given to a collection of Latin biographies of the Roman bishops (popes), probably the work of a series of anonymous compilers. The edition of the *Lib. Pont.* that we have dates from the middle of the 6th c. and was then added to and extended at some point in the 7th c. up until the late 9th c. (*ca.* A.D. 870).[7] Then there are the chronicles of Marcellinus Comes[8] and John Malalas,[9] and, of course, Procopius' *History of the Wars*, which remains the main historical written source for the events of this war as for most of Justinian's reign.

It should be noted at the outset that the other contemporary or near-contemporary sources contribute virtually no additional information to Procopius' account of the Gothic war. There is very little corroborating coverage of the events narrated in Procopius, and for the main part, the other sources are silent. Most of the sources end their account at the beginning of the Gothic war or continue only as far as the first few years. The remainder post-date the war, having been composed after the final outcome of the campaigns, and, therefore, the value of the information

---

[5] For selective English translations of the *Variae*: *The Letters of Cassiodorus* (Cassiod. *Var.*), see Hodgkin (1886); and Barnish (1992). O'Donnell (1979) remains the only available complete study of Cassiodorus and his work. There is also an online version of this book at the following website with extensive bibliographical and footnote supplements to the 1979 print edition: http://www9.georgetown.edu/faculty/jod/texts/cassbook/toc.html.

[6] The *Getica* (Jord *Get.*) is the only work of Jordanes that has been translated into English (Mierow (1960) with introduction and notes); for a biography of Jordanes: Goffart (1988) 42–47; Heather (1991) 43; and Martindale *et al.* (1971–92) *PLRE* IIIa 713 (Iordanes 1).

[7] For the compilation and dating of *Lib. Pont.*, see the introduction and notes of the French edition: Duchesne (1886–92); Vogel (1955–57); and the English translation of Davis (2000), along with Davis (1976).

[8] Croke (2001). Croke (1995), for the only study and translation available in English of Marcellinus with a reproduction of Mommsen's edition of the text. Martindale *et al.* (1971–1992) *PLRE* II, 711 (Marcellinus 9).

[9] For English translation and study of Malalas and his work, see trans. Jeffreys *et al.* (1986) and (1990).

provided is further undermined by the distance in time, and by the various problems surrounding their composition and credibility.

However, these problems in no way suggest that these other literary sources should be dismissed out of hand. Although they offer hardly any original contributions additional to what is known from Procopius, they nevertheless allow confirmation of Procopius' account of some of the events. Most importantly, though, some of them do afford important insights into the contemporary life of the period, which cannot be gained from Procopius' works alone. This is especially true of the sources written from the western Italian perspective. But it does mean that the modern historian is forced to rely almost entirely upon Procopius' account for the reconstruction of the sequence of the events of the war, and for the examination of the issue of relations between the three noted parties in Italy: Italians, Goths and Romans.

Procopius devotes the greater part of his *Wars*—in sum, three entire books and almost half of a fourth—to narrating the events in Italy (Books 5–7 and 8.21 onwards). The first part of the narrative covers events preceding the outbreak of hostilities from *ca.* A.D. 474 to the first phase of the war from 535 to 540 (Books 5 and 6). This first war phase is characterised by the swift Roman victory against the Goths and the capture of Ravenna by Belisarius in 540. The second phase of the war covers the period from 540/41 to 548/49, and can be further divided into two sub-phases, the first from 540/41 to 544 and the second from 545 to 548/49 (Book 7–7.35). During the second phase, the recall of Belisarius to the capital after the capitulation of Ravenna, and the apparent inability of the remaining Roman commanders to confront and counter the swift revival of the Gothic army under Totila (540–544), is followed by the return of Belisarius to the Italian front, but without significant impact for the Roman side (545–548/49). The third phase of the war spans the years from 550 to 552/53 (Book 7.36–Book 8.21–35). After a number of failed attempts to provide an effective leader for the Roman army, the General Narses is sent from Constantinople with reinforcements, and leads the Romans to their eventual victory over the Goths and their king, Teias. Procopius' account breaks off at this point and the remaining battles between Narses and the various Gothic forces scattered throughout Italy until *ca.* 563 are covered in the *History* of Agathias of Myrina.[10]

---

[10] *Agathiae Myrinaei Historiarum*, ed. Keydell (1967); Cameron (1970) on Agathias and his work.

Procopius is, by no means, an objective source. Despite the insistence of most scholars on placing a greater degree of trust in his account than those of the other written sources, he displays many of the same limitations that these other sources present. He is a biased reporter of select events and often fails to appreciate the significance of certain episodes in the war, while being unable to arrive at conclusions that display a profound understanding of the complex political, military and social reality of his time. In addition, it can be argued that he was probably in Italy only during the first 5 years of the war (535–540), and, although we cannot be sure of his exact whereabouts after this time, it is unlikely that he accompanied Belisarius to the Italian front during the general's second stint (545–548/49). However, there is a marked change in the tone and pace of his account of the Italian campaign after 540 (evident from the first chapter of Book 7 onwards), from which point he becomes far more negative and critical of the Roman side, especially with regard to both Emperor Justinian and General Narses, while at the same time recounting in fuller detail the successes of the Goths and even portraying Totila in a favourable light. He appears not to have agreed with Belisarius' recall to Constantinople in 540. It is a matter of scholarly speculation whether his changed stance is due to the protracted and bitter struggle of the war instead of the swift capitulation of Gothic forces in Italy that had been hoped for after the fall of Ravenna, or whether he had other, personal reasons.[11]

The Archaeological Record

The limitations and problems of the written source material are usually balanced by the evidence of archaeology. However, there is very little evidence that the archaeological record of late antique Italy directly provides for the particular topic of this article. The written sources, although providing more detail on geography and topography, remain singularly uninformative and selective concerning the peninsula's urban and rural infrastructure. Until recently, historians were further encumbered by the conspicuous absence of a general study of late antique Italian archaeology. This has been tidily addressed by Neil Christie (2006), who offers a

---

[11] For Procopius' life, works and discussion of the problems, the best study is still Cameron (1985), esp. chapters. 1, 3 and 8. Kaldellis (2005) is thought-provoking but, at times, far-fetched. Building on Cameron, I have offered a reappraisal of several aspects of Procopius' life and historiographical methods in my (as yet unpublished) 2005 Oxford D.Phil. thesis, esp. chapters. 1, 2 and 7.

broad and synthetic overview of the subject based on individual archaeological reports of excavations in Italy and the plethora of secondary literature on the subject.[12] However, the archaeological evidence also has its limitations, as the crucial years of the Gothic war are often absent from the concerns of the archaeological record.

There are, of course, a number of explanations for this apparent oversight. First, this was a period of instability and turmoil which would naturally prohibit the erection of important new monuments. It is evident that the two opposing armies would be concerned with the power struggle between each other rather than building projects of the type which can be readily identifiable in the archaeological record and easily dated, such as churches. The exception is Ravenna, but this city, as the imperial capital of the West since the 5th c, is a special case. Ravenna also enjoyed a more stable fate than other cities in late antique Italy, since it remained in Byzantine hands from 540 onwards, and served as the seat of the Byzantine exarchate established in Italy after the end of the war.[13] Ravenna is famous for both its well-preserved Gothic and Roman/Byzantine monuments, primarily ecclesiastical, such as the church of San Vitale, but also unique buildings, such as the Mausoleum of Theoderic. However, the existence of these monuments cannot really contribute much to the discussion of relations between the three parties in this article.

Secondly, the uncertainty which surrounds the dating of many excavated archaeological remains due to the continuity of architectural and structural forms (e.g. the continued maintenance, re-construction and re-decoration of buildings) complicates the issue even further. This is also a very short time span, and being able to date activity (whether of buildings or demolitions or destruction) precisely is rarely feasible. This difficulty is further enhanced by the uncritical use of Procopius, which has led modern scholars to take for granted that the Gothic war was almost solely responsible for every destruction, site abandonment or defensive wall from this period. Thirdly, precise techniques and care are needed to distinguish and record the different archaeological layers on a site, and in urban contexts especially, the stratigraphy—fragile at best for this time

---

[12] Christie (2006). Other contributions include articles in edited volumes by Francovich and Noyé (1992); Rich (1993); and Christie and Loseby (1996), to name but a few. See also the very useful Brogiolo and Gelichi (1998). An earlier summary on Byzantine Italy is Christie (1989) 249–93.

[13] Deichmann (1976) and (1989); and Deliyannis (2009) are thorough on the churches. See also Brown (1984) and (1988). Christie and Gibson (1988) 156–97 on Ravenna's city walls.

period—is rarely coherent. Structures such as fortifications, roads and
bridges were continuously in use since they were important to the military operations. While they often bear signs of repair which could well
date to the 6th c., proving such dates is never easy.[14]

As importantly, one must remember that in Italy there is an abundance
of classical and Early Roman remains, which further complicates attempts
to form a clear picture. The cities mentioned in Procopius' account certainly did not spring up in the 6th c., but were, on the contrary, originally Roman or even earlier Etruscan and Greek foundations, most with a
continuous existence and evolving character. No one would suggest that
the Italian cities remained unaltered in form since there were fundamental changes beginning as early as the 2nd and 3rd c., and which became
more marked with the advent of Christianity in the mid-4th c. The overall general picture is that the Roman town, once the object of patronage by the local governors and prominent citizens, became subject to the
general, but less regular, patronage of the emperor, the local bishop and
the informal group of local notables which replaced the old group of the
curiales. With the shift in political circumstances, which involved more
centralised administration, and the development of the imperial bureaucracy to oversee the far-reaching implications of imperial policy, the city
councils, governors and individual wealthy citizens no longer aspired to
endow their hometowns with splendid and expensive public buildings, or
to offer funds for maintenance, games and the like. By A.D. 450/500, much
of the 'classical' monumental fabric of towns—theatres, baths, etc.—was
gone, redundant or in severe decay.[15]

We need to be very cautious in assuming that the rise of Christianity
was a prime factor in changing the face of these towns. As Bryan Ward-
Perkins has convincingly shown in his work,[16] most changes in building
policies had already been implemented. Nonetheless, churches slowly
became the new foci for congregation, and their placement did impact
on the organisation of many towns. By the time the Gothic War broke
out, churches inside and outside—but mainly inside—fortified cities
were prominent built features, and the bishop had risen in social prominence; by this date, while there were still noble families, many of these

---

[14] Ward-Perkins (1996) 4–17.
[15] Christie (2006) for more detailed studies of individual cities and towns throughout
Italy; Arthur (2002) for Naples; Brogiolo (1993) for Brescia.
[16] Ward-Perkins (1984), which remains an indispensable source, exploiting chiefly
textual/epigraphic data.

were already starting to compete for clerical office. Bishops could even be found organising maintenance of the water supply, and urban granaries may have relied greatly on goods produced on Church lands. By this time, there may have been fewer divisions in the social hierarchy of towns, and all citizens were Christians.

Finally, the material and textual evidence shows that Italy remained strongly urban-oriented in the 5th and 6th c: despite losses of buildings, bathing establishments and games, the archaeological record shows that people still lived, worked and worshipped in these towns. When the Goths arrived, there was even an enhancement of some towns in the reign of Theoderic, and even an encouragement of Roman or 'imperial' culture.[17] And, at the same time, the landscape, despite some upheavals, especially in the 5th c., was still heavily farmed to serve the towns.[18] On these levels, the archaeology is valuable in showing an Italian population in town and country. However, what is almost impossible to observe from the archaeology is how these natives viewed the Goths when they came and established themselves on a permanent basis; and then their reactions and allegiances when the Romans attempted to wrest Italy away from these Goths.

Relations of Italians with Goths and Romans

As noted, my concern here is with trying to identify the attitude and allegiance of the Italians towards both Goths and Romans. Some scholars have previously addressed this question, but with differing results. The prevailing view is that the Italians were pro-Roman, although this opinion is based almost exclusively on the attitudes of certain figures of authority, such as Pope Vigilius and Cassiodorus, and does not involve a detailed examination of the evidence in Procopius. Moorhead, in particular, arrived at this conclusion by looking exclusively at prominent Italians before and during the Gothic war. In the first of two articles, he maintains that *all* prominent Italians were pro-Roman. In the second, he argues for a division of the sympathies of prominent Italians: Cassiodorus and Ennodius were pro-Gothic, as opposed to the pro-Roman stance of Arator, Boethius

---

[17] Moorhead (1992); Brown (1993); Settia (1993); Christie (2006) 273–75.
[18] Christie (2006) 452–58; see also papers in Christie (2004) and useful summary of the changing landscapes in Central Italy, especially in Francovich and Hodges (2003).

and Vigilius. The reason for the differing support of these figures was to be found in their family backgrounds. Ennodius and Cassiodorus belonged to self-made, wealthy families, and their prestige and authority owed much to the Goths; in contrast, Arator, Boethius and Vigilius were members of ancient senatorial families, long pre-dating the presence of Ostrogothic rule in Italy.

However, in both of Moorhead's articles, the evidence is examined cursorily and uncritically, leading to his rather unconvincing conclusions. He also makes rather broad assumptions about the general Italian population on the basis of the actions of these authority figures.[19] A more balanced view has been advanced more recently, albeit briefly, arguing for the use of the Italians by both sides to further their own interests in the war.[20] Therefore, to arrive at a conclusion regarding the exact nature of the relations between the three sides, especially those of the general population, it is necessary to look at the evidence preserved, primarily in Procopius, diachronically during the war.

As already noted, the other sources do not offer a great deal of evidence, but, whenever relevant, will be included. On the whole, Procopius has few things to say about the Italians and their relations with the two opposing sides. One can even say that they only feature incidentally in the narrative. Despite this paucity of evidence and the limitations implied by the use of only one main source, the roles in which the citizens of Italy appear in Procopius' account should be noted, as they afford some insight into the relationship between Italians, Goths and Romans during the Gothic war. One would naturally expect the indigenous population, members of the original home of the Roman Empire, with half a millennium of their historical past ingrained in their memories, to be favourably predisposed towards the incoming Roman forces. However, the Ostrogoths were largely Romanised before their arrival in Italy, and, as observed, once there, had made a considerable effort to maintain and strengthen this image during their half century of rule. It becomes apparent that the issue is far from straightforward, and there is reason to suggest that the Italians had no strong ideological predisposition towards one side or the other. We need

---

[19] Moorhead (1983) 575–96 and (1987) 161–68; Thompson (1982) ch. 6. It is worthwhile noting that Thompson, despite presenting some evidence from Procopius which points towards Italian neutrality, arrives at the somewhat arbitrary conclusion that the Italians were pro-Roman.

[20] Heather (1996) esp. 272–73; Liebeschuetz (2001) 363–66 and (1996) 230–39, at 233–34 briefly refers to Procopius' evidence on the response of cities to the Roman army without a detailed examination of this evidence.

to take a closer look at specific passages in Procopius in order to probe deeper the attitude of the Italians, and thereby reconstruct a clearer picture of their relationship to the two opponents.

1. *The Case of Naples*

During the siege of Naples by the Romans, Belisarius received Stephanus the Neapolitan, the envoy of the citizens, who expressed their request for the Romans to abandon the siege. Belisarius denied the request and instead asked for the surrender of the city. Privately, he bribed Stephanus to support his course of action. Stephanus managed to persuade the Neapolitans to surrender, but was unexpectedly opposed by two other eminent citizens, Pastor and Asclepiodotus, who argued that the Neapolitans should remain loyal to the Goths. If they were to consider surrender, they should at least receive a series of concessions from the Romans. This was, indeed, what happened, and Belisarius acceded to the demands of the citizens, even though, as Procopius states without offering any details as to the exact nature of the demands, the concessions were considerable. The population was ready to surrender, while the Gothic garrison stationed in the city was prepared to allow the citizens to do whatever they wished, albeit reluctantly. Once again, though, Pastor and Asclepiodotus opposed the surrender, and were supported in this by the Jews of the city and the Gothic garrison. The citizens were finally swayed by the two, and decided to fight against the Romans. A final attempt on the part of Belisarius and Stephanus to persuade the Neapolitans to surrender failed, with the result that the city was captured and sacked.[21]

This is an example of the results of divided loyalties within a city. The native population initially would have preferred to remain outside the Roman—Gothic confrontation. When this was not possible, they decided on the basis of the arguments presented by each side, Stephanus for the Romans and Pastor and Asclepiodotus for the Goths. Stephanus, on the one hand, was driven by personal interest and perhaps by fear of Roman military superiority. On the other hand, Pastor and Asclepiodotus appear to have wanted to preserve the existing status quo. Neither side, though, seems to have been driven by primary concern for the ideological

---

[21] Procop. *Goth.* 5.8.19; *Lib. Pont.* Silverius 3 (trans. Davis (2000) 55–56): confirms the refusal of the citizens to accept Belisarius in the city and notes the sacking of Naples, attributing it to Belisarius' fury at being refused entrance.

implications of the proposals, i.e. support of Roman imperial authority as opposed to the Ostrogothic regime.

The only exception was the stance of the Jews, who were probably actively pro-Gothic in light of the tolerant religious policy of the Goths, in contrast to Justinian's intolerant one. The Goths were Christian Arians, but unlike the Vandals in Chalcedonian Africa, Theoderic had shown the utmost consideration for the Chalcedonian Italians. During most of his reign (thus pre-war), Italy was the paragon of Orthodoxy as the East Roman Empire was plagued by contentions between the Monophysites and Chalcedonians.

For the major part of his rule, Theoderic chose to allow the Church to conduct its own affairs, and there was no persecution of Chalcedonians or enforced conversion. Indeed, if Procopius is to be believed, the opposite was often the case. During the siege of Rome, in a debate between the Gothic envoys and Belisarius,[22] the former mentioned that Goths had become Chalcedonian, while Chalcedonians did not convert to Arianism. This tolerant attitude extended to other minority groups such as the Jews, and Cassiodorus credits Theoderic with the infamous quote: *quia nemo cogitur ut credit invitus*.[23] Only during the Laurentian Schism did Theoderic clearly intervene on behalf of Pope Symmachus, and then probably because the disturbances and riots in Rome not only disrupted the fabric of everyday life, but were also extended among many prominent senators, who supported one candidate against the other. One could also conceivably see behind this intervention of Theoderic the beginnings of a break with the East, which was to become more pronounced towards the end of his reign with the harsh treatment he displayed towards Pope John.[24]

The main preoccupation for the remaining Neapolitans, therefore, was the minimising of the impact of the war on their life and the interests of their city. The prevailing attitude was to side with the eventual winner of the war, thereby safeguarding their continuing prosperity with the least direct involvement.

---

[22] Procop. *Goth.* 6.6.18.

[23] Cassiod. *Var.* 2.27.2: 'We cannot order a religion, because no one is forced to believe against his will' (transl. Hodgkin (1886)).

[24] Moorhead (1992) ch.4; and Noble (1993) 395–423: for a detailed analysis of the schism.

2. *The Case of Milan*

Datius, the bishop of the city, alongside other notables, arrived at Rome in late 537 to ask Belisarius for military assistance, and promised him the surrender of Milan and the rest of Liguria.[25] This is the only case amongst the cities that surrendered to the Romans where the citizens, or, more accurately, the leading citizens, of their own initiative, requested help from Belisarius in order to capitulate. The Milanese envoys were also exceptional in that they appeared to have sided with the emperor's cause without immediate external pressures, since Belisarius was still at that time besieged in Rome, and the outcome of his campaign far from conclusive.

We are not given any reason for this move on their part. One can only speculate that perhaps the close links between the nobility of the city and Fidelius, a native of Milan and a strong enough supporter of the Romans to be appointed their praetorian prefect in Italy, might have prompted this action. Fidelius was, after all, an ex-quaestor of Athalaric, known to Cassiodorus and the Gothic court, and he may well have retained ties to the authorities of his native city, including perhaps with Bishop Datius.[26] It is possible that Fidelius encouraged his compatriots to shift their allegiance to the Roman cause. Their links to the Goths might have been tenuous, as Milan had an ongoing rivalry with Ravenna for dominance in northern Italy. Although it was one of the great northern cities, and the former capital of the Western Roman Empire, it was not one of the cities favoured by the Goths, such as Pavia or Verona. Whatever the reasons for the Milanese siding with the Romans, their decision brought upon them the severest punishment from the Goths as will be seen below.

3. *Other Italian Cities*

We have few references to the attitude of the remaining strategic cities of Italy towards the two opponents. Some of the strongholds in Umbria, Tuscany and the Marche surrendered (Chiusi, Narni, Spoleto and Perugia

---

[25] Procop. *Goth.* 6.7.35–38.

[26] Cassiod. *Var.* 8.18–19: These letters refer to Fidelius' appointment to the position of quaestor under Athalaric; Martindale *et al.* (1971–1992) *PLRE* II 469–70 (Fidelis), for other references. Fidelius' pro-Roman attitude will also be seen below. The information we have on Datius is meagre. In addition to the evidence in Procopius, he is also mentioned in passing in the *Lib. Pont.* Silverius 5 (trans. Davis (2000) 56): there he recounts, in an otherwise unattested report, that the consequences of the famine in Italy (537) had forced some of his parishioners to eat their own children. Finally, he is the recipient of one of Cassiodorus' letters (Cassiod. *Var.* 12.27), detailing relief measures for the alleviation of this same famine. There is no direct evidence linking Fidelius to Datius, but both were known to the Gothic court and could conceivably have had a personal acquaintance.

in Umbria and Tuscany; Ascoli Piceno and Osimo in the Marche), and the
rest capitulated after sustained military action and sieges by either side. In
each case, their allegiance was usually influenced by military superiority
rather than any fervent support towards either the Romans or Goths. Due
to their strategic military importance, these sites feature prominently in
the attempts to gain dominance, and are traded back and forth between
the warring sides. The sentiments of their populations, hapless victims
in the conflict and the ones most affected by food shortages, were probably disregarded, and it is often the Gothic or Roman garrisons in these
strategic locations which surrender to the other side with no mention of
the stance and fates of their citizens.

4. *Participation of Italians in Roman or Gothic Armies*

Evidence for the commitment of the Italians to one side or the other may
also be derived from examining whether they actually took part in the
fighting or not. We have general references to the population of towns
or cities as a whole. Both sides made use of those populations, according
to need. Thus we find the citizens of Rome and Milan forced to guard
the circuit walls of their respective cities because there were an insufficient number of troops.[27] Even though the citizens of these cities had
surrendered to the Romans, they had not offered to participate in their
cities' defence, but were conscripted into doing so by their new Roman
overlords. The Neapolitans were also obliged to help the Gothic garrison
defend their city since they refused to surrender to Belisarius. Liebeschuetz believes that the Goths replenished their casualties by recruiting amongst the population of Italy, not only during, but even before the
war, while the Romans were unable or unwilling to recruit Italians. I find
this unlikely as there are several references in Procopius which reveal the
inexperience of the civilian population in military training, and instead
point to the disruption and possible negative consequences of their participation in battle.[28]

  These latter examples indicate that civilian recruits were only used to
either fool the Goths into believing there were more Roman forces than
was the case, or as a last resort, where there was a severe lack of defending troops available during sieges. Liebeschuetz also notes these references, but deduces that the Romans were unwilling to give the Italians

---

[27] Procop. *Goth.* 5.15.11–12 (Rome) and 6.12.41 (Milan).
[28] See esp. Procop. *Goth.* 5.29.25 and 6.3.23–29.

the necessary military training or that the Italians themselves refused to become part of the expeditionary force so as not to abandon their homes. It is hard to see why they would have chosen to follow the Goths, since that would certainly have entailed equal disadvantages and the abandonment of their homes, or why the Romans would not have taken advantage of their availability and trained them when they seemed perfectly capable of coercing them to defend their own cities. As far as I am aware, there is no evidence to support the notion of large numbers of Italian recruits amongst the Gothic army during Theoderic's time or subsequently, and, in Procopius' account, most additions to the Gothic side during the war were deserters from the Roman army or slaves, who had probably seized the opportunity to escape their masters by tagging along behind the Gothic army.[29]

The fact that the citizens were usually coerced into service, rather than undertaking military initiatives, did not render them immune to the consequences. Both sides punished the population as a whole for opposing them, for changing sides and for disloyalty. This happened in Naples, when only Belisarius' intervention prevented the wholesale slaughter of the population,[30] and in Milan, where the Roman soldiers were allowed to depart without problems, but, according to Procopius, the entire male population was killed and the town razed to the ground.[31]

5. The Attitude of Romans and Goths towards the Italians

We should also not assume that the attitudes of the opponents towards the native population remained unchanged during the war. We have to allow that one side or the other introduced a different policy in order to shift the balance in their favour. It is particularly important to examine the Gothic King Totila's policies, because there has been considerable debate regarding his attitude towards the population of Italy. Several scholars believe that at a certain point he proposed a social and economic revolution, and see him as the liberator of slaves and the defender of the peasantry against the landowners.[32] The evidence used in support of this

---

[29] For the latter, Procop. *Goth.* 7.16.4–32. Liebeschuetz (1996) 233.

[30] *Lib. Pont.* Silverius 3 (trans. Davis (2000) 55): where Belisarius is blamed for the slaughter.

[31] Procop. *Goth.* 6.20: Procopius gives a grossly exaggerated figure of 300,000 male inhabitants for Milan.

[32] Amongst others: Stein (1949) 569–71; Jones (1964) 288 onwards; Oudalzova (1971a) and (1971b), respectively. The latter's insistence on viewing Totila as a noble defender of the poor, and her acceptance of Procopius' idealised portrait of him at face value,

view derives primarily from a few references in Procopius, and the provisions of the Pragmatic Sanction of A.D. 554, Justinian's legislative directive for the government of Italy, although mention is also made of a brief statement in the *Liber Pontificalis*, which, referring to Totila's occupation of Rome in 549/50, states:

> The king [after his entry] stayed with the Romans like a father with his children. (*Lib. Pont.* Vigilius).

However, this is a rather romantic reference to what was in reality a strategic decision for Totila. According to Procopius, he was concerned to secure Rome from the imperial forces as he had been refused an alliance by the Franks on the basis of his inability to capture and maintain Rome without letting it fall into the hands of the Romans in 546, a sure indication, to their minds, that he was incapable of ever becoming king of Italy.[33] It is obvious that Totila, thwarted in 547 by Belisarius' ingenious ploy to re-occupy Rome, was reluctant to repeat the same mistake. His actions after re-taking the city indicate that he wished to underline his claim to be the legal king of both Italians and Goths. He re-settled both Goths and the citizens of Rome in the city, recalled the Italian hostage notables, and re-built what he had previously destroyed. These actions, along with his organisation and celebration of games, all point to his desire to appear and to act as the benevolent ruler, interested in returning Rome to its former prestige and position as the ancient capital of the Roman Empire.[34]

This view of Totila as instigator of social and economic reforms seems far-fetched and can be refuted if one re-examines the relevant references in Procopius and the Pragmatic Sanction, as well as the impressions of Totila's actions contained in other contemporary and later sources, such as the Continuator of Marcellinus and the *Dialogues* of Gregory the Great, which prove to be extremely hostile to him.[35] The Pragmatic Sanction of

---

unfortunately, distort some of her observations on the military events of the war, based as they are on a misleading supposition that the population of Italy was fervently in support of Totila and the Goths. Her perspective is, of course, influenced by the Marxist view of history as a socio-economic phenomenon, as she was one of the most prominent Soviet-Marxist historians of the second part of the 20th c. For the particular Soviet approach to medieval history, see Kahzdan (1982) 1–19.

[33] Procop. *Goth.* 7.36.29–37.1–4.

[34] *Lib. Pont.* Vigilius 1.7 (trans. Davis (2000) 60).

[35] Moorhead (2000) 382–86 for the full re-examination of Totila's role, successful to my mind; Marcell. com. 542.2; 543.1; 544.1; 545.1, 4; 546.2; 547.5; 548.1–2 and Greg. *Dial.* (trans. Zimmerman (1959)), esp. Books 2.14–15 and 3.12–13, where the adjectives used to describe Totila are very harsh.

August 13, 554 re-extended the laws of the Eastern Roman Empire to Italy, and, in particular, made a point of reversing every financial and administrative decision enacted by Totila, although it maintains the legality of the regulations of the previous Gothic kings.[36]

Totila adopted different approaches towards civilians depending on the circumstances. Thus, to take but a few examples, the citizens of Naples agreed to surrender to him and in return were treated with remarkable kindness.[37] Procopius devotes a whole chapter to narrate the details of how Totila tenderly led the inhabitants, who were exhausted by famine and the hardships of the siege, back to health. He also punished one of his own men who had raped a native girl. In stark contrast to this gentlemanly performance was the capture of the city of Tibur,[38] which was razed to the ground and all of its inhabitants killed, along with the priest of the city. Procopius refuses to narrate this capture in detail so that he may 'not leave records of inhuman cruelty to future times'. Similarly, the cities of Spoleto and Rome and those of the island of Sicily suffered destruction and devastation to varying degrees.[39] Rome escaped complete destruction thanks to a letter from Belisarius,[40] but was left uninhabited by Totila.[41] Sicily meanwhile was plundered throughout by Totila and the Goths.[42]

In general, Totila seems to have behaved towards the civilian population in the very same manner he displayed in his treatment of Rome's senators, which we shall see below. Despite Procopius' calculated reasons to present Totila in a mostly positive light, it is undeniable that the Gothic king was quite ruthless and intolerant when angered by the resistance of the citizens, and by their refusals to comply with his demands. Naples and Rome only highlight the fact that he was prepared to be considerate when he achieved his purpose without undue effort, or when he had some other goal in mind, as in the case of Rome in 549/50.

---

[36] *Sanctio pragmatica pro petitione Vigilii* 2 (commonly known as the Pragmatic Sanction or Constitution), see Appendix VII of *Nov. Iust.*: Totila is referred to as a 'tyrant' and his reign as 'tyranny.'

[37] Procop. *Goth.* 7.8.

[38] Procop. *Goth.* 7.10.22–23.

[39] Procop. *Goth.* 7.23 (Spoleto's walls destroyed), 7.22.7 and 7.24.3 (walls of Rome partially destroyed).

[40] Procop. *Goth.* 7.22.8–17.

[41] Procop. *Goth.* 7.22.19.

[42] Procop. *Goth.* 7.39.4–40.19.

6. *Italians as Ambassadors*

Another way of gauging attitudes is to examine episodes when Italians are used as ambassadors in the various phases of the war.[43] These episodes feature citizens, especially priests, being used as envoys by the Goths and once by the Romans (e.g. two priests sent as envoys by the Goths to the Persian King Chosroes in 539, to encourage him to attack the Romans;[44] Pelagius, the deacon of Rome, is sent to Justinian along with Theodorus the orator, to beg for peace once Totila has captured Rome during his first occupation of the city in December 546).[45] We are not told whether these envoys were willing or not in the text, but we can surmise that they probably were not presented with an alternative choice; nor in this and other instances can we state if the selection of envoys—or the messages being delivered by such—were 'democratic' ones. The envoys were not always well-received, as the case of one Stephanus sent to Justinian by Totila, reveals. He arrived in Constantinople, but was refused an audience by the emperor.[46] Procopius does not state the reason for the choice of priests as envoys. It was, however, a long-established practice to use clergy (bishops, priests and deacons) as imperial envoys in both East and West prior to the Gothic War, and, as the evidence in the *Lib. Pont.* shows, not only to resolve theological matters.[47] It should be assumed that clergy would command greater respect and authority, especially when sent to emperors such as Justin and Justinian, concerned with resolving the thorny theological issues of the time.

The Case of Rome and the Senators

Thus far, we have an emerging picture of the relationship between the three parties, consisting of a mostly neutral indigenous population in terms of allegiance to either side, while the Romans and, even more evidently, the Goths attempted to make use of the Italians in accordance with their needs, whether by coercion or inducement. This becomes more apparent if we observe the numerous passages referring to Rome. This

---

[43] Procop. *Goth.* 6.7–21; 6.6.3, 7.3.5–6, 21.3–4 and 22.17–20; 7.21.18–19, 30.8 and 37.6–7; these examples are in contrast to the episodes of Naples, Rome and Milan, where the citizens send envoys of their own initiative.

[44] Procop. *Goth.* 6.22.17–20.

[45] Procop. *Goth.* 7.21.13–25.

[46] Procop. *Goth.* 7.37.6.

[47] *Lib. Pont.*: the actions of popes Hormisdas, John, Silverius and Vigilius.

great city, the bygone capital of the Roman Empire, remained the base of the senatorial aristocracy and the elite. Rome changed hands many times during the Gothic War, as each side looked upon its occupation as essential to maintaining their superiority because of the prestige associated with the former heart of the empire. Rome thus merits a closer look, with particular emphasis on the attitudes and allegiance of the senators and nobles. The considerable evidence offered by Procopius will be assembled and examined in detail as this has not been done so by previous scholars, who, when addressing the issue, have instead focused on a more selective presentation of the actions of prominent individual figures, such as Pope Vigilius and Cassiodorus.

After King Wittigis departed for Ravenna with the majority of the Gothic army in 536, leaving behind only a Gothic garrison to guard Rome, the citizens of Rome decided to send an envoy to Belisarius in order to surrender the city. They did this because they were afraid of suffering as the Neapolitans had if they chose to resist, and they were urged to do so by Pope Silverius.[48] They disregarded their promises to Wittigis that they would safeguard the city in his absence without much thought. Here again we have the familiar phenomenon of wanting to avoid trouble. The main concern of the population was to escape the consequences of a violent occupation of the city. The repercussions of an approaching Roman military force and its impact on their lives were more important than any allegiance to imperial or Gothic authority.

The same concern was evident when Pelagius was sent, on behalf of the citizens of Rome, to negotiate with Totila during the siege of Rome by the latter in 546.[49] The citizens, being hard-pressed by the famine, sent the deacon (and later pope) Pelagius to negotiate an armistice of a few days. If no help arrived from the Roman side during that time, they would surrender the city to Totila and the Goths. The petition was unsuccessful, and Totila eventually captured the city by betrayal, but, again, it is important to note that the population was intent on avoiding the hardships of war rather than proclaiming support for the Gothic cause.

---

[48] Procop. *Goth.* 5.14.4–6. *Lib. Pont.* Silverius 6 (trans. Davis (2000) 56–57), mentions Belisarius being received courteously by Silverius, although the same source, further along in the account (7–9), describes the deposition and exile of Silverius by Belisarius on the basis of maliciously contrived reports that the pope was in secret agreement with the Goths to hand over the city and the Roman general to them.

[49] Procop. *Goth.* 7.16.4–32.

The examination of the attitude of Rome's citizens toward the Goths
and Romans and vice versa would be incomplete if we overlooked the
references to members of Rome's Senate and prominent citizens. Procopius provides us with no information on the Senate. Rather, he takes it for
granted that his audience knew of the Senate and its functions.[50] Even
though the Senate, in both parts of the Roman Empire, did not command
the authority of the Early Imperial period, and the senators themselves
were no longer directly involved in governance, the prestige associated
with their title undoubtedly must have helped them influence the urban
population. On the other hand, Procopius' references to the Senate and its
members are revealing in several respects. Not only do they reveal senatorial attitudes, but they also present the policy of the Goths and Romans
towards them and their subsequent reactions to it. They are a testimony
to the continuing importance of the nobility during the war.

At 5.20.19–20 of Procopius' *Wars*, the members of the Senate were
present when the Goths sent envoys to Belisarius. They were accused by
the Goths of treason and remained silent except for Fidelius, who had
been made the praetorian prefect, and who taunted the Gothic envoys.
This same Fidelius was also the envoy sent to Belisarius to invite him to
enter Rome,[51] and he later reappears, accompanying the soldiers sent by
Belisarius to take control of Milan, and in the embassy from Milan upon
their return to the city. According to Procopius, he was a native of Milan
and was murdered by the Goths in 538 outside Ticinum (Pavia) when he
remained behind the main body of the army in a church.[52]

At 5.25.14–15, some of the Senators were banished by Belisarius along
with Pope Silverius. They were reinstated again when the Siege of Rome
ended. Wittigis also interfered vindictively with the Senate, killing most
of its members according to Procopius, with only a few managing to
escape to Ravenna, amongst them Reparatus, the brother of the new
Pope Vigilius. However, Procopius' exaggeration of this slaughter is shown
by later statements, which point to more than a few senatorial members
surviving. At 7.6.4, Totila is shown releasing the Senators' wives, and, later,
at 7.9.7–21, he writes a long letter to the Senate, urging the assembly to
remember their prosperity under Theoderic, and thereby attempting to
gain their allegiance. The Senators were prevented from answering by

---

[50] Jones (1964) 329–33: on the senate.
[51] Procop. *Goth.* 5.14.5.
[52] Procop. *Goth.* 6.12.28–29.

John, the nephew of Vitalian. Although Procopius does not give a reason for John's refusal to allow a reply, we can speculate that John would have been concerned to stop any signs of loyalties shifting back to the Gothic side, especially since the attitude of the nobles could influence the collective stance of the besieged population of Rome by persuading them to throw in their lot with the Goths once more, thereby compromising the defence of the city. No doubt, Totila had this in mind when he did not give up after the first rebuttal, but continued to pester the Senators with numerous short letters, all to no avail, as John ensured they did not answer and removed the remaining Arian priests, who were suspected of conveying these letters to the Senators and people of Rome.

The continuing influence of the Senate is to be seen in a further episode at 7.21.12–17, when Totila berates the assembly for treason in a long speech. When he abandoned Rome, he took the senators as hostages with him,[53] and arranged for them to be held in Campania,[54] from where they were rescued by John and sent to Sicily.[55] Finally, we hear of prominent citizens one final time at 8.34.5–8. Procopius here makes a general reference to the fate of the Senate as he finishes his description of Narses' recapture of Rome in 552 after the defeat and death of Totila at Busta Gallorum. The Goths, being pushed back by the victorious Roman army, were intent on mercilessly persecuting the Italians, while the same treatment was reserved for the Italians by the barbarians of the Roman army, as our author specifically notes. The heaviest toll was extracted from the members of the Senate, who, having been held captive by Totila in Campania, were now returning to Rome as soon as they heard it was again in the hands of imperial troops. The Goths in the area, hearing of this, searched them out and killed them. Totila had also gathered many of the children of the Italian notables throughout Italy—a total of 300 in number according to Procopius—ostensibly to live with him north of the Po River, but, in reality, as additional hostages, presumably to guarantee the neutrality of their parents' behaviour. These children were now discovered and murdered by King Teias in vengeance against the Italians.

Individual members of the Senate and other high elite figures appear to be known to Procopius as specific names, and their circumstances are mentioned on occasion. We must envisage the historian becoming

---

[53] Procop. *Goth.* 7.22.19.
[54] Procop. *Goth.* 7.23.18.
[55] Procop. *Goth.* 7.26.10–14.

acquainted with several of them during his long sojourn in Rome in the first phase of the Gothic War. A few examples can be recounted in order to consider the attitude of the two opponents towards such individuals.[56]

Two senators, Maximus and Orestes,[57] sought refuge in the Church of the Apostles when Totila captured Rome in 546.[58] The first of these, Maximus, was amongst the senators banished by Belisarius under suspicion of treason when Silverius was deposed,[59] but he was later reinstated. He was finally killed by the Goths sometime in 552 during the vengeance killing of any Italian patrician the Goths came across after the Battle of Busta Gallorum.[60] Orestes had in fact been a consul, and was later unable to flee with John during the rescue of the hostage senators held in Campania by Totila.[61]

The senator Vergentinus was fortunate enough to escape death at the hands of the Goths twice, once by going to Liguria, when Wittigis executed those Roman senators he held as hostages in Ravenna,[62] and later by avoiding slaughter in the sack of Milan by the Goths. He managed to reach Constantinople with his followers, travelling through Dalmatia, and informed Justinian of the fate of the city.[63] The Reparatus (praetorian prefect),[64] who was also brother of Pope Vigilius, had eluded Wittigis by leaving for Liguria at the same time as Vergentinus.[65] However, he was much less fortunate since he was cut into pieces and thrown to the dogs by the enraged Gothic army in the atrocity at Milan.[66]

The noble lady Rusticiana,[67] the daughter of Symmachus and widow of Boethius, was reduced to poverty after the vicissitudes of the consecutive sieges of Rome by the Goths. When Totila occupied Rome, she was at risk of being killed by certain Goths, but was protected by Totila himself along with other Roman women.[68] The patrician and leader of the Senate,

---

[56] Barnish (1988) 120–55: for more details on individual aristocratic families in Italy.
[57] Rufius Gennadius Probus Orestes, Martindale *et al.* (1971–92) *PLRE* IIIb, 956.
[58] Procop. *Goth.* 7.20.19.
[59] Procop. *Goth.* 5.25.15.
[60] Procop. *Goth.* 8.34.6.
[61] Procop. *Goth.* 7.26.13.
[62] Procop. *Goth.* 5.26.2.
[63] Procop. *Goth.* 6.21.41.
[64] Martindale *et al.* (1971–92) Reparatus 1, *PLRE* II, 939–40.
[65] Procop. *Goth.* 5.26.2.
[66] Procop. *Goth.* 6.21.40.
[67] Martindale *et al.* (1971–92) Rusticiana 1, *PLRE* II, 961.
[68] Procop. *Goth.* 7.20.27–30.

Cethegus,[69] suspected of treason by the imperial commanders in Rome, was hastily forced to leave the city for Centumcellae.[70]

In addition to the above, we have the rather more detailed story of Spinus,[71] native of Spoleto and personal advisor of Totila, who was captured by the Romans in Sicily. Totila was anxious to have him released, and offered to exchange a notable's wife for him. The Romans, however, refused, as they did not want to trade a woman for a man, especially one who held the position of quaestor. Spinus, becoming fearful of his fate at the hands of the Romans, promised them he would persuade the Goths and Totila to abandon Sicily and return to Italy in exchange for his freedom. The Romans agreed to this, and Spinus somehow convinced the Goths that their best interests lay in crossing over to Italy and preparing for an alleged Roman attack from the north.[72]

Finally, the powerful Italian landowner Tullianus[73] approached the imperial army under John, the nephew of Vitalian, and protested against the treatment of the locals by the Roman army. He did agree, though, to hand over Bruttium and Lucania to the Romans, if they respected the Italians and treated them with consideration forthwith. He maintained that they had not willingly yielded to the Goths—these 'men who were both barbarians and Arians', as Procopius has him say—but had been forced to do so by the dire pressure placed on them by the Goths and the injustice they had suffered at the hands of the Romans. John gave him the promises he required, and, thereafter, these areas were subject to the Romans.[74] Tullianus later gathered together native farmers and organised resistance against Totila, to prevent him from invading Lucania, by guarding the narrow pass into the district, being helped in this by a force of Antae left to him by John. But, when John decided to leave Apulia and go to Dryus, these rustics detached themselves from the Roman army at the request of their masters, who were held hostage by Totila, and returned to work in

---

[69] Martindale *et al.* (1971–92) Fl. Rufius Petronius Nicomachus Cethegus, *PLRE* II, 281–82.

[70] Procop. *Goth.* 7.13.12.

[71] Martindale *et al.* (1971–92) Spinus, *PLRE* IIIb, 1182.

[72] Procop. *Goth.* 7.40.20–21, 24–25 and 26–29.

[73] Martindale *et al.* (1971–1992) *PLRE* IIIb 1344 (Tullianus 1). This Tullianus was the brother of another Italian notable, Deopheron, who was one of the prominent Italians besieged by the Goths in the fortress near Rusciane in 548, and who was later sent as one of the envoys to Totila to negotiate their safety and pardon for their resistance against the Goths (Procop. *Goth.* 7.30.2 and 19).

[74] Procop. *Goth.* 7.18.20–22.

the fields. Therefore, Tullianus fled from the area and is not mentioned again in Procopius' *Wars*.[75]

From all of the above, we can deduce that each side was anxious to secure the support of the senators because of their social power and the prestige and influence which their position conveyed. This effort was made regardless of the fact that the warring sides quite obviously controlled all military and other resources in comparison to the defenceless aristocracy. According to the circumstances in each instance, these leading nobles were used as pawns by the two opponents in the wider context of the war. Their support was more essential for the outward preservation of appearances than for any real influence the senators would have on military events. They were, however, still the aristocracy of Rome, with nominal authority and voice, and, as such, were perceived as important to both Goths and Romans, who wished to preserve continuity with the political structures of the past.

We are not given enough information to decide the senators' own prevailing allegiance. Most of them would probably have been motivated by the same concerns as the rest of the Italians, i.e. to safeguard their lives, properties, lands and fortunes. With the exceptions of Fidelius and Tullianus, both of whom blatantly display anti-Gothic sentiments, the latter, (as previously mentioned), going so far as to organise direct action against Totila, the remaining cases indicate that the majority of senators were understandably concerned to remain on the winning side. They were very rarely given a free choice of allegiance and were usually held captive by whichever side held the upper hand at any given moment.

It is difficult to speculate as to whether there was a developing change in attitude on the senators' part over the course of the war, i.e. from support of their Ostrogothic overlords to imperial sympathy. A letter from the Senate addressed to Justinian around 535, at a time of growing tension between the two sides, is preserved in the *Variae* of Cassiodorus.[76] In this, the Senate entreated the emperor to maintain the peace towards the Goths. The letter is full of Cassiodorus' flowery praise and flattery towards the Goths and their benevolent rule of the Italians. Even if not the product of outright threat, as Bury has suggested,[77] the letter is highly unlikely to have been a genuine expression of the Senate's sentiments.

---

[75] Procop. *Goth.* 7.22.2, 4–6 and 21.
[76] Cassiod. *Var.* 11.13.
[77] Bury (1923) 168.

Other letters in the *Variae* indicate that, in writing at least, the Ostrogothic State, such as it was during the war, maintained the outward impression of caring for the well-being of the Italians.[78]

All the evidence in Procopius, however, points to the often brutal mistreatment of senators and notables by the Goths, who were often held hostage, and many of whom were executed, sometimes out of sheer vengeance. In contrast, the Romans, although by no means innocent from exploiting the senators' position and using them to further their own means, certainly treated them better than the Goths, and were more concerned with respecting their wishes and ensuring their safety, as is evident from the efforts made to rescue them from imprisonment by John. Even in the cases of suspected traitors, such as Cethegus and Maximus, the penalty of exile imposed by the Romans was considerably less harsh than the summary executions inflicted by the Goths.

Totila's occasional sympathetic overtures were not enough to correct this impression, especially since they were often temporary and belied by subsequent acts of brutal retaliation. The Goths believed that they had treated the Italians and the Italian aristocracy, in particular, benevolently. Consequently, they viewed the senators' neutrality or tolerance of the Romans as lack of support and betrayal of their own cause, and became enraged at their ingratitude. The Romans, on the other hand, were, undoubtedly, more astute in maintaining warmer relations with the nobility of Italy. Whatever the real reasons for this difference in treatment, the result was that the senators might have been prompted by the Goths' hostility to decide that their better interests, or at least their physical safety, as often as not, lay with the Roman side, while the court in Constantinople provided a haven for those fortunate enough to escape Gothic revenge from 540 onwards. Even so, we certainly do not have any outright expressions of support for Roman imperial authority in the narrative of Procopius, apart from the reference at 7.35.9–11, in which the notables of Italy and Pope Vigilius pressure Justinian to prevail in Italy.

Finally, we may compare the evidence given by Procopius with his own explicit observations of the relationship between the three sides. Procopius, on occasion, directly expresses the attitude of the Italians and the

---

[78] E.g. Cassiod. *Var.* 12.5, redressing the results of the raids in Lucania and Bruttium by the Gothic army; 12.26, remitting supplies which had been ordered for the Gothic army from the area of the Veneti, and detailing plans for the relief of the scarcity of resources there; 12.27, in similar vein, for the provision of the distribution of corn to the famished population of Liguria.

treatment they received. Thus, in Books 5 and 6, he presents two instances where the people of Rome complain vehemently to Belisarius because they are suffering from the famine and hardships of the siege.[79] At 7.4.16, the Italians are said to repent of betraying the Goths, and at 7.6.7, they appear unruly and dejected—small wonder as they had been enduring six years of warfare and hardships.

This bleak picture is further reinforced and explained by 7.1.32 and 7.9.2–5, namely the oppression of the Italians by Alexander the Logothete, and the portrayal of the Roman army as lawless wastrels who inflicted suffering on the Italian population. Naturally, this is influenced by the darkened tone which Procopius adopts from Book 7 onwards, following the recall of Belisarius to Constantinople, and his evident disappointment at the shabby treatment the general received from the emperor. It is, however, at 8.34.1–5 where he makes his concluding remark on the treatment of the Italian population:

> Both sides treated them badly; the Goths because they were losing the dominion of Italy and therefore destroyed them without mercy, and the Roman army because its barbarian (sic) contingent treated everyone whom they chanced to fall upon as enemies. (Procop. *Goth.* 8.34.3–5).

It would be hard not to agree with this last statement. From what we have seen above, this would be the most accurate summary of the emerging picture of the relations between Italians, Goths and Romans. Procopius presents a population caught between two warring powers, each concerned with military operations and predominance. Under such conditions, the civilians sided with whoever would provide them with protection, some economic stability and relative peace. The Italians were, of course, subject to contradictory ideological influences, but the evidence points to their stance being one of neutrality and avoidance of involvement in so far as that was possible. It would seem that they were no more than pawns in this war, their particular interests interpreted according to each side's needs and purposes as is always the case with political and military authorities.

---

[79] Procop. *Goth.* 5.20.5–7 and 6.3.8–32.

BIBLIOGRAPHY

Primary Sources

Cassiod. *Var.* = Mommsen T. (1894) ed. *MGH AA* XII (Berlin 1894); Hodgkin T. (1886) trans. *The Letters of Cassiodorus* (London 1886); Barnish S. J. B. (1992) trans. *The Variae of Magnus Aurelius Cassiodorus Senator, the right honourable and illustrious ex-quaestor of the palace, ex-ordinary consul, ex-master of the offices, praetorian prefect and patrician: being documents of the Kingdom of the Ostrogoths in Italy chosen to illustrate the life of the author and the history of his family* (Translated Texts for Historians 12) (Liverpool 1992).

Cod. Iust. and *Nov. Iust.* = Schöll R. and Kroll W. (1982–95) edd. *Corpus Juris Civilis* III: *Novellae* (Berlin 1892–1895, repr. 1945–1963); Mommsen T., Krueger P. and Watson A. (1985) edd. and trans. *The Digest of Justinian*, vols. 1–4 (Philadelphia 1985); Scott S. P. (1932) trans. *The Civil Law Including the Twelve Tables* (Cincinnati 1932).

Greg. *Dial.* = de Vogüé A. (1978–80) ed. and trans. *Grégoire le Grand, Dialogues*, vols. 1–3 (Paris 1978–80); Zimmerman O. J. (1959) trans. St Gregory the Great, *Dialogues* (Washington, D.C. 1959).

Jord. *Get.* = Mommsen T. (1882) ed. *De origine actibusque Getarum* (Berlin 1882); Mierow C. C. (1960) trans. *The Gothic History of Jordanes* (New York 1960).

Jord. *Rom.* = Mommsen T. (1961) ed. *De summa temporum vel origine actibusque gentis Romanorum MGH AA* V (1) (Berlin 1961).

Lib. Pont. = Duchesne L. and Vogel C. (1886–1957) edd. *Le Liber Pontificalis*, vols. 1–3 (Paris 1886–1957); Davis R. (2000) trans. Liber Pontificalis. *The Book of Pontiffs: The Ancient Biographies of the First Ninety Roman Bishops to AD 715* (2nd ed., Liverpool 2000).

Malalas = Thurn I. (2000) ed. *Ionnis Malalae Chronographia* (Berlin 2000); Jeffreys E., Jeffreys M. and Scott R. (1986) trans. *The Chronicle of John Malalas* (Byzantina Australiensia 4) (Melbourne and Sydney 1986).

Marcell. com. = Mommsen T. (1894) ed. *Chronica Minora saec. IV–VII/2, MGH AA IX*, 2 (Berlin 1894); Croke B. (1995) ed. and trans. *The Chronicle of Marcellinus: a Translation and Commentary with a Reproduction of Mommsen's Edition of the Text* (Sydney 1995).

Procop. *Goth.*, Procop. *Vand.*, Procop. *Pers.*, Procop. *Anec.* and Procop. *Aed.* = Dewing H. B. (1914–54) ed. and trans. Procopius, *History of the Wars, The Secret History, The Buildings*, volumes 1–7 (Cambridge, Mass. and London 1914–54); Haury J. (1962–64) ed. rev. G. Wirth, Procopius of Ceasarea, *Opera Omnia* (Leipzig 1962–64).

Secondary Works

Arcamone M. G. (1984) ed. *Magistra Barbaritas: i Barbari in Italia* (Milan 1984).

Archi G. G. (1978) "Pragmatica Sanctio pro petitione Vigili" in *Festschrift für Franz Wieacker zum 70. Geburtstag*, edd. F. Wieacker and O. Behrends (Göttingen 1978) 11–36.

Arthur P. R. (2002) *Naples: from Roman Town to City State: an Archaeological Perspective* (London 2002).

Ashby T. (1935) *The Aqueducts of Ancient Rome* (Oxford 1935).

Augenti A. and Conconi M. (2000) edd. *Art and Archaeology of Rome: from Ancient Times to the Baroque* (Firenze and New York 2000).

Barnish S. J. B. (1988) "Transformation and survival of the western senatorial aristocracy, c. AD 400–700", *PBSR* 56 (1988) 120–55.

Barnwell P. S. (1992) *Emperors, Prefects and Kings: the Roman West, 395–565* (London 1992).

Bierbrauer V. (1975) *Die Ostgotischen Grab- und Schatzfunde in Italien* (Spoleto 1975).

Bowden W. and Hodges R. (1998) edd. *The Sixth Century: Production, Distribution and Demand* (Transformation of the Roman World 3) (Leiden 1998).

Brogiolo G. P. (1993) *Brescia Altomedievale: urbanistica ed edilizia dal IV al IX secolo* (Mantova 1993).

—— (1999) "Ideas of the town in Italy during the transition from antiquity to the Middle Ages" in *The Idea and Ideal of the Town between Late Antiquity and the Early Middle Ages*, edd. G. P. Brogiolo and B. Ward-Perkins (Transformation of the Roman World 4) (Leiden 1999) 99–126.

Brogiolo G. P. and Gelichi S. (1998) *La città nell' alto medioevo italiano: archeologia e storia* (Rome and Bari 1998).

Brogiolo G. P. and Ward-Perkins B. (1999) edd. *The Idea and Ideal of the Town between Late Antiquity and the Early Middle Ages* (Transformation of the Roman World 4) (Leiden 1999).

Brogiolo G. P., Gauthier N. and Christie N. (2000) edd. *Towns and their Territories between Late Antiquity and the Early Middle Ages* (Transformation of the Roman World 9) (Leiden 2000).

Brown T. S. (1984) *Gentlemen and Officers: Imperial Administration and Aristocratic Power in Byzantine Italy, AD 554–800* (London 1984).

—— (1993) "Everyday life in Ravenna under Theoderic: an example of his tolerance and prosperity?" in *Teoderico il grande e i Goti d'Italia: Atti del XIII congresso internazionale di studi sull'Alto Medioevo, Milano, 2–6 novembre 1992* (Spoleto 1993) 77–99.

Burns T. S. (1980) *The Ostrogoths: Kingship and Society* (Wiesbaden 1980).

——(1984) *A History of the Ostrogoths* (Indiana 1984).

——(1994) *Barbarians within the Gates of Rome* (Indiana 1994).

Bury J. B. (1923) *History of the Later Roman Empire from the Death of Theodosius to the Death of Justinian (395–565 AD)*, 2 vols. (London 1923).

Cameron A. M. (1985) *Procopius and the Sixth Century* (London 1985).

Christie N. (1989) "The archaeology of Byzantine Italy: a synthesis of recent research" *JMA* 2 (1989) 249–93.

——(1995) *The Lombards* (Oxford 1995).

—— (2004) ed. *Landscapes of Change: Rural Evolution in Late Antiquity and the Early Middle ages* (Aldershot 2004).

——(2006) *From Constantine to Charlemagne: an Archaeology of Italy, AD 300–800* (Aldershot 2006).

Christie N. and Gibson S. (1988) "The city walls of Ravenna", *PBSR* 56 (1988) 156–97.

Christie N. and Loseby S. T. (1996) edd. *Towns in Transition: Urban Evolution in Late Antiquity and the Early Middle Ages* (Aldershot 1996).

Chrysos E. K. (1997) "Conclusion: '*De foederatis iterum*'", in *Kingdoms of the Empire: the Integration of Barbarians in Late Antiquity*, ed. W. Pohl (Transformation of the Roman World 1) (Leiden 1997) 185–206.

—— (2003) "The empire, the *gentes* and the *regna*", in *Regna and Gentes: the Relationship between Late Antique and Early Medieval Peoples and Kingdoms in the Transformation of the Roman World*, edd. H.-W. Goetz, J. Jarnut and W. Pohl (Transformation of the Roman World 13) (Leiden 2003) 13–19.

Chrysos E. K. and Wood I. N. (1999) edd. *East and West: Modes of Communication: Proceedings of the First Plenary Conference at Merida* (Transformation of the Roman World 5) (Leiden 1999).

Coates-Stevens R. (1998) "The walls and aqueducts of Rome in the Early Middle Ages, AD 500–1000", *JRS* 88 (1998) 166–78.

Francovich R. and Noyé G. (1992) edd. *La storia dell'Alto Medioevo italiano (VI–X secolo) alla luce dell'archeologia* (Florence 1992).

Heather P. J. (1989) "Cassiodorus and the rise of the Amals: genealogy and the Goths under Hun domination" *JRS* 79 (1989) 103–28.

——(1991) *Goths and Romans: 332–489* (Oxford 1991).

—— (1993) "The historical culture of Ostrogothic Italy", in *Teoderico il grande e i Goti d'Italia: Atti del XIII congresso internazionale di studi sull'Alto Medioevo, Milano, 2–6 novembre 1992* (Spoleto 1993) 317–53.

—— (1995) "Theoderic, king of the Goths", *Early Medieval Europe* 4.2 (1995) 145–73.

—— (1996) *The Goths* (Oxford 1996).

——(1997) "Foedera and Foederati of the fourth century", in *Kingdoms of the Empire: the Integration of Barbarians in Late Antiquity*, ed. W. Pohl (Transformation of the Roman World 1) (Leiden 1997) 57–74.

——(1998) "Disappearing and reappearing tribes", in *Strategies of Distinction: the Construction of Ethnic Communities, 300–800*, edd. W. Pohl and H. Reimitz (Transformation of the Roman World 2) (Leiden 1998) 95–111.

—— (1999) "The barbarian in Late Antiquity", in *Constructing Identities in Late Antiquity*, ed. R. Miles (London 1999) 234–58.

—— (2001) "The Late Roman art of client management: imperial defence in the fourth century west', in *The Transformation of Frontiers from Late Antiquity to the Carolingians*, edd. W. Pohl, I. Wood and H. Reimitz (Transformation of the Roman World 10) (Leiden 2001) 15–68.

—— (2003) "*Gens* and *Regnum* among the Ostrogoths", in *Regna and Gentes: the Relationship between Late Antique and Early Medieval Peoples and Kingdoms in the Transformation of the Roman World*, edd. H.-W. Goetz, J. Jarnut and W. Pohl (Transformation of the Roman World 13) (Leiden 2003) 85–133.

Hedeager L. (2000) "Migration period Europe: the formation of a political mentality", in *Rituals of Power: from Late Antiquity to the Early Middle Ages*, edd. F. Theuws and J. L. Nelson (Transformation of the Roman World 8) (Leiden 2000) 15–57.

Hendy M. F. (1998) "From public to private: the western barbarian coinages as a mirror of the disintegration of Late Roman structures", *Viator* 19 (1988) 29–78.

Hodges R. and Francovich R. (2003) *Villa to Village: the Transformation of the Roman Countryside in Italy, c. 400–1000* (London 2003).

Johnson S. (1983) *Late Roman Fortifications* (London 1983).

Jones A. H. M. (1964) *The Later Roman Empire, 284–602: a Social and Economic Survey*, 3 vols. (Oxford 1964).

Kahzdan A. (1982) "Soviet studies on medieval western Europe: a brief survey", *Speculum* 57.1 (1982) 1–19.

Kouroumali M. (2005) *Procopius and the Gothic War* (D.Phil. diss., Univ. of Oxford 2005).

Krautheimer R. (1980) *Rome: Profile of a City, 312–1308* (Princeton 1980).

—— (1982) *Three Christian Capitals: Topography and Politics* (London 1982).

La Rocca C. (2002) ed. *Italy in the Early Middle Ages, 476–1000* (Oxford 2002).

Laurence R. (1999) *The Roads of Roman Italy: Mobility and Cultural Change* (London 1999).

Liebeschuetz J. H. W. G. (1992) "The end of the ancient city", in *The City in Late Antiquity*, ed. J. Rich (London 1992) 1–49.

—— (1996) "The Romans demilitarised: the evidence of Procopius", *Scripta Classica Israelica* 15 (1996) 230–39.

—— (1997) "Cities, taxes and the accommodation of the barbarians: the theories of Durliat and Goffart", in *Kingdoms of the Empire: the Integration of Barbarians in Late Antiquity*, ed. W. Pohl (Transformation of the Roman World 1) (Leiden 1997) 135–51.

—— (1998) "Citizen states and law in the Roman Empire and the Visigothic Kingdom", in *Strategies of Distinction: the Construction of Ethnic Communities, 300–800*, edd. W. Pohl and H. Reimitz (Transformation of the Roman World 2) (Leiden 1998) 131–52.

—— (2001) *The Decline and Fall of the Roman City* (Oxford 2001).

Marazzi F. (1998) "The destinies of late antique Italies", in *The Sixth Century: Production, Distribution and Demand*, edd. R. Hodges and W. Bowden (Transformation of the Roman World 3) (Leiden 1998) 119–59.

Markus R. (1998) Review of Amory, *People and Identity in Ostrogothic Italy 489–554* in *JThS* 49 (1998) 414–17.

Martindale J. R., Jones A. H. M. and Morris J. (1971–1992) edd. *The Prosopography of the Later Roman Empire I–III a–b, AD 395–527* (Cambridge 1971–1992).

Moorhead J. (1978) "Boethius and Romans in Ostrogothic service", *Historia* 27 (1978) 604–12.

—— (1983) "Italian loyalties during Justinian's Gothic War", *Byzantion* 53 (1983) 575–96.

—— (1987) "*Libertas* and *Nomen Romanum* in Ostrogothic Italy", *Latomus* 46 (1987) 161–68.

—— (1992) *Theoderic in Italy* (Oxford 1992).

—— (1994) *Justinian* (London 1994).

—— (2000) "Totila the revolutionary", *Historia* 49 (2000) 382–86.

—— (2001) *The Roman Empire Divided, 400–700* (London 2001).

Noble T. F. X. (1993) "Theoderic and the Papacy", in *Teoderico il grande e i Goti d' Italia: Atti del XIII congresso internazionale di studi sull'Alto Medioevo, Milano, 2–6 novembre 1992* (Spoleto 1993) 395–423.

Oudalzova Z. V. (1971a) "L' Italie et Byzance au VI siècle", *Corso cultura sull'arte ravennate e bizantina* 18 (1971) 547–55.

—— (1971b) "La campagne de Narses et l'écrasement de Totila", *Corso di cultura sull'arte ravennate e bizantina* 18 (1971) 557–64.

Pohl W. (1997) ed. *Kingdoms of the Empire: the Integration of Barbarians in Late Antiquity* (Transformation of the Roman World 1) (Leiden 1997).

—— (1997) "Introduction: the empire and the integration of barbarians", in *Kingdoms of the Empire: the Integration of Barbarians in Late Antiquity*, ed. W. Pohl (Transformation of the Roman World 1) (Leiden 1997) 1–11.

—— (1998a) "Introduction: strategies of distinction", in *Strategies of Distinction: the Construction of Ethnic Communities, 300–800*, edd. W. Pohl and H. Reimitz (Transformation of the Roman World 2) (Leiden 1998) 1–15.

—— (1998b) "Telling the difference: signs of ethnic identity", in *Strategies of Distinction: the Construction of Ethnic Communities, 300–800*, edd. W. Pohl and H. Reimitz (Transformation of the Roman World 2) (Leiden 1998) 17–69.

—— (1999) "Social language, identities, control of discourse", in *East and West: Modes of Communication, Proceedings of the First Plenary Conference at Merida*, edd. E. Chrysos and I. Wood (Transformation of the Roman World 5) (Leiden 1999) 127–41.

—— (2001) "The transformation of frontiers", in *The Transformation of Frontiers from Late Antiquity to the Carolingians*, edd. W. Pohl, I. Wood and H. Reimitz (Transformation of the Roman World 10) (Leiden 2001) 247–60.

—— (2002) "Invasions and ethnic identity", in *Italy in the early Middle Ages, 476–1000*, ed. C. La Rocca (Oxford 2002) 11–33.

Pohl W. and Reimitz H. (1998) edd. *Strategies of Distinction: the Construction of Ethnic Communities, 300–800* (Transformation of the Roman World 2) (Leiden 1998).

Pohl W., Wood I. and Reimitz H. (2001) edd. *The Transformation of Frontiers from Late Antiquity to the Carolingians* (Transformation of the Roman World 10) (Leiden 2001).

Rich J. (1992) ed. *The City in Late Antiquity* (London 1992).

Schäfer C. (1991) *Der weströmische Senat als Träger antiker Kontinuität unter den Ostgotenkönigen, 490–540 n. Chr.* (St. Katharinen 1991).

Schwarcz A. (1997) "Die Liguria zwischen Goten, Byzantinen, Langobarden und Franken im 6. Jahrhundert", in *Oriente e Occidente tra Medioevo ed età moderna, Studi in onore di G. Pistarino*, ed. L. Balleto (Genoa 1997) 1109–31.

Settia A. A. (2000) "Le fortificazioni dei Goti in Italia", in *Teoderico il grande e i Goti d' Italia: Atti del XIII congresso internazionale di studi sull'Alto Medioevo, Milano, 2–6 novembre 1992* (Spoleto 1993) 101–31.

Stein E. (1949) *Histoire du Bas-Empire II: de la disparition de l' Empire d' Occident à la mort de Justinian (476–565)* ed. J.-R. Palanque (Paris 1949).

Theuws F. and Nelson J. L. (2000) edd. *Rituals of Power: from Late Antiquity to the Early Middle Ages* (Transformation of the Roman World 8) (Leiden 2000).

Thompson E. A. (1982) *Romans and Barbarians: the Decline of the Western Empire* (Madison, WI 1982).

Wallace-Hadrill J. M. (1967) *The Barbarian West, 400–1000* (London 1967).

Ward-Perkins B. (1984) *From Classical Antiquity to the Middle Ages: Urban Public Building in Northern and Central Italy, AD 300–850* (Oxford 1984).

—— (1996) "Urban continuity?", in *Towns in Transition: Urban Evolution in Late Antiquity and the Early Middle Ages*, edd. N. Christie and S. T. Loseby (London 1996) 4–17.

Wilson A. I. (2000) "The water-mills on the Janiculum", *MAAR* 45 (2000) 219–46.

Wolfram H. (1987) *History of the Goths* (Berkeley 1987).

—— (1994) "Origo et religio", *Early Medieval Europe* 3 (1994) 19–38.

—— (1997) *The Roman Empire and its Germanic Peoples* (Berkeley 1997).

Wood I. (1998a) "Conclusion: strategies of distinction", in *Strategies of Distinction: the Construction of Ethnic Communities, 300–800*, edd. W. Pohl and H. Reimitz (Transformation of the Roman World 2) (Leiden 1998) 297–303.

—— (1998b) "The frontiers of western Europe: developments east of the Rhine in the 6th century", in *The Sixth Century: Production, Distribution and Demand*, edd. R. Hodges and W. Bowden (Leiden 1998) 231–53.

—— (2001) "Drawing frontiers", in *The Transformation of Frontiers from Late Antiquity to the Carolingians*, edd. W. Pohl, I. Wood and H. Reimitz (Transformation of the Roman World 10) (Leiden 2001) 1–4.

Wormald P. (2003) "The *Leges Barbarorum*: law and ethnicity in the post-Roman West", in *Regna and Gentes: the Relationship between Late Antique and Early Medieval Peoples and Kingdoms in the Transformation of the Roman World*, edd. H.-W. Goetz, J. Jarnut and W. Pohl (Transformation of the Roman World 13) (Leiden 2003) 21–53.

ABSTRACTS IN FRENCH

Sarantis

Cet article cherche à identifier les facteurs décisifs dans le déroulement et l'issue des guerres durant l'Antiquité tardive. Bon nombre de ces facteurs sont également valables pour les guerres ayant eu lieu à d'autres époques, mais, selon l'auteur de cet article, c'est dans l'importance des travaux de fortification menés par des empereurs successifs que réside la caractéristique distinctive des guerres de l'Antiquité tardive. Ces cités fortifiées, ces forts, ces tours de garde et ces murailles n'étaient pas simplement des structures purement défensives, mais ils servaient pour les Romains de bases pour des campagnes offensives à l'intérieur de l'empire et au-delà de ses frontières. Ces défenses permirent aux Romains de contrôler le renseignement, l'approvisionnement, la main-d'œuvre, mais aussi les esprits et les cœurs au sein des zones de campagnes militaires.

Haldon

Cet article examine les relations qui existent entre les informations concernant le paysage et la géographie de l'Anatolie entre le 7ème et le 11ème siècles après Jésus-Christ. Il s'intéresse également aux dispositifs stratégiques concrets mis en place par le gouvernement de l'empire d'Orient pour faire face à ses ennemis ainsi qu'aux voies de communications reliant les régions frontalières et opérationnelles avec leur arrière-pays, source d'approvisionnements et réserve de troupes. Cet article démontre qu'il existe une relation entre les structures physiques par lesquelles les informations étaient collectées et le type d'informations diffusées et il conclut que les dispositifs défensifs byzantins pouvaient être à la fois sophistiqués et efficaces.

Crow

Les fortifications sont des structures majeures du monde de l'Antiquité tardive encore visibles. Cet article détaille le vaste éventail des structures défensives construites à travers l'empire romain d'Orient. Il commence par

A. Sarantis, N. Christie (edd.) *War and Warfare in Late Antiquity: Current Perspectives* (Late Antique Archaeology 8.1–8.2 – 2010–11) (Leiden 2013), pp. 1001–1008

une étude de cas portant sur les murailles d'Antioche, à partir de gravures de la fin du 18ème siècle, et révèle l'ampleur d'un projet impérial majeur du 5ème siècle en grande partie perdu de nos jours. L'article examine ensuite les données concernant l'Asie mineure, où les signes de l'édification de nouvelles défenses sont plus limités. Les grandes cités fortifiées de la frontière orientale sont bien connues, mais l'article attire notre attention sur les hameaux fortifiés situés dans les régions frontalières, en Mésopotamie romaine et dans les Balkans. Dans cette dernière région, on rencontre une solution plus élaborée aux problèmes de sécurité à travers la construction d'un certain nombre de murailles internes, comme le Mur d'Anastase en Thrace et la muraille de 'Portes Haemus' récemment découverte. La conclusion de cet article évalue le rôle des fortifications dans le monde de l'Antiquité tardive et souligne l'importance d'envisager des interprétations multiples à travers les frontières de l'Empire romain d'Orient, qui prennent en considération à la fois les sources archéologiques et les données textuelles.

Whitby

Bien qu'il existe de nombreux vestiges de murailles et d'autres structures défensives de l'Antiquité tardive, il se trouve qu'ils ne donnent que peu d'informations sur la manière dont les sièges se déroulaient; nos connaissances des opérations de siège dans l'Antiquité tardive proviennent de sources littéraires qui, pour différentes raisons, sont des puits d'information. Les tactiques et les techniques étaient en substance identiques à celles des époques romaine et hellénistique précédentes, ce qui justifie une étude comparative. Le principal point de débat est le passage de l'artillerie utilisant la propulsion par torsion à celle qui emploie la traction.

Coulston

Cet article explore les composantes culturelles de l'équipement militaire de l'Antiquité tardive romaine à travers l'examen de catégories spécifiques: les ceintures, les casques, les boucliers et les armes. Des éléments hellénistiques, romains, mésopotamiens-iraniens, de l'Europe de l'Age de fer et de l'Asie centrale nomadique jouèrent tous un rôle dans son élaboration. L'article conclut que toute l'histoire de l'équipement militaire romain est celle d'une intégration culturelle et, en particulier, que le développement de l'équipement tardo-antique n'était pas une nouvelle forme de dégénérescence ou de « barbarisation », mais une acculturation positive.

KAZANSKI

L'équipement militaire et, partant, les types de combat, connurent des changements significatifs entre le 3ème et le 6ème siècles après Jésus-Christ. Les armes des peuples germaniques et de leurs voisins devinrent plus adaptées à des manœuvres rapides et rapprochées au sein de rangs dispersés. La propagation des armes germaniques au sein du territoire romain et dans la région du Pont indique que les troupes barbares de l'armée romaine et les fédérés employaient les mêmes tactiques. Une évolution similaire eut lieu dans les armées des peuplades des steppes, y compris celles qui combattaient pour l'empire. La cavalerie en armure du Haut-Empire fut tout d'abord remplacée par une cavalerie alanique plus légère puis par des archers montés huns. Enfin, l'infanterie légère slave, utilisant des tactiques de guérilla, vainquit les armées de l'empire romain d'Orient et conquit la péninsule des Balkans.

CONYARD

Cet article tente de donner un aperçu de la contribution que peut apporter la recherche touchant à la reconstitution de l'armée romaine et à la compréhension de l'équipement militaire romain de l'Antiquité tardive. Cet article ne peut offrir qu'une brève introduction à certains éléments de cet équipement; le livre de Bishop et Coulston *Roman Military Equipment*, publié en 1993 (2ème édition publiée en 2006), reste l'ouvrage de référence. L'objectif principal de l'article est d'examiner la manière dont certaines pièces de l'équipement militaire étaient fabriquées et, surtout, la façon dont elles étaient utilisées.

COLVIN

Cet article établit que les sources des récits de Procope et d'Agathias sur la guerre lazique menée par Justinien entre 548 et 557 sont des documents spécifiques et archivés. L'utilisation de ces documents par ces auteurs explique certaines caractéristiques frappantes de leurs comptes-rendus des batailles et des campagnes non seulement en Lazique, mais aussi dans d'autres parties de leurs histoires. L'auteur en conclut que l'opinion généralement partagée par les spécialistes, selon laquelle Procope et Agathias, ainsi que d'autres historiens classicisants, dépendaient largement de sources orales et, dans le cas de Procope, de résultats d'autopsies, devrait être rééxaminée.

LILLINGTON-MARTIN

Cet article se penche sur les descriptions par Procope des stratégies développées par les Romains et les Perses pour contrôler Dara en 530 et de celles des Romains et des Goths pour contrôler Rome en 537–38. Pour cela, il réconcilie les textes avec les paysages des zones concernées, en tirant parti de l'imagerie satellite, la cartographie et de visites des sites. L'approche traditionnelle a été de ne s'appuyer que sur les sources textuelles, mais celles-ci, comme on le verra, se prêtent à de multiples interprétations. L'étude du paysage permet d'obtenir une perspective différente et complémentaire, qui est parfois plus fiable, dans la mesure où les caractéristiques physiques du paysage n'ont pas tellement changé au cours des siècles et que les nouvelles technologies ont créé de nouvelles manières de les lire. Ces deux études de cas suggèrent fortement que Procope est fiable quand il est interprété avec soin, ce qui a des répercussions pour l'étude des nombreux autres événements pour la connaissance desquels il est la source principale.

BELCHER

Cet article se penche sur la reddition de Nisibe au roi perse Shapur II en 363. Cet événement est présenté par un témoin oculaire, Ammien Marcellin, comme un moment crucial dans l'histoire de l'Etat romain : celui où la survie de l'empire n'obéit plus à son pacte ancien avec Justitia (qu'il définit comme la divinité président à la Cause) mais dépend d'actions qui contreviennent à la vision idéale de Rome de l'historien et à la responsabilité de ses dirigeants de défendre ses intérêts. Parallèlement à l'examen de cette interprétation, cet article considère le traumatisme causé par la reddition pour les citoyens de Nisibe, une cité d'une grande importance stratégique, et le tableau très différent peint par Ephrem.

Elton

Cet article se concentre sur les données archéologiques concernant les campagnes de l'Empire d'Occident entre les règnes de Dioclétien (284–305) et d'Honorius (395–423). Les campagnes militaires constituent un processus éphémère caractérisé par une évolution rapide et de multiples interactions humaines. Bien que les campagnes romaines soient souvent bien documentées, les données archéologiques ne sont pas bien adaptées à la compréhension d'événements ayant eu lieu au cours d'une année particulière, même si elles sont très utiles pour améliorer notre connaissance des ressources et des processus. Cet article analyse les actions de l'armée, puis se demande comment les données archéologiques contribuent à notre compréhension de ces actions. Il établit qu'il y avait d'énormes différences entre les ressources dont disposait Rome et celles de ses ennemis dans l'Occident du 4ème siècle, même si les cultures frontalières étaient similaires.

Kulikowski

Dans cet article, l'auteur se demande à quel point l'état de guerre est caractéristique du 5ème siècle, et si l'attention particulière portée par les spécialistes aux invasions barbares durant cette période est justifiée par les données recueillies. Il étudie les façons dont l'archéologie et les sources littéraires sont, ou non, complémentaires dans la compréhension de la guerre au 5ème siècle, à partir d'une série d'exemples spécifiques tels que la réoccupation de sites élevés dans le Nord de l'Espagne, l'interprétation d'un point de vue ethnique d'objets dans les cimetières de la Meseta et les traces de violence à Emerita Augusta dans l'Antiquité tardive.

Oriol Olesti

On a découvert en 2001, dans le site des Colomines (Llívia), les vestiges de la tombe d'un primate (un macaque de Barbarie, *macaca sylvanus*) comprenant le squelette de l'animal accompagné de quelques offrandes. Parmi celles-ci, on a trouvé des objets métalliques ornés et quelques ceintures militaires en bronze typique de la période tardo-antique. Cette tombe peut être associée à la période d'occupation de Iulia Libica au 5ème et 6ème siècle ainsi qu'à plusieurs épisodes militaires qui prirent place dans les Pyrénées à cette époque. Il est possible que le macaque ait appartenu à un officier. Quelques-unes des études ostéologiques et biométriques menées sur l'animal sont présentées à la fin de l'article.

WILKES

Entre les 3ème et 6ème siècles après Jésus-Christ, les menaces de l'extérieur et les tensions à l'intérieur conduisirent à une prolifération de fortifications dans le Sud-Ouest des Balkans, de chaque côté de la ligne de partage des eaux des mers Adriatique et Egée, dans la région autrefois unifiée de la Macédoine romaine. Les études récentes ont distingué deux phases dans ce processus. La première correspond à un programme, ordonné par le pouvoir central, de construction de nouvelles bases militaires, de murailles urbaines et d'autres fortifications, suivant le réseau des routes romaines. La seconde phase eut lieu après la séparation des empires d'Occident et d'Orient, lorsque la région devint une zone frontalière incontrôlée, et que de nombreux groupes cherchèrent à se mettre à l'abri dans des habitats fortifiés en altitude, entourés d'un réseau de pistes et de sentiers qui remplacèrent les routes.

SARANTIS

L'histoire des Balkans de la fin du 5ème siècle au 6ème siècle est perçue par les spécialistes, au mieux, comme un répit après une série de raids barbares dévastateurs ou, au pire, comme un pas de plus en direction de l'inévitable perte de contrôle du pouvoir impérial sur la région. Cet article veut rectifier cette perception en présentant les règnes d'Anastase et de Justinien comme une période durant laquelle les romains / byzantins prenaient l'initiative et l'emportaient dans leurs relations militaires et diplomatiques avec les barbares. Ces empereurs consacrèrent une énergie politique ainsi que des ressources économiques et militaires considérables à la restauration de l'autorité militaire impériale dans le Nord des Balkans.

CURTA

On remarque une absence flagrante d'étriers et d'autres éléments accompagnant la présence de troupes de cavalerie dans les sites fortifiés des Balkans du 6ème siècle au début du 7ème siècle. On a commis une erreur en

datant de l'Antiquité tardive des trésors d'ustensiles en fer contenant des
étriers; ils appartiennent en fait à une époque bien plus tardive (du 9ème
au 11ème siècle). Les trésors qui peuvent être attribués au 6ème siècle avec
quelque certitude ne contiennent aucun des outils agricoles associés à
une culture des champs à grande échelle. Dans la mesure où la plupart des
trésors semblables que l'on a trouvés dans les forts situés sur des collines
durant la première période byzantine incluent des outils destinés à la
culture de petits lopins de terre (jardinage), ils révèlent qu'aucune activité
agricole ne pouvait être pratiquée à l'intérieur ou à l'extérieur des forts du
6ème siècle, qui puisse satisfaire les besoins d'une population existante. Ces
sites n'étaient donc pas des villages fortifiés, mais des forts.

Howard-Johnston

Les structures défensives de la frontière orientale de l'empire furent modi-
fiées et étendues à partir du 3ème siècle, afin de faire face à la puissance
grandissante de la Perse sous la dynastie sassanide. On compte quatre
phases principales de développement : sous la Tétrarchie; au 4ème siècle; au
début puis à la fin du 6ème siècle. Le système défensif était bien adapté
au terrain et comptait plusieurs éléments distincts: des cités fortifiées, des
forteresses, des forts, des redoutes en altitude, des cols défendus, des routes de secours et des routes latérales. La dernière phase fut caractérisée
par un déplacement de l'attention vers le Nord du Taurus arménien et par
un recours croissant aux Bédouins dans le Sud.

Whately

Cet article réexamine certaines des conclusions du rapport de fouilles
final, récemment publié, sur la forteresse de el-Lejjūn en Jordanie, parti-
culièrement en ce qui concerne son occupation durant la première moitié
du 6ème siècle. L'auteur pense que s'y trouvait toujours une présence militaire importante à cette époque, probablement composée de *limitanei*, et
que leur nourriture était principalement locale. Cette pratique correspond
à ce que nous savons de l'approvisionnement des forteresses frontalières romaines dans d'autres parties de l'empire et des tendances dans les
réseaux commerciaux de l'Orient du 6ème siècle en général. En outre, cet
article souligne l'importance des rapports archéologiques détaillés dans
l'élucidation de la logistique militaire romaine de l'Antiquité tardive.

CHRISTIE

L'archéologie ne nous donne que trop peu de renseignements sur la guerre civile, au contraire des textes. Le monde romain de l'Antiquité tardive fut souvent affligé par les conflits civils et les luttes de pouvoir entre empereurs rivaux, généraux et troupes, qui eurent de lourdes répercussions sur les communautés, les régions, les économies et les frontières. De quelles façons l'archéologie peut-elle néanmoins nous proposer une grille de lecture ou une meilleure connaissance de ces nombreux conflits ? Cet article considère les types de données matérielles, depuis les murailles jusqu'aux pièces de monnaies, qui pourraient lever le voile sur ces guerres du 3ème au 5ème siècle qui ravagèrent l'Occident romain en particulier, et soutient qu'il faudrait prêter une attention beaucoup plus grande à ces conflits internes.

KOUROUMALI

Dans cet article, l'auteur se penche sur un aspect particulier des campagnes de Justinien contre les Ostrogoths en Italie, aspect souvent négligé et pourtant essentiel à la compréhension de ces guerres: la nature des relations entre les trois parties aux prises dans ce conflit (Romains, Goths et Italiens). Cette étude montre, grâce à un examen minutieux des sources primaires et notamment du récit de Procope, que les relations entre les habitants de l'Italie et les deux côtés belligérants dépendaient des besoins des Italiens et de leur souci de préserver leur sécurité plutôt que de choix idéologiques.

INDEX

Editors' note: In this index, sub entries are in most cases structured thematically according to the logic underlying the subject, rather than alphabetically.

LATE ANTIQUE ARCHAEOLOGY

Series Editor

LUKE LAVAN

Late Antique Archaeology is published annually by Brill, based on papers given at the conference series of the same title, which meets annually in London. Contributions generally aim to present broad syntheses on topics relating to the year's theme, discussions of key issues, or try to provide summaries of relevant new fieldwork. Although papers from the conference meetings will form the core of each volume, relevant articles, especially syntheses, are welcome from other scholars. All papers are subject to satisfying the comments of two anonymous referees, managed by the discretion of the editors. The editorial committee includes Albrecht Berger, Will Bowden, Kim Bowes, Averil Cameron, Beatrice Caseau, Alexandra Chavarria, James Crow, Jitse Dijkstra, Sauro Gelichi, Lale Ozgenel, Jean-Pierre Sodini, Emanuele Vaccaro, Bryan Ward-Perkins and Enrico Zanini. The next volume, based on papers given at a conference in 2010, will consider *Local Economies? Production and Exchange in Inland Regions in Late Antiquity*. Journal abbreviations follow those used by the *American Journal of Archaeology*, whilst literary sources are abbreviated according to the *Oxford Classical Dictionary* (3rd ed., Oxford 1999) xxix–liv and when not given here, following A. H. M. Jones *The Later Roman Empire* (Oxford 1964) vol.2, 1462–76, then G. W. H. Lampe *A Patristic Greek Lexicon* (Oxford 1961).

For programme information and notes for contributors, with contact details, visit: www.lateantiquearchaeology.wordpress.com

A. Sarantis, N. Christie (edd.) *War and Warfare in Late Antiquity: Current Perspectives* (Late Antique Archaeology 8.1–8.2 – 2010–11) (Leiden 2013), p. 1085